Paul's SAT
Vocabulary

저자 Paul Kim(김동현)

SAT 단어학습 필수교재!

2016 Redesigned SAT 소개
SAT Novel
SAT Vocabulary

Contributors

Written and edited by the talented test prep professionals at PaulAcademy

PaulAcademy is the publishing arm of one of the industry-leading test prep organizations in Asia. PaulAcademy is a dedicated test prep organization that has helped thousands of students to realize their potentials and achieve their dreams. As a leader in test prep & strategy development specializing in SAT, ACT and AP preparation, PaulAcademy teaches pragmatic problem-solving skills that will ultimately help students obtain successful academic results. PaulAcademy aims to spread the expert knowledge to students worldwide.

Editor-in-Chief
Paul Kim

Head of Publishing
Andrew Park

Material Development & Editing
Niles, Eric Kim, Puck Lee

Marketing
Byeong Kook Kim

Email: books@paulacademy.net   Website: http://www.paulacademy.net

Copyright © 2015 All rights reserved by PaulAcademy.
The contents of the book may not be copied or reused without the expressed written consent of PaulAcademy.

SAT® is a registered trademark of the College Board, which is not affiliated with and does not endorse this product.

ISBN: 979-11-86461-06-8 (53740)

Paul's SAT® Vocabulary

Paul Academy

...ours is a mongrel language which started with a child's vocabulary of three hundred words, and now consists of two hundred and twenty-five thousand; the whole lot, with the exception of the original and legitimate three hundred, borrowed, stolen, smouched from every unwatched language under the sun, the spelling of each individual word of the lot locating the source of the theft and preserving the memory of the revered crime.

- Mark Twain's Autobiography

Paul's SAT Vocabulary 서문

10여 년 전 "한국의 Test Prep이 세계 최고"라는 가능성을 보고 유학길에 올라 공부를 마치고 귀국 후 강남의 모 SAT 학원 팀장으로 매년 20%씩 성장을 이룬 후, 그 학원을 나와서 '친절한 폴샘'의 SAT 서문을 쓴 지도 이제 2년이 지났다. 그 당시에는 "아마존 Test Prep 분야 넘버원"이라는 꿈을 위해서 한국의 SAT 교재 1등을 달성한 후에 미국에 진출하고 싶다"고 이야기했는데, 그 2년 간 수많은 동역자들의 도움으로 한국 SAT 교재 베스트셀러(교보문고 기준)를 달성했고, 미국 Amazon.com에 진출하여 SAT Grammar 분야 4위, SAT Math 분야 15위를 기록했다. (2015년 5월 25일 기준) 글로벌 시장 진출을 위해서 시리즈 제목도 '친절한 폴샘의 SAT' 시리즈에서 'Paul's SAT', 'Paul's ACT' 시리즈로 정비하고 본격적인 미국 진출에 박차를 가하고 있다.

저자의 고교 시절에는 교과서, 학교 수업과 참고서만으로도 충분히 자기주도학습이 가능했지만, 지금은 학원에서 공부하지 않으면 효율적인 학습과 시험준비가 불가능하다는 견해가 이 사회에 팽배해 있는 것 같다. 저자는 좋은 교재와 콘텐츠를 만들어 사교육에 의존하지 않고도 자기주도학습이 가능하다는 것을 증명하고, 학습에 대한 잘못된 사회인식을 바로잡고, 더 나아가 미국 아마존의 Test Prep 분야에서 세계최고가 되어 '교육한류'의 한 축이 되고 싶다.

만일 누군가 독학이 힘들어 학원의 도움이 필요하다면, 폴아카데미에서 도움을 받기를 바란다. 폴아카데미에서는 본 교재를 사용하여 학생들이 빠른 시간 내에 고득점을 받을 수 있도록 도와주고, 혼자서 해결하기 힘든 부분들에 대한 해결책을 제시해 주고 있다.

이 책은 2016년 3월부터 본격적으로 시행되는 Redesigned SAT를 효과적으로 대비할 수 있게 해 주는 단어학습교재다. SAT Reading이라고 하면 단어학습을 빼놓고 얘기할 수 없고, Redesigned SAT Reading에서는 Sentence Completion이 없음에도 불구하고 별도로 단어학습을 해야 할 필요가 여전히 있고, 또한 중요하다. 이 교재는 69개 에피소드로 전개되는 소설 형식으로 구성되어 있으며, 그 안에서 context-based 단어학습이 이루어지도록 설계되었다. 각 에피소드의 끝에는 Vocabulary Study 섹션을 마련하여 집중적으로 단어학습을 할 수 있도록 했으며, 각 단어마다 mnemonic approach에 입각한 효과적인 암기법을 제공하여 단어들을 쉽게 외울 수 있도록 도와준다. 또한 SAT Official Guide를 포함하여 최근 20년간 SAT Reading Passage에 나온 기출단어를 총망라, Paul's Vocab Algorithm을 통한 분석으로 단어빈도의 우선순위 가중치를 숫자 형태로 각 단어에 표시하였다. 말 그대로 이 책 하나만 있으면 SAT Vocabulary 학습은 끝이라고 하겠다.

본 교재와 콘텐츠를 통해 단기간에 고득점을 가능하게 하고, 그렇게 확보된 소중한 시간을 본인이 진정으로 하고 싶은 것을 하면서 사는 세상을 만드는데 기여하는데 이 책이 좋은 첫걸음이 되길 바란다. "Paul's SAT Vocabulary"가 빛을 볼 수 있도록 많은 사람들이 도움을 주었다. 내게 "best place to work"의 꿈을 심어주신 하늘에 계신 사랑하는 아버지, 못난 아들을 위해 항상 기도해 주시는 사랑하는 어머니, 부족한 남편임에도 열심히 섬겨주는 사랑하는 아내, 그리고 바쁘다는 이유로 함께 시간을 갖지 못해도 바르게 자라주고 있는 사랑하는 두 아들 영준, 경준에게 너무나 고맙고 사랑한다는 말을 전하고 싶다. 마지막으로 길가의 돌멩이보다 못한 나에게 비전을 주시고 여건을 허락해 주신 하나님께 감사를 드린다.

Paul Kim

NYU에서 영어교육을 전공하였으며 실력 있는 SAT, ACT 부문 최고의 전문강사로서 세한아카데미에서 수많은 학생을 가르치며 큰 명성을 쌓아온 Paul Kim은 현재 Test Prep 전문기관 Paul Academy의 대표로 재직하고 있다. Paul Academy에서는 SAT 및 ACT 교재 시리즈 출간, 온라인 교육 콘텐츠 개발, 자기주도학습과 수험생을 위한 영어교육 전반에 힘을 쏟고 있다.

CONTENTS

2016 Redesigned SAT 소개 8

SAT Novel & Vocabulary 15

- Episode 01   Trepidation 16
- Episode 02   Audio Attack 24
- Episode 03   De-composition 31
- Episode 04   TJ's Arrival 36
- Episode 05   The Actor, My Uncle 44
- Episode 06   Enemy, Unexpected 51
- Episode 07   The Vocab Blues 56
- Episode 08   Reading Jail 62
- Episode 09   Some People Say the First Test is the Hardest 68
- Episode 10   Family Time 74
- Episode 11   Just Another Monday Morning 80
- Episode 12   Heart Strings and Vocab Quizzes 87
- Episode 13   Disappointment 92
- Episode 14   The Empty Chair 98
- Episode 15   Study Group 103
- Episode 16   The Game 110
- Episode 17   Maternal Criticism 117
- Episode 18   Lingerie and Roses Are Not Good Ideas for a First Date 123
- Episode 19   Women, The Grand Riddle 128
- Episode 20   The Date 134
- Episode 21   In the Study 140
- Episode 22   A Brief Visit 147

CONTENTS

Episode 23	An Uncertain Return	153
Episode 24	Guess This!	157
Episode 25	Coincidence	161
Episode 26	The Summit	166
Episode 27	Disappointment: The Other Side of the Coin	173
Episode 28	Money, Or the Pain of Being Poor	178
Episode 29	Family Spirit(s)	183
Episode 30	The Karaoke Gang	191
Episode 31	The Drinking	198
Episode 32	The Hangover	207
Episode 33	The New Class	212
Episode 34	Woo-Time	218
Episode 35	The College Board = Awful	225
Episode 36	The Lecture	229
Episode 37	Making Fun	234
Episode 38	A Release or 'Kick Out Thursday'	240
Episode 39	The Hamburger Mafia	248
Episode 40	Cleave Means Two Things	253
Episode 41	Fear	257
Episode 42	Social Mobility	262
Episode 43	Alas, Fair Jessica, I Knew Her Well	268
Episode 44	The Whims of the Gods	274
Episode 45	The Story of the Bear	279
Episode 46	Hands Across the Table Top	284
Episode 47	Home Stay Sickness	289

Episode 48	Sam's Story	294
Episode 49	Classroom Prank (Again)	300
Episode 50	A New Member, and a Proposal	306
Episode 51	A Tragic Ending	312
Episode 52	The Socratic Method of Making Friends	318
Episode 53	The Boat Race	327
Episode 54	Dog Days	334
Episode 55	Loss	342
Episode 56	Grief	348
Episode 57	After the Destruction, a Reckoning	353
Episode 58	The Academic Recovery	359
Episode 59	Postmodernism	365
Episode 60	Back to School	370
Episode 61	A Future Foreshadowed	374
Episode 62	(Just Like) Starting Over	381
Episode 63	Touchdown	388
Episode 64	An Unexpected Friend	398
Episode 65	A Dream of Mimes	406
Episode 66	Curry Disease	414
Episode 67	Crimes and Sin	421
Episode 68	The Cousin Clause	427
Episode 69	Night in the Zoo	433

기출 예상 단어 443
Index 451

SAT 시험, 이렇게 바뀐다!

2016 Redesigned SAT 소개

시행일시 : 2016년 3월부터 시행될 예정

1. Redesigned SAT 주요변화

A. 점수
- 전체 2,400점 만점 → 1,600점 만점 (Reading + Writing & Language 800점, Math 800점)
- 에세이는 선택사항으로 변경되고 점수도 독자적으로 매겨진다. Reading, analysis, writing 각 항목에 대해서 2~8점 배점되고 총점은 24점
- 에세이가 선택사항으로 바뀌었지만 상위권 대학을 희망하는 학생들은 필수적으로 점수를 받아놓아야 한다.

B. 영역
Essay, Critical Reading, Writing, Math 였던 영역구분이
→ Evidence-based Reading & Writing(Reading + Writing & Language), Math, Essay(선택사항) 으로 변경됨

C. 시험시간
전체 3시간 45분이었던 것이 3시간으로 축소. (에세이를 선택할 경우에는 3시간 50분)

1. Evidence-based Reading & Writing: Reading 65분, Writing 35분

2. Math: 55분 계산기 허용, 25분 계산기 사용불가

D. 시험 문제수
- Critical Reading: 67문제 → 52문제
- Writing: 49문제 → 44문제
- Essay: 1문제 그대로
- Math: 54문제 → 58문제

E. 시험 출제방식
- 오지선다에서 사지선다 방식으로 변경
- 지필시험방식을 유지

F. 채점방식 및 기준
- Essay: 글의 일관성보다는 학생의 분석능력과 논증과정을 중시
- 오답에 대한 감점제도 폐지: 틀린 문제와 풀지 않은 문제가 성적에 영향을 주지 않음

G. 기존 SAT와 새로운 SAT 비교표

현재 SAT			2016 Redesigned SAT			
과목	시험시간	문제 수	과목	시험시간	문제 수	시험방식
Critical Reading	70분	67문제	Reading	65분	52문제	4 LP 1 DP
Writing	60분	49문제	Writing & Language	35분	44문제	4 Passages
Essay	25분	1문제	Essay	50분	1문제	1 EP 1 RP
Math	70분	54문제	Math	80분	58문제	계산기/ 38문제 NO계산기/ 20문제
계	225분	171문제	계	180분 (에세이 포함시 230분)	154문제 (에세이 포함시 155문제)	

※참고 – LP: Long Passages, DP: Double Passages, EP: Essay Prompt, RP: Reading Passage

2. 과목별 구체적인 변화

A. Reading Test (독해)
1. 단어의 난이도 보다는 context에 집중
   - 기존의 단어 뜻 모르면 풀 수 없는 obscure한 문제 폐지
   - Extended context에서 단어 톤 찾기
     예) how word choice shapes tone/impact
   - Sentence Completion 폐지
   - 단편적인 정보, 직접적으로 단어 뜻을 물어보는 문제는 축소

2. Analysis & evidence use (분석, 근거 사용)
   - 답을 찾아내는 것뿐 아니라 텍스트의 어느 부분이 그 답을 support하는지 찾아야 한다
     예) Which portion of the passage best supports the answer to the text?
     CB: "There will be at least one question asking them to select a quote from the text that best supports the answer they have chosen in response to the preceding question."

3. Real-world에 관한 지문
   - 기존의 임의적인 토픽의 essay와 fiction은 나오지 않음

- 차트, 그래프, 인포그래픽이 포함된 지문 (reading, writing, math 모두 동일하게 적용됨)
- 1개의 역사/사회 지문과 1개의 과학지문

4. 새로운 지문

> **학습전략**
>
> 2016 Revised SAT는 Evidence-based reading을 강조하므로 글의 paragraph summary, main idea, tone을 꼼꼼히 체크해가면서 글을 읽고 이해를 하며, 리딩문제를 풀 때 더 이상 '감'에 의존해서 푸는 것이 아니라 몇 번째 line을 통해서 답을 유추했는지를 항상 확인하면서 공부를 해야 한다. 혼자 하기 어려운 학생은 친절한 폴샘의 기출해설서의 CR 영역을 공부하면 된다.
>
>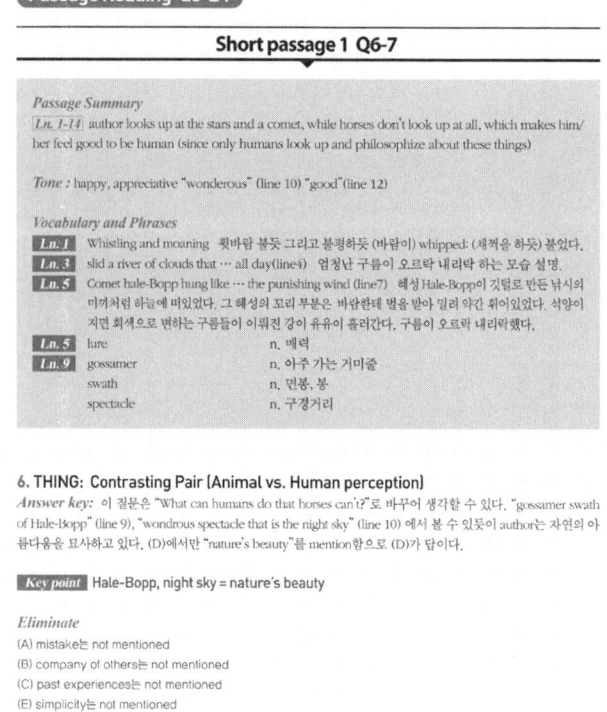
>
> 특별히 CR이 600점대 이하의, 유학 3년차 이하의 학생들은 찍기 식으로 가르치는 학원보다는 지문을 잘 이해시켜 주는 curriculum을 제공하는 학원과 교재를 선정하여 공부하는 것이 좋다. 그리고 SAT는 미국대학에 진학하려는 학생을 위한 시험이므로, 평소에 미국적 사고에 필요한 역사, 문학, 사회이슈들에 대한 배경지식을 잘 정리해 놓으면 지문을 이해하고 문제풀이 시간을 줄이는데 도움이 된다.

B. Writing and Language Test (문법)

1. Real-world에 관한 지문
   - 역사/사회, 과학, 인문학, Career 관련 지문

- 그래프, 도표 문제 한 개 이상 출제: 주어진 정보들을 어떻게 잘 연결해서 자연스럽고 논리적인 글로 만들어 낼 수 있는가에 대한 문제 출제

2. 문법적 오류 관련문제는 크게 변화 없음
    - Development of idea
        예) adding relevant supporting details, improving focus and cohesion
    - Careful & purposeful use of words
        예) improving precision or concision
    - Rhetoricals and conventions
        예) fragments & run-ons, parallel structure, modifier, tense, pronoun & number, verb agreement, logical comparison, idiom, punctuation
    - Diction

3. 주어진 텍스트와 차트 또는 도표 간의 연관 찾기
    예) 차트에 대한 잘못된 해석 고치기

4. 지문 길이 증가
    - 기존의 한 문장 짜리 문법 문제 폐지
    - Extended context를 제공하는 문단 제공

> **학습전략**
>
> 기존 SAT Grammar 섹션에서 나오는 Improving Paragraph 유형에 Grammar 요소가 조금 더 가미되었다고 보면 된다. 너무 걱정하지 말고 조만간 출간될 Paul' SAT Writing and Language로 준비하면 된다. 아직 교재가 출간되지 않아 조바심이 나는 경우는 친절한 폴샘의 SAT Grammar 기본서로 공부를 해도 대부분 커버할 수 있으니 너무 걱정하지 말자.

C. Essay (에세이)

1. 요구사항에서 선택사항으로 변경

2. 짧게 자신의 의견을 요구하는 prompt 폐지
    - 기존의 prompt는 배경지식과 경험에 의존; 논리구조만 맞으면 fact는 상관 없었지만 새로운 SAT Essay 에서는 600~700 단어로 주어진 글을 읽고 그 주장을 분석해서 설명해야 함 → 자기 마음대로 예시를 쓰거나, 단순히 자신의 주장을 펼치는 것이 아니라는 점에 주의
        예) 작가가 어떻게 주장을 이끌어 나가는지 텍스트 속 객관적 근거를 제시하여 설명하여야 하며, 자신의 의견은 쓰지 않음
    - 글쓴이의 주장과 논리를 분석하여 그 논리전개에 대하여, 또한 그 주장에 대한 찬성 또는 반대의 관점을 어떻게 자기의 말로 잘 풀어내는지가 포인트

3. 채점방식 및 기준
    - 기존의 0~12점대의 scale은 폐지되고 criteria에 따른 점수로 0~24점까지 채점
    - Reading: Source text와 main idea에 대한 이해가 중요하며, 얼마나 디테일이 정확한지, 텍스트 속의 근거를 얼마나 잘 사용하는지 등이 중요한 포인트

- Analysis: 주어진 과제를 얼마나 잘 이해했는지, 작가가 논거를 펼치며 사용한 각종 element가 얼마나 효과적인지, 그리고 자신의 주장에 대한 근거를 잘 제시하고 있는지 부분에 중점
- Writing: Central claim 사용, 효과적인 organization과 progression이 되고 있는지, 문장구조가 varied한지, 정확한 뜻의 단어를 사용하는지, 그리고 consistent한 스타일과 톤을 유지하는지, 문법적인 오류는 없는지 등이 중점채점사항

4. 에세이 시간이 25분에서 50분으로 길어졌기 때문에, 체계적인 논리와 전개과정이 필수적이다. 시간이 길어지면서 그만큼 평가도 정확하고 가혹하게 될 것이라 예상된다.

> **학습전략**
>
> 기존 SAT는 내용을 '지어낼' 수 있었던 반면, Redesigned SAT는 fact-based essay이다. 2016 Redesigned Reading처럼 저자의 main idea와 argument를 잘 파악하여 fact-based argument를 하는 연습이 매우 중요해졌다. 이 연습만 잘 된다면 해외 유학생들이 국내대학의 영어특기자 입시를 준비할 경우에 많은 도움이 될 것이다.

D. Math Test (수학)

*출제범위 및 비중이 조정되었기 때문에 일단 전반적으로 수학문제의 난이도가 올라가게 되며, 일부 문제는 AP 시험유형과 수준의 문제라고 생각하고 준비해야 한다.

1. Data Analysis에 중점
   - Reading과 Writing에서 Real-world에 중점을 둔 것과 같은 맥락
   - 실제 상황에 적용해서 푸는 문제들이 출제된다는 뜻

2. Real-world context 사용한 문제 출제
   예) 사회/역사/과학과 관련된 시나리오를 보여준 후 그것에 대한 문제 여러 개 출제

3. Pre-Calculus 영역이 추가됨
   - Trigonometry, Complex Number, Radians 등의 상급개념 추가

4. 일부 섹션에서 계산기 사용이 제한됨
   - 복잡한 계산은 아니고 유리수 산술계산 정도의 수준
   - Grid-ins 형태의 주관식이 총 12문제 출제

〈출제범위〉

범위	문제 개수	출제비중
Heart of Algebra (Creating, Solving, Interpreting Linear Expressions)	21	36%
Problem Solving and Data Analysis	16	27%
Passport to Advanced Math (Quadratic/Exponential Functions)	15	26%
Additional Topics (Area/Volume Calculation, Investigation of Lines, Angles, Triangles and Circles Using Theorem, Working with Trigonometric Functions)	6	11%
계	58	100%

〈계산기 사용에 따른 구분〉

구분	유형	시험시간
계산기 사용가능	객관식 30문제 Grid-ins 8문제	55분
계산기 사용불가	객관식 15문제 Grid-ins 5문제	25분
계	총 58문제	총 80분

> **학습전략**
>
> Pre-Calculus 영역을 중점 학습하고, 특히 trigonometry(삼각함수), complex number(복소수), radians(호도법) 등의 개념학습을 충실히 한다. 그리고 계산기를 사용할 수 없는 section이 하나 있으므로, 평소 계산연습을 많이 해 두도록 하고, real-world situation에 입각한 문제에 대비하기 위해 관련 응용문제 풀이를 많이 하도록 한다. 여름방학에 2016 SAT 학원수강을 하게 되면 꼭 꼭 Math수업을 수강하여서 고득점의 발판을 마련하여야 한다. 더 이상 SAT 1 Math는 유학생들에게 쉬운 과목이 아니라는 점을 꼭 명심하도록 하자.

SAT Vocabulary

Episode 1 ~ 69

Episode 01

Trepidation

001 trepidation [2]
n. 두려움
nervousness; fear

002 solicitous [1]
a. 배려하는
worried or concerned
(about someone else)
cf. oversolicitous

003 devoid [6]
adj. 전혀 없는
without; empty

The summer morning, as usual, was cool and blue. The street, apart from a single lonely businessman and a group of partiers from the evening before, was empty. Jake took out his phone and finally selected a good morning song, since the subway had been too full to even reach down to his pockets. He decided upon The Zombies' "She's Not There." He always had been a bit old-fashioned.

Jake, our hero, was a quiet sort of boy, humble yet often frightened that he was doing something wrong. Occasionally, laughter on a crowded street made him feel nervous. He had just landed in the big city the previous Friday. It was faster, somehow. There was so much more to see than he remembered.

His mother had over-**solicitously** prepared his materials for his first day of classes, and so he took out her carefully-written list of instructions. It was written in her usual business-like style.

Paul Academy building. Out of Seolleung Station, exit 2. Up the hill, first left, up the steep hill. Keep walking straight until you see a GS 25 on your right. It is across the street. Take the elevator to the second floor.
Love Mom.

PS: Please eat a sensible lunch. Nothing chocolate or fried.
PPS: Make friends but come home on time. Make sure the class is organized and be polite.

He looked up to see that his destination, the SAT prep school building, was dark, and seemed as empty of life as the street it sat upon. It was 8:30 on a Monday. What was he doing here and why couldn't he still be sleeping? Who studies the SAT this early anyway?

Maybe I'll be the only student here, he thought. He was, by nature, an imaginative boy, and his thoughts suddenly jumped to a well-lit classroom, clean and completely **devoid** of other students, with only himself in the very center and a teacher at the front, asking him

incessantly about the meaning of a word he'd never seen before. He shook his head. Somehow he'd gotten to the third floor without noticing his feet moving nor the elevator's slow ascent.

When the elevator door opened, he could see that the dark and unwelcoming **aesthetic** the **edifice** presented from the street completely **belied** the activity **enclosed** within. Turning to his left, he looked down the hallway and saw a vast **profusion** of students **wandering** from classroom to classroom, with a few walking through the group with **clusters** of paper and concerned glances. One such person nearly ran straight into him, and to be polite he stepped out of her way, only to step heavily on the toes of someone a girl coming up the stairs. She grabbed the railing to avoid falling backwards.

She let out a yell, steadied herself and gave Jake a cold look. Her cheeks had become bright pink.

"Sorry, I — " Jake took out his earphones to show how sorry he was, and that he was trying to be as polite as possible, but without a word she walked to the second floor.

So much for making friends, he thought.

He turned back toward the hallway and looked for someone he knew. No one. He was beginning to think of taking the elevator back down to the first floor and sitting in a café until he could go home when one of the many faces amongst the crowd turned toward him. Her eyebrow was raised slightly. She had the official look of someone responsible for keeping things running smoothly, not to mention a very important looking clipboard.

"Name?" she said, removing a pencil from behind her ear.

"Huh?"

"Your name. We need to know what class you should go to."

What was his name? He looked at her and noticed she had a pencil stuck vertically into the gathering of hair at the back of her head, looking to him as though it was **embedded** into her skull. He told her.

"Ok..." she checked her register and directed him toward a classroom at the end of the hallway. "You will go there every morning

---

[004] **aesthetic** [40]
adj. 심미적, 미학적인
related to appearance and beauty

[005] **edifice** [4]
n. 큰 건물, 빌딩
building, structure

[006] **belie** [2]
v. 거짓임을 보여주다
create a false impression; contradict

[007] **enclose** [3]
v. 둘러싸다
close in all sides

[008] **profusion** [3]
n. 풍부, 부유
multitude; great number of something, abundance

[009] **wander** [15]
v. 떠돌아다니다
ramble without a definite purpose or objective

[010] **cluster** [5]
n. 묶음, 뭉치
bundle, group, bunch

[011] **embedded** [7]
a. 단단히 박아 넣은
sunk deeply; inserted

012 inconspicuous [1]
a. 이목을 끌지 못하는
unnoticeable; hidden

013 diffident [2]
a. 자신 없는, 수줍은
quiet; shy

to take a vocab test. Be here by 8:30 every day, no exceptions. You understand?"

She's got a pen in her brain, he thought. She handed him a piece of paper, the class schedule that day. Pencilhead turned and disappeared into the crowd. Jake blinked, realized he was in everyone's way, and went where the paper told him to go.

The classroom was about two-thirds full, with many students just like him trying to be **inconspicuous** and disappear. One particularly **diffident**-looking girl was sitting near the wall, her legs turned away from the room so that she was looking more at the wall than she was at anything else. He set his facial expression to what he thought of as "James Bond" and approached. *Make friends*, his mother had said. If she only knew how strange that request was.

"Is this seat taken?" he asked with a smile, using a phrase he'd heard used in the movies.

"What a horrible saying," the girl told the wallpaper.

"Sorry?"

"That phrase." She did not look at him. "Did you hear it in a movie or something? How boring."

"What's...that —"

"It means 'flat statement' and it's a longer way of saying something is so common that it means nothing."

"So —"

"So it means you're using a very old, very lame expression. And you think you're being clever about it, too."

"What, I —"

"Did you think you were saying something smooth? Did I detect a hint of James Bond?"

Jake blinked once, and a long time seemed to pass. Outside, for some reason, a man yelled about five dollar oranges. The girl finally turned toward him, her expression a mixture of **disdain** and boredom.

"Why haven't you sat down yet?"

He sat, watching her eyes as she turned again toward the wall. She rolled them so deeply and fully into the back of her head that Jake thought she might hurt herself. Suddenly, she turned towards him again, and he **averted** his gaze quickly.

"Your name?"

He got nervous. More name requests? He was beginning to feel like he was escaping an **oppressive** dictatorship.

"Jake," he managed.

"Well, Jake, nice to meet you." Her gaze shifted downward and then slowly back toward the wall, as though wanting to return to an old friend. Jake made his move.

"And you?" he said quickly, clearing his throat.

"Me what?" she said carefully. Her eyes were locked on his, focused with laser-like intensity. Jake thought he could feel the back of his eyes burning. He blinked three whole eternities before he remembered to speak **obliquely**.

"Uh, what's yours?"

She turned at once back to the wall.

"Ashley."

Jake decided that making friends and pleasing his mother were just not worth the cost. He crossed his arms, turned toward the front of the classroom and let his anger reactors overload.

"So very nice to meet you, too, you strange wall woman. Tell me, do you ever let strangers finish their sentences?"

She turned to him with a smile of hesitant respect.

"Obviously, Mr. Bond, I just did."

---

014 **disdain** [21]
n. 경멸
strong dislike

015 **avert** [4]
v. 외면하다
look away from something

016 **oppressive** [11]
a. 탄압하는
burdening with cruel or unjust impositions or restraints
v. oppress

017 **oblique** [2]
a. 완곡한, 간접적인
indirectly stated or expressed; not straightforward

Vocabulary

0001
trepidation [2]
[ˈtrepɪdeɪʃn]

n. 두려움   nervousness; fear
Intrepid is fearless, so Trepid is fearful
I was full of **trepidation** when I faced my first class. (*n.*)

0002
solicitous [1]
[səlísətəs]

adj. 배려하는, 염려하는   worried or concerned (about someone else)
'solicit'은 '간청하다, 부탁하다'라는 뜻이다.
The **solicitous** mother watched her child closely at the swimming pool. (*adj.*)

0003
devoid [6]
[dɪvɔ́ɪd]

adj. 전혀 없는, ~이 없는, 결여된   without; empty
de(없는)과 emptiness를 의미하는 void 가 합쳐져 '결여된'의 의미
Nobody laughed because your jokes are **devoid** of humor. (*adj.*)

0004
aesthetic [40]
[esˈθetɪk]

adj. 심미적, 미학적인   related to appearance and beauty
aesthetic에서 첫 글자가 art처럼 a로 시작한다고 외우세요.
The decision to add a belt to my outfit is **aesthetic** rather than practical: I don't need it, it just makes me look prettier. (*adj.*)

0005
edifice [4]
[ˈedɪfɪs]

n. 큰 건물, 빌딩; 건축하다   building, structure
edify는 즉, 지식을 한 사람의 정신에 'build'하다, '건축하다'라는 단어에서 만들어진 edifice는 '건물, 빌딩'이라는 뜻
A group of men are erecting a monstrous copper **edifice**. (*n.*)

0006
belie [2]
[bilái]

v. 거짓임을 보여주다   create a false impression; contradict
lie가 거짓말이라는데서 파생된 단어.
Contrary evidence **belied** his claim. (*v.*)

0007
enclose ³

[ɪnˈkloʊz]

v. 둘러싸다   close in all sides
enclose하면 어떤 closed(닫힌) 공간에 넣는 거겠지?
The witch **enclosed** her garden with thick stone walls so nobody could get in. (*v.*)

0008
profusion ³

[prəˈfjuːʒən]

n. 풍부, 부유, 대량   multitude; great number of something, abundance
핵 융합(fusion)은 대량의 에너지를 생성해낸다.
Giving a **profusion** of flowers may give her a burden. (*n.*)

0009
wander ¹⁵

[ˈwɑːndə(r)]

v. 떠돌아다니다   ramble without a definite purpose or objective
[WAN+ DUR] He accidently enter into WAN(wide area networking), so he is feeling DUR.
She **wandered** aimlessly around the streets. (*v.*)

0010
cluster ⁵

[ˈklʌstər]

n. 묶음, 뭉치   bundle, group, bunch
비슷한 말인 clot은 blood clot처럼 응고된 피덩어리를 말할때 쓰인다. 이를 연관시켜 '뭉쳐진 무리'를 연상하자.
The penguins **clustered** together until they looked like a big black and white blob from the distance. (*v.*)

0011
embedded ⁷

[ɪmˈbedɪd]

adj. 단단히 박아 넣은   sunk deeply; inserted
embedded system fix all things together/enclose.
These attitudes are deeply **embedded** in our society. (*a.*)

0012
inconspicuous ¹

[ˌɪnkənˈspɪkjuəs]

adj. 이목을 끌지 못하는   unnoticeable; hidden
conspicuous는 '눈에 띄는' 것이다.
When the **inconspicuous** celebrity slipped into the grocery store, none of her fans noticed. (*adj.*)

0013
diffident [2]

[dífədənt]

adj. 자신 없는, 수줍은　　quiet; shy
no confidence '자신이 없는'이란 뜻이다.
The **diffident** girl only shuffled her feet and stared at the ground while the teacher talked to her. (*adj.*)

0014
disdain [21]

[disdéin]

n. 경멸, 경멸하다　　strong dislike
des(do the opposite of), deignier(treat as worthy)가 합쳐진 단어.
The vain woman **disdained** everyone who was uglier than her. (*v.*)

0015
avert [4]

[əvə́:rt]

v. 외면하다, 회피하다　　look away from something
avert는 going around 라고 생각하면 쉽다.
He did his best to **avert** suspicion. (*v.*)

0016
oppressive [11]

[əpresɪv]

adj. 탄압하는　　burdening with cruel or unjust impositions or restraints　　*v.* oppress
ob는 '~에 반해', press는 '누르다'는 뜻으로 반하는 자들을 찍어 누른다는 의미이다.
The boss was very **oppressive** to us. (*adj.*)

0017
oblique [2]

[əblí:k]

adj. 비스듬한; 완곡한, (간접적으로) 우회적인　　indirectly stated or expressed; not straightforward
oblique는 '비스듬한'이라고 알고 있지? 원래 말하려고 하는것을 비스듬히 말하면 '우회적으로 돌려 말하는'이 될 수 있다.
Timmy tilted his head sideways to look properly at the **oblique** rectangle. (*adj.*)

Note :

Episode 1

MATCHING Quiz

1. trepidation
2. solicitous
3. devoid
4. aesthetic
5. edifice
6. belie
7. enclose
8. profusion
9. wander
10. cluster
11. embedded
12. inconspicuous
13. diffident
14. disdain
15. avert
16. oppressive
17. oblique

A. multitude; great number of something, abundance
B. bundle, group, bunch
C. create a false impression; contradict
D. indirectly stated or expressed; not straightforward
E. unnoticeable; hidden
F. without; empty
G. burdening with cruel or unjust impositions or restraints
H. nervousness; fear
I. sunk deeply; inserted
J. worried or concerned (about someone else)
K. ramble without a definite purpose or objective
L. building, structure
M. look away from something
N. related to appearance and beauty
O. quiet; shy
P. close in all sides
Q. strong dislike

1-H, 2-J, 3-F, 4-N, 5-L, 6-C, 7-P, 8-A, 9-K, 10-B, 11-I, 12-E, 13-O, 14-Q, 15-M, 16-G, 17-D

더 많은 문제를 풀고자 한다면 www.quizlet.com에서 'paul academy seoul' class를 검색

Episode 02 — Audio Attack

018 **baffle** 7
v. 당황하게 만들다
confuse

019 **witty** 4
a. 익살스러운
comic

020 **anticipated** 33
a. 예상된
expected or predicted

021 **onslaught** 2
n. 맹공격
an onset, assault, or attack

022 **alignment** 5
n. 가지런함
the correct relationship of things with each other

023 **pelt** 3
n. 전력질주
running very fast

Interested and **baffled** by his first official classmate, Jake wished he were the sort of person to whom casual replies and **witty** comments came easily. But he wasn't. He could only turn away, toward the rest of the classroom, as his desk partner began unpacking her bag and setting her things around her as if constructing defenses for some **anticipated onslaught**. Out of the corner of his eye, he saw her stack four notebooks in the centre of the desk, a metal pencil case on the right side (out of which she withdrew a mechanical pencil and an unused black eraser), a fresh pack of post-it notes, and a blue water bottle with "Your Favorite Band Sucks" printed on the front in a clear white font. As a seeming final touch, she placed a tiny teddy bear carefully on the corner nearest to Jake.

He looked at her with little trust. Surely a girl of her intensity wouldn't keep a cute teddy bear on her desk, would she? She noticed him watching her and sighed. Without glancing at Jake, she pushed the corners of her books to bring them into **alignment**.

"It's not what you think."

"I wasn't thinking anything."

"You're a horrible liar. You were thinking 'why would a girl like that keep a cute little teddy bear on her desk?'"

"OK, I was thinking that a little bit," he admitted.

"I knew it."

Again, Jake tried to think of something clever to say, but his anger reactor had shut down completely. Maybe he should try to find a normal person to sit by… he turned around to find another empty seat, but just as soon as he'd done so, he realized in horror that he'd stuck his head directly in the path of someone coming up the central aisle with great **pelt**. As the form avoided the sudden appearance of Jake's head with a quick movement, he noticed that the pattern of her dress was familiar. When the woman had reached the slightly raised platform at the front of the room, he saw her pink cheeks and grew afraid. Had he already made an accidental enemy?

Luckily, Pink Face (the girl he'd nearly killed on the stairs just a few minutes earlier) didn't seem to have noticed him. Once she'd got to the front of the room, she greeted the class.

"Good morning everybody! I am the TA for this class. I'm just going to take attendance and take your phones and mp3s before the teacher gets here."

Her first words had been greeted with the teenage indifference typical in such a setting. Jake, of course, had tried to keep out of sight to avoid blame for the incident on the stairs. The mention of no cell phones sent the classroom up in angry **grunts** of **consternation**.

"Yes, yes, I know," Pink Cheeks said. "You will get them back at the end of the day. This is just to make sure that you are focused throughout the class."

She smiled uneasily but took action quickly to **vanquish** the **dissent** beginning to **propagate** throughout the room. She picked up an empty cardboard box on the **pedestal** and balanced it on her hip as she took attendance.

"Now, when I say your name, you are going to say 'here' or 'present' or make some sort of noise that isn't a cough or a bad word, and drop your appliances into this box. OK?" Each name she called **elicited** an **abashed** 'here,' and a self-conscious look around the room to make sure others weren't laughing at her. With every syllable, a few seconds after she'd shuffled over to its point of origin, came the hollow sound of an electronic rectangle hitting the bottom of the box. Jake **clutched** his earphones tightly and tried to think of an **appropriately** sad song for the moment he would part with his connection to the outside world.

"Jake!" she called just as he selected Chicago's. "If You Leave Me Now".

He sighed, and could have sworn he saw a look of hurt and confusion pass briefly over his beloved's display as it tumbled into the box.

---

024 grunt [2]
n. 꿀꿀거리는 소리
a deep guttural sound (as a pig does)

025 consternation [2]
n. 실망
panic; confused worry

026 vanquish [3]
v. 완파하다
defeat, overcome

027 dissent [6]
n. 반대
disorder and disagreement

028 pedestal [2]
n. 받침대
a base or foundation

029 elicit [7]
v. 끌어내다
withdraw; cause to be released

030 abashed [1]
a. 창피한, 겸연쩍은
shy; embarrassed

031 clutch [2]
v. 움켜쥐다
held tightly

032 appropriately [20]
adv. 적당하게, 알맞게
suitable or probable in given circumstances

| 033 | **reap** ²
v. 수확하다
gather or take

| 034 | **connoisseur** ³
n. 전문가
expert

| 035 | **prudent** ¹⁰
a. 신중한
wise or judicious in practical affairs

| 036 | **acquiescence** ¹⁰
n. 묵인
to be in agreement; consent; submission
v. acquiesce
a. acquiescent

| 037 | **confine** ¹¹
v. 국한시키다
enclose with bounds; limit or restrict

Once all the cellphones had been **reaped**, the TA left as quickly as she had come. Jake imagined Strawberry Jaws and Pencil-Head running to the elevator with all the other TAs, gathering outside in a market of their own making, and selling the equipment like criminals to passing Turks and traders like in some Constantinople market. His dearest treasure would travel down the street and out of his life forever and someone living in a desert community somewhere would give it to one of his children for Christmas (do they have Christmas in the desert?) and the little boy or girl would delight at the excellent choice of songs, the diverse taste of the music **connoisseur** who'd owned that device before, maybe someday writing letters to world newspapers in the hopes of finding that mysterious man who'd been such an inspiration.

His dream was interrupted by another form entering the room and brushing by his desk, this one taller and masculine, with a bundle of papers instead of a box. Jake slowly drew his own notebook out of his bag, along with a faded old pencil case which had a slit in one end through which pencils could slip if he wasn't **prudent**.

"Morning everyone," the strange shadow said as he passed. "Please take one of these packets and follow along."

He wanted to scream out in protest of his stolen music, but instead he followed the rest of the class and shifted his facial expression into one of pleasant **acquiescence**, the image of the good student. Class had begun for the summer, and he was **confined** without music next to a girl who had a teddy bear on her desk and an attitude like a bitter 40 year-old woman.

Jake calculated how many seconds there were in a summer, and began counting them down.

Vocabulary

0018
baffle [7]
[|bæfl]

v. 당황하게 만들다 confuse
낙담의 의성어인 'Bah!'를 떠올리면 외우기 편하다.
Everyone was **baffled** by the riddle until finally a young child pointed out the obvious answer. (*v.*)

0019
witty [4]
[|wɪti]

a. 익살스러운 comic
우리가 유재석은 '위트가 있다'고 말한다.
His **witty** speech set the audience roaring with laughter. (*adj.*)

0020
anticipated [33]
[æn|tɪsɪpeɪtɪd]

a. 예상된 expected or predicted *v.* anticipate
우리 고모는(aunt)는 항상 애완동물(pet)이 어디에 있는지 보고(see) 어디로 갈지 예측하는 걸 좋아해.
No effects on the sucking child are **anticipated**. (*adj.*)

0021
onslaught [2]
[|ɑːnslɔːt;|ɔːn-]

n. 맹공격 an onset, assault, or attack
slaughter(대량학살)이 이제 막 on 되었으니 맹공격이 시작된 것이라고 생각하자.
The town survives the **onslaught** of tourists every summer. (*n.*)

0022
alignment [5]
[ə|laɪmənt]

n. 가지런함 the correct relationship of things with each other
[a < ad(to) + lign(line, 선, 줄, 열) + ment (명사형): → 일렬로 정렬하다, 정돈하다
The troops were in perfect **alignment**. (*n.*)

0023
pelt [3]
[pelt]

n. 전력질주 running very fast
라틴어 pellere (push, drive, strike)에서 온 단어인데, 축구황제 펠레를 생각해서 외우자.
I'm told: "Work is proceeding at full **pelt**. (*n.*)

0024
grunt ²
[grʌ́nt]

n. 꿀꿀거리는 소리; 기분 상하게 만들다   a deep guttural sound (as a pig does)
dis– "very" 와 gruntle "grumble, 불평하다"가 합쳐져 '매우 불만스럽게 하다' 는 의미
His only answer was a **grunt**. (*n.*)

0025
consternation ²
[kànstərnéiʃən]

n. 실망, 대경실색, 경악   panic; confused worry
불어 'consternation' 즉, '깜짝 놀란, 당황한'에서 유래했다.
While solving a problem, he faced **consternation** as the problem dealt with many complex concepts. (*n.*)

0026
vanquish ³
[|væŋkwɪʃ]

v. 완파하다   defeat, overcome
victory라는 뜻의 라틴어 vincere에서 유래했다.
We'd have to **vanquish** the demon first. (*v.*)

0027
dissent ⁶
[disént]

n. 반대, 반대하다   disorder and disagreement
dis(not)와 sent(feel)가 이 합쳐져 not feel the same way, 즉 '반대의견'이란 뜻이다.
The king and his advisor **dissented** at first, but eventually they reached an agreement. (*v.*)

0028
pedestal ²
[|pedɪstl]

n. 받침대   a base or foundation
pie "foot" + di "of" + stallo "stall, place, seat". 즉 어떤 물건이나 장소의 하부, 아랫부분을 가리킨다.
I replaced the vase carefully on its **pedestal**. (*n.*)

0029
elicit ⁷
[i|lɪsɪt]

v. 끌어내다   withdraw; cause to be released
집이 깨끗하지 않으면 벼룩(lice)이 나올(elicit) 수도 있다.
Daniel tried to **elicit** a smile from his gloomy girlfriend by saying that she was very pretty today. (*v.*)

0030
abashed ¹
[əbǽʃt]

a. 창피한, 겸연쩍은   shy; embarrassed
얼굴이 bashed(강타당한)되면 창피하고 부끄럽다.
She stood to sing, but was **abashed** by the large crowd. (*adj.*)

0031
clutch [klʌtʃ]

v. 움켜쥐다; 움켜짐   hold tightly
자동차의 clutch는 원래 두 장의 판이 서로 꽉 움켜잡는 장치를 말한다.
A drowning man will **clutch** at a straw. (v.)

0032
appropriately [ə|proʊpriətli]

adv. 적당하게, 알맞게   suitably or probably in given circumstances
ad(to)+proper(own)이 합쳐져 "~ 자기 것으로 만드는"이란 뜻으로 "적절한, 어울리는"이라는 뜻이다.
He was dressed **appropriately** for the time of year. (ad.)

0033
reap [riːp]

v. 수확하다   gather or take
농사와 관련된 단어로 동식물을 모으다는 의미에서 '파생', 즉 '어떤 일의 결과를 거두다'는 뜻이다.
If you plant acts of kindness in many parts of your life, you will **reap** much joy from them later. (v.)

0034
connoisseur [kànəsə́ːr]

n. 전문가   expert
라틴어 gno는 알다는 뜻이다. con(-com함께) + noiss(=gno=know) + eur(=er사람) 전문가는 여러 가지를 함께 아는 사람이다.
The museum requested the most famous **connoisseur** to give a lecture about their paintings. (n.)

0035
prudent [prúːdnt]

a. 신중한, 조심성 있는   wise or judicious in practical affairs
provdent 의 축약형. 즉, prudent = pru < pre(전에) + dent < vdent (vd(see) + ent) : "미리 앞을 내다보는" → 〈사람, 행위 등이〉신중한, 분별있는, 현명한 → 빈틈없는, 타산적인(self-interested) → 절약하는
It's not a **prudent** course of action. (adj.)

0036
acquiescence [|ækwi|esns]

n. 묵인   to be in agreement; consent; submission
ac(=to) + quiesc(=quiet) + ent, 즉 '조용하게 따르는'의 뜻으로 나누어서 외우자.
There was general **acquiescence** in the UN sanctions. (n.)

0037
confine [kən|faɪn]

v. 국한시키다   enclose with bounds; limit or restrict
confine 되면 fine하지 않다.
Don't use your credit card for every single thing; instead, **confine** its use to emergencies only. (v.)

Note :

Episode 2

MATCHING Quiz

1. baffle
2. witty
3. anticipated
4. onslaught
5. alignment
6. pelt
7. grunt
8. consternation
9. vanquish
10. dissent
11. pedestal
12. elicit
13. abashed
14. clutch
15. appropriately
16. reap
17. connoisseur
18. prudent
19. acquiescence
20. confine

A. gather or take
B. an onset, assault, or attack
C. comic
D. panic; confused worry
E. expected or predicted
F. .shy; embarrassed
G. suitable or probable in given circumstances
H. wise or judicious in practical affairs
I. enclose with bounds; limit or restrict
J. the correct relationship of things with each other
K. defeat, overcome
L. a base or foundation
M. running very fast
N. disorder and disagreement
O. a deep guttural sound (as a pig does)
P. confuse
Q. held tightly
R. withdraw; cause to be released
S. expert
T. to be in agreement; consent; submission

1-P, 2-C, 3-E, 4-B, 5-I, 6-M, 7-O, 8-D, 9-K, 10-N, 11-L, 12-R, 13-F, 14-Q, 15-G, 16-A, 17-S, 18-H, 19-T, 20-I

더 많은 문제를 풀고자 한다면 www.quizlet.com에서 'paul academy seoul' class를 검색

Episode 03

De-Composition

Jake had hardly heard the first teacher's breathless lecture, and the stack of notes, vocabulary lists, and brand new textbooks sat fatly on his desk like a fat white insect. Just one class and he felt as though he had learned more than enough for one summer. He reached for his pocket to check the time on his phone and felt another feeling of sadness. No more music in my life, he **lamented**. No more music forever. He rolled his eyes even at himself and drummed his hands a little on his desk with bored yawns. Ashley coughed, looked at Jake's hands, then up at him. He stopped drumming.

When the teacher was in the room, it allowed the newly-**forged** class to sit in each other's company without awkwardness for a while, but now that he was gone, teenage insecurities and passions took center stage. Boys began looking at girls and the girls pretended not to notice. **Furtive** glances crossed through the narrow room before students shamefully turned their eyes away to avoid being seen. There was much more fidgeting, coughing, and chair sliding than one would normally expect from a five minute break.

Jake was tempted to start up the conversation with Ashley for a third time, but was again **abruptly** cut off when the loud sound of the door **decreed** a new arrival.

The teacher entered as the last one had, with an **earnest** grin on his face and **myriad** papers to further worsen the students' evenings. He marched up to the board and began speaking as he walked.

"Morning everyone. Please take your seats again. It's time…" he left here an **ominous** pause, even though he was smiling, "For the essay section!"

The groans he had expected from this announcement were **emitted** by a few of the returning students, who seemed familiar with this playful tone. The new students merely looked at one another with **apprehension**. Jake feared this class most of all, especially if the

---

038 lament [7]
v. 한탄하다
mourn; regret

039 forged [10]
a. 구축된
to be formed or made

040 furtive [5]
a. 은밀한
secretive

041 abruptly [3]
adv. 갑자기
suddenly

042 decree [2]
v. 선언하다
command, ordain

043 earnest [4]
a. 성실한
showing sincerity or serious dedication

044 myriad [5]
a. 무수히 많은
abundant, a very large number of

045 ominous [8]
a. 불길한
having bad signs for the future; threatening

046 emit [3]
v. 내다, 내뿜다
send-out; release

047 apprehension [4]
n. 우려, 불안
nervousness; trepidation

048 quintessential [7]
a. 정수의, 본질적인
typical, classic

049 delineate [3]
v. 기술/설명하다
outline, describe

050 stupefied [9]
a. 얼이 빠진
to be put into a state of little or no sensibility

051 pupil [7]
n. 학생
student, the children who go to school

052 convoluted [2]
a. 대단히 난해한
complex and confusing

053 vernacular [2]
n. 토착어, 방언
language used by a particular or specialized group

054 fathom [7]
v. 헤아리다, 가늠하다
understand; grasp the meaning

teacher seemed to be so playfully horrible, taking pleasure in their difficulty with the material.

"Now, I know some of you know me, and for that I'm very sorry," he continued, writing his name on the board. "For the rest, my name is Greg and I'll be teaching this section for the summer. So, the essay…" he turned and looked out across the room.

"First of all, it's not as bad as you think. It follows a **quintessential** pattern, and I've give you all a comprehensive packet which **delineates** everything you need to know. Today we are going to talk about exactly what the essay graders are looking for. So, if you would turn to page one…"

He spoke almost without a break, letting his words wash over his **stupefied pupils** like a wave of **convoluted** text and confusing concepts. Jake kept underlining words and phrases in the packet, but they seemed like islands of ink in a vast sea of **vernacular** which he knew he would never quite **fathom**. To his right, Ashley nodded enthusiastically every few seconds, and smiled unironically at the teacher's jokes.

Vocabulary

0038
lament [7]
[ləˈment]

v. 한탄하다 mourn; regret
weep, mourn이라는 뜻의 라틴어 lamentari에서 온 단어.
Ken began to **lament** the death of his only son. (*v.*)

0039
forged [10]
[fɔːrdʒɪd]

a. 구축된 to be formed or made
뭔가 만들려면 force가 필요하지? forge가 바로 그 force에서 온 말이다.
There was a move to **forge** new links between management and workers. (*v.*)

0040
furtive [5]
[ˈfɜːrtɪv]

a. 은밀한, 몰래 하는 secretive; stealthy or sly, like the actions of a thief
fur(thief) + tive에서 유래한 말로, "도둑과 같은"이라는 뜻
He did something unseen and **furtive**. (*adj.*)

0041
abruptly [3]
[əˈbrʌptli]

adv. 갑자기 suddenly
ab (="off") + rumpere (="break")
The cliff recedes **abruptly** from its base upward. (*ad.*)

0042
decree [2]
[dɪˈkriː]

v. 선언하다, 명령 command, ordain; ruling
It's a decree to get a degree in Korea. 한국에서는 대학 졸업증을 따는 것이 의무에 가깝다.
The people didn't like the king's **decree** to raise taxes, but there was nothing they could do about it. (*n.*)

0043
earnest [4]
[ˈɜːrnɪst]

a. 성실한 showing sincerity or serious dedication
성실한(earnest) 사람은 너의 믿음을 얻고 싶어한다(earn your trust).
When you love someone, tell her your **earnest** feelings. (*adj.*)

0044
myriad [5]
[ˈmɪriəd]

a. 무수히 많은; 무수함 abundant, a very large number of; a vast indefinite number of
myriad는 그리스어로 '일만'이란 뜻이며 '무수한'을 나타낸다.
Parents face **myriad** problems raising their children. (*adj.*)

0045
ominous [8]
[άmənəs]

a. 불길한, 험악한   having bad signs for the future; threatening
'불길한 예고'를 뜻하는 'omen'에서 온 말이다.
The number 13 is considered **ominous** in the Western world. (*adj.*)

0046
emit [3]
[iˈmɪt]

v. 내다, 내뿜다   send-out; release
ex− (="out") + mittere (="to send") : 속에 있는 것이 '밖으로 나오는' 것이다.
When fire burns, it **emits** both light and heat. (*v.*)

0047
apprehension [4]
[ˌæprɪˈhenʃn]

n. 우려, 불안   nervousness; trepidation
apprehend는 '경찰에 체포되다'. 경찰에 체포될까봐 불안한 거지.
I noticed the look of **apprehension** on her face. (*n.*)

0048
quintessential [7]
[kwɪntəˈsénʃəl]

a. 정수의, 본질적인   typical, classic, essential essence of something
essential의 queen이라고 생각해 보면 이해하기 쉽다.
His work embodies the **quintessential** Korean art. (*adj.*)

0049
delineate [3]
[dɪˈlɪnièɪt]

v. 기술/설명하다, 묘사하다   outline, to describe
line 위에 정렬하다 (lay out in a line)라는 뜻으로 직역하면 '묘사하다'라는 뜻을 쉽게 유추할 수 있다.
If you clearly **delineate** the tasks, your kids will know what to do. (*v.*)

0050
stupefied [9]
[ˈstuːpɪfaɪd]

a. 얼이 빠진   to be put into a state of little or no sensibility
stupid하게 만드는 것이니까 '얼이 빠진, 정신이 나간'의 뜻이다.
It's the double standard that is so **stupefying**. (*adj.*)

0051
pupil [7]
[ˈpjuːpl]

n. 학생   student, the children who go to school
'orphan child'라는 뜻의 라틴어 pupillus에서 온 단어로, 'disciple, student'로 뜻이 확대되었다.
Jesse is a **pupil** in the high school. (*n.*)

0052
convoluted [2]

[|kɑ:nvəlu:tɪd]

a. **대단히 난해한, 복잡한**   complex and confusing; intricate
con(together) + volu ⟨ volve(roll, 굴리다) + ted : "함께 구르는" → 둘둘 감긴 → 나선상의 → 복잡한, 뒤얽힌
A lot of people don't understand old literature because it contains **convoluted** sentences. (*adj.*)

0053
vernacular [2]

[vərnækjulər]

n. **토착어, 방언**   dialect that is most widely spoken by ordinary people in a region
verna는 라틴어의 전신인 고대 Etruria 말에서 'native, home-born slave'를 뜻하는 말이었다.
They study the history of different forms of **vernacular** in North America. (*n.*)

0054
fathom [7]

[|fæðəm]

v. **헤아리다, 가늠하다**   understand; grasp the meaning
고대 영어에서는 'length of the outstretched arm'을 뜻했다. 팔을 뻗어 보면 길이를 가늠할 수 있다.
It is hard to **fathom** the pain felt at the death of a child. (*v.*)

Episode 3

MATCHING Quiz

1. lament	A. having bad signs for the future; threatening
2. forged	B. send-out; release
3. furtive	C. showing sincerity or serious dedication
4. abruptly	D. command, ordain
5. decree	E. mourn; regret
6. earnest	F. secretive
7. myriad	G. to be formed or made
8. ominous	H. outline, describe
9. emit	I. complex and confusing
10. apprehension	J. abundant, a very large number of
11. quintessential	K. suddenly
12. delineate	L. language used by a particular or specialized group
13. stupefied	M. typical, classic
14. pupil	N. nervousness; trepidation
15. convoluted	O. understand; grasp the meaning
16. vernacular	P. to be put into a state of little or no sensibility
17. fathom	Q. student, the children who go to school

1-E, 2-G, 3-F, 4-K, 5-D, 6-C, 7-J, 8-A, 9-B, 10-N, 11-M, 12-H, 13-P, 14-Q, 15-I, 16-L, 17-O

더 많은 문제를 풀고자 한다면 www.quizlet.com에서 'paul academy seoul' class를 검색

Episode 04 — TJ's Arrival

055 debased ³
a. 품질이 저하된
reduced in quality or value

056 cardinal ²
a. 가장 중요한
central, important, key

057 demagogue ²
n. 선동 정치가, 리더
a person, especially an orator or political leader

058 dominant ⁶
a. 우세한
main, superior, powerful

059 assorted ²
a. 여러 가지 종류의
various

060 meander ²
v. 이리저리 거닐다
walk (usually slowly)

061 faction ²
n. 파벌, 파당
a group or clique within a larger group

062 impulsively ⁶
adv. 충동적으로
instinctively, without thought

After the other three classes had finished, a flood of students streamed out of the building onto the street, stretching their legs on the way, all of them taking deep lungfuls of sweet, **debased** street air as they smiled up into the sunshine. Jake walked out in the middle of the pack, suddenly aware of how hungry he was. How long had it been since that roll of bread this morning? At least a thousand years.

As with any large group of people without a primary leader, or a **cardinal demagogue** as the SAT might say, the students suddenly stopped on the steps since no one knew quite what to do or where to go, and so gathered around the doorway in groups of three or four like sheep who don't want to stray off alone from the **dominant** pack. To make matters worse, the street itself, so empty of life in the morning, was now full of activity as office workers, students from a nearby high school, and other **assorted** members of the neighborhood now filled the sidewalks and **meandered** in **faction**s of four or five, walking, talking, laughing or doing all at once. **Impulsively**, Jake moved nearer the group to avoid being too noticeable and was thinking of just eating something from the convenience store at his desk when he was tapped on the shoulder.

He turned to see another boy his same age who had just put a cigarette into his mouth, despite looking like he was twelve years old. He had a wide nose and chubby round cheeks. The boy put a cigarette into his mouth and smiled crookedly as he extended a hand to Jake for introduction. Jake looked at him with a weary expression suggesting he'd just been through a war, rather than a few hours of fairly harmless education. The other boy's smile didn't move.

"You're Jake aren't you?" the boy asked

"Yes," Jake replied, shaking the boy's hand as though it might explode if handled too roughly. "Who are you?"

Questions Jake wanted to ask but did not: *how do you know my name, what is going on here, why are you smiling so much?*

"TJ. Does your mother go to a book club near the park every Saturday?"

Jake, for the second time that day, had the feeling of being **interrogated** by a secret policeman. However, as he was an **intrinsically** honest person, he felt **impelled** to tell the truth.

"Yes."

"Oh that explains it," the boy said as he tried to flick the wheel on a plastic lighter. "Hey, how do you work this thing?"

Another boy came up and, swearing to himself, turned it properly and lit TJ's cigarette. This misbehavior, the low cement wall around them **adorned** with a messy graffiti, and the general atmosphere of secrecy and personal questions, combined to make Jake felt like he had wandered into a prison yard. It was quite clear after a few seconds of loud, coughing that TJ had not yet **inured** himself to the practice of smoking. Despite his comical lack of skill, the round-faced boy pulled his chin low and sucked in his cheeks, making his face look thinner and attempting to adopt the appearance of a **solemn** poet. Jake had never seen anyone try so hard to look serious and end up looking so ridiculous.

"Explains what?" He finally asked when he realized the other boy would not resume the conversation without some help.

"Hmm?" the boy said, trying unsuccessfully not to cough.

"What does it explain?"

"Oh right. Our mothers know each other, and my mom told me you'd be here. That we should be friends or that I should show you around. I dunno."

"Well how did you know it was me? There are like sixty students here."

"Well I asked quite a few, until one of them told me that you'd been in his class, and pointed me this way. I wouldn't have tried so hard

---

063 interrogate [2]
v. 심문하다
question very intensely

064 intrinsically [7]
adv. 본질적으로
naturally, fundamentally

065 impelled [4]
a. ~해야만 하는
compelled

066 adorned [5]
a. 꾸민, 장식된
to be made more attractive or beautiful

067 inure [2]
v. 익히다, 단련하다
accustom, habituate

068 solemn [8]
a. 근엄한
very serious

069 succinct [2]
a. 간단명료한, 간단한
concise, blunt

070 appraisal [3]
n. 평가
judgment of value

071 derisive [7]
a. 조롱하는
mocking, contemptuous
v. deride

072 prophesy [6]
v. 예언하다
predict, foretell, forecast

073 imperative [3]
a. 반드시 해야 하는
necessary, compulsory

074 alluring [5]
a. 매력적인
attractive, charming

075 courtier [2]
n. (왕을 보필하던) 조신
an attendant at a sovereign's court

except that my mother's expecting me to do this. Don't feel that we have to be friendly with each other or anything, but maybe I could help you anyway. I was here last summer. Let's go eat something."

Jake immediately was reminded of his mother's note and its concise **succinct** style. TJ spoke a lot, but he seemed to get to the point pretty quickly. He moved speedily too, turning as he finished speaking to gather a few other boys and then suddenly heading down the street as they all hurried to catch up. A few of the other lost sheep among the flock outside the doors followed behind as they went into the road.

Gesturing to the taco stand across the road as he walked, TJ said only "3 bucks, not terrible". Other establishments received equally brief **appraisals**. A small noodle shop was "so incredibly cheap you'd think they stole the food to sell it to you." The sandwich shop was for "idiots who don't eat much...but good coffee".

After a few more shops and a few more **derisive** evaluations, the boys reached a modern looking italian restaurant and without warning TJ turned sharply and entered the bright interior. The others seem to have **prophesied** this, and so turned in as well. Jake had not, however, and ran into one of the pack quite forcefully, causing the slightly older boy, who clearly felt it **imperative** to prove his power the lower ranks as often as possible, to swear angrily. Jake apologized and followed the others.

Once inside, TJ said "order the lunch special. You won't be disappointed," and then leaned back in his chair, nearly falling over backwards. It was hard to understand why the others associated with him, Jake thought. He's just a loser. Nonetheless, the food soon arrived and the boys hastily started talking of this matter and that, girls that were particularly **alluring** that year, games they had discovered, hobbies they had enjoyed, and love affairs that existed only in their minds or they had made up entirely.

"Oh my God, this girl was so in love with me," the older boy said, "but her face...let's just say she was more like this guy" — gesturing to Jake — "than any woman." He laughed too loudly, and a few of the other boys joined in as if they were his **courtiers**. Jake tried to laugh politely, but looking around the table, he got the feeling he was in some smoky men's club, where whiskey was served in large glasses and everyone smoked cigars. He was being polite and making friends, as his mother had instructed, but it seemed as though he had aged 30 years in the last 20 minutes.

Looking over at TJ, however, he noticed that the loser was not laughing much either, just looking out the window onto the passing walkers, looking as bored and tired as they did. After the laughter slowed to a stop, the older boy turned to the **pensive**, chubby-cheeked street gazer..

"So, TJ," the other boy began. "What's your uncle been doing lately?"

TJ's lonely thinking stopped at once, and he turned round to the boy who'd asked the question, his eyes shining for an instant, as if to say *Finally!*

"I mean, is he making any movies these days?"

The loser smiled and took a deep breath as though thinking about some pretty big issue. Jake knew now why the other boys bothered to hang out with him.

076 **pensive** [6]
a. 수심 어린
deep in thought

Vocabulary

0055
debased ³
[dɪˈbeɪst]

a. 품질이 저하된   reduced in quality or value
base는 '맨 아랫부분'을 지칭하는 단어로, de(=of, from)를 붙이면 '저하시키다, 품질을 떨어뜨리다'는 뜻이 된다.
Sport is being **debased** by commercial sponsorship. (*v.*)

0056
cardinal ²
[káːrdənl]

a. 가장 중요한, 주요한, 기본적인   central, important, key, of prime or special importance
Pierre Cardin(피엘 카르뎅)은 디자인 계통에서 가장 '중요한' 사람이었지.
The **cardinal** rule in the school is to obey the teachers. (*adj.*)

0057
demagogue ²
[déməgɑ̀g]

n. 선동 정치가, 리더   a person, especially an orator or political leader; one who tries to win people's support by appealing to their emotions
dem < demo(people) + agogue(leader) : "사람들을 이끄는 사람" → 선동 정치가, 민중 지도자
Hitler was a successful **demagogue** in the sense that he made thousands of people believe and follow him. (*n.*)

0058
dominant ⁶
[dámənənt]

a. 우세한, 유력한, 우성 유전자   main, superior, powerful; the one in a pair of alleles that masks the effect of the other when both are present in the same cell or organism
라틴어 domin이 '주인이 되어 다스리다'의 뜻이라는데서 파생된 단어이다.
Don's **dominant** hand is his left hand, so he almost never uses his right hand. (*adj.*)

0059
assorted ²
[əsɔ́ːrtəd]

a. 여러 가지 종류의   various
sort of 라는 표현에서 sort가 kind처럼 사용되지? 그래서 assign의 as랑 sort(종류)가 합쳐진 것이라고 생각하자. 종류를 주는 것이니까 분류하다라는 뜻.
An economy pack containing 150 **assorted** screws (*adj.*)

0060
meander ²
[miˈændə(r)]

v. 이리저리 거닐다; 목적없이 떠돌다   walk (usually slowly); to wander aimlessly
a MEan person wANDERs 라는 문장을 외우자!
The film was boring because the plot seemed to **meander** along with no resolution. (v.)

0061
faction ²
[fækʃən]

n. 파벌, 파당, 무리   a group or clique within a larger group
fraction처럼 더 큰 그룹의 일부
One **faction** was strongly opposed to the rest of the group. (n.)

0062
impulsively ⁶
[ɪmˈpʌlsɪvli]

adv. 충동적으로   instinctively, without thought
impulse의 뜻이 '갑작스러운 충동'이니까 그것에서 파생된 단어라고 외우면 된다.
The marriage was an **impulsive** decision. (adj.)

0063
interrogate ²
[ɪnˈterəgeɪt]

v. 심문하다   question very intensely
inter(='between') + rogare(='ask')
He was **interrogated** by the police for over 12 hours. (v.)

0064
intrinsically ⁷
[ɪnˈtrɪnsɪkli;ɪnˈtrɪnzɪkli]

adv. 본질적으로   naturally, fundamentally
twin(쌍둥이들)은 intrinsic하게 닮았다.
Humans are **intrinsically** social and are not able to live by themselves. (adj.)

0065
impelled ⁴
[ɪmˈpeld]

a. ~해야만 하는   compelled
impala(임팔라)는 살기 위해 뛰어야만 한다.
There are various reasons that **impel** me to that conclusion. (v.)

0066
adorned ⁵
[əˈdɔːrn]

a. 꾸민, 장식된   to be made more attractive or beautiful
장식이나 장신구를 ornament라고 하지? ornament를 add한다고 생각하면 외우기 쉽다.
His watercolor designs **adorn** a wide range of books. (v.)

0067
inure ² [injúər]

v. 익히다, 단련하다　accustom, habituate to accustom to hardship, difficulty, pain, etc
in + use. 계속 써서 익히는, 단련하는 것이라고 외우자.
Inured to violence, he wasn't afraid of the gangs who threatened him. (*adj.*)

0068
solemn ⁸ [|sɑ:ləm]

a. 근엄한　very serious
church ceremony는 serious하고 solemn하다.
The funeral was **solemnly** conducted by the priest. (*adv.*)

0069
succinct ² [sək|sɪŋkt]

a. 간단명료한, 간단한　concise, blunt
single을 연상하면 하나 또는 단순함을 생각할 수 있다.
Keep your answers as **succinct** as possible. (*adj.*)

0070
appraisal ³ [ə|preɪzl]

n. 평가　judgment of value
ap(='to') + praise(='price') 즉 '값을 매겨보는' 것을 뜻한다.
He had read many detailed critical **appraisals** of her work. (*n.*)

0071
derisive ⁷ [dɪ|raɪsɪv]

a. 조롱하는　mocking, contemptuous
de('=down') + ridere(='ridicule') 이니까 '깔보는' 것을 말한다.
His **derisive** way of talking gets on my nerve. (*adj.*)

0072
prophesy ⁶ [|prɑ:fəsaɪ]

v. 예언하다　predict, foretell, forecast
pro('=before') + phesy('=talk')
She **prophesied** that she would win a gold medal. (*v.*)

0073
imperative ³ [impérətiv]

a. 반드시 해야 하는　necessary, compulsory, absolutely required
in(in)+pera(command) 라고 나누어서 연상하면 '명령적인' 이라는 뜻을 가지고 있다는 것을 알 수 있다
The soldier could not rebel against his general's **imperative** orders. (*adj.*)

0074
alluring [əlúəriŋ]

a. 매력적인, 유인하는, 마음을 홀리는   very attractive, charming
lure가 '꾀다, 유혹하다'는 뜻이다.
You must look demure, but at the same time **alluring**. (*adj.*)

0075
courtier [kɔ́ːrtiər]

n. (왕을 보필하던) 조신   an attendant at a sovereign's court
court라는 단어가 있으므로 court에 있는 신하들이라고 추론이 가능하다.
The king was surrounded by his **courtiers**. (*n.*)

0076
pensive [ǁpensɪv]

a. 수심 어린   deep in thought
pension(연금)이 적어 깊이 수심에 빠진(pensive) 노인이 있다고 생각하자.
On Monday on the flight out he sat alone and **pensive**. (*adj.*)

Episode 4

MATCHING Quiz

1. debased	A. predict, foretell, forecast
2. cardinal	B. naturally, fundamentally
3. demagogue	C. very serious
4. dominant	D. a group or clique within a larger group
5. assorted	E. to be made more attractive or beautiful
6. meander	F. question very intensely
7. faction	G. reduced in quality or value
8. impulsively	H. mocking, contemptuous
9. interrogate	I. walk (usually slowly)
10. intrinsically	J. a person, especially an orator or political leader
11. impelled	K. instinctively, without thought
12. adorned	L. attractive, charming
13. inure	M. concise, blunt
14. solemn	N. accustom, habituate
15. succinct	O. compelled
16. appraisal	P. main, superior, powerful
17. derisive	Q. necessary, compulsory
18. prophesy	R. judgment of value
19. imperative	S. central, important, key
20. alluring	T. various

1-G, 2-S, 3-J, 4-P, 5-T, 6-I, 7-D, 8-K, 9-F, 10-B, 11-O, 12-E, 13-N, 14-C, 15-M, 16-R, 17-H, 18-A, 19-Q, 20-L.

더 많은 문제를 풀고자 한다면 www.quizlet.com에서 'paul academy seoul' class를 검색

Episode 05

The Actor, My Uncle

077 venerated [6]
a. 존경 받는, 추앙 받는
respected, prestigious

078 improbable [4]
a. 있을 것 같지 않은
unlikely to be true or to happen

079 legitimate [7]
a. 합법적인
authentic

080 opulent [2]
a. 호화로운
fancy; well-decorated

081 incongruous [3]
a. 어울리지 않는
not matching or fitting in

082 fallacious [5]
a. 잘못된
false; untrue

083 cerebral [2]
a. 뇌의
brainy; scholarly, smart

084 garish [2]
a. 야한, 화려한
decorated in a tasteless, cheap way; overly showy

"Yes, it's true," TJ started to say as they left the restaurant. "You recognize the name, anyway, don't you?"

Jake admitted he had, but the still had a hard time believing it. After all, how often does one meet someone related to such a **venerated** figure? And while studying for the SAT, no less?

"I know it seems **improbable**, but he's more of a family friend than a **legitimate** uncle. He knew my father from university and he keeps in touch from time to time. Enough to give me a few stories to tell. He gave me this, for instance." He shook his wrist and a massive, **opulent** watch fell over his hand, almost leaving his arm completely. As with everything else TJ presented to the world, it was **incongruous** with his face and mannerisms, which were so childlike it was hard to believe he was old enough to study the SAT at all.

"Nice," said Jake.

"Did you see his last movie?"

"Yes," Jake lied. He was thinking about getting back without being late. Lunch had gone on for such a long time, with the boys trying a bit too hard to pretend about their school-year activities. Too many falsehoods about girls and **fallacious** drinks they had had and, finally, this supposed actor. Why didn't the boys simply ask TJ for an autograph and be done with it? He didn't understand why people got so worked up. Jake thought about his own uncle, a **cerebral** older man who had had the bad luck of having been his father's older brother, but who had introduced him to so much music and literature he treasured far more than any **garish** watch. He looked over at the watch to see its minute hand slip up to the top of the dial. It was 2 o'clock on his first day and he wasn't back in class.

"Maybe we should hurry," he said quickly.

A few of the other boys chuckled.

"You're not going to the afternoon session, are you?" one of them asked with disbelief.

"Well, aren't you guys?"

Another of them swore and the others laughed. They gestured to the singing room across the street. That's where they'd decided to spend their afternoon.

TJ smiled apologetically.

"I'll walk back with you. See you guys in a bit," he called out to the other impassive faces as they sucked on their cigarettes.

They walked along the emptier street — the other restaurant **patrons** having returned to their **arduous** tasks in the **ubiquitous** office blocks and others having presumably resumed their studies. Jake wondered about his new acquaintances, and how much older they seemed. Was this what maturity **purported**? He tried to imagine himself in their shoes, dressed in the garb of the young gangster, **callously** cursing insults at other boys and **blatantly** ignoring his studies. Somehow the image wouldn't come.

"They're nice guys, really," TJ said, almost trying to give himself comfort as much as persuade his new friend.

"I'm sure they are. But why don't you study in the afternoon?"

TJ looked uncomfortable.

"Can't you join me just for today?" Jake suggested nicely, noticing his **companion**'s obvious lack of enthusiasm for **collaborating** with the outlaws. "I don't want to be a **misfit** in there. You could tell me a bit more about how I can persevere in this place."

The other boy's features brightened a little, but he tried hard to remain as uninterested as the other boys had pretended to be.

---

085 patron [14]
n. 고객; 후원자
customer; financial supporter

086 arduous [9]
a. 몹시 힘든, 고된
requiring great effort; taxing

087 ubiquitous [12]
a. 어디에나 있는
occurring everywhere

088 purported [3]
a. ~라고 알려진
alleged, supposed

089 callous [4]
a. 냉담한
emotionally cold; unfeeling (often cruel)

090 blatant [6]
a. 노골적인, 뻔한
very obvious in an offensive or shameless way

091 companion [7]
n. 동반자, 동행
a person who is frequently in the company of another

092 collaborate [11]
v. 협력하다
work, one with another; cooperate

093 misfit [2]
n. 부적응자
a person who is suited to adjust to the circumstances

094 albeit ³
conj. 비록 ~일지라도
although, even though, despite

095 flustered ²
a. 갈팡질팡하는
confused and slightly annoyed

"OK, but just for today," he agreed.

They got up to the classroom at 2:10, and Pink Face was suitably annoyed.

"Where have you been? Smoking again?"

"No, ma'am," TJ responded. "Just a bit of fresh air to prepare our passionate young minds. Here," he took out a chocolate bar out of his back pocket, and held it out to her with two hands to show his respect. "Tribute!"

She laughed, **albeit** obviously a bit irked by their late arrival, taking the chocolate with a smile. "So you learned *one* of the vocabulary words for tomorrow?"

"I'm really a better student than you think," he replied with a wink. She immediately stopped smiling.

"If you came here to study, that's great, TJ. If you came to flirt, you can —" she was about to say something rude when one of the teachers looked in to ask a question about paperwork. "You can sit quietly," she finished.

TJ turned to his friend and gestured to two seats near the back, smiling playfully as the **flustered** TA walked back to the front of the classroom.

Vocabulary

0077

venerated [6]

[ˈvenəreɪtɪd]

a. 존경 받는, 추앙 받는   respected, prestigious
venus '아름다움'의 어원을 갖고 있는 단어로 '아름다움을 숭배/존경한다'는 뜻에서 파생되었다.
Accepted into the **venerated** Actors Studio, he began finding theater work in off-Broadway productions. (*adj.*)

0078

improbable [4]

[ɪmˈprɑːbəbl]

a. 있을 것 같지 않은   unlikely to be true or to happen
probable이 '있을 것 같은'이지? 그 반대니까 '있을 것 같지 않은'.
It seems **improbable** that the current situation will continue. (*adj.*)

0079

legitimate [7]

[lɪˈdʒɪtɪmət]

a. 합법적인   authentic; according to law, lawful
legal(합법적인) 또는 law(법)을 연상하자.
To get into this bar you need **legitimate** proof of your age, like your passport or driver's license. (*adj.*)

0080

opulent [2]

[ápjulənt]

a. 호화로운, 부유(풍부)한   fancy; well-decorated; wealthy
돈을 lent 빌려줄 수 있는것은 opulent한 사람들이다.
The **opulent** king wore opals on his fingers, his throat, his wrists, and even his toes. (*adj.*)

0081

incongruous [3]

[ɪnˈkɑːŋɡruəs]

a. 어울리지 않는   not matching or fitting in; inconsonant
con '같이' + gruo 그룹이 안(in) 되니까 '어울리지 않는'이라는 뜻이다.
The **incongruous** decoration of the room made it clear that he didn't like harmony and similarity at all. (*adj.*)

0082

fallacious [5]

[fəˈleɪʃəs]

a. 잘못된   false; untrue
false와 fallacy는 같은 부류.
Therefore the whole argument is **fallacious**. (*adj.*)

0083
cerebral [2]
[sərí:brəl]

a. 뇌의; 지적인   brainy; scholarly, smart, using intellect rather than intuition
의학 용어 'cerebellum' 과 'cerebrum'과 같은 어원을 가진다. "뇌를 잘 사용하는, 똑똑한" 이라는 의미이다.
The **cerebral** cortex is a key element inside a brain. (*adj.*)

0084
garish [2]
[|gerɪʃ]

a. 야한, 화려한   decorated in a tasteless, cheap way; overly showy
Gary는 항상 garish하게 옷을 입어.
I like it, but the green is a little **garish**. (*adj.*)

0085
patron [14]
[|peɪtrən]

n. 고객; 후원자   customer; financial supporter
해리포터의 마법주문 Expecto Patronum을 기억하지? 강력한 수호주문으로 수호자 Patronus를 만들어낸다.
I have agreed to become **patron** of the year. (*n.*)

0086
arduous [9]
[ɑ́:rdʒuəs]

a. 몹시 힘든, 고된; 끈기있는   taxing, requiring great effort; strenuous
hard-uous라고 외울 수 있다.
The lazy worker hated the **arduous** job, and wished he had an easier one. (*adj.*)

0087
ubiquitous [12]
[ju:bíkwətəs]

a. 어디에나 있는, 흔한   occurring everywhere, existing or being everywhere, especially at the same time
ubi는 where(어디)란 뜻이고, qui는 any(어떤), 즉 '어느 곳에서나 존재하는'이란 뜻이다.
USBs used to be **ubiquitous**, but now hardly anybody carries them around. (*adj.*)

0088
purported [3]
[pər|pɔ:rtɪd]

a. ~라고 알려진   alleged, supposed
purport는 '진술하다'는 뜻이니까 '~라고 진술된, 그렇게 말하는', 즉 '~라고 알려진'이라는 뜻이다.
Scientific research on its **purported** benefits has had conflicting results. (*adj.*)

0089
callous [4]
[kæləs]

a. 냉담한　emotionally cold; unfeeling (often cruel), indifferent
call + us로 외워서 우리에게 전화하면 반응이 냉담하다라고 외우자.
The **callous** man made a joke about the disabled child right in front of her parents on purpose. (*adj.*)

0090
blatant [6]
[bléitənt]

a. 노골적인, 뻔한, 시끄러운　very obvious in an offensive or shameless way; noisily
우리 안에서 수십 마리의 양들이 동시에 울어대며 시끄러운 소리를 낸다는 뜻에서 왔다.
"I didn't eat the cookies," he said, which was a **blatant** lie, as crumbs were falling from his lips. (*adj.*)

0091
companion [7]
[kəmˈpæniən]

n. 동반자, 동행　a person who is frequently in the company of another
com('=with') + panis(='bread') 같이 빵을 먹는 사이니까 '동반자, 동행하는 사람'
He was a good friend, a dependable **companion**. (*n.*)

0092
collaborate [11]
[kəˈlæbəreɪt]

v. 협력하다　work, one with another; cooperate
co '같이' + labor '일하다' 같이 일하니까 '협력한다'는 뜻.
We have **collaborated** on many projects over the years. (*v.*)

0093
bmisfit [2]
[ˈmɪsfɪt]

n. 부적응자　a person who is suited to adjust to the circumstances
fit해야 하는데 맞지 않으니까(mis) 적응하지 못한다는 뜻.
The problem was, that I was a social **misfit**. (*n.*)

0094
albeit [3]
[ɔːlˈbiːɪt]

conj. 비록 ~일지라도　although, even though, despite, even if
운동은 알 배일(albeit)지라도 열심히 해야 되는 것처럼 albeit은 '비록~할지라도'라는 뜻이다.
You have to eat something stay alive, **albeit** not hungry. (*conj.*)

0095
flustered [2]
[ˈflʌstərd]

a. 갈팡질팡하는　confused and slightly annoyed
flurry(광풍)가 몰아치면 이리저리 마구 흔들리고 flustered된다.
He was so **flustered** that he didn't know what to do. (*adj.*)

Note :

Episode 5

MATCHING Quiz

1. venerated
2. improbable
3. legitimate
4. opulent
5. incongruous
6. fallacious
7. cerebral
8. garish
9. patron
10. arduous
11. ubiquitous
12. purported
13. callous
14. blatant
15. companion
16. collaborate
17. misfit
18. albeit
19. flustered

A. decorated in a tasteless, cheap way; overly showy
B. brainy; scholarly, smart
C. fancy; well-decorated
D. unlikely to be true or to happen
E. false; untrue
F. a person who is frequently in the company of another
G. customer; financial supporter
H. a person who is suited to adjust to the circumstances
I. requiring great effort; taxing
J. alleged, supposed
K. work, one with another; cooperate
L. although, even though, despite
M. authentic
N. not matching or fitting in
O. occurring everywhere
P. confused and slightly annoyed
Q. emotionally cold; unfeeling (often cruel)
R. very obvious in an offensive or shameless way
S. respected, prestigious

1-S, 2-D, 3-M, 4-C, 5-N, 6-E, 7-B, 8-A, 9-G, 10-I, 11-O, 12-J, 13-Q, 14-R, 15-F, 16-K, 17-H, 18-L, 19-P

더 많은 문제를 풀고자 한다면 www.quizlet.com에서 'paul academy seoul' class를 검색

Episode 06

Enemy, Unexpected

The second morning had all the hallmarks of a beautiful day, and the clear blue light that filled the empty street reminded Jake of a morning during the vacation he'd taken a few weeks earlier. Then, too, he'd been walking lazily down a road listening to The Velvet Underground's "Sunday Morning" and thinking about nothing. Now, however, he was reminded by the turn toward the school and the typical crush of morning commuters that he wouldn't be ending the walk with a refreshing swim in the ocean, but rather would have to sit in a chair for four hours straight and try to stay awake while learning how to take a test. In all, however, the weather was so **tranquil** that nothing seemed at all **premonitory** about the rest of the day, which shows how wrong we usually are.

Sliding into his usual seat, he noticed the teddy bear was sitting in it the corner of Ashley's desk, but the usual occupant was nowhere to be seen. He imagined for some reason that she'd run away with a secret international organization of angry teens, travelling all over the globe and making **snide** remarks at world leaders, when suddenly he felt a presence standing over him and he looked up. It was Terry, the older boy from lunch.

"So, Jake, right?" he asked, as though he was **scrutinizing** his ID.

"Yeah."

"I never asked you — how do you know TJ?"

"Oh, our mothers met at book club apparently. He came up to me yesterday saying that his mother had told him to talk to me, make me feel welcome and all that." Jake realized he was speaking quickly, slightly nervously, and louder than usual to try to avoid the older boy's cold, **clinical** gaze.

"Hmm. Well he never showed up yesterday. He was going to pay for us to sing with him." He said the last part as though he were **conferring**

---

096 tranquil [11]
a. 고요한
quiet, peaceful

097 premonitory [2]
a. 예고의, 전조의
having bad signs for the future, ominous
n. premonition

098 snide [5]
a. (은근히) 헐뜯는
sarcastic, hateful

097 scrutinize [7]
v. 면밀히 조사하다
inspect, examine

100 clinical [5]
a. 냉담한
cold, unemotional

| 101 | **confer** [63]
v. 수여하다
bestow upon as a gift or honor

| 102 | **eminent** [7]
a. 유명한, 저명한
famous, distinguished

| 103 | **parsimonious** [3]
a. 인색한, 쩨쩨한
miserly, frugal, avaricious

| 104 | **conviction** [4]
n. 신념, 의견; 유죄선고
strong belief; a declaration that a person is guilty

| 105 | **dearth** [4]
n. 부족, 결핍
lack/shortage of something

| 106 | **salvage** [7]
v. 구조하다
save from destruction

| 107 | **relish** [4]
v. 즐기다
enjoy greatly

an honor on TJ, allowing him to pay for the honor of singing with such an **eminent** figure, rather than just being **parsimonious** and too stubborn to ask for money.

"Oh, yeah. I think he wanted to stay with me and show me around a bit more."

"Really?" he said without **conviction**, clearly not believing the excuse. "He's our friend, so why don't you just hang out with your classmates," Here he gestured to the empty chair and the teddy bear, "and let us hang out with him?" It was clear from his **dearth** of synonyms that the his vocabulary was as limited as his manners were poor.

"Ok..." Jake wasn't sure how to conclude the conversation without being killed. Just at that fortunate moment, right before he was sure the knife would enter his kidney, the door opened and Pink Face appeared, forcing Terry to retreat to wherever he went during the day (it turned out he wasn't a student at all but just hung out near the building in the afternoon). Jake had never noticed how angelic the TA looked until the moment she was **salvaging** his internal organs just in time.

"What's the matter with you?" Ashley asked as she came in a second later. "You look as if you've seen a ghost."

"Nothing. Maybe. Anyway I think I've made a *nemesis*," he said casually, knowing she'd **relish** his use of SAT vocabulary.

"Really? Such drama in the classroom on the second day? You *are* going to be popular."

Vocabulary

0096
tranquil [11]

[ˈtræŋkwɪl]

a. 고요한, 조용한   quiet, peaceful, calm
tran은 '통과하는'이란 뜻이고 qui는 quiet, 즉 '조용하다'라는 뜻이므로 '고요한'의 의미를 가진다.
It feels nice and calm to walk inside a **tranquil** forest. (*adj.*)

0097
premonitory [2]

[priˈmɑnətɔːri]

a. 예고의, 전조의   having bad signs for the future, ominous
n. premonition
pre(미리), monitory(권고의, 훈계의)에서 premonitory는 '나쁜 일이 일어날 것에 대해 미리 권고'를 준다는 뜻이다.
They pulled on in silence till Tess, without any **premonitory** symptoms, burst out crying. (*adj.*)

0098
snide [5]

[snaɪd]

a. (은근히) 헐뜯는   sarcastic, hateful
sneer하는 사람은 snide한 비평을 많이 하지.
You might say I'm a fine one to talk about **snide** remarks. (*adj.*)

0099
scrutinize [7]

[ˈskruːtənaɪz]

v. 면밀히 조사하다   inspect, examine, to look something closely
screwdriver를 써서 computer의 내부를 면밀히 뜯어보고 조사하는 것을 생각하자.
She leaned forward to **scrutinize** their faces. (*v.*)

0100
clinical [5]

[ˈklɪnɪkl]

a. 냉담한   cold, unemotional
clinic에서 주는 medical report는 warm하지 않고 cold한 말로 가득하다.
He watched her suffering with **clinical** detachment. (*adj.*)

0101
confer [63]

[kənˈfɔːr]

v. 수여하다, 주다   bestow upon as a gift or honor
conference에서 우리는 주는 것을 배운다.
The president **conferred** a medal to the general who won the most recent overseas battle. (*v.*)

0102
eminent [7]
[ˈemɪnənt]

a. 유명한, 저명한   famous, distinguished
Eminem은 힙합가수로 아주 유명하지? Eminem은 eminent한 가수라고 외우자.
That view is supported by **eminent** people. (*adj.*)

0103
parsimonious [3]
[pɑ̀ːrsəmóuniəs]

a. 인색한, 쩨쩨한, 지나치게 알뜰한   miserly, frugal, avaricious, stingy
pars는 '줄이다', moni는 '돈'을 뜻하는 어원으로 돈을 줄이다, 즉 '인색한'이란 뜻이다.
The **parsimonious** man never paid for his dinner to save every penny he could. (*adj.*)

0104
conviction [4]
[kənvíkʃən]

n. 신념, 의견, 확신; 유죄선고   strong belief; a declaration that a person is guilty
conviction은 평결이라고 알고 있지? 한 사람을 감옥에도 넣을 수 있는 것인데 거의 100% 확실해야겠지?
He had such **conviction** that he could fly, that he jumped off a cliff flapping his arms. (*n.*)

0105
dearth [4]
[dɜːrθ]

n. 부족, 결핍   lack/shortage of something, an inadequate supply
de가 "없다" 로 많이 쓰이니까 dearth도 부족하다는걸로 기억해.
Her **dearth** of time to relax made Cecilia very tired. (*n.*)

0106
salvage [7]
[ˈsælvɪdʒ]

v. (특히 조난, 화재 등에서) 구조하다   save from destruction, to rescue or save, especially from wreckage or ruin
salvage는 비슷하게 생긴 단어 'save'와 뜻이 같다.
A rescue party was sent to the forest to **salvage** any animals that might have survived the forest fire. (*n.*)

0107
relish [4]
[rélɪʃ]

v. 즐기다, 큰 기쁨   enjoy greatly, enjoyment (particularly of the taste of something)
release(자유, 해방)되면 relish하지.
He ate the delicious food with **relish**. (*n.*)

Note :

Episode 6

MATCHING
Quiz

1. tranquil
2. premonitory
3. snide
4. scrutinize
5. clinical
6. confer
7. eminent
8. parsimonious
9. conviction
10. dearth
11. salvage
12. relish

A. bestow upon as a gift or honor
B. strong belief; a declaration that a person is guilty
C. quiet, peaceful
D. enjoy greatly
E. save from destruction
F. having bad signs for the future, ominous
G. cold, unemotional
H. sarcastic, hateful
I. inspect, examine
J. famous, distinguished
K. miserly, frugal, avaricious
L. lack/shortage of something

1-C, 2-F, 3-H, 4-I, 5-G, 6-A, 7-J, 8-K, 9-B, 10-L, 11-E, 12-D

더 많은 문제를 풀고자 한다면 www.quizlet.com에서 'paul academy seoul' class를 검색

55

Episode 07

The Vocab Blues

108 invade [4]
v. 침입하다
enter and encroach, infiltrate
a. invasive

109 disintegrate [5]
v. 해체하다
break apart

110 verify [11]
v. 확인하다
confirm as to accuracy or truth by acceptable evidence

111 pedantic [6]
a. 지나치게 규칙을 찾는
overly-fixated on small academic details
n. pedant

112 serendipitous [4]
a. 시기 적절한
happening at a good time, opportune

113 elate [7]
v. 우쭐대다
make very happy or proud

114 subdued [9]
a. (기분이) 가라앉은
quiet; suppressed or limited

115 teeter [2]
v. 불안정하게 움직이다
move unsteadily; tremble

116 detonate [5]
v. 폭발하다
explode

Vocab class, the third hour of Jake's day, had come again, and he was in the mood for sleep (coincidence? no). The snack he'd purchased at 10 o'clock had now **invaded** his digestive system and sat in his stomach, **disintegrating** into life-sustaining chemicals with a sleep-inducing effect. Clearly, this would be a long hour.

The teacher, Matt, stepped to the front of the room. He was in his mid-twenties, shorter than some of the taller male students, and had **verified** over the past three days (it was Thursday) that he didn't appreciate stupid answers. Mildly **pedantic**, he insisted on accuracy, and was, incidentally, the essay teacher's brother. He began by pointing at the front row to Jana, a nervous yet studious girl who took the class very seriously.

"OK Jana," he began, seeming to enjoy the fear he had caused in his first victim. "Tell me what '**serendipitous**' means."

The girl looked at him blankly for a moment, and then seemed to draw the word from nowhere.

"Um..timely!" she almost shouted, **elated** at having remembered correctly.

"That's correct, and, I suppose you could say, *serendipitous* that you remembered it at the right time," he said in a **subdued**, self-satisfied tone. He allowed a few of the student-victims a moment of nervous laughter before continuing. "Now, Ashley, tell me what *fastidious* means."

After a long pause, Jake looked at his desk-mate with some nervousness. For the first three days of classes, she had always had the right answer. What was wrong this time? The girl's face had paled somewhat, and she looked to Jake like a broken computer, **teetering** slightly as if about to suddenly **detonate**.

"Come on, Ashley, give us an answer please. Otherwise you'll have to stand up." The man showed neither pity nor **aversion** toward the girl, but was **relentless** in his search for an answer. "Today would be fine, if you don't mind," he said cynically.

"Um…*fastidious*…" she smiled a bit at her fellow students, the usual tactic of those who don't know the right answer but want others' **approbation** for being **benighted** and foolish. Jake couldn't believe it…was she going to get it wrong?

"It means careless," she said finally.

"Um…no," he said finally, a tone of real disappointment in his voice. "You'll have to stand up, I'm afraid."

The girl stood, and swore under her breath. The teacher didn't hear her clearly, and asked her to **reiterate**, but she stared rudely ahead, refused to **paraphrase** what she said and remained silent for the remainder of the class.

Ashley was, as Jake knew, one of the smartest people in the academy, but he was still amazed that she was so **defiant**. Maybe, he thought, she wasn't really following the study **regimen** at all but rather depending on her **preexistent** knowledge to answer the questions? It seemed this strategy had worked for the first few classes, where the teachers rewarded her continually for her **penetrating** insights, but this was an unexpected development.

---

117 aversion [6]
n. 혐오, 적대감
dislike, antipathy

118 relentless [2]
a. 끈질긴; 가차 없는
incessant, without giving up

119 approbation [2]
n. 승인, 찬성
approval; praise

120 benighted [2]
a. 무지몽매한
intellectually or morally ignorant

121 reiterate [4]
v. 반복하다
state something again, repeat

122 paraphrase [3]
v. 달리 표현하다
restate or reword

123 defiant [9]
a. 반항하는
rejecting, refusing to follow

124 regimen [8]
n. (결과를 얻기 위한) 요법
a regulated course intended to restore health; a systematic plan

125 preexistent [2]
a. 이전부터 존재하는
existing beforehand

126 penetrating [11]
a. 날카로운; 꿰뚫어보는
sharp; discerning

Vocabulary

0108
invade [4]
[ɪnˈveɪd]

v. 침입하다, 침략하다   enter and encroach, infiltrate
     a. invasive
in + vadere(='go, walk') 남의 집 안으로 걸어들어가니까 '침입, 침략'하는 것이다.
Troops **invaded** on August 9th that year. (v.)

0109
disintegrate [5]
[dɪsˈɪntəɡreɪt]

v. 해체하다, 분해시키다; 허물다   break apart; to crumble
dis 'not' + integrate '통합하다'. 즉 분해하다라는 뜻.
The used car shop **disintegrated** the car and sold the parts to different people. (v.)

0110
verify [11]
[ˈverɪfaɪ]

v. 확인하다   confirm as to accuracy or truth by acceptable evidence
veritas(진리)가 맞는지 아닌지는 verify(확인)해 봐야 알겠지?
I need to **verify** your identity. (v.)

0111
pedantic [6]
[pɪˈdæntɪk]

a. 지나치게 규칙을 찾는   overly-fixated on small academic details   n. pedant
이탈리아어의 pedante('schoolmaster')에서 온 말로 '좀 짜증나게 규칙을 강조하는 사람'이라는 뜻이다.
His writing is too **pedantic** to understand. (adj.)

0112
serendipitous [4]
[ˌserənˈdɪpətəs]

a. 시기 적절한; 뜻밖의 발견을 하는 능력의(에 의해 얻은)   happening at a good time, opportune; found by accident
영국의 Horace가 쓴 동화 'three Princes of Serendip'에서 만든 단어. 그 왕자들은 '미처 몰랐던 것들을 항상 우연히, 지혜롭게 발견'하곤 했다.
It was a **serendipitous** move, she now realizes. (adj.)

0113
elate [7]
[ɪˈleɪt]

v. 우쭐대다   make very happy or proud
elevator를 생각하면서 외우자.
The youth council session was fantastic and the most **elating** part of the day. (adj.)

0114
subdued [9]
[səbdjúːd]

a. (기분이) 가라앉은, 은은한   quiet; suppressed or limited
강도를 줄일 때 쓰이는 단어이다.
Once the officer **subdued** the large man with a stun gun, he was finally able to apply the handcuffs. (*adj.*)

0115
teeter [2]
[|tiːtə(r)]

v. 불안정하게 움직이다   move unsteadily; tremble
teeth가 빠질 때가 되어서 teeter하다고 생각하자.
He **teetered** after him in her high-heeled shoes. (*v.*)

0116
detonate [5]
[|detəneɪt]

v. 폭발하다   explode
de(='down') + tonare(='thunder') 천둥소리는 폭발하는 것 같은 소리.
I have to **detonate** it manually. (*v.*)

0117
aversion [6]
[ə|vɜːrʒn]

n. 혐오, 적대감   dislike, antipathy
avert의 명사형으로 a(to)와 vert(turn)이 합쳐져 '얼굴이나 눈을 다른 곳으로 돌리다'는 의미를 갖고 있다.
I have an **aversion** to traveling during the heat of August. (*n.*)

0118
relentless [2]
[riléntlis]

a. 끈질긴; 가차 없는   persistent, incessant, without giving up
relent는 '포기하다'라는 뜻으로 끈질기게 포기하지 않는다는 의미이다.
He worked **relentlessly** on his chemistry test; even when his mother peeked in and asked if he wanted a snack, he shook his head no and just kept studying. (*ad.*)

0119
approbation [2]
[|æprə|beɪʃn]

n. 승인, 찬성   approval; praise
approve의 뜻인 approbare에서 만들어진 단어.
I am grateful for the **approbation** of the House. (*n.*)

0120
benighted [2]
[bɪ|naɪtɪd]

a. 무지몽매한   intellectually or morally ignorant
night는 어두워. dark하니까 보이지 않고, 알 수가 없어서 무지몽매해진다고 생각하자.
Last year, under the previous **benighted** Government, not one council house was built. (*adj.*)

0121
reiterate [4]
[ri|ɪtəreɪt]

v. 반복하다　　state something again, repeat
iterate가 '반복하다'는 뜻인데 re가 붙어서 더 강조되었다.
Let me **reiterate** that we are fully committed to this policy. (*v.*)

0122
paraphrase [3]
[|pærəfreɪz]

v. 달리 표현하다　　restate or reword
para(='beside') + phrazein(='to tell') 원래 있는 말 '옆에' 또 말하니까 '달리 표현한다'는 뜻.
The following is a **paraphrase** of what was said. (*n.*)

0123
defiant [9]
[dɪ|faɪənt]

a. 반항하는　　rejecting, refusing to follow
반항아(defiant)는 법을 따르지않고 부정하는 사람이겠지.
The **defiant** dog refused to fetch anything that his owner threw. (*adj.*)

0124
regimen [8]
[|redʒɪmən]

n. (결과를 얻기 위한) 요법; 식이 요법　　a regulated course intended to restore health; a systematic plan
좋은 'REGImen'을 위해서는 'VEGGIes'를 많이 먹어야 한다 라고 외우자.
The doctor recommended a healthy **regimen** of vegetables to lower my cholesterol level. (*n.*)

0125
preexistent [2]
[prìːigzístənt]

a. 이전부터 존재하는　　existing beforehand
exist가 '존재한다'는 뜻이니까 쉽게 외울 수 있다.
They reinforced a **preexistent** practice of the church. (*adj.*)

0126
penetrating [11]
[pénətrèitiŋ]

a. 날카로운; 꿰뚫어보는, 꿰뚫는　　sharp; discerning
원래는 '관통하다'라는 뜻으로 어떤것의 이면적인것만을 보는것이 아니라 내재된 것도 '관통해서' 볼 수 있는 능력을 말한다.
His **penetrating** insight allowed him to see through the lies and find the truth. (*adj.*)

Note :

Episode 7

MATCHING Quiz

1. invade
2. disintegrate
3. verify
4. pedantic
5. serendipitous
6. elate
7. subdued
8. teeter
9. detonate
10. aversion
11. relentless
12. approbation
13. benighted
14. reiterate
15. paraphrase
16. defiant
17. regimen
18. preexistent
19. penetrating

A. break apart
B. confirm as to accuracy or truth by acceptable evidence
C. happening at a good time, opportune
D. enter and encroach, infiltrate
E. move unsteadily; tremble
F. intellectually or morally ignorant
G. rejecting, refusing to follow
H. quiet; suppressed or limited
I. make very happy or proud
J. incessant, without giving up
K. explode
L. overly-fixated on small academic details
M. existing beforehand
N. sharp; discerning
O. approval; praise
P. state something again, repeat
Q. restate or reword
R. dislike, antipathy
S. a regulated course intended to restore health; a systematic plan

1-D, 2-A, 3-B, 4-L, 5-C, 6-I, 7-H, 8-E, 9-K, 10-R, 11-J, 12-O, 13-F, 14-P, 15-Q, 16-G, 17-S, 18-M, 19-N

더 많은 문제를 풀고자 한다면 www.quizlet.com에서 'paul academy seoul' class를 검색

Episode 08 — Reading Jail

127 versatile [3]
a. 다재다능한, 능숙한
skillful

128 perpetual [8]
a. 끊임없이 계속되는
continuing forever, everlasting

129 novice [3]
n. 초심자
beginner

130 lapse [3]
n. 실수
mistake

131 palpable [3]
a. 감지할 수 있는
able to be touched or physically felt; tangible

The reading teacher was very **versatile**, but Jake **perpetually** struggled with the often difficult nature of the passages she attempted to explain every day and this one was no exception. It concerned an experiment by Louis Pasteur.

"What have you done to label this passage?" the teacher began, her earnest expression betraying a certain degree of nervousness as she knew it was a difficult one. She was, it should be mentioned, a first time teacher, her **novice** status and the difficulty of the passage working together to fully confuse her students.

The wall of silence that greeted her question was painful. No one made eye contact. Students knew that to look directly at the teacher was to invite a conversation, and they weren't about to make that **lapse**.

"Jake, what did you write for the second paragraph?" she called suddenly.

Jake looked down at a blank space where his labeling should have gone. His embarrassed silence was almost **palpable**, like a smell in the air.

"Jake? Hello? Are you are awake? You look like you've been punched." She said playfully, as though his pain should be a source of pleasure.

"I'm awake," he announced, without matching her friendly tone.

"Good. So, tell us what you labeled for the second paragraph." Her insistent stare only increased his nervousness and made it even more difficult for him to find the right words. He stared down at the passage. It said "chance rewards the scientist who is prepared."

"Chance," he said tentatively, "rewards the scientist who is prepared." He looked at her intensely, begging her with his eyes to turn to someone else.

"Nice reading, Jake, but that doesn't count as an answer. We label the main idea of each paragraph, yes? Where is that information usually found?"

"In the middle of the paragraph?" Oh, man, he was really messing up.

"No. In the first sentence. Look at it please and tell me what you see."

He felt the eyes of every student in the room absorbing and **indicting** his stupidity. Even Ashley, who usually sat **obliviously** through this section (she didn't label passages, and saved her energy for arguing why her answer was not right when they talked about the questions) turned her attention on him.

"It's...his...plan," he announced finally, as though he had just completed a particularly **burdensome** task.

"Very good," she said. "Label that, then, Jake." She then turned her attention to another poor victim.

Although relieved, Jake was nonetheless **disconcerted** by the reading passages in general. He tried to label the passages, but the questions were so confusing. Sometimes he looked at the options of ABC and D and they *all* looked right. What was he to do? He usually just **culled** answers without careful consideration in those cases, since he knew the teacher would explain the answer anyway.

She got to the questions pretty soon thereafter, and Ashley immediately looked up, dropping the good-natured attitude she usually gave authority in favor of the stubborn one she adopted any time the correct answer clashed with her own.

"Number thirty-three," the teacher began, "is E." This, obviously, was not acceptable to Ashley.

"Um, why not C?" she began.

"Well, first of all C adds information to the passage." the **valiant** and

---

132 indicting [2]
a. 기소하는
accusing of a crime or wrongdoing

133 oblivious [10]
a. 의식하지 못하는
unmindful; unconscious; unaware

134 burdensome [4]
a. 아주 힘든
requiring great effort; arduous; taxing

135 disconcert [5]
v. 당혹스럽게 하다
disturb the self-possession of; perturb; frustrate

136 cull [2]
v. 고르다; 도태시키다
pick, choose

137 valiant [2]
a. 용감한
brave, courageous

138 omnipotent [2]
a. 전능한
almighty or infinite in power, as God

139 perverse [3]
a. 비뚤어진
willfully determined to go counter to what is expected

140 rake [2]
v. 샅샅이 뒤지다, 찾아내다
scour, scrape up

141 recalcitrant [2]
a. 저항하는; 다루기 힘든
resisting authority or control; stubborn, obstinate

omnipotent teacher began. Jake almost pitied her for questioning such a stubborn and **perverse** mind as Ashley's. "It never suggests that the *critics* question his Alps experiment. However, it does mention E in line thirty-six."

"But it's right here! It says — "

"I know what it says," the instructor said shortly. "The question asks what the critics said, so to find their views we have to go all the way back to line thirty-six. I'm sorry, but that's the way it works. You look at the question, **rake** the passage for keywords, and find a sentence which explains the answer. Usually it's easier than this question, but sometimes we have to go backwards and find something earlier in the passage."

"A swear word," was all Ashley said, under her breath.

"What was that?" the teacher asked, pretending not to have heard. "You have another question, Ashley?"

"No, not at all," came the **recalcitrant** response.

Jake looked down at the passage, still unsure of the teacher's explanation. He obviously had a lot to learn about reading passages.

Vocabulary

0127
versatile [ˈvɜːrsətl]

a. 다재다능한, 능숙한; 다목적의   skillful, capable of doing different things competently
vers−는 turning 이란 뜻으로 '여러 가지 방향으로 돌 수 있는, 여러 가지 일을 할 수 있는'이라는 의미이다.
A T-shirt is a **versatile** piece of clothing and can be worn with anything. (*adj.*)

0128
perpetual [pərpétʃuəl]

a. 끊임없이 계속되는, 영구한   continuing forever, everlasting
영화 설국열차에 나오는 것 같은 never-ending engine에서 유래된 단어이다.
Perpetual motion is impossible. (*adj.*)

0129
novice [ˈnɑːvɪs]

n. 초심자   beginner
nov− 는 new를 뜻하기 때문에 한 분야를 새로 접하는 사람을 말한다.
Although she was a political **novice**, she entered the House. (*n.*)

0130
lapse [læps]

n. 실수; (두 사건 사이의 시간적) 경과; 일탈, 탈선; 소멸되다   mistake; time gap between two incidents; an accidental or temporary decline or deviation from an expected or accepted condition or state; to be gone
lap + se 로 보자. lap(무릎)을 세게(se) 치는 것이니까 실수했을 때 하는 행동이다. 고로 lapse는 실수이다.
His small **lapse** in the last round led to his defeat in the match. (*n.*)

0131
palpable [ˈpælpəbl]

a. 감지할 수 있는   able to be touched or physically felt; tangible
palpus는 곤충의 '촉수'를 말하는데, palpus가 하는 일은 'touch, sense'이다.
The atmosphere of violence is **palpable** in other ways. (*adj.*)

0132
indicting [ɪnˈdaɪtɪŋ]

a. 기소하는   accusing of a crime or wrongdoing
'말하다'라는 의미를 가진 dict 에서 유래되었다.
A federal grand jury seated in San Francisco expired without **indicting** Barry Bonds on perjury charges. (*adj.*)

0133
oblivious [10]
[əblíviəs]

a. 의식하지 못하는   unmindful; unconscious; unaware
'잘 잊는'을 의미하는 라틴어 obliviosus에서 파생된 단어이다.
Oblivious to his surroundings, he fell into a hole. (*adj.*)

0134
burdensome [4]
[bə́:rdnsəm]

a. 아주 힘든, 부담스러운   requiring great effort, distressing; arduous; taxing
burden은 '짐'을 뜻하므로 짐처럼 부담스럽다는 의미이다.
Burt's job was too **burdensome** for him: he had to work twenty hours a day and never had time to rest. (*adj.*)

0135
disconcert [5]
[|dɪskən|sɜ:rt]

v. 당혹스럽게 하다   disturb the self-possession of; perturb; frustrate
콘서트(concert)가 당일날 취소(dis)되면 당황스럽겠지?
The confident woman was **disconcerted** by how well he knew her flaws. (*v.*)

0136
cull [2]
[kʌl]

v. 고르다; (특정 동물을 그 수를 제한하기 위해)도태시키다   pick, choose
colligere는 'gather together'란 뜻을 가진 라틴어로 collect나 cull의 어원이라고 할 수 있다.
Examples have been **culled** from around the world. (*v.*)

0137
valiant [2]
[væljənt]

a. 용감한, 영웅적인   brave, courageous; boldly courageous
bold와 valiant의 어원은 valdr- 로서 같은 말이다.
He mourned for his **valiant** men. (*adj.*)

0138
omnipotent [2]
[ɑ:m|nɪpətənt]

a. 전능한   almighty or infinite in power, as God
omni(='all') + potens(='powerful')
The Party is omniscient and **omnipotent**. (*adj.*)

0139
perverse [3]
[pər|vɜ:rs]

a. 비뚤어진   willfully determined to go counter to what is expected
'turned away, contrary, askew'라는 뜻의 라틴어 perversus에서 온 말이다.
It's a **perverse** effect of socialism. (*adj.*)

0140
rake [reɪk]

v. 샅샅이 뒤지다, 찾아내다   scour, scrape up

rake(갈퀴)로 밭을 갈 때에는 대충 하지 말고 샅샅이 뒤지듯 해야 한다고 생각하자.

That way I don't have to **rake** the yard more than once. (*v.*)

0141
recalcitrant [rikǽlsitrənt]

a. 저항[반항]하는; 다루기 힘든, 고집 센   resisting authority or control, not obedient or compliant; stubborn, obstinate

'calc'는 뼈를 더 튼튼하게 하는 calcium에 나오는 단어. 따라서, 자기의 주관이 '튼튼'해져 반항을 하게 되는 것을 말한다.

The more people tried to persuade her, the more **recalcitrant** she became. (*adj.*)

Episode 8

MATCHING Quiz

1. versatile	A. willfully determined to go counter to what is expected
2. perpetual	B. accusing of a crime or wrongdoing
3. novice	C. beginner
4. lapse	D. requiring great effort; arduous; taxing
5. palpable	E. mistake
6. indicting	F. resisting authority or control; stubborn, obstinate
7. oblivious	G. continuing forever, everlasting
8. burdensome	H. pick, choose
9. disconcert	I. brave, courageous
10. cull	J. almighty or infinite in power, as God
11. valiant	K. skillful
12. omnipotent	L. unmindful; unconscious; unaware
13. perverse	M. able to be touched or physically felt; tangible
14. rake	N. disturb the self-possession of; perturb; frustrate
15. recalcitrant	O. scour, scrape up

1-K, 2-G, 3-C, 4-E, 5-M, 6-B, 7-L, 8-D, 9-N, 10-H, 11-I, 12-J, 13-A, 14-O, 15-F

더 많은 문제를 풀고자 한다면 www.quizlet.com에서 'paul academy seoul' class를 검색

Episode 09
Some People Say the First Test is the Hardest

142 raiding [5]
a. 습격하는, 급습하는
suddenly assaulting or attacking

143 meticulousness [5]
n. 꼼꼼함
paying close attention to details

144 dissipate [5]
v. 낭비하다
spend or use wastefully

145 emancipation [7]
n. 해방
the act of being free from restraint, influence, or the like

146 poignant [4]
a. 가슴 아픈
causing great pain, agonizingly

147 inanimate [2]
a. 무생물의, 죽은
not alive, not moving (used of physical objects)

148 jumble [4]
n. 뒤죽박죽 뒤섞인 것
a mixed or disordered heap or mass

149 toil [3]
n. 노역, 고역
hard work

150 indispensable [2]
a. 필요한
necessary, basic, crucial

151 facet [2]
n. 측면
aspect, phase

Seven o'clock on Saturday morning came without warning, rudely interrupting Jake's peaceful dream of crossing a fantastic winter landscape home to **raiding** Vikings from whom he had to flee. For some reason, he always was being chased in his dreams these days.

The morning meal was prepared with his mother's usual **meticulousness**. There was French toast she had woken up early to grill, with fried eggs, sausage and orange juice. He wished he could **dissipate** his entire morning here, in the comforting cool of the kitchen, maybe watching some TV and chatting with his friends online. But Saturday was no longer a day of **emancipation** from the world. He had to accept that fact.

He remembered the test he'd taken the prior weekend. It was remarkable to even have received that 470 in reading. Now there was the whole question of *improvement*, the word that everyone, including his own mother, spent a **poignantly** long time discussing, as though he lived now not to enjoy life as a human, but rather to sit without feeling as an **inanimate** statistic, which would receive smiles or frowns depending on his relative size.

The subway on Saturday mornings is an odd **jumble** of people, some freshly-brushed for another day's **toil**, others clearly suffering the effects of a long night out. The rest were students pushing sleep dusts from their tired eyes, looking lost. As always (an **indispensable facet** of every subway car), there was an old woman with a child. Where they go, no one knows, but they rarely look happy.

A few minutes later, Jake found himself in the same large room, everyone settling into their seats as Pink Face and Pencil-Head (along with a few other TAs who had yet to earn any nicknames) stood at the front, looking agitated as they always did. Packets were distributed and numbers were drawn on the board, announcing the time **allotted** for each section. Jake tasted the orange juice from that morning, and felt the cool of the kitchen.

The time had started for the first section, and as nervous eyes started reading the essay question, pencils began dancing along pages, underlining words and writing down notes. Jake stared hard, but the passage still seemed **impenetrably** difficult.

What did it mean? he thought. He thought of what they had discussed in class the week before. What had it been? The thesis! he thought excitedly. Think of the **premise**.

Being original, he thought. That was like being something really good, right? He thought of the **propagandists** with their "original recipe" or "original flavor" slogans. So what did they mean? He looked at the girl next to him. She had already started her introduction and was writing **fervently**. His page was blank.

Then, with a moment of inspiration, he remembered some of the strategies they had discussed in class. He knew that the correct side of the **dichotomy** would always be the individual. And that being original could be like being **pioneering**, or creative. Ok, then.

So how does the essay start? "In this passage…" he wrote at the top of the page. In this passage the author argues that too much innovation is bad. Who would think that? Pink-Face for one, but he couldn't write that. Why would they think that new ways of thinking were bad? How did they make their argument. He thought of his mother, who wanted him to be financially successful like other people's children. She thought being original would be useless and unproductive, because people who are original don't **subordinate** themselves to society's rules. "It would be **anarchy**," she would say simply, "if everyone **contravened** the rules, there would be no law or order."

Thinking of his mother at the front of a church, dressed in a bishop's costume and holding her staff high over the worshippers, delivering a **homily** on the **lurking** dangers of individual thought, Jake began to write his first essay. The rest of the test passed like the dream, but with fewer Vikings.

---

[152] **allotted** [2]
a. 할당된, 정해진
divided

[153] **impenetrable** [5]
a. 들어갈 수 없는
unable to be penetrated; also used for anything which cannot be understood easily (abstruse)

[154] **premise** [6]
a. 전제, 주장
argument, assertion

[155] **propagandist** [16]
n. 선전원
a person who deliberately spread information, rumors, etc.
a. propagandizing

[156] **fervently** [2]
adv. 열렬하게
with great passion

[157] **dichotomy** [2]
n. 양분
a pair of opposites
a. dichotomous

[158] **pioneer** [8]
v. 개척하다
be the first person to open or prepare

[159] **subordinate** [8]
v. 경시하다
place in a lower rank

[160] **anarchy** [6]
n. 난장판, 무정부 상태
lawlessness, chaos

[161] **contravene** [3]
v. 위반하다
come or be in conflict with

[162] **homily** [2]
n. 설교, 훈계
a sermon, an admonitory discourse

[163] **lurking** [2]
a. 숨어 있는
existing unperceived or unsuspected

Vocabulary

0142
raiding [5]
[ˈreɪdɪŋ]

a. 습격하는, 급습하는　suddenly assaulting or attacking
Indiana Jones의 Raiders 시리즈를 기억하자. 무덤을 raide해서 보물을 훔쳐가는 사람이 raider이다.
Alcohol, an addictive drug that is **raiding** the minds of teens all over the world. (*adj.*)

0143
meticulousness [5]
[məˈtɪkjələsnɪs]

n. 꼼꼼함　paying close attention to details
meti '두려움', culous '가득 찬' 이라는 뜻으로 '사소한 일에 마음을 쓰고, 꼼꼼한'이라는 의미이다.
Their **meticulousness** proved much too minimal. (*n.*)

0144
dissipate [5]
[ˈdɪsɪpeɪt]

v. 낭비하다; 소멸하다　spend or use wastefully; to scatter in various directions
diss (디쓰)를 계속 하고 다니면 친구들이 다 dissipate하겠지?
They **dissipated** the smoke by flapping their arms and opening all the windows. (*v.*)

0145
emancipation [7]
[ɪˌmænsəˈpeɪʃən]

n. 해방, 이탈　the act of being free from restraint, influence, or the like; freedom
e(out)+man(hand)+cip(take)+ate "잡힌 손을 풀어 자유롭게 하다"라는 뜻에서 유래
Slavery became illegal when Abraham Lincoln became the president and ordered the **emancipation** of slaves. (*n.*)

0146
poignant [4]
[ˈpɔɪnjənt]

a. 가슴 아픈　causing great pain, agonizingly, severely painful or acute to the spirit
poig는 '날카로운', '찌르는'이란 뜻으로 '가슴을 찌르는'의 의미이다.
When the **poignant** story was over, everyone cried. (*adj.*)

0147
inanimate [2]
[ɪnˈænɪmət]

a. 무생물의, 죽은　not alive, not moving (used of physical objects), not animate; lifeless
animal 은 동물이다. 동물은 활발하게 돌아다니는 것이 특징이므로 animate는 '생기를 불어넣는다'는 뜻이고, inanimate는 '죽은, 무생물의'이라는 뜻이다.
Unlike the animals around it, the stone is an **inanimate** object. (*adj.*)

0148
jumble ⁴

[dʒʌ́mbl]

n. 뒤죽박죽 뒤섞인 것, 혼잡   a mixed or disordered heap or mass, junk; muddle
jumble jungle. 정글에는 모든 동식물이 섞여있지? 그렇게 외우자.
He has a **jumble** of papers on his desk so he isn't able to fully focus on his work. (*n.*)

0149
toil ³

[tɔil]

n. 노역, 고역   hard work
conspiration(변비)이 있어서 toilet에 오래 앉아있는 것은 힘든 일이다.
There is no reward without **toil**. (*n.*)

0150
indispensable ²

[ìndispénsəbl]

a. 필요한, 필수의, 없어서는 안 될   necessary, basic, crucial, necessary for the purpose
dispense는 버리다, 처분하다라는 의미가 있다. in 'not' 즉 '처분할 수 없는, 꼭 필요한'의 뜻이다.
The company offered anything it could to stop the **indispensable** engineers from leaving. (*adj.*)

0151
facet ²

[ǀfæsɪt]

n. 측면, 양상   aspect, phase
facet은 face라고 생각하면 된다.
Now let's look at another **facet** of the problem. (*n.*)

0152
allotted ²

[əǀlɑ:tɪd]

a. 할당된, 정해진   divided
지정된 lot에 집어넣는 것이 allot.
A share was **allotted** to each. (*v.*)

0153
impenetrable ⁵

[impénətrəbl]

a. 들어갈 수 없는, 뚫을 수 없는   unable to be penetrated; also used for anything which cannot be understood easily (abstruse), not penetrable
im(not), penetrate(뚫다)가 합쳐져 '속을 알 수 없는, 알기 어려운' 등의 뜻으로 해석될 수 있다.
We thought the door was **impenetrable** until he smashed it open with a sledgehammer. (*adj.*)

0154
premise ⁶

[ǀpremɪs]

n. 전제, 주장   argument, assertion
pre '앞에, 미리' mise 'to send' 즉 어떤 얘기를 하기 전에 미리 내보내거나 말하는 것이 '전제'라고 볼 수 있다.
The law is based upon a **premise** that is inaccurate. (*n.*)

0155
propagandist [16]

[ˌprɑːpəˈɡændɪst]

n. 선전원   a person who deliberately spread information, rumors, etc.   *a.* propagandizing
propaganda가 '선전, 홍보'라는 뜻이니까 그런 일을 하는 사람을 말한다.
In 1975, The New York Times said, 'In a sense, he has been a **propagandist** ever. (*n.*)

0156
fervently [2]

[ˈfɜːvəntli]

adv. 열렬하게, 강렬하게   with great passion
fervere는 '끓다'는 뜻으로 '열정이 끓어오른다'는 의미이다.
He studied **fervently** and passed the exam. (*adv.*)

0157
dichotomy [2]

[daikátəmi]

n. 양분, 이분법, 대생   a pair of opposites, contrast
a. dichotomous
di '두 갈래로' cut '자르다'.
The **dichotomy** between what we have and what we want is often the cause of much unhappiness. (*n.*)

0158
pioneer [8]

[ˌpaɪəˈnɪr]

v. 개척하다   be the first person to open or prepare
엔지니어(engineer)는 산업사회의 곳곳에서 선구적인 역할을 한다.
He was a **pioneer** who was ahead of his time. (*n.*)

0159
subordinate [8]

[səˈbɔːrdɪnət]

v. 경시하다   place in a lower rank
sub 'under' + ordinate 'order, arrange' 누군가를 또는 무언가를 아래쪽에 놔두니까 '경시하다, 깔보다'.
In many societies women are **subordinate** to men. (*adj.*)

0160
anarchy [6]

[ˈænərki]

n. 난장판, 무정부 상태   lawlessness, chaos
an '없는' + anarchia '지도자'. 지도자가 없으니 혼란에 빠져있다는 뜻이다.
Loss of faith leads to intellectual and moral **anarchy**. (*n.*)

0161
contravene [3]

[ˌkɑːntrəˈviːn]

v. 위반하다   come or be in conflict with, To go against
무엇인가를 contravene하면, 그것에 contrary (반대) 방향으로 가는 것이다.
The company was found guilty of **contravening** safety regulations. (*adj.*)

0162
homily [ˈhɑːməli]

n. 설교, 훈계 a sermon, an admonitory discourse
이 단어의 옛말인 homilia는 'speaking with'라는 뜻으로, 옛날부터 sermon과 동일하게 쓰던 단어이다.
She delivered a **homily** on the virtues of family life. (*n.*)

0163
lurking [ˈlɔːrkiŋ]

a. 숨어 있는 existing unperceived or unsuspected
lurk에서 r 이| k 뒤에 살짝 숨어있는 것처럼 보이지?
Why are you **lurking** around outside my house? (*adj.*)

Voca Hamburger
Episode 9
MATCHING Quiz

1. raiding	A. argument, assertion
2. meticulousness	B. aspect, phase
3. dissipate	C. be the first person to open or prepare
4. emancipation	D. place in a lower rank
5. poignant	E. causing great pain, agonizingly
6. inanimate	F. the act of being free from restraint, influence, or the like
7. jumble	G. a pair of opposites
8. toil	H. a mixed or disordered heap or mass
9. indispensable	I. lawlessness, chaos
10. facet	J. hard work
11. allotted	K. not alive, not moving (used of physical objects)
12. impenetrable	L. necessary, basic, crucial
13. premise	M. come or be in conflict with
14. propagandist	N. paying close attention to details
15. fervently	O. unable to be penetrated; also used for anything which cannot be understood easily (abstruse)
16. dichotomy	P. a person who deliberately spread information, rumors, etc.
17. pioneer	Q. divided
18. subordinate	R. with great passion
19. anarchy	S. suddenly assaulting or attacking
20. contravene	T. spend or use wastefully

1-S, 2-N, 3-T, 4-F, 5-E, 6-K, 7-H, 8-J, 9-L, 10-B, 11-Q, 12-O, 13-A, 14-P, 15-R, 16-G, 17-C, 18-D, 19-I, 20-M

더 많은 문제를 풀고자 한다면 www.quizlet.com에서 'paul academy seoul' class를 검색

Episode 10

Family Time

164 concede [11]
v. 인정하다
give in

165 succumb [2]
v. 굴복하다
give in; surrender; concede

166 fatigue [2]
n. 피로
tiredness
a. indefatigable

167 gritty [2]
a. 불쾌한 현실을 보여주는
consisting of, containing, or resembling grit

168 vanity [3]
n. 자만심
excessive pride

169 surreptitious [2]
a. 은밀한
secretive; furtive

170 accustomed [4]
a. 익숙한
habituated, used to

It was 3 AM later that Saturday night, and Jake was trying to improve himself. The words from the test were fading from his mind just as quickly as he tried to push them in. He was about to **concede** defeat when he suddenly heard the front door open in the outer hall.

His father entered the house, heavily, slipping his shoes off after a few attempts and letting his umbrella slap against the floor. Though he was only wearing socks, he made about as much noise coming into the living room as two professional wrestlers trying to wear high heeled shoes. When he finally got where he was going, he looked in to see Jake reading on the floor, the TV on mute. The older man's confused expression clearly showed that he had not anticipated anyone being awake at three o'clock in the morning.

Jake's father, it should be mentioned, was a bank manager. In the eyes of his son, he always had been, and would continue to be until he **succumbed** to **fatigue** and finally retired, as all old people did. Hidden to his son, however, was the **gritty** fact that his high position, which was envied by many other men, had always been a source of boredom to him, a so-called profession about which he felt little **vanity**.

Jake did not know all of this, of course, only that his father worked very hard, wore suits his mother bought by the dozen every year or so, smoked occasionally (though **surreptitiously**) in the laundry room, and drank with his colleagues. On Saturdays he used to take him to the park, but not anymore.

"Hiya, son," his father said, in slightly too harsh a tone.

"Hello, Dad. Did you have a fun night?" Jake had long gotten **accustomed** to the sound of his father entering the apartment at night, but had seldom actually seen him do so.

"Ugh. Weekend training workshop," the older man said with a slight

jeer in his voice. "So many young people, now, clicking away on their phones without paying attention to the conversation, or caring. Too bad they couldn't be as attentive to their responsibilities as you are." He smiled lovingly and gestured to Jake's book as he fell onto the sofa, barely managing to stay upright.

"Oh, I'm just trying to memorize some vocab," Jake said. "It's not exactly hard work, just **tedious**."

"Well, don't let me interrupt you." The old man sighed heavily and the smell of alcohol and cigarettes wafted like a fog across the room toward Jake's seat. Jake looked back at the list of words and tried to make connections between them. It was a useless effort, and his eyes had been feeling tired for the last hour anyway. He looked up and found his father's gaze, which had evidently rested on him for the last five minutes. Having come home **intoxicated**, he was now beyond that point. Even though he usually spoke very **coherently** during the day, at this moment, his mind was barely aware of what his mouth was saying.

"You work so very hard, Jake," he said, a slight suggestion of emotion in his voice. "You know we're proud of you, right?"

"Dad, you don't have to —"

The older man fell forwards onto his knees and approached his son on the floor, sitting sloppily across the table from him. He glanced over to the vocabulary book that rested near Jake, but the words might as well have been Martian to him. After a moment, he raised one hand (the other resting on the floor to keep himself upright) and gestured around the half-lit room.

"Look, son. See this apartment, this room?"

"Yes…" Jake answered uneasily. He was quickly becoming embarrassed for both of them.

"You like it, don't you?"

"Yeah, of course, Dad."

"Well, this has always been for you. Everything has been for you. You understand?" His voice cracked slightly as if remembering a

---

171 jeer 3
n. 야유, 조롱
ridicule, scoff

172 tedious 4
a. 지루한, 싫증나는
boring, dull

173 intoxicated 2
a. 취한
drunk, inebriated

174 coherently 13
adv. 일관성 있게
making sense

175 anecdote [50]
n. 일화, 알려지지 않은 얘기
a short, amusing story

particularly sad memory, and he closed his eyes.

Jake didn't know what to do. His father had never addressed him in this way before. A long silence passed uncomfortably.

"Just make sure you do something for me, will you?"

"What, Dad?"

"Just make something beautiful, OK? Don't ever forget your own happiness."

Jake looked at his father, unsure of the proper response. In ten minutes or less, his father had changed immeasurably in front of him. Something told him that he would someday be telling this **anecdote** to a psychotherapist.

"OK, Dad. I'll try."

His father, pleased with his little speech but still melancholy nonetheless, nodded and rose to his feet unsteadily. He looked down at Jake and then turned toward the darkened hallway where his bedroom lay. Jake heard him loosen his belt and then fall into bed.

It was too late for any more vocab after that.

Vocabulary

0164
concede [11]
[kənsíːd]

v. 인정하다; 양보하다, 용인하다   give in; to surrender
cedere는 '가다'라는 뜻의 라틴어로 '상대가 가도록 양보하다'라는 의미이다.
Although he **conceded** that there were few errors in the plan, he refused to admit that the plan was completely ridiculous. (v.)

0165
succumb [2]
[səkʌ́m]

v. 굴복하다, 압도되다   give in; surrender; concede; to yield
압도당해서(succumb) 엄지손가락이나 빨고 있게 되다(suck thumb).
The country **succumbed** to its enemies and gave them what they wanted. (v.)

0166
fatigue [2]
[fətíːg]

n. 피로   tiredness, exhaustion
'tired'를 연상하자!
To overcome his **fatigue**, the runner slept for five more hours than usual. (n.)

0167
gritty [2]
[|grɪti]

a. 모래를 씹는 듯 불쾌한   consisting of, containing, or resembling grit
grit은 'tiny particles of crushed rock'을 가리킨다.
It's kind of **gritty** urban. (adj.)

0168
vanity [3]
[|vænəti]

n. 자만심, 허영심   excessive pride
'empty'라는 뜻의 라틴어 vanus에서 온 단어. 자만심은 곧 vain(헛된 것)이다.
She is a woman full of **vanity**. (n.)

0169
surreptitious [2]
[sə̀ːrəptíʃəs]

a. 은밀한, 비밀의, 내밀의   secretive; furtive, clandestine
sub(under)+rapt(seize)+it(go)가 합쳐서 "아래로 낚아채서 가는"이라는 뜻에서 유래.
Drug dealers involve **surreptitious** business dealings. (adj.)

77

0170
accustomed ⁴
[əˈkʌstəmd]

a. **익숙한**　habituated, used to
custom에 맞추면 익숙해지겠지?
They're **accustomed** to the rigors of army life. (v.)

0171
jeer ³
[dʒíər]

n. **야유, 조롱[하다]**　ridicule, scoff; to hiss, to boo
cheer를 살짝 비틀어서 조롱하듯 사용하는 단어.
The police were **jeered** at by the waiting crowd. (v.)

0172
tedious ⁴
[tíːdiəs]

a. **지루한, 싫증나는; 장황한**　boring, dull
원래 의미 : "싫증난" → (일이) 지루한, 따분한 → (말하는 사람이) 진저리가
날 만큼 말 많은, 장황한
The principal's **tedious** speech made all the students go to sleep. (adj.)

0173
intoxicated ²
[inˈtɑːksikeitid]

a. **취한**　drunk, inebriated
toxic은 '중독'이라는 뜻인데 이것을 술과 연관지어 생각하면 외우기 쉽다.
The **intoxicated** people were spaced out. (adj.)

0174
coherently ¹³
[kouˈhirəntli]

adv. **일관성 있게**　making sense
co 'together' + haerere 'to stick'. 같이 나란히 붙여놓으니 일관성이 있지.
When she calmed down, she did her work more **coherently**. (adv.)

0175
anecdote ⁵⁰
[ˈænikdout]

n. **일화, 알려지지 않은 얘기**　a short, amusing story
주장을 하기 위해 내세우는 짧은 이야기이다.
He told several humorous **anecdotes** about the troubles of being a film composer. (n.)

Note :

Voca Hamburger

Episode 10

MATCHING **Quiz**

1. concede	•	• A. habituated, used to
2. succumb	•	• B. consisting of, containing, or resembling grit
3. fatigue	•	• C. drunk, inebriated
4. gritty	•	• D. give in
5. vanity	•	• E. making sense
6. surreptitious	•	• F. tiredness
7. accustomed	•	• G. excessive pride
8. jeer	•	• H. a short, amusing story
9. tedious	•	• I. secretive; furtive
10. intoxicated	•	• J. ridicule, scoff
11. coherently	•	• K. boring, dull
12. anecdote	•	• L. give in; surrender; concede

1-D, 2-L, 3-F, 4-B, 5-G, 6-I, 7-A, 8-J, 9-K, 10-C, 11-E, 12-H

더 많은 문제를 풀고자 한다면 www.quizlet.com에서 'paul academy seoul' class를 검색

Episode 11: Just Another Monday Morning

176 civilized [2]
a. 문명화된, 교양 있는
having a high state of culture and development both socially and technologically

177 inexorable [3]
a. 멈출 수 없는, 거침없는
relentless, unyielding

178 sloth [2]
n. 나태
laziness, idleness, indolence

179 cease [3]
v. 중단되다
bring to an end

After a sleepy Sunday, Monday morning of Week Two had come all too soon for Jake. His mother welcomed him with a wide smile as he came into the kitchen.

"Week two, huh? Ready for it? Do your homework?" For some reason, just as the rest of the **civilized** world hated conversation in the morning, Jake's mother delighted in it, asking questions as he tried to eat his breakfast as quickly as possible to escape her **inexorable** questions.

"You're like a dentist!" he finally shouted out, his mouth half-full of eggs so that it sounded more like an angry talk.

"A dentist? What do you mean?"

"Always asking questions when a person's mouth is full. It isn't practical, Mom. Yes, I am ready. There was no homework."

"You sure?"

"Yeah, we're just doing test review today."

"What about the vocabulary?"

He froze, suddenly feeling a chill. How had he forgotten in the comfortable **sloth** of his Sunday day of rest? Even the words from Saturday night had long **ceased** to occupy any of his brain. He took another large spoonful of eggs so his mother wouldn't hear what he was about to say to himself.

"What was that, dear? I didn't hear you."

"Sorry, Mom. I've got to go." He swallowed what he had left and ran towards the door with his bag flying behind him.

The subway was unusually **clamorous** that morning, and its constant **lurching** motion completely **thwarted** his attempt to study. To make matters worse, a particularly **garrulous** girl from his school had gotten on a few stops after him, and, having noticed him trying to study, tried to get his attention.

"Hey, Jake!" she **exclaimed**. He pretended very hard that he had gone deaf in the time since they had last seen each other.

"Over here! Can you hear me?" Think of the words, he thought… oh these words are impossible to understand!

She had given up shouting and had decided to navigate through the crowd of unresponsive commuters as **deftly** as she could, finally sliding out between two tourists like a rat from its hole. At least the **analogy** that seemed **apt** to him.

The voice **recurred**. "Hey Jake!" She was one of those over-**zealous** people who always had to speak as though it was the best day of her life and that everyone else should be in **jubilation** with her. He now had no choice but to look up.

"Oh, hey Susan," he said, in no mood for her mindless good cheer.

"Studying, huh? You've changed! Where are you going this summer?"

"I'm at a place called —"

"I'm at this place downtown called 'SAT A-OK'. It's fun. Only fifty vocab words a day. Of course, they let you study more if you want, but still, it's not too stressful."

He prayed for some near-**apocalyptic** event. Please let the train run off the tracks, he thought. Let me save a child from the danger so they'll let me avoid the vocab test and this **atrocious** girl. He'd be a hero, he thought, **vaunted** throughout the land. Mothers would give him babies to kiss, and girls would throw their phone numbers at his feet. He'd forever be **lauded** as the 'train disaster savior'. He'd be free of this irritating girl as well.

"Hey, are you listening to me?" She had the irritating smile of someone who assumes the attention should always be placed on her

---

180 clamorous [3]
a. 떠들썩한
loud noise; usually from many voices

181 lurching [2]
a. 흔들리는, 동요시키는
stagger, jerk

182 thwart [3]
v. 방해하다
prevent or stop from happening

183 garrulous [2]
a. 말이 많은
talkative; sociable

184 exclaim [3]
v. 소리치다, 외치다
cry out or speak suddenly and vehemently

185 deftly [3]
adv. 솜씨 좋게
skillfully; adeptly

186 analogy [43]
n. 비유
similarity or comparability

187 apt [9]
a. 적절한
appropriate (also used to describe a skilled person)

188 recur [7]
v. 마음에 다시 떠오르다
happen again, repeat in one's mind

189 zealous [5]
a. 열성적인
passionate; fervent
n. zeal

190 jubilation [2]
n. 환희, 환호
rejoice, exult

191 apocalyptic [2]
a. 종말론의
catastrophic; destructive
n. apocalypse

192 atrocious [8]
a. 형편없는, 끔찍한
awful, outrageous

193 vaunt [2]
v. 자랑하다, 허풍 떨다
speak vaingloriously of, boast of

194 lauded [3]
a. 칭찬받는
praised; lionized
a. laudable

195 gregarious [3]
a. 사교적인
sociable

196 engulfing [2]
a. 에워싸는
completely surround

197 gibberish [4]
n. 횡설수설
meaningless talk, babble, prattle

198 apex [2]
n. 정점, 꼭대기
highest point

alone.

"Of course. SAT A-OK. Sounds fun."

"Well, I heard your school is pretty fun, too. Sociable"

"Yeah, **gregarious**," he muttered, looking at a few other passengers who'd noticed the girl's strident voice as it echoed through the subway car.

"Idiot. You can't use gregarious for a place. Only for people. Maybe I should let you study. Oh! Too late!"

The train had arrived. With every step he prayed he'd arrive to find a massive firestorm **engulfing** the building. Everyone surviving, of course, but a terrible blaze nonetheless, which would consume all the available vocab quizzes with it.

He knew her academy was right next to his, and so dreaded the long walk up the stairs with her. She continued talking in **gibberish** about the other students she knew, stopping occasionally to draw breath.

"And of course there's Jessica. We study together, but sometimes she's so mean —" the girl paused dramatically as they continued up the stairs. At the **apex** of their climb, he noticed a shadow had blocked the doorway at the top of the stairs. It was a small shadow, with a skirt.

"Oh," Susan whispered. "That's her."

As they approached, the shadow took shape. It was a girl, as he'd guessed from the skirt. She was small, though not weak-looking, and wore a large pair of sunglasses. Her thighs sat right in his path as he looked up, however, and he tried as politely as he could to focus on the glasses. It wasn't easy.

"Hey, Jessica!" Susan called out in forced friendliness. The girl at the top looked down at them both, figuratively and literally.

Vocabulary

0176

civilized [²]

[ˈsɪvəlaɪzd]

a. 문명화된, 교양 있는   having a high state of culture and development both socially and technologically
civil한 사람이 된다는 것은 문명화된 사람으로 교양이 있다는 뜻이다.
We are **civilized** people. (*adj.*)

0177

inexorable [³]

[inéksərəbl]

a. 멈출 수 없는, 거침없는; 냉혹한   relentless, unyielding; cold-blooded
in(not) + ex(out) + ora(speak). '애원의 말을 밖으로 내뱉을 수 없을 정도로 냉정한'이란 뜻이다.
Alexander, the **inexorable** warrior, showered attacks on his enemies until they surrendered. (*adj.*)

0178

sloth [²]

[sloʊθ]

n. 나태, 나태한   laziness, idleness, indolence, characteristically slow
sloth는 나무늘보이다. 나무늘보는 slow하지?
It is **said** that sloth is the mother of poverty. (*n.*)

0179

cease [³]

[siːs]

v. 중단되다   bring to an end
승승장구하던 로마황제 Julius Caesar의 정치는 Brutus에 의해 cease 되었다. 라틴어 cessare 'to stop, end'에서 온 단어.
Welfare payments **cease** as soon as an individual starts a job. (*v.*)

0180

clamorous [³]

[klǽmərəs]

a. 떠들썩한, 소란한   loud noise; usually from many voices, talking loudly or shouting
라틴어 clamare 'cry out'에서 온 단어.
The alarm was so **clamorous** that everybody woke up within a second. (*adj.*)

0181

lurching [²]

[lɜːrtʃɪŋ]

a. 흔들리는, 동요시키는   stagger, jerk
원래 left에서 변형된 말이라고 함. right 방향으로 가야 하는데 left로 lurch하는 거지.
I don't wanna leave anyone in the **lurch**. (*n.*)

0182
thwart [3]
[θwɔ́:rt]

v. 방해하다, 좌절시키다   prevent or stop from happening, to prevent success
throat와 연관지어서 설명할 수 있다. 만약 throat(목구멍이) thwarted 되면 숨을 쉴 수 없으니 thwart의 의미를 잘 살릴 수 있다.
The rain **thwarted** his plan to go to a picnic. (*v.*)

0183
garrulous [2]
[gǽrələs]

a. 말이 많은, 수다스러운; 장황한   talkative, given to constant trivial talking; sociable
약간 careless처럼 들리므로 부주의하게 말을 막 한다고 해석할 수 있다.
Garrulous drunks talk in the street. (*adj.*)

0184
exclaim [3]
[ɪk|skleɪm]

v. 소리치다, 외치다   cry out or speak suddenly and vehemently
기본적으로는 cry와 비슷한 뜻이지만, ex(='out')가 붙어있으므로 '특히 감정이 격해져서 소리를 지르는' 것을 말한다.
They all **exclaimed** over her beautiful clothes. (*v.*)

0185
deftly [3]
[déftli]

adv. 솜씨 좋게   skillfully; adeptly
'left'와 비슷한 발음. 왼(left)손을 잘 쓰는 사람을 생각하자.
Jake handles a soccer ball **deftly**. (*adv.*)

0186
analogy [43]
[ə|nælədʒi]

n. 비유   similarity or comparability, A comparison of two different things that are similar in some way
Ana는 항상 2개의 사물을 비교하는 logic(논리)를 사용한다.
We made an **analogy** between Igor and a fart by saying that they were both deadliest when they were silent. (*n.*)

0187
apt [9]
[æpt]

a. 적절한   appropriate (also used to describe a skilled person), inclined; disposed
아파트(apt)는 가족들이 생활하기 적절한 공간이지?
A particularly **apt** description/name/comment (*adj.*)

0188
recur [7]
[rikə́:r]

v. 마음에 다시 떠오르다   happen again, repeat in one's mind
cur는 happen이라는 뜻인데, re(='again') cur하니까 '(뭔가) 다시 일어나는' 것을 가리킨다.
A theme that was to **recur** frequently in his work (*adj.*)

0189
zealous [5]
[zéləs]

a. 열성적인, 열심인, 열렬한   passionate, enthusiastic; fervent
zeal은 '열정'을 뜻하므로 열렬하다는 의미이다.
The **zealous** fan burst into tears of joy when the popstar signed her t-shirt. (*adj.*)

0190
jubilation [2]
[dʒùːbəléiʃən]

n. 환희, 환호   rejoice, exultation
베스킨라빈스 아이스크림 중에서 체리쥬빌레 알지? 바로 이 단어야. 너무 맛있어서 환호한다고 기억해.
Everyone shouted and laughed in **jubilation** for finishing the year-long project. (*n.*)

0191
apocalyptic [2]
[əˌpɑːkəˈlɪptɪk]

a. 종말론의   catastrophic; destructive   *n.* apocalypse
apocalypse는 apo(='from') + calyp(='kalyptein: to cover; uncover')
즉 '감춰진 미래를 드러낸다'는 뜻으로 외우자.
An **apocalyptic** view of history (*adj.*)

0192
atrocious [8]
[əˈtroʊʃəs]

a. 형편없는, 끔찍한; 흉악한 잔인한   awful, outrageous;
Outrageously or wantonly wicked, criminal, vile, or cruel
atrocious에서 제일 뒤에 있는 cious는 '써쓰'로 센 쌍시옷 발음을 낸다. 그만큼 흉악하다는 것이다.
It is now nearly a year since those **atrocious** attacks. (*adj.*)

0193
vaunt [2]
[vɔːnt, vɑːnt]

v. 자랑하다, 허풍 떨다   speak vaingloriously of, boast of
vault '금고'를 생각하면 금고를 열고 자랑하는 모습을 연상할 수 있다.
He **vaunted** his big new boat to others. (*v.*)

0194
lauded [3]
[lɔːdɪd]

a. 칭찬받는   praised; lionized   *a.* laudable
applaud '박수 치다, 갈채를 보내다'를 생각하면 laud의 뜻을 짐작할 수 있다.
There are times when people **laud** the children of working mothers for being more academically motivated and ambitious. (*v.*)

0195
gregarious [3]
[grigέəriəs]

a. 사교적인   sociable
greg는 '여러 사람'을 뜻하니까, '사람들과 어울리기를 좋아하는'.
The **gregarious** manager soon made friends with everyone. (*adj.*)

0196
engulfing [2]

[ɪnˈɡʌlfɪŋ]

a. 에워싸는   completely surround
en(='make')과 gulf(만: 바다로 둘러싸인 육지)가 합쳐져서 에워싸다는 의미.
He was **engulfed** by a crowd of reporters. (*v.*)

0197
gibberish [4]

[ˈdʒɪbərɪʃ]

n. 횡설수설   meaningless talk, babble, prattle
gibber jabber는 횡설수설할 때 흔히 쓰인다. 거기서 gibber가 이 단어이다.
You were talking **gibberish** in your sleep. (*v.*)

0198
apex [2]

[éipeks]

n. 정점, 꼭대기, 절정   The highest point, as of a mountain
A의 peak는 apex라고 외우자.
All presidents use people to climb to the **apex**. (*n.*)

Episode 11
MATCHING Quiz

1. civilized • • A. similarity or comparability
2. inexorable • • B. laziness, idleness, indolence
3. sloth • • C. appropriate (also used to describe a skilled person)
4. cease • • D. speak vaingloriously of, boast of
5. clamorous • • E. awful, outrageous
6. lurching • • F. cry out or speak suddenly and vehemently
7. thwart • • G. catastrophic; destructive
8. garrulous • • H. loud noise; usually from many voices
9. exclaim • • I. bring to an end
10. deftly • • J. sociable
11. analogy • • K. prevent or stop from happening
12. apt • • L. skillfully; adeptly
13. recur • • M. having a high state of culture and development both socially and technologically
14. zealous • • N. relentless, unyielding
15. jubilation • • O. talkative; sociable
16. apocalyptic • • P. stagger, jerk
17. atrocious • • Q. happen again, repeat in one's mind
18. vaunt • • R. passionate; fervent
19. lauded • • S. rejoice, exult
20. gregarious • • T. praised; lionized

1-M, 2-N, 3-B, 4-I, 5-H, 6-P, 7-K, 8-O, 9-F, 10-L, 11-A, 12-C, 13-Q, 14-R, 15-S, 16-G, 17-E, 18-D, 19-T, 20-J

더 많은 문제를 풀고자 한다면 www.quizlet.com에서 'paul academy seoul' class를 검색

Episode 12

Heart Strings and Vocab Quizzes

"You're late," Jessica, the girl in the skirt, shouted down, her voice playful in the morning light.

"Yeah, I guess I was talking to Jake here…" said Susan as she and Jake passed the halfway mark of the long staircase.

"Is he a friend of yours?"

"Yeah, we go to school together."

"Hello, Jake, whoever you are!"

Jake got to the top step, annoyed at how out of breath the staircase conversation had **rendered** him. He simply stared and nodded weakly.

"Where are you going?"

"Uh, to the SAT academy at the top of the hill."

"Nice. Let's walk together."

Jake had never in his life walked with a girl like this, even on friendly terms. He was careful to breathe as normally as possible, which he took to be once every thirty seconds, leading to an overly-loud intake of breath accompanied by a long sigh when he realized he'd taken too much air. Nothing in his body seemed to work properly. His feet slapped the pavement in the most awkward way possible. Luckily, Susan ran inside a convenience store for a drink. He paused, looking down at the ground to avoid the Jessica's eyes, which were piercing even when **obscured** by her glasses.

"How's your score?" she asked suddenly.

Jake considered how high he ought to lie. Numbers near 700 danced in his mind, as if guided by a man crazed with test scores and

---

199 render [17]
v. 만들다
cause to become

200 obscured [23]
a. 무명의, 잘 알려지지 않은
covered or blocked;
occluded

201 commodity [4]
n. 상품, 물자
something that is sold for money

202 facilitate [7]
v. 가능하게 하다
make it easier or more likely to happen

203 linger [2]
v. 어슬렁거리다
hang around

impressing women with fake emotions.

"No need to lie. I'm 350," she said with humility. She was looking down the road as she said it, and he saw her eyes through the colored plastic for the first time. They were wide, and beautiful.

"Well, it was 470 last weekend," he admitted.

"Oh, nice job! You like studying?"

"Uh...not really, but I guess that's our job, now, isn't it?"

"Yeah, I guess it is." Through the store window he could see Susan paying for her **commodities**. Jake wished she would spent half a day in there to **facilitate** his having a longer conversation with this girl. Why did she have to be such an efficient shopper!

"You're friends with her?" Jessica asked pointedly. A slightly sharp tone made him feel that she did not particularly like their mutual acquaintance either.

"I know her, but..." he stopped talking to indicate there was more to say on the subject, all of it negative.

"Got it. Well, we're studying together if you ever want to join. Could be fun..."

"Like a broken leg," he said without humor, nodding towards the emerging SJ. The girl laughed.

Her laughter obscured everything Susan began to say on the subject of paper clips and vocabulary. It was brief, lasting only for a second, but it shot through his grey morning fog like a beam from a lighthouse. He had made her laugh, and wanted nothing more than to hear that sound again. And just like that, Jake was in love.

"Well, this is your place," he heard Susan say, although her words reached his brain as though traveling through cloth.

"What?" he said, suddenly unaware of where precisely he was.

"This is your school, isn't it?" Susan looked at him strangely, as several older boys **lingered** around the entrance, smoking and gazing at Jessica. A few **snobby** remarks were made in whispers, but mostly they just stood, as amazed as Jake had been for the previous five minutes by her beauty.

"Oh, yes," he said faintly, remembering with **haste** about the vocab quiz, his mother's **injunction** during breakfast, the fear of failure. All that had been wiped away by sunshine and laughter now became clear again with renewed energy.

"I should get going," he said suddenly. He turned toward the darkened doorway and they began wandering away, the **reciprocal** goodbyes exchanged quickly. Reaching the elevator, however, he realized what **folly** it would be to let this opportunity go to waste. "Wait!" he shouted at their distant backs. He jogged up behind them.

"What time do you guys study?"

Jessica laughed again at his reddened face and breathing, which was now quicker thanks to nervousness, worry about vocabulary, and running to catch them.

"Six o'clock at Starbucks," she said. "The one on the way to the next station, do you know it?"

"Yes," he said, unsure if he could tell her his own name. At least Susan had served that function. "You'll be there tonight?"

"Should be. Will you?"

"I will," he promised.

"Well...we can't really go any farther than this right now, Jake."

"What do you mean?"

"We're at our school." Another laugh, this time amused by his awkwardness. "But do join us, OK?"

"Of course." They entered their building, and he wandered back to his own school, realizing once and for all that his vocabulary score would definitely not be high that day. At least it was sacrificed for a good cause, he told himself.

---

204 snobby [6]
a. 거만한, 버릇없는
impertinent, haughty
a. snobbish

205 haste [3]
n. 서두름
speed; alacrity
a. hasty

206 injunction [2]
n. 경고
telling someone not to do something

207 reciprocal [4]
a. 상호간의
mutual; a command, order, admonition

208 folly [8]
n. 판단력 부족, 어리석음
a foolish action, practice, idea

Vocabulary

0199
render [17]
[|rendə(r)|]

v. (어떤 상태가 되게) 만들다　to cause to be or become; make
그는 적이 항복(surrender) 하게 'render' 했다 라고 외우자.
The terrible car accident **rendered** everyone unable to walk. (*v.*)

0200
obscured [23]
[əb|skjʊrd]

a. 무명의, 잘 알려지지 않은; 이해하기 힘든, 모호한　covered or blocked; occluded
ob는 '~위', scurus는 '덮은'이란 뜻으로, '뭔가에 덮여서 모호하다'는 의미이다.
It has become even more complicated and **obscure**. (*adj.*)

0201
commodity [4]
[kə|mɑːdəti]

n. 상품, 물자　something that is sold for money
commodity가 있으면 "Come on! Enjoy the party!"라고 말하기가 훨씬 쉽겠지?
Life is not a **commodity** that can be bought and sold. (*n.*)

0202
facilitate [7]
[fə|sɪlɪteɪt]

v. 가능하게 하다　make it easier or more likely to happen
예쁜 얼굴 (face)를 가지면 웬만한 건 다 facilitate되지.
Henry moved next to his school to **facilitate** his ride there every day. (*v.*)

0203
linger [2]
[líŋgər]

v. 어슬렁거리다, 오래 머무르다　hang around, to stay on in a place longer than is usual
병원에서 링거 맞을 때 오랫동안 링거를 달고 있으라고 하는 걸 생각해.
The smell of the garlic **lingered** in the house.

0204
snobby [6]
[snábi]

a. 거만한, 버릇없는　impertinent, haughty　*a.* snobbish
잘난 척하는 사람을 고깝게 생각하면서 표현할 때 snob이라고 부른다.
She looks kind of **snobby**, but actually, she's outgoing and a people person. (*adj.*)

0205
haste ³ [heɪst]

n. 서두름   speed; alacrity   *a.* hasty

'Haste makes waste.'라는 속담 들어봤지? 성급하면 일을 그르친다는 뜻이야.

In her **haste** to complete the work on time, she made a number of mistakes. (*n.*)

0206
injunction ² [ɪndʒʌ́ŋkʃən]

n. 경고, (법원의)명령, 훈령   telling someone not to do something; decree, admonition

라틴어 injunctionem에서 온 말로 'command'라는 뜻이다.

A judge has granted an **injunction** request by Mattel Inc. (*n.*)

0207
reciprocal ⁴ [rɪsíprəkl]

a. 상호간의   mutual; a command, order, admonition

이쪽에서도 되돌려주고 저쪽에서도 되돌려주니까 '상호간의'.

The two colleges have a **reciprocal** arrangement whereby students from one college can attend classes at the other. (*adj.*)

0208
folly ⁸ [fάːli]

n. 판단력 부족, 어리석음   a foolish action, practice, idea

fool에서 하나가(o) 더 빠졌으니 얼마나 어리석겠어.

I wish he'd wake up to his **folly**. (*n.*)

Episode 12
MATCHING Quiz

1. render •   • A. something that is sold for money
2. obscured •   • B. make it easier or more likely to happen
3. commodity •   • C. hang around
4. facilitate •   • D. cause to become
5. linger •   • E. telling someone not to do something
6. snobby •   • F. mutual; a command, order, admonition
7. haste •   • G. a foolish action, practice, idea
8. injunction •   • H. speed; alacrity
9. reciprocal •   • I. impertinent, haughty
10. folly •   • J. covered or blocked; occluded

1-D, 2-J, 3-A, 4-B, 5-C, 6-I, 7-H, 8-E, 9-F, 10-G

더 많은 문제를 풀고자 한다면 www.quizlet.com에서 'paul academy seoul' class를 검색

Episode 13

Disappointment

209 deplore [5]
v. 깊이 개탄하다, 슬퍼하다
regret with great passion

210 personnel [3]
n. 직원
staff, employee

211 nonchalant [3]
a. 차분한
coolly unconcerned, indifferent, or unexcited

212 preempt [5]
v. 못하게 하다
prevent

213 repugnant [3]
a. 불쾌한, 혐오스러운
nasty, obnoxious, disgusting

In the second hour of classes on Monday, after having completely failed the vocab test, Jake was surprised to find someone more disappointed than himself. Ashley had decided that, following her results on Saturday, she could not contain how much she **deplored** the results and, at the same time, how much she hated the teaching **personnel** for having disappointed her.

"How could my score have gone down?" she said angrily, obviously directing her comments to the teacher at the front of the room. "I did everything I could!"

She frowned at Jake, as though looking angry could change the results she held in her hands.

He looked over at them. They read:

Math - 780
Reading and Writing - 640
Essay - 8

TOTAL: 1420

"Wow," he whispered, in disbelief at her anger.

"Eight! It's insultingly low! There's no way the College Board would give me that score!"

This caught Greg's attention.

"Do you have a question about the essay grade, Ashley?" he asked **nonchalantly**, obviously trying to **preempt** any sort of drama.

"Well, this score is obviously too low," she said angrily, giving him a **repugnant** look. "Tell me, what's wrong with this example?"

"The comments are on the page, Ashley," the teacher said with the same **dispassionate** tone, hardly looking up from the papers he was shuffling at the table.

Obviously, she was not satisfied with this level of attention. She rose and walked straight up to the front of the room, pushing the essay paper under his nose.

"Explain, please," she said shortly.

Greg, calm under normal **circumstances**, seemed unusually irritated by this. He gave the page a **cursory** glance and said that she had "had only read the first and last sentences of the paragraphs."

"Well, they're not going to know that, are they?" she spat back.

"Yes, they are. You no specific examples from the passage, so that it sounds like something someone told you in a bar."

"A bar?!? I can't even go into a bar! What does that mean?"

"It means that it sounds like someone told you something **equivocally credible**, and you repeated it without adding any or any specific details from the passage to answer the question. Now, we're going to start the class. Take your seat."

Jake had never seen someone trying to sit down angrily before, but Ashley tried as hard as she could to make the contact of her body with the chair an expression of her **rage**. As it was, it just seemed like she hurt herself.

"This freaking guy doesn't know anything. Neither does his brother. No improvement. No *improvement!*" This last she said so forcefully that a few surrounding students gasped. "I'm leaving this stupid factory."

Then go, Jake thought. But he didn't dare say it. Who could challenge a girl with so much hatred?

For the rest of the class, Ashley expressed her rage to her deskmate and to others as often as she could, saying at various times how hard she had studied and how **vehemently** she hated the quality of the teaching staff.

---

[214] **dispassionate** [7]
a. 감정에 좌우되지 않는
phlegmatic, calm, impartial

[215] **circumstance** [22]
n. 환경, 상황, 정황
a condition

[216] **cursory** [3]
a. 대충 하는
hasty, superficial

[217] **equivocally** [3]
adv. 모호하게
vaguely

[218] **credible** [4]
a. 믿을 수 있는
believable; tenable; feasible

[219] **rage** [5]
n. 격렬한 분, 격노
pure anger/fury

[220] **vehemently** [4]
adv. 격렬하게
with great passion; zealously

221 methodically [3]
adv. 체계적으로
with great attention paid to details; meticulously

222 assemble [4]
v. 집합시키다, 모이다
bring together or gather into one place

"I mean, this is our future we're talking about here," she complained. "Why don't we go to another place?"

"What, are you talking to me?" Jake felt like he'd been seated on a long bus trip next to the only crazy person.

"Yeah. That place down the street has much more capable teachers. My friend studied TOEFL there in the winter and she improved so much. I really need that 1500."

"I'm staying," he said quietly.

"Fine. Good luck I guess." Then, to the rest of the class, including the nervous reading teacher, she said, "no one will improve in this stupid place. You all should leave if you want to actually get better!"

The class ended and she **methodically** placed her belongings into her bag, even though there were several classes to go. The teddy bear, Jake noticed for the first time, had a special pocket to itself. What an unlucky bear to belong to her, he thought. After everything was **assembled**, she pulled her seat back and went upstairs to get her phone.

Vocabulary

0209
deplore [5]
[dɪˈplɔː(r)]

v. 깊이 개탄하다, 슬퍼하다　regret with great passion
어딘가를 탐험(ex'plore')하면 그 곳을 가고 싶지만, 어딘가를 싫어하면 (de'plore')하면 그 곳에 가고 싶지 않다.
Like everyone else, I **deplore** and condemn this killing. (v.)

0210
personnel [3]
[ˌpɜːrsəˈnel]

n. 직원들　staffs, employees
person이 여럿 모여서 일하고 있다고 생각하자.
What are administrative **personnel** asked to do? (n.)

0211
nonchalant [3]
[nɑ̀nʃəlάːnt]

a. 차분한, 무관심한　coolly unconcerned, indifferent, or unexcited
non(없는)–care(관심)–ant, 즉 '관심없다'고 해석할 수 있다.
His **nonchalant** attitude was calming but sometimes frustrating. (adj.)

0212
preempt [5]
[priˈempt]

v. 못하게 하다; 선매권에 의하여(공유지를) 획득하다　prevent
pre(먼저) empty(빈), 즉 먼저 빈 곳을 획득하다.
When the president's speech **preempted** the TV show, many fans were furious.

0213
repugnant [3]
[rɪˈpʌɡnənt]

a. 불쾌한, 혐오스러운　nasty, obnoxious, disgusting
re(='again') + pugnare(='to fight') 보기만 하면 또다시 싸우고 싶어지니 얼마나 불쾌하면 그럴까.
We found his suggestion absolutely **repugnant**. (adj.)

0214
dispassionate [7]
[dɪsˈpæʃənət]

a. 감정에 좌우되지 않는, 침착한　phlegmatic, calm; impartial, rather composed
말 그대로 열정적이지(passionate) 않다(dis)는 뜻이다.
The **dispassionate** queen waited calmly for the screaming woman to quiet down. (adj.)

0215
circumstance [22]

[ˈsɜːrkəmstæns]

n. 환경, 상황, 정황 a condition, detail, part, or attribute, with respect to time, place, manner, agent, etc., that accompanies, determines, or modifies a fact or event
주어지는 조건(circumstance)에 따라서 너의 태도(stance)를 바꿔야지.
As Theresa is having a baby, I don't think the **circumstances** allow her to practice skydiving. (*n.*)

0216
cursory [3]

[ˈkɜːrsəri]

a. 대충 하는, 서두른; 조잡한 hasty, superficial; rapid and superficial
마우스 커서(cursor)가 빨리빨리 스크린을 왔다갔다하는 모습을 떠올려보라.
Cursory greeting (*adj.*)

0217
equivocally [3]

[ɪˈkwɪvəkli]

adv. 모호하게 vaguely
equi는 '동일한', voc는 '말하다'라는 뜻이므로 양쪽에 대하여 비슷하게 얘기 해서 '모호하다'는 뜻이 된다.
Heather **equivocally** answered her question. (*adv*)

0218
credible [4]

[ˈkredəbl]

a. 믿을 수 있는 believable; tenable; feasible
credit '신용거래'를 할 수 있는 사람이니까 '믿을 수 있는'.
He doesn't think she's very **credible**. (*adj.*)

0219
rage [5]

[reɪdʒ]

n. 격렬한 분, 격노 pure anger/fury
rage에 가득 차서 옷을 rag '넝마, 누더기'가 되도록 찢어버렸다고 외우자.
His face was dark with **rage**. (*n.*)

0220
vehemently [4]

[ˈviːəməntli]

adv. 격렬하게 with great passion; zealously
vehicle을 vehement하게 타고 가는 모습.
Some international leaders, however, **vehemently** disagree. (*adv.*)

0221
methodically [3]

[məˈθɑːdɪkli]

adv. 체계적으로 with great attention paid to details; meticulously
뭔가를 하는 데 method가 있으면 대충 하지 않고 체계적으로 잘 하겠지?
To build a sturdy model, you must follow the instructions **methodically**. (*adv.*)

0222

assemble [əˈsembl]

v. **집합시키다, 모이다**   bring together or gather into one place
as(='to') + similare(='to make like') 비슷하게 만들려면 일단 한 곳에 모아놓아야 한다.
Did you **assemble** this by yourself? (v.)

Episode 13

MATCHING Quiz

1. deplore
2. personnel
3. nonchalant
4. preempt
5. repugnant
6. dispassionate
7. circumstance
8. cursory
9. equivocally
10. credible
11. rage
12. vehemently
13. methodically
14. assemble

A. a condition
B. regret with great passion
C. coolly unconcerned, indifferent, or unexcited
D. hasty, superficial
E. staff, employee
F. with great passion; zealously
G. vaguely
H. bring together or gather into one place
I. prevent
J. nasty, obnoxious, disgusting
K. phlegmatic, calm, impartial
L. believable; tenable; feasible
M. pure anger/fury
N. with great attention paid to details; meticulously

1-B, 2-E, 3-C, 4-I, 5-J, 6-K, 7-A, 8-D, 9-G, 10-L, 11-M, 12-F, 13-N, 14-H

더 많은 문제를 풀고자 한다면 www.quizlet.com에서 'paul academy seoul' class를 검색

Episode 14

The Empty Chair

223 omniscient [7]
a. 모든 것을 다 아는
knowing everything

224 appalled [9]
a. 간담이 서늘한, 끔찍해 하는
filled or overcome with horror, consternation, or fear

225 renounce [3]
v. 포기하다
give up (usually disdainfully)

226 microcosm [2]
n. 소우주 (더 큰 것의 축소판)
a little world, a world in miniature

227 hyperbole [5]
n. 과장
exaggeration

228 astounded [5]
a. 경악한, 충격 받은
amazed, shocked

229 foolhardiness [2]
n. 무모함
reckless and thoughtless boldness; foolish rash
a. foolhardy

230 petulant [5]
a. 심통 사나운
cranky, moody

231 morose [3]
a. 시무룩한
sad; melancholy

After her brief comment, Ashley had disappeared, not waiting for the afternoon session. Thinking herself already near-**omniscient**, she had expected her score to have been enhanced by staying at the academy for a week, but she was **appalled** by her lack of improvement. She **renounced** the school and disappeared, leaving an empty space next to Jake's seat and rushing away like some 19 year-old country girl desperate to escape her uncivilized **microcosm**.

After the first hour of her absence, Jake felt sure that he'd never see her again, even though her perfectionism confused him. Surely her anger had been **hyperbole**? He had been **astounded** at the **foolhardiness** with which she had spoken to the teacher. She had even sworn, which he had thought only boys did. Well, he thought, at least there's some room next to me. He looked over to her desk, where she had taken down her wall and departed. 'The empty chair,' he whispered to himself, thinking that, if this was a movie, a sad song would play over a long shot of the seat, as if she'd died. Nothing about the last week seemed real, suddenly.

Of course, the teachers had not been surprised by her anger, knowing that children had a tendency to act angry and **petulant**. Adults always said these sorts of things, he thought. "Those teenagers, always **morose** about something," he'd hear. His mother sometimes complained about his 'teenage hormones,' but he'd brushed her comments aside as adult ignorance and **paranoia**. How could they know what it was like to live like this?

She wasn't the only one to be annoyed by her scores, however, and by lunchtime a number of other unhappy students had begun **vilifying** teachers and TAs for their lack of improvement. Many of them falsely **alleged** to have studied.

"I **transcribed** all the vocab words into my notebook!" they'd say.
"I spent all night memorizing those essay examples," another chorus would sing.

It was all the same. They had bombed on the test, and now sought someone to **censure** for their **mischief**. TJ and Sam, luckily, were also unconcerned. Both of them had shown slight improvement.

"I mean, it's one week," Sam said practically. "How much do you really expect to improve so quickly?"

Having **canvassed** a number of his classmates, Jake found many of them had been disappointed, but none as much as his former seat mate, whose displeasure in the few early classes had changed into **acute** hatred. The chair, it seemed would stay empty.

232 paranoia [2]
n. 편집증
baseless or excessive suspicion of the motives of others

233 vilify [4]
v. 비난하다
criticize

234 allege [4]
v. 주장하다
assert, claim

235 transcribe [5]
v. 기록하다, 옮겨 쓰다
copy, rewrite

236 censure [2]
v. 비난하다, 책망하다
reproach or criticize harshly, blame

237 mischief [2]
n. 나쁜 짓, 못된 장난
misconduct, wrongdoing
a. mischievous

238 canvass [6]
v. 여론조사를 하다
poll; question a group of people to understand the majority opinion

239 acute [2]
a. 극심한, 격심한
intense, crucial

Vocabulary

0223
omniscient [7]
[ɑ:m|nɪsɪənt]

a. 모든 것을 다 아는   knowing everything, perceiving all things, all-knowing
omniscient sounds like omni + scientist so a scientist knows about all the things
The **omniscient** narrator knows all of the characters' thoughts. (*adj.*)

0224
appalled [9]
[əpɔːld]

a. 간담이 서늘한, 끔찍해 하는   filled or overcome with horror, consternation, or fear
스마트폰 초창기에 모든(all) 앱(app)을 배우려고 했을 때 얼마나 경악했는지 기억해?
Mrs. Ford was **appalled** when she saw how badly her beloved son had been beaten. (*v.*)

0225
renounce [3]
[rɪnáuns]

v. 포기하다   give up (usually disdainfully), to give up voluntarily
re(back) + nounce(announce, 공표하다, 선언하다) : "선언하여 뒤로 하다"로 직역된다.
She **renounced** what she previously loved. (*v.*)

0226
microcosm [2]
[|maɪkroʊkɑ:zəm]

n. 소우주 (더 큰 것의 축소판)   a little world, a world in miniature
microcosmos와 같은 말이다.
The family is a **microcosm** of society. (*n.*)

0227
hyperbole [5]
[haɪpə́ːrbəli]

n. 과장(법), 과장 어구   exaggeration; overstatement
라틴어 'hyper' beyond, 란 뜻으로 원래것보다 더 크게, 과장하는 것을 의미.
"I have a million things to do" is a **hyperbole**– you actually have only fifteen things to do. (*n.*)

0228
astounded [5]
[əstáundɪd]

a. 경악한, 충격 받은, 몹시 놀란   amazed, shocked
'stun', 어리벙벙하게 하다와 연관되어 있다.
The child was **astounded** by the magic trick at first, but he soon figured out the secret. (*adj.*)

0229
foolhardiness ²

[ˈfuːlhɑːdinəs]

n. 무모함   reckless and thoughtless boldness; foolish rash
a. foolhardy
fool은 머리가 hard해서 겁이 없고 무모하다.
There's no excuse for such **foolhardiness**. (*n.*)

0230
petulant ⁵

[pétʃulənt]

a. 심통 사나운, 발끈하는, 성마른   cranky, moody, showing sudden, impatient irritation
Usually related to acting like an angry child, argumentative for petty reasons.
The child was **petulant** after his punishment and took revenge by refusing to eat his dinner. (*adj.*)

0231
morose ³

[məróus]

a. 시무룩한, 뚱한   sad; melancholy, gloomy
mori는 '죽음'을 뜻하는 라틴어이다.
The **morose** young woman never stopped crying. (*adj.*)

0232
paranoia ²

[ˌpærəˈnɔiə]

n. 편집증, 피해망상   baseless or excessive suspicion of the motives of others
para(='beside') + noos(='mind') 생각이 엉뚱한 쪽으로만 가니까 paranoia.
Has his **paranoia** deepened over time? (*n.*)

0233
vilify ⁴

[víləfài]

v. 비난하다, 중상하다   criticize, slander
villain(악당)들이 주로 하는 일이 vilify하는 것이라고 외우자.
Prejudiced or interested writers **vilify** other nations. (*v.*)

0234
allege ⁴

[əlédʒ]

v. 주장하다, 단언하다   claim, to assert without proof
allege 는 ad(to)+leg(law)+e가 합쳐져 "법 쪽으로 가다" → "법정에서 증언하다" → "충분한 증거없이 단언하다, 주장하다"로 발전
The rock star sued the magazines that **alleged** he was using drugs, and won in court. (*adj.*)

0235
transcribe ⁵

[trænskráib]

v. 기록하다, 옮겨 쓰다, 베끼다   copy, rewrite, to write over again (something already written)
trans- "over" 와 scribere "쓰다".
In the old days, people **transcribed** the king's words on a paper to carry out his orders as accurately as possible. (*v.*)

0236
censure ²
[|senʃə(r)]

v. **비난하다, 책망하다**   reproach or criticize harshly, blame
census(인구조사), censor(검사관, 검열관)는 고대 로마의 귀족이나 시민의 국세를 조사하고 풍기단속을 관장했던 데서 온 말이다.
A vote of **censure** on the government's foreign policy (*adj.*)

0237
mischief ²
[|mɪstʃɪf]

n. **(심각하지 않은)나쁜 짓, 못된 장난**   misconduct, wrongdoing
a. mischievous
공포영화에서는 mischief가 misfortune 으로 이어지는 일이 잦다.
Those children are always getting into **mischief**. (*n.*)

0238
canvass ⁶
[|kænvəs]

v. **여론조사를 하다, 유세를 하다**   poll; question a group of people to understand the majority opinion, to solicit votes, opinions
어떤 화가의 스타일은 항상 유화(canvas)에 자기의 의견을 나타내는 것이야.
The candidate **canvassed** enough votes and won the election. (*v.*)

0239
acute ²
[ə|kju:t]

a. **극심한, 격심한**   intense, crucial
라틴어 acuere는 '예리하게 하다'는 뜻. 참고로 acupuncture는 '침술'.
There is an **acute** shortage of water. (*adj.*)

Voca Hamburger
Episode 14
MATCHING Quiz

1. omniscient — A. filled or overcome with horror, consternation, or fear
2. appalled — B. baseless or excessive suspicion of the motives of others
3. renounce — C. exaggeration
4. microcosm — D. reproach or criticize harshly, blame
5. hyperbole — E. cranky, moody
6. astounded — F. a little world, a world in miniature
7. foolhardiness — G. knowing everything
8. petulant — H. copy, rewrite
9. morose — I. reckless and thoughtless boldness; foolish rash
10. paranoia — J. intense, crucial
11. vilify — K. amazed, shocked
12. allege — L. sad; melancholy
13. transcribe — M. poll; question a group of people to understand the majority opinion
14. censure — N. assert, claim
15. mischief — O. misconduct, wrongdoing
16. canvass — P. give up (usually disdainfully)
17. acute — Q. criticize

1-G, 2-A, 3-P, 4-F, 5-C, 6-K, 7-I, 8-E, 9-L, 10-B, 11-Q, 12-N, 13-H, 14-D, 15-O, 16-M, 17-J

더 많은 문제를 풀고자 한다면 www.quizlet.com에서 'paul academy seoul' class를 검색

Episode 15: Study Group

Even with all the drama in the classroom, Jake had other things on his mind as he left the school that Monday afternoon.

After leaving the afternoon study session, Jake knew that his mother would be expecting him home promptly, so he decided to call her and tell her the truth, rather than **foray** some **elusive** story that would only get him into further trouble.

"What do you mean, a 'study group'?" she replied cynically. "You know that's a **notorious euphemism** for going out and wasting time, don't you?"

"Of course, Mom, but this is a real group."

"Who's in it? TJ?"

"No, he's got his own group," Jake said, a half-lie. He thought of his friend's strange circle of **intimidating** acquaintances and thought it would be best not to get him in trouble by revealing such a fact, especially since their mothers were friends as well.

"Well, who's in this one?" she asked warily.

"Well, this morning I ran into this girl Susan from school, and —"

"Oh, the short girl with the round glasses? She's lovely. Volunteers at homeless shelters, actually. I didn't know you were interested in her!"

Even though she must have been five miles away, his mother still knew how to make him turn red. However, this **revelation** had shown unexpectedly good results. Of course Susan would be a devoted volunteer. How couldn't she be?

---

240 foray [4]
v. 약탈하다
ravage in search of plunder; pillage

241 elusive [15]
a. 찾기 힘든
cleverly or skillfully evasive

242 notorious [5]
a. 악명 높은
famous in a bad way

243 euphemism [3]
n. 완곡어법
'good' word used in place of a bad one

244 intimidating [2]
a. 위협하는, 협박하는
frightening especially by threatening someone

245 revelation [13]
a. 폭로
something revealed; also, a realization

246 imply [23]
v. 암시하다
hint, insinuate
n. implication

247 pious [3]
a. 경건한
religious

248 timid [3]
a. 소심한
lacking in self-assurance, courage, or bravery; shy

249 sanction [3]
n. 허가, 인가
approval, permission

250 bliss [7]
n. 더 없는 행복
state of euphoria or heavenly happiness

251 deity [2]
n. 신
God

252 discrepant [6]
a. 모순되는
differing, not matching
n. discrepancy

253 exemplary [2]
a. 모범적인
serving as an example (very good)

254 inadvertent [2]
a. 고의가 아닌, 우연의
without intending; accidental

255 circumscribe [6]
v. 제한하다, 억제하다
limit, confine

256 colloquial [6]
a. 구어의
involving or using conversation; informal

"Mom, I'm not interested in her. This isn't some drama. I'm trying to be a good student."

"Sure you are, son," she replied in the same suspicious tone as before, but this time **implying** some happiness at the thought of her son having such a safe and **pious** crush. At least it was better than the truth, he thought. "Just tell her that I say hello to her mother?"

"Sure thing, Mom," he responded **timidly**, but overjoyed that he had been given **sanction** to see his newfound love. While his mother was doubtlessly hearing wedding bells in her post-conversation **bliss**, he was hearing Jessica's laugh from the morning's conversation.

The laugh greeted him as soon as he walked into the cafe twenty minutes later. She was sitting in the back, against the wall, with Susan at her right and an empty chair to her left, and Jake breathed a sigh of joy. Maybe there was some sort of **deity** up there after all.

The study session, like their first meeting that morning, was made worse as always by Susan, who constantly interrupted with questions about various vocabulary words, wondering why the definition in her dictionary gave her a **discrepant** definition of a word to that provided by her academy's vocab list. She was obviously someone whom teachers would call an **exemplary** student, but one who unfortunately had not learned much charm or social skills. Several times, she **inadvertently** revealed her own ignorance, as when she claimed 'curtail' was something one hung in window frames. Jake had to point out that she had misspelled it in her translator.

Curtail was an appropriate word, however, as she seemed to **circumscribe** any attempt Jake made at a joke or **colloquial** conversation with Jessica, as in this exchange:

Jake: What's '**flagrant** mean'?
Jessica: I'm not sure.
Jake: It sounds like someone's shouting about a national symbol.
Jessica: What do you mean?
Jake: Well, a rant is an **acrimonious** speech, right? So flag plus rant, like you're just screaming at a piece of cloth. I wonder if that helps with the definition.
Jessica: (laughing) I hope that's right. It would be so easy to remember.

Susan: (seriously) It means obviously wrong. Like that flag image. It won't help you, Jake.

At the end of the night, Jake was reminded by his mother to come home quickly after making sure Susan had got to the subway safely. He wondered how long he could continue this **swindle**, but for now it had bought him two free hours with Jessica and that was enough for now. He did walk them both to the station, but it was mostly to hear the laugh as often as he could before heading home.

---

257 flagrant [2]
a. 노골적인
intentionally harmful; obviously wrong; blatant

258 acrimonious [2]
a. 신랄한, 험악한
caustic, stinging, bitter

259 swindle [5]
n. 속임수, 사기
deceit, deception

Vocabulary

0240
foray [4]
[|fɔːreɪ|fɑː-]

v. 약탈하다   ravage in search of plunder; pillage
적들이 fortress를 넘어서 foray하고 있다고 생각하자.
He whets his knife today, sharp for the **foray**. (*n.*)

0241
elusive [15]
[ilúːsiv]

a. 찾기 힘든, (교묘히) 회피하는   cleverly or skillfully evasive, hard to grasp
'elude' 피하다라는 뜻의 파생형이다.
The cops never caught the **elusive** criminal. (*adj.*)

0242
notorious [5]
[noutɔ́ːriəs]

a. 악명 높은, (보통 나쁜 의미로) 유명한   famous in a bad way, unfavorably known
knowtorious라고 기억하자. 사람들이 알지만 좋은 의미로 아는 것은 아니라는 뜻.
Everyone knows the name of the **notorious** criminal, but nobody is brave enough to say it out loud. (*adj.*)

0243
euphemism [3]
[|juːfəmɪzəm]

n. 완곡어법   'good' word used in place of a bad one
eu(='good, well') + pheme(='speech, voice') 좋은 말로 얘기하니까 완곡어법.
'Pass away' is a **euphemism** for 'die'. (*n.*)

0244
intimidating [2]
[ɪn|tɪmɪdeɪtɪŋ]

a. 위협하는, 협박하는   frightening especially by threatening someone
intimate과 반대되는 뜻이라고 외워두자.
They have a pretty thuggish and **intimidating** past. (*adj.*)

0245
revelation [13]
[|revə|leɪʃn]

n. 폭로   something revealed; also, a realization
re(='opposite of') + velare(='to cover, veil') 감춰졌던 facts를 unveil 하는 것이다.
The **revelation** of the thief's hiding place (*n.*)

0246
imply [23]

[ımǀplaı]

v. 암시하다   hint, insinuate   *n.* implication
'감싸다'는 뜻의 라틴어 implien에서 온 단어이다.
Are you **implying** (that) I am wrong? (*adj.*)

0247
pious [3]

[páiəs]

a. 경건한   religious
'purus' 는 pure와 같은 어원이다. 마음이 순수해서 경건한 마음으로 신을 믿는 것.
The **pious** pastor always lifted his hands and said, "It is all thanks to God!" whenever people complimented him. (*adj.*)

0248
timid [3]

[ǀtımıd]

a. 소심한, 용기[자신감]가 없는   lacking in self-assurance, courage, or bravery; shy
intimidate (겁주다)에서 보듯이 timid는 겁먹은, 소심한 이란 뜻이다.
The man was too **timid** to say hi to the woman he liked. (*adj.*)

0249
sanction [3]

[sǽŋkʃən]

n. 허가, 인가, 제재   approval, permission, authoritative approval
sanct(holy)+ion이 합쳐져 "신성하게 함" → "허용, 찬성하다".
The government had **sanctions** against trade. (*n.*)

0250
bliss [7]

[blís]

n. 더 없는 행복, 다시 없는 기쁨   state of euphoria or heavenly happiness, ecstasy
bless(축복)를 받으면 bliss해져.
Bliss on a warm and peaceful day. (*n.*)

0251
deity [2]

[ǀdeıəti:ǀdi:əti]

n. 신   God
divine한 entity를 줄였다고 생각하자.
People are treating him like a **deity** in death. (*n.*)

0252
discrepant [6]

[diskrépənt]

a. 모순되는   differing, not matching   *n.* discrepancy
dis를 'kept'로 바꾸어서 생각해보면 '똑같은 상태로 있지 않는다'라고 생각하며 외울 수 있다.
But no government has ever offered any explanation or justification for the **discrepant** treatment. (*adj.*)

0253
exemplary [2]

[ɪɡ|zempləri]

a. **모범적인**   serving as an example (very good)
example(예시)에서 유래한 단어.
The **exemplary** woman was awarded Employee of The Month. (*adj.*)

0254
inadvertent [2]

[inədvə́ːrtnt]

a. **고의가 아닌, 우연의, 의도하지 않은**   without intending; accidental, not on purpose
advertent는 '주의가 깊다'는 뜻이다. 반대로 주의를 주지않으면(in-) 의도하지 않은 상황이 생길 수 있다.
I happily accept that it was **inadvertent**. (*adj.*)

0255
circumscribe [6]

[|sɜːrkəmskraɪb]

v. **제한하다, 억제하다, ~의 둘레에 선을 긋다**   limit, confine; to draw a line around
만약 원(circle) 안에 게(crab, sounds like cribe)를 가둔다면 게들의 의지를 억제하는 행동이겠지?
The scope of the chickens' movements are **circumscribed** by their cages. (*v.*)

0256
colloquial [6]

[kəlóukwiəl]

a. **구어(체)의, 일상회화의**   involving or using conversational speech; informal
co-(함께)와 loq (speaking, 말하는) 가 합쳐져 함께 말하는, "구어체의"란 뜻이다.
"Ain't" is a **colloquial** form of "isn't", so we shouldn't use it in formal writing. (*adj.*)

0257
flagrant [2]

[fléigrənt]

a. **노골적인, 명백한**   intentionally harmful; obviously wrong; blatant, openly scandalous; shameless
flagrant fragrance '명백한 향기'.
The criminal was caught due to the **flagrant** evidence he left at the scene-his knife with his fingerprints. (*adj.*)

0258
acrimonious [2]

[æ̀krəmóuniəs]

a. **신랄한, 험악한, 호된**   caustic, stinging, bitter
우리 팀 ace, 컴퓨터회사 acer 등 모두 뾰족한 것의 윗부분(top)을 상상하면 된다. acri(shart)+monious도 뾰족한 부분으로 찌르니까 '신랄한'처럼 외우면 되겠다.
Their relationship grew **acrimonious** after the fight. (*adj.*)

0259

swindle [swíndl]

n. 속임수, 사기, 속이다   deceit, deception; to deceive; to cheat

wind와 비슷한 발음이니까 '바람둥이'라고 연상하면 '속이다'는 뜻을 유추할 수 있다.

They **swindled** him out of hundreds of dollars. (*v.*)

Voca Hamburger
Episode 15
MATCHING Quiz

1. foray
2. elusive
3. notorious
4. euphemism
5. intimidating
6. revelation
7. imply
8. pious
9. timid
10. sanction
11. bliss
12. deity
13. discrepant
14. exemplary
15. inadvertent
16. circumscribe
17. colloquial
18. flagrant
19. acrimonious
20. swindle

A. frightening especially by threatening someone
B. serving as an example (very good)
C. caustic, stinging, bitter
D. 'good' word used in place of a bad one
E. differing, not matching
F. without intending; accidental
G. famous in a bad way
H. cleverly or skillfully evasive
I. something revealed; also, a realization
J. hint, insinuate
K. religious
L. ravage in search of plunder; pillage
M. intentionally harmful; obviously wrong; blatant
N. limit, confine
O. God
P. state of euphoria or heavenly happiness
Q. lacking in self-assurance, courage, or bravery; shy
R. approval, permission
S. involving or using conversation; informal
T. deceit, deception

1-L, 2-H, 3-G, 4-D, 5-A, 6-I, 7-J, 8-K, 9-Q, 10-R, 11-P, 12-O, 13-E, 14-B, 15-F, 16-N, 17-S, 18-M, 19-C, 20-T

더 많은 문제를 풀고자 한다면 www.quizlet.com에서 'paul academy seoul' class를 검색

Episode 16

The Game

260 boisterously [2]
adv. 떠들썩하게
loudly

261 console [2]
v. 위로하다, 위안을 주다
soothe, comfort, assuage
a. consolatory

262 evade [4]
v. 피하다
avoid, circumvent

263 devious [5]
a. 정직하지 못한, 기만적인
with evil or deceitful intention

264 deferential [9]
a. 공손한
respectful; reverential

265 hunched [4]
a. 구부린
bent; not standing straight

266 skulk [2]
v. 몰래 숨다
lie or keep in hiding, as for some evil reason

267 unequivocally [4]
adv. 명백히, 분명히
undeniably

268 halting [5]
a. 멈칫거리는
faltering or hesitating

On Thursday morning Jake was early, with the sound of The Cure's "Friday I'm in Love" playing **boisterously** in his ears to comfort his morning's hunger and to **console** his growing hatred of waking up so early.

Coming around the usual corner, **evading** the small pine bush which grew on the street, he was nearly splashed by the cleaning woman's hose as she cleaned the sidewalk outside the front door. She smiled **deviously**, as if to say "next time, young man, I'll get you," but answered his **deferential** 'good morning' as though he was a young prince returning to his castle. He was about to enter into the hallway's blackness when he heard the nearby fall of coins, followed by a familiar voice.

"Why can't I win just once?"

Startled, he looked for the source of the voice, and noticed a pair of **hunched** figures **skulking** on the other side of a table of the cafe next door, where they would be mostly hidden from view. The figure nearest him Jake recognized as Sam from TJ's lunches — he'd started eating with the other boy more frequently since the first day, though they were no longer bothered by the frightening older boys — and the farther one, rocking slightly to keep his balance, was **unequivocally** the chief Poseur himself, TJ.

"Hello!" Jake called out as he approached. Sam rose to his unusually awkward height, and approached Jake with the **halting** walk of a young deer who had only recently mastered walking.

"Hey Sam. What are you guys doing?" Jake turned his neck around to see TJ still squatting down, tossing a coin impatiently up and down in his right hand. The lower figure spun around when he heard Jake speak, and looked a bit embarrassed.

"Jake! What are you doing here so early?"

"I was going to ask you the same question," Jake replied.

"Oh, it's just a game we invented. Wanna see?" TJ was obviously eager to return to playing.

"Sure."

TJ began to explain the rules, which were **ingeniously** simple and just the sort of thing that one **contrives** when one has too much time to think and too little to do. The game was called "The Toss," but its **nomenclature** didn't matter, since normally one of the boys just hit a few coins in his hand as an invitation to play. Players had to sit, resting on their heels with knees off the ground at all times. A large coffee cup filled with **distilled** water using a **conduit** nearby was placed in its customary place about 7 meters away, just far enough to require a forceful throw. They threw quarters toward the cup. If you missed, you had to pay two coins. If you hit the cup without making it in, you had to pay five coins. Only the player who got the coin into the bottom of the cup could claim the pot.

Jake, who had been **fostered** in a conservative home and taught the **heinous** danger of gambling, looked on uneasily, slightly worried about TJ's unappealing interest in coin throwing. Nonetheless, he was curious to see how it worked and sat down to pass the few moments before class began.

TJ was set to throw, and there were about fifteen or twenty coins on the paper between them. He showed almost comedic concentration, his boyish forehead wrinkled as he **squinted** toward the darkness where the cup had been set. He drew his arm back, and tossed his coin about ten centimeters above the cup. Sam started laughing.

"Two more, my friend," he said, taking his position. He took a coin from his pocket and tossed it in the air a few times to **assess** its weight. He held his finger in the air as if to **gauge** the air pressure. He repeated TJ's motion of taking his arm backwards and threw the coin higher into the air. It seemed to hang there for a minute before coming down, right into the middle of the cup. A little water splashed out onto the iron floor.

---

269 ingeniously [11]
adv. 재치 있게
cleverly

270 contrive [2]
v. 고안하다, 창안하다
devise, create, invent

271 nomenclature [3]
n. (학술적) 이름
naming

272 distilled [5]
a. 증류된
processed through vaporization and subsequent condensation, as for purification

273 conduit [2]
n. 도관
a pipe or channel for conveying fluids

274 foster [8]
v. 양육하다, 조성하다
promote the growth of, raise

275 heinous [2]
a. 악랄한, 극악무도한
abhorrent, horrifying

276 squint [3]
v. 눈을 가늘게 뜨고 보다
look with the eyes partly closed

277 assess [14]
v. 재다, 평가하다
estimate officially the value of

278 gauge [4]
v. 측정하다
measure

"Ha! All mine!" he took an empty coffee cup that had been sitting beside him and poured the coins into it. TJ looked disappointed, but by then a few other students had gathered and it seemed a good time to enter the classroom.

Vocabulary

0260

boisterously [2]

[ˈbɔɪstərəsli]

adv. 떠들썩하게   loudly
'boys'terous. 남자애들은 모이면 시끄럽고 떠들썩하다고 외우자.
Although the students had been asked to keep their voices down, they continued to talk **boisterously**. (*adv.*)

0261

console [2]

[kənˈsoʊl]

v. 위로하다, 위안을 주다   soothe, comfort, assuage, to allievate or lessen the grief   *a.* consolatory
만약 연인과 헤어진 친구가 솔로(solo)가 되면 위로가 필요하겠지?
Stephen **consoled** his disappointed friend by saying, "Hey, at least you have a higher score than me." (*v.*)

0262

evade [4]

[ɪˈveɪd]

v. 피하다   avoid, circumvent, to escape from by trickery
자만심이 강한 (vain)사람들은 자기 잘못을 회피 (evade)하려고 하죠.
He **evaded** her questions by saying, "Ask no questions, Hermione, and we'll tell no lies." (*v.*)

0263

devious [5]

[ˈdiːviəs]

a. 정직하지 못한, 기만적인   with evil or deceitful intention, departing from the most direct way
명확한(obvious)과 de가 합쳐져서 devious(정직하지 못한)란 단어가 나왔다고 암기하자!
The **devious** villain said smoothly, "Oh, children, I'm not trying to hurt you." (*adj.*)

0264

deferential [9]

[dèfərénʃəl]

a. 공손한   respectful; reverential
de(down) + fer(carry) 로 자기 자신을 남의 아래로 이끈다. 즉 '복종하고 존경을 표한다'는 뜻이다.
He has a **deferential** attitude toward important customers. (*adj.*)

0265

hunched [4]

[hʌntʃt]

a. 구부린   bent; not standing straight
유명한 Hunchback of Notre Dame을 기억하자.
He **hunched** his shoulders and thrust his hands deep into his pockets. (*v.*)

0266
skulk ²
[skʌ́lk]

v. 몰래 숨다; 숨은　　lie or keep in hiding, as for some evil reason, lurking; hidden
너의 skull 안에서만 생각해서, '숨다'라는 뜻.
There was someone **skulking** behind the bushes. (v.)

0267
unequivocally ⁴
[|ʌnɪ|kwɪvəkli]

adv. 명백히, 분명히　　undeniably
un은 '아닌', equi는 '동일한', voc는 '말하다'라는 뜻이므로 양쪽에 대하여 비슷하게 얘기하지 않는, 즉 '명백한'이란 의미를 가진다.
We found them most **unequivocally** in the Russian camp. (adv.)

0268
halting ⁵
[|hɔ:ltɪŋ]

a. 멈칫거리는　　faltering or hesitating
hal 헐떡이면 멈춰서 쉬어야 한다.
I talked with him in **halting** English. (adj.)

0269
ingeniously ¹¹
[ɪn|dʒi:niəsli]

adv. 재치 있게　　cleverly
genius의 머릿속은 똑똑하고 재치 있지.
This book is **ingeniously** edited. (adv.)

0270
contrive ²
[kən|traɪv]

v. 고안하다, 창안하다　　devise, create, invent
con(='with') + tropus(='song, musical code') 음표를 같이 모아서 놔두는 것은 새로운 음악을 '창안'해 내는 것.
They **contrived** a plan to defraud the company. (v.)

0271
nomenclature ³
[nə|menklətʃə(r)]

n. (학술적) 이름　　naming
name을 classic하게 부른다고 생각하자.
We are merely talking about a change in **nomenclature**. (n.)

0272
distilled ⁵
[dɪstíld]

a. 증류된　　processed through vaporization and subsequent condensation, as for purification, purified; extracted
화학시간에 distilled water 들어본 적 있지? 물을 가열했을 때 발생하는 수증기를 냉각시켜 정제된 물을 말해.
Drinking any water can be very dangerous; you should drink only **distilled** water. (adj.)

0273
conduit [2]
[|kɑːnduɪt]

n. 도관   a pipe or channel for conveying fluids
duct '배관'이라는 말과 duit는 같은 어원이다.
They are an important **conduit** for training and recruitment. (*n.*)

0274
foster [8]
[fɔ́ːstər]

v. 양육하다; 조성하다, [육성]촉진하다   raise; to promote growth
드라마에서 'foster mom, dad'라고 들어본적 있지? 즉, 친모/부는 아니지만 길러준 부모를 말하는 것이다.
Plenty of light and water are necessary to **foster** potted plants. (*v.*)

0275
heinous [2]
[|heɪnəs]

a. 악랄한, 극악무도한, 가증스러운   abhorrent, horrifying
'증오하다'라는 의미를 가진 hate와 같은 어원을 쓰며 말 그대로 hateable의 의미를 가진다.
While laughing, the **heinous** murderer killed the victims extremely painfully. (*adj.*)

0276
squint [3]
[skwɪnt]

v. 눈을 가늘게 뜨고 보다, 사시, 사팔뜨기   look with the eyes partly closed
눈을 가늘게 뜨면 약간 기울어진듯 보이지? slant에서 변형된 단어야.
She was **squinting** through the keyhole. (*v.*)

0277
assess [14]
[əses]

v. 재다, 평가하다   estimate officially the value of
asset(자산)은 assess해 봐야 제 맛.
It's difficult to **assess** the effects of these changes. (*adj.*)

0278
gauge [4]
[géidʒ]

v. 측정하다, 알아내다   to measure an amount, often by using a device
정확한 측정을 통해 확인하다는 의미인 프랑스 고어 gauger에서 유래한 단어이다.
They distributed a survey to **gauge** the public's reaction to the news. (*v.*)

Note :

Episode 16

MATCHING Quiz

1. boisterously
2. console
3. evade
4. devious
5. deferential
6. hunched
7. skulk
8. unequivocally
9. halting
10. ingeniously
11. contrive
12. nomenclature
13. distilled
14. conduit
15. foster
16. heinous
17. squint
18. assess
19. gauge

A. lie or keep in hiding, as for some evil reason
B. bent; not standing straight
C. loudly
D. devise, create, invent
E. faltering or hesitating
F. measure
G. respectful; reverential
H. avoid, circumvent
I. estimate officially the value of
J. look with the eyes partly closed
K. with evil or deceitful intention
L. abhorrent, horrifying
M. soothe, comfort, assuage
N. cleverly
O. naming
P. undeniably
Q. processed through vaporization and subsequent condensation, as for purification
R. promote the growth of, raise
S. a pipe or channel for conveying fluids

1-C, 2-M, 3-K, 4-K, 5-G, 6-B, 7-A, 8-P, 9-E, 10-N, 11-D, 12-O, 13-Q, 14-S, 15-R, 16-L, 17-J, 18-I, 19-F

더 많은 문제를 풀고자 한다면 www.quizlet.com에서 'paul academy seoul' class를 검색

Episode 17 — Maternal Criticism

Jake returned home on Thursday to find his mother waiting for him in the kitchen. Her face bore a serious expression, and she wore a cooking apron to **bolster** her motherly authority.

"Excuse me? Do you want to go out or would you rather stay in this boring **sanctuary** all day? Look at me!"

Adults were always asking you to look at them, he thought. He regretfully took out his earphones and looked at her, thinking that it was strange that people **ascribe** so much value to eyes. After all, they're just little objects of white and color. He looked at her, but he was really just **delving** into thoughts on Darwinian evolution. At that moment, Jake could see how his mother was related to fish.

"I'm listening," he said with as much anger as he could manage.

"Well, never mind your teenage pain. I got a text from the school yesterday." Her tone was **portentous**, he thought, as though she was about to **conjure** a black cloud over their heads.

"Do you know what they told me?" she asked **rhetorically**. Of course he knew. Monday. Love. Forgotten vocab quiz. Et cetera. But he couldn't talk to her about all of that. He stayed quiet, hoping that his silence could **vindicate** him from her **ruthless** questioning.

"A failed vocabulary test hurts me, Jake, it really does, and no **pharmaceutical** product could cure me." She would be the first to admit that her metaphors needed work, but she continued anyway. "After all the work your father does, at that office all day, and you ruin your chances of a good education by **foiling** every opportunity you get." Jake had to give her credit for her acting. She seemed to have tears in her eyes.

The chances his father had given him? '*You see this room*?' He thought about his father's face as he had said these words, and then

---

279 bolster [3]
v. 강화하다
reinforce, strengthen

280 sanctuary [3]
n. 성소, 성역
a sacred or holy place

281 ascribe [8]
v. 돌리다, 탓하다
give credit to; attribute

282 delve [2]
v. 조사하다, 연구하다
investigate, examine

283 portentous [1]
a. (불길한) 징후가 있는
having bad signs for the future; foreboding

284 conjure [6]
v. 마술을 부리다
magically make something appear

285 rhetorically [27]
adv. 수사적으로
related to public speaking

286 vindicate [3]
v. 정당성을 입증하다
free from blame/guilt

287 ruthless [13]
a. 무자비한
without pity
cf. ruth

288 **pharmaceutical** [2]
a. 약학의
pertaining to pharmacy or pharmacists

289 **foil** [2]
v. 좌절시키다
prevent success of

290 **nostalgically** [42]
adv. 향수에 젖어
desiring to return to the past

291 **cryptic** [2]
a. 수수께끼 같은
mysterious, difficult to understand; inscrutable

292 **rebel** [8]
n. 반역자
a person who resists any authority, control, or tradition

293 **conventional** [15]
a. 관습적인
conforming or adhering to accepted standards

294 **refute** [28]
v. 논박하다
contradict, deny

295 **indulgent** [3]
a. 관대한
lenient, permissive

296 **subversion** [11]
n. 전복, 파괴
the state of being subverted; destruction
v. subvert

looked back at his mother. How the two had stayed married so long, he had no idea. He **nostalgically** thought of how he had wished, as a child, that his parents had divorced and that he'd be allowed to live with his father, no matter how **cryptic** the man was in real life. At least it would be better than this difficult woman.

She stared at him, trying to induce some emotional response.

"What about all of those heroes you have? Don't you want to be like them?" she asked after a long pause. Jake smiled. His heroes were all **rebels**, people who probably all dropped out of high school or who had genius that didn't need **conventional** education.

"Of course, Mom, but —"

"*But*?" she cried, as though no one in the history of conversation had ever used such a term before. "You're going to **refute** me? Good God, do I have to hit you now, too? That's two vocabulary quizzes you've failed. I allowed the first one because I'm an **indulgent** person. I know it's difficult to adjust a new environment, but this is inexcusable. How exactly were you planning to make an excuse for yourself?"

Jake burned with rage. Couldn't she, at least once, understand? But he said nothing again, merely looking at the ground. He knew that some children talked back to their parents. He wondered how many were left alive after their **subversion**.

"Go to your room, Jake, if you're not going to answer me. You can eat in there tonight."

He went to his room and texted Jessica about this injustice. She responded a minute later:

Parents don't really get it, do they?

Vocabulary

0279

bolster [3]

[bóulstər]

v. 강화하다　reinforce, strengthen, to support, as something wrong
베개 밑에 까는 기다란 덧베개를 일컫는 말로 기계의 받침대나 덧대는 물건을 가리킬 때 쓴다.
The nervous man took several deep breaths to **bolster** his confidence before going into the interview. (v.)

0280

sanctuary [3]

[sǽŋktʃuèri]

n. 성소, 성역　a sacred or holy place
sanct '신성한'이란 뜻이다.
When the Christian **sanctuary** was invaded by nomads, the citizens got extremely mad. (n.)

0281

ascribe [8]

[əskráib]

v. 돌리다, ~의 탓으로 돌리다　give credit to; to attribute to a specific cause
오스카(Oscar, sounds like Ascr)상을 받으면 주변 사람들에게 감사를 돌려야(ascribe)한다고 기억하자.
He **ascribed** his cold to the thinness of his winter jacket. (v.)

0282

delve [2]

[délv]

v. 조사하다, 연구하다, 탐구하다, 찾다　to investigate, examine
dig around for의 의미이다.
The anthropologist **delved** into the ruins to find hidden mysteries. (v.)

0283

portentous [1]

[pɔːrténtəs]

a. (불길한) 징후가 있는　having bad signs for the future; foreboding, an indication of something important or calamitous
portent가 불길한 예고를 의미한다.
The coffee spilled on his shirt was **portentous** for the rest of his terrible day. (adj.)

0284
conjure [6]
[|kʌndʒə(r)|]

v. 마술을 부리다　magically make something appear, to influence by invocation or spell
con이라는 prefix(접두사)는 agree(동의하다)라는 뜻이다. 이길수 없는 재판에서 배심원(jury)에게 동의(con)를 받으려면 마술(magical power)이 필요하겠지?
The magician **conjured** up a bunny eating a carrot out of thin air. (*v.*)

0285
rhetorically [27]
[rɪ|tɔːrɪkli]

adv. 수사적으로　related to public speaking
love letter는 최대한 rhetorical하게 쓰면 더 좋겠지?
"Do these kids know how lucky they are?" Jackson asked **rhetorically**. (*adv.*)

0286
vindicate [3]
[víndəkèit]

v. 정당성을 입증하다;정당한, 무죄가 입증된
free from blame/guilt, proved to be innocent
vin(win) + di(the) + cate(case), 즉 법정에서 승소해서 혐의에서 풀려났다.
The **vindicated** one has been freed from his wrongful charges. (*adj.*)

0287
ruthless [13]
[rúːθlis]

a. 무자비한, 무정한　without pity, pitiless; cruel　*cf.* ruth
rut(regret) + less
The **ruthless** dictator killed everyone who failed without giving a second chance. (*adj.*)

0288
pharmaceutical [2]
[|fɑːrmə|suːtɪkl]

a. 약학의　pertaining to pharmacy or pharmacists
pharmacy는 '약국, 약학'을 말한다.
I worked at a **pharmaceutical** company in Minneapolis. (*adj.*)

0289
foil [2]
[fɔɪl]

v. 좌절시키다　prevent success of; frustrate
알루미늄 호일 (foil)로 꽁꽁 싸매면 아무것도 못하겠지? 그래서 상대방의 계략을 좌절시키다 라는 동사로 쓰인다.
CIA found out about the terrorists' plan of bombing New York and **foiled** it beforehand. (*v.*)

0290
nostalgically [42]

[nɒˈstældʒɪkli]

adv. 향수에 젖어   desiring to return to the past
향수병, 고향을 그리워하는 마음을 nostalgia라고 한다.
People look back **nostalgically** on the war period, simply because everyone pulled together. (*adv.*)

0291
cryptic [2]

[kríptik]

a. 수수께끼 같은, 비밀스러운   mysterious, difficult to understand; inscrutable
crypt(hidden)를 어원으로 갖고 있다.
It took hours for the agents to solve the **cryptic** code. (*adj.*)

0292
rebel [8]

[rɪ|bel]

n. 반역자   a person who resists any authority, control, or tradition
revolution을 하려면 일단 rebel부터 해야지.
Armed **rebels** advanced towards the capital. (*n.*)

0293
conventional [15]

[kənvénʃən]

a. 관습적인   conforming or adhering to accepted standards, traditional
con은 '합치다'의 의미로 합쳐진 사회의 관습이라고 생각하자.
It is **conventional** for a bride to wear a wedding dress. (*adj.*)

0294
refute [28]

[rifjúːt]

v. 논박하다   contradict, deny, to prove to be wrong
re는 '되돌려', futare는 '때리다'는 뜻으로 반박하다라는 뜻이다.
He tried to **refute** the rumors with contrary evidence. (*v.*)

0295
indulgent [3]

[indʌ́ldʒənt]

a. 관대한, 멋대로 하게 하는   benignly lenient or permissive
마음 속('in'side')이 'dul'l해질 때까지 하고 싶은것을 마음껏 한다고 해석하자.
The chocolate cake was an **indulgent** treat. (*adj.*)

0296
subversion [11]

[səbvə́ːrʒən,-ʃən]

n. 전복, 파괴   the state of being subverted; destruction
sub(under), vertere(to turn)의 어원을 갖고 있다.
He was arrested on charges of **subversion** for organizing the demonstration. (*n.*)

Note :

Episode 17

MATCHING Quiz

1. bolster
2. sanctuary
3. ascribe
4. delve
5. portentous
6. conjure
7. rhetorically
8. vindicate
9. ruthless
10. pharmaceutical
11. foil
12. nostalgically
13. cryptic
14. rebel
15. conventional
16. refute
17. indulgent
18. subversion

A. a sacred or holy place
B. pertaining to pharmacy or pharmacists
C. lenient, permissive
D. investigate, examine
E. prevent success of
F. without pity
G. related to public speaking
H. magically make something appear
I. desiring to return to the past
J. free from blame/guilt
K. reinforce, strengthen
L. conforming or adhering to accepted standards
M. give credit to; attribute
N. contradict, deny
O. a person who resists any authority, control, or tradition
P. the state of being subverted; destruction
Q. mysterious, difficult to understand; inscrutable
R. having bad signs for the future; foreboding

1-K, 2-A, 3-M, 4-D, 5-R, 6-H, 7-G, 8-J, 9-F, 10-B, 11-E, 12-I, 13-Q, 14-O, 15-L, 16-N, 17-C, 18-P

더 많은 문제를 풀고자 한다면 www.quizlet.com에서 'paul academy seoul' class를 검색

Episode 18: Lingerie and Roses are Not Good Ideas for a First Date

A few days after the study session, Jake still returned to thoughts of Jessica, and brief **snatches** of conversation interrupted his concentration during the essay class especially, when the students were asked to sit in silence for at least half an hour to write. He hadn't been able to finish the **preamble** for the last three classes.

The cafe sessions themselves weren't every day, since Susan had a math tutor she met on Tuesdays and Thursdays, and they all had agreed that Friday nights were better spent "studying vocab" separately, rather than engaging in their usual scholarly **symbiosis**. This meant different things for each of them. Jake usually did try to study for an hour or so, but his phone would start vibrating, and he and a distant friend would fall into a conversation that would **diverge** from the subject of the SAT very quickly. He found it difficult to keep his focus **straddled** between two topics, and usually ended up just talking with his friends.

He had a friend studying as an exchange student abroad who chatted with him regularly during this time, as Jake's Friday night was his Friday morning, and he told stories full of news of horrible home-stay families, homesickness, or new relationships with local girls or sometimes (scandalously) college girls, who were **deemed** more mysterious. Since these stories were usually fictional on his end, it seemed improper to Jake to **disclose** his current love of with a very real human girl.

To his friends at the academy, however, it was a different story. To begin with, the older boys had seen Jessica, and so he had proof of she existed. He decided to tell a few of them, but since TJ couldn't keep a secret, nearly half the school knew about it before lunchtime.

During lunch on Friday, after a second study session with her, Jake met the boys for their now-usual lunch meeting (Jake enjoyed their company, and TJ seemed to enjoy it much more than his old habit of hanging out with the older boys), but this time it was focused not on

---

297 snatch [3]
n. 조각, 단편
a bit, piece, fragment

298 preamble [3]
n. 서문
introduction, preface

299 symbiosis [2]
n. 공생
the living together of two dissimilar organisms, as in mutualism

300 diverge [2]
v. 갈라지다
depart from; go down a different path

301 straddle [2]
v. 걸터앉다
sit or stand with the legs wide apart

302 deem [3]
v. 여기다, 간주하다
think, regard

303 disclose [4]
v. 밝히다, 드러내다
reveal; betray

| 304 | **innate** ³
a. 타고난
in-built; something one is born with, rather than acquired

| 305 | **outlandish** ⁵
a. 기이한
strange; not normal

| 306 | **shard** ²
n. 조각, 파편
a fragment, especially of broken earthenware

| 307 | **pivotal** ³
a. 중심적인
central, key, essential

| 308 | **stellar** ⁵
a. 별의; 뛰어난
of or relating to the stars; like a star, as in brilliance

| 309 | **haphazardly** ²
adv. 우연히
by chance; randomly; indiscriminately

---

sports or pop stars or cars but on something more serious: getting Jake involved romantically with Jessica. When a car breaks down, men have an **innate** need to stand around the engine block and offer their advice, no matter how **outlandish** or unprofessional it might be. New relationships are the same way, and Jake's team of strategists sat around him like he had a broken radiator, offering their own wildly contradictory **shards** of "wisdom."

"You've got to get her flowers, man," said the usually-quiet Sam, who had surprised everyone when it had been discovered a few days earlier that he had a girlfriend he saw on the weekends. "Girls love flowers."

"No, no, only old men do that. Underwear is the best gift. Girls love it." TJ, it surprised no one, had no girlfriend, but believed underwear to be a **pivotal** part to any attempt to win a girl's heart.

"Absolutely not. Here's what I would do —"

"Oh come on, man. Something sexy, you know, let her know you're serious."

Jake put up his hands in protest. "I'm not buying her underwear, TJ. What's your plan, Sam?"

"Well, I've never done it, but it's a **stellar** idea. Call her up ask her to **haphazardly** pick a number between one and nine. Then you go out and buy the same number of roses. Nice, huh?" The tall and awkward boy smiled widely, clearly waiting for their approval.

"Nope," sad TJ, before he began a long talk about lace and patterns which was interrupted when they realized they were already five minutes late to afternoon class.

Vocabulary

0297
snatch [snætʃ]
n. 조각, 단편, 와락 붙잡다, 잡아채다   a bit, piece, fragment
smack은 '찰싹 때리는' 것이고, snatch는 '확 잡아채는' 것이라고 비교해서 외우자.
The man **snatched** the paper bag from[out of] my hand. (v.)

0298
preamble [priˈæmbl]
n. 서문   introduction, preface
amble은 '천천히 걷는' 것을 말한다. 걷기 대회를 하기 전에는 preamble부터 읽어야겠지?
The aims of the treaty are stated in its **preamble**. (n.)

0299
symbiosis [ˌsɪmbaɪˈoʊsɪs]
n. 공생, 협력 관계   the living together of two dissimilar organisms, as in mutualism; collaboration
sync를 생각하면 외우기 쉽다.
Some beneficial bacteria live in **symbiosis** with their hosts. (n.)

0300
diverge [dɪvˈɜːrdʒ, daɪ-]
v. 갈라지다; 차이   depart from; go down a different path; difference between
두 개로 나뉘어질 때 사용하는 단어이다.
The parallel lines appear to **diverge**.(n.)

0301
straddle [ˈstrædl]
v. 걸터앉다   sit or stand with the legs wide apart
stride '성큼성큼 걷다'가 지치면 잠깐 straddle하면 좋다.
He swung his leg over the motorcycle, **straddling** it easily. (v.)

0302
deem [diːm]
v. ...로 여기다, 간주하다   to form or have an opinion, think, regard
dim (멍청한) 사람은 deem하기도 어렵지.
I thought my answers were right, but my teacher **deemed** them wrong. (v.)

0303
disclose [4]
[disklóuz]

v. 밝히다, 드러내다   to reveal; betray
'dis' not 'close' 닫지 않는다의 의미로 '보여주다, 공개하다'라는 뜻.
Finally, after months of secrecy, Apple **disclosed** the design for the new iPhone. (*v.*)

0304
innate [3]
[inéit]

a. 타고난, 천성의   in-built; something one is born with, rather than acquired, existing in one from birth
'~에서 유래한, 태어난'의 의미인 라틴어 innatus에서 유래했다.
His lack of **innate** talent is not a problem, because he practices more than anybody else. (*adj.*)

0305
outlandish [5]
[autlǽndiʃ]

a. 기이한, 이국풍의   strange; not normal, very unusual
out + land 먼 나라 이야기같이 이상한.
The dancer dressed **outlandishly**: he had a green beard, red scarf, and a sparkly gold suit. (*adv.*)

0306
shard [2]
[ʃɑːrd]

n. 조각, 파편   a fragment, especially of broken earthenware
유리의 shard는 sharp하지.
There is a **shard** of glass in his finger. (*n.*)

0307
pivotal [3]
[pívətl]

a. 중심적인, 중심이 되는   central, key, essential, crucial; vital
pivot은 '축, 중심'을 말한다.
Bismarck was a **pivotal** figure in history, because he changed the way people view countries. (*adj.*)

0308
stellar [5]
[ˈstelə(r)]

a. 별의; 뛰어난   of or relating to the stars; like a star, as in brilliance
star like한 것이 stellar라고 생각하자.
All we have to do is correct for **stellar** drift. (*adj.*)

0309
haphazardly [2]
[hæpˈhæzərdli]

adv. 우연히   by chance; randomly; indiscriminately
haphazard하면 많은 위험들 (hazard)이 있을 수도 있다.
She looked at the books jammed **haphazardly** in the shelves. (*adv.*)

Note :

Voca Hamburger

Episode 18

MATCHING Quiz

1. snatch	A. a fragment, especially of broken earthenware
2. preamble	B. introduction, preface
3. symbiosis	C. by chance; randomly; indiscriminately
4. diverge	D. depart from; go down a different path
5. straddle	E. of or relating to the stars; like a star, as in brilliance
6. deem	F. a bit, piece, fragment
7. disclose	G. the living together of two dissimilar organisms, as in mutualism
8. innate	H. reveal; betray
9. outlandish	I. strange; not normal
10. shard	J. in-built; something one is born with, rather than acquired
11. pivotal	K. think, regard
12. stellar	L. sit or stand with the legs wide apart
13. haphazardly	M. central, key, essential

1-F, 2-B, 3-G, 4-D, 5-L, 6-K, 7-H, 8-J, 9-I, 10-A, 11-M, 12-E, 13-C

더 많은 문제를 풀고자 한다면 www.quizlet.com에서 'paul academy seoul' class를 검색

Episode 19

Women, the Grand Riddle

310 riddle ³
n. 수수께끼, 미스터리
a puzzling question, problem; enigma, conundrum

311 array ⁸
v. 배치하다, 진열하다
place in a proper order

312 lurid ⁵
a. 섬뜩한, 소름 끼치는
gruesome; horrible; shocking

    On the way back to the academy, the boys passed the Starbucks, all checking their reflections in the window as young people do. As he stared past his own reflection, Jake noticed a familiar face in the window. It was Ashley, the academy drop-out. She had **arrayed** her books over the countertop and who was now staring right back at him, her expression blank yet looking somewhat concerned. The boys made a few of the usual jokes about her craziness, but Jake felt the need to go inside. After all, they had been desk-mates for her brief time in class.

    "Hey," he said as he approached her.

    She looked horrified to have been discovered, and he regretted coming in. He was just about to turn back and leave her in silence when TJ burst in and walked straight towards her.

    "How's it going Ashley? We've missed you," he said, extending his hand.

    She grew even more embarrassed, but stayed dumb.

    "Well, just don't fall in love with our Jake here," he said, ignoring her discomfort. "He's got a girlfriend now." TJ smiled **luridly** at this and then departed, saying he'd see Jake in class a few minutes later.

    Now it was Jake's turn to feel embarrassed, and he just stood there awkwardly until she broke the silence, finally.

    "Off the market, huh?" she said, with a slight smile sprouting at the corners of her lips.

    He looked down at his feet, but still nodded.

    "Got a date, or is this just one of those teenage imaginary crushes?"

Crush! To speak of his profound love for Jessica in these terms was **heresy**! Ashley didn't seem to notice his rage.

"Well, just say something nice when you see her," she said warmly. "I'm sure she'll like you." She smiled **benevolently**, a complete departure from her usual quietness.

This friendliness was completely unexpected. Wasn't she supposed to say something **demoralizing**?

"Thanks," he said suspiciously, before their conversation was **abridged** by the two o'clock alarm ringing on his watch. He left as quickly as he'd come in, but he was glad that all the rumors he'd heard weren't true about his **estranged** classmate.

That afternoon, standing just outside the academy's entrance and after having pressed 'send' a dozen times and then hanging up instantly, Jake finally summoned the courage to call Jessica to let her know of his intentions. The phone rang an awfully long time, and he was too **absorbed** in what he was going to say to notice the laughter rising behind him.

"Hey Jake!" she called, causing him to turn suddenly, blush, and almost wet himself with fear simultaneously. "You rang?"

"Oh, yeah," he said uncomfortably, almost throwing his phone to the ground to **exterminate** and **obliterate** the evidence.

"Well, I'm here. What's up?"

Apart from my heart rate?, he thought. This was going to be awfully embarrassing on the phone. How could he do it now in person? He felt **pessimistic** about what would **befall** him if he opened his mouth again.

"Well, I was just going to ask if there's a study session tomorrow," he said, stalling.

"Of course not. It's Friday. We'll be there on Monday though."

A long silence followed, as Jake tried to remember how to speak.

---

313 heresy [8]
n. 이단; 신성모독
blasphemy, fallacy

314 benevolent [8]
a. 자애로운
generous; with good intentions

315 demoralizing [2]
a. 사기를 떨어뜨리는
discouraging, debasing

316 abridge [7]
v. 요약하다, 줄이다
shorten by omissions; diminish

317 estranged [4]
a. 소원해진
alienated; separated

318 absorb [3]
v. 빨아들이다; 빠지게 만들다
suck up or drink in; engross or engage wholly
n. absorption

319 exterminate [3]
v. 몰살시키다
get rid of destroying

320 obliterate [2]
v. 흔적을 없애다
destroy completely

321 pessimistic [18]
a. 비관적인
having negative thoughts about the future
opp. optimistic
n. pessimism

322 befall [2]
v. ~에게 일어나다
occur to, happen to

323 meddle [4]
v. 간섭하다
intervene, interfere

324 constrain [7]
v. 제한하다
restrain; suppress
n. constraint

325 exuberance [8]
n. 풍부함, 무성함
abundancy

326 gloat [4]
v. 흡족해하다, 고소해하다
relish, rejoice

"Doing anything?" he said quickly hoping that someone else would **meddle** in his business and just do this for him.

"Tomorrow night? I was going to go to the movies with friends, but one of them's sick, and the others decided not to go. Why?"

Why? He could answer that, but barely.

"Well…I was thinking of seeing a movie too. Maybe you could see it after all."

"With you?" she laughed innocently.

"I…guess so."

"Why not?" She said lightly, flipping her hair a bit obviously. Jake was stunned. She continued.

"Will you be wearing a tuxedo?" Jake blinked.

"What?"

"Oh, so it's not a wedding, then. Ok, I was worried by your seriousness. Yes, Jake, a movie sounds great, thanks for asking me."

"Well…great!" He was barely able to **constrain** his **exuberance**.

"Now you ask me what time and where we should meet," she proposed, clearly **gloating** at his nervousness.

"Yes…what time and where should we meet?" he echoed, beginning to relax.

"How about seven at the park?"

"Perfect."

Vocabulary

0310

riddle [3]

[rídl]

n. 수수께끼, 미스터리, 구멍을 뚫다, 벌집같이 만들다   a puzzling question, problem; enigma, conundrum, to pierce with many holes
riddle은 '수수께끼'라는 뜻을 가지고 있는데 수수께끼는 알 수 없는 점이 많을 때 쓰인다. 이와 연관지어서 '벌집 같이 만들다'라는 뜻으로 외울 수 있다.
His essay was **riddled** with so many grammatical mistakes that his teacher had to give him a C. (*v.*)

0311

array [8]

[əǀreɪ]

v. 배치하다, 진열하다   place in a proper order
ad(='to') + raed(='ready') to place in order라는 뜻이다.
Jars of all shapes and sizes were **arrayed** on the shelves. (*v.*)

0312

lurid [5]

[ǀlʊrɪd]

a. 섬뜩한, 소름 끼치는   gruesome; horrible; shocking
라틴어 luridus는 '창백한 노란색'을 말한다. 생각만 해도 소름 끼치지 않는가?
The paper gave all the **lurid** details of the murder. (*adj.*)

0313

heresy [8]

[ǀherəsi]

n. 이단; 신성모독   blasphemy, fallacy
heresy 이교도 알지?
Other times, christianity was considered **heresy**. (*n.*)

0314

benevolent [8]

[bənévələnt]

a. 자애로운, 인정 많은   generous; with good intentions
bene는 '좋은', vol은 '의지'란 뜻으로 '인정많은'이라는 의미이다.
The **benevolent** ruler chose to let the slaves go. (*adj.*)

0315

demoralizing [2]

[dɪǀmɔːrəlaɪzɪŋ]

a. 사기를 떨어뜨리는   discouraging, debasing
morale이 let down 됐다.
Constant criticism is enough to **demoralize** anybody. (*v.*)

0316

abridge [7]

[əbrídʒ]

v. 요약하다, 줄이다, 단축하다   to shorten by omissions; diminish
bridge(다리)를 세우면 거리를 단축시킬수 있다.
He read an **abridged** version of the classic novel because he didn't have enough time. (*adj.*)

0317
estranged [4]
[ɪ|streɪndʒd]

a. 소원해진　alienated; separated
친했던 사람이 strange하게 만드는 것이니까 '소원해지다'.
He became **estranged** from his family after the argument. (*adj.*)

0318
absorb [3]
[əb|sɔːrb;əb|zɔːrb]

v. 빨아들이다; 빠지게 만들다　suck up or drink in; engross or engage wholly　*n.* absorption
라틴어 sorbere는 'suck in'이라는 뜻이다.
This work had **absorbed** him for several years. (*v.*)

0319
exterminate [3]
[ɪkstɜ́ːrmənèɪt]

v. 몰살시키다, 근절시키다, 전멸시키다　get rid of, destroying, to kill
termin은 '끝'을 뜻하므로 끝을 낸다는 의미이다.
When the scientist developed a spray that would **exterminate** cockroaches permanently; everyone was happy that they would never have to see cockroaches again. (*v.*)

0320
obliterate [2]
[əblítərèɪt]

v. 흔적을 없애다, 지우다, 말살하다　destroy completely, to remove all traces
liter는 letter, 즉 '글자'를 뜻하므로 '글자를 지우다'에서 유래되었다.
As a result of the deadly missile strike, the city was completely **obliterated**. (*v.*)

0321
pessimistic [18]
[|pesɪ|mɪstɪk]

a. 비관적인　having negative thoughts about the future
opp. optimistic　*n.* pessimism
중세 시대에는 pest 때문에 많은 사람들이 pessimistic한 삶을 살았죠.
Business and other analysts are **pessimistic**. (*adj.*)

0322
befall [2]
[bɪ|fɔːl]

v. ~에게 일어나다　occur to, happen to
무언가가 일어날 때 쓰인다.
What is the worst that may **befall**? (*v.*)

0323
meddle [4]
[|medl]

v. 간섭하다　intervene, interfere, to involve oneself in a matter without right or invitation
meddle이 middle이랑 소리가 비슷하지? 중간(middle)에 껴서 양쪽을 간섭(meddle)하는 것을 생각하자.
We all hate Tim **meddling** in everyone's affairs that have nothing to do with him. (*v.*)

0324
constrain [kən|streɪn]

v. 제한하다   restrain; suppress   *n.* constraint
strain(부담)이 될만한 것을 함께 주니까 '강요하다, 제한하다'.
You cannot **constrain** public debate in that way. (*v.*)

0325
exuberance [igzúːbərəns(i)]

n. 풍부함, 무성함   abundancy
엄청 exuberant한 사람은 beret(프랑스모자)를 쓰고 춤출 수도 있지.
Her burst of **exuberance** and her brightness overwhelmed me. (*n.*)

0326
gloat [glóut]

v. 흡족해하다, 고소해하다; 흡족해하는   relish, rejoice; reveling, rejoiced
무지한 사람들은 goat를 죽이고도 gloat '자랑스러워한다'고 연상하면 외우기 쉽다.
After winning the Premier League, the Chelsea players **gloated** with joy. (*v.*)

Episode 19
MATCHING Quiz

1. riddle
2. array
3. lurid
4. heresy
5. benevolent
6. demoralizing
7. abridge
8. estranged
9. absorb
10. exterminate
11. obliterate
12. pessimistic
13. befall
14. meddle
15. constrain
16. exuberance
17. gloat

A. restrain; suppress n. constraint
B. place in a proper order
C. relish, rejoice
D. blasphemy, fallacy
E. gruesome; horrible; shocking
F. a puzzling question, problem; enigma, conundrum
G. generous; with good intentions
H. alienated; separated
I. discouraging, debasing
J. shorten by omissions; diminish
K. destroy completely
L. having negative thoughts about the future opp. optimistic n. pessimism
M. suck up or drink in; engross or engage wholly n. absorption
N. get rid of destroying
O. intervene, interfere
P. occur to, happen to
Q. abundancy

1-F, 2-B, 3-E, 4-D, 5-G, 6-I, 7-J, 8-H, 9-M, 10-N, 11-K, 12-L, 13-P, 14-O, 15-A, 16-Q, 17-C

더 많은 문제를 풀고자 한다면 www.quizlet.com에서 'paul academy seoul' class를 검색

Episode 20: The Date

[327] consent [3]
n. 허락, 동의
permission, approval

[328] austere [2]
a. 냉정한, 근엄한
severe in manner or appearance; uncompromising; strict

[329] undermine [9]
v. 약화시키다
weaken, reduce the intensity of

[330] urge [10]
v. 촉구하다, 강권하다
push or force along; impel with force or vigor

[331] dreary [3]
a. 음울한, 따분한
depressingly dull; bleak

[332] abyss [3]
n. 심연, 깊은 구렁
a deep, immeasurable space, gulf, or cavity

[333] refracting [4]
a. 굴절되는
changing the direction of a ray of light, sound, or heat

Jake received special **consent** from his mother. Her **austere** response temporarily **undermined** his enthusiasm, but he was allowed to go out for the evening. The advice he received the day before still rang in his ears. He still hadn't worn any scent product, though Sam had **urged** him to. The smell of it on subways always made him feel like he was under attack, so he decided to do without.

Ah Jessica! Her name resounded in his ears as he stepped onto the sidewalk outside his building. It shone in his mind like a glowing light, erasing the **dreary** nonsense of his daily routine. The sound of Chet Baker's "I Fall in Love Too Easily," recommended by his uncle, drowned out his inner monologue and focused his mind.

Arriving at the agreed-upon subway station, he felt his hands begin to sweat like microwaved beef patties, and, alternatively, his mouth shrink into a useless hole, lacking all moisture or words worth speaking. Words! He'd forgotten almost any of those now in the **abyss** of despair.

Just say something nice to her, Ashley had said.

Coming up the stairs, he saw her at the top, just as he had the first time, only now she was lit not by the harsh light of morning but the soft orange street lamps, her black hair **refracting** it into a light wave so powerful he thought it might tan his skin. She wasn't especially dressed up, but her profile was just as striking as it had been the first time he'd seen her. He wanted to say how good she looked, but remembered TJ's warning against comments on physical attributes.

Don't be a weird! he had warned seriously.

Finally reaching the sidewalk, he called her name and she turned slowly to greet him. She didn't even have makeup on, he thought, and she still looked beautiful. He walked up to her and tried to sound charming.

"Hello," he said.

That's the best you can do, man?

"Oh, hey," she half-whispered. They stood for what seemed like ten minutes as he summoned the courage to say something original.

"Feel like a movie?"

"Sure."

"Ok. Which way do we go?"

"You've never been here before?"

"I have, but I can't seem to remember the way to the cinema," he admitted quietly.

She laughed and then grabbed his sleeve, pulling him away from the subway entrance toward the legions **aggregated** on the sidewalk. She forced her way ahead, her small frame quick in the **congested** crowd. Every so often, she turned back and smiled at him, obviously enjoying his **ineptitude** as he **reeled** behind her. Once they had reached the theater, she stopped and turned toward him completely.

"Now's the part where you ask me what I want to see and then we argue about the decision for a while," she said.

"Well, I really want to see a girly romance," he said cynically, "and I'm not going to see anything else."

She laughed genuinely this time, and then began, in contrast to the usual stereotype, to **advocate** a recently-released action movie about robots. With every sentence she spoke, and every laugh, Jake began to feel more comfortable with making jokes and with enjoying her company.

"Are they robots in love?" he **improvised**.

"Of course," she said, giving as good as she got. "They're French robots, designed with emotions and everything. They mostly sit in cafés and **converse** about labor laws and 19th century poetry."

---

[334] **aggregated** [2]
a. 전체의, 합쳐진
cumulative, amassed

[335] **congested** [3]
a. 혼잡한
crowded, blocked

[336] **ineptitude** [4]
n. 기량 부족
lack of skill or proficiency

[337] **reel** [2]
v. 비틀거리다
falter, lurch

[338] **advocate** [36]
v. 지지하다
speak in favor; support or urge

[339] **improvise** [10]
v. 즉석에서 짓다
made or said without previous preparation

340 converse [5]
v. 대화를 나누다
talk, chat

"Perfect," he said as she led him, once more by the sleeve, toward the smell of popcorn.

Vocabulary

0327
consent ³
[kənˈsent]

n. 허락, 동의　permission, approval
핸드폰 충전기를 꽂는 콘센트 알지? 콘센트랑 충전기가 서로 '합의된' 상태여서 전기가 통해야 충전이 되는 것과 비슷한 의미로 해석하자.
The written **consent** of a parent is required. (*n.*)

0328
austere ²
[ɔːstíər]

a. 냉정한, 근엄한; 꾸밈없는, 소박한　severe in manner or appearance, uncompromising, strict; severely, simple; unadorned
acid '산'처럼 장식, 가구들이 녹아내려서 acid-ere '꾸밈없다'라는 뜻이다.
The company is famous for its **austere** designs that use only dark colors and minimalist shapes. (*adj.*)

0329
undermine ⁹
[ʌ̀ndərmáin]

v. 약화시키다　to weaken, reduce the intensity of
undermine은 "under" + "mine"(굴을 파다) : "아래에 굴을 파다" → ~의 토대를 허물다, 토대를 약하게 하다 → 〈명성 등을〉 몰래 손상시키다, 음흉한 수단으로 훼손하다.
Harsh comments **undermine** confidence. (*v.*)

0330
urge ¹⁰
[ɜːrdʒ]

v. 촉구하다, 강권하다　push or force along; impel with force or vigor
라틴어 urgere는 'press hard, push forward, force'라는 뜻이다.
The situation is dangerous and the UN is **urging** caution. (*v.*)

0331
dreary ³
[dríəri]

a. 음울한, 따분한, 쓸쓸한, 황량한　depressingly dull; bleak
drop, drip과 같은 어원으로 '쓸쓸하고, 외롭고 황량해서 눈물이 떨어진다'로 외우자.
The castle was so cold and **dreary** that nobody wanted to live in it. (*adj.*)

0332
abyss ³
[əbís]

n. 심연, 깊은 구렁　a deep, immeasurable space, gulf, or cavity
a(='without') + byssos(='bottom') base가 없어서 '깊은'이라고 외우자.
The country is stepping back from the edge of an **abyss**. (*n.*)

0333
refracting [4]

[rɪ|fræktɪŋ]

a. 굴절되는   changing the direction of a ray of light, sound, or heat
fract는 '금, 쪼개진 것'을 말하는데, re '다시' 쪼개졌으니 '굴절'을 뜻한다.
The sunlight should **refract** and form a rainbow of colors on the paper. (*v.*)

0334
aggregated [2]

[|ægrɪgeɪtɪd]

a. 전체의, 합쳐진   cumulative, amassed
aggregate는 ad(to)+gregare(herd) 즉 '모두 모이다'라는 뜻이다.
We made estimates using the **aggregated** data. (*adj.*)

0335
congested [3]

[kən|dʒestɪd]

a. 혼잡한   crowded, blocked
너무 음식을 많이 먹으면 소화(di'gest')에 혼잡(con'gest')이 생긴다.
Many of Europe's airports are heavily **congested**. (*adj.*)

0336
ineptitude [4]

[ɪ|neptɪtuːd]

n. 기량 부족   lack of skill or proficiency
apt와 ept는 비슷한 뜻. 그런데 'ept하지 못한 것'이니까 솜씨가 부족하다는 뜻이다.
The **ineptitude** of the police in handling the situation (*n.*)

0337
reel [2]

[riːl]

v. 비틀거리다   falter, lurch
reel이 돌아가면서 실이 감길 때 덜컹거리며 흔들리는 것을 연상하면 외우기 쉽다.
She was **reeling** after several glasses of wine. (*v.*)

0338
advocate [36]

[ædvəkèit]

v. 지지하다, 옹호하다; 옹호자   speak in favor; support or urge; who supports an idea publicly
ad(='toward') + voc '말하다'. 어떤 한 쪽에 찬성하는 말을 하다.
Ellie wore a shirt that said "Save the Whales!" to **advocate** protecting ocean life. (*v.*)

0339
improvise [10]

[|ɪmprəvaɪz]

v. 즉석에서 짓다   made or said without previous preparation
improv는 '즉흥연주', '애드리브'라는 뜻이다.
Wise people know how to **improvise**. (*v.*)

0340

converse [5]

[kən|vɜːrs]

v. ~와 대화를 나누다   talk, chat, to exchange views by talking

컨버스(converse) 신발을 고른 다음에 사려고 카운터에 가면 점원과 대화를 나눠야겠지?

If you have something to say to your friend, don't just think about it; **converse** with her! (v.)

Voca Hamburger
Episode 20
MATCHING Quiz

1. consent	A. made or said without previous preparation
2. austere	B. weaken, reduce the intensity of
3. undermine	C. depressingly dull; bleak
4. urge	D. permission, approval
5. dreary	E. lack of skill or proficiency
6. abyss	F. push or force along; impel with force or vigor
7. refracting	G. changing the direction of a ray of light, sound, or heat
8. aggregated	H. cumulative, amassed
9. congested	I. a deep, immeasurable space, gulf, or cavity
10. ineptitude	J. talk, chat
11. reel	K. crowded, blocked
12. advocate	L. speak in favor; support or urge
13. improvise	M. falter, lurch
14. converse	N. severe in manner or appearance; uncompromising; strict

1-D, 2-N, 3-B, 4-F, 5-C, 6-I, 7-G, 8-H, 9-K, 10-E, 11-M, 12-L, 13-A, 14-J

더 많은 문제를 풀고자 한다면 www.quizlet.com에서 'paul academy seoul' class를 검색

Episode 21: In the Study

341 intersperse [2]
v. 흩어 배치하다
scatter here and there or place at intervals among other things

342 abide [2]
v. 머무르다, 깃들다
dwell; reside; stay

343 beckon [2]
v. 손짓하다
signal, summon, or direct by a gesture of the head or hand

344 hamper [2]
v. 막다, 방해하다
block, hinder

345 admonish [10]
v. 꾸짖다, 책망하다
criticize for wrongdoing

Still floating after his evening with Jessica, Jake found himself the next morning, a Sunday, in the study.

Jake sang the tune of Bob Dylan's "Desolation Row" as he gazed at the books that lined the walls. Here and there were **interspersed** framed photographs of the same smiling pair of eyes, shining from behind circular spectacles, with a few other people **abiding** alongside. The room smelled like old paper, and perhaps a few sandwiches which had gone missing during the man in the picture's time at the university. While occupied by scholarly concerns their owner had simply forgotten about them in the midst of absent-minded daydreams.

Unlike his younger brother, the Professor (as Jake's mother called him, derisively) had few desires concerning money or family. He had no children of his own, and had not married his long-time partner (whose existence was never fully proved to Jake, as he had never seen her in person or even in photographic form). He once overheard his father remark about the "two women" whom his uncle was simultaneously "entertaining" but nothing more was said on the subject as the two men had realized he was listening.

"You're not going over to that old creep's house are you?" his mother had asked him that morning, arching an eyebrow cynically while pouring milk into his cereal bowl.

"You mean your husband's brother, my uncle? Yes, I am going to see him. Is that alright, Mother?" Jake seldom felt very angry towards her, but this morning was sunny through the windows and the light seemed to **beckon** him away to freedom. Anyone trying to **hamper** his escape today would regret it.

She **admonished** him strongly, but after a little convincing, she finally agreed and told him to be home by eight that evening.

Jake watched the old yellowing clock on the wall ticking its way toward 11 AM. His uncle had told him that he had a meeting that morning, and that he might be late. Jake had been sitting in the office for twenty minutes, checking his phone for messages from Jessica, when suddenly the door burst open with short noise from its **hinge** and the old familiar figure walked into the room. He was losing hair, with the middle of his head now reflecting light brightly and the edges a mess of grey hair which his hands were constantly trying to flatten against his head. His white jacket was dirty around the wrists and stuffed with pens and other assorted odds and ends in its **capacious** pockets. His trousers were surprisingly clean, although they were **luminous** yellow, as though he habitually dressed in the dark.

"My boy! How are you? You look enormous! Haven't been waiting too long, have you?" His youthful energy belied his age and he seemed to say the everything in one or two excited syllables. He put a large hand in Jake's and flew behind his desk, his jacket tail flying up behind him. Sitting down, Jake couldn't help thinking he was seated across from a large bird of some kind.

"How is everything? Your father is well, I hope?"

Everything has been for you. Make something beautiful. Jake **shuddered** slightly as he couldn't help comparing the two men. Luckily, his reaction was not noticed.

"Oh, of course," came the gloomy reply.

"You're studying for the SAT now, right?" the old man's eyes sparkled as he spoke. "English truly is a fantastic language, isn't it. Delightful to figure out the meanings of its **conjugated** parts. Have you spent much time on the roots of words?"

"Actually, we did talk about that a few days ago —" Jake began.

"Excellent!" his uncle's voice boomed. "My favorite has always been *anthro*. Just like the sound of it I suppose."

Anthro. Anthro. Anthro. The word whistled through Jake's mind like wind in an empty tunnel. Oh yes! He thought. Humans!

"Man," he said quietly.

---

346 hinge [2]
n. 경첩
a jointed device or flexible piece on which a door swings

347 capacious [3]
a. 널찍한
able to hold many things; large (as in a space)

348 luminous [4]
a. 선명한, 빛을 발하는
bright, glowing

349 shudder [2]
v. 몸서리치다
tremble with a sudden movement, as from horror or cold

350 conjugated [5]
a. 합쳐진
joined together

| 351 | **exultant** [2]
a. 기뻐서 어쩔 줄 모르는
very happy, delighted

| 352 | **loathe** [3]
v. 혐오하다, 싫어하다
hate, abhor

| 353 | **erroneous** [7]
a. 잘못된
wrong, incorrect

| 354 | **obsolete** [14]
a. 더 이상 쓸모가 없는
no longer in general use

| 355 | **predate** [7]
v. ~보다 (시간에) 앞서다
precede in date

| 356 | **inextricable** [4]
a. 떼어 놓을 수 없는
unable to be separated from

| 357 | **aspect** [38]
n. 측면
part, attribute

| 358 | **permeate** [6]
v. 침투하다, 퍼지다
pass into or through every part of

"Exactly right!" the old man exclaimed, clearly **exultant** by such talk of words and learning.

Don't ever forget your own happiness, he heard again.

"Phil*anthro*py, *anthro*pology, *anthro*pocentrism," the syllables were each pronounced carefully, slowly tasting the words as one might a piece of chocolate. "What does a *misanthrope* do, do you think?"

"Well, *mis* would be negative…"

"Yes, yes," his uncle prompted.

"So…someone who **loathes** people?" Jake hoped he was right. It would certainly be nice to get something right after so many **erroneous** answers lately.

"Perfecto! Well, I can see that you're doing well. But have you heard any good jazz lately?"

Jake had listened exclusively to love pop for the last week, for obvious reasons. He shook his head.

"Here, let's listen to something I bought this morning." He took a CD out of one of his many pockets and put it into an **obsolete** old stereo behind the desk, which probably **predated** Jake himself. the song was another by the same artist he had given Jake the last time they had met. The sound of Chet Baker's soft voice and heartbroken trumpet harmonies, now **inextricably** an **aspect** of the soundtrack of his date with Jessica the previous night, **permeated** the room.

In the midst of the lovely sounds, Jake realized why his mother didn't like her brother-in-law: he enjoyed life too much to pass for normal.

Vocabulary

0341

intersperse ²

[|ɪntər|spɜːrs]

v. 흩어 배치하다   scatter here and there or place at intervals among other things
inters는 'between', sperse는 disperse처럼 '흩어놓다'는 뜻이다. 사이사이에 흩어서 놔둔다는 얘기.
Lectures will be **interspersed** with practical demonstrations. (*v.*)

0342

abide ²

[əbáid]

v. 머무르다, 깃들다, 견디다   dwell; reside; stay, to put up with
abide by는 '견디다'라는 뜻으로 자주 쓰인다.
She **abided** by his jokes even though they are not funny at all. (*v.*)

0343

beckon ²

[|bekən]

v. (오라고)손짓하다   signal, summon, or direct by a gesture of the head or hand.
beckon을 보면 뭔가 back + on 같지? 손가락이 뒤로 갔다 올라오는 것을 생각해 보자. 손가락 까딱거리면서 누구를 부르는 것 같지? 손짓으로 남을 부른다는 뜻이다.
I **beckoned** to the waiter, because he was far away and I didn't want to shout to call him. (*v.*)

0344

hamper ²

[hǽmpər]

v. 막다, 방해하다   block, hinder; to prevent the free movement or action
hamper는 큰 바구니란 뜻이기 때문에 바구니 안에서 들어가면 움직임이 제한되는 상황을 나타낸다. 잘 안 외워지면 'hammer로 때려서 나의 진로가 hampered 되었다'고 외우면 되겠다.
Hamper movement through imprisonment. (*v.*)

0345

admonish ¹⁰

[ædmάniʃ]

v. 꾸짖다, 책망하다, 충고하다, 경고하다   criticize for wrongdoing; to warn of a fault
monitor는 '충고자, 감시자, 선도위원'의 뜻이고 라틴어 monitus '상기시키다, 경고하다'에서 온 말이다. 앞에 쓰인 접두어 ad는 to(~에 대하여) 정도가 된다.
Her father **admonished** her for not taking out the garbage. (*v.*)

143

0346
hinge [2]
[hɪndʒ]

n. 경첩   a jointed device or flexible piece on which a door swings
문이 매달려(hang) 있게 해 주는 것은 hinge.
We must keep the front door on the **hinge**. (*n.*)

0347
capacious [3]
[kəˈpeɪʃəs]

a. 널찍한   able to hold many things; large (as in a space)
'capture할만한 공간이 충분히 있는' 것이라고 생각하자.
I usually choose a bag with **capacious** pockets. (*adj.*)

0348
luminous [4]
[ˈluːmənəs]

a. 선명한, 빛을 발하는, 반짝이는   bright, glowing
lumin은 '빛'이라는 뜻이니까 luminous는 '반짝이다'는 뜻이다.
I was scared of how dark the night sky was, but thankfully a few **luminous** insects appeared and I felt much better. (*adj.*)

0349
shudder [2]
[ˈʃʌdə(r)d]

v. 몸서리치다   tremble with a sudden movement, as from horror or cold
문이 shut되면 겁이 나서 shudder하게 되겠지?
Just thinking about the accident makes me **shudder**. (*v.*)

0350
conjugated [5]
[ˈkɑndʒugèitid]

a. 합쳐진   joined together
함께 (con) 합쳤다고 (join = ju) 외워보자.
How does this verb **conjugate**? (*v.*)

0351
exultant [2]
[ɪɡˈzʌltənt]

a. 기뻐서 어쩔 줄 모르는   very happy, delighted
궁극기(ult)를 배우면 매우 기뻐서 exult하게 된다.
The fans were **exultant** at their team's victory. (*adj.*)

0352
loathe [3]
[loʊð]

v. 혐오하다, 싫어하다   hate, abhor
평생 싫어하기로 맹세할(oath) 정도로 혐오한다고 외워보자.
The two men **loathe** each other. (*v.*)

0353
erroneous [7]
[ɪˈroʊniəs]

a. 잘못된   wrong, incorrect
오류(error)와 연결시켜서 외워보자.
The teacher fixed Eric's **erroneous** sentences with a red pen. (*adj.*)

0354
obsolete [14]
[|ɑ:bsəlli:t]

a. 더 이상 쓸모가 없는   no longer in general use
OB + SO + LETE = obviously so late... Something so late is outmoded
Telegraph became an **obsolete** technology when the telephone was invented because no one would prefer the slower and more complex machine over.a much simpler one. (*adj.*)

0355
predate [7]
[pri:déit]

v. ~보다 (시간이) 앞서다   precede in date
시간(date)을 앞선다고 (pre) 외워보자.
The oldest fossils of sharks found actually **predate** the dinosaurs by more than 200 million years!

0356
inextricable [4]
[|ınık|strıkəbl]

a. 떼어 놓을 수 없는   unable to be separated from
extricate(떼어놓다)를 나무(tri = tree)에서 꺼낸다고 (ex) 외워보자.
An **inextricable** connection between the past and the present (*adj.*)

0357
aspect [38]
[|æspekt]

n. 측면   part, attribute
스펙(spec)은 한 사람을 판단할 때 봐야 하는 측면(aspect)이기도 하다.
The book aims to cover all **aspects** of city life. (*n.*)

0358
permeate [6]
[|p3:rmieıt]

v. 침투하다, 퍼지다   pass into or through every part of
어디에 나가는 게 허락돼서(permit = permeat) 퍼질 수 있다. (permeate)
The smell of leather **permeated** the room. (*v.*)

Note :

Episode 21
MATCHING Quiz

1. intersperse — A. block, hinder
2. abide — B. dwell; reside; stay
3. beckon — C. pass into or through every part of
4. hamper — D. unable to be separated from
5. admonish — E. precede in date
6. hinge — F. signal, summon, or direct by a gesture of the head or hand a door swings
7. capacious — G. tremble with a sudden movement, as from horror or cold
8. luminous — H. a jointed device or flexible piece on which
9. shudder — I. wrong, incorrect
10. conjugated — J. part, attribute
11. exultant — K. bright, glowing
12. loathe — L. joined together
13. erroneous — M. able to hold many things; large (as in a space)
14. obsolete — N. very happy, delighted
15. predate — O. criticize for wrongdoing
16. inextricable — P. no longer in general use
17. aspect — Q. scatter here and there or place at intervals among other things
18. permeate — R. hate, abhor

1-Q, 2-B, 3-F, 4-A, 5-O, 6-H, 7-M, 8-K, 9-G, 10-L, 11-N, 12-R, 13-I, 14-P, 15-E, 16-D, 17-J, 18-C

더 많은 문제를 풀고자 한다면 www.quizlet.com에서 'paul academy seoul' class를 검색

Episode 22

A Brief Visit

Every day by this point, the three boys sat at their usual table in the Mexican restaurant, but without the drama of Jake's love affair or their usual game (the teachers had warned them against playing it, so it had to be conducted only in the early morning hours), they found themselves facing an unexpected boredom. Their conversation was always enjoyable, but seemed to revolve around the same dull topics, and offered little that was new. In the third week of classes, however, a new boy entered Jake's class from the lower level, and had followed their group out into the street after the morning session. Recognizing the newcomer's lost expression, Jake invited him to join them for their afternoon meal.

Initially, the other two reacted negatively, making their **chagrin** apparent with some rude gestures behind the other boy's back. However, Jake had sympathy, and as the conversation progressed they began to **grudgingly** accept him, at least for one day.

The one thing that truly changed their opinions of him was how **pliable** the boy seemed. His name was Sean, and, being younger (only in 10th grade), he seemed instantly to adapt to their expectations or change his opinion to suit the **vagaries** of others' perspectives. He was also, for the same reason, **servile**, admiring Jake's good manners and the fact he had a girlfriend and marveling at TJ's less academic (but still **didactic**) use of bad words, for which TJ had become well-known.

"Really?" he said after hearing the news of Jake's romance. "That's so cool. You must be quite a romantic guy, huh?" He also declared TJ a swearing **artisan**, capable of crafting curses **infallible** in any situation.

"I never thought of using those words together before!" he said with wonder, following an especially **articulate** turn of phrase. "Do you mind if I use that one?"

---

359 chagrin [3]
n. 분함
displeasure, annoyance

360 grudgingly [7]
adv. 마지못해
reluctantly

361 pliable [2]
a. 유연한
flexible; easy to persuade or control

362 vagary [4]
n. 예측 불허의 변화[변동]
an unpredictable or erratic action, occurrence, course

363 servile [4]
a. 아부하는, 굽실거리는
obsequious, subservient

364 didactic [6]
a. 교훈적인
educational, teaching

365 artisan [2]
n. 장인, 기능 보유자
a person skilled in an applied art

366 infallible [4]
a. 결코 실패하지 않는
unfailing in effectiveness or operation

367 articulate [13]
a. 분명히 표현된
uttered clearly in distinct syllables

368 assimilate [3]
v. 완전히 이해하다, 동화되다
change oneself to fit into an unfamiliar or different place
n. assimilation

369 demise [4]
n. 죽음, 사망
death

370 candid [2]
a. 정직한
completely honest, straightforward

"Not at all," TJ allowed. When the boy rose to get the boys more water, TJ said he was willing to accept Sean, so long as he didn't "bring any more kids around here."

However nice Sean was, though, he wasn't too shy about saying that he was probably going to leave the academy after his first day.

"Where were you before this?" Jake asked the boy.

"Oh, China," he replied. It seemed that he had been at a homestay himself for the summer, staying with a nice middle-class family and trying to **assimilate** to their lifestyle and habits. He was, generally, a personable fellow, and got along pretty well. But then, an unexpected **demise** in the family made his mother recall him home, where he was currently 'shopping around' academies to find somewhere he fit in.

"What do you think of our little place?" Jake asked, feeling a little pride in the academy by this point, though he didn't want to admit it.

"It's…OK," the boy said. "Just…I'm not sure I like all the vocabulary study. At this other place you only have to study fifty words a day. Seems easier."

Jake recognized the same claim that had been made by his former classmate Susan a few weeks earlier. It was Jessica's academy he was discussing.

"So I might go there tomorrow. My friend says they have a much better essay program, too. They're famous for it."

"Oh," Sam said suddenly, feeling slightly discouraged by the boy's lack of loyalty. He might have been a loser, but it was clear he would never be a regular member of the group.

"But it was really nice of you guys to let me join you for lunch. It's kind of scary coming out here all alone."

"Any time," Jake said, glad that his group was strong enough to accommodate another member, even for an afternoon. The older boys, feeling oddly responsible for the **candid** little guy, argued with him about paying for lunch, eventually convincing him to let them pay. Even if the boy was going to go to another institute, he promised to see them again, and pay them back for their kindness.

Afterwards, Sam and TJ teased Jake a bit about letting another member **intrude** on their now-regular lunch sessions, but Jake had already been thinking about inviting another person to the group, even though he felt strange about talking to them about it. He now thought daily about how much better it would be to have Jessica there with him in the afternoon, but he wasn't sure how to **broach** the subject. Maybe tomorrow, he thought as they accompanied Sean back to the academy to collect his cell phone and bid him good luck.

371 intrude [2]
v. 방해하다
come or go without permission or welcome

372 broach [2]
v. 이야기를 꺼내다
bring up a topic in conversation

Vocabulary

0359
chagrin [3]
[ʃəgrin]

n. 분함   displeasure, annoyance
not 'grin'으로 외우자. 웃지 않으면 분하거나 원통해서다.
Much to his **chagrin**, he came out bottom in the race. (*n.*)

0360
grudgingly [7]
[ˈɡrʌdʒɪŋli]

adv. 마지못해   reluctantly
공포영화를 싫어하지만 친구의 부탁해 마지못해 (grudgingly) 영화 'the Grudge'를 봤다고 외워보자.
Grudgingly, I put on a cap and walked to the airport. (*adv.*)

0361
pliable [2]
[pláiəbl]

a. 유연한, 휘기 쉬운; 유순한   flexible; easy to persuade or control, easily influenced
ply- 는 '구부리다'라는 뜻이 있다.
The thin plastic rod was **pliable**. (*adj.*)

0362
vagary [4]
[véigəri]

n. 예측 불허의 변화[변동], 변덕   an unpredictable or erratic action, occurrence, course, whim
variable과 같이 변덕스러운 것을 지칭할 때 쓰인다.
His character is full of vagary that his decision **varies** every time. (*n.*)

0363
servile [4]
[sə́ːrvil]

a. 아부하는, 굽실거리는, 노예(근성)의, 비굴한   obsequious, subservient, slavish; cringing
slave와 serve는 같은 어원을 갖고 있고, servile은 slave-like라고 생각하면 된다.
His **servile** nature made him a useful but irritating employee. (*adj.*)

0364
didactic [6]
[daidǽktik]

a. 교훈적인   educational, teaching
didact 는 가르치는 사람, 도학자를 말한다. 따라서, 그들의 말은 교훈적이다.
His **didactic** tone made him sound like a teacher. (*adj.*)

0365
artisan ²
[|ɑːrtəzn]

n. **장인, 기능 보유자**   a person skilled in an applied art
하나의 예술에 (art) 통달한 사람이라고 외워보자.
The **artisan** lived by his fingers' ends. (*n.*)

0366
infallible ⁴
[ɪn|fæləbl]

a. **결코 실패하지 않는, 절대 오류가 없는** unfailing in effectiveness or operation, perfect; without error
fall할 수 없다는 뜻으로 해석하면 된다.
The time-accuracy of the Greenwich tower is **infallible**. (*adj.*)

0367
articulate ¹³
[ɑːrtíkjulèit]

a. **분명히 표현된, 또렷이 표현된**   uttered clearly in distinct syllables, to speak clearly
라틴어 "articulatus"는 '부분이 합쳐진'이란 뜻으로 '한 부분마다 잘 설명한'이란 뜻이된다.
An **articulate** description helps us understand a difficult subject better. (*adj.*)

0368
assimilate ³
[ə|sɪmə leɪt]

v. **완전히 이해하다, 동화되다**   change oneself to fit into an unfamiliar or different place   *n.* assimilation
비슷하게(simila = similar) 만들어서 동화된다고 외워보자.
The committee will need time to **assimilate** this report. (*v.*)

0369
demise ⁴
[dɪ|maɪz]

n. **죽음, 사망; 종말**   death or termination
de + mise로 읽자. 디+마이스. 뒤(de)에 쥐들 (mice=마이스)가 있으면 어떡해? 죽여야지. 그래서 demise는 죽음이다.
After the rock star's untimely **demise**, thousands of people gathered at his funeral and paid their respect. (*v.*)

0370
candid ²
[kǽndid]

a. **정직한, 솔직한, 숨김없는**   completely honest, straightforward
candidum(하얀, 깨끗한)의 뜻을 갖고 있는 라틴어에서 파생되었다.
A **candid** discussion of one's faults (*adj.*)

0371
intrude ²
[intrúːd]

v. **방해하다, 침입하다**   come or go without permission or welcome; to come in without leave or license
in(안으로) rude(무례)하게 들어오다.
My sister **intrudes** into my room all the time, no matter how many times I tell her to knock first. (*v.*)

0372
broach ²

[broʊtʃ]

v. **(하기 힘든) 이야기를 꺼내다** bring up a topic in conversation, to mention or suggest a subject for the first time

하기 힘든 고민이나 이야기를 형에게(brother)에게 하려면 먼저 접근(approach)를 해야 해.

I was afraid to **broach** the subject of money to my parents who were going through a hard time because of debts. (*v.*)

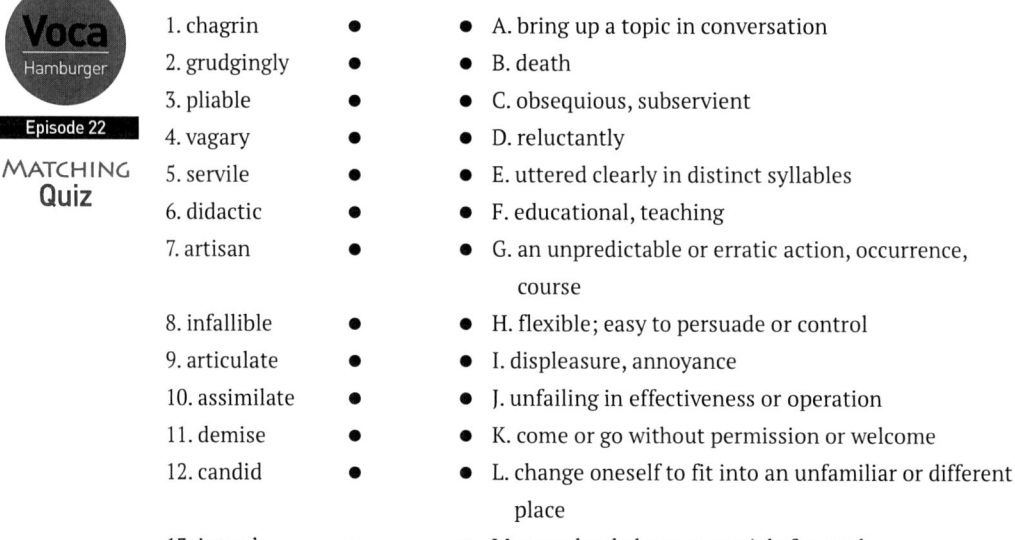

Voca Hamburger
Episode 22
MATCHING Quiz

1. chagrin
2. grudgingly
3. pliable
4. vagary
5. servile
6. didactic
7. artisan
8. infallible
9. articulate
10. assimilate
11. demise
12. candid
13. intrude
14. broach

A. bring up a topic in conversation
B. death
C. obsequious, subservient
D. reluctantly
E. uttered clearly in distinct syllables
F. educational, teaching
G. an unpredictable or erratic action, occurrence, course
H. flexible; easy to persuade or control
I. displeasure, annoyance
J. unfailing in effectiveness or operation
K. come or go without permission or welcome
L. change oneself to fit into an unfamiliar or different place
M. completely honest, straightforward
N. a person skilled in an applied art

1-I, 2-D, 3-H, 4-G, 5-C, 6-F, 7-N, 8-J, 9-E, 10-L, 11-B, 12-M, 13-K, 14-A

더 많은 문제를 풀고자 한다면 www.quizlet.com에서 'paul academy seoul' class를 검색

Episode 23 — An Uncertain Return

Having been so wrapped up in love and the continual pressure to improve, Jake had begun to recognize the empty seat next to him as normal, Ashley's absence as a certainty. It had been more than a week since her **precipitate** departure and her attempt to **engender** protest from the other students by claiming that the academy had failed them. This **calumnious** claim, overheard by a few of the TAs, was as unproductive as her own attempts to improve without properly studying, as many of them perceived (rightly) that she was too unrealistic in her expectations.

Still, her anger and the bravery which she had shown in her outspoken complaints were still spoken of by other students, and her still-empty chair had taken on an unmistakable **taint** of darkness. Various specious remarks were made about her, that she had somehow started her own school, or had been a spy for a rival program, and so on. All were lies, of course, but often such stories are more reasonable than **verity** among small groups of people. Regardless, the last thing Jake or anyone else expected was to see her sitting there, with perfect posture and tightly pursed lips, ready to begin class on Tuesday morning of their third week.

"Where have you been?" someone asked from the back of the room.

"I went to another place, but the classes were…" she said, trailing off as she realized she was about to admit how wrong she was "…the other students were annoying. So much playing around. So I came back."

She had again constructed her desk fortress, and assumed the **adamant** look of a runner about to begin a marathon. Despite her multiple offenses (swearing at a teacher, cursing at the TAs), she had been allowed back when she promised to do as the teachers requested and make her complaints to the teaching staff in private.

"You sure you won't be bothered by the classes here, too?" he asked

---

373 precipitate [4]
a. 느닷없는
exceedingly sudden or abrupt

374 engender [2]
v. 발생시키다, 불러 일으키다
produce, arouse, foment

375 calumnious [2]
a. 중상의
of or relating vicious or untruthful statement; slanderous
n. calumny

376 taint [5]
n. 오명, 오점
stigma, contamination

377 verity [3]
n. 진리, 진실
truth

378 adamant [3]
a. 단호한, 요지부동의
determined

379 unease [9]
n. 불안감, 우려
not being easy in body or mind

380 wrench [2]
n. (마음의) 쓰라림
ache, pain

381 conceited [7]
a. 자만하는
excessively proud of oneself; arrogant

382 magnificent [3]
a. 훌륭한, 웅장한
glorious

smartly. He had become 'the boy who sat beside the crazy girl,' and had suffered a little due to his association with her.

"I will work harder," she said firmly. "I suppose, in the end, the responsibility for my score is mine."

"Well, next time, don't involve me in your nonsense," he said. "I don't want to be associated with you bad-mouthing the academy."

"I'm sorry, Jake. I promise won't cause you any more **unease**."

Jake momentarily felt a **wrench** of pity as he heard these words. She was more fragile than he realized, and less **conceited** than she had seemed before. To improve (that great and **magnificent** thing, they were told), she would have to apply herself much more than she had done before. Stopping short of apologizing, he nonetheless said he was glad to have her back.

Vocabulary

0373
precipitate [4]
[prisípətèit]

a. 느닷없는, 갑자기 어떤 상태로 치닫게 하다   exceedingly sudden or abrupt, to force forward prematurely
precip이라는 '빨리 떨어지다'라는 뜻의 라틴어 어원에서 유래했다.
The fall of Roman Empire **precipitated** the cultural drawback in Western society. (*v.*)

0374
engender [2]
[indʒéndər]

v. (상태 등을)발생시키다, 불러 일으키다   to produce, arouse, foment
genesis와 같은 어원을 가진다.
The large fire **engendered** the destruction of the forest. (*v.*)

0375
calumnious [2]
[kəlʌ́mniəs]

a. 중상의   of or relating vicious or untruthful statement; slanderous   *n.* calumny
신문 기사(column)에 중상(calumny)을 하는 기사가 실렸다고 외워보자.
His **calumnious** words have no basis in fact whatsoever. (*adj.*)

0376
taint [5]
[téint]

n. 오명, 오점; 더럽히다, 오명을 남기다   stigma, contamination; to spoil the status or reputation
tainted by a stain. '얼룩으로 더럽혀지다'라고 외우자.
Clear water was **tainted** by poison. (*v.*)

0377
verity [3]
[vérəti]

n. 진리, 진실(성)   truth
ver은 '진실'이라는 뜻으로, 진실성을 뜻한다.
The **verity** of his claim was obvious. (*n.*)

0378
adamant [3]
[ǽdəmənt]

a. 단호한, 요지부동의   determined not to change their mind
'돌처럼 단단한'이란 뜻으로 완고하다라는 의미다.
Mother was **adamant** about the babies going to bed at 8 o'clock. (*adj.*)

0379
unease [9]
[ʌníːz]

n. 불안감, 우려 not being easy in body or mind
편안하지(easy) 않은(un) 상태이다.
He was unable to hide his **unease** at the way the situation was developing. (*n.*)

0380
wrench [2]
[rentʃ]

n. (마음의) 쓰라림 ache, pain
렌치(wrench)로 한 대 맞은 것처럼 쓰라리다고 외워보자.
Leaving home was a terrible **wrench** for me. (*n.*)

0381
conceited [7]
[kənsíːtid]

a. 자만하는, 잘난 체하는 excessively proud of oneself; arrogant, self-important
self-conceit에서 줄여진 단어로 원래 자기만을(self) 생각한다는(conceit) 의미이다.
A **conceited** person won't have many friends. (*adj.*)

0382
magnificent [3]
[mægnífəsnt]

a. 훌륭한, 웅장한, 장대한, 당당한 glorious, grand or majestic
maximum, magnify, majestic에서 max, mag, maj는 great의 뜻이다.
magna는 'great'을 뜻하고 fic는 '만들다'를 뜻하므로 '굉장하게 만들어진'의 의미를 가진다.
The beautiful city lights at night are a **magnificent** sight. (*adj.*)

Episode 23

MATCHING Quiz

1. precipitate — A. glorious
2. engender — B. produce, arouse, foment
3. calumnious — C. truth
4. taint — D. excessively proud of oneself; arrogant
5. verity — E. of or relating vicious or untruthful statement; slanderous
6. adamant — F. exceedingly sudden or abrupt
7. unease — G. determined
8. wrench — H. not being easy in body or mind
9. conceited — I. stigma, contamination
10. magnificent — J. ache, pain

1-F, 2-B, 3-E, 4-I, 5-C, 6-G, 7-H, 8-J, 9-D, 10-A

더 많은 문제를 풀고자 한다면 www.quizlet.com에서 'paul academy seoul' class를 검색

Episode 24

Guess This!

After all the complaining of the first few weeks, it was clear to many of the students that there was only one way to improve. It wasn't especially easy, nor was it quick, but the gradual practice of repeating vocabulary words, applying essay examples, memorizing grammar idioms, and labeling the passages seemed to have had a great effect. Others, after weeks of being subjected to the same routine of classes, were given to sitting almost unconscious in their chairs until being awakened by a teacher's question.

Even Ashley's usual whining had lessened as she began seeing more of the teachers' logic. She even had fewer **disputes** with the reading teacher, though Jake still felt many of her explanations were **dissonant** to *his* interpretation of the readings.

The reading teacher, who clearly treated the job seriously, had prepared an activity to help some of those still struggling with labeling and **discarding** incorrect answer choices. She handed it out and some members of the class began shifting slightly in their seats, always nervous when it came to activities in which their lack of preparation might be made clear.

"Now, this little activity is meant to review the way we interpret those inference questions and their **considerable** difficulty, "she said, hoping that her explanation would prove the educational intentions of the activity, and deflect any criticisms some discontented students might make about a 'waste of time.'

The activity **comprises** a number of statements taken from reading passages, after which the students were asked which available option was the proper **postulation** to make from the information provided. The first excerpt looked like this:

That morning, Mayella woke up at six and prayed before going to the factory, where she had worked for ten years.

---

383 dispute [7]
n. 논란, 분쟁
a debate, controversy, or difference of opinion

384 dissonant [2]
a. 조화되지 않은
disagreeing, discordant

385 discard [3]
v. 버리다, 제거하다
eliminate, get rid of

386 considerable [9]
a. 상당한, 많은
rather large or great in size, distance, extent, etc.

387 comprise [5]
v. ~로 구성되다
consist of

388 postulation [4]
n. 가정
assumption, hypothesis, inference

389 predisposed [3]
a. 성향이 있는
having a tendency toward some activity or particular object

390 deduce [8]
v. 추론하다
logically infer; surmise

391 capitulate [4]
v. 굴복하다
surrender; succumb

Jake, who was **predisposed** to getting such questions wrong, tried to **deduce** from the available information which option seemed appropriate. They looked like this:

    A. Mayella always woke up early
    B. Mayella woke up earlier than the other factory workers
    C. Mayella prayed as a habit
    D. Mayella had not always been a factory worker

The question was pretty easy, and most of the students had gotten it right.

"You see?" the teacher said cheerfully. "If you can do it here, you can do it on the test. Don't just **capitulate** to these questions and think you're just going to get them wrong."

Jake wasn't sure about her wisdom here (after all, the test questions were harder than this exercise had been), but it felt good to get something right for once, and to feel that, perhaps, he was improving after all.

Vocabulary

0383
dispute [7]
[dɪ|spjuːt]

n. 논란, 분쟁　a debate, controversy, or difference of opinion
debate와 발음이 비슷하니까 비슷한 뜻이라고 외우자.
Sometimes people will **dispute** your release. (*v.*)

0384
dissonant [2]
[dísənənt]

a. 조화되지 않은　disagreeing, discordant
소리가(sound = son) 좋지 않다고(dis), 조화되지 않는다고 외워보자.
There were a few **dissonant** voices. (*adj.*)

0385
discard [3]
[dɪs|kɑːrd]

v. 버리다, 제거하다　eliminate, get rid of
필요없는 패(card)를 없앤다고(dis) 외워보자.
We must **discard** those old ideas. (*v.*)

0386
considerable [9]
[kən|sɪdərəbl]

a. 상당한, 많은　rather large or great in size, distance, extent, etc.
생각해 볼(consider) 여지가 충분히 있을 정도로 상당하다고 외워보자.
Damage to the building was **considerable**. (*adj.*)

0387
comprise [5]
[kəm|praɪz]

v. ~로 구성되다　consist of, to include
상품(prise = prize)이 여러 개로 구성되어 있다고 외워보자.
A soccer team **comprises** eleven players. (*v.*)

0388
postulation [4]
[pàstʃuléɪʃən]

n. 가정　assumption, hypothesis, inference
항상 우편이(post) 늦을(late) 거라고 가정한다고(postulate) 외워보자.
They **postulated** a 500-year lifespan for a plastic container. (*v.*)

0389
predisposed [3]
[priːdɪspóuzd]

a. 성향이 있는, ~하는 경향이 있는　having a tendency toward some activity or particular object, inclined to take certain action
pre(미리) 형성된 자신의 disposition(성격)을 통해서 ~하는 경향이 있다고 생각하자.
He was **predisposed** to a life of gambling. (*adj.*)

0390
deduce [8]
[didjúːs]

v. 추론하다, 연역하다   logically infer; surmise, to derive or to draw as a conclusion by reasoning from given premises or principles
What was that!!?!? 'did you see'(deduce) that? 그게 뭔지 추론해보자.
Without being told, she **deduced** that the criminal had been wearing boots from mud on the floor. (v.)

0391
capitulate [4]
[kəpítʃulèit]

v. 굴복하다; (조건부로) 성을 내주다, 항복하다   to surrender; succumb
붙잡히기(capture) 전에 항복하다(capitulate).
They were finally forced to **capitulate** to the terrorists' demands after a huge number of casualties. (v.)

Episode 24
MATCHING Quiz

1. dispute • • A. eliminate, get rid of
2. dissonant • • B. disagreeing, discordant
3. discard • • C. consist of
4. considerable • • D. a debate, controversy, or difference of opinion
5. comprise • • E. logically infer; surmise
6. postulation • • F. rather large or great in size, distance, extent, etc.
7. predisposed • • G. having a tendency toward some activity or particular object
8. deduce • • H. surrender; succumb
9. capitulate • • I. assumption, hypothesis, inference

1-D, 2-B, 3-A, 4-F, 5-C, 6-I, 7-G, 8-E, 9-H

더 많은 문제를 풀고자 한다면 www.quizlet.com에서 'paul academy seoul' class를 검색

Episode 25

Coincidence

After the date, and the **proliferation** of text messages that were required of lovers (apparently), Jake felt almost lifted off the ground. Every morning and afternoon, the music was some selection of pop songs which matched his **ennobled** mood. This morning, it was 'Something' by the Beatles, which was a song TJ would certainly **denigrate** as "lame", but which seemed to match Jake's **ineffable gaiety**. He'd had a date with a girl, a proper one with a movie and long chats in the cafe afterwards. The film itself had been pretty stupid, but somehow Jake and Jessica had found things to talk about. It was almost as if she was an actual human being and not just a fantasy in his mind.

Jessica, the date had confirmed, was simply **exquisite**. She dressed perfectly, laughed **delightfully**, and not just out of pity. She laughed with her whole body sometimes, and her eyes sparkled as they met his. Of course, they didn't look directly at each other very often, as Jake thought this would be a mistake (like he was trying too hard to be a hero in some movie) and also because he felt a strong desire to turn red when their eyes met.

Among their many messages back and forth, there was one which Jake again dreaded sending, though not as much as the first time. How was he going to ask her for *another* date? Should *she* do it so things would be more **egalitarian**? He again consulted his friends, but TJ only said that he should try to bring his date to somewhere **intimate** and Sam was a bit hurt since Jake hadn't listened to his advice on the roses so he just frowned.

On Monday night, walking the half mile or so toward the café where they held their study group meetings, he thought again about what he should do, and then it turned out that a miracle had happened.

Susan was sick.

When he **prowled** into the café, not believing his good luck, he saw

---

392 proliferation [6]
n. 급증
spread; large amount
a. proliferate

393 ennobled [2]
a. 기품이 있는
elevated in degree, excellence, or respect; exalted

394 denigrate [2]
v. 폄하하다
mock or speak badly of

395 ineffable [4]
a. 형언할 수 없는
unable to be expressed in words

396 gaiety [3]
n. 흥겨움, 유쾌함
happiness, hilarity

397 exquisite [5]
a. 매우 아름다운, 정교한
beautiful; superb; of high quality

398 delightful [12]
a. 정말 기분 좋은
giving great pleasure or delight

399 egalitarian [2]
a. 평등주의의
equal or fair

400 intimate [9]
a. 친밀한, 분위기 있는
characterized by an atmosphere conducive to privacy

401 prowl [3]
v. 서성거리다
rove or go about stealthily

402 sprawl [2]
v. 큰 대자로 뻗다
spread out (often covering a wide area)

403 vulnerable [5]
a. 취약한, 연약한
susceptible to being wounded or hurt

404 exhilarated [13]
a. 쾌활하게 하는
extremely excited; exuberant

405 intuition [12]
n. 직감
direct perception of truth, fact, etc.
a. intuitive

406 gallant [2]
a. 용감한, 용맹한
brave, courageous

Jessica at her usual table, the part in her hair directed towards him as her face was buried in an exercise book. Her coffee sat at the edge of the table, and her arms **sprawled** over the book's edge, leading Jake to wonder what was wrong. He looked around for the other girl, and realized her books weren't on the table. Jessica was alone.

He felt **vulnerable** and yet **exhilarated**. The second feeling was obvious, since he would again be able to talk to Jessica alone. The first, however, was caused by a panicked **intuition** that he was unprepared to do so. Trying not to think of this uncertainty, he decided instead to try a **gallant** strategy, but was unsure if it would work. He just hoped that he would be able to speak clearly for once.

Vocabulary

0392

proliferation [6]

[prəlɪfəreɪʃn]

n. 급증　spread; large amount　　*a.* proliferate
새 생명이(life) 막 솟아난다(pro)고 외워보자.
Attempts to prevent cancer cell **proliferation** (*n.*)

0393

ennobled [2]

[ɪnoʊbld]

a. 기품이 있는　elevated in degree, excellence, or respect; exalted
고귀해서(noble) 기품이 있다고 외워보자.
In a strange way she seemed **ennobled** by her grief. (*v.*)

0394

denigrate [2]

[dénigrèit]

v. 폄하하다　mock or speak badly of, belittle
nego '검은 색을 바르다'. 즉, '사람을 먹칠하다, 폄하하다'.
She **denigrated** everyone with less money than her by calling them lazy and stupid. (*v.*)

0395

ineffable [4]

[ɪnefəbl]

a. 형언할 수 없는　unable to be expressed in words
한국 사람들이 f 발음(eff)을 잘 못하는(in) 것이 대체 왜 그런지 말로 '형언할 수 없다'고 외워보자.
The **ineffable** joys of heaven (*adj.*)

0396

gaiety [3]

[géiəti]

n. 흥겨움, 유쾌함　happiness, hilarity, festivity
gay는 원래 '행복하다'라는 뜻으로 유쾌함을 의미한다.
Gaiety at the grand ball (*n.*)

0397

exquisite [5]

[ɪkskwɪzɪt]

a. 매우 아름다운, 정교한　beautiful; superb; of high quality, of special beauty or charm, or rare and appealing excellence
Exquisite라는 잡지가 있다. 그것을 기억하자. 그 잡지 표면에는 exquisite라는 단어와 함께 아름다운 모델들 사진이 나오겠지? 그래서 exquisite은 '매우 아름다운, 정교한'이라는 뜻이다.
His **exquisite** art pieces prove that he is a genius. (*adj.*)

0398
delightful [12]
[dɪ|laɪtfl]

a. 정말 기분 좋은   giving great pleasure or delight
heavy한 사람이 다이어트를 하는데 몸무게가 엄청 많이 빠져서 light해졌어. 기분이 어떻겠지? 정말 좋겠지? 기분이 delightful해질거야.
The weather was **delightful** - clear skies, soft winds, and warm sunlight everywhere. (*adj.*)

0399
egalitarian [2]
[ɪgæ̀lətέəriən]

a. 평등주의의, 평등주의자   equal or fair, democratic; democrat
equal(동일한)–itarian이라고 해석할 수 있다.
According to the **egalitarian** principle, everyone should have equal rights and duties. (*adj.*)

0400
intimate [9]
[|ɪntɪmət]

a. 친밀한, 분위기 있는   characterized by an atmosphere conducive to privacy
하나의 팀 (tim = team) 안에 (in) 있는 친구 (mate)처럼 친밀하다고 외워보자.
We're not on **intimate** terms with our neighbours. (*adj.*)

0401
prowl [3]
[praʊl]

v. 서성거리다   rove or go about stealthily
으르렁(roar → rowl)거리는 동물이 서성거리고 있다고 외우자.
A man was seen **prowling** around outside the factory just before the fire started. (*v.*)

0402
sprawl [2]
[sprɔːl]

v. 큰 대자로 뻗다   spread out (often covering a wide area)
'여기저기 자라나다'라는 뜻의 sprout와 연결해서 외워보자.
People **sprawl** in beach chairs or sit under umbrellas. (*v.*)

0403
vulnerable [5]
[|vʌlnərəbl]

a. 취약한, 연약한   susceptible to being wounded or hurt, capable of being wounded or hurt
vulner(wound, 상처) + able : '상처 입을 수 있는' → 상처 입기 쉬운, 공격 당하기 쉬운
As the walls were destroyed, the castle was now **vulnerable** to attacks. (*adj.*)

0404
exhilarated [13]
[ɪgzɪ̀ləreɪtɪd]

a. 쾌활하게 하는   extremely excited; exuberant
매우 웃긴(hilarious) 걸 봐서 기분이 좋아졌다고 외워보자.
When do you feel most happy, relaxed, and **exhilarated**? (*adj.*)

0405

intuition [12]

[ɪntuˈɪʃn]

n. 직감　　direct perception of truth, fact, etc.　　*a.* intuitive

웬만한 학비(tuition)는 비쌀 거라고 우리는 '직감'할 수 있다.

I had an **intuition** that something awful was about to happen. (*n.*)

0406

gallant [2]

[ɡǽlənt]

a. 용감한, 용맹한　　brave, courageous, spirited

프랑스어 galant(용맹한)에서 유래한 단어이다.

Gallant knight in shining armor (*adj.*)

Episode 25

MATCHING Quiz

1. proliferation	A. mock or speak badly of
2. ennobled	B. elevated in degree, excellence, or respect; exalted
3. denigrate	C. beautiful; superb; of high quality
4. ineffable	D. spread; large amount
5. gaiety	E. happiness, hilarity
6. exquisite	F. equal or fair
7. delightful	G. unable to be expressed in words
8. egalitarian	H. spread out (often covering a wide area)
9. intimate	I. characterized by an atmosphere conducive to privacy
10. prowl	J. giving great pleasure or delight
11. sprawl	K. direct perception of truth, fact, etc.
12. vulnerable	L. susceptible to being wounded or hurt
13. exhilarated	M. rove or go about stealthily
14. intuition	N. brave, courageous
15. gallant	O. extremely excited; exuberant

1-D, 2-B, 3-A, 4-G, 5-E, 6-C, 7-J, 8-F, 9-I, 10-M, 11-H, 12-L, 13-O, 14-K, 15-N

더 많은 문제를 풀고자 한다면 www.quizlet.com에서 'paul academy seoul' class를 검색

Episode 26 — The Summit

407 compatriot [2]
n. 동포
fellow member of a group or country

408 banal [2]
a. 지극히 평범한
devoid of freshness or originality; trite

"Ahem," he coughed slightly. She looked up, at first angry that someone would disturb her, and then delighted to see him.

"Hello stranger! As you can see, we're missing one **compatriot** today."

"I see that. How's your stuff going?"

"Ugh. This stuff is terribly boring. So…" she searched for a word.

"**Banal**?" he offered, happy that he had paid attention in vocabulary class that morning.

"Exactly… I think," she said, unsure.

"Well, now *I'm* not so sure," he joked, wondering how he would begin.

"Are you gonna study?" she asked, noticing that he hadn't sat down.

He had been focusing on making a very challenging sentence come out of his face, but it didn't seem to want to come. Finally, the awkwardness of the silence forced him to speak.

"Um, actually, I was wondering if we should have dinner instead," he said much too quickly. What was so hard about this? It was just words!

"You mean, like, not study?" she asked unsurely.

"Well…yes, I guess. I haven't eaten anything yet, and I was wondering if we could get something to eat nearby."

"Sure, that's fine," she said, and made a few final marks in her book before closing it and putting it into her bag. She stood up with a smile.

They moved to a nearby restaurant and ate in near silence. Jake felt embarrassed by how **voracious** he actually had been, and glad that the food gave him an excuse to have his mouth full. Still, once his appetite had been **gratified**, he was happier when they finally left and took to the streets. Although she didn't know it, he was executing a plan.

He headed up the hill, carrying her bag like a gentleman and **flaunted** that he knew a café nearby that she might like. As they climbed, he worried that she would start doubting the truth of this claim, but she continued on silently.

At last, they reached the top, and he dove into a small clearing, where a darkened path led up through a little park. Again they climbed, and a few times she grabbed his arm to steady herself.

"Where are we going, Jake?"

"Sorry, I thought maybe we could take a brief rest first."

When they got to the top, they found the park deserted. Even the tennis courts were empty, and an unusual quiet had fallen over the entire grounds.

"I just really like this park, and thought well...I guess I wanted to show it to someone," he said as he regained his breath.

She looked around and then straight at him, brushing hair out of her eyes with a teasing flourish.

"It's lovely, Jake. But you should probably tell someone you're going to make them climb like this."

"Sorry, I guess it was supposed to be a surprise. It's just —" What could he say but the truth? "I wanted to ask you out to another movie or something, but I didn't know how I should."

She was silent for a moment, and then began laughing with her usual full-bodied laugh.

---

409 voracious [2]
a. 배가 고파 죽을 지경인
very hungry, ravenous

410 gratified [10]
a. 만족스러운
satisfied, as a desire

411 flaunt [2]
v. 과시하다, 자랑하다
show off, boast

| 412 | **forbear** ²
v. 참다, 삼가다
refrain or abstain from

| 413 | **sublime** ²²
a. 숭고한
heavenly; near-perfect

| 414 | **trite** ³
a. 진부한
clichéd; overly-common; banal

| 415 | **hobble** ³
v. 다리를 절뚝거리다
stumble, limp

"You could have just asked me, idiot! What, you want to see another romantic robot movie?"

"It doesn't really matter what we see," he said, sure that this was the sort of cliché he should definitely **forbear**. She didn't seem to notice, but just stepped towards him and grabbed his hand.

"You're very sweet, Jake."

To Jake's lovestruck gaze, at that moment she had a ghostly quality, the moon hanging above them both and running white across her face (or it could have been a street light — he preferred imagining it was the moon). She looked like a marble statue, her head held still against the black night behind her. It was hard to imagine that she was human at times like this. He allowed himself to look into her eyes, which stared back intensely. A sudden violent attack of anxiety filled his chest, as though he would drop dead then and there. But he didn't, and knew it would be alright. He felt **sublime** in that silent space, and in those few seconds, there was nothing in his mind but the starlight glinting of the city lights and the moon and Jessica and… and then he did something he never expected to do. He stooped somewhat (she was a few inches shorter in her flat shoes) and kissed her on the mouth.

Of all the things written about kissing, or the **trite** Klimt painting, nothing really prepares one for their first experience. Jake's shock at his own boldness and the awkward angle caused him to **hobble** a bit as they broke contact. Blinking and steadying himself, he wondered if anything could have been better at that moment. Her lips were warm, and as they broke off their brief connection with his, they seemed to have left an impression, which felt nice.

"Sorry," he murmured.

"Nothing to be sorry about, Jake. I was hoping you'd do that." She smiled again, still holding his hand.

"Well, I'm glad the mind-reading worked that time," he whispered jokingly.

"Oh, you can read my thoughts? It certainly seems like it."

They walked slowly through the park, almost entering a public platform until they realized it was already occupied by a pair of older lovers who looked like they didn't want to be disturbed. Jake took her up further near the very top, where a large circle of sharp fence housed a small police station. Staying by the edge, and **attentive** that a large dog **tramped** the interior of the compound at night, he took her beyond the path to a small area overlooking the white lights of the train station. They sat very close on a fallen tree and she spoke. This time, her voice seemed distant, as though she was almost asleep.

"You know what I learned today, Jake?"
"No, what did you learn?"
"You know the word 'cleave?'"
He shook his head.
"Well, it means two things apparently, totally opposite."
"Oh yeah?"
"Yeah, one meaning is to **amputate** something into two **discrete** pieces. Like a cleaver knife."
"Uh-huh," he said uncertainly.
"The other is weird though, because you can say 'he cleaved to an idea or person,' which means he stuck very closely together with it. Isn't that odd?"
"That cleave means two things? I guess so."

She was quiet again, and they sat like that for a number of minutes, **ruminating** the expanse of metropolitan space lying beneath them, when both realized that their study session had ended. Standing up, Jessica approached him, and again kissed him forcefully, and they **adhered** to one another for a minute or so until they had to part ways down opposite sides of the hill.

---

416 attentive [3]
a. 주의를 기울이는
mindful, considerate

417 tramp [6]
v. 떠돌다
patrol, wander

418 amputate [3]
v. 절단하다
cut off

419 discrete [8]
a. 별개의
separate, distinct

420 ruminate [3]
v. 심사숙고하다
think seriously, contemplate

421 adhere [6]
v. 들러붙다
cling, stick fast

Vocabulary

0407
compatriot [2]
[kəmˈpeɪtriət]

n. 동포   fellow member of a group or country, fellow countryman or countrywoman
com은 '같이'라는 뜻이고 patriot은 '애국자'라는 뜻이다. 그래서 같이 애국자니까 같은 나라의 동포라고 볼 수 있다. 그래서 동포이다.
Because both of the finalists were Greek, John had to fight his **compatriot** to win the competition. (*n.*)

0408
banal [2]
[bənǽl]

a. 지극히 평범한, 진부한   devoid of freshness or originality; trite
너무 진부한 (banal) 아이디어들은 금지하기로 (ban) 했다고 외워보자.
Everyone disliked the **banal** comments from the boring woman. (*adj.*)

0409
voracious [2]
[vɔːréiʃəs]

a. 배가 고파 죽을 지경인, 게걸스레 먹는   very hungry, ravenous, eating with greediness or in very large quantities
vor는 '먹는다'는 의미의 어원이다.
Football players had a **voracious** appetite after the long and exhausting game. (*adj.*)

0410
gratified [10]
[grǽtəfàid]

a. 만족스러운   satisfied, as a desire
매우 훌륭해서(great = grat) 만족스러웠다고 외워보자.
I was **gratified** to hear the news. (*adj.*)

0411
flaunt [2]
[flɔːnt]

v. 과시하다, 자랑하다   show off, boast
이모께서(aunt) 꽃을(flower → fla) 받았다고 자랑했다고 외워보자.
He did not believe in **flaunting** his wealth. (*v.*)

0412
forbear [2]
[fɔːrbέər]

v. 참다, 삼가다   refrain or abstain from
bear가 '참다'라는 데서 유래.
The alcoholic made the very difficult choice to **forbear** from drinking. (*v.*)

0413
sublime [22]
[səbláim]

a. 숭고한   heavenly; near-perfect, elevated in thought, language, etc
거대한 라임(lime) 아래(sub)에 있는 것을 상상해보라. 너무 환상적이고 신비로운 기분이 들 것이다.
The **sublime** beauty of a saint's statue made everyone respect him. (*adj.*)

0414
trite [3]
[tráit]

a. 진부한, 흔해빠진   clichéd; overly-common; banal, dull because it has been told too many times
라틴어 tritus에서 온 말로 '써서 닳아빠진, 길 따위가 밟아 다져진'이란 뜻으로 '더 이상 신선미가 없는, 케케묵은, 진부한'의 뜻이다.
After eating at the five-star restaurant everyday for a week, his mother's food tasted **trite** to him. (*adj.*)

0415
hobble [3]
[hábl]

v. 다리를 절뚝거리다   stumble, to limp; to make one limp
hop은 '뛴다'는 의미로 뛰다 다쳤다고 생각하자.
The injury **hobbled** the runner. (*v.*)

0416
attentive [3]
[ətentɪv]

a. 주의를 기울이는   mindful, considerate
주의(attention)를 많이 기울인다고 외워보자.
The hotel staff are friendly and **attentive**. (*adj.*)

0417
tramp [6]
[træmp]

v. 떠돌다   patrol, wander
트램펄린(trampoline) 위에서 방방 뛰다 보면 여기저기 왔다갔다(tramp)하게 된다.
An old **tramp** was sitting on a bench. (*n.*)

0418
amputate [3]
[ǽmpjuteɪt]

v. (수술로)절단하다   cut off
팔을(arm → am) 절단한 것으로 외우자.
He had to have both legs **amputated**. (*v.*)

0419
discrete [8]
[dɪskríːt]

a. 별개의   separate, distinct, apart from others
discrete에서 e 2개 사이를 막는 t가 있는것처럼, discrete도 따로따로 분리되어 있는 거야.
Her song was a constant flow of melody rather than many **discrete** notes. (*adj.*)

0420
ruminate [rúːmənèit]

v. 심사 숙고하다, 되새기다 — to think seriously, contemplate, to think very carefully about
소처럼 계속 곱씹다는 의미를 가진 어원에서 유래한 단어이다.
They **ruminate** about the meaning of life. (v.)

0421
adhere [ədhír]

v. 들러붙다 — cling, stick fast
여기에(here) 더해서(add → ad) 붙인다고 생각하자.
Once in the bloodstream, the bacteria **adhere** to the surface of the red cells. (v.)

Episode 26 — MATCHING Quiz

1. compatriot — A. satisfied, as a desire
2. banal — B. devoid of freshness or originality; trite
3. voracious — C. fellow member of a group or country
4. gratified — D. show off, boast
5. flaunt — E. heavenly; near-perfect
6. forbear — F. very hungry, ravenous
7. sublime — G. stumble, limp
8. trite — H. refrain or abstain from
9. hobble — I. patrol, wander
10. attentive — J. mindful, considerate
11. tramp — K. separate, distinct
12. amputate — L. clichéd; overly-common; banal
13. discrete — M. cling, stick fast
14. ruminate — N. cut off
15. adhere — O. think seriously, contemplate

1-C, 2-B, 3-F, 4-D, 5-H, 6-H, 7-E, 8-L, 9-G, 10-J, 11-I, 12-N, 13-K, 14-O, 15-M

더 많은 문제를 풀고자 한다면 www.quizlet.com에서 'paul academy seoul' class를 검색

Episode 27

The Other Side of the Coin

Though she had returned, Ashley was still the nervous girl she had been before, and when Jake got into the school the next morning (their fourth Thursday), she was sitting alone at her desk, crying. Jake, in his short life, had never learned how to **unravel** the cause of a girl's melancholy without her **despising** him for some reason and then becoming more upset. There was cure for it, apparently, so he decided to spend the few minutes he had before class looking for TJ or Sam to play The Toss.

They, as he had expected, were deeply-invested in their game, sitting near the coffee shop patio, tossing coins into a coffee cup partially-filled with water. Needless to say, with their competitive **propensity,** they took it quite seriously.

This sense of gravity was shown on TJ's face as he stared hard at the cup, cursing to himself and trying to **downplay** Sam's taunts about his poor throwing ability. Jake noticed they had about 40 coins between them. It was a great throw. With some fear, TJ drew his arm back and flung the coin quite high with a nice arc, as though the **trajectory** of the coin had been set electronically to fit the middle of the cup. Down it came in a perfect arc, revolving slowly on its descent. From behind, Jake could see his friend's cheeks spreading wider into a smile.

Then the coin landed on the edge of the cup, and pulled the whole thing down.

"Ha ha! That's five more coins you owe me!" Sam cried. Jake dug into his pockets and found only fabric.

"I guess I'm finished," he sighed, and rose to leave. Seeing Jake, his face brightened. "Hey brother, can you spare a quarter?"

"Or five?" Jake asked.

---

422 unravel [5]
v. 풀다
figure out, solve

423 despise [2]
v. 경멸하다, 깔보다
look down on with contempt; loathe

424 propensity [3]
n. 기질, 경향
inclination, disposition

425 downplay [6]
v. 대단치 않게 생각하다
treat or speak of so as to reduce emphasis on its importance, value, strength, etc.

426 trajectory [2]
n. 탄도, 궤적
a curve described by a projectile, rocket, or the like in its flight

427 **chronic** [15]
a. 만성적인
constant, habitual, inveterate

428 **prevail** [24]
v. 승리하다
win, triumph

429 **despondent** [4]
a. 낙담한
very depressed or hopeless

430 **disillusioned** [3]
a. 실망한, 환멸을 느낀
disappointed

431 **demur** [1]
v. 이의를 제기하다
refuse or deny

430 **maxim** [2]
n. 격언
a principle or rule of conduct

433 **antidote** [4]
n. 해독제
medicine or remedy

434 **rigorous** [14]
a. 철저한, 엄격한
rigidly severe or harsh, as people, rules, or discipline

TJ approached him with the casual yet awkward smile of the **chronic** gambler, trying to get another few dollars to rebuild his fortunes.

"Come on, man, if I don't **prevail** this morning, I've got no money for lunch."

Sighing, Jake took out a few bills and dropped them in his friend's hands.

"Good luck."

But Sam had already thrown his coin into the cup by the time the boys returned to play, and the stack of coins that rested on the ground now sat in his overflowing coffee cup, ready to be used again for the next game. **Despondent** and **disillusioned** by the letdown, TJ raised the bills toward Jake's hands and tried to return the money he'd so recently borrowed.

"No, no," Jake **demurred**. "You need to eat something."

"Not at all," came the shamefaced reply. "It'll teach me a lesson. A **maxim** if you will: No gambling anymore."

"I think you can learn that without all the self-denial, don't you?"

"Not sure, but maybe I should try this **antidote** and see what works. Such a **rigorous** lifestyle might have an 'easing' effect on my behavior, as the vocab book might say."

He walked past Jake, his shoulders bent forward and his over-serious, yet still childishly round, face facing the ground ahead of him. The two friends took the elevator up in silence.

Vocabulary

0422
unravel [5]
[ʌnrǽvl]

v. 풀다   figure out, solve, to make clear
twist, tangle, ravel 은 모두 '꼬여있는'이라는 뜻으로 unravel은 '풀다'는 뜻이다.
The mysterious murder case was **unravelled** when the witness appeared. (*v.*)

0423
despise [2]
[dispáiz]

v. 경멸하다, 깔보다   look down on with contempt; loathe, to regard with contempt, disdain
spi 는 '보다'라는 뜻이어서 '어떤 사람에 대해서 보지 않는다'. 그러니까 미워하는 사람은 보려고 하지 않겠지?
Honest people tend to **despise** lies. (*v.*)

0424
propensity [3]
[prəpénsəti]

n. 기질, 경향, 버릇   natural inclination, disposition
pro는 '앞으로'라는 뜻이고 pendere는 '매달리다'는 뜻이므로 무언가에 계속 매달려있으려는 성질, 즉 버릇을 뜻한다.
The gambler had a **propensity** for losing money. (*n.*)

0425
downplay [6]
[dáunplèi]

v. 대단치 않게 생각하다, 경시하다   treat or speak of so as to reduce emphasis on its importance, value, strength, etc., to play down
너는 down 아래에서 play 놀아! 라고 무시하는 것이다.
The president tried to **downplay** his mistake to keep the people's support. (*v.*)

0426
trajectory [2]
[trədʒéktəri]

n. 탄도, 궤적   a curve described by a projectile, rocket, or the like in its flight
제트기(jet → ject)가 움직일 때 (travel → tra) 따라가는 궤적을 생각하자.
My career seemed to be on a downward **trajectory**. (*n.*)

0427
chronic [15]
[kránik]

a. 만성적의, 만성적인   constant, habitual, inveterate
chrono는 '시간'을 뜻하므로 '항상'이라는 의미를 지닌다.
I've been trying to get rid of the **chronic** pain in my knees for years, but it just won't go away. (*adj.*)

0428
prevail [24]
[prɪvéɪl]

v. 승리하다   win, triumph
용감하다(valiant)라는 단어에서 기원한 단어로 '용기있는 자가 승리한다'고 외우자.
Justice will **prevail** over tyranny. (*v.*)

0429
despondent [4]
[dɪspάndənt]

a. 낙담한, 기죽은   very depressed or hopeless, disheartened
너무 기가 죽어서 대답하지(respond) 못한다고(de) 해석할 수 있다.
He was **despondent** after his mother died. (*adj.*)

0430
disillusioned [3]
[dìsɪlúːʒənd]

a. 실망한, 환멸을 느낀   disappointed, disenchanted
환상이(illusion) '깨진'(dis)의 의미이다.
People were **disillusioned** about the politician as soon as the scandal broke out. (*adj.*)

0431
demur [1]
[dɪmə́ːr]

v. 이의를 제기하다   refuse or deny, object (because of doubts, scruples); hesitate
demur 는 라틴어 demorari 에서 나온 말이다. de(완전히) + mur(지연) = '완전히 지연시키다' → 망설이다, 주저하다 → 이의를 제기하다.
When Dimitri offered her a bite of his awful soup, she **demurred** and said she would try the salad instead. (*v.*)

0432
maxim [2]
[mǽksim]

n. 격언, 금언   a principle accepted as true and acted on as a rule or guide
maximum + saying 가장 크고 좋은 말, 즉 격언이다.
Confucius is famous for his numerous **maxims**. (*n.*)

0433
antidote [4]
[ǽntidòʊt]

n. 해독제   medicine or remedy
독(dot)에 반대되므로(anti) 해독제이다.
There is no known **antidote** to the poison. (*n.*)

0434
rigorous [rígərəs]

a. **철저한, 엄격한, 가혹한**   rigidly severe or harsh, as people, rules, or discipline, exact

rigor 는 라틴어로 '뻣뻣하다'는 뜻으로 '일이 뻣뻣하게 진행되어 가혹하다'는 의미이다.

In order to join the CIA, one must go through a **rigorous** training. (*adj.*)

Episode 27
MATCHING Quiz

1. unravel	A. look down on with contempt; loathe
2. despise	B. a curve described by a projectile, rocket, or the like in its flight
3. propensity	C. inclination, disposition
4. downplay	D. figure out, solve
5. trajectory	E. constant, habitual, inveterate
6. chronic	F. very depressed or hopeless
7. prevail	G. treat or speak of so as to reduce emphasis on its importance, value, strength, etc.
8. despondent	H. disappointed
9. disillusioned	I. rigidly severe or harsh, as people, rules, or discipline
10. demur	J. win, triumph
11. maxim	K. medicine or remedy
12. antidote	L. refuse or deny
13. rigorous	M. a principle or rule of conduct

1-D, 2-A, 3-C, 4-G, 5-B, 6-E, 7-J, 8-F, 9-H, 10-L, 11-M, 12-K, 13-I

더 많은 문제를 풀고자 한다면 www.quizlet.com에서 'paul academy seoul' class를 검색

Episode 28

Money, or the Pain of Being Poor

435 ordeal ²
n. 시련
an extremely severe or trying test, experience, or trial

436 forsake ⁵
v. 버리다, 저버리다
give up; eschew

437 pastime ²
n. 취미
something that serves to make time pass agreeably; recreation

438 omnipresence ²
n. 어디에나 있음
occurrence everywhere; ubiquity

439 preeminent ⁵
a. 아주 뛰어난
superior or extremely important

440 crucial ⁹
a. 중대한, 결정적인
involving an extremely important decision or result; critical

441 benefactor ³
n. 후원자
one who gives a charitable donation

442 guise ²
n. 겉모습
style of dress, general external appearance

Following TJ's disastrous **ordeal** the day before, the round-faced boy had **forsaken** gambling as promised and had gotten more money from his mother, to be used exclusively for **pastimes** outside of the Game. However, the subject of money was still very much on Jake's mind for other reasons.

All throughout the wealthy neighborhood, there were reminders of the **omnipresence** of wealth: the prices of food, clothes, alcohol, the quality of life itself there. Money, everyone had decided, was the **preeminent** feature of modern life. It made the world go round, and, yet, oddly, was also the source of all evil. Regardless, it also bought movie tickets and food and flowers and everything else that is thought **crucial** by high school boys for impressing a pretty girl. Jake needed more of it.

"What am I going to do?" he asked TJ after lunch.

"About what?" TJ asked innocently, enjoying his meal.

"Money. Jessica's rich, you know? How am I supposed to buy her something nice?" He had been fantasizing lately that one day, on his way home, he might be approached by a rich **benefactor**, perhaps some tech CEO, who liked his smart **guise** and promised to leave a fortune to him. He was never sure why this fictional billionaire would do such a thing, but at the moment it was his only hope.

"Dunno," TJ answered. "You could **deprive** a wealthy old lady of her jewels, or rob a bank perhaps. If ever you need help, just let me know." He laughed and then gestured toward the clock to indicate it was time to get to the afternoon study.

On the street, Jake felt the few bills he had in his pocket. He tried hard to be **frugal**, eating cheaply and restricting himself to a few visits to the arcade with his friends. Occasionally he bought coffee but it seemed he still never had money. His mother was, to say the least, unsympathetic.

"Maybe I should get a job," he **meditated**.

"Doing what?"

"Well, I have a cousin who works in a convenience store. Maybe I could do that."

"They work six-hour shifts, man. And usually the only one available is from midnight to six in the morning. You think your mother's going to allow that?"

Jake had to admit his friend's **rebuttal** was sensible, but the idea of steady work with steady pay seemed like a **notion** he couldn't easily dismiss.

"What we need is a plan," he said, trying to affect the concentrated look of a movie character just as he was about to have a breakthrough.

"We?" TJ said disbelievingly as they rode the elevator up to the third floor. "What do I have to do with this?"

"Well…don't you wanna make some extra money?"

"My mom gives me enough, I think, as long as I don't do anything stupid with it. Maybe you could persuade yours to —"

"Or my Dad! Maybe he could help me!" Jake again dreamt of his imaginary billionaire, and the idea of being independent — an **entity** entirely separate from his parents. He would buy a house (or at least become a **tenant**), and marry Jessica, and they would have children who would never be sent to academies. Oh well, perhaps his father would be **unstinting** when he asked him that night.

---

443 deprive [12]
v. 면직하다
remove or withhold something from the enjoyment or possession of

444 frugal [3]
a. 검소한
spending little money

445 meditate [7]
v. 사색하다, 명상하다
muse, contemplate

446 rebuttal [8]
a. 반박
argument against another
v. rebut

447 notion [16]
n. 개념, 관념
a general understanding, an opinion, view

448 entity [4]
n. 독립체
being or existence considered as independent

449 tenant [6]
n. 세입자
a person or group that rents and occupies land or a house

450 unstinting [2]
a. 아낌없이 주는
generous, magnanimous

Vocabulary

0435
ordeal ²
[ɔːrˈdiːl]

n. **시련**   an extremely severe or trying test, experience, or trial
뭔가를 deal해야 한다는 얘기니까, '시련을 겪어야한다'는 뜻으로 설명할 수 있다.
He became CEO after many **ordeals** and troubles. (*n.*)

0436
forsake ⁵
[fərséik]

v. **버리다, (친구 등을)저버리다**   give up; eschew, leave entirely
God-forsaken이란 말 들어봤지? 어떤 안 좋은 일이 생겼을때 '하나님이 나를 떠났어!' 또는 '나를 버렸어!'라는 뜻으로 많이 쓴다.
Teacher, please do not **forsake** us; if you leave, there is no one left at school to teach us. (*v.*)

0437
pastime ²
[pǽstàim]

n. **취미, 기분전환, 오락**   something that serves to make time pass agreeably; recreation, activity
공부, 일할 시간(time)이 지난후에(past)는 오락, 여가시간을 즐기는 것이다.
His **pastime** was reading Japanese manga. (*n.*)

0438
omnipresence ²
[ὰmniprézns]

n. **어디에나 있음**   occurrence everywhere; ubiquity
모든 곳에(omni) 존재하므로(presence) 어디에나 있다.
The **omnipresence** of the secret police made it impossible to do anything without the authorities finding out. (*n.*)

0439
preeminent ⁵
[priːéminənt]

a. **아주 뛰어난**   superior or extremely important
힙합 가수 에미넴(Eminem → eminen)보다도 앞섰으므로(pre) 매우 뛰어나다고 외워보자.
He played a **preeminent** role in the peace talks. (*adj.*)

0440
crucial ⁹
[ˈkruːʃl]

a. **중대한, 결정적인**   involving an extremely important decision or result; critical
보트 크루즈(cruise)에서 벌어지는 행사는 정말 중대한 행사겠지? 불참하지 말고 꼭 참석해야 해!
A **crucial** ingredient in every sandwich is bread; without bread, a sandwich is not a sandwich. (*adj.*)

0441
benefactor [3]
[|benɪfæktə(r)|]

n. 후원자　one who gives a charitable donation
혜택을(benefit → benefa)을 가져다 주는 후원자라고 외워보자.
In his old age he became a **benefactor** of the arts. (*n.*)

0442
guise [2]
[gaɪz]

n. (가장된)겉모습　style of dress, general external appearance
disguise(속이다)는 결국 가짜(dis), 겉모습(guise)이라는 의미이다.
His speech presented racist ideas under the **guise** of nationalism. (*n.*)

0443
deprive [12]
[dipráiv]

v. 면직하다, 빼앗다, 박탈하다　remove or withhold something from the enjoyment or possession of, to divest
de(없는) private(사적인 것). 즉 '결여된'.
When he arrived at the prison, the prisoner was **deprived** of his freedom. (*v.*)

0444
frugal [3]
[|fruːgl|]

a. 검소한　spending little money
과일(fruit → fru) 하나도 모두(all → al) 나눠먹을 정도로 검소하다고 외우자.
I think you really are **frugal**. (*adj.*)

0445
meditate [7]
[|medɪteɪt|]

v. 사색하다, 명상하다　muse, contemplate
자신의 중심을(middle = medi) 찾기 위해 명상한다고 외워보자.
You **meditate** constantly until you simply have clear thought. (*v.*)

0446
rebuttal [8]
[rɪbʌtl]

n. 반박　argument against another　*v.* rebut
다시(re) '하지만'(but) 이라고 말하며 반박을 제기한다고 외워보자.
Ashley's last **rebuttal** was very effective. (*n.*)

0447
notion [16]
[|noʊʃn|]

n. 개념, 관념　a general understanding, an opinion, view
개념은 무언가를 아는(know → no) 것이다.
That was an interesting **notion**. (*n.*)

0448
entity [4]
[|entəti|]

n. 독립체　being or existence considered as independent, something that has a real existence
title(제목, 이름)이 있어야 entity로 취급될 때가 많아.
Each ant acts like part of a larger machine rather than like a separate **entity**. (*n.*)

0449
tenant 6

[ǀtenənt]

n. 세입자   a person or group that rents and occupies land, an office, or the like
미국에서 집을 구한다는 것은 보통 tenant 상태가 되는 것을 말해.
The owner of the building evicted the loud **tenants** from the building because other tenants were complaining about them. (*n.*)

0450
unstinting 2

[ʌnstíntiŋ]

a. 아낌없이 주는   giving generously, magnanimous
stint는 '멈추다'라는 뜻으로 멈추지 않고 계속해서 준다고 해석할 수 있다.
With **unstinting** generosity, he bought his little sisters chicken, cake, fruit juice, teddy bears, and whatever they asked for. (*adj.*)

Voca Hamburger
Episode 28
MATCHING Quiz

1. ordeal
2. forsake
3. pastime
4. omnipresence
5. preeminent
6. crucial
7. benefactor
8. guise
9. deprive
10. frugal
11. meditate
12. rebuttal
13. notion
14. entity
15. tenant
16. unstinting

A. something that serves to make time pass agreeably; recreation
B. give up; eschew
C. superior or extremely important
D. an extremely severe or trying test, experience, or trial
E. one who gives a charitable donation
F. occurrence everywhere; ubiquity
G. remove or withhold something from the enjoyment or possession of
H. involving an extremely important decision or result; critical
I. spending little money
J. argument against another
K. style of dress, general external appearance
L. generous, magnanimous
M. a general understanding, an opinion, view
N. muse, contemplate
O. a person or group that rents and occupies land or a house
P. being or existence considered as independent

1-D, 2-B, 3-A, 4-F, 5-C, 6-H, 7-E, 8-K, 9-G, 10-I, 11-N, 12-J, 13-M, 14-P, 15-O, 16-L.

더 많은 문제를 풀고자 한다면 www.quizlet.com에서 'paul academy seoul' class를 검색

Episode 29

Family Spirit(s)

Later that night, at 2:17 AM to be precise, Jake's father arrived home after having spent much of the night trying to prepare quarterly finance reports for the bank's head office. He was totally exhausted, and the sight of his son in the living room brought him less joy than it had the last time they'd met this way.

"Hey Dad," Jake said happily.

"Hey son. Don't you sleep anymore?"

"Well, I had some vocabulary to memorize again, so I thought I'd stay up till three to see if it helps." He had prepared his vocabulary book on the coffee table to **attest** to his **conscientiousness**, but had actually spent much of the night texting Jessica and watching TV.

"Good work, son," the **patriarch** said wearily. He was desperate for an evening whiskey and some quiet time.

"Sorry, I'll go to my room." Jake decided he would have to give up before even trying to ask. After their last meeting, the two had resumed their previous **aloofness**, rarely seeing each other for more than ten minutes at the time, usually when one or both of them had food in his mouth, which naturally **impeded** too much discussion. However, thoughts of another date with Jessica appeared, and Jake remembered his empty pockets.

"Hey, Dad, I know it's late and everything, but I wanted to ask you, well …" he was unsure of the best tactic at this point. "It's just that I've got this study group."

"Uh huh," his father responded, sitting down heavily as the boy rose.

"Well, the other people in this group always pay for coffee and stuff, and sometimes they go to movies to celebrate their scores…but

---

451 attest [4]
v. 증명하다
give evidence of

452 conscientious [12]
a. 양심적인
controlled by one's inner sense of what is right

453 patriarch [6]
n. 족장
the male head of a family or tribal line

454 aloof [6]
a. 무관심한, 냉담한
indifferent; disinterested

455 impede [5]
v. 방해하다, 막다
prevent, hinder, obstruct

456 superfluous [5]
a. 필요치 않은
unnecessarily extra

457 expenditure [4]
n. 지출, 비용
the act of expending something, especially funds

458 fabricate [5]
v. 만들어 내다, 제작하다
devise, construct

459 impart [17]
v. 전하다, 주다
make known, tell

460 judicious [4]
a. 신중한
using good judgment; careful

461 omit [2]
v. 생략하다
leave out

462 peculiar [13]
a. 이상한
strange, queer, odd

I can't always pay."

"What? Isn't your mother giving you enough money?"

"Not really. She says movies and things are '**superfluous** waste of time.'"

"She's probably talking about that Susan girl. The over-enthusiastic one. Never liked her much myself, but I guess it's your type."

"What? What do you mean 'my type?'"

"You're dating her, right? Your mother told me."

"No, Dad! God, no! It's a study group. No dating, whatsoever."

"But you still need **expenditures** for 'activities'?"

"Yeah."

At this point, Jake had no way of knowing that his father understood a great deal more about he **fabricated** story than he Jake would have liked. Of course, the older man had suspected there was a girl involved in this somehow, and was delighted that it wasn't Susan. Having relaxed into his chair, and having forgotten the work he had only recently left, he asked his son to bring a bottle of whiskey from the small collection in his office. He undid his tie, and sat back wondering how to **impart** to his wife about what was about to happen, and how much to **judiciously omit**.

"Two glasses, son!" he whispered to Jake as the boy returned with the bottle and his father's customary glass.

"Two? But you —"

"Just get another one from the kitchen. Quietly, if you don't mind."

Once he had the necessary accessories, his father poured a small measure in one glass and a considerably bigger measure into the other. They clashed the glasses and his father brought the glass to his mouth, sniffed appreciatively, and sipped it, letting a small sigh of satisfaction escape. Trying to do things as perfectly as possible, Jake copied the older man's actions, sniffed at the **peculiar** brownish liquid, and his nostrils burned with the smell. He took a small sip and **flinched**. Immediately, his gums and his tongue seemed on fire. This is what men spent so much money and time pretending to enjoy? It was **repellent**!

His father laughed at Jake's expression, and told him to sit down.

"It's a bit strong, huh?" he said with a laugh. "That's the point. It'll taste better when you get a bit older," he added like it was an old **adage**. "Get some ice if you like."

Jake tried to answer but his vocal cords had been burnt by the whiskey. He spoke **incoherently**, trying to say that he'd drink it as his father did, and **perched** on the other end of the sofa.

"So, you're not dating this Susan, but you need some money, right?"

"Yes."

"And you don't want your mother to know about it?" He flashed a **conspiratorial** smile, as though they were peers sharing a **clandestine** secret.

"It's not for anything secret, Dad. Just so I can spend some time with friends when we're not studying…"

"OK, OK. You're young obviously and you have been working hard. How much should I give you?" From his inside jacket pocket, he produced a fat wallet, from which a large number of bills and checks **spewed** out visibly.

"Well, I dunno…" Jake had not expected this to be quite so straightforward. Perhaps the sleeplessness had **impaired** his father's judgment, but the man didn't seem that insane. In fact, he seemed exactly as Jake remembered him from their trips to the park in his youth, happy to share a moment which wasn't **overborne** by questions of tax law or corporate finances.

His father finished his glass quickly, and fished two 100 dollar bills from the wallet, putting up a nicotine-stained finger to his lips to insist on the boy's silence. Jake took another burning sip as his father had done, and pocketed the money quickly, as though the old man were **volatile** and might change his mind at any second. He began to

---

463 flinch [2]
v. 움츠러들다, 움찔하다
shy away, wince

464 repellent [3]
a. 역겨운
disgusting; driving one away
v. repel

465 adage [3]
n. 속담, 격언
a traditional saying expressing a common experience or observation; proverb

466 incoherent [3]
a. 앞뒤가 안 맞는
without logical or meaningful connection; unintelligible

467 perch [13]
v. 걸터앉다
take a seat

468 conspiratorial [5]
a. 음모를 꾸미는
sharing a secret; acting as accomplices
v. conspire

469 clandestine [2]
a. 은밀한
secretive; furtive

470 spew [2]
v. 토해내다
vomit

471 impair [3]
v. 손상을 입히다
weaken; damage

472 overborne [2]
a. 압도당한
dominated, overpowered
v. overbear

473 volatile [2]
a. 변덕스러운
changeable; tending to fluctuate

474 **consummate** ³
v. 완료하다
fully complete; bring to a perfect state of completion

thank him, but his father rejected him and poured himself another drink. Jake was not invited to do the same.

"What do you think of the whiskey?" his father asked after the secret transaction had been **consummated**.

"I'm not sure I'll drink it again," Jake admitted.

He didn't know how wrong he was.

Vocabulary

0451
attest [4]
[ətést]

v. 증명하다　give evidence of, to certify as accurate, genuine, or true
testify와 동일한 어원을 가지므로 '증명하다'란 의미이다.
A government stamp **attests** the document's reliability and credibility. (*v.*)

0452
conscientious [12]
[kànʃiénʃəs]

a. 양심적인, 성실한　controlled by one's inner sense of what is right, careful and painstaking, meticulous
conscious는 '정신'을 뜻하므로 정신차리고 성실하게 일한다고 해석할 수 있다.
The company favors **conscientious** individuals because they can finish their work on time. (*adj.*)

0453
patriarch [6]
[ǀpeɪtriɑːrk]

n. (공동체의) 족장, (가정의) 가장　the male head of a family or tribal line
아빠(papa → pa)로써 가정의 가장 중요한(arch) 존재이므로 '가장'을 의미한다.
Paul has burdensome duties as a **patriarch**. (*n.*)

0454
aloof [6]
[əlúːf]

a. 무관심한, 냉담한, 떨어진　indifferent; disinterested, not in sympathy with or desiring to associate with others; indifferent
지붕(roof) 위에서 멀리 떨어져 보고 있다고 해석할 수 있다.
I wish my **aloof** cat showed me more affection. (*adj.*)

0455
impede [5]
[impíːd]

v. 방해하다, 막다, 지연시키다　prevent, hinder, obstruct, to interfere in the way
자전거 pedal에서 알다시피 ped-는 '발'을 뜻하므로 im(in) + pede(foot) '가는 길에 발을 걸어서 방해한다'고 생각하면 된다.
The traffic was **impeded** by the construction work in the middle of the road. (*v.*)

0456
superfluous [5]
[suːpɜːrfluəs]

a. 필요치 않은, 남는, 여분의　unnecessarily extra, excessive
가득 차서 위로(super) 넘쳐흐르다(flu)는 뜻이다.
Isn't it **superfluous** to have 20 pairs of shoes when you only wear the same 5 pairs? (*adj.*)

0457
expenditure [4]
[ɪk|spendɪtʃə(r)]

n. 지출, 비용　the act of expending something, especially funds
비싼(expensive) 물건을 많이 사면 당연히 지출이 많을 것이다.
The budget provided for a total **expenditure** of $27 billion. (*n.*)

0458
fabricate [5]
[|fæbrɪkeɪt]

v. (거짓 정보를) 만들어 내다, 제작하다　devise, construct
인공으로 가짜 천조각(fabric)을 만들어낸다고 외워보자.
The evidence was totally **fabricated**. (*v.*)

0459
impart [17]
[ɪmpάːrt]

v. 전하다, (나누어)주다　make known, tell, to reveal or tell; to grant
in과 partire(to divide, part)가 합쳐져 'to share in, divide with another'의 뜻을 갖게 되었다.
A sage usually **imparts** knowledge to his/her followers. (*v.*)

0460
judicious [4]
[dʒuːdíʃəs]

a. 신중한, 사리분별이 있는　using good judgment; careful, prudent
judge에서 파생되었다.
Judicious **judgement**. (*adj.*)

0461
omit [2]
[oumít]

v. 생략하다, 빠뜨리다　leave out, to bypass; to overlook
SAT 문제 중에 정말 모르는 문제가 있으면 '오밋'하는 것도 방법이다.
The school's performance of the play strictly **omitted** swear words. (*v.*)

0462
peculiar [13]
[pɪ|kjuːliə(r)]

a. 이상한　strange, queer, odd
특별한(particular) 장점이나 단점은 없이 그냥 이상하다고(peculiar) 외워보자.
I had a **peculiar** feeling we'd met before. (*adj.*)

0463
flinch [2]
[flɪntʃ]

v. 움츠러들다, 움찔하다　shy away, wince
소설 '해리포터'에서 경비원인 핀치(finch)가 다가오면 학생들은 움츠러든다(flinch).
He **flinched** at the sight of the blood. (*v.*)

0464
repellent [3]
[rɪ|pelənt]

a. 역겨운　disgusting; driving one away　*v.* repel
re (back) + pellere (strike)가 합쳐서 '쳐내다'라는 뜻에서 유래.
Their political ideas are **repellent** to most people. (*adj.*)

0465
adage ³

[ǽdidʒ]

n. 속담, 격언   a traditional saying expressing a common experience or observation; proverb, wise saying
나이가(age) 많아질수록(ad) 속담을 많이 알게 된다.
There's an **adage** in my business. (*n.*)

0466
incoherent ³

[ìnkouhírənt]

a. 앞뒤가 안 맞는   without logical or meaningful connection; unintelligible
듣고 나서(hear → here) 바로 머리에 들어올 수 (in) 있을 정도로 일관성이 있다 (coherent)고 외워보자. 따라서 incoherent는 '앞뒤가 맞지 않다'는 뜻이라고 볼 수 있다.
The little boy was so scared that his speech was **incoherent**. (*adj.*)

0467
perch ¹³

[pɜːrtʃ]

v. (특히 무엇의 끝에) 걸터앉다   take a seat
의자(chair → ch) 끝에 고양이가 pur(→ per) 하고 울며 앉았다고 외워보자.
We **perched** on a couple of high stools at the bar. (*v.*)

0468
conspiratorial ⁵

[kənspìrətɔ́ːriəl]

a. 음모를 꾸미는   sharing a secret; acting as accomplices
v. conspire
해적이(piracy) 되기로 음모를(conspiracy) 꾸몄다고 외워보자.
'I know you understand,' he said and gave a **conspiratorial** wink. (*adj.*)

0469
clandestine ²

[klændéstin]

a. 은밀한, 내밀의   secretive; furtive, surreptitious
불어에서 파생된 말. clam(secret) + intestine(내부)이 합쳐져 '내부의 비밀'이라는 뜻에서 유래.
Clandestine spy activities (*adj.*)

0470
spew ²

[spjuː]

v. 토해내다   vomit
먹은 스튜(stew)가 상해서 토했다고(spew) 외워보자.
Flames **spewed** from the aircraft's engine. (*v.*)

0471
impair ³

[impέər]

v. 손상을 입히다, 해치다   weaken; damage, to harm; to debilitate
impair되면 repair(수리)를 해야 한다.
The injury **impaired** his ability to walk properly. (*v.*)

0472
overborne ²
[òuvərbɔ́ːrn]

a. 압도당한　　dominated, overpowered　　*v.* overbear
앞서(over) 태어난(born) 형한테 압도당하고 말았다.
The merit principle could be **overborne** by people feeling that they have to secure a particular outcome. (*adj.*)

0473
volatile ²
[vάlətl]

a. 변덕스러운　　changeable; tending to fluctuate
vola < volare(fly) + tile 은 '날고 있는'으로 직역이 되는데, 한 곳에 가만히 있지 않고 하늘에 둥둥 떠다니면 차분하지 않고 변덕스럽겠지?
The explosive was highly **volatile**. (*adj.*)

0474
consummate ³
[|kɑːnsəmeɪt]

v. 완료하다; 완벽하게[완전하게] 하다　　fully complete; bring to a perfect state of completion
모든 것을 완벽하게 먹어치웠다고(consum → consume) 외우자.
The man is a **consummate** actor. (*adj.*)

Voca Hamburger
Episode 29
MATCHING Quiz

1. attest　　　　　　● ● A. prevent, hinder, obstruct
2. conscientious　　● ● B. controlled by one's inner sense of what is right
3. patriarch　　　　 ● ● C. vomit
4. aloof　　　　　　 ● ● D. give evidence of
5. impede　　　　　● ● E. unnecessarily extra
6. superfluous　　　● ● F. make known, tell
7. expenditure　　　● ● G. the act of expending something, especially funds
8. fabricate　　　　 ● ● H. indifferent; disinterested
9. impart　　　　　 ● ● I. strange, queer, odd
10. judicious　　　　● ● J. using good judgment; careful
11. omit　　　　　　● ● K. shy away, wince
12. peculiar　　　　 ● ● L. disgusting; driving one away
13. flinch　　　　　 ● ● M. devise, construct
14. repellent　　　　● ● N. without logical or meaningful connection; unintelligible
15. adage　　　　　 ● ● O. leave out
16. incoherent　　　● ● P. secretive; furtive
17. perch　　　　　 ● ● Q. a traditional saying expressing a common experience or observation; proverb
18. conspiratorial　● ● R. sharing a secret; acting as accomplices
19. clandestine　　 ● ● S. the male head of a family or tribal line
20. spew　　　　　 ● ● T. take a seat

1-D, 2-B, 3-S, 4-H, 5-A, 6-E, 7-G, 8-M, 9-F, 10-J, 11-O, 12-I, 13-K, 14-L, 15-Q, 16-N, 17-T, 18-R, 19-P, 20-C

더 많은 문제를 풀고자 한다면 www.quizlet.com에서 'paul academy seoul' class를 검색

Episode 30: The Karaoke Gang

It was Saturday and Terry, the boy who had **menaced** Jake at the academy a few weeks earlier, was sitting on the smoking place of the coffee shop with a few of the older boys, some of whom attended other academies but most who frequented arcades during the day while claiming to be studying. He was waiting for TJ to show up, as had been their habit the previous summer, to hang out with them and pay for their time out.

Unfortunately, TJ had not returned his calls since that first day, which caused him to have some serious **scruples** about the whole situation. In the winter, the younger boy had been insecure enough to require their approval. They, the Karaoke Gang, as they liked to call themselves, **exploited** this **deficiency** in his personality, and kept his loyalty **intact** by supplying him with cigarettes and light friendship alternated with light abuse, **manipulating** him to accept their demands upon his time and money.

TJ, actually, was not much more **affluent** than most students, but his mother, who paid most of her attention to his younger, more academically successful brother, gave him a large allowance without asking too many questions. Most often he was left without supervision, brought in occasionally to his father's office in their apartment to be **castigated** for his various **transgressions**. He was told that he had to attain decent scores to get at least the **rudiments** of a resume for finding a university, but these were empty threats. He had been 'studying' for two years, with little effect.

Terry was in much the same position, though his mother was not so generous and left him usually just enough for a sandwich, with the rest of his allowance supplemented by "friendly help" from boys like TJ. As with most bullies, he didn't consider himself a **villain**, and had grown up as a **mediocre** student in classrooms where little attention was paid to anyone but the very strong or the very weak. If he had thought about it seriously, and had been a more **considerate** person

---

[475] **menace** 8
v. 위협하다
threaten, imperil

[476] **scruple** 2
n. 양심, 양심의 가책
a moral or ethical consideration or standard

[477] **exploit** 15
v. (부당하게) 이용하다
use in an abusive way; take advantage of

[478] **deficiency** 6
n. 결점, 결함
weakness, flaw
a. deficient

[479] **intact** 2
a. 온전한
not changed or broken; complete or whole

[480] **manipulate** 22
v. 조작하다
manage or influence skillfully in an unfair manner

[481] **affluent** 8
a. 부유한
wealthy

[482] **castigate** 4
v. 꾸짖다, 책망하다
scold or criticize for wrongdoing

483 transgression [3]
n. 위반
violation of law, command, etc.; infraction
v. transgress

484 rudiment [6]
n. 기본, 기초
basis, foundation

485 villain [6]
n. 악당, 악인
evil person

486 mediocre [6]
a. 평범한
of average value; not overly positive or negative

487 considerate [2]
a. 사려 깊은
thoughtful, mindful

488 precarious [3]
a. 불안정한, 위태로운
uncertain; unstable; insecure

489 puffery [3]
n. 과찬
exaggerated praise; adulation

490 endorsement [7]
n. 지지, 승인
support, backing, approval

491 indulge [4]
v. 마음껏 하다
treat oneself; give in to a temptation

492 appease [3]
v. 진정시키다, 달래다
make peaceful; pacify

493 apprentice [10]
n. 견습생, 도제
a person who works for another in order to learn a trade

in general, he would probably have seen quite quickly that TJ was not the only kid in a **precarious** position between the two, and that he needed the younger boy's **puffery** and **endorsement** just as the TJ needed his approval.

While Terry was waiting, the academy students who had finished their practice tests and were emerging from the building into the light of day. Jake, TJ, and Sam were walking toward the subway station, ready to go Sam's house and **indulge** in some computerized combat for the rest of their free evening. After several weeks of little improvement, Jake was feeling quietly confident about the result, having scored 540 in the reading and having received a seven on the essay. In total, he was up to 1820 overall, and this would at least **appease** some of his mother's rage about his vocabulary scores.

As they came down the hill, TJ saw Terry sitting lazily on his cafe chair, and almost stopped walking. The senior boy stood up and stretched his arms wide as though preparing for an embrace.

"TJ, my little **apprentice**!" he began with his usual confidence. "There you are! Don't you want to hang out with us?" he gestured toward a few of the other boys, who were **frenetically** texting various girls in the hopes of finding dates for the evening.

TJ stood uncertainly and began to make excuses for not hanging out, an effort that was quickly **truncated** into silence as Terry jumped down to the sidewalk and approached them like a predator **ravening** for **timorous** prey.

"Come on, you little dork. You've hardly hung out with us at all after he you met these—" he referred to Jake and Sam with several unprintable words.

"But, Terry, I've got to get home. My mom's expecting me…"

"Yeah right. She's never cared much about you. You told me that yourself. You should spend more time with your friends," he made scary noises. "And that's me, isn't it, little guy?"

"That's right, big guy," TJ sighed resentfully. "What are you guys doing tonight?"

Terry called back to the assembled group, and a few dropped down to the street level.

"First, we're gonna get lunch. We're hungry."

494 frenetic [2]
a. 정신 없이 바쁜, 부산한
frantic, frenzied

495 truncate [2]
v. 줄이다, 짧게 만들다
shorten; abridge

496 raven [5]
v. 먹이를 찾아 다니다
seek prey

497 timorous [3]
a. 겁이 많은
full of fear; fearful

Vocabulary

0475
menace [ménəs]

v. 위협하다; 위험한 존재   to threaten, imperil; a person whose actions, attitudes, or ideas are considered dangerous
사람(men)은 상대편을 위협할 때 보통 그 팀 ace를 협박한다.
The lion **menaced** the antelope with a big roar. (v.)

0476
scruple [ˈskruːpl]

n. 양심, 양심의 가책   a moral or ethical consideration or standard
양심의 가책은 무언가가 마음을 긁는 것처럼(scrub) 사람을 불편하게 만든다.
I overcame my moral **scruples**. (n.)

0477
exploit [ɪkˈsplɔɪt]

v. (부당하게) 이용하다   use in an abusive way; take advantage of, to use selfishly for one's own ends
exploit를 해서 점점 부당하게 돈을 모으다 보면 explode '터질' 수도 있다.
Bobbly **exploited** his little sister by forcing her to clean his room for him. (v.)

0478
deficiency [dɪˈfɪʃnsi]

n. 결점, 결함   weakness, flaw   a. deficient
sufficient가 '충분하다'는 뜻이므로 deficient는 '불충분하다'는 뜻이다.
Vitamin **deficiency** in the diet can cause illness. (n.)

0479
intact [ɪnˈtækt]

a. 온전한, 손을 대지 않은   not changed or broken; complete or whole
아무도 행동을(act) 취하지 않고(in) 가만히 내버려두니까 '온전하다'.
Most of the house remains **intact** even after two hundred years. (adj.)

0480
manipulate [məˈnɪpjuleɪt]

v. 조작하다, 조종하다   to manage or influence skillfully in an unfair manner
manipulate는 mani(hand) + pul(drive, 몰다) + ate. 즉 '손으로 몰다, 다루다'라는 뜻이다.
The believers of the pseudo-religion were **manipulated** by their leader to do everything he asked them to do. (v.)

0481
affluent [8]
[ǽfluənt]

a. 부유한, 풍부한   wealthy, rich
정말 부자라서 돈이 'flow(흐르다)'라고 생각하자.
Only **affluent** families could afford such an expensive tuition. (*adj.*)

0482
castigate [4]
[kǽstəgèit]

v. 꾸짖다, 책망하다, 매질하다, 혹평하다   scold or criticize for wrongdoing, to criticize severely
castus(='pure') + agere(='to do') 혹평하고 매질하며 한 사람을 순수하게 만드는 것이다.
The newspaper **castigated** the politician as a liar who didn't care at all about the public good. (*v.*)

0483
transgression [3]
[trænsgréʃən, trænz-]

n. 위반   violation of law, command, etc.; infraction
v. transgress
잔디밭을(grass → gress) 넘어가는(trans) 것은 위반행위다.
Where there is no law there is no **transgression**. (*n.*)

0484
rudiment [6]
[rúːdəmənt]

n. 기본, 기초   basis, foundation
길을(road → rud) 만들 때 시멘트(ciment → diment)를 발라서 기초 공사를 탄탄히 해야 한다.
She mastered the **rudiments** of grammar. (*n.*)

0485
villain [6]
[|vɪlən]

n. 악당, 악인   evil person
사악한(evil → vil) 악당이라고 외워보자.
He often plays the part of the **villain**. (*n.*)

0486
mediocre [6]
[|miːdioʊkər]

a. 평범한, 보통 정도의   of average value; not overly positive or negative; of an ordinary or moderate quality
mediocre와 medium이 소리가 비슷하지?
It is not sufficient for an artist to have a **mediocre** level of talent in order to succeed. He or she must be exceptional. (*adj.*)

0487
considerate [2]
[kən|sɪdərət]

a. 사려 깊은   thoughtful, mindful
콜라를(cola → con) 마실지 사이다를(cider → sider)를 마실지 생각한다고 (consider) 외워보자.
She is always polite and **considerate** towards her employees. (*adj.*)

0488
precarious [3]

[prikέəriəs]

a. 불안정한, 위태로운   uncertain; unstable; insecure
care 받지 못하는 '불안정한 상태'라고 외우자.
Although the coffee cup had a **precarious** balance at the edge of the table, it did not fall for 10 days. (*adj.*)

0489
puffery [3]

[pʌ́fəri]

n. 과찬   exaggerated praise; adulation
지나친 과찬은 사람을 부풀어오르게(puff) 만든다.
Right now, all he is is a bag of self-**puffery** and arrogance. (*n.*)

0490
endorsement [7]

[inǀdɔ́:rsmənt]

n. 지지, 승인   support, backing, approval
승인을 함으로써(endorse) 문 (door = dorse) 안으로 (in = en) 들여보내 준다고 외워보자.
The election victory is a clear **endorsement** of their policies. (*n.*)

0491
indulge [4]

[indʌ́ldʒ]

v. 마음껏 하다, 충족시키다   treat oneself; give in to a temptation, to satiate
마음 속('in'side)이 'dul'l해질 때까지 하고 싶은 것을 마음껏 한다고 해석하자.
Sometimes it's okay to **indulge** in unhealthy activities. (*v.*)

0492
appease [3]

[əpí:z]

v. 진정시키다, 달래다, 요구를 들어주다
make peaceful; pacify, to soothe by quieting anger or indignation
ap-please, 즉 요구를 들어줘서 기분이 좋게 한다고 볼 수 있다.
The changes did not **appease** rights groups. (*v.*)

0493
apprentice [10]

[əpréntis]

n. 견습생, 도제   one who works for another in order to learn a trade
중세시대에 장인들에게 전문적인 기술을 배우려고 하는 견습생들을 apprentice 라고 한 것에서 유래했다.
The sorcerer's **apprentice** was not good at magic yet. (*n.*)

0494
frenetic [2]

[frənétik]

a. 정신 없이 바쁜, 부산한, 열광적인, 발광한   frantic, frenzied
'제어력을 잃은'이란 뜻의 frantic과 매우 비슷하게 들리며 '발광한'의 의미를 가진다.
The young people's energy and abundant supply of alcohol made the party **frenetic**. (*adj.*)

0495
truncate ² [trʌ́ŋkeit]

v. 줄이다, 짧게 만들다, 꼭대기를 자르다   to cut short, shorten; abridge

trunk는 나무 몸통이란 뜻이다. 그러니까 '나무 몸통을 자르는' 것이라고 외우자.

The tv station **truncated** the overly long movie. (v.)

0496
raven ⁵ [rǽvən]

v. 먹이를 찾아 다니다   seek prey

raven은 '까마귀'라는 뜻도 있다. 까마귀가 먹이를 찾아다니는 걸 생각해보자.

The rat **ravened** the poisoned bait just as we had hoped. (v.)

0497
timorous ³ [tíməres]

a. 겁이 많은, 마음 약한   full of fear; fearful, nervous of other people and situations

timid(소심한)라는 단어에서 유래.

Timorous voice of the shy child (adj.)

Voca Hamburger
Episode 30
MATCHING Quiz

1. menace
2. scruple
3. exploit
4. deficiency
5. intact
6. manipulate
7. affluent
8. castigate
9. transgression
10. rudiment
11. villain
12. mediocre
13. considerate
14. precarious
15. puffery
16. endorsement
17. indulge
18. appease
19. apprentice
20. frenetic

A. use in an abusive way; take advantage of
B. a moral or ethical consideration or standard
C. weakness, flaw
D. wealthy
E. threaten, imperil
F. manage or influence skillfully in an unfair manner
G. violation of law, command, etc.; infraction
H. not changed or broken; complete or whole
I. of average value; not overly positive or negative
J. basis, foundation
K. scold or criticize for wrongdoing
L. uncertain; unstable; insecure
M. evil person
N. support, backing, approval
O. thoughtful, mindful
P. make peaceful; pacify
Q. exaggerated praise; adulation
R. frantic, frenzied
S. treat oneself; give in to a temptation
T. a person who works for another in order to learn a trade

1-E, 2-B, 3-A, 4-C, 5-H, 6-F, 7-D, 8-K, 9-G, 10-J, 11-M, 12-I, 13-O, 14-L, 15-O, 16-N, 17-S, 18-P, 19-T, 20-R

더 많은 문제를 풀고자 한다면 www.quizlet.com에서 'paul academy seoul' class를 검색

Episode 31 — The Drinking

498 rambunctious [4]
a. 난폭한
loud and (usually) destructive

499 amoral [2]
a. 도덕 관념이 없는
without moral quality; neither moral nor immoral

500 condone [3]
v. 용납하다
to allow; sanction

501 treachery [7]
n. 배반
disloyalty

502 parlor [3]
n. 방, 점, 건물
a room, apartment, or building serving as a place of business

503 invariable [5]
a. 변함없는
without change or deviation

504 paramount [2]
a. 다른 무엇보다 중요한
important, supreme

505 demolished [4]
a. 철거된, 무너진
dilapidated, destroyed

506 ailment [4]
n. 질병
a physical disorder or illness

507 grieving [10]
a. 비통해하는
feeling grief or sorrow

They walked back to the usual restaurant, where the three younger boys were forced into a silence by their **rambunctious** companions. They decided they should play some pool, which the younger group thought was a good idea, until it was suggested that they keep score. They played there for two hours or so, during which time Sam went to the bathroom and never came back. He texted TJ to say that he was sorry but that he was too frightened by the **amoral** plans the older group seemed to have for later and that he had to meet someone anyway. Jake couldn't **condone** this **treachery**, but at the same time was somewhat jealous that he hadn't thought of it himself.

"Now, boys, it's getting darker outside, so you know what that means…" said Terry's equally-scary friend after they had killed more time at the café. "…It's time to sing!"

Jake looked back at his friend with dread. This was why Sam had fled so quickly. It was well-known that this group of boys had an uncle who owned a Karaoke **parlor** and let them use it whenever they wanted. Singing **invariably** meant drinking, and older boys drinking meant drinking younger boys, in the 'friendship' that was **paramount** to these 'friends'.

They got to the nearly-**demolished** karaoke bar a few minutes later, and were greeted by an attendant who seemed in equally poor condition. Terry's uncle wasn't around, but apparently there was a standing order. They obviously came often, and their regular order of beer was brought quickly. After the old man had gone, a few of the boys produced some tiny vodka bottles they'd stolen from a convenience store and hidden in their bags, a total of twelve for the six of them. With the beer included, Jake felt certain he would die of some alcohol-induced **ailment** before the night was over. He imagined his **grieving** mother, and a legion of his academy classmates dressed in black, throwing carnations on his grave. "He was such a great guy," they'd say, shaking their heads at the life of drinking which had **annihilated** his future. In the midst of his terrible daydream, he felt a glass being placed into his hand. Tiny bubbles rose slowly and mixed the mixture. It looked like soda, but smelled much more **potent** than any soda he'd ever drank before. The whiskey his father had given him was stronger, but not by much.

He'd had beer before, of course, but he had only had beer when allowed by his parents, most often when the Professor came to visit. It was never forced on him, and certainly two glasses were never offered at the same time. Vodka, or any other liquor, had never even been mentioned.

Now, those innocent sips of beer belonged to an **idyllic** past, **supplanted** by the orders of Terry and his followers as they watched **maliciously** as the two young friends stood awkwardly with their glasses in hand.

"Bottoms up, boys!" one of them shouted.

They looked at each other, and TJ tried to smile **repentantly**, but one of the older boys taunted them and the two simultaneously drank from their glasses. Jake almost threw up at once as the unfamiliar flood of spirits met his throat, only managing to suppress it to **retain** his **dignity** (whatever dignity there was in a place like that).

The older boys began drinking their **concoctions**, and every so often **beseeched** Jake and TJ to perform the same trick, leaving some time in between for them to recover from the previous round. After the first two, Jake was surprised not to feel any worse, thinking that perhaps he had acquired an immunity to alcohol. This thought was instantly **dispelled** when he stood up to go to the **communal** toilet.

As he stepped down the narrow, yellow hallway, he became aware that the usual stability that guided his steps was beginning to **falter**. He didn't fall over, but a few times had to grab the wall as a **hedge** against falling over. When he got to the bathroom, the face in the mirror seemed much the same as it had that morning, though its eyes were slightly unfocused.

"This is what I look like drunk," he said, aloud for some reason. Returning to the room he found a fresh beverage waiting for him, and after that things became increasingly **ambiguous**.

He did remember singing, with the lyrics half-wrong and his voice

---

508 annihilate [3]
v. 전멸시키다
to destroy the collective existence or main body of

509 potent [2]
a. 강한
powerful
cf. omnipotent 전지전능한

510 idyllic [6]
a. 목가적인; 아주 편안한
rustic; extremely pleasant, simple, and peaceful

511 supplant [2]
v. 대신하다
to replace; push away

512 malicious [4]
a. 악의적인
with harmful intentions

513 repentantly [3]
adv. 뉘우치며
apologetically, regretfully
v. repent

514 retain [10]
v. 유지하다, 보유하다
to preserve, keep

515 dignity [1]
n. 위엄, 품위
honor, nobility
opp. indignity

516 concoction [6]
n. 혼합물
mixture of liquids

517 beseech [2]
v. 애원하다
to beg or request; entreat

518 dispel [2]
v. 떨쳐버리다
to disprove (as a theory)

519 communal [5]
a. 공동의
used or shared in common by everyone in a group

520 **falter** [2]
v. 흔들리다
to stumble; move without confidence or skill

521 **hedge** [3]
n. 울타리
any barrier or boundary

522 **ambiguous** [10]
a. 애매모호한
of doubtful or uncertain nature, difficult to comprehend

523 **fortitude** [2]
n. 불굴의 용기
bravery, boldness

524 **fray** [5]
n. 싸움, 소동
fight, battle

525 **corollary** [10]
n. 필연적인 결과
a natural consequence or result

526 **negate** [3]
v. 부인하다
to deny the existence, evidence, or truth of

527 **proclaim** [4]
v. 선언하다
to announce or declare in an open manner

528 **nebulous** [3]
a. 모호한, 애매한
vague, unclear

529 **hedonist** [4]
n. 쾌락주의자
lover of pleasure (usually immorally); a licentious person

530 **contend** [3]
v. 주장하다
to assert

terribly off-key, The Rolling Stones' "Street Fighting Man". He also remembered leaving the karaoke room after TJ finally gathered the **fortitude** to curse at Terry and try to hit him, which had predictably disastrous effects. There was a brief **fray**, the **corollary** being a black eye for TJ. Terry formally **negated** any future offers to 'allow' TJ to hang out with the older boys, who **proclaimed** that the young fighter was 'psycho'. After that, his memory was somewhat **nebulous**, until he found himself walking unsteadily through the streets with TJ as they looked for a taxi that would accept them, counting the remaining money they had to ensure that they both would be able to get home. The older boys had left just enough and then ran away, not eager to be seen with two young **hedonists** who would presumably blame them for their black eyes (in TJ's case) and vomit-stained trousers (in Jake's). Jake was just glad he'd left his father's money safely at home.

When they finally found a taxi, they rode in silence to Jake's house, where TJ decided to get out anyway even though he lived five minutes further down the road. They walked, steadying each other with joined arms.

"Those guys are assholes," TJ **contended** defiantly.
"Yeah, and drinking's not as fun as I expected it to be," Jake responded.
"At least they won't bother us anymore," his friend added certainly. "Anyway, thanks for sticking around."

They stopped outside Jake's apartment building, where his mother would no doubt be waiting with much less kind words. He wasn't sure how many times she'd called, since Terry had taken their cell phones for much of the evening, but she wouldn't be pleased. Still, as he looked at his friend stumbling around the building and onto the shadowy street towards his own home, he was glad to have been there, if only to ensure that TJ would be back at the academy and studying by Monday.

Vocabulary

0498

rambunctious [4]

[ræmbʌ́ŋkʃəs]

a. 난폭한, 제멋대로의   loud and (usually) destructive, difficult to control
ram(양)이 어딘가에 bonking(머리를 부딪힌다)는 뜻으로 생각하면 '난폭한'이라는 뜻을 쉽게 유추해 낼 수 있다.
Rambunctious teenagers ignored their teachers' order to be quiet. (*adj.*)

0499

amoral [2]

[|eɪ|mɔːrəl;-|mɑːr-]

a. 도덕 관념이 없는   without moral quality; neither moral nor immoral
도덕(moral)이 없다(a-).
I disagree with an **amoral** approach to politics. (*adj.*)

0500

condone [3]

[kəndóun]

v. 용납하다; 용납된   to allow; sanction; accepted and allowed to take an action
con(함께) + done(완료하다). 모두에게 인정 받고 승인되어서 완료되었다.
Corn dogs are **condoned** at the baseball stadium, but alcohol is not allowed. (*adj.*)

0501

treachery [7]

[|tretʃəri]

n. 배반   disloyalty
보물을(treasure → treacher) 들고 도망치는 배반을 저질렀다고 외우자.
King Arthur's kingdom was destroyed by **treachery**. (*n.*)

0502

parlor [3]

[pάːrlər]

n. 방, 점, 건물   a room, apartment, or building serving as a place of business
'강당, 법정'을 뜻하는 12세기 프랑스 단어 parleor에서 유래.
The funeral **parlor** was crowded with too many people. (*n.*)

0503

invariable [5]

[ɪnvέəriəbl]

a. 변함없는, 불변의   without change or deviation, unchangeable
in(='not') + vary(바뀌다). '바뀌지 않는'의 의미이다.
Although people think that the law of science is **invariable**, they do change as our understanding of science grows. (*adj.*)

0504
paramount ²
[pǽrəmàunt]

a. **다른 무엇보다 중요한, 최고의**　important, supreme in authority
primary 의 동의어이며 ancillary의 반대어다. par(by) + ad(up) + mount가 합쳐져서 '산 위에 의해서'라는 의미로 '최고의, 중요한'이라는 뜻으로 발전했다.
Hiding the spies' identities is of **paramount** importance in spying activities. (*adj.*)

0505
demolished ⁴
[dɪ|mɑːlɪʃt]

a. **철거된, 무너진**　dilapidated, destroyed, disease
악마(demon → demo)는 모든 것을 부순다고(demolish) 외워보자.
The factory is due to be **demolished** next year. (*adj.*)

0506
ailment ⁴
[|eɪlmənt]

n. **질병**　a physical disorder or illness
ill과 연결해서 외워보자.
Cold, when not cared enough, is not just a simple **ailment**. (*n.*)

0507
grieving ¹⁰
[griːvɪŋ]

a. **비통해하는**　feeling grief or sorrow
무덤(grave) 앞에서 비탄에 빠져있다(grieve).
He is **grieving** over his dead wife and son. (*adj.*)

0508
annihilate ³
[ənáiəlèit]

v. **전멸시키다**　to destroy the collective existence or main body of, to destroy absolutely
nihil은 '아무 것도 없다'. 즉 아무 것도 없는 것처럼 만든다는 의미이다.
The car's windshield **annihilated** the insect. (*v.*)

0509
potent ²
[|poʊtnt]

a. **강한**　powerful　*cf.* omnipotent 전지전능한
강한(potent) 사람은 잠재력(potential)이 많다.
Environment is a **potent** influence on character. (*adj.*)

0510
idyllic ⁶
[aidílik]

a. **목가적인; 아주 편안한, 전원시(풍)의**　rustic; extremely pleasant, simple, and peaceful; picturesque
은퇴 후 아름다운 전원생활을 하는 것이 모두의 ideal이다.
Isabel lived in an **idyllic** countryside, with gently flowing streams, soft green meadows, and lovely sunsets. (*adj.*)

0511
supplant ²

[səplǽnt]

v. 대신[대체]하다   to replaced by something else; push away
supplant와 implants가 소리가 비슷하고, implant는 원래의 이빨을 대신한다.
When the little boy loses his tooth, a new one would grow and **supplant** it. (*v.*)

0512
malicious ⁴

[məlíʃəs]

a. 악의적인   with harmful intentions
mal- 이 '나쁘다'는 뜻을 가지고 있으므로 malicious는 '악의적인'이라는 뜻이다.
I don't think they are that **malicious**. (*adj.*)

0513
repentantly ³

[rɪpéntəntli]

adv. 뉘우치며   apologetically, regretfully   *v.* repent
다시금(re) 숨을 헐떡이며(pent) 잘못을 뉘우친다고(repent) 외워보자.
He **repentantly** admitted he was wrong. (*adv.*)

0514
retain ¹⁰

[rɪtéɪn]

v. 유지하다, 보유하다   to preserve, keep
교정할 때 끼는 리테이너(retainer)는 교정 후 치아의 모습을 유지(retain)하기 위해 끼는 도구다.
She **retained** her tennis title for the third year. (*v.*)

0515
dignity ¹

[dígnəti]

n. 위엄, 품위   honor, nobility   opp. indignity
품위를 저버리지 않기 위해 땅을 파는(dig) 걸 거부한다고(no → ni) 외워보자.
She accepted the criticism with quiet **dignity**. (*n.*)

0516
concoction ⁶

[kənkɑ́kʃən]

n. 혼합물; 조합   mixture of liquids; invention
합쳐서(con) 요리하니까(cook → coc) 섞어 만든다고(concoct) 외우자.
I could eat their bizarre vegetable **concoctions** all day. (*n.*)

0517
beseech ²

[bɪsíːtʃ]

v. 애원하다, 간청하다   to beg or request; entreat, to beg eagerly for; solicit.
거머리처럼 (leech = seech) 달라붙어서 간청한다고 (beseech) 외워보자.
I **beseeched** my mother to buy me an IPad, and she did, impressed by how sincere I was. (*v.*)

0518
dispel [2]
[dispél]

v. 떨쳐버리다, 쫓아버리다, 흐트러뜨리다   to stop, to push away
to disprove (as a theory), dis(away)와 pel(pulse: to push에서 유래한 단어)이 합쳐져 '밀어서 쫓다'.
The child ran toward the pigeons and **dispelled** them all, leaving only a few feathers behind. (v.)

0519
communal [5]
[kəmjúːnəl]

a. 공동의, 자치체의   used or shared in common by everyone in a group, held in common; of a group of people
commun(common) + al에서 온 것으로 community의 다른 형태 정도로 외우면 된다.
The chief commanded the **communal** jug of wine be passed around the circle of friends. (adj.)

0520
falter [2]
[ǁfɔːltə(r)]

v. 흔들리다   to stumble; move without confidence or skill
떨어질 것처럼(fall → fal) 흔들린다고 외워보자.
The economy shows no signs of **faltering**. (v.)

0521
hedge [3]
[hedʒ]

n. (생)울타리   any barrier or boundary
디즈니영화 Hedge를 보면, 울타리를 사이에 두고 동물과 인간이 대적한다.
A **hedge** of rose bushes encircled the house. (n.)

0522
ambiguous [10]
[æmǀbɪgjuəs]

a. 애매모호한   of doubtful or uncertain nature, difficult to comprehend
ambi-는 '둘 다'라는 의미를 가지고 있다. 두 개의 뜻이 다 되므로 애매모호하다는 뜻이다.
I don't like things fuzzy and vague and **ambiguous**. (adj.)

0523
fortitude [2]
[fɔ́ːrtətjùːd]

n. 불굴의 용기, 꿋꿋함   bravery, boldness, strength
'fortification'(요새)와 관련되 있는 단어. 요새는 극심한 공격에도 꿋꿋하게 버텨낸다.
The movie '300' portrays the Spartan's **fortitude** to withstand the battle. (n.)

0524
fray [5]
[fréi]

n. 싸움, 소동   fight, battle
싸움은 항상 두려움(afraid = a'fray'd) 때문에 일어난다.
At 71, he has now retired from the political **fray**. (n.)

0525
corollary [10]
[kɔ́ːrəlèri]

n. 필연적인 결과, 계, 추론   a natural consequence or result
correlated와 발음이 비슷하니까 연관지어서 생각하면 기억하기 쉽다.
Scientists found a **corollary** between sleep and feeling rested. (*n.*)

0526
negate [3]
[nɪ|ɡeɪt]

v. 부인하다   to deny the existence, evidence, or truth of
negative는 '반대, 음수'를 뜻하므로 negate는 '반대하다, 부인하다'라는 의미이다.
Medical conditions don't **negate** the human condition. (*v.*)

0527
proclaim [4]
[prə|kleɪm]

v. 선언하다   to announce or declare in an open manner
사람들 앞에(pro) 서서 주장하는(claim) 것이니까 '선언하다'.
The president **proclaimed** a state of emergency. (*v.*)

0528
nebulous [3]
[nébjuləs]

a. 모호한, 애매한, 흐린   vague, unclear, indistinct and cloudy
nebulous의 어원은 cloud를 의미한다. 따라서 '구름처럼 흐린, 일정한 모양이 없는'이란 뜻이다.
His idea was so **nebulous**, we couldn't understand what he was saying at all. (*adj.*)

0529
hedonist [4]
[|hiːdənɪst]

n. 쾌락주의(자)   lover of pleasure (usually immorally); a licentious person, self-indulgent; self-indulgent
hedone은 그리스어로 '즐거움'을 뜻하므로 쾌락을 찾는 사람을 뜻한다.
Hedonists think that pleasure is the only thing good for a person. (*n.*)

0530
contend [3]
[kənténd]

v. 주장하다, 싸우다, 논쟁하다   to assert, to struggle; compete
contest와 연관되어 있지만 '~에 반해' 싸우는 대신 '~을 위해' 싸운다는 의미이다.
Connie had difficulty trying to **contend** with her son's tantrums. (*v.*)

Note :

Episode 31

MATCHING Quiz

1. rambunctious
2. amoral
3. condone
4. treachery
5. parlor
6. invariable
7. paramount
8. demolished business
9. ailment
10. grieving
11. annihilate
12. potent
13. idyllic
14. supplant
15. malicious
16. repentantly
17. retain
18. dignity
19. concoction
20. beseech

A. to allow; sanction
B. without moral quality; neither moral nor immoral
C. disloyalty
D. important, supreme
E. loud and (usually) destructive
F. without change or deviation
G. a physical disorder or illness
H. a room, apartment, or building serving as a place of
I. to destroy the collective existence or main body of
J. dilapidated, destroyed
K. to replace; push away
L. feeling grief or sorrow
M. rustic; extremely pleasant, simple, and peaceful
N. to preserve, keep
O. with harmful intentions
P. powerful
Q. to beg or request; entreat
R. honor, nobility
S. apologetically, regretfully
T. mixture of liquids

1-E, 2-B, 3-A, 4-C, 5-H, 6-F, 7-D, 8-J, 9-G, 10-L, 11-I, 12-P, 13-M, 14-K, 15-O, 16-S, 17-N, 18-R, 19-T, 20-Q

더 많은 문제를 풀고자 한다면 www.quizlet.com에서 'paul academy seoul' class를 검색

Episode 32

The Hangover

When Jake awoke the next morning, the goodwill and warmth he had felt for TJ the night before had been **transmuted** into a powerful headache and a strong desire never to get out of bed again. As he attempted to open his eyes, the beams of light pouring through the windows felt like knives, and the sudden realization of just what had happened hit him hard, and he wondered what his mother would say. She had been there the night before, waiting up in the living room, uncharacteristically drinking a glass of wine. He had stumbled in, and - he could remember it clearly now - yell-singing Elvis Presley's "**Hound** Dog" at her. "You ain't nothing but a hound dog! Crying all the time!" After that first verse he had broken down into tears. As he remembered this, he was filled with overwhelming shame. She had said nothing but "we'll talk about this in the morning," and had helped him to bed as though he'd been five years old once more. He noticed as he stretched that he had taken off his vomit-covered trousers. He could still smell the cigarette smoke on his shirt and the taste of death in his **arid** mouth.

He checked the clock. 10:45 AM. He had reached home at around midnight, he seemed to remember. As he stretched again, it seemed that his legs had stopped working during the night, a condition he could only **impute** to the thirsty effects of alcohol (as he'd been told in chemistry class, as well as in **innumerable** films). Also, his bloodstream seemed to have hardened in his body, making each heart beat feel like a gun fired very close. Still, he knew he had to present himself for his parents' **reproach**, and it would be better to confront them in the living room than have them stand over him as he lay crying in his bed.

Walking uncertainly into the living room, he was actually pleased to find only his mother sitting there, even though his father would certainly have been more friendly (at any rate, one asker was preferable to two). She sat in nearly the same position as she had the night before, though the wine glass had now been **outmoded** by a Starbucks cup. She had placed a glass of water on the table across

---

531 transmute [2]
v. 변화시키다
to transform completely

532 hound [2]
n. 사냥개
a dog trained to hunt a game by sight or by scent

533 arid [6]
a. 건조한
dry; desiccated

534 impute [3]
v. ~에게 돌리다, 전가하다
to ascribe, attribute

535 innumerable [3]
a. 많은
many, numerous

536 reproach [4]
n. 비난
blame or criticism

537 outmoded [3]
a. 유행에 뒤떨어진
gone out of style; no longer fashionable

538 coerced [6]
a. 강요된
compelled by force

from her. She told him to sit.

"How do you feel?" she asked as he tried to sit upright on the couch.

"Terrible," he admitted.

"Good. You know you've done a horrible thing, don't you? How angry I am?"

He had no response for this, other than to look down at the floor.

"And I'm not just talking about the drinking. You never once texted or called last night, even yesterday afternoon. I was so worried I nearly called the police."

He looked up for a second to see her worried expression. She hadn't looked so sad since her uncle had died nearly five years earlier.

"I'm sorry," he said blankly, trying to look as apologetic as possible.

"Well, I talked to TJ's mother about it. She called me at around nine when he hadn't shown up, and we both guessed you had run off somewhere. He's always been a bit of a troublemaker, I suppose, according to his own mother, but I kept saying, 'no, no. There's no way my Jake could be doing anything so bad.' You made me a liar, Jake."

For the second time in the last twelve hours, he started to cry. He felt stupid, but it came uncontrollably. She told him to take a drink after he'd stopped. It wasn't water, but cold flat cider. The sugar was heavenly to his dried mouth.

"Now, TJ confirmed what his mother guessed: you two were stopped by a few older boys and **coerced** into joining them. And then your cell phones were taken. Is this all true?"

"Yes," he said, still sniffing.

"Well, at least you didn't do this on purpose. I was just so worried about you." She too had started to cry slightly, but her natural seriousness kept the tears from her voice. "I know you're under a lot of pressure, Jake, and I just want you to know that I want you to be happy. But you must know also that, when something like this happens, other people have to deal with your trouble. You hurt more than just yourself with these actions."

He nodded, unsure of what else he could say.

"We love you, Jake. That's all I wanted to say. And I figured that the feeling you're having now is punishment enough for the rest of the day."

He agreed it was. She told him that it was called a hangover, which he knew already. He was allowed to return to bed, and lay weak in the warm covers for the remainder of the day.

Dinner, when he finally felt able to digest more than Sprite, was a double bacon cheeseburger. His father, when he returned from golfing, looked at him seriously, but winked at him when his mother's back was turned.

"If you ever steal any of my whiskey, buddy, I'll beat you till your backside's blue," he said with a sly smile.

But Jake had already admitted that the horrors of drinking were far behind him. He promised himself to stay **sober** forever. He slept the rest of the night until waking for class the next morning.

---

539 sober ²
a. 술 취하지 않은
not intoxicated or drunk

Vocabulary

0531
transmute [2]
[trænz|mju:t]

v. 변화시키다   to transform completely
돌연변이로(mutate) 이전시켜버렸으므로(trans) '변화'시켰다고 외우자.
It is possible to **transmute** one form of energy into another. (*v.*)

0532
hound [2]
[haʊnd]

n. 사냥개   a dog trained to hunt a game by sight or by scent
셜록 홈즈에 나오는 The hounds of baskerville(바스커빌의 사냥개들)을 생각해보자.
A **hound** chases a rabbit out of the bush. (*n.*)

0533
arid [6]
[ǽrid]

a. (토지가)건조한   very dry; desiccated
the land is a'rid' of water 물이 부족한 땅.
Ariel's mermaid tail dried up in the **arid** air. (*adj.*)

0534
impute [3]
[impjú:t]

v. (죄, 불명예 등을)~에게 돌리다, 전가하다   to ascribe, attribute
in + put 이라고 생각하자. 'in put in jail'을 연상하면 된다.
Members do not **impute** dishonour to each other. (*v.*)

0535
innumerable [3]
[ɪ|nu:mərəbl]

a. 많은, 셀 수 없이 많은   many, very numerous
innumerable은 in(없다) + number(숫자, 세다). 즉 '셀 수 없이 많은'이란 뜻이다.
It was easy to write a paper on World War II as there were **innumerable** books written on that subject. (*adj.*)

0536
reproach [4]
[ripróutʃ]

n. 비난; 책망하다   blame or criticism; express disapproval or disappointment
옛 불어로 reprochier 'upbraid, blame, accuse'라는 뜻에서 왔다.
He **reproached** the taxi driver for his rudeness: "If you treat every passenger like that, you won't be driving for long." (*v.*)

0537
outmoded [àutmóudid]

a. 유행에 뒤떨어진, 구식의   gone out of style; no longer fashionable, old-fashioned
old model로 외우자.
His **outmoded** fashion style made him look older than he was. (*adj.*)

0538
coerced [kəʊˈɜːst]

a. 강요된   compelled by force
coerce와 force(강요하다)를 연관지어서 외워보자.
Do not **coerce** me into doing this. (*v.*)

0539
sober [sóubər]

a. 술 취하지 않은   not intoxicated or drunk, abstemious; serious
흐느껴 울(sob) 때에는 보통 취하지 않고 맑은 정신일 경우가 많다.
The **sober** man never drinks in his life. (*adj.*)

Episode 32

MATCHING Quiz

1. transmute	A. dry; desiccated
2. hound	B. a dog trained to hunt a game by sight or by scent
3. arid	C. to transform completely
4. impute	D. blame or criticism
5. innumerable	E. to ascribe, attribute
6. reproach	F. not intoxicated or drunk
7. outmoded	G. many, numerous
8. coerced	H. compelled by force
9. sober	I. gone out of style; no longer fashionable

1-C, 2-B, 3-A, 4-E, 5-G, 6-D, 7-I, 8-H, 9-F

더 많은 문제를 풀고자 한다면 www.quizlet.com에서 'paul academy seoul' class를 검색

Episode 33

The New Class

540 extraterrestrial [6]
n. 외계인
an alien

541 docile [2]
a. 유순한, 고분고분한
meek, gentle

542 juxtapose [4]
v. 병치하다, 나란히 놓다
to place close together or side by side

543 raucous [2]
a. 요란하고 거친
loud and potentially destructive; rambunctious

544 resilient [6]
a. 회복력 있는
springing back, rebounding

545 complacent [5]
a. 자기만족적인
self-satisfied, often not aware of potential danger

546 avarice [3]
n. 탐욕
insatiable greed for riches

547 disregard [8]
v. 무시하다, 묵살하다
to ignore, pay no attention to

548 concur [2]
v. 동의하다
to agree

On Monday, after the boys had awkwardly reunited following their unfortunate evening, it was revealed that a new class had joined the academy. Having been **inured** to the usual routine for the last three weeks, the regular students, Jake included, looked upon the recruits with an arrogant yet curious gaze. They — the new class — occupied the farthest classroom of the hallway, and seemed almost **extraterrestrial** with their quiet, **docile** look **juxtaposed** with the **raucous** sounds that echoed in the hallway before, between, and sometimes during class from the veteran students.

TJ, who announced that he had a very discriminating taste in people (and who was surprisingly **resilient** from his misadventures a few nights prior) decided at lunch that they should try to befriend a select few of the new students in order to instruct them in the ways of the academy. He argued that the current classes had become too **complacent**, and that they needed to adapt in order to keep improving. Sam remarked that TJ was just trying to find more people to steal money from at the toss, to target with his **avarice**. TJ **disregarded** this.

"I mean, we don't have to ignore them because they're new, do we? It's not like they're diseased or something. We've been here the longest, so we are the leadership of the classroom. We have a responsibility."

Sam was not sure.

"Why are you so keen to make new friends, huh?"

TJ smiled but said nothing. Sam shot Jake a quick look as though to say 'there's something fishy here,' with which Jake **concurred**.

"Yeah, TJ," Jake started, "don't be shy. What's up?"

TJ, known for his talkativeness (the boy could keep a secret for ten minutes at most) looked at them **serenely**. He kept this poker face for about ten seconds this time.

"Ok, Jake, you've got your grand passion, so you're not going to be impressed by this, but…" he paused for dramatic effect, "I've fallen in love."

The other customers of the restaurant were alarmed by the enormous blasts of laughter TJ's friends couldn't stop themselves from releasing.

"You? You've fallen in love? Who is the unlucky girl?" Sam asked, once his laughter had **waned**.

Now that his secret was exposed, TJ spent the rest of the lunch hour recounting his adventures in romance. Though it wasn't much of a story yet, he was somehow **fascinated** by personal **intricacies** only a man in love would remember.

The girl, it turned out, was quiet and smart and had come back from abroad for the summer, having spent almost her entire life out of the country. In short, she know much about popular culture, which was tough because TJ knew little else. However, having been **mesmerized** by her beauty, TJ claimed he was now powerless to stop his **ardor**, and had to somehow **defraud** this girl into a social setting so he could chat with her under the **pretext** of helping her adjust to the new strange environment.

"What's her name, TJ?" Sam interrupted at one point.

"Oh, that. I don't know," he admitted. More laughter **ensued**. "But I *will* find out soon, because you guys are gonna help me."

They hadn't expected this, but afterwards Sam **confided** to Jake that he was secretly hoping to see what TJ's style of teasing **entailed**. They agreed to help, and agreed **covertly** that whatever TJ had planned was bound to fail.

---

549 serenely [13]
adv. 차분하게
calmly, peacefully

550 wane [5]
v. 줄어들다, 약해지다
to subside, diminish

551 fascinate [45]
v. 매료시키다
to attract and hold attentively

552 intricacy [10]
n. 복잡한 사항들
complicated matter
a. intricate

553 mesmerized [2]
a. 마음이 사로잡힌, 매료된
hypnotized, captivated

554 ardor [3]
n. 열정
passion; vehemence

555 defraud [2]
v. 속이다, 사기 치다
to cheat or deceive

556 pretext [5]
n. 구실
something to conceal a true purpose; an ostensible reason

557 ensue [4]
v. 뒤따르다
to follow; happen as a result

558 confide [4]
v. 털어놓다
to tell a secret to a trusted friend

559 entail [2]
v. 수반하다, 포함하다
to involve, require

560 covert [2]
a. 은밀한
concealed; secret; disguised

Vocabulary

0540
extraterrestrial [6]
[|ekstrətə|restriəl]

n. 외계인   an alien
영화 ET에서 외계인 ET의 이름은 Extra Terrestrial의 줄임말이다.
The boy fell in a faint when he saw a **extraterrestrial**. (*n.*)

0541
docile [2]
[dásəl]

a. 유순한, 고분고분한   meek, gentle, easily managed
doc는 '이끄는, 가르치는'이라는 뜻을 가지고 있는데 이와 연관지어서 '가르치기 쉽다'라고 외울 수 있다. 온순하거나 다루기쉬우면 가르치기 쉽기 때문이다.
Thankfully, the kids were **docile** as lambs. (*adj.*)

0542
juxtapose [4]
[dʒʌ̀kstəpóuz]

v. 병치하다, (비교를 위해)나란히 놓다   to place close together or side by side
just next + position '바로 옆에 두다'.
It is easy to see when you **juxtapose** one with the other and see what is different and the same. (*v.*)

0543
raucous [2]
[|rɔːkəs]

a. 요란하고 거친   loud and potentially destructive; rambunctious
울부짖으며(roar → rau) 요란하고 거친 소리를 낸다고 외우자.
A group of **raucous** young men (*adj.*)

0544
resilient [6]
[rizíljənt]

a. 회복력 있는; 원상태로 돌아가는; 탄력있는   springing back, rebounding from damage, flexible
're-seal'iant로 변형시켜서 읽으면 '구멍을 메꾸어 원상태로 돌리는'이라는 뜻으로 외울 수 있다.
Ronaldo was **resilient** and recovered from his injury just in time for the season. (*adj.*)

0545
complacent [5]
[kəm|pleɪsnt]

a. 자기만족적인   self-satisfied, often not aware of potential danger, pleased, especially with oneself or one's merits, advantages, situation, etc
사무실에서 내가 원하는 위치에 컴퓨터(computer)를 놓고(place) 좋은 향(scent, sounds like cent)을 뿌린다면 만족스럽겠지?
"Don't take too many pictures of me, no matter how handsome I am," said Joey **complacently**. (*adv.*)

0546
avarice [3]

[|ævərɪs]

n. 탐욕　insatiable greed for riches
옛날 탐관오리들은 탐욕스럽게(avarice) 쌀을(rice) 독차지하려고 했다.
The **avarice** of the country's dictator had no end. (*n.*)

0547
disregard [8]

[|dɪsrɪ|gɑːrd]

v. 무시하다, 묵살하다　to ignore, pay no attention to
누군가를 존중하지(regard) 않으면(dis), 무시하는 것과 다름 없겠지?
Jason **disregarded** his mother's request to help with the dishes, and played video games instead. (*v.*)

0548
concur [2]

[kənkə́ːr]

v. 동의하다, 동시에 일어나다　to agree; to coincide
'con'with 'cur'는 occur. 같이 일어나는, 동시에 일어나는.
I suggested pizza for dinner and my brother gladly **concurred**. (*v.*)

0549
serenely [13]

[səri:nli]

adv. 차분하게　calmly, peacefully
바다(sea → se) 한 가운데는 매우 조용하고 차분하다(serene).
We sailed **serenely** down the river. (*adv.*)

0550
wane [5]

[wéin]

v. 줄어들다, 약해지다　to subside, diminish, to lessen; shrink; fade
wax and wane이라는 표현 들어본 적 있지? 달이 찼다가 다시 이지러지는 것을 말한다.
His popularity began to **wane** when he said he hates his fans. (*v.*)

0551
fascinate [45]

[|fæsɪneɪt]

v. 매료시키다　to attract and hold attentively
영화에서 요정이(fairy → fa) 나오는 장면(scene → scin)은 아이들을 매료시킨다.
I'm a writer, and extreme characters always **fascinate** me. (*v.*)

0552
intricacy [10]

[|ɪntrɪkəsi]

n. 복잡한 사항들　complicated matter　*a.* intricate
나무의(tree → tri) 속은(in) 생각보다 복잡하다.
The price depends on the **intricacy** of the work. (*n.*)

0553
mesmerized [2]

[|mezməraɪzd]

a. **마음이 사로잡힌, 매료된**   hypnotized, captivated
mermaid (인어)와 스펠링이 살짝 비슷한 것 같지? 인어를 만나서 마음이 사로잡혔다고 생각하자.
Their performances were thrilling enough to **mesmerize** their 100,000 fans. (*v.*)

0554
ardor [3]

[ɑ́:rdər]

n. **열정**   passion; vehemence
자신의 꿈을 위해 모든 (all = ar) 문을 (dor = door) 열어볼 정도의 열정 (ardor)이라고 외워보자.
He shows great **ardor** for music. (*n.*)

0555
defraud [2]

[dɪ|frɔ:d]

v. **속이다, 사기 치다**   to cheat or deceive
fraud가 '사기꾼'이라는 뜻이므로 defraud는 '사기 치다'라는 뜻이다.
They were accused of **defrauding** the company of $14,000. (*v.*)

0556
pretext [5]

[prí:tekst]

n. **구실, 변명**   something to conceal a true purpose; an ostensible reason; excuse
pre(미리) + text(글을 쓰다). '변명을 위해 미리 준비하다'라는 뜻으로 외울 수 있다.
She left her coat in the car as a **pretext** to see him again later. (*n.*)

0557
ensue [4]

[ɪn|su:]

v. **뒤따르다**   to follow; happen as a result
미국에선 조그만 잘못을 해도 소송이(sue) 뒤따를(ensue) 것이라 예상할 수 있다.
I will accept any consequences which may **ensue**. (*v.*)

0558
confide [4]

[kən|faɪd]

v. **털어놓다**   to tell a secret to a trusted friend
함께(con) 하는 친구에게(friend → fide) 모든 걸 털어놓는다고 외우자.
She **confided** all her secrets to her best friend. (*v.*)

0559
entail [2]

[ɪn|teɪl]

v. **수반하다, 포함하다**   to involve, require
무언가에 꼬리가(tail) 매달려 따라다닌다고 외우자.
The job **entails** a lot of hard work. (*v.*)

0560
covert [kóuvərt]

a. 은밀한, 숨은   concealed; secret; disguised, especially for an evil purpose
덮여져 있어서(cover) 숨겨져 있다고 외우자.
Spies had a **covert** plan to steal secrets. (*adj.*)

Episode 33
MATCHING Quiz

1. extraterrestrial
2. docile
3. juxtapose
4. raucous
5. resilient
6. complacent
7. avarice
8. disregard
9. concur
10. serenely
11. wane
12. fascinate
13. intricacy
14. mesmerized
15. ardor
16. defraud
17. pretext
18. ensue
19. confide
20. entail

A. to place close together or side by side
B. to ignore, pay no attention to
C. springing back, rebounding
D. to agree
E. passion; vehemence
F. calmly, peacefully
G. self-satisfied, often not aware of potential danger
H. to attract and hold attentively
I. cheat or deceive
J. hypnotized, captivated
K. something to conceal a true purpose; an ostensible reason
L. to follow; happen as a result
M. insatiable greed for riches
N. to tell a secret to a trusted friend
O. to involve, require
P. to subside, diminish
Q. meek, gentle
R. complicated matter
S. an alien
T. loud and potentially destructive; rambunctious

1-S, 2-Q, 3-A, 4-T, 5-C, 6-G, 7-M, 8-B, 9-D, 10-F, 11-P, 12-H, 13-R, 14-J, 15-E, 16-I, 17-K, 18-L, 19-N, 20-O

더 많은 문제를 풀고자 한다면 www.quizlet.com 에서 'paul academy seoul' class를 검색

Episode 34

Woo-Time

561 indistinct ³
a. 또렷하지 않은
not clearly marked or defined

562 derive ⁷
v. 얻다, 끌어내다
to obtain, glean

563 peregrine ²
a. 외국의, 외래의
foreign, alien, coming from abroad

564 expatriate ³
n. 국외 거주자
someone who is living in a country which is not their own

565 pastoral ⁶
a. 시골의, 소박한
related to the countryside, outside of the city; rural

566 parochial ³
a. 편협한
narrow-minded (used for those from rural areas)

567 habituated ⁶
a. 길들여진, 익숙한
used to, accustomed to

568 immobile ³
a. 움직이지 않는
incapable of being moved or moving

The next day, TJ's strategy was still **indistinct** at best, but Sam kept an eye on the girl, **deriving** what information he could from a few brief trips into the classroom or from a few quick glances through the window.

This is what he had found out in the few hours before lunch:

She was indeed decidedly **peregrine**, having travelled the globe, living as an **expatriate** and spoke almost exclusively about things which the boys knew nothing about. Owing to her sheltered existence in a **pastoral** area while living abroad, she was decidedly **parochial**, and not **habituated** to the crowd of the subways or the strange rituals of academy life. As people poured into the hallways between classes, she stayed **immobile**, seeming to find the whole thing completely **incomprehensible**.

But to TJ she was beautiful, and to make matters even better, she lived with a mean old aunt who also happened to be in the book club with his mother.

"I tell you that club is fantastic," he said outside the convenience store during their morning break. "It's practically a social network for me." He took a long victorious drink of Coke as though he had already secured an engagement from a girl whose name he still didn't know.

His plan was still in its early stages, but it seemed that the boy, who was never **coy** about expressing himself, was planning to act as smooth as he could and ask her to join them for lunch. This caused Sam's shoulders to **heave** with laughter once more, but he remained **undeterred**.

"TJ, no offense, but you're as charming as a toad," Sam said finally. "You lack even the smallest measure of charm. When have you even tried talking to a girl?"

"Well, never really. But I've seen enough films to know the usual format. Plus, I've been studying more vocabulary so I can talk to her using the good-old SAT vocab."

"Sounds good, TJ," added Jake helpfully. "What's your opening **artifice** going to be?"

"Well, I was thinking that you two could accompany me up to the third floor between classes, and I could talk to her briefly and invite her to lunch."

Sam, as previously mentioned, had a more terrible feeling about TJ's immature courtship, believing that his friend was **inherently** incapable of romance. But he was willing to lend a hand, if only to see the results. After the classes had concluded, they walked into the new class's room try to bring the boy's plans to perfection.

She was sitting, as usual, at her desk, poking unenthusiastically at some french fries while a few of the other students were sleeping over their books. TJ, full of nervous courage, headed straight over to her desk.

"Ahem," he coughed loudly. "How are you?" he asked in his most confident tone.

She turned quickly, her face registering an expression of pure confusion as the three strange boys (one of whom sported a recovering black eye) stood over her. Jake pulled Sam back so that they wouldn't **tamper** too much.

"You are a new student, right?" he asked again. They were standing in the new classroom.

"Um...yes. Can I help you with something?" she asked innocently. Sam almost **snorted** with laughter.

"Well..." TJ searched for the words. "Maybe you looked lonely. We will eat at the cafe. Do you want to join our threesome?"

Sam's eyes went wide with shock.

---

569 incomprehensible [9]
a. 이해할 수 없는
impossible to understand or comprehend

570 heave [2]
v. 들썩거리다
to cause to rise and fall with a swelling motion

571 undeterred [3]
a. 단념[좌절]하지 않는
not discouraged

572 artifice [7]
n. 책략, 계략
hoax, gimmick

573 inherent [24]
a. 타고난
in-born or innate; something one has as part of one's nature

574 tamper [4]
v. 간섭하다, 참견하다
to meddle, interfere

575 snort [2]
v. 콧방귀를 뀌다
to express contempt, indignation

576 tempestuous [2]
a. 격렬한
wild, stormy

577 egregious [2]
a. 지독하게 나쁜
outstandingly bad

578 extrapolate [3]
v. 추론하다
to deduce, infer

She looked at TJ suspiciously again, as he turned back to the other boys with a look of **tempestuous** panic.

"We are not bad guys," Sam offered, not realizing that the claim of 'I'm not bad' sounds a lot like one is covering up a lot of **egregiousness**.

"Yeah, we're…real…benevolent!" TJ said quickly having taken a pause to remember the word.

She laughed slightly. A good sign, Jake **extrapolated**.

"But I'm already eating," she said, smiling.

"Oh, you don't want that garbage," he said..

"Oh, it's bad?" she said with some concern.

"Oh, definitely. It's…" another pause for a good vocabulary word. "…disgusting," he said..

"What does that mean?"

Jake now felt it was his turn to get involved.

"It's gross, bad food."

"Oh," she said. "Well, what are you going to eat?"

"Italian."

"Sounds great!" she said with a smile. "I'm so glad you guys came over and talked to me, but I think you should probably not refer to yourselves as 'a threesome'. Let's go!"

She laughed and tossed the remainder of her offensive french fries into the trash. As they headed out the door, while she wasn't looking, Sam hit TJ so hard in the back of his head that his glasses fell off.

Vocabulary

0561
indistinct [3]

[|ɪndɪ|stɪŋkt]

a. 또렷하지 않은   not clearly marked or defined
이(this → dis) 냄새는(stink → stinc) 너무 뚜렷다하고(distinct) 외워보자.
따라서 indistinct는 '또렷하지 않다'는 뜻이다.
His voice was **indistinct** because of the loud music. (*adj.*)

0562
derive [7]

[diráiv]

v. 얻다, (이끌어) 끌어내다   to obtain, glean, to deduce, as from a premise
'de-'는 from, of 이고 'riv'는 river에서 나온 말로 '물의 원천으로부터 물을 이끌어 내다, 끌어내다'라는 뜻이다.
From the frown on her face, David **derived** that his mother was unhappy. (*v.*)

0563
peregrine [2]

[|perɪgrɪn]

a. 외국의, 외래의   foreign, alien, coming from abroad
미소를 잘 짓는 (grin) 서양인을 생각해보자.
The **peregrine** falcon was imported from the US.

0564
expatriate [3]

[|eks|peɪtriət]

n. 국외 거주자   someone who is living in a country which is not their own, a person who lives outside of his country
ex + patriate로 보자. patriate은 뭔가 애국자(patriot)랑 비슷하다. 그런데 애국자면 국내에 살도록 노력하겠지? 근데 ex니까 전에는 patriot으로 국내에서 살았는데 이제 더 이상은 아니다. 그래서 '국외 거주자'를 뜻한다.
Jim is an **expatriate**, because he lives in Korea, despite the fact that he is a US citizen. (*n.*)

0565
pastoral [6]

[pǽstərəl]

a. 시골의, 소박한, 목가적인, 전원시(풍)의   related to the countryside, outside of the city; rural, having the spirit or sentiment of rural life "pasture," a field where farm animals are kept
시골에서는 심심풀이로 (pasttime → past) 이야기를 (story → stor) 주고받는다고 외워보자.
As a shepherd, I love **pastoral** scene of farm animals and sunshine. (*adj.*)

0566
parochial [3]
[pəróukiəl]

a. 편협한   narrow-minded (used for those from rural areas), narrow in outlook; provincial
작은 시골 지방 → 좁은 → 시각이 편협한
The **parochial** man always votes for the politician from his own hometown without considering about his promises. *(adj.)*

0567
habituated [6]
[həˈbɪtʃueɪtɪd]

a. 길들여진, 익숙한   used to, accustomed to
habit이 습관이라는 뜻이니까 habituate는 '무언가가 습관이 되어 익숙해졌다'는 의미이다.
He is **habituated** to get up early. *(adj.)*

0568
immobile [3]
[ɪˈmoʊbl]

a. 움직이지 않는   incapable of being moved or moving
휴대폰은 영어로 mobile phone이다. mobile은 움직일 수 있다는 뜻이므로 immobile은 '움직이지 않는다'는 의미이다.
She stood **immobile** by the window. *(adj.)*

0569
incomprehensible [9]
[ɪnˌkɑːmprɪˈhensəbl]

a. 이해할 수 없는   impossible to understand or comprehend
학생들이 항상 하는 듣기 평가 시간에 listen comprehension이라는 표현을 자주 들어봤을 것이다. 즉 comprehend는 이해한다는 뜻이므로 incomprehensible은 '이해할 수 없다'는 의미이다.
He found his son's actions totally **incomprehensible**. *(adj.)*

0570
heave [2]
[hiːv]

v. 들썩거리다   to cause to rise and fall with a swelling motion
엉덩이가(hip → heave) 들썩거리는 걸 떠올려보자.
Her shoulders **heaved** with laughter. *(v.)*

0571
undeterred [3]
[ˌʌndɪˈtɜːrd]

a. 단념[좌절]하지 않는   not discouraged
죽음(death)의 공포는 사람들을 좌절시키기도(deter) 한다. 따라서 undeterred는 '좌절하지 않는다'는 의미이다.
His career as a child actor was a failure, but he was **undeterred**. *(adj.)*

0572
artifice [7]
[ˈɑːrtɪfɪs]

n. 책략, 계략   hoax, gimmick
계략은(artifice) 예술적으로(art) 실행되었다고 외우자.
The **artifice** is being stripped away. *(n.)*

0573
inherent [24]
[inhíərənt]

a. 타고난, 태생의, 고유한   in-born or innate; something one has as part of one's nature
in(안에)과 here(여기)가 합쳐진 말로 원래 안에 있는, 즉 '태생의, 고유한'이라는 뜻을 가진다.
Her **inherent** talents made her a good singer, but it was the hours of practice that made her a true diva. (*adj.*)

0574
tamper [4]
[tǽmpər]

v. 간섭하다, 참견하다   to meddle, interfere
그는 성질이(temper) 나빠서 항상 참견을 한다고(tamper) 외워보자.
The government will not directly **tamper** with prices.

0575
snort [2]
[snɔ:rt]

v. 콧방귀를 뀌다   to express contempt, indignation
코로(nose → nor) 콧방귀를 뀐다고(snort) 생각해보자.
The horse **snorted** and tossed its head. (*v.*)

0576
tempestuous [2]
[tem|pestʃuəs]

a. 격렬한   wild, stormy
성질이 나빠서(temper) 격렬한 행동을 취했다고 외우자.
Ivan is a man of foul moods, of **tempestuous** rage, of wild, ungovernable caprice. (*adj.*)

0577
egregious [2]
[ɪ|gri:dʒiəs]

a. 지독하게 나쁜   outstandingly bad, extraordinary in some bad way
영어이름 Greg은 sheep의 group을 관리하는 목동이다. group에서 볼 수 있듯이, e(out) + greg(group) + ious는 나쁜사람이어서 그룹에서 쫓겨나는 사람을 뜻한다.
His mistake was so **egregious** that people wondered if he was drunk. (*adj.*)

0578
extrapolate [3]
[ɪk|stræpəleɪt]

v. 추론하다   to deduce, infer
극지방에는(pole) 어떤 다른(extra) 생명체가 사는지 추론한다고 생각하자.
We have **extrapolated** these results from research done in other countries. (*v.*)

Note :

Voca Hamburger
Episode 34
MATCHING Quiz

1. indistinct
2. derive
3. peregrine
4. expatriate
5. pastoral
6. parochial
7. habituated
8. immobile
9. incomprehensible
10. heave
11. undeterred
12. artifice
13. inherent
14. tamper
15. snort
16. tempestuous
17. egregious
18. extrapolate

A. used to, accustomed to
B. to meddle, interfere
C. to express contempt, indignation
D. related to the countryside, outside of the city; rura
E. someone who is living in a country which is not their own
F. foreign, alien, coming from abroad
G. not clearly marked or defined
H. to deduce, infer
I. to cause to rise and fall with a swelling motion
J. impossible to understand or comprehend
K. narrow-minded (used for those from rural areas) not discouraged
L. incapable of being moved or moving
M. wild, stormy
N. not discouraged
O. hoax, gimmick
P. in-born or innate; something one has as part of one's nature
Q. outstandingly bad
R. to obtain, glean

1-G, 2-R, 3-F, 4-E, 5-D, 6-K, 7-A, 8-L, 9-J, 10-I, 11-N, 12-O, 13-P, 14-B, 15-C, 16-M, 17-Q, 18-H

더 많은 문제를 풀고자 한다면 www.quizlet.com에서 'paul academy seoul' class를 검색

Episode 35: College Board = Awful

Greg, the essay teacher, was a very **placid** man, keeping his calm even as young **insolent** students tried to confuse him with interesting but **irrelevant** and **peripheral** questions.

"But Greg," they might begin, "where does logic come from? How do we know what is true?"

He dismissed these tempting treats like a well-behaved golden retriever. The only thing he cared about was how to get the more stubborn minds in the classroom to absorb the proper essay strategy. Today, the subject was theses.

"So, JW," he began, standing over the same **hapless** girl who seemed always to be the first one annoyed by the teachers when looking for **foible**. "How would you summarize the thesis of this passage?"

Her head turned from the question written on the board back to the teacher's waiting face. She was locked in **ambivalent** panic between two answers she was equally unsure of.

"Um…We shouldn't…not…recycle?" she asked rather than answered.

"Ok, that's not wrong, but it doesn't fully cover the whole passage?" He gestured to the board again, on which was written a big collection of different notes to his lecture.

The girl glanced again at the board, fearing that she would be unable to give an **unerring** response. A few more of the students who had been struggling on the essay section were silently hoping she'd get the answer right so the question would not pass to them. Finally, she gave up and admitted that she wasn't sure.

"Well," Greg said in his usual measured way. "How does the author frame his argument? Isaiah?"

---

579 placid [5]
a. 차분한, 얌전한
calm, tranquil

580 insolent [2]
a. 무례한, 버릇없는
rude; impudent

581 irrelevant [12]
a. 무관한
not applicable or pertinent

582 peripheral [3]
a. 주변적인
concerned with relatively minor, irrelevant aspects of the subject

583 hapless [2]
a. 불운한
unlucky

584 foible [3]
n. 약점
weakness, flaw

585 ambivalent [23]
a. 결정할 수 없는
being unable to choose between the two

586 unerring [3]
a. 틀림없는, 정확한
accurate

587 abysmal [2]
a. 심히 나쁜, 끔찍한
extremely hopeless, wretched

588 cognitive [7]
a. 인식의
of or relating to the mental processes of perception, memory, judgment, and reasoning

589 cohesion [2]
n. 화합, 결합
the act or state of uniting or sticking together
a. cohesive

The similarly-confused student, known more for his strong arms and body building than his brains, was equally unsure, as he had not actually read the passage.

"Umm...he says recycling is...**abysmal**?" he offered, apparently hoping the vocab word would distract the teacher.

"Isaiah, did you even read the passage?" The beefy boy shrugged.

Sighing, the brave teacher (who demanded answers with exact information and hated words like "some" or "thing") did not give up, however, and finally found his answer from Ashley, who had actually given the passage some thought. He thanked her, and remarked to the class that being able to accurately summarize a thesis was probably the most important part of the SAT essay. The very concept seemed cruel to many of the students, who just couldn't wrap their heads around it yet. As a result, the teacher assigned five passages for dissection.

"Every teacher thinks that they are the only ones who give homework," TJ said at lunchtime.

But it didn't matter how much one complained. As far as they were concerned, the brain's **cognitive** power for **cohesion** of information had to be stretched, and so would their free time.

Vocabulary

0579
placid [5]
[ˈplæsɪd]
a. **차분한, 얌전한** calm, tranquil
매우 평평해서(flat → pla) '차분하고 얌전하다'고 외우자.
The heat is searing and the mood **placid**. (*adj.*)

0580
insolent [2]
[ˈɪnsələnt]
a. **무례한, 버릇없는** rude; impudent
욕을 (insult → insol) 마구 해대며 버릇없게 (insolent) 군다고 외워보자.
The **insolent** son slammed the door in his parents' face. (*adj.*)

0581
irrelevant [12]
[ɪˈreləvənt]
a. **무관한** not applicable or pertinent
relevant는 '연관이 있다'는 뜻이므로 irrelevant는 '무관하다'는 의미이다.
That evidence is **irrelevant** to the case. (*adj.*)

0582
peripheral [3]
[pəˈrɪfərəl]
a. **주변적인, (신경이) 말초의** concerned with relatively minor, irrelevant aspects of the subject, marginal; outer
peri- 는 '원 밖에, ~ 밖에'를 뜻하니까 peripheral은 '중심의 주변'을 뜻한다.
Rather than focusing on the core issues, he focuses too much attention on **peripheral** problems. (*adj.*)

0583
hapless [2]
[ˈhæpləs]
a. **불운한** unlucky
너무 불운해서(hapless) 속수무책으로(helpless) 당한다고 생각하자.
Many children are **hapless** victims of this war. (*adj.*)

0584
foible [3]
[ˈfɔɪbl]
n. **약점** a personal weakness or failing, flaw
'fail'ble 로 연상해서 생각하면 '실패하기 쉬운 약점'으로 외울 수 있다.
His laziness is his biggest **foible**; without that, he would be such a likable person! (*n.*)

0585
ambivalent [23]
[æmˈbɪvələnt]
a. **결정할 수 없는, 반대 감정이 병존하는**
being unable to choose between the two, having mixed feelings
ambi(both) + val(value) + ant 는 양쪽에 가치를 지니므로 애매모호한 입장을 뜻한다.
He was **ambivalent** about whether to eat a pizza or a burger. (*adj.*)

0586
unerring ³
[ʌnəːrɪŋ]

a. 틀림없는, 정확한   accurate, certain; without error
un + no + 'err'or. '에러가 없는, 틀림없는'이란 뜻이다.
As the international champion, she has **unerring** aim at the target and which never misses. *(adj.)*

0587
abysmal ²
[əˈbɪzməl]

a. 심히 나쁜, 끔찍한   extremely hopeless, wretched
abyss는 '심연'이란 뜻으로 '심연에 갇힌 것처럼 끔찍하다'는 의미이다.
Nutrition is **abysmal** at this school. *(adj.)*

0588
cognitive ⁷
[ˈkɑːgnətɪv]

a. 인식(인지)의   of or relating to the mental processes of perception, memory, judgment, and reasoning
뇌가 공장이고 톱니바퀴(cog)들이 열심히 돌아가고 있다고 기억하자.
To develop their brains, children should do a lot of **cognitive** exercises, like puzzles or memory games. *(adj.)*

0589
cohesion ²
[kouˈhiːʒn]

n. 화합, 결합   the act or state of uniting or sticking together
a. cohesive
cohere는 '응집하다'라는 의미로 다 같이(co) 여기에(here) 모인다고 외우자.
따라서 명사 cohesion은 '결합'이란 뜻이다.
Another major issue is employment and social **cohesion**. *(n.)*

Episode 35
MATCHING Quiz

1. placid   • • A. calm, tranquil
2. insolent   • • B. of or relating to the mental processes of perception, memory, judgment, and reasoning
3. irrelevant   • • C. rude; impudent
4. peripheral   • • D. the act or state of uniting or sticking together
5. hapless   • • E. unlucky
6. foible   • • F. weakness, flaw
7. ambivalent   • • G. being unable to choose between the two
8. unerring   • • H. extremely hopeless, wretched
9. abysmal   • • I. concerned with relatively minor, irrelevant aspects of the subject
10. cognitive   • • J. accurate
11. cohesion   • • K. not applicable or pertinent

1-G, 2-C, 3-K, 4-I, 5-A, 6-E, 7-E, 8-J, 9-H, 10-B, 11-D

더 많은 문제를 풀고자 한다면 www.quizlet.com에서 'paul academy seoul' class를 검색

Episode 36

The Lecture

Seeking **refuge** from the academy once more, Jake skipped the afternoon session (with surprising permission from his mother) to meet his uncle at the campus. The old man had told him that he would be teaching, and that Jake should either wait in the office until four or observe the first lecture of the semester. Jake enthusiastically chose the second option, and slipped into the darkened lecture hall just as the Professor took the stage.

"Some people are happy to let their minds rest, almost **sluggish**, while promising themselves that tomorrow they will resume their activity. Indeed, they might **feign erudition** by buying books with glossy covers and 'guaranteed success' on the cover, but as soon as those volumes are open, their minds close. They stop learning and begin to drift. They will be confused by a cell phone full of **tame** texts, a dialog on that same piece of machinery on **fragmentary** matters of social gossip, mere **natter**. They first put a bookmark in the page, saying 'when I have time, I'll really devote myself to this.' But once the book is closed, it is closed forever. If there is one **immutable** law of academic study, it is this: books must be read, not bought. A purchased book unread—or, I should say, unstudied, since people often associate the movement of their eyes across the page with learning—will **deteriorate** and expire without fail, as will the critical abilities of the mind **diminish**, **wilt**, and die. Don't take this course unless you intend to read and discuss. Anything less will be a **stark** waste of your time and mine."

Jake had never heard anyone so impassioned by the idea of learning as his uncle. From the back of the lecture hall, he noticed a few heads nodding in **accord**, one or two eyes held in attention, but the majority turning to each other to roll their eyes **irreverently**, making the same childish, funny expressions as his own friends. He **condemned** their lack of interest, and wanted to **spout** praise in his poor uncle's defense, but instead he watched as the old man, wearing the same jacket and faded, though still loud, canary-yellow trousers, turned to

---

590 refuge [4]
n. 피난처
protection; a safe place

591 sluggish [3]
a. 느릿느릿한
inactive, lethargic

592 feign [3]
v. 가장하다
to fake; affect

593 erudition [3]
n. 학식
academic knowledge
a. erudite

594 tame [2]
a. 재미없는, 밋밋한
dull, insipid

595 fragmentary [2]
a. 부분적인
consisting of or reduced to fragments, incomplete

596 natter [2]
n. 수다
foolish and vapid conversation; chatter

597 immutable [4]
a. 변경할 수 없는
unchangeable; eternal

598 deteriorate [3]
v. 악화되다
to degenerate, languish

229

599 diminish 15
v. 줄어들다
to make or cause to seem smaller

600 wilt 2
v. 말라 죽다, 시들다
to weaken, fade, wither

601 stark 3
a. 완전한, 극명한
blunt, utter

602 accord 6
n. 합의
agreement

603 irreverently 9
adv. 비웃듯이
without respect; impiously

604 condemn 12
v. 규탄하다
to pronounce to be guilty

605 spout 3
v. 지껄이다, 반복하다
to talk or speak at some length or in an oratorical manner

606 amplify 4
v. 더 자세히 설명하다
to expand in stating or describing

the first assigned reading and began **amplifying** the importance of the author, whose name was unrecognizable to Jake as it must have been to many of the sleeping attendees in the hall.

Vocabulary

0590

refuge [4]

[réfju:dʒ]

n. 피난처, 피난　　protection; a safe place, shelter from danger
Syrian refugees 들어봤지? 즉 '시리아 난민'을 말하는데 refugee(난민)들이 피난할 수 있는 공간이 refuge이다.
Forests are a **refuge** for wild animals. (*n.*)

0591

sluggish [3]

[slʌ́giʃ]

a. 느릿느릿한, 부진한　　inactive, lethargic, unusually slow
slug(민달팽이)를 기억하자.
He felt very heavy and **sluggish** after the meal. (*adj.*)

0592

feign [3]

[feɪn]

v. 가장하다　　to fake; affect; to represent fictitiously
소풍 가는 날 비(rain)가 온다고 친구들을 속이면(feign) 재밌지.
She **feigned** amusement, even though his jokes were very boring. (*v.*)

0593

erudition [3]

[ˌeruˈdɪʃn]

n. 학식　　academic knowledge
ex (out) + rudis (배운 게 없는), 즉 '무지에서 벗어나다'라는 뜻에서 유래.
His range of **erudition** is wide. (*n.*)

0594

tame [2]

[téim]

a. 재미없는, 밋밋한; 길든　　dull, insipid; domesticated
team에 넣으면 tame '길든' 상태가 된다.
Humans have **tamed** dogs from the very beginning of history. (*adj.*)

0595

fragmentary [2]

[ˈfrægmənteri]

a. 부분적인　　consisting of or reduced to fragments, incomplete
'사금파리 한 조각'이라는 책을 모두 읽어봤지? fragment는 '조각'이라는 의미다. 따라서 fragmentary는 '부분적인'이라는 뜻이다.
There is only **fragmentary** evidence to support this theory. (*adj.*)

0596

natter [2]

[ˈnætə(r)]

n. 수다　　foolish and vapid conversation; chatter
chat(수다)와 모양이 비슷한데, 뜻도 같다고 외우자.
You **natter** all day long at the hospital. (*v.*)

0597
immutable [imjúːtəbl]

a. 변경할 수 없는   unchangeable; eternal
mutation은 '돌연변이', 유전자에 이상한 변화가 생긴 것을 말한다. 따라서, im (not) +mutable 이라고 하면, '변화가 생길수 없는'이 된다.
Even after forty years of marriage, my love for my husband has remained **immutable**. (*adj.*)

0598
deteriorate [ditíəriərèit]

v. 악화되다   to degenerate, languish
deter는 '좌절시키다'라는 의미이다. 그러니까 계속 좌절당해서 '악화됐다'고 외우자.
Her health **deteriorated** rapidly, and she died shortly afterwards. (*v.*)

0599
diminish [dimíniʃ]

v. 줄어들다, 감소하다   to make or cause to seem smaller, to decrease
de- '완전히', minuere '작게 만들다'에서 유래했다.
When your stress level **diminishes**, a smile appears on your face. (*v.*)

0600
wilt [wɪlt]

v. 말라 죽다, 시들다   to weaken, fade, wither
살려는 의지가(will)가 없어져 시들어 버렸다(wilt)고 외우자.
He was **wilting** under the pressure of work. (*v.*)

0601
stark [stάːrk]

a. 완전한, 극명한   blunt, utter, unambiguous; complete
star가 밤에 완전히(stark) 선명하게 잘 보인다고 생각하자.
The snow was **starkly** white. (*adv.*)

0602
accord [əkɔ́ːrd]

n. 합의; 부합하다   agreement, harmony; to be in agreement; to correspond
cord는 '마음'을 뜻하므로 마음이 일치하는 상태이다.
We always fight each other, because her opinion does not **accord** with mine. (*v.*)

0603
irreverently [ɪ|revərəntli]

adv. 비웃듯이   without respect; impiously
revere은 '존경하다'라는 의미이다 (respect와 연결해서 외워보자).
따라서 irreverently는 존경하지 않고 '비웃듯이'라는 의미이다.
Teachers deal with spoiled **irreverent** children every day. (*adj.*)

0604
condemn [12]
[kən|dem]

v. **규탄하다** to pronounce to be guilty, to express an unfavorable judgement on

우리 마음에 안 드는 상황에 처하면 Damn! 이렇게 말하지? 그거와 condemn을 같이 외워보자.

Jack **condemned** Jill for dropping the bucket of water, and Jill said sorry. (v.)

0605
spout [3]
[spaʊt]

v. **지껄이다, 반복하다** to talk or speak at some length or in an oratorical manner

잡초가 계속해서 솟아나듯이(sprout) 반복해서 지껄인다고(spout) 외우자.

He's always **spouting** off about being a vegetarian. (v.)

0606
amplify [4]
[ǽmpləfài]

v. **더 자세히 설명하다, 확대하다** to expand in stating or describing, to increase in size or effect

공연장에 가면 amplifier 옆 자리에 앉은 사람은 귀가 멍멍하다고 말하지? amplifier는 '소리를 크게 해주는, 증폭시켜 주는' 장치이다.

The equipment **amplified** the sound until it became very loud. (v.)

Episode 36
MATCHING Quiz

1. erudition	A. to expand in stating or describing
2. refuge	B. protection; a safe place
3. sluggish	C. dull, insipid
4. feign	D. academic knowledge
5. tame	E. to degenerate, languish
6. fragmentary	F. to fake; affect
7. natter	G. foolish and vapid conversation; chatter
8. immutable	H. consisting of or reduced to fragments, incomplete
9. deteriorate	I. blunt, utter
10. diminish	J. to make or cause to seem smaller
11. wilt	K. unchangeable; eternal
12. stark	L without respect; impiously
13. accord	M. to weaken, fade, wither
14. irreverently	N. to talk or speak at some length or in an oratorical manner
15. condemn	O. to pronounce to be guilty
16. spout	P. agreement
17. amplify	Q. inactive, lethargic

1-D, 2-B, 3-Q, 4-F, 5-C, 6-H, 7-G, 8-K, 9-E, 10-J, 11-M, 12-I, 13-P, 14-L, 15-O, 16-N, 17-A

더 많은 문제를 풀고자 한다면 www.quizlet.com에서 'paul academy seoul' class를 검색

Episode 37

Making Fun

607 recede [7]
v. 사라지다, 물러나다
to go or move away;
retreat; withdraw

608 empirical [6]
a. 경험에 의한
derived from or guided by experience

609 drudgery [8]
n. 힘들고 단조로운 일
menial, distasteful, dull, or hard work
v. drudge

610 dilute [2]
v. 약화시키다
to reduce the strength or force

611 quirk [4]
n. 별난 성격
a peculiarity of action, behavior, or personality

612 manifest [12]
v. 분명해지다, 나타내다
to make clear or evident; show plainly

613 voluptuous [2]
a. 풍만한
full of luxury, pleasure, and sensuous enjoyment

614 opine [2]
v. 의견을 밝히다
to hold or express an opinion

615 caricature [3]
n. 희화/풍자화한 그림
a picture, ludicrously exaggerating the peculiarities of person or things

After a few weeks, as excitement **recedes** and is replaced by bored, the new fun of **empirical** knowledge learned in class among friends becomes a **drudgery**. Luckily, however, human nature **dilutes** this by providing students an easy tactic in times of boredom: making fun of teachers.

The teachers at the academy were all equipped with a number of **quirks** and mannerisms, all of which **manifested** themselves in various ways. When Greg got annoyed, his voice would become booming, not quite shouting but resonating through the room in **voluptuous** bass tones.

Matt, the vocabulary teacher, spoke quickly and was fond of rolling his eyes at trivial questions, making him unpopular with students who struggled. He continually talked about using bigger words more often than smaller ones, complaining about the "madness of commonplace language" and the "easiness" of using simplistic words for answer choices (whereas the other teachers would say "B as in boy", for example, in place of which he would propose "B as in ballet").

Paul, the grammar teacher, was endlessly upbeat, and tried to motivate the students with stories about successful athletes and Harvard graduates who never gave up and kept trying, laughing happily at his own jokes.

The reading teacher *had* gone to Harvard, and usually talked about how if you didn't study, you'd end up working at McDonald's. Jake tended to **opine** that this approach was slightly elitist, but didn't say so, as many of the students claimed it gave them 'great motivation' from someone who had actually gone to a good school.

All this meant, of course, only one thing to most students: **caricatures**. In between classes, when many escaped to the street to buy sandwiches or smoke, most would stay behind, some napping and others gathering around the board at the front, drawing pictures of various teachers, or making fun of the teachers and their vocal **idiosyncrasies**. One such day, TJ **leapt** up to the front of the room after Matt had left, and began copying the teacher's **eloquent** style of speaking.

"Now, hmmm... That's an interesting **conundrum**... let's see now... perhaps if we...," he said quickly. Then, making fun of Matt's tendency to dismiss **frivolous** questions, he said, "Well... huh... well that's a stupid comment... and general blahblahblah... funny joke, etc, and of course..." copying all of the pauses and gestures that Matt used when explaining the answers to questions, even his tendency for **pattering**, which he did on occasion with difficult questions. However, on this day, TJ had done much of this facing the board, making **miscellaneous** quick and illegible notes with the marker while speaking. He didn't notice as the **tumultuous** laughter stopped suddenly, nor was he aware that the teacher had entered the room.

"TJ!" Matt called out darkly.

The boy turned, and his face went white.

"Yes, sorry. I—it was a little—game I guess. Sorry." He backed down slowly, embarrassed beyond belief. The man just stood there watching this little show of **belittlement** and smiled his usual smile.

"Surely my writing's not that bad," he said after a long pause. "Anyway, I presume you'll wipe down that board now that you've finished using it."

TJ rose quietly, **rehashed** a few more apologies, and the rest of the class began laughing just as they had before, telling returning students about the encounter as the slightly embarrassed **pedant bustled** away.

---

616 idiosyncrasy [10]
n. 특별한 점
a characteristic, habit, mannerism

617 leap [11]
v. 서둘러 ~ 하다
to move or act quickly or suddenly

618 eloquent [7]
a. 유창한
articulate, distinctive

619 conundrum [4]
n. 수수께끼
problem or puzzle

620 frivolous [6]
a. 바보 같은, 까부는
foolish

621 patter [3]
v. 재잘거리다
to babble

622 miscellaneous [2]
a. 이것 저것 다양한
having various qualities, aspects, or subjects

623 tumultuous [3]
a. 떠들썩한
boisterous, raucous

624 belittlement [3]
n. 비하, 업신여김
depreciation; abasement, disparagement

625 rehash [2]
v. 반복하다
to repeat

626 pedant [6]
n. 세세한 것에 얽매이는 사람
a person who overemphasizes rules or minor details

627 bustle [2]
v. 바삐 움직이다
to move with a great show of energy

235

Vocabulary

0607
recede [7]
[risíːd]

v. 사라지다, 물러나다   to go or move away; retreat; to withdraw
re(back) + cede(go). precede(먼저 가다), concede(함께 가다 → 동의하다) 모두 같은 어원.
The waters passed and the flood **receded**. (v.)

0608
empirical [6]
[impírikəl]

a. 경험에 의한, 경험적인   derived from or guided by experience, based on experiment
많은 경험을 쌓은 황제(emperor)를 떠올려보라.
Empirical and scientific evidence (adj.)

0609
drudgery [8]
[|drʌdʒəri]

n. 힘들고 단조로운 일   menial, distasteful, dull, or hard work
v. drudge
drudgery를 열심히 하면 마약(drug)처럼 중독되어서 일 중독이 될 수도 있어.
After a day full of **drudgery**, Cinderella did not want to wash another dish or fold another load of laundry. (n.)

0610
dilute [2]
[dailúːt]

v. 약화시키다; 묽게 하다   to reduce the strength or force, to make more fluid or less concentrated by admixture with something
di(de = 더(more)) + loose(풀어진)이라고 생각하자.
The water **diluted** the grape juice, until I couldn't taste any grapes in the juice at all. (v.)

0611
quirk [4]
[kwə́ːrki]

n. 별난 성격, 꾀바른, 변덕스러운   a peculiarity of action, behavior, or personality, unpredictable
돈키호테(Don 'Qui'xote)는 변덕스러운('qui'rky) 성격이다.
Only he knew how to work his **quirky** car. (adj.)

0612
manifest [12]
[mǽnəfèst]

v. 분명해지다, 나타내다; 분명한; 화물목록   to make clear or evident; show plainly; a list of the cargo carried by a ship, made for the use of various agents and officials at the ports of destination
'선언, 성명'을 뜻하는 manifesto를 생각해서 외우자.
The storm **manifested** itself through lightning and thunder. (v.)

0613
voluptuous [vəlʌptʃuəs]

a. 풍만한, 육감적인   full of luxury, pleasure, and sensuous enjoyment, sensuously pleasing or delightful
볼륨 있는 사람은 sensuous하다.
Women exercise to obtain a **voluptuous** body. (*adj.*)

0614
opine [oʊpaɪn]

v. 의견을 밝히다   to hold or express an opinion
opinion이 의견이니까 opine은 '의견을 밝히다'라는 의미이다.
He **opined** that Prague was the most beautiful city in Europe. (*v.*)

0615
caricature [kǽrikətʃər]

n. 희화/풍자화한 그림   a picture, ludicrously exaggerating the peculiarities of person or things, a picture or description in which natural characteristics are exaggerated or distorted
이탈리아어로 caricare는 '과장하다'라는 뜻이다.
Caricature artist. (*n.*)

0616
idiosyncrasy [ˌɪdiəˈsɪŋkrəsi]

n. 특별한 점   a characteristic, habit, mannerism
얼간이라고(idiot) 불리우는 사람들은 거의 그들이 하는 하나의 특이한 행동 (idiosyncrasy) 때문에 그렇게 불리우곤 한다.
It is an **idiosyncrasy** of hers that she always smells a book before opening it. (*n.*)

0617
leap [liːp]

v. 서둘러 ~ 하다   to move or act quickly or suddenly
leap은 '점프하다'라는 의미도 있으므로 무언가를 듣자마자 서둘러 점프해서 행동에 옮긴다고 생각해보자.
She **leapt** out of bed. (*v.*)

0618
eloquent [éləkwənt]

a. 유창한, 웅변의, 웅변에 능한   articulate, distinctive, having the ability to express emotion or feeling in lofty and impassioned speech
어원 eu- 는 'good'이라는 뜻이고 loq 는 speaking과 관련이 있어서 '웅변의'라는 뜻이 자연스럽게 연상된다.
He won the "Best Speaker of the Year" Award with his **eloquent** speech. (*adj.*)

0619
conundrum [kənʌ́ndrəm]

n. 수수께끼, 어려운 문제 — problem or puzzle, a riddle; anything that puzzles
코난(Conan)이 수수께끼를 푼다고 생각해.
It took a long time to come up with a good solution to the **conundrum**. (*n.*)

0620
frivolous [frívələs]

a. 바보 같은, 까부는, 천박한 — foolish, lacking seriousness and dealt lightly
flippant와 같은 의미로 생각하면 된다.
The immature boys continue their **frivolous** discussion even when they have to be serious and respectful. (*adj.*)

0621
patter [|pætə(r)]

v. 재잘거리다 — to babble
chatter, natter처럼 모두 '수다를 떨다, 재잘거리다'라는 의미이다.
Sales **patter** (*n.*)

0622
miscellaneous [|mɪsə|leɪniəs]

a. 이것 저것 다양한 — having various qualities, aspects, or subjects
게임이나 책 부록 등을 보면 기타 잡동사니에 대한 정보들을 모아놓은 곳을 miscellaneous라고 부른다. 즉 '이것 저것 다양한 것들이 모아져 있다'는 의미이다.
She keeps all sorts of **miscellaneous** items in her garage. (*adj.*)

0623
tumultuous [tjumʌ́ltʃuəs]

a. 떠들썩한, 시끄러운, 동요한 — boisterous, raucous, involving many exciting events
tum(swell, 부풀다) + ult + uous : '부풀어 일어나는'의 뜻으로 '소동을 일으키는, 흥분하다'라는 의미가 있다.
The **tumultuous** thunderstorm woke the whole neighborhood. (*adj.*)

0624
belittlement [bɪ|lɪtlmənt]

n. 비하, 업신여김 — depreciation; abasement, disparagement
누군가를 작다고(little) 업신여긴다는 의미이다.
Within the ghettos, there was **belittlement** of life. (*n.*)

0625
rehash ²
[riːhǽʃ]

v. 반복하다, 다시 만들다, 재탕하다   to repeat
'hash' is leftover food chopped up
Her friend **rehashed** last night's episode for her. (*v.*)

0626
pedant ⁶
[ˈpednt]

n. 세세한 것에 얽매이는 사람   a person who overemphasizes rules or minor details
개미의(ant) 발(ped)처럼 세세한 것에까지 신경을 쓰는 사람이라고 외우자.
I know: I'm a **pedant** and a snob. (*n.*)

0627
bustle ²
[ˈbʌsl]

v. 바삐 움직이다   to move with a great show of energy
출근길 버스(bus)에 탄 사람들은 어딘가를 가기 위해 모두 바삐 움직이고 있다(bustle).
She **bustled** around in the kitchen. (*v.*)

Episode 37
MATCHING Quiz

1. recede
2. empirical
3. drudgery
4. dilute
5. quirk
6. manifest
7. voluptuous
8. opine
9. caricature
10. idiosyncrasy
11. leap
12. eloquent
13. conundrum
14. frivolous
15. patter
16. miscellaneous
17. tumultuous
18. belittlement
19. rehash
20. pedant

A. derived from or guided by experience
B. to reduce the strength or force
C. to go or move away; retreat; withdraw
D. to make clear or evident; show plainly
E. a peculiarity of action, behavior, or personality
F. a picture, ludicrously exaggerating the peculiarities of person or things
G. menial, distasteful, dull, or hard work
H. full of luxury, pleasure, and sensuous enjoyment
I. articulate, distinctive
J. a characteristic, habit, mannerism
K. to hold or express an opinion
L foolish
M. to move or act quickly or suddenly
N. having various qualities, aspects, or subjects
O. problem or puzzle
P. to repeat
Q. boisterous, raucous
R. to babble
S. a person who overemphasizes rules or minor details
T. depreciation; abasement, disparagement

1-C, 2-A, 3-G, 4-B, 5-E, 6-D, 7-H, 8-K, 9-F, 10-J, 11-M, 12-I, 13-O, 14-L, 15-R, 16-N, 17-Q, 18-T, 19-P, 20-S

더 많은 문제를 풀고자 한다면 www.quizlet.com에서 'paul academy seoul' class를 검색

Episode 38: A Release or 'Kick Out Thursday'

628 aggressive ²
a. 공격적인, 적대적인
hostile, contentious
n. aggression

629 exile ³
n. 망명, 추방
expulsion from one's native land by authoritative decree

630 beget ⁴
v. 야기하다, 일으키다
to create, cause

631 turbulence ⁸
n. 격동, 난기류
trouble and chaos

632 disruptive ⁹
a. 지장을 주는
preventing something from acting in a normal way

633 partisan ²
n. 열렬한 신봉자
an adherent or supporter of a person, group, party, or cause

634 reticent ⁴
a. 말이 없는
disposed to be silent or not to speak freely

635 exemplify ⁵
v. 예를 들다
to illustrate by example; typify

While some of the more wholesome and innocent students relieved their stress by making fun of the teachers, others had slightly more **aggressive** means of showing their frustration, leading to the event known by many students as 'Kick Out Thursday,' or 'the **Exile**'.

At this point, some of the students who clearly hadn't been trying very hard were beginning to **beget** some **turbulence** in some of the classes. They didn't study for the vocab quizzes, preferring to play games at home, and when asked a question by a teacher, they tended to remain silent and just stand up.

However, one boy, known as Danny, was more **disruptive** than others. He had come in from another academy, from which he had been ejected for cheating. There were also rumors of a fight he had started. He was a tall boy, and spoke loudly in classes, often swearing in front of the teachers and complaining of unfair treatment by the teachers, accusing them of being **partisans**.

One of the things that students don't know, however, is that even though they are under pressure to improve their scores, teachers face the same pressure for ensuring that improvement and guaranteeing to their parents that the scores will go up. Of course, one of the bad sides of having two sets of people under different pressure is that, sometimes, they don't exactly communicate as they should.

This was seen one day, Thursday of Week Six, as Matt was asking the students about words from the previous class, and he got to Danny. He asked him the word, as carefully as he could, knowing that he might create a bit of uproar if he chose a difficult word. Matt chose the easiest word he could think of.

"Danny, what does ***reticent*** mean?"

The boy looked blankly, and stood up with the usual smile to the other students which **exemplified** those who didn't know and didn't care.

"Danny? *Reticent*?" He had raised his voice a little now, to sound more commanding.

"I don't know, sorry," Danny said quietly, gesturing to the next student as if to say "ask her."

But the teacher, who had withstood a great deal of Danny's silence and ignorance for the
previous weeks, was not prepared to allow Danny this refusal.

"I asked *you* the question, Danny," he said, raising his voice. "So you can at least guess at the meaning if you like."

The boy did not care.

"Fine," the angry teacher now said. "Come to the hallway with me right now."

The other students started whispering as the teacher marched to the back of the room, the student beginning to follow him. However, feeling he had been **disparaged** and **affronted** by this **exotic** foreigner, he decided to take **vengeance**, at least in verbal form.

"Flashing gas pole!" he said, or at least something that sounded like it, and **rashly** kicked an empty desk so hard it fell over.

The teacher turned around quickly, red in the face and **bristling** with anger.

"Right," he said, his voice nearly shaking. "Pick up your bag."

"Why? What have I done?" the boy asked innocently, pretending to be **righteous**.

"You know what you did," came the response. "Pick up your bags."

They stood looking at each other for a few seconds, until the student finally accepted and went back to get his belongings. He walked angrily out of the classroom and was heard swearing loudly

---

636 disparage [16]
v. 폄하하다
to speak of or treat slightly

637 affront [4]
v. 모욕하다
to offend

638 exotic [4]
a. 외국의, 이국적인
of foreign origin or character

639 vengeance [2]
n. 복수
violent revenge

640 rashly [5]
adv. 성급하게
too hastily; without thinking of the consequences

641 bristling [2]
a. ~으로 꽉 찬
to be thickly set or filled with something

642 righteous [4]
a. 도덕적으로 옳은
morally right or justifiable

643 polarized [2]
a. 양극화된, 나뉜
divided, separated

644 repress [7]
v. 억누르다
to put pressure on; control

645 pragmatic [10]
a. 실용적인
of a practical point of view or practical considerations

646 premature [2]
a. 너무 이른, 시기상조의
mature or ripe before the proper time

647 infringe [2]
v. 위반하다
to violate, disobey

648 verdict [4]
n. 판결
a judgment, decision

649 irrevocable [2]
a. 변경할 수 없는
not to be revoked or recalled

650 preside [4]
v. 통제하다
to control, have authority over

651 noxious [3]
a. 해로운
harmful

652 contaminating [4]
a. 오염시키는
affecting negatively

653 conjecture [3]
v. 추측하다
to assume, guess

654 roguish [2]
a. 악당 같은
acting like a rogue; knavish

in the hallway.

For the rest of the day, all that was discussed was the issue of the 'kick out' as the students called it. They were **polarized** on their opinions. However, by afternoon, Paul decided to speak to every class and let them know about what had happened from an objective point of view.

"Look, I know some of you think that we're **repressing** you sometimes with our rules, making you stand up and everything, but I promise you we're not trying to be cruel, just **pragmatic**. Sometimes you might think we make questionable or **premature** decisions that aren't logical, and for that I can understand, but you must know that any student who **infringes** the rules in the way we saw this morning cannot be tolerated. It isn't a **verdict** we pass happily, but it's more of a last and **irrevocable** resort for those whom we can no longer **preside** in our school. We don't want their **noxious** influence **contaminating** the rest of you. Our decision will have to stand."

In all four classes, this speech—which was pretty much the same all four times it was given—was met by silence. The teachers had **conjectured** that this was teenage **roguishness** or anger. The students knew better: they were just tired of being talked to, or talked at, by anyone at the front of the room.

Vocabulary

0628

aggressive [2]
[əgrésɪv]

a. **공격적인, 적대적인**   hostile, contentious   *n.* aggression
어그로를(aggro) 끌기위해 공격적으로(aggressive) 행동하는 사람들이 인터넷에는 많이 존재한다.
He gets **aggressive** when he's angry. (*adj.*)

0629

exile [3]
[éksaɪl]

n. **망명, 추방**   expulsion from one's native land by authoritative decree
영원히 바깥으로 내보낸다고(exit) 외우자.
The former president was in **exile**. (*n.*)

0630

beget [4]
[bigét]

v. **야기하다, 일으키다, 자식을 보다**   to create, cause; to procreate
get이 '얻다'는 의미니까 '자식을 얻다'라고 외워보자.
It helped to **beget** various fantastic rumors. (*v.*)

0631

turbulence [8]
[tə́ːrbjuləns]

n. **격동, 난기류, 격변**   trouble and chaos, state of violent agitation
turbulent ambulance '격동하는 앰뷸런스'라고 생각해 보자.
Passengers should wear seat belts to protect themselves from **turbulence** during the flight. (*n.*)

0632

disruptive [9]
[dɪsrʌ́ptɪv]

a. **지장을 주는**   preventing something from acting in a normal way
disrupt가 '방해하다'라는 의미니까 disruptive는 방해를 해서 '지장을 주는'이라는 의미이다.
She had a **disruptive** influence on the rest of the class. (*adj.*)

0633
partisan [2]
[pάːrtizən]

n. 열렬한 신봉자[지지자]   an adherent or supporter of a person, group, party, or cause
parti 〈 party(모임, 일행, 정당, 파벌) + san : '모임에 있는 (사람)' → 일당, 도당, 패거리, 당파심이 강한 사람 → 동지, 지지자(↔ opponent) → [군대] 유격병, 게릴라 대원, 빨치산(guerrilla). 〈정책, 논의, 입장 등이〉 당파심이 강한, 당파에 치우친 → 〈공격 등이〉 유격병에 의한]
He was a **partisan** of Mr. Costa's political party, and told everyone to vote for Mr. Costa at least a hundred times a day. (*n.*)

0634
reticent [4]
[rétəsənt]

a. 말이 없는, 과묵한, 입이 무거운   disposed to be silent or not to speak freely, taciturn; reserved
re 는 '다시', tic 은 silent이다. 즉 tacit(speechless)를 이해하면 reticent는 '또 다시 말이 없는'의 뜻이라는 것을 알 수 있다.
The **reticent** general only said one word while accepting the honor. (*adj.*)

0635
exemplify [5]
[ɪɡǀzemplɪfaɪ]

v. 예를 들다   to illustrate by example; typify
example이 '예시'라는 의미니까 exemplify는 '예를 들다'는 의미이다.
Her early work is **exemplified** in her book. (*v.*)

0636
disparage [16]
[dɪspǽrɪdʒ]

v. 폄하하다   to speak of or treat slightly, depreciate
dis(away) + par(equal) + age : '동등하게 보지 않다' → 깔보다, 경시하다 → ~을 헐뜯다, 험담하다, 비난하다
She made critical remarks that **disparaged** his cooking skills. (*v.*)

0637
affront [4]
[əǀfrʌnt]

v. 모욕하다   to offend
면전에(front) 대고 바로 f (af) word를 쓰며 모욕했다고 외워보자.
He hoped they would not feel **affronted** if they were not invited. (*v.*)

0638
exotic [4]
[ɪɡǀzɑːtɪk]

a. 외국의, 이국적인   of foreign origin or character
밖에서(exit → exot) 온 이국적인(exotic) 것들이라고 외워보자.
She travels to all kinds of **exotic** locations all over the world. (*adj.*)

0639
vengeance [²]
[véndʒəns]

n. 복수   violent revenge
revenge가 '복수'라는 뜻이므로 vengeance는 '복수'라는 의미이다.
A desire for **vengeance** (n.)

0640
rashly [⁵]
[rǽʃli]

adv. 성급하게, 분별없게   too hastily; without thinking of the consequences
rush가 '돌진하다, 급히 움직이다'의 뜻이니까, 급하게 움직이면(rush) 경솔한 (rash) 결정을 내리게 된다.
After **rashly** agreeing to marry him, Tiffany became so scared and regretful about her decision that she ran away from the wedding. (*adv.*)

0641
bristling [²]
[brísliŋ]

a. ~으로 꽉 찬   to be thickly set or filled with something
bristle은 동물의 뻣뻣한 털을 의미한다. 동물의 겉표면이 털로 꽉 차 있다고 외워보자.
He is **bristling** with energy and sheer force now. (*adj.*)

0642
righteous [⁴]
[|raɪtʃəs]

a. 도덕적으로 옳은   morally right or justifiable
right가 '옳다'는 의미이므로 도덕적으로 옳다고 외워보자.
His motive was to do the **righteous** thing. (*adj.*)

0643
polarized [²]
[|poʊləraɪzd]

a. 양극화된, 나뉜   divided, separated
polar이 '극'을 뜻하므로 polarized는 '양극화된'이라는 의미이다.
Public opinion has **polarized** on this issue. (*adj.*)

0644
repress [⁷]
[rɪ|pres]

v. 억누르다   to put pressure on; control
다시(re) 눌러서(press) 억누른다고(repress) 외워보자.
He burst in, making no effort to **repress** his fury. (*v.*)

0645
pragmatic [¹⁰]
[præg|mætɪk]

a. 실용적인   of a practical point of view or practical considerations
practical (현실성 있는)과 연관지어 외워보자.
We use it in a pretty **pragmatic** way. (*adj.*)

0646
premature ²
[prìːmətjúər]

a. 너무 이른, 시기상조의, 때 아닌   mature or ripe before the proper time, coming too soon
성숙하기(mature) 전(pre)이라는 의미이다.
It is easy to take **premature** action. (*adj.*)

0647
infringe ²
[infríndʒ]

v. 위반하다   to violate, disobey
사람의 자유를 (free → fri) 침범하는 것은 인간의 권리를 위반하는 짓이다.
The material can be copied without **infringing** copyright. (*v.*)

0648
verdict ⁴
[vɚ́ːrdikt]

n. 판결, (배심원의) 답신, 평결   a judgment, decision
ver 는 진실을 말한다. 따라서 진실을 가리는 평결을 뜻한다.
The judge's **verdict** for the accused was the death sentence. (*n.*)

0649
irrevocable ²
[irévəkəbl]

a. 변경할 수 없는   not to be revoked or recalled, unalterable; irreversible
in(not) + revocable(취소할 수 있는)
Use a pencil when writing a rough draft; if you make a mistake in pen, it's **irrevocable**. (*adj.*)

0650
preside ⁴
[prizáid]

v. 통제하다   to control, have authority over
한 쪽 편에(side) 서지 않고 자유롭게(free → pre) 모임을 통제한다고 외워보자.
They asked if I would **preside** at the committee meeting. (*v.*)

0651
noxious ³
[nákʃəs]

a. 해로운, 해독한   harmful, poisonous
'to harm'이란 어원을 가진 nocere 에서 파생된 단어다.
Noxious mushrooms can look and taste just like harmless ones. (*adj.*)

0652
contaminating ⁴
[kəntǽmineitiŋ]

a. 오염시키는   affecting negatively
사방이 막혀있는 컨테이너를(container → contami) 잘못 건드리면 안에 있는 걸 오염시킬(contaminate) 수 있다고 외워보자.
You are **contaminating** a crime scene. (*adj.*)

0653

conjecture ³

[kən|dʒektʃə(r)]

v. 추측하다; 추측(한 내용)   to assume, guess

과학 시간에 실험을 하기 전 결과를 미리 추측하는 것을 conjecture라고 하는 때가 있다.

The truth of his **conjecture** was confirmed by the newspaper report. (*n.*)

0654

roguish ²

[|roʊgɪʃ]

a. 악당 같은   acting like a rogue; knavish

도적이나 무법자를 rogue라고 한다. 따라서 roguish는 '악당 같은'이라는 의미이다.

Meanwhile, the **roguish** Jackson may be seeking more than just retribution. (*adj.*)

Episode 38
MATCHING Quiz

1. aggressive
2. exile
3. beget
4. turbulence
5. disruptive
6. partisan
7. reticent
8. exemplify
9. disparage
10. affront
11. exotic
12. vengeance
13. rashly
14. bristling
15. righteous
16. polarized
17. repress
18. pragmatic
19. premature
20. infringe

A. to create, cause
B. expulsion from one's native land by authoritative decree
C. preventing something from acting in a normal way
D. hostile, contentious
E. to illustrate by example; typify
F. trouble and chaos
G. an adherent or supporter of a person, group, party, or cause
H. of foreign origin or character
I. to speak of or treat slightly
J. disposed to be silent or not to speak freely
K. too hastily; without thinking of the consequences
L. to offend
M. to be thickly set or filled with something
N. morally right or justifiable
O. to put pressure on; control
P. violent revenge
Q. mature or ripe before the proper time
R. divided, separated
S. to violate, disobey
T. of a practical point of view or practical considerations

1-D, 2-B, 3-A, 4-F, 5-C, 6-G, 7-J, 8-E, 9-I, 10-L, 11-H, 12-P, 13-K, 14-M, 15-N, 16-R, 17-O, 18-T, 19-Q, 20-S

더 많은 문제를 풀고자 한다면 www.quizlet.com에서 'paul academy seoul' class를 검색

Episode 39: The Hamburger Mafia

655 desolate [4]
a. 적막한 empty and gloomy

656 forgo [1]
v. 포기하다 to give up

657 stern [7]
a. 엄격한, 단호한 strict, harsh

658 resolute [14]
a. 단호한 firmly resolved or determined

659 mergence [3]
n. 합체, 융합 coming together or uniting; coalescence
v. merge

660 reaffirmed [2]
a. 확인된, 확언된 acknowledged, affirmed

661 profane [2]
a. 불경한 impious or irreverent

662 stifle [4]
v. 억누르다 to suppress

663 intermittently [6]
adv. 간간이 occasionally

664 relegated [4]
a. 좌천[강등]당한 sent down to a lower level

665 foremost [3]
a. 가장 중요한 primary, most important

666 embodied [7]
a. 구현된, 표현된 represented, manifested

After five weeks of daily study, crammed into the same classrooms and breathing the same air, after having nearly been killed by Terry and the demons of alcohol and gambling, Jake and TJ were now close friends, each relying on the other for friendship and support. The company of TJ made Jake feel like the summer was not quite as **desolate** as he had expected it to be, even if he had been forced to **forgo** his phone to the **stern** guards each day.

TJ, too, clearly enjoyed the company of such a **resolute** companion and a soulmate, spirit, and his scores seemed to be climbing, much to his surprise. Had they been older and featured in a sitcom, they would probably have had a tear-filled conversation about how much they valued each other, but this was the real world (or as real as any academy could be), and the **mergence** of their little social circle was merely **reaffirmed** by **profane** conversations and private jokes.

Their daily routine featured the same run down the stairs to the street at ten o'clock, after the first class had ended, to **stifle** their hunger with junk food purchased at the convenience store. TJ still smoked **intermittently**, but one of the teachers had caught him at it one day, and had warned him that his mother would be told if he were caught again, and that if that happened he'd be sent to a lower class. He decided that he didn't want to be **relegated** to the lowest class, and so smoked secretly if at all. Still, the **foremost** motivation for their morning trips was the boys' breakfast, which was almost always **embodied** in the microwaveable hamburgers sold for a dollar in the sandwich section. The two of them, accompanied by the ever-silent Sam, would throw their brunches in together and watch the plastic bags fill with steam before running back to avoid being scolded by the next hour's teacher.

This routine gained the three of them the title of "the Hamburger Mafia", though the second part was not fully accurate, since their interests were mostly **innocuous** and they had so far not attempted to murder anyone or steal any **lucrative** business funds. They all **deputed** themselves the role of "President for Life," and decided that their children could continue their **reign** in the style of ancient kings.

667 **innocuous** [3]
a. 악의 없는 harmless

668 **lucrative** [5]
a. 수익성이 좋은 profitable

669 **depute** [2]
v. 위임[위탁]하다 to appoint, instruct

670 **reign** [5]
n. 통치기간 the period during a king or queen rules a country

Vocabulary

0655
desolate [4]
[désəlǝt]

a. 적막한, 고독한 empty and gloomy, rob of joy; lay waste to; forsake
isolate 된 땅은 desolate하다.
Robinson felt **desolate** on the deserted island because there was nobody to talk to. (*adj.*)

0656
forgo [1]
[fɔːrgóu]

v. 포기하다, 없이 지내다 to give up, do without
forgo는 for-(away)와 go가 합쳐져 go away → 떠나서 ~없이 지내다
If you are in a hurry, please **forgo** the usual morning routine. (*v.*)

0657
stern [7]
[stɜːrn]

a. 엄격한, 단호한 strict, harsh
strict(엄격한), stiff(빳빳한)과 함께 외워보자.
Her voice was **stern**. (*adj.*)

0658
resolute [14]
[ǀrezəluːt]

a. 단호한 firmly resolved or determined
새해 결심을 New Year's resolution이라고 하는 걸 들어봤을 것이다.
단호하게 새해 결심을 해야 한다고 외워보자.
Even the **resolute** officer began to feel hopeless. (*adj.*)

0659
mergence [3]
[mɜ́ːrdʒəns]

n. 합체, 융합 coming together or uniting; coalescence
v. merge
남자와 (man → mer) 여자가 (girl → ge) 하나로 합쳐졌다고 외워보자.
The **mergence** of the two companies resulted in a monopoly.

0660
reaffirmed [2]
[ǀriːəǀfɜːrmd]

a. 확인된, 확언된 acknowledged, affirmed
회사에서 서류 컨펌을(confirm) 받는다는 말을 들어봤을 것이다. confirm은 affirm과 같이 '확인하다'라는 뜻으로 reaffirm은 다시 확인했으므로 확실히 확인됐다는 뜻이다.
We **reaffirm** our most strident protests against this position. (*v.*)

0661
profane [prəˈfeɪn]

a. **불경한**　impious or irreverent
교회에서 불을 자연스러운 방법으로 피우지 않고 프로페인을(propane) 사용해 피웠다고 불경하다는 (profane) 소리를 들었다.
He uses too much **profane** language. (*adj.*)

0662
stifle [stáifl]

v. **억누르다**　to suppress, to quiet down
silencing과 비슷하다.
Stifle a noise. (*v.*)

0663
intermittently [ˌɪntərˈmɪtəntli]

adv. **간간이**　occasionally
연극이나 뮤지컬 중간에 인터미션이(intermission) 나온 적이 있을 것이다. 무언가 도중에 간간히(intermittently) 나오는 것이 인터미션이다.
It has been raining **intermittently** for a week. (*adv.*)

0664
relegated [ˈrelɪɡeɪtɪd]

a. **좌천[강등] 당한**　sent down to a lower level
원래 정상에 섰다가 다시(re) 리그에서 경쟁하게(league → leg) 강등당했다고(relegate) 외워보자.
She was then **relegated** to the role of assistant. (*adj.*)

0665
foremost [ˈfɔːrmoʊst]

a. **가장 중요한, 첫번째의**　primary, most important, first in place, order, rank, etc
most가 '가장, 제일'이니까, foremost는 가장 중요한 거지.
The **foremost** reason I cannot eat broccoli is because I'm fatally allergic. (*adj.*)

0666
embodied [ɪmˈbɑːdid]

a. **구현된, 표현된**　represented, manifested
무언가에 몸(body → bodi)을 주어서 표현되었다고 외워보자.
These ideals were **embodied** in the constitution. (*adj.*)

0667
innocuous [ɪˈnɑːkjuəs]

a. **악의 없는**　harmless
innocent '결백한'과 연결해서 외워보자.
It seemed so **innocuous** at the time. (*adj.*)

0668
lucrative [⁵]

[ˈluːkrətɪv]

a. 수익성이 좋은   profitable
운(luck → luc)이 많으면 수익성이 좋은(lucrative) 사업을 할 수 있다.
A **lucrative** business/contract/market (*adj.*)

0669
depute [²]

[dɪˈpjuːt]

v. 위임[위탁]하다   to appoint as one's representative, instruct
deputy로 세우는 거니까 deputed가 되겠지.
The babysitter was **deputed** to look after Jack-Jack while his parents were away. (*v.*)

0670
reign [⁵]

[reɪn]

n. 통치기간   the period during a king or queen rules a country
rule '통치하다'와 연결해서 외워보자.
The **reign** of Queen Victoria (*n.*)

Episode 39

MATCHING Quiz

1. desolate
2. forgo
3. stern
4. resolute
5. mergence
6. reaffirmed
7. profane
8. stifle
9. intermittently
10. relegated
11. foremost
12. embodied
13. innocuous
14. lucrative
15. depute
16. reign

A. to give up
B. strict, harsh
C. coming together or uniting; coalescence
D. firmly resolved or determined
E. acknowledged, affirmed
F. occasionally
G. impious or irreverent
H. to suppress
I. sent down to a lower level
J. to appoint, instruct
K. empty and gloomy
L. represented, manifested
M. primary, most important
N. profitable
O. the period during a king or queen rules a country
P. harmless

1-K, 2-A, 3-B, 4-D, 5-C, 6-E, 7-G, 8-H, 9-F, 10-I, 11-M, 12-L, 13-P, 14-N, 15-J, 16-O

더 많은 문제를 풀고자 한다면 www.quizlet.com에서 'paul academy seoul' class를 검색

Episode 40: Cleave Means Two Things

It was Friday night of week five, and after a few dates and two powerful but nothing-more-than kisses after first meeting Jessica, Jake was enjoying the peace which love brings. He was just generally satisfied, he decided, even with all the other ups and downs of the past few weeks. Lost in that peaceful focus, he had not noticed that the once innocent tone of their conversations had become somewhat more focused on studying. He accepted her renewed **vigor** for a better score, and had actually enjoyed having fewer problems with his homework questions. Even his reading comprehension seemed to have improved.

However, the **counterfeit** image of innocence was beginning to fade, even if he was unaware of the gathering storm clouds which were hidden in the **connotations** of her conversations with him. Jake did not know, but Jessica had grown **disenchanted** with his lack of interest in her studying. "Why can't I do better?" she'd sometimes mutter under her breath, then, looking at him, ask why he was improving and she wasn't. The tone had grown more obvious as the days had drawn on.

In truth, he had a **fuzzy** idea of why he was doing well. More and more words were coming to his mind more easily, and he had decided a little **bombastically** to use them in conversation. He found that she could do much better if he said the words in his own context, or **explicated** them to her. She, on the other hand, was not doing as well, and didn't enjoy his amateur scholarship as much as he did.

He had arranged a meeting at a Chinese restaurant near the academy, where he sat staring anxiously out the window. He was just beginning to think that the world of love and scholarship were not entirely mutually exclusive when she came in the door.

"Hello!" he called cheerfully. "I was just about to send the police to find you."

---

671 vigor [10]
n. 활력
liveliness or energy; earnestness

672 counterfeit [3]
a. 위조의, 모조의
made in imitation; not genuine

673 connotation [7]
n. 함축된 의미
the associated or secondary meaning
v. connote

674 disenchanted [3]
a. 환상에서 깨어난
free from enchantment, illusion, or credulity

675 fuzzy [2]
a. 어렴풋한
indistinct, blurred

676 bombastically [2]
adv. 과장되게, 허풍스럽게
pretentiously
n. bombast

677 explicate [5]
v. 설명하다
to explain, expound

678 colossal [3]
a. 거대한, 엄청난
enormous, huge

679 abject [3]
a. 아주 비참한
hopeless or very low

She dropped her **colossal** bags on the opposite chair and greeted his innocent comment with little happiness.

"What are you so happy about?" she asked sharply.

"Nothing, I guess. Just happy to see you," he said, calmly. "I ordered some spring rolls for you. Is that OK?"

"Ugh, I never asked you to do that. We're not married, Jake." She stared icily at him as she delivered this anger, showing none of the affection she had shown before.

"Well, I'm sorry. What happened?" Jake was justifiably hurt by this slight, but decided everything could be remedied by some conversation.

"Nothing *happened*. It's just… you don't really pay attention, do you?"

"What do you mean?" He had not expected this drama tonight. Had he done something wrong?

"I *mean*," she said, "that these study sessions haven't been that productive, have they? I mean, we've had fun, but it's just… my scores are still so low."

"Well, they'll go up," he said.

"Not while we're hanging out like this," she said flatly. "I'm gonna go home now. I'll text you later. *Don't* follow me out."

She walked out just as the waitress brought over two trays of steaming porridge. It might as well have been prison food to Jake, though. He thought about following her anyway, but she had been pretty clear. He looked out the window as she hurried down the sidewalk, and turned back to take a few **abject** bites before deciding he was in no mood for dinner.

Vocabulary

0671
vigor [10]
[vígər]

n. 활력, 원기   liveliness or energy; earnestness, vitality; energy
vit- 'life'를 뜻한다. 즉, '활력'이란 뜻이다.
After drinking four cups of coffee, he recovered his original **vigor**. (*n.*)

0672
counterfeit [3]
[káuntərfit]

a. 위조의, 모조의, 허위의   made in imitation; not genuine, unreal; imitated
'counter' 반대의 fit '원조에 어울리지 못하는, 속하지 못하는', 즉 '모조의'란 뜻이다.
The **counterfeit** painting was so skilled that some art experts thought it was real. (*adj.*)

0673
connotation [7]
[|kɑːnəteɪʃn]

n. 함축된 의미   the associated or secondary meaning
v. connote
코난이 하는 말에는 항상 함축된 의미가 있다고 외워보자.
I do not think it has a political **connotation**. (*n.*)

0674
disenchanted [3]
[|dɪsɪn|tʃæntɪd]

a. 환상에서 깨어난   free from enchantment, illusion, or credulity
enchant가 마법을 걸다는 의미이므로 마법으로부터 풀려나서(dis) 환상에서 깨어났다는(disenchant) 뜻이다.
He was becoming **disenchanted** with his job as a lawyer. (*adj.*)

0675
fuzzy [2]
[|fʌzi]

a. 어렴풋한   indistinct, blurred
f 나 z 발음은 입술이 떨리게 한다. 계속 떨려서 확실하게 보이거나 들리지 않고 어렴풋하다고 외우자.
The soundtrack is **fuzzy** in places. (*adj.*)

0676
bombastically [2]
[bɑmbǽstikəli]

adv. 과장되게, 허풍스럽게   pretentiously   *n.* bombast
폭탄이(bomb) 터진 것처럼 과장시켜서 얘기한다고 외워보자.
A **bombastic** speaker (*adj.*)

0677
explicate [|ekspləkeɪt] 5

v. 설명하다   to explain, expound
explain과 연결해서 외워보자.
They've been working hard to **explicate** Marx's theory. (*v.*)

0678
colossal [kəlásəl] 3

a. 거대한, 엄청난   enormous, huge, gigantic
로마에 있는 colosseum(콜로세움)처럼 엄청나다고 해석할 수 있다.
The Great Wall of China is so **colossal** that you can see it even from outer space. (*adj.*)

0679
abject [|æbdʒekt] 3

a. 아주 비참한   hopeless or very low
고백했다고 거절당해서(reject) 매우 비참한(abject) 상황이라고 외워보자.
The family lived in **abject** poverty. (*adj.*)

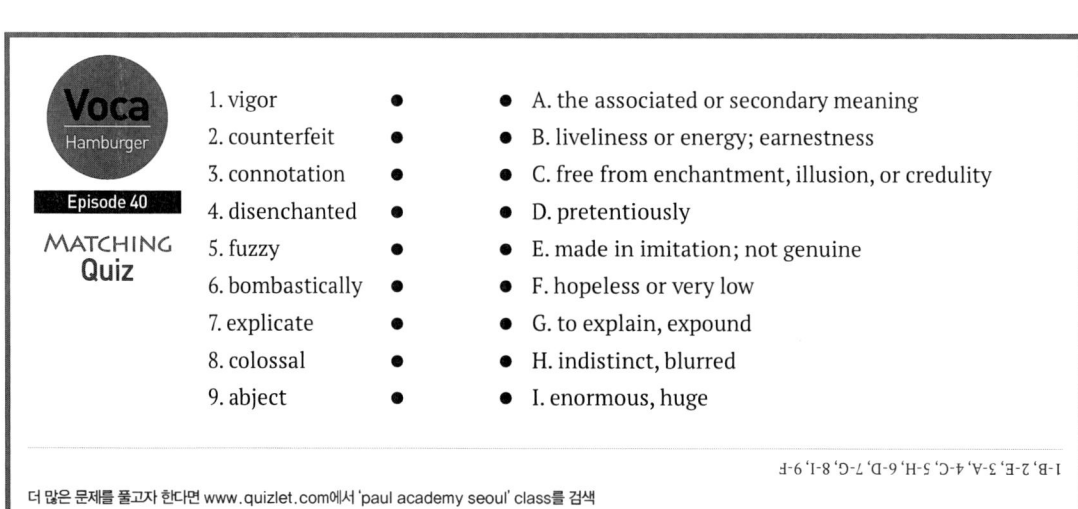

Episode 40 — MATCHING Quiz

1. vigor — A. the associated or secondary meaning
2. counterfeit — B. liveliness or energy; earnestness
3. connotation — C. free from enchantment, illusion, or credulity
4. disenchanted — D. pretentiously
5. fuzzy — E. made in imitation; not genuine
6. bombastically — F. hopeless or very low
7. explicate — G. to explain, expound
8. colossal — H. indistinct, blurred
9. abject — I. enormous, huge

1-B, 2-E, 3-A, 4-C, 5-H, 6-D, 7-G, 8-I, 9-F

더 많은 문제를 풀고자 한다면 www.quizlet.com에서 'paul academy seoul' class를 검색

Episode 41

Fear

The next day, a Saturday, Jake did not have a good practice test, and had done much worse than the previous few weeks. He knew why, though, and it all centered on that damned conversation the night before. Once he had received the bad news (490 in reading, 1120 overall), he dashed up the stairs two at a time to the fourth floor, wondering what sort of message Jessica had sent. However, the surly Pink Face, who had **patently** never been in love, was overly slow when getting his phone and beloved iPod from the box.

"Come on, TA. I've got places to go to," he complained.

"Where are you in such a hurry to get to?" she asked playfully.

"Important places," he said quickly.

"Oh?" she asked with a laugh. "Got a date tonight, Jake?" she **probed**. The girl behind him laughed noisily and a few of the other students glanced over.

"None of your business," he said finally. "Just give me those."

"Fine," she said, looking a bit hurt. "Just joking around."

Jake, red-faced from embarrassment and impatience, finally had his phone. He needed to know why she had acted so coldly the night before, why his relationship seemed to have ended before it had begun.

When he turned the phone on, there was only one message, which was from a salesman, trying to offer him an easy loan for all his housing needs. He was deeply disappointed, and unfortunately it must have showed.

"What's bugging you?" Ashley asked as they took the elevator down together.

---

680 patently [4]
adv. 명백히, 틀림없이
obviously; blatantly

681 probe [11]
v. 캐묻다, 조사하다
to search into or examine thoroughly

682 deceit [3]
n. 속임수, 기만
duplicity, deception

683 pompous [2]
a. 거만한
arrogant, pretentious

684 contemptuous [20]
a. 경멸하는
feeling something is inferior or worthy of hatred; dismissive

685 abnormal [4]
a. 비정상의
not normal; deviating from what is usual

686 complicity [2]
n. 공모
partnership in wrongdoing (as accomplices)

"Oh, nothing."

"It's funny. For a boy, you are a really bad liar."

"What do you mean, 'for a boy?'?"

"Well, aren't boys supposed to be better than girls at that stuff? Cheating and lying and all of that **deceit**? My feminist friend once said that you can't spell 'mendacious' without 'men.'"

Jake looked at her blankly.

"Maybe that's just a stereotype, though," she said, looking apologetic.

"You know, you have a bad habit of being too **pompous**," he said finally, as the doors were opening at the first floor. He ran out into the dying sunlight without waiting for a reply.

"Jake, wait!" she called as he reached the miniature fir tree. When he looked back, she appeared much smaller against the black of the doorway, wearing white shorts and a blue shirt. Almost pretty.

"What?" he yelled, trying to act more **contemptuous** than he felt. Sometimes it feels good to be mad.

"Well, it seemed like you got upset when you checked your messages. I think I might understand."

"Oh yeah?" he looked at her suspiciously. "What do you know about it?"

"Well..." She hesitated. This kind of personal connection was **abnormal** to her. "You were waiting for a message from that girl, right?"

"Yeah, I guess so."

"It's annoying when people don't message, huh?"

Jake looked at her. There was something that she wasn't talking about, but she was feeling it anyway. He dropped his anger.

"It is," he said finally, sincerely. He waited to see if she would add anything more. Whatever it was, he hoped that she could handle it herself. Friends are friends, but love is love.

The mystery girl with the teddy bear just stood there, however, without giving any further explanation for herself.

"Never mind. I hope everything's OK," she finally finished.

"Thanks." He meant it, but he was soon on his way regardless, looking at his phone to see if he had any emails waiting for him. On the way to the subway, his phone buzzed once more and he saw the familiar name at the top of the text:

I'm at home. Sorry about earlier. Why don't you come over? We can talk here.

He responded instantly and then called his mother to say that his study group was having an emergency meeting to review some particularly difficult grammar rules they had learned that day. Luckily, Susan's **complicity** in his lie had kept his mother ignorant of his romance, and she allowed him to go. As he was waiting for directions to Jessica's house, he received another text:

The car's coming to you now. Just stand outside the Starbucks and wait. It's a black Bentley.

He waited at that fateful point where they had first met, looking down the long stairwell as office workers, students, teachers, and other more mysterious travelers headed down toward the colorful blur of the evening commute. He, on the other hand, was moving in a different direction. As the car approached, he wondered for a moment why Ashley had said that to him, and what her suddenly sad tone was meant to communicate. But as the automatic car door opened to accept him, and he slid in the back seat to be greeted as 'sir' by the respectful driver, he quickly forgot all about it.

Vocabulary

0680
patently [4]
[ˈpætəntli]

adv. **명백히, 틀림없이**   obviously; blatantly
우리는 우리의 부모님이(parent → patent) 누구인지 명백하게(patently) 알 수 있다.
Her explanation was **patently** ridiculous. (*adv.*)

0681
probe [11]
[próub]

v. **캐묻다, 조사하다; 우주탐색기**   to search into or examine thoroughly; an unmanned spacecraft designed to explore the solar system
어떠한 것을 prove '증명'하기 위해서는 probe해야 한다.
A government **probed** into the cause of the disaster. (*v.*)

0682
deceit [3]
[dɪˈsiːt]

n. **속임수, 기만**   duplicity, deception
속임수로(deceit) 여럿을 죽음에(death → dec) 빠뜨렸다고 외워보자.
He was accused of lies and **deceit**. (*n.*)

0683
pompous [2]
[pámpəs]

a. **거만한**   arrogant, pretentious, marked by an assumed stateliness and impressiveness of manner
너무 거만해서(pompous) 가슴에 힘이 잔뜩 들어간 상태(pumped).
The **pompous** politician wouldn't stop boasting. (*adj.*)

0684
contemptuous [20]
[kənˈtemptʃuəs]

a. **경멸하는, 업신여기는**   feeling something is inferior or worthy of hatred; dismissive
누군가를 경멸하며(contempt) 가짜로(con) 유혹했다고(tempt) 외워보자.
Don't be **contemptuous** of the poor. (*adj.*)

0685
abnormal [4]
[æbˈnɔːrml]

a. **비정상의**   not normal; deviating from what is usual
정상이(normal) 아니라는(ab) 뜻이다.
Abnormal levels of sugar in the blood (*adj.*)

0686
complicity [kəm|plɪsəti]

n. 공모 partnership in wrongdoing (as accomplices)

범죄에서 공범을 accomplice라고 하는 걸 들어봤을 것이다. 같은 단어가 들어간 complicity는 공모라는 의미를 가지고 있다.

He was taken up on a charge of **complicity** in the riot. (*n.*)

Episode 41
MATCHING Quiz

1. patently
2. probe
3. deceit
4. pompous
5. contemptuous
6. abnormal
7. complicity

A. arrogant, pretentious
B. to search into or examine thoroughly
C. not normal; deviating from what is usual
D. feeling something is inferior or worthy of hatred; dismissive
E. partnership in wrongdoing (as accomplices)
F. duplicity, deception
G. obviously; blatantly

1-G, 2-B, 3-F, 4-A, 5-D, 6-C, 7-E

더 많은 문제를 풀고자 한다면 www.quizlet.com에서 'paul academy seoul' class를 검색

Episode 42 — Social Mobility

687 pristine ⁴
a. 완전 새 것 같은
having its original purity; uncorrupted

688 alternative ⁴⁰
a. 대안적인
(of one or more things) available as another possibility

689 overshadow ⁴
v. 그늘을 드리우다
to make obscure or dim

690 furnish ⁵
v. 비치하다
to decorate, supply

691 configured ²
a. 구성된, 배열된
arranged, structured

692 elaborate ¹⁰
a. 정교한
worked out with great care and nicety of detail

693 designated ²
a. 지정된
nominated; selected for duty

694 impoverished ⁴
a. 빈약한, 형편 없는
poor, deprived of strength

695 envisage ²
v. 예상, 상상하다
to imagine

To say that Jessica's family was wealthy would be an understatement. In truth, they were the richest people with whom Jake had ever been associated, and their living style reflected this. Upon being picked up by their private Bentley (driven, of course, by a driver in a **pristine** black suit), he felt like he had entered an **alternative** city, one in which the street was **overshadowed** by tinted windows and in which personal duties could all be handled by the private car, the call-service, or the helpful servant.

The house was another issue altogether. As the car sped down the road, Jake was aware that the regular neighborhood of the academy with its generic middle class apartment buildings was fading into the background. They were climbing into an area which he'd always assumed to be off-limits: where Jessica had grown up, where large walls hid the view of massive homes. They were **furnished** with large, beautifully-cut hedges, **configured** in sheer walls or pleasantly uneven shapes, with **elaborate** security systems and private guards **designated** outside. One such of these, a red brick mansion with a matching wall in a colonial English style, was what Jake faced when the driver told him that this was the place, and that someone would let him in through the front gate.

Stepping out and letting the car door close automatically behind him (the driver having told him not to close it with his dirty and **impoverished** fingers), Jake felt small next to the high walls and the three stories of house that towered over him. He suddenly became aware that, to anyone else who might be on this street at this hour, he might look like he was trespassing. He hurried over to the gate and hid in the shadows.

Pressing the buzzer near the garden gate, he **envisaged** what their living arrangement must be. The inside must be like some **palatial**, **ostentatious** English country house, he decided, with rows of animal heads adorning the walls and a collection of servants assigned to various tasks. Her parents, she had said, were **fickle** people, always fighting and arguing over little things in the most immature way. Maybe rather than shouting, they call each other on telephones from either side of the house? Suddenly, the buzzer sounded and the door swung open, opening onto a patch of grass where a few broad flat rocks were scattered to walk on, each **illuminated** by a small light. A set of stairs led up to a small balcony, on which Jessica stood, her eyes, as usual, covered by a large pair of sunglasses.

"You know it's nighttime, right?" Jake called up to her. "You don't look cool with those things on, just blind."

It was too dim to see whether or not she was smiling, but she called out "come up and take them, then!" in a **disinterested** tone.

He looked down to get a good footing on the rocks, and skipped across the lawn. Leaping up the steps two-by-two, he appeared next to her in about ten seconds, out of breath. After looking at her, he followed her gaze to the city below them, blinking in the twilight, with lines of cars reaching to the horizon, sitting quietly in the evening rush hour. It seemed that they were on Olympus, merely surveying the pointless comings and goings of the human world from their **celestial** tower.

"How was the drive?" she asked without changing her position.

"Ok, but the car was so cheap. Really, I expected something a bit more **sumptuous**." He tried to pull a funny expression but noticed that she still hadn't faced him.

"You alright?" he asked nervously.

"Yeah, of course," she said, her face again **depicting** no clear emotion.

"Nothing... happened?"

"Just parents stuff," she replied, in a voice that sounded decades older than she was.

"Oh," he said, and they stood in silence a while, contemplating age and adulthood and cars and houses as the city rolled out beneath them.

---

696 palatial [2]
a. 으리으리한
grand, opulent

697 ostentatious [4]
a. 호사스러운
very showy or expensive-looking

698 fickle [2]
a. 변덕스러운
temperamental, capricious

699 illuminated [10]
a. 빛이 비춰지는
supplied or brightened with light

700 disinterested [3]
a. 객관적인, 무관심한
neutral

701 celestial [4]
a. 하늘의, 천체의
heavenly; sublime; ethereal

702 sumptuous [5]
a. 호화스러운
fancy, luxurious

703 depict [17]
v. 그리다
to represent by or as if by painting

Vocabulary

0687
pristine [4]
[prístiːn]

a. 완전 새 것 같은, 본래의 — having its original purity; uncorrupted, primitive
pri(before)를 어원으로 갖고 있어 'pertaining to the earliest period'의 뜻을 갖고 있다.
My uncle's **pristine** car looks as though it were made yesterday. (*adj.*)

0688
alternative [40]
[ɔːltɜːrnətɪv]

a. 대안적인 — (of one or more things) available as another possibility
alter는 '바꾸다'는 뜻이다. 그러니까 alternative는 원래 계획이 실패했을 때 바꿀 수 있는 대안적인 계획이 있다고 외워보자.
Do you have an **alternative** solution? (*adj.*)

0689
overshadow [4]
[òuvərʃǽdou]

v. 그늘을 드리우다, 그늘지게 하다 — to make obscure or dim
shadow가 '그림자'라는 데서 유래한 단어이다.
The garden is **overshadowed** by tall trees. (*v.*)

0690
furnish [5]
[ˈfɜːrnɪʃ]

v. 비치하다 — to decorate, supply
가구를(furniture) 비치했다고(furnish) 외우자.
The room was **furnished** with antiques. (*v.*)

0691
configured [2]
[kənˈfɪɡjərd]

a. 구성된, 배열된 — arranged, structured
특정한 모양(figure)으로 배열했다고(configure) 외워보자.
Please enter the e-mail address you would like to **configure**. (*v.*)

0692
elaborate [10]
[ɪˈlæbərət]

a. 정교한, 정성을 들인, 자세히 설명하다 — worked out with great care and nicety of detail, to work out carefully or minutely, involving many carefully arranged parts or details
열심히 노동하여(labor) 정성을 들인(elaborate) 것이라고 외워보자.
The instructions on the test were unclear, so I asked the teacher to **elaborate**. (*v.*)

0693
designated ²
[dézignèitid]

a. **지정된**　nominated; selected for duty
무대 디자인을(design) 하기 전에 모두에게 역할을 지정해 준다고 (designate) 외워보자.
The officer was **designated** for[to] the command. (*v.*)

0694
impoverished ⁴
[impávəriʃt]

a. **빈약한, 형편 없는, 가난해진, 힘을 잃은**　poor, deprived of strength
poverty '가난'에서 파생된 단어이다.
The **impoverished** family had to burn newspapers for heat and look for food in public trashcans. (*adj.*)

0695
envisage ²
[inǀvizidʒ]

v. **예상, 상상하다**　to imagine, to contemplate; visualize
sage는 '현자'인데 envi는 '부럽다'라는 envy와 비슷하다. 그래서 현자가 부러운 가장 큰 이유는 무엇? 바로 미래를 예측한다는 것이다. 즉 envisage는 '미래를 상상하다'는 뜻.
Although he **envisaged** a great profit, he actually faced a great loss. (*v.*)

0696
palatial ²
[pəǀleiʃl]

a. **으리으리한**　grand, opulent
궁전처럼(palace → palati) 으리으리하다는 의미이다.
Palatial family house with high ceilings and grand balcony. (*adj.*)

0697
ostentatious ⁴
[ὰstentéiʃəs]

a. **호사스러운, 허세를 부리는**　very showy or expensive-looking, expensive and intended to impress people
'보여주다'의 의미를 가진 어원 ostentare에서 유래한 단어이다.
It was too clear that the **ostentatious** man bought the new car just to show-off and brag.(*adj.*)

0698
fickle ²
[fĭkl]

a. **변덕스러운, 변하기 쉬운**　temperamental, capricious, casually changeable
고대 영어로는 'ficol' 인데 tricky(교활한, 음흉한)의 뜻이다.
The **fickle** child hated pickles one day, then loved them the next day (*adj.*)

0699
illuminated [10]

[ɪ|luːmɪneɪtɪd]

a. 빛이 비춰지는   supplied or brightened with light

영화 해리포터에서 lumos는 빛을 밝히는 주문이다. 이것과 비슷한 illuminate는 '빛을 밝히다'라는 의미이다.

The bright moon **illuminated** the night sky so the lovers could see each other's faces. (*v.*)

0700
disinterested [3]

[dɪsíntərèstɪd]

a. 객관적인, 무관심한, 사심이 없는, 공평한   neutral, impartial

이익(interest)를 원하지 않는(dis)이란 의미이다.

We should invite a **disinterested** judge if we want a fair verdict on this case. (*adj.*)

0701
celestial [4]

[səlestʃl]

a. 하늘의, 천체의   heavenly; sublime; ethereal

고대 그리스 달의 여신인 셀레네(Selene → cele)와 연결해서 외워보자.

The moon is a mysterious **celestial** body.

0702
sumptuous [5]

[sʌ́mptʃuəs]

a. 호화스러운, , 사치스러운   fancy, luxurious, splendid and expensive-looking

sumpt(take) + uous : '많이 취하는'이란 뜻으로 '사치스러운, 호화스러운'이라는 의미이다.

King Joffrey likes **sumptuous** clothes made of expensive silk and furs.(*adj.*)

0703
depict [17]

[dipíkt]

v. 그리다; 묘사하다, 서술하다   to represent by or as if by painting, to portray

'the picture 를 묘사하다'라고 생각하자.

The painting "Last Supper" depicts Jesus's last meal with his **disciples**. (*v.*)

Note :

Episode 42

MATCHING Quiz

1. pristine • • A. having its original purity; uncorrupted
2. alternative • • B. to decorate, supply
3. overshadow • • C. very showy or expensive-looking
4. furnish • • D. arranged, structured
5. configured • • E. (of one or more things) available as another possibility
6. elaborate • • F. worked out with great care and nicety of detail
7. designated • • G. poor, deprived of strength
8. impoverished • • H. grand, opulent
9. envisage • • I. nominated; selected for duty
10. palatial • • J. temperamental, capricious
11. ostentatious • • K. to make obscure or dim
12. fickle • • L. to represent by or as if by painting
13. illuminated • • M. to imagine
14. disinterested • • N. fancy, luxurious
15. celestial • • O. heavenly; sublime; ethereal
16. sumptuous • • P. supplied or brightened with light
17. depict • • Q. neutral

1-A, 2-E, 3-K, 4-B, 5-D, 6-F, 7-I, 8-G, 9-M, 10-H, 11-C, 12-J, 13-P, 14-Q, 15-O, 16-N, 17-L

더 많은 문제를 풀고자 한다면 www.quizlet.com에서 'paul academy seoul' class를 검색

Episode 43: Alas, Fair Jessica, I Knew Her Well

704 sardonically [4]
adv. 냉소적으로
sarcastically

705 despair [11]
n. 절망
feeling of hopelessness

706 ruptured [2]
a. 파열된
broken apart; exploded

707 sterile [3]
a. 아무 소득이 없는
not productive of results, ideas, etc.

708 feasible [3]
a. 실현 가능한
possible

709 inadequate [13]
a. 불충분한
not adequate or sufficient

710 catastrophically [3]
adv. 파멸로, 비극으로
disastrously

711 empathy [16]
n. 감정이입, 공감
feeling of pity or sadness for another person's distress

"I don't know what to do about my parents, Jake. My father went to Harvard, so he thinks the sun shines out of his butt, and he's always telling me that I need to go to a top school like him. My mother, too. She went to a famous liberal arts college, and keeps looking at my scores with the same disappointed look. 'Why can't you just try harder?' she'll say, and then nothing else. She's got other things to do, I guess."

Jake looked over at her again. She had been crying behind her glasses, and her voice was light.

"You could kill them, I guess," he offered **sardonically**, trying to cut through her sadness and **despair**.

"Ugh. Why can't you be serious about this, huh?"

"What? As serious as your parents? As serious as my mother? You think I want to die of a heart attack before I'm forty?"

"My heart feels **ruptured** already." She finally looked at him, her forehead changed into a frown. She still looked incredible, he thought, but there was something he couldn't quite help, no matter how hard he tried. To please a parent was **sterile**.

"Come on, it's **feasible**. You're improving, right?"

"But not enough! To them, I am **inadequate**. How am I supposed to get to a top school by next year if I can't even get a 600 in reading?"

"Well, I can't do that, either. Not yet, but —" he offered his hand over to her side of the balcony in a **catastrophically** ill-timed gesture of **empathy**.

She brushed his hand away as if it were an unwelcome insect.

"You're not me, Jake, alright? Don't compare us as if you have the same problems."

"What, because I'm not rich?" He looked back at the house, with its medieval design and **anachronistic** construction. Nonetheless, wasn't he entitled to treat her as an equal? Weren't they both just students?

"Don't be an idiot," she said, her tone acid. "You don't have parents who went to schools like that, do you? And at least you talk to your father. I barely even see mine."

"I talked to him one time! And you know what he said? He said that I shouldn't **squander** my life doing something I don't want to do. He understood. Just for a second. Maybe he was drunk, but at least his face looked honest."

"So what? You think that means he wants you to quit school and join the circus?"

"Well, no, but at least I know that he won't stop loving me."

"Oh, of course they won't do that!" She seemed on the **verge** of tears once more. "They'll never stop loving you, but at some point that love becomes a horrible **encumbrance**, a burden you have to deal with, a pressure. 'We love you, honey, and we want you to succeed. We don't want to see you fail by not trying.' You hear that sentence? My mother said that to *me*. Fail or try. They never say anything about failing WHILE trying. They don't think it's possible."

She broke down into a **havoc** of tears, sobs, and cursing. Jake felt far away from her suddenly, like she'd cut him **adrift** from her ship so he could float among the flotsam of the '**inferior** people' who couldn't understand a rich girl's problems. He put his arm around her shoulders but felt none of the love he'd felt a few days before. She didn't brush him off this time, but let his hand lie still on her. He felt useless to her, and he realized that was actually ok with him now.

After she had stopped crying quite so hard, he decided it was time to say, "Maybe I should go."

---

712 anachronistic [4]
a. 시대착오적인
not fitting the times; from the wrong time period

713 squander [4]
v. 낭비하다
to waste, use up

714 verge [3]
n. 가장자리, 맨 끝
the limit or point beyond which something occurs; brink

715 encumbrance [5]
n. 짐, 폐
burden or hardship

716 havoc [3]
n. 대파괴, 큰 피해
great destruction of devastation

717 adrift [2]
a. 표류하는, 떠내려가는
floating without control; drifting

718 inferior [5]
a. 낮은, 열등한
lower, less in rank

719 fissure [5]
n. 길게 갈라진 틈
a narrow opening produced by cleavage or separation of parts

She rose and his arm fell down her back.

"Yes, perhaps you should." she began. He felt a **fissure** opening between them, uncrossable.

"Sorry I couldn't help, but you know where to find me if you want to hang out with poor people again."

"Hey! Asshole! Why do you keep bringing that up?"

"Well, obviously I'm not like you, so…"

"Come on, don't be an idiot."

"No, no, Jessica. I'm gonna go." He left the balcony, looked back down from a height he'd never again command, and stepped down toward the darkened lawn.

"Well, if that's the way you feel, you'll never hear from me again!" she shouted after him, before turning towards the house and slamming the door.

He himself had reached the garden gate, and let it electronic lock click behind him as he stepped onto the street. Obviously, he'd be going home in a taxi rather than a Bentley.

Vocabulary

0704
sardonically [4]
[sɑːrˈdɑːnɪkli]

adv. **냉소적으로**   sarcastically
sardonic과 sarcastic을 연결해서 외워보자.
"Pink is the color of pigs, hippo sweat, and weakness," he said **sardonically**. (*adv.*)

0705
despair [11]
[dɪˈsper]

n. **절망**   feeling of hopelessness, loss of hope
출근 5분 전에 양말을 신으려고 했는데 한 짝(pair)이 없으면 절망에 빠지겠지?
"My life will never, ever, ever get better!" Sheila screamed with **despair**. (*n.*)

0706
ruptured [2]
[ˈrʌptʃə(r)d]

a. **파열된**   broken apart; exploded
찢어져서(rip → rup) 파열됐다고(rupture) 외워보자.
A pipe **ruptured**, leaking water all over the house. (*v.*)

0707
sterile [3]
[ˈsterɪl]

a. **아무 소득이 없는, 불모의**   not productive of results, ideas, etc.
멈춰버리고(stop → st) 아픈(ill → il) 상태라서 아무 소득이 없다고 생각하자.
What do the people of this **sterile** land eat? (*adj.*)

0708
feasible [3]
[ˈfiːzəbl]

a. **실현 가능한**   possible
매 끼니마다 잔치를(feast → feas) 여는 건 실현 가능하지(feasible) 않아.
I don't know whether it is **feasible** or not. (*adj.*)

0709
inadequate [13]
[ɪnˈædɪkwət]

a. **불충분한, 부적당한**   not adequate or sufficient; inept or unsuitable
adequate이 적당하다는 뜻이다.
Tanya's muttered "oops" after breaking five of her brother's bones was an **inadequate** apology. (*adj.*)

0710
catastrophically [3]
[kæˌtəˈstræfɪkəli]

adv. **파멸로, 비극으로**   disastrously
고양이가(cat) 트로피를(trophy) 떨어뜨려서 깨뜨리는 비극이(catastrophe) 일어났다고 외우자.
The record on productivity is **catastrophically** bad. (*adv.*)

0711
empathy [16]

[émpəθi]

n. 감정이입, 공감   feeling of pity or sadness for another person's distress, ability to identify with others' feelings or ideas
pathy는 '감정'을 의미한다.
The woman felt **empathy** to the beggar and donated money.(n.)

0712
anachronistic [4]

[ənæ̀krənístik]

a. 시대착오적인(의)   not fitting the times; from the wrong time period, having an error involving time in a story
어원 ana- 는 against, chronos는 '시간'을 의미한다. '시간을 반하는, 거스르는'의 의미다.
A digital watch in a 15th century picture is a perfect **anachronistic** example. (adj.)

0713
squander [4]

[skwάndər]

v. 낭비하다   to waste, use up
squander는 '목적 없이 떠돌아다니다'라는 의미의 wander와 비슷하게 들리므로 '목적 없이 돈을 낭비한다'고 해석할 수 있다.
The overconfident team **squandered** their lead and eventually lost. (adj.)

0714
verge [3]

[v3:rdʒ]

n. 가장자리, 맨 끝, 변두리 직전   the limit or point beyond which something occurs; brink, the edge, rim, or margin of something
verge는 이렇게 외워보자! VER(very) + ge(edge) = very edge
The baby was on the **verge** of crying but managed to stay calm. (n.)

0715
encumbrance [5]

[ɪn|kʌmbrəns]

n. 짐, 폐   burden or hardship
cumber이라는 단어가 보이면 일단 오이가(cucumber) 자동적으로 떠오를 것이다. 계속해서 오이가 떠오르는게 얼마나 방해되는지(encumber) 생각해보며 외워보자.
I felt like I was being an **encumbrance** to them. (n.)

0716
havoc [3]

[hǽvək]

n. 대파괴, 큰 피해, 황폐   great destruction of devastation, destroy
have, all, chaos 로 나누어서 외우면 '황폐'의 뜻을 잘 외울 수 있다.
The **havoc** on the battlefield was terrifying. (n.)

0717
adrift ² [əˈdrɪft]

a. **표류하는, 떠내려가는**   floating without control; drifting
drift는 흘러간다는 의미이므로 흘러가는 물에 떠내려간다고(adrift) 외워보자.
The survivors were **adrift** in a lifeboat for six days. (*adj.*)

0718
inferior ⁵ [ɪnˈfɪriə(r)]

a. **(~보다)낮은, 열등한**   lower, less in rank, lower in station, rank, degree or grade
inferior하면 상대방에게 두려움(fear)를 주기 어렵다.
The arrogant genius thought that everyone in the class was intellectually **inferior** to him.(*adj.*)

0719
fissure ⁵ [ˈfɪʃər]

n. **길게 갈라진 틈**   a narrow opening produced by cleavage or separation of parts; a long, narrow opening or line of breakage made by cracking or splitting
너무나도 당연하게(sure) 생각했던 믿음에 틈이(fissure) 생겼다고 외우자.
It's that **fissure** that causes the entire house to shake. (*n.*)

Voca Hamburger — Episode 43
MATCHING Quiz

1. sardonically	A. feeling of hopelessness
2. despair	B. sarcastically
3. ruptured	C. possible
4. sterile	D. not productive of results, ideas, etc.
5. feasible	E. feeling of pity or sadness for another person's distress
6. inadequate	F. broken apart; exploded
7. catastrophically	G. disastrously
8. empathy	H. to waste, use up
9. anachronistic	I. not fitting the times; from the wrong time period
10. squander	J. floating without control; drifting
11. verge	K. not adequate or sufficient
12. encumbrance	L. the limit or point beyond which something occurs; brink
13. havoc	M. great destruction of devastation
14. adrift	N. a narrow opening produced by cleavage or separation of parts
15. inferior	O. burden or hardship
16. fissure	P. lower, less in rank

1-B, 2-A, 3-F, 4-D, 5-C, 6-K, 7-G, 8-E, 9-I, 10-H, 11-L, 12-O, 13-M, 14-J, 15-P, 16-N

더 많은 문제를 풀고자 한다면 www.quizlet.com에서 'paul academy seoul' class를 검색

Episode 44

The **Whims** of the Gods

720 whim [10]
n. 일시적인 변덕
an odd or capricious notion or desire; a freakish fancy

721 lore [2]
n. 설화, 전통
folklore, myth

722 capricious [5]
a. 변덕스러운
unpredictable, whimsical, mercurial

723 sinister [10]
a. 사악한
evil; destructive

724 haughty [7]
a. 거만한, 오만한
overly proud of oneself; supercilious

725 throes [5]
n. 고통, 고투
pain, suffering, misery (mostly in a plural form)

726 fatal [3]
a. 치명적인, 해로운
deleterious, deadly

727 ephemeral [3]
a. 일시적인
momentary, short-lived

728 sojourn [3]
n. 체류
a temporary stay

According to the **lore** of ancient Greece, Jake's uncle had told him once, the Greek gods, like humans, were incredibly **capricious**, and that their blessings could very quickly become **sinister** curses depending on their mood. Just a week earlier, Jake had been in love, and had walked around with the **haughty** attitude of the alpha male. Things had been going well, and now, on Monday morning, he realized that life was unfair and the sun would never shine again. Things looked decidedly more horrible than they had since the summer began.

One of the dangers of being in such a bad mood was that the mixture of mid-summer **throes**, a sudden lack of a study partner, and little motivation to improve had a **fatal** effect on his studies as well. His **ephemeral** improvement, which had offered so much promise of future success, now had ended, and his scores started to drop. Coincidentally, TJ's family had decided to spend a brief **sojourn** abroad for the week, leaving him in the unusual situation of having nobody to talk to.

"Jake, what does a **quagmire** mean?" Matt asked. Jake was thinking of Bentleys and large houses filled with miserable rich girls.

"Jake? Quagmire?" he repeated in the **exasperated** tone everyone had **espoused** after too many weeks in each other's daily company.

"Oh, I don't know," he finally answered, rising to his feet as a gesture of his ignorance.

"That's not an answer, Jake," the man replied. "We learned this word yesterday. At least guess."

Jake looked down at his shoes. He wanted to **elucidate** for this man, for the entire world, the **drastic** nature of his sadness, but of course that couldn't be done under the normal **criteria** of high school rules. He remained frozen and silent.

"Fine, never mind. Anyone else?"

Ashley put up her hand so her thin fingers reached up very near to Jake's nose.

"It means an insolvable problem, a great **quandary**," she said confidently.

"Very good," came the reply. "It's nice to see you trying again Ashley."

She looked up at Jake and then slyly took a piece of paper from her notebook, broke it cleanly along its perforated edge, and wrote a message in large enough letters for him to see:

You wanna have coffee together?

Jake didn't, at all, want to do that, but he remembered her standing in the doorway the week prior, and her teddy bear. With no friends around, a lonely lunch would have made the day even worse. He nodded.

---

729 quagmire [3]
n. 수렁;역경
very difficult problem; conundrum

730 exasperated [9]
a. 몹시 화가 난
annoyed and vexed

731 espouse [3]
v. 쓰다, 채택하다
to adopt

732 elucidate [2]
v. 설명하다
to clarify and explain

733 drastic [4]
a. 극단적인
extreme, intense

734 criteria [7]
n. 기준
standards of judgment

735 quandary [3]
n. 진퇴양난, 곤경
dilemma, difficulty

Vocabulary

0720
whim [10]
[wɪm]

n. **일시적인 변덕** an odd or capricious notion or desire; a freakish fancy
바람처럼(wind → whim) 마구 변하는 변덕이라고 외워보자.
My duties seem to change daily at the **whim** of the boss. (*n.*)

0721
lore [2]
[lɔː(r)]

n. **설화, 전통** folklore, myth
여러 설화에는(lore) 울부짖는(roar → lore) 짐승들이 등장한다.
The place abounds in legendary **lore**. (*n.*)

0722
capricious [5]
[kəprɪʃəs]

a. **변덕스러운** unpredictable, whimsical, mercurial; fickle
라틴어 capri 는 goat '염소'를 말한다. 즉 사람의 마음이나 날씨 등의 미리 알 수 없는 상태를 변덕스러운 염소에 비유한 말이다.
The taste of that drink is **capricious**: sometimes it's good, sometimes it's bad. (*adj.*)

0723
sinister [10]
[sínəstər]

a. **사악한, 악의 있는, 불길한** evil; destructive, bad, evil
'왼쪽'을 뜻하는 라틴어에서 유래되었는데, 당시 왼쪽은 불길하다는 의미를 지녔다.
Sinister plans. (*a.*)

0724
haughty [7]
[|hɔːti]

a. **거만한, 오만한** overly proud of oneself; supercilious
"Ho ho" (haugh) 웃으며 거만하게 군다고 외워보자.
He speaks in a **haughty** tone. (*a.*)

0725
throes [5]
[θroʊz]

n. **고통, 고투** pain, suffering, misery (mostly in a plural form)
몸에 가시가(thorn → throe) 박혀서 받는 고통을 생각해보자.
It sounds like it's in its final death **throes**. (*n.*)

0726
fatal [3]
[|feɪtl]

a. **치명적인, 해로운** deleterious, deadly
운명을(fate → fat) 끝낼만큼 치명적인 상처라고 생각해보자.
A potentially **fatal** form of cancer (*adj.*)

0727
ephemeral [3]
[ifémərəl]

a. 일시적인, 수명이 짧은, 단명하는   momentary, short-lived
hemera는 그리스어로 '하루'라는 뜻으로 하루 밖에 못 사는, 즉 '단명하는'이란 의미이다.
The **ephemeral** war lasted only two days. (*adj.*)

0728
sojourn [3]
[ǁsoʊdʒɜːrn]

n. 체류   a temporary stay
짧게 머물렀지만(sojourn) 매우 즐거웠다고(joy → jou) 외워보자.
We also met an amateur musical group during our **sojourn**. (*n.*)

0729
quagmire [3]
[kwǽgmàiər]

n. 수렁; 역경, 진창   very difficult problem; conundrum, complicated, or unpleasant situation
quagmire의 본래 뜻은 '늪'으로, quack quack (quag)거리는 오리들과 개구리들이 사는 곳을 떠올려보자. 늪에서 빠져나오기 어려운 역경, 진창이라는 의미를 가진다.
At the end of the match, the pitch was real **quagmire**. (*n.*)

0730
exasperated [9]
[igzǽspərèitid]

a. 몹시 화가 난   greatly annoyed and vexed, frustrated
ex- 'thoroughly' + asper 'rough'. 즉, '완전히 거칠어진다'라는 뜻.
The **exasperated** man tore at his hair but there was nothing he could do. (*adj.*)

0731
espouse [3]
[ispáuz]

v. 쓰다, 채택하다, 옹호하다   to adopt; to support
spouse는 '배우자'를 뜻하므로, 결혼한 것처럼 무언가를 옹호한다는 의미이다.
I **espouse** the idea that people should have respect for each other's opinions! (*v.*)

0732
elucidate [2]
[ilúːsədèit]

v. 설명하다, (사실 등을) 밝히다   to clarify and explain, to make clear
lucid는 '빛'을 뜻하는 라틴어로 '밝히다'는 의미이다.
Elucidating an idea. (*adj.*)

0733
drastic [4]
[ǁdrǽstɪk]

a. 극단적인, 과감한   extreme, intense, violent; extremely severe
drastic이랑 dramatic 드라마틱이랑 비슷하지?
Draco, taking **drastic** measures, set the house on fire to get rid of one cockroach. (*adj.*)

0734

criteria [krai]

n. 기준   standards of judgment

오디션에서 심사위원들의 기준에(criteria) 못 미치는 사람들은 울면서 (cry → cri) 떨어지곤 한다.

The **criteria** is diverse and its applications broad. (*n.*)

0735

quandary [kwɑ́ndəri]

n. 진퇴양난, 곤경   dilemma, difficulty, a state of perplexity or uncertainty

수렁을 뜻하는 quagmire와 연관지으면 기억하기 쉬워.

After graduation, she had a real **quandary** about what to do next. (*n.*)

Episode 44

MATCHING Quiz

1. whim	A. dilemma, difficulty
2. lore	B. standards of judgment
3. capricious	C. folklore, myth
4. sinister	D. an odd or capricious notion or desire; a freakish fancy
5. haughty	E. unpredictable, whimsical, mercurial
6. throes	F. pain, suffering, misery (mostly in a plural form)
7. fatal	G. evil; destructive
8. ephemeral	H. overly proud of oneself; supercilious
9. sojourn	I. a temporary stay
10. quagmire	J. very difficult problem; conundrum
11. exasperated	K. momentary, short-lived
12. espouse	L. to adopt
13. elucidate	M. deleterious, deadly
14. drastic	N. annoyed and vexed
15. criteria	O. to clarify and explain
16. quandary	P. extreme, intense

1-D, 2-C, 3-E, 4-E, 5-H, 6-F, 7-M, 8-K, 9-I, 10-J, 11-N, 12-L, 13-O, 14-P, 15-B, 16-A

더 많은 문제를 풀고자 한다면 www.quizlet.com에서 'paul academy seoul' class를 검색

Episode 45

The Story of the Bear

After an **excruciating** series of classes, during each of which he was required to stand, Jake was ready for any kind of relief from the blues which had been bothering him for the last several days. Ashley's offer wasn't perfect, but perhaps even an uneventful lunch with her might improve his condition. After all, she was **perspicacious**, and had even suggested that they run away together, although this hadn't exactly been a romantic offer as much as an attempt to escape the academy.

She was waiting down the road, outside the Starbucks. This had been planned in a whispered **discourse** between classes. She had agreed to wait there, and then walk behind him as he **plodded** down the hill. They would be able to walk together once they had **traversed** the main avenue, and would have coffee at the little independent coffee shop across from the park, where no student of the academy or any other academy was likely to go, and they could avoid gossip.

Once there, they bought their coffees individually and she ate a small chocolate muffin as he drank his black with three sugars while trying to appear sad.

"So, Jake," she began. "Why have you suddenly become an angry young man?"

"Same reason you act like a bitter middle-aged woman, I guess."

"You think I **enact** that as a show?"

"You seem to, yes, but I don't ask you *why*; I don't like **prying** into other people's lives."

He expected her to be hurt by this, but she pushed on.

"I think I understand what you're going through more than you think," she said quickly before nervously taking a sip of her coffee. Jake was interested in her **opacity**.

---

736 excruciating [2]
a. 몹시 고통스러운
incredibly painful; arduous

737 perspicacious [4]
a. 총명한, 명민한
shrewd, astute

738 discourse [15]
n. 담론, 대화
conversation or dialogue

739 plod [2]
v. 터벅터벅 걷다
to walk heavily

740 traverse [2]
v. 가로지르다
to cross

741 enact [3]
v. 상연[연기]하다
to represent or perform in or as if in a play

742 pry [3]
v. 캐묻다
to inquire impertinently or unnecessarily into something

743 opacity [2]
n. 불투명함, 불분명함
lack of clarity; cloudiness
a. opaque

744 **contour** [3]
n. 윤곽
silhouette, outline

745 **fugitive** [2]
a. 도피하는; 순간적인
fleeting; lasting a short time

746 **seep** [4]
v. 스미다, 배다
to permeate, soak

747 **inaccessible** [4]
a. 가까워지기 어려운, 먼
distant, out of reach

"Yes?" he said, prodding her on.

"Well, I guess you don't remember that day you were waiting for a text message, and I asked you about it, do you?"

"Of course; it was only last week." He remembered her sad eyes and the **contour** she formed against the black of the dark, her prettiness then, as now. But he didn't say any of that, of course.

"Well, I didn't expect that you'd remember such a small moment. Anyway, I know about people not keeping in touch. My bear…" she started sniffling slightly, and Jake looked about nervously, worried that the few other customers would think he was breaking her heart or somehow abusing her. Quickly, she regained her senses.

"It was a gift, that's why I kept it on my desk. My boyfriend… my ex-boyfriend now, I guess, he gave it to me the day before he went to college in Australia. I bought him a little pendant to wear around his neck. I put my picture in it. I promised I'd keep the bear on my desk throughout the summer. And I did, until…" again, she released a **fugitive** cry, taking a large breath and looking across the road to the trees the park, which shone from the moisture that had **seeped** onto their leaves from the humid air.

"I mean, I kept emailing him, and then calling him, and writing these stupid letters to his dorm. And I got nothing! He never answered my calls, and I don't know if he got any of my letters, but whatever happened, he seemed to cast me into some **inaccessible** nothingness. He just disappeared."

Vocabulary

0736

excruciating [2]

[ikskrúːʃièitiŋ]

a. 몹시 고통스러운   incredibly painful; arduous, causing intense suffering
해리포터에 나오는 크루시오('crucˈio)라는 주문은 사람을 매우 고통스럽게 만드는 주문이다.
The surgery was **excruciating**, but Father endured it bravely and said, "It's not so bad." (*adj.*)

0737

perspicacious [4]

[pə̀ːrspəkéiʃəs]

a. 총명한, 명민한   shrewd, astute, having keen mental perception and understanding
per(through) + spic(see). 따라서 어려운 상황에서 진실을 볼 수 있다는 의미로 '총명하다'는 뜻이다.
Sherlock Holmes was **perspicacious** and solved many cases. (*adj.*)

0738

discourse [15]

[dískɔːrs]

n. 담론, 대화   conversation or dialogue, formal discussion
discourse는 discuss(회의하다)와 비슷하게 들리며 똑같은 뜻이다.
The old ladies always found their **discourse** so funny their laughter and shrieks could be heard all around the neighborhood. (*n.*)

0739

plod [2]

[plɑːd]

v. 터벅터벅 걷다   to walk heavily
비에 젖은 흙길을 걷는 소리에서 따온 단어이다.
Our horses **plodded** down the muddy track. (*v.*)

0740

traverse [2]

[trə|vɜːrs]

v. 가로지르다   to cross
1절에서(verse 1) 2절로(verse 2) 가로지른다고 외워보자.
Many cars **traverse** the bridge daily. (*v.*)

0741

enact [3]

[ɪ|nækt]

v. 상연[연기]하다, 제정하다   to represent or perform in or as if in a play, to make into an act
act를 만들다.
When the government **enacted** the Freedom Act, all former slaves celebrated the occasion. (*v.*)

0742
pry ³ [praɪ]

v. 캐묻다　　to inquire impertinently or unnecessarily into something
스파이가(spy) 마구 캐묻고(pry) 다니는 걸 떠올려보자.
I'm sick of you **prying** into my personal life! (*v.*)

0743
opacity ² [oʊ|pæsəti]

n. 불투명함, 불분명함　　lack of clarity; cloudiness　　*a.* opaque
보석 오팔은(opal → opa) 내부가 잘 보이지 않는 불투명한 보석이다.
Even those who support it point out at least two problems: haste and **opacity**. (*n.*)

0744
contour ³ [|kɑːntʊr]

n. (사물의) 윤곽　　silhouette, the outline of an object
conto + ur라고 보자. conto 라고 하면 콘티(미술에서 대략적으로 그리는 것) 같다. contour는 그렇게 콘티처럼 대략적인 윤곽을 뜻한다.
The blind man figured out the **contour** of the object by touching it with his hands. (*n.*)

0745
fugitive ² [|fjuːdʒətɪv]

a. 도피하는; 순간적인　　fleeting; lasting a short time
티비에서(tv → tive) 도망치는(fugitive) 범죄자 사진이 나왔다고 외워보자.
A **fugitive** criminal (*adj.*)

0746
seep ⁴ [siːp]

v. 스미다, 배다　　to permeate, soak
빨대로 음료수를 조금씩 빨아마시는(sip → seep) 것처럼 스며든다고(seep) 외워보자.
Water **seeped** from a crack in the pipe. (*v.*)

0747
inaccessible ⁴ [|ɪnæk|sesəbl]

a. 가까워지기 어려운, 먼, 접근하기 어려운　　distant, out of reach, unapproachable; not accessible
in은 '없다' 라는 뜻을 가지고 있으니까 access '접근'을 할 수 없다는거지.
The ATM was not used much since it was located at an **inaccessible** place.(*adj.*)

Note :

Episode 45

MATCHING Quiz

1. excruciating
2. perspicacious
3. discourse
4. plod
5. traverse
6. enact
7. pry
8. opacity
9. contour
10. fugitive
11. seep
12. inaccessible

A. distant, out of reach
B. to permeate, soak
C. incredibly painful; arduous
D. to walk heavily
E. shrewd, astute
F. conversation or dialogue
G. to cross
H. lack of clarity; cloudiness
I. to represent or perform in or as if in a play
J. fleeting; lasting a short time
K. to inquire impertinently or unnecessarily into something
L. silhouette, outline

1-C, 2-E, 3-F, 4-D, 5-G, 6-I, 7-K, 8-H, 9-L, 10-J, 11-B, 12-A

더 많은 문제를 풀고자 한다면 www.quizlet.com에서 'paul academy seoul' class를 검색

Episode 46

Hands across the Table Top

748 moribund [2]
a. 빈사 상태의
in a dying state, near death

749 mundane [3]
a. 재미없는, 일상의
ordinary or common (often with negative connotation)

750 afflicted [5]
a. 괴로워하는, 고통 받는
suffering, tormented

751 contempt [20]
n. 경멸
disdain

752 perpetrate [8]
v. (범죄를) 저지르다
to commit (used for crimes)

753 distress [10]
n. 고통, 괴로움
great pain, anxiety, or sorrow; acute physical or mental suffering

754 clasp [3]
v. 움켜쥐다
to seize, grip, or grasp with the hand

755 premeditate [2]
v. 미리 숙고하다
to plan, propose

"What happened to him?" Jake asked innocently. He assumed that the young man had died or became **moribund** in some accident. He pictured the many ways in which one could die in Australia. Maybe kangaroo boxing, he thought, or sharks! But again, his young imagination couldn't account for the **mundane** changes of heart undergone by a traveler far from home. The boy had 'fallen head over heels' (to use Ashley's words) for a homesick girl who went to the same sun-drenched school. The two had begun posting pictures on facebook as Ashley felt more and more **afflicted** by his horribleness and her stupidity at having loved him in the first place.

"I mean, I guess I knew it would happen. He's handsome, and obviously I wasn't as exciting as *she* was." She pronounced the pronoun with **contempt**, as though this girl had made it difficult for her family or **perpetrated** some horror against humankind.

"That's horrible, Ashley," her Jake offered, unsure of what one should do to comfort a woman in **distress**. In the movies, the man puts his hand on the table and gets it **clasped** in hers, but he wasn't about to do something so melodramatic. A few seconds later, though, he was forced to do something. She was crying uncontrollably within moments, hardly able to draw breath between deep sobs.

"I've—got—no one—to talk—to" she cried sadly, and just as she said it, Jake felt his hand glide across the table top. It wasn't something he **premeditated**, but he felt like he had to comfort her pain. She grabbed it hard. Her hand was sweaty and hot. Again, she felt like the day outside, from her shining eyes to her wet skin. She looked past him to the street and he waited for her tears to pass.

Finally, they did, and he felt like her confession required one of his own. He realized he hadn't really told anyone this either, and the weight of it would be nice to unload.

"I'm not pretending it's the same thing, but I guess I was hurt by this girl. She didn't fall in love with anyone else, but…" But what? he thought **frantically**. She couldn't deal with her parents' expectations, and she was too rich to notice other people's **multifaceted** problems. It simply wasn't a similar situation, but it was all he had. So he told it, from Monday meeting to the Bentley to the house, leaving out the kiss in the park. That felt **extraneous**.

"I could see you were in love with her, Jake," she said after he'd finished, neither of them noticed the LED clock outside telling them it was 5:55 in the afternoon.

"Thanks, Ashley. I *am* sorry about your teddy bear. But that guy sounds like a bad person anyway."

"Yeah, he is." She even seemed to smile when she said this, and seemed about to say something else before she got a text from her mother, telling her to come home quickly after class.

"Oh!" she said suddenly. "It's six already!"

"Crap!" he didn't quite say suddenly, before adding a "sorry." (She was a girl, after all, and rules had to be followed).

"No problem," she responded drily, though she didn't use the word printed her, she **harnessed** the full power of the original word. "But I do have to go."

The two of them walked back to the school together, not bothering with any secrecy. In the elevator, Ashley thanked him again, but it was Jake who felt like he'd gotten more out of the experience. With their phones retrieved, they headed down the road towards home, he heading east and she west.

---

756 frantic ³
a. 정신 없이 서두르는
desperate or wild with excitement, passion, fear, pain, etc.

757 multifaceted ²
a. 다면적인
having many facets, as a gem

758 extraneous ³
a. 관련 없는
unnecessarily extra; superfluous

759 harness ²
v. 이용하다
to bring under conditions for effective use

Vocabulary

0748
moribund [2]
[mɔ́ːrəbʌ̀nd]

a. 빈사 상태의, 소멸해가는   in a dying state, near death
bound for death라는 뜻으로 곧 죽을 상태를 뜻한다.
He felt his company was **moribund**, so he decided to quit and find a company with a better future.

0749
mundane [3]
[mʌndéin]

a. 재미없는, 일상의   ordinary or common (often with negative connotation)
mund(world 세상, 현세, 속세)의 뜻에서 '평범한, 흔히 있는'이 나오게 되었다.
I want an adventure instead of this **mundane** life! (*adj.*)

0750
afflicted [5]
[əflíktid]

a. 괴로워하는, 고통 받는   suffering, tormented
둘 사이에 껴서 갈등하며(conflict) 괴로워하는(afflicted) 모습을 생각해보자.
Don't be **afflicted** at such a trivial thing. (*adj.*)

0751
contempt [20]
[kəntémpt]

n. 경멸, 모욕   disdain, scorn; disgrace
contempt of court 라고 들어봤지? 법정 모독으로 법정에서 쫓겨나거나 벌금을 무는 장면도 본 적이 있을 거야.
Tim showed his **contempt** for reading by ripping the book in half and spitting on it.(*n.*)

0752
perpetrate [8]
[ǀpɜːrpətreɪt]

v. (범죄를) 저지르다   to commit (used for crimes)
금고를 뚫고(penetrate → perpetrate) 돈을 훔쳐 달아나는 범죄를 저질렀다고 외워보자.
Those who **perpetrate** it are criminals. (*v.*)

0753
distress [10]
[dɪǀstres]

n. 고통, 괴로움   great pain, anxiety, or sorrow; acute physical or mental suffering
고통에(distress) 빠져 스트레스를(stress) 많이 받는다고 외워보자.
The newspaper article caused the actor considerable **distress**. (*n.*)

0754
clasp ³
[klæsp]

v. 움켜쥐다   to seize, grip, or grasp with the hand
박수(clap → clasp) 치는 것이 두 손을 사용하는 것처럼, 두 손에 꽉 움켜쥐었다고 외워보자.
He leaned forward, his hands **clasped** tightly together. (*v.*)

0755
premeditate ²
[priːmédətèit, pri-]

v. 미리 숙고하다   to plan, propose
meditate는 '명상'이라는 뜻이다. 따라서 미리(pre) 생각해본다는 의미이다.
I rarely **premeditate**, which is a mistake. (*v.*)

0756
frantic ³
[ǀfræntɪk]

a. 정신 없이 서두르는   desperate or wild with excitement, passion, fear, pain, etc.
친구들이(friend → fran) 온다는 말에 정신 없이 서둘러(frantic) 만날 준비를 한다고 외워보자.
Things are **frantic** in the office right now. (*adj.*)

0757
multifaceted ²
[mʌ̀ltifǽsitid]

a. 다면적인, 많은 면을 가진   having many facets, as a gem
multi 는 '여럿', facet 는 '얼굴'을 뜻하므로 여러 면을 가졌다는 의미이다.
Josiah had a **multifaceted** personality; sometimes he was extremely kind, and at other times he could be nasty and careless. (*adj.*)

0758
extraneous ³
[ikstréiniəs]

a. 관련 없는, 외부로부터의, 무관계한   unnecessarily extra; superfluous, unrelated
extra가 많아서 관계 없는 것들이 많이 생겼다고 생각하자.
It is not necessary to have **extraneous** information. (*adj.*)

0759
harness ²
[ǀhɑːrnɪs]

v. 이용하다; 마구(馬具)   to bring under conditions for effective use; armor for horses
harness가 있어야 말을 거칠게 탈 수 있다. (ride hard)
They put a **harness** on the horse and rode him down the street. (*n.*)

Note :

Episode 46

MATCHING Quiz

1. moribund
2. mundane
3. afflicted
4. contempt
5. perpetrate
6. distress
7. clasp
8. premeditate
9. frantic
10. multifaceted
11. extraneous
12. harness

A. unnecessarily extra; superfluous
B. to bring under conditions for effective use
C. in a dying state, near death
D. ordinary or common (often with negative connotation)
E. to commit (used for crimes)
F. suffering, tormented
G. disdain
H. to plan, propose
I. desperate or wild with excitement, passion, fear, pain, etc.
J. to seize, grip, or grasp with the hand
K. great pain, anxiety, or sorrow; acute physical or mental suffering
L. having many facets, as a gem

1-C, 2-D, 3-F, 4-G, 5-E, 6-K, 7-J, 8-H, 9-I, 10-L, 11-A, 12-B

더 많은 문제를 풀고자 한다면 www.quizlet.com에서 'paul academy seoul' class를 검색

288 | Paul's SAT Vocabulary

Episode 47

Home Stay Sickness

The next day, with a **lull** in the drama which seemed to have **pervaded** the summer so far, the Hamburger Mafia had met at a busy food cart, where a number of other academy students had gathered to eat and drink. It was Tuesday of Week Six.

It was easy for Jake to forget, **amid** all of the distractions, that there *were* other people at the academy, and it struck him that he had never really learned much about these **anonymous** shadows in the six or seven weeks that he'd been at the academy. A few of them were in his class, a few others were friends of theirs from school or other academies. There was a group of kids who had been in foreign exchange programs, and they were talking about their home-stay experiences.

"It was horrible, you guys. This family was so annoying. First of all, the kids were my age, but they were like little **nuisances**, so rude to their parents and to anyone they talked to, so the old folks kept leaning toward me, as though I was the good daughter they should have had, the nice silent one."

A few knowing laughs passed through the group. Many of them had similar stories. The mostly silent and always nervous Korean student Yujin, whom the teachers always picked on, spoke next, alarming everyone with her sudden passion.

"Ugh, I know. My family was so unruly. The kids would go out late, partying with their friends, and I'd either be at home studying or be forced to join them. You know, standing on the edge of a conversation or being the butt of a joke is not very fun. They would always say "oh, she's an Asian **prodigy**!" or "you should sit next to her in math class." I mean, it was funny sometimes, but they kept saying **bigoted** stuff, and then they'd offer me drugs or drinks. Just... horrible!"

---

760 lull ²
n. 소강상태
pause; moment of inactivity

761 pervade ¹⁴
v. 팽배하다
to spread throughout

762 amid ²
prep. ~의 한가운데에
in the middle of, surrounded by

763 anonymous ⁷
a. 익명의
not identified by name

764 nuisance ²
n. 성가신 사람
an obnoxious person, annoyance, pest

765 prodigy ⁶
n. 영재
genius at a young age; precocious person

766 bigoted ⁵
a. 편견이 심한
prejudiced or racist

767 paternal [3]
a. 아버지의
characteristic or befitting of a father

768 anomaly [7]
n. 변칙
something which doesn't fit a pattern or rule; abnormality

769 consigned [2]
a. 위임된, 위탁된, 맡겨진
assigned, handed over for care

770 encompass [2]
v. 둘러싸다, 에워싸다
to surround, encircle

771 caucus [2]
n. 회의, 모임
gathering, meeting, assembly

772 paltry [3]
a. 하찮은 사소한
of little importance; insignificant

Again, the group knowingly nodded like old retirees recounting stories at a wedding dinner. The agreement seemed to be (among many of them) that they had been brought into houses as targets for **paternal** affection (or as examples for struggling teenage troublemakers), or sometimes as easy meal-tickets for those seeking the high fees paid by concerned parents.

The next participant in the dialogue seemed to be the **anomaly** in the pattern. His experience, it seems, had been quite nice. He had been treated almost as another son, brought to baseball games and movies, and he really seemed to have liked the evening dinners his family had eaten together. Of course, it then turned out that he had been **consigned** to an older couple whose children had all left home already, drawing jealous remarks from the others arranged in the tiny space of the small food stall (by this time, a few more had joined and completely **encompassed** the small aluminum table).

"Oh, that's just luck, though," Isaiah said flatly. "They were one of the good ones."

Sam, usually timid in large **caucuses** such as this, (he almost never spoke in class, even to ask to go to the bathroom), agreed. "Yeah," he said, "I think my family was worse than any of yours."

A few students groaned at this attempt at comparison, and decided to leave at that moment, drifting either toward the academy or the subway. The remaining crowd, however, pressed in a bit closer, lengthening their necks to hear the horror story that would have to follow (it was a lot to promise, but if Sam had opened his mouth to speak, it wouldn't be a **paltry** matter.)

He did not disappoint.

Vocabulary

0760
lull [lʌl]

n. 소강상태   pause; moment of inactivity
lullaby는 자장가라는 의미이다. 즉 자장가는 아기를 수면상태에(lull) 빠지게 하는 노래이다.
A **lull** in the conversation/fighting (*n.*)

0761
pervade [pərˈveɪd]

v. 팽배하다, 만연하다   to spread throughout
invade가 침략하다는 의미이니까 모든 곳에 100퍼센트(per) 침략해서 (invade) 팽배해졌다고 외워보자.
The entire house was **pervaded** by a sour smell. (*v.*)

0762
amid [əˈmɪd]

prep. ~의 한가운데에   in the middle of, surrounded by
Ana는 튀는 걸 좋아해서 항상 가운데(middle) 자리만 앉아.
Amid the bustling crowd, Bella thought she saw a familiar face. (*n.*)

0763
anonymous [əˈnɑːnɪməs]

a. 익명의   not identified by name
no name(no nym), 즉 이름이 없다고 외워보자.
An **anonymous** donor (*adj.*)

0764
nuisance [ˈnjuːsns]

n. 성가신 사람, 골칫거리   an obnoxious person, annoyance, pest, that which annoys, vexes, or irritates
nocere는 라틴어로 '해를 주다'라는 뜻으로 '골칫거리'라는 뜻이다.
Noise at night is a **nuisance** to anyone. (*n.*)

0765
prodigy [ˈprɑdədʒi]

n. 영재   genius at a young age; precocious person, a person or thing of very remarkable gifts or qualities
pro(forth)의 어원을 갖고 있다.
Mozart was a **prodigy**. (*n.*)

0766
bigoted [bígətid]

a. 편견이 (아주) 심한   prejudiced or racist
편견이 아주 심한 big idiot(엄청난 멍청이)를 떠올려라.
bigoted racist (*adj.*)

0767
paternal [pə|tɜ:rnl]

a. 아버지의   characteristic or befitting of a father
아빠(father → pater), 즉 '아버지의'라는 의미라고 외우자.
He gave me a piece of **paternal** advice. (*adj.*)

0768
anomaly [ə|nɑ:məli]

n. 변칙   something which doesn't fit a pattern or rule; abnormality
정상적이지(normal → nomal) 않은(a), 즉 규칙을 벗어나는 변칙을 의미한다.
the many **anomalies** in the tax system (*n.*)

0769
consigned [kən|saɪnd]

a. 위임된, 위탁된, 맡겨진   assigned, handed over for care
다른 곳에서 맡겨지기로(consign) 이미 사인을 받았다(sign) 라고 외워보자.
The goods are to be **consigned** by train. (*v.*)

0770
encompass [ɪn|kʌmpəs]

v. 둘러싸다, 에워싸다, 포함하다   to surround, to encircle
나침반(compass) 하나만 가지고 있어도 세계여행을 손 안에 encompass 하고 있지.
Dad's strong arms **encompass** my body when he hugs me tight. (*v.*)

0771
caucus [|kɔ:kəs]

n. 회의, 모임   gathering, meeting, assembly
많은 회의들이(caucus) 꼭 서커스처럼(circus) 난장판이 되는 일이 많다고 외우자.
The **caucus** has split into factions. (*n.*)

0772
paltry [pɔ́:ltri]

a. 하찮은 사소한, 무가치한   of little importance; insignificant, utterly worthless; insultingly small
시도하기도(try) 전에 패스할(pass → pal) 정도로 하찮은 것이라고 생각하자.
This account offers a **paltry** 1% return on your investment. (*adj.*)

Note :

Episode 47

MATCHING Quiz

1. lull	A. not identified by name
2. pervade	B. in the middle of, surrounded by
3. amid	C. gathering, meeting, assembly
4. anonymous	D. characteristic or befitting of a father
5. nuisance	E. an obnoxious person, annoyance, pest
6. prodigy	F. genius at a young age; precocious person
7. bigoted	G. assigned, handed over for care
8. paternal	H. to surround, encircle
9. anomaly abnormality	I. something which doesn't fit a pattern or rule;
10. consigned	J. prejudiced or racist
11. encompass	K. of little importance; insignificant
12. caucus	L. to spread throughout
13. paltry	M. pause; moment of inactivity

1-M, 2-L, 3-B, 4-A, 5-E, 6-F, 7-J, 8-D, 9-I, 10-G, 11-H, 12-C, 13-K

더 많은 문제를 풀고자 한다면 www.quizlet.com에서 'paul academy seoul' class를 검색

Episode 48: Sam's Story

773 chronicle ²
n. 연대기
an extended account in prose presented in chronological order

774 insuperable ²
a. 난공불락의
unable to be defeated

775 defy ²
v. 반항[거역]하다
to challenge the power of; confront

776 ascertain ⁸
v. 확인하다
to check for accuracy

775 gnaw ⁴
v. 갉아먹다
to wear away, erode

778 crumble ⁶
v. 바스러지다
to break into small fragments or crumbs

779 hone ⁴
v. 연마하다
to make more acute or effective; improve; perfect

780 dreadful ⁹
a. 끔찍한, 지독한
extremely bad, unpleasant, or ugly

781 raconteur ²
n. 이야기꾼
storyteller (one who recounts)

Now we must say something about Sam, who has so far escaped the attention of this **chronicle**. What has been said could be printed on a matchbox: he was fairly shy (particularly in large groups), was great at throwing coins (as evidenced by his **insuperable** conquests against TJ in their game), and he had a girlfriend (so he said. Neither of his two best friends ever **defied** this fact, nor did they try to **ascertain** its truthfulness). But there is much more to relate.

Sam was a child of divorce, though didn't make a habit of telling people. His parents—one a heart surgeon, the other a former teacher—had fallen in love in university, and had been passionate. But children and the demands of work and responsibility began to slowly **gnaw** and **crumble** their relationship, and by time he was ten, their increasingly-tall and awkward eldest son was being shuttled between aunt's houses and being cared for by his maternal grandmother, hearing his parents shouting at each other sometimes, but mostly kept away from their fighting. They divorced when he was thirteen, and shortly thereafter he was sent to a middle school in Minnesota, where he was told he would **hone** his English in anticipation of high school and the **dreadful** SAT.

Standing on the corner of the food stand, the young **raconteur** began his story.

He had always been a quiet boy, and had arrived in Minnesota shy and quite unskilled in social situations. He was picked up by a very **coarse** older cousin, who drove them both in his broken-down old car to a house outside town. He lived there with his younger wife, who was unused to the habits of marital life, and was, as he later found out, a drug user.

The two ushered their young responsibility into his small closet-sized room, which had very few **amenities**, just a small bed, an **archaic** school desk from an old elementary school, and a broken clock on the wall. Sam, feeling that he had been kidnapped, still didn't have the language skills to **decry** this **fraudulent** situation, and spent the rest of his first night in that room, unpacking his bag in neat piles of clothes and books against the wall as the couple began listening to loud music and occasionally arguing next door. Around midnight, the wife brought him several cold pieces of pizza and a can of Coke. It seemed an unsolvable situation, particularly as his parents were **grappling** with their own personal problems and didn't really listen to their son's complaints when he talked to them over the next few months.

Over the few minutes of this story, everyone had leaned in, including the usually angry serving lady, all of them silent as the boy kept speaking.

"Every day, I would catch the bus to school, and just hang out with my classmates. They would **collude** to help me cheat at tests since a few of them were older and had taken the classes before. I had to fight a couple of boys who kept referring to me with these **minimizing** terms, but mostly I would just stay with as many friends as I could, and then play soccer after school. Sometimes I would stay at friends' houses, but then the man would come and pick me up, and bring me back home. After a few months, my mom sent me a care package of snacks, but most of it got eaten by those horrible people. They kept going into my room when I was gone, taking things that looked valuable, then back to that dirty little living room. I think they were doing drugs in there, but they never did it in front of me. They were just bad people, only doing it for the **pittance** my parents sent them."

A few sympathetic mutterings greeted this, and Jake realized why Sam was so quiet. He had never heard him talk about anything for so long, and when the boy had finished he felt a **seismic** shift of feeling toward his poor friend.

---

782 **coarse** [3]
a. 거친; 불손한
rude and unsociable; vulgar

783 **amenity** [4]
n. 편의시설
a feature of a house which gives comfort

784 **archaic** [4]
a. 낡은, 구식의
antiquated, ancient

785 **decry** [3]
v. 헐뜯다, 매도하다
to criticize

786 **fraudulent** [8]
a. 기만하는, 사기를 치는
cheating, dishonest

787 **grapple** [3]
v. (해결책을 찾아) 고심하다
to deal with, cope

788 **collude** [5]
v. 공모하다
to co-operate

789 **minimize** [13]
v. 최소화하다
to reduce to smallest possible amount

790 **pittance** [3]
n. 아주 적은 보수
a small salary

791 **seismic** [5]
a. (영향, 규모가) 엄청난
of enormous proportions or having highly significant consequences

Vocabulary

0773
chronicle [2]
[kránikl]

n. 연대기   an extended account in prose presented in chronological order, report; record (in chronological order)
chronicles of Narnia '나니아 연대기' 알지? 그 때 그 단어야. chron(time) + ic : '시간의' → 장기간에 걸친, 만성적인.
The boy wrote a **chronicle** of the group's adventures in his diary. (*n.*)

0774
insuperable [2]
[insú:pərəbl]

a. 난공불락의, 이겨내기 어려운   unable to be defeated, incapable of being passed over
in(not) + super(over) + able(있는) = 올라갈 수 없는.
No obstacle is **insuperable** if you believe in yourself. (*adj.*)

0775
defy [2]
[difái]

v. 반항[거역]하다   to challenge the power of; confront, to disobey
de는 '취소하다', fy는 fid-, 즉 '충성심'이라는 뜻으로 누군가를 거역해 충성심을 취소하다 라는 뜻이다.
The rebellious soldiers **defied** the order to fight in the war. (*v.*)

0776
ascertain [8]
[ǽsərtein]

v. 확인하다   to check for accuracy
확실한지(certain) 물어보니까(ask → as) 확인한다고 외우자.
It can be difficult to **ascertain** the facts. (*v.*)

0777
gnaw [4]
[nɔ:]

v. 갉아먹다   to wear away, erode
턱을(jaw) 계속 움직이며 갉아먹는다고(gnaw) 생각하자.
The dog was **gnawing** a bone. (*v.*)

0778
crumble [6]
[ˈkrʌmbl]

v. 바스러지다   to break into small fragments or crumbs
crumb은 부스러기라는 뜻이고, 빵 부스러기 등을 말할 때 많이 쓰인다. 그러므로 동사형인 crumble은 '바스러지다'라는 뜻이다.
The wall **crumbled** into dust when the earthquake started. (*v.*)

0779
hone [hoʊn]

v. 연마하다　to make more acute or effective; improve; perfect
뿔처럼(horn → hone) 뾰족해지도록 계속해서 연마한다고 생각하자.
She **honed** her debating skills at college. (*v.*)

0780
dreadful [drédfəl]

a. 끔찍한, 지독한, 무서운, 지긋지긋한　extremely bad, unpleasant, or ugly, terrible
dead + red. 죽음과 붉은색이 합쳐지면 무서울 것 같지?
Surprisingly, the child was not scared of the **dreadful** monster at all. (*adj.*)

0781
raconteur [ǁrækɑːnˈtɜː(r)]

n. 이야기꾼　storyteller (one who recounts)
이야기꾼이(raconteur) 숲에서 너구리(racoon → racon) 한 마리를 만난 얘기를 하며 듣는 이의 눈물을(teur → tear) 자아냈다고 외워보자.
He knew many jokes and was an excellent **raconteur**. (*n.*)

0782
coarse [kɔːrs]

a. 거친; 불손한　rude and unsociable; vulgar
매우 거친(coarse) 경주 코스를(course) 떠올려보자.
The bottom of the swimming pool is so **coarse**. (*adj.*)

0783
amenity [əˈmenəti]

n. 편의시설　a feature of a house which gives comfort
아멘이라는(amen) 말이 저절로 나올 정도로 편의시설이 잘 되어 있는 곳이라고 외우자.
The campsite is close to all local **amenities**. (*n.*)

0784
archaic [ɑːrˈkeɪɪk]

a. 낡은, 구식의　antiquated, ancient, forming the earliest stage
archaic의 root 'archae'는 'old'의 뜻을 가지고 있다.
The system is **archaic** and needs to be updated. (*adj.*)

0785
decry [dɪkráɪ]

v. 헐뜯다, 매도하다, 비방하다　to criticize, to express strong disapproval of; disparage
decry는 de(down) + cry(울다, 소리치다, 외치다) : '소리질러 내리다' → 깎아내리다.
The animal rights group **decried** the use of animals in product testing. (*v.*)

0786
fraudulent [8]
[frɔ́ːdʒulənt]

a. 기만하는, 사기를 치는, 부정의   cheating, dishonest, counterfeit
fraud가 '사기'니까 frudulent 는 '사기의'란 뜻이 된다.
The criminals made **fraudulent** claims to the government. (*adj.*)

0787
grapple [3]
[ǀgræpl]

v. (해결책을 찾아) 고심하다   to deal with, cope
그리스 로마 신화에서 시지포스가 자기 위에 있는 사과를(apple) 잡기(grab → gra) 위해 고심하는 모습을 떠올려보자.
The new government has yet to **grapple** with the problem of air pollution. (*v.*)

0788
collude [5]
[kəǀluːd]

v. 공모하다   to co-operate
무례한(rude → lude) 신하를 어떻게 내쫓을지 같이(co) 공모한다고 (collude) 생각하자.
Several people had **colluded** in the crime. (*v.*)

0789
minimize [13]
[ǀmɪnɪmaɪz]

v. 최소화하다   to reduce to smallest possible amount
미니(mini), 즉 '작게 만든다'는 의미이다.
Good hygiene helps to **minimize** the risk of infection. (*v.*)

0790
pittance [3]
[ǀpɪtns]

n. 아주 적은 보수   a small salary
애처로울 정도로(pity → pitt) 적은 보수라고 외우자.
He is supported on a **pittance**. (*n.*)

0791
seismic [5]
[ǀsaɪzmɪk]

a. (영향, 규모가) 엄청난   of enormous proportions or having highly significant consequences
마이크에(mic) 대고 말을 하면(say → sei) 목소리가 엄청나게 크게(seismic) 들린다고 외워보자.
A **seismic** shift in the political process (*adj.*)

Note :

Episode 48

MATCHING Quiz

1. chronicle	A. of enormous proportions or having highly significant consequences
2. insuperable	B. a small salary
3. defy	C. to reduce to smallest possible amount
4. ascertain	D. to co-operate
5. gnaw	E. to deal with, cope
6. crumble	F. cheating, dishonest
7. hone	G. to criticize
8. dreadful	H. antiquated, ancient
9. raconteur	I. a feature of a house which gives comfort
10. coarse	J. rude and unsociable; vulgar
11. amenity	K. storyteller (one who recounts)
12. archaic	L. extremely bad, unpleasant, or ugly
13. decry	M. to make more acute or effective; improve; perfect
14. fraudulent	N. to break into small fragments or crumbs
15. grapple	O. to wear away, erode
16. collude	P. to check for accuracy
17. minimize	Q. to challenge the power of; confront
18. pittance	R. unable to be defeated
19. seismic	S. an extended account in prose presented in chronological order

1-S, 2-R, 3-Q, 4-P, 5-O, 6-N, 7-M, 8-L, 9-K, 10-J, 11-I, 12-H, 13-G, 14-F, 15-E, 16-D, 17-C, 18-B, 19-A

더 많은 문제를 풀고자 한다면 www.quizlet.com에서 'paul academy seoul' class를 검색

Episode 49

Classroom Prank

792 obfuscated [2]
a. 어리둥절한, 혼란스러운
perplexed and confused

793 arbitrary [10]
a. 임의적인, 제멋대로의
despotic or tyrannical;
referring to randomness

794 enraged [5]
a. 격분한, 화가 난
exasperated, angered

795 muster [2]
v. 모으다, 소집하다
to gather or bring together
for a service

796 benign [5]
a. 상냥한
benevolent

Words, words, words, Hamlet had once answered when asked what he was reading. While he had gained quite a large glossary in the time he'd been at the academy (some of which he felt he would never forget due to the ties the words had to moments in his recent life), Jake nonetheless felt like the word in vocab class **obfuscated** things rather than make them clear. And while he had apologized for his failure in vocabulary a week earlier, the many thoughts of recent heartbreak caused him continual trouble.

At the same time, many of the other students were starting to grow frustrated at Matt's **arbitrary** control, especially since the teacher had become increasingly bitter toward students who hadn't done the homework or who could not define words they had so recently studied. Occasionally, he gave congratulations to the students who gave the right answer, but more often he acted frustrated when people couldn't get something right. Even TJ's attempts to bow before him with chocolate bars for had no effect on his steely expression. Today, the Wednesday of Week Six, was no exception.

"Come on, Jake!" the **enraged** teacher said. "What does *maverick* mean?"

Jake stared at the word with every bit of concentration he could **muster**. A wave of words filled his head, but no definitions seemed appropriate. While most of the class was already standing, he had attained a good reputation in the vocabulary class, but today he couldn't come up with the correct answer. He stared back at the teacher, wishing he could dismiss him in some dramatic rebellion, taking over the class and ruling as a more **benign** ruler than the cynical man that currently controlled the class from behind the desk. He stood without speaking.

"So that's it, huh Jake? You're just going to stand without even trying to give the answer? Again?"

Jake burned with rage at this suggestion of ignorance and lack of a good work ethic.

"I just can't remember. I'm sorry."

"We have talked about this word so many times!"

Though the teacher had a point, Jake didn't feel like acting that **conciliatory** to his demands.

"Listen," he said with his most revolutionary and angry **timbre**, "we've studied a lot of words this summer. I guess I can't remember all of them." At this point, he couldn't completely control his anger and swore under his breath while kicking at the chair beneath his feet.

"We don't need the attitude, Jake, but, ironically, you have shown the definition in your attitude. *Maverick*, of course, means …" he waited for an answer, but the class, together with Jake, refused to answer, looking at the teacher with the same tough expressions.

"Fine," he said, somewhat **dismayed**. "It refers to a rebellious person." He stared at his watch. There were five minutes left in the hour. "I guess we should stop there," he said as the students started their usual practice of jumping toward the doorway or **slumping** over their desks. Jake was turning toward the exit when he heard the teacher call his name.

"Jake! Can I have a minute of your time, please?" Matt called out darkly.

He shuffled back to the front of the classroom, which had all but emptied in the last thirty seconds.

"OK, Jake, what's the problem?"

He stared at his feet.

"I know I was kind of angry there, but your attitude worries me. Is everything OK?"

"Yeah, sure," Jake said, still refusing to meet the teachers' gaze.

---

797 conciliatory 2
a. 달래는
attempting to placate or behave in an acquiescent manner
v. conciliate

798 timbre 2
n. 음색
tone

799 dismayed 8
a. 낭패한
thoroughly disheartened

800 slump 2
v. 털썩 앉다
to fall heavily or collapse

801 ferocious [4]
a. 흉포한, 난폭한
violent, brutal, truculent

802 anguish [2]
n. 고민, 고뇌
great suffering or acute distress; pain

803 preoccupation [6]
n. 집착
obsession or fixation

804 quasi [2]
a. 외견상[표면상]의
seeming; virtual

805 esoteric [4]
a. 소수만 이해하는
understood by only the select few who have special knowledge

806 ludicrous [7]
a. 터무니없는
causing laughter because of absurdity

"OK, whatever Jake. If you don't want to be honest, then I guess you can go, but you know you have great potential, and your scores have been improving. I just don't want you to slide back to where you were before. Once you start doing better, you have to keep pushing, you understand?"

"Yeah, OK," he said, feeling the heat of an angry tear in his eye. He looked up at the teacher, who was frowning with concern.

"OK, you can go."

He walked out, and the teacher hastily passed him in the hallway on the way to the fourth floor. He heard him say something to the TA with a grave expression. Something about "too much pressure," and Jake felt a bit sorry for having been so **ferocious**. Still, there were a great many things which even teachers don't understand.

He thought back over the summer up to that point, his father's prescription to 'make something beautiful' and Jessica's parental **anguish**, Ashley's empty chair and his own continual **preoccupation** with the scores he received each week. All that work for a number, he thought. And the definition of *maverick*. And the interpretation of a thousand **quasi**-garbled passages, their meanings always hidden by complexity and **esoteric** language. It was too important and too **ludicrous** all at the same time.

Vocabulary

0792
obfuscated [ábfəskèitid]

a. **어리둥절한, 혼란스러운, 애매한**   perplexed and confused
발음이 비슷한 obscure '불투명한, 애매한'과 연관지어 기억하자.
The crash of the Soviet Union made many countries **obfuscated**. (*adj.*)

0793
arbitrary [á:rbətrèri]

a. **임의적인, 제멋대로의**   despotic or tyrannical; referring to randomness, random, inconsistent
라틴어 arbitrarius 는 arbiter '중재자'의 판단력에 맡긴다는 뜻이다. 즉 옳고 그름이 딱 정해져 있지 않고 '임의적'이란 뜻이다.
The choice of players for the team seemed completely **arbitrary**. (*adj.*)

0794
enraged [ɪn|reɪdʒd]

a. **격분한, 화가 난**   exasperated, angered
rage가 '분노'라는 의미이므로 화가 났다는 뜻이다.
Her mother was just **enraged** when she came home drunk. (*adj.*)

0795
muster [|mʌstə(r)]

v. **모으다, 소집하다**   to gather or bring together for a service; to assemble for inspection, service, etc
cluster 와 muster 가 발음이 비슷하니까 같이 외우자! 뜻도 같다.
The political candidate **mustered** all the support he could for the election. (*v.*)

0796
benign [bɪ|naɪn]

a. **상냥한**   benevolent, gracious
상냥한 선생님은 똑같은 문제를 nine(아홉 번, sounds like nign)이라도 설명해 줄 거야.
The **benign** grandfather let his grandchildren tug his beard and kiss him whenever they wanted to. (*adj.*)

0797
conciliatory [kən|sɪliətɔ:ri]

a. **달래는**   attempting to placate or behave in an acquiescent manner   *v.* conciliate
아기가 무서워하는 것을 숨기고(conceal → concil) 달랬다고(conciliate) 외우자.
The next time he spoke, he used a more **conciliatory** tone. (*adj.*)

0798
timbre [|tæmbə(r)]

n. 음색　tone
노래방에서 탬버린을(tambourine → timbre) 흔들며 목소리를 낼 때의 음색을(timbre) 떠올려보자.
I recognise the **timbre** of her voice. (*n.*)

0799
dismayed [disméid]

a. 낭패한, 깜짝 놀란　thoroughly disheartened, discouraged; distressed
옛 불어 esmaier 는 '문제되게 하다, 방해하게 하다'라는 뜻이다.
She was **dismayed** to hear that she had been fired from her dream job. (*adj.*)

0800
slump [slʌmp]

v. 털썩 앉다　to fall heavily or collapse
털썩 주저앉고 싶은 힘든 시기를 슬럼프라고 한다.
The old man **slumped** down in his chair. (*v.*)

0801
ferocious [fəróuʃəs]

a. 흉포한, 난폭한, 포악한, 잔인한　violent, brutal, truculent, of a wild, fierce, and savage nature
ferox(savage, wild)가 어원. feral, fierce가 모두 같은 어원이다.
Ferocious attack. (*adj.*)

0802
anguish [ǽŋgwiʃ]

n. 고민, 고뇌; 심한 고통　great suffering or acute distress; acute pain
화가(anger → ang) 날 정도로 큰 고민이라고 외워보자.
He groaned in **anguish**. (*n.*)

0803
preoccupation [pri|ɑ:kju|peɪʃn]

n. 집착　obsession or fixation
occupation은 직업이라는 의미인데, 직업보다도 먼저(pre) 생각할 정도로 집착한다고(preoccupy) 생각하자.
She found his **preoccupation** with money irritating. (*n.*)

0804
quasi [kwéizai]

a. 외견상[표면상]의; 유사의; 준(準)…, 반(半)…　seeming; virtual
노트르담의 꼽추에 나오는 주인공 콰지모도(Quasimodo)의 이름의 뜻은 '거의 인간이다'라는 뜻으로, quasi는 '비슷하다'라는 의미를 가지고 있다.
We are talking about a **quasi**-judicial role. (*adj.*)

0805
esoteric [èsətérik]

a. 소수만 이해하는   understood by only the select few who have special knowledge, hard to understand; known only to the chosen

eso(within → within the circle)를 어원으로 가진 단어로, 'known only within a certain circle'이란 뜻을 내포하고 있다.

Terry, the **esoteric**, liked to speak in a made-up language that only a few can understand. (*adj.*)

0806
ludicrous [lúːdəkrəs]

a. 터무니없는, 익살맞은, 바보 같은   causing laughter because of absurdity, laughable

ludo는 '놀다, 즐기다'라는 뜻으로 너무 익살맞아서 즐겁다는 의미로 해석할 수 있다.

When the small girl wore such a huge hat, people laughed and thought that her looks were **ludicrous**. (*adj.*)

Episode 49
MATCHING Quiz

1. obfuscated
2. arbitrary
3. enraged
4. muster
5. benign
6. conciliatory
7. timbre
8. dismayed
9. slump
10. ferocious
11. anguish
12. preoccupation
13. quasi
14. esoteric
15. ludicrous

A. causing laughter because of absurdity
B. understood by only the select few who have special knowledge
C. great suffering or acute distress; pain
D. perplexed and confused
E. despotic or tyrannical; referring to randomness
F. exasperated, angered
G. tone
H. thoroughly disheartened
I. to gather or bring together for a service
J. benevolent
K. attempting to placate or behave in an acquiescent manner
L. obsession or fixation
M. seeming; virtual
N. violent, brutal, truculent
O. to fall heavily or collapse

1-D, 2-E, 3-F, 4-I, 5-J, 6-K, 7-G, 8-H, 9-O, 10-N, 11-C, 12-L, 13-M, 14-B, 15-A

더 많은 문제를 풀고자 한다면 www.quizlet.com에서 'paul academy seoul' class를 검색

Episode 50

A New Member, and a Proposal

807 recuperate [2]
v. 회복하다
to recover, improve in health

808 temper [21]
v. 완화시키다
to moderate

809 contentious [2]
a. 논란의 소지가 있는
tending to argue; quarrelsome

810 erudite [3]
a. 학식 있는
learned; scholarly

811 catalyst [2]
n. 촉매
something that motivates or causes activity to occur

812 affirmation [6]
n. 확언
agreement or 'yes' response

On Thursday, having **recuperated** noticeably from the mood he'd had since the weekend, Jake decided that he ought to do something following the surprising conversation he'd had on Monday afternoon. With this in mind, he made a sudden proposal to his usual lunchtime companions: that a new member be initiated into the Mafia.

After some debate, then, Ashley was allowed to become a member of the group. Sam was concerned that he would have to **temper** his **contentious** language around her, but after Ashley first sat down with a heavy sigh followed by a heavier swear word, he felt much more comfortable. TJ, predictably, blinded by the light of love, thought it a perfect opportunity to get his 'girlfriend' to join the now-mixed group, though she had not accepted any of his recent requests to join them. (This, of course, didn't stop him from referring to her as his 'future wife').

For Jake, ever since he had realized that the people who gathered regularly at lunch had become his friends, harbored a secret desire to introduce them to his uncle, and now that the most **erudite** (though still nervous) girl in the academy was sitting alongside him at lunch as well as in class, he felt it was the perfect **catalyst** for a meeting.

"You guys free on Saturday afternoon?" he asked innocently, as they finished their lunch.

They all were, though qualified their **affirmations**, as there was always the perpetual danger of their parents' planning to make them 'unfree' for the purposes of family reunions or some other stupid activity.

"I was thinking of going to visit my uncle."

"Yes?" Sam asked indifferently. "So?"

"Well, I was wondering if you wanted to come with me. He's really cool. I mean," he added quickly, **envisioning** the **juxtaposition** between uncles, "he's no movie actor, but he's really interesting and he might even help us with SAT."

TJ groaned. After the mention of his uncle during that first lunch, little attention had been paid to his celebrity connection, which previously had been his primary means of making friends or convincing **fawning** boys to follow and **revere** him. Jake had noticed that he no longer wore the huge watch, which had at first seemed too big. However, the other boy was clearly a bit jealous, and his **peevish** expression was noticeable for the remainder of lunch. In truth, he had not heard anything from the man in months, apart from a suggestion his father had made during one of his evening **vituperations** that his uncle "was deeply concerned with your performance," which was a patent lie that the old man never bothered to back up with evidence.

Ignorant of TJ's sadness regarding the question of uncles, Jake began to tell them all about his uncle: his unusual character, the fact that he never married and yet seemed to have acquired a few female admirers, his **morbid** interest in music, his love of learning. For most of the descriptions, Sam and TJ were pretty bored, but as the descriptions continued, Ashley seemed more and more **enthralled**. Her eyes shone with interest.

"Sounds great, Jake. What time are you going?" she said eagerly.

"Well, he offered to have lunch with me after the test. I was thinking of asking him about some of the vocab."

"Hmm. Does he read a lot?"

"He does. And he reads classic literature."

"Oh really? What books?"

This was a question he hadn't **foreseen**, and he had a **scanty** knowledge of the subject (his uncle had encouraged him to read a few of the classics of English literature, but he had always declined and just read their descriptions online, along with a half-hearted attempt to make it through the opening chapters). He thought of any authors he knew, but could only think of Shakespeare.

---

813 envision [2]
v. 마음 속에 그리다, 상상하다
to imagine or picture mentally

814 fawning [3]
a. 아양떠는
flattering or sycophantic; trying to gain favor by praising or following

815 revere [21]
v. 숭배하다
to respect, worship

816 peevish [2]
a. 짜증을 잘 내는
argumentative or annoyed; fractious

817 vituperation [2]
n. 혹평
severe criticism, castigation

818 morbid [2]
a. 병적인
suggesting an unhealthy mental state or attitude

819 enthralled [5]
a. 마음을 사로잡는
deeply attracted or fixated on something

820 foreseen [2]
a. 예견된
anticipated, predicted
opp. unforeseen

821 scanty [7]
a. 얼마 안 되는
very little; insufficient

"Honestly, there's too many to count," he said apologetically.

"Well, regardless, I'm excited to meet him," Ashley replied.

"I know he feels the same."

Vocabulary

0807
recuperate [2]

[rɪ|kuːpəreɪt]

v. 회복하다, 건강해지다   to recover, improve in health, to restore health
recover와 비슷한 뜻으로, 없어진 것을 원래 상태로 되돌릴 때 쓰인다.
He went to the beach to **recuperate**.

0808
temper [21]

[témpər]

v. 완화시키다, 누그러뜨리다   to moderate, to mitigate
temperate '차분한'이라는 단어를 생각하자.
She **tempered** his rudeness by saying sweetly, "Oh, my dear, he just got fired from his job today; it's nothing personal." (v.)

0809
contentious [2]

[kənténʃəs]

a. 논란의 소지가 있는, 다투기(논쟁)를 좋아하는   tending to argue; quarrelsome
contend '싸우다'라는 뜻의 단어에서 유래.
The highly **contentious** presidential race created a tense atmosphere.(adj.)

0810
erudite [3]

[érjudàit]

a. 학식 있는, 박식한   learned; scholarly
접두사 e- (out of) 과 rude(거친, 수준이 낮은)가 합쳐진 단어로 '거치거나 수준이 낮지 않은', 즉 '학식이 있는'을 뜻한다.
The **erudite** English professor impressed his students with his extensive knowledge.(adj.)

0811
catalyst [2]

[kǽtəlist]

n. 촉매(제), 기폭제   something that motivates or causes activity to occur; agent which brings about a chemical change; stimulant
화학실험을 할 때 결과를 빨리 내기 위해서 catalyst(촉매제)를 넣는 걸 본 적이 있을 거야.
A simple misunderstanding became the **catalyst** for full-blown war between the cats and dogs.(n.)

0812
affirmation [6]

[æfərméiʃən]

n. 확언   agreement or 'yes' response
confirm(확인하다)와 연결해서 외워보자.
The ruling was a welcome **affirmation** of the constitutional right to free speech. (n.)

0813
envision ²

[ɪn|vɪʒn]

v. 마음 속에 그리다, 상상하다   to imagine or picture mentally
vision이 시야라는 뜻이므로, 안에서(in → en) 보다, 즉 '상상한다'고 외우자.
They **envision** an equal society, free of poverty and disease. (*v.*)

0814
fawning ³

[fɔ́:nɪŋ]

a. 아양 떠는, 알랑거리는   flattering or sycophantic; trying to gain favor by praising or following, courting favor by cringing and flattering
'개가 꼬리치다'는 뜻을 갖고 있다.
The fans **fawned** over the celebrity. (*v.*)

0815
revere ²¹

[rɪ|vɪr]

v. 숭배하다   to respect, worship
respect(존경하다)보다 한 단계 더 높은 감정이라고 외워보자.
I'm sure he'll **revere** you as much as I do. (*v.*)

0816
peevish ²

[pí:vɪʃ]

a. 짜증을 잘 내는, 투정부리는, 성마른   argumentative or annoyed; fractious, bad-tempered
pee는 urine의 뜻을 가지고 있고 화장실이 가고싶을 때는 투정을 부리므로 peevish의 뜻을 유추해낼 수 있다.
The **peevish** kid threw food on the floor and cried to ask for candy. (*adj.*)

0817
vituperation ²

[vaɪ|tu:pə|reɪʃn]

n. 혹평   severe criticism, castigation
물어뜯고(bite → vit) 어퍼컷을(upper → uper) 날리는 것처럼 혹평을 퍼부었다고 외워보자.
His speech was full of **vituperation**. (*n.*)

0818
morbid ²

[mɔ́:rbɪd]

a. 병적인, 불건전한   suggesting an unhealthy mental state or attitude, affected by, caused by, causing, or characteristic of disease
mori는 '죽음'을 뜻하는 라틴어이다.
"Don't be so **morbid**," said Samantha when her sister Rose remarked that the tree branches looked like broken fingers waving for help. (*adj.*)

0819
enthralled [5]
[ɪn|θrɔːld]

a. **마음을 사로잡는**   deeply attracted or fixated on something
너무나 스릴 있어서(thrill → thrall) 마음을 사로잡는다고(enthrall) 생각하자.
The dancer **enthralls** her audiences with the beauty of her movements.

0820
foreseen [2]
[fɔːr|siː]

a. **예견된**   anticipated, predicted   *opp.* unforeseen
미리 앞에서(fore) 본(seen), 즉 '예견됐다'는 의미다.
The fate of a battle cannot be **foreseen**. (*v.*)

0821
scanty [7]
[|skænti]

a. **얼마 안 되는, 빈약한**   very little; insufficient
대충 스캔을(scan) 해 봐도 딱 빈약한 게 보인다고 외우자.
This country has a **scanty** public security. (*adj.*)

Episode 50

MATCHING Quiz

1. recuperate
2. temper
3. contentious
4. erudite
5. catalyst
6. affirmation
7. envision
8. fawning
9. revere
10. peevish
11. vituperation
12. morbid
13. enthralled
14. foreseen
15. scanty

A. to moderate
B. agreement or 'yes' response
C. anticipated, predicted
D. learned; scholarly
E. tending to argue; quarrelsome
F. argumentative or annoyed; fractious
G. to imagine or picture mentally
H. something that motivates or causes activity to occur
I. to respect, worship
J. deeply attracted or fixated on something
K. flattering or sycophantic; trying to gain favor by praising or following
L. severe criticism, castigation
M. very little; insufficient
N. suggesting an unhealthy mental state or attitude
O. to recover, improve in health

1-O, 2-A, 3-E, 4-D, 5-H, 6-B, 7-G, 8-K, 9-I, 10-F, 11-L, 12-N, 13-J, 14-C, 15-M

더 많은 문제를 풀고자 한다면 www.quizlet.com에서 'paul academy seoul' class를 검색

Episode 51

A Tragic Ending

822 discredit ⁹
v. 존경심을 떨어뜨리다
to injure the credit or reputation of

823 refined ⁶
a. 세련된, 교양 있는
sophisticated, polished, cultivated

824 enchant ⁵
v. 황홀하게 하다
to delight, to the point where it seems magical

825 detach ⁶
v. 떼다, 분리하다
to cut off, sever

826 repudiate ²
v. 거절하다, 거부하다
to reject

827 slur ²
n. 비방, 중상하는 말
disparaging remark; slander, innuendo

828 sordid ³
a. 비도덕적인
dirty or vulgar (not sophisticated); lurid

829 tenet ³
n. 주의, 교리
statement of belief

830 chasm ³
n. 아주 깊은 틈
wide space; gulf

The other members of the Mafia (now including Ashley) had begun to forget about TJ's romance, particularly since he had done nothing to initiate further contact with the object of his affection. On the day he tried to restore this connection, however, TJ unfortunately obtained evidence that his chance of love at the academy was doomed.

His fears were difficult to **discredit**. To begin with, his style, which was supposed to be smooth and **refined,** was not as **enchanting** as he'd imagined, and anyway Chastity (as her name turned out to be) generally avoided later lunch dates by making friends with a few girls from her class, effectively **detaching** ties from the Mafia for the time being.

Much of this seemed to stem from one central problem, which arose during Chastity's second lunch date with the group on the Friday of that week. She had **repudiated** many such offers, but now the presence of Ashley reassured her with the promise of another female supporter against the male majority.

Unfortunately, TJ, a fan of casual **slurs** regarding sex and taboo topics, tried to introduce his sense of humor to his beloved, who misunderstood almost every joke as some **sordid** insult to her gender.

As the lunch wore on, TJ seemingly violated every one of the **tenets** of Chastity's personal **ideology**. He didn't do it on purpose, but the **chasm** between the both of them and their understanding of the world was just too large to overcome. For example, when the food arrived, TJ pointed out the similarities between the consistencies of the sweet and sour sauce and snot. It was a harmless joke for a young boy, but Jake nearly went red with embarrassment, and Chastity sank in her seat and seemed genuinely to think the boy insane. Even Sam and Ashley (who didn't mind the humor so much) were put off by this **breach** of **protocol**.

Of course, on learning how sensitive the object of his affection was, TJ spent the rest of the meal trying desperately to use the rest of lunch to **assure** her that he was just as serious as she was. These attempts, too, went bad, as he reverted to his usual vocabulary when he got nervous, which meant, naturally, that he began to swear. **Abundantly**. His ability to succeed at romance, it seemed, had been **excised**.

Jake was worried that his friend would be denied his former **assertiveness** by this brief romance, but it seemed that TJ bounced back quite quickly, and was soon walking around academy once more, continuing to study vocabulary with the same enthusiasm, if only to have more words with which to make jokes and **rag** the TAs.

He would simply have more words for the next girl he met, he said at the next lunch.

831 breach [3]
n. 위반
break or transgression (as in a set of rules)

832 protocol [2]
n. 외교 의례, 프로토콜
the customs and regulations dealing with diplomatic formality

833 assure [3]
v. 장담하다, 확언하다
to convince, persuade

834 abundantly [15]
adv. 아주 분명하게
very

835 excised [2]
a. 삭제된
deleted

836 assertiveness [16]
n. 적극성
confident aggression or self-assurance

837 rag [2]
v. 놀리다
to tease

Vocabulary

0822
discredit [9]
[diskrédit]

v. 존경심을 떨어뜨리다, 신임을 떨어뜨리다   to injure the credit or reputation of
dis + credit '신뢰, 신임을 떨어뜨리다'.
The politician **discredited** the president by pointing out his various scandals. (v.)

0823
refined [6]
[riːfáind]

a. 세련된, 교양 있는, 정제된   sophisticated, polished, cultivated; improved
re(again) + fin(end)가 합쳐져 '다시 마무리하다'라는 뜻으로 '정교하게 하다, 품위있게 하다'로 발전된 단어이다.
Simplicity and beauty is the two key-words to build a **refined** watch.(adj.)

0824
enchant [5]
[ɪnˈtʃænt]

v. 황홀하게 하다   to delight, to the point where it seems magical; to delight to a high degree
enchant가 '마법에 걸리게 하다'는 의미도 있는 걸 기억해.
Her smile was so **enchanting** that the teacher did not punish her for being late. (adj.)

0825
detach [6]
[dɪˈtætʃ]

v. 떼다, 분리하다   to cut off, sever
attach가 '붙이다' 의미이므로, detach는 '떼어내다'는 의미이다.
Detach the coupon and return it as soon as possible. (v.)

0826
repudiate [2]
[rɪpjúːdièit]

v. 거절하다, 거부하다   to reject, to refuse
refuse와 비슷하게 들리므로 '거절하다'라는 의미를 가진다고 생각하자.
The company **repudiated** the other company's offer to settle, which made the other company very angry.(adj.)

0827
slur [slɜː(r)]

n. 비방, 중상하는 말; 불분명하게 발음하다   disparaging remark; slander, innuendo; to pronounce (a syllable, word, etc.) indistinctly by combining, reducing, or omitting sounds, as in hurried or careless manner
졸려서(sleepy → slu) 발음이 제대로 안 나온다고(slur) 외우자.
Because he **slurred** his words, nobody could understand what exactly he said. (*v.*)

0828
sordid [sɔ́ːrdid]

a. 비도덕적인, 더러운, 야비한   dirty or vulgar (not sophisticated); lurid, filthy
SOR(ry) I DID this DIRTY, FILTHY thing. 이라는 문장을 외우면 기억하기 쉽다.
The **sordid** details of the politician's life made everyone gasp in horror.

0829
tenet [|tenɪt]

n. 주의, 교리   statement of belief
십(ten) 계명은 기독교의 가장 오래된 교리(tenet) 중 하나이다.
Ethics has been a central **tenet** of our Institute for years. (*n.*)

0830
chasm [kǽzm]

n. 아주 깊은 틈, 갈라진 틈   wide space; gulf, wide gap in the earth
chasm의 'ch'와 'sm'은 '자르다, 갈라지다(scissor)'에 의미를 두고 있다.
Chasm between mountains. (*n.*)

0831
breach [briːtʃ]

n. 위반   break or transgression (as in a set of rules)
해변에(beach) 쓰레기를 버리는 것은 법에 위반(breach)되는 행위이다.
A **breach** of contract (*n.*)

0832
protocol [próutəkɔ̀ːl]

n. 외교 의례, 프로토콜; 의정서   the customs and regulations dealing with diplomatic formality, A declaration or memorandum of agreement less solemn and formal than a treaty
라틴어의 'protocollum'과 그리스어의 'protokollon'이란 어원에서 유래하였으며 그 의미는 문서, 교황 칙서, 외교 의례 등 서류, 문서의 총체적인 것을 포함한다.
Many countries signed the Kyoto **protocol** to declare the importance of nature and decrease the amount of gas released. (*n.*)

0833
assure [3]
[əʃʊr]

v. 장담하다, 확언하다   to convince, persuade
assure '확실하다, 보증하다'의 명사형이다.
She's perfectly safe, I can **assure** you. (*v.*)

0834
abundantly [15]
[əˈbʌndəntli]

adv. 아주 분명하게   very
abundant는 '충분하다'는 의미이다. 한 꾸러미만큼(bundle → bund) 충분히 있다고 생각해보자. 따라서 abundantly는 충분히 말했으므로 분명하다는 의미이다.
She made her wishes **abundantly** clear. (*adv.*)

0835
excised [2]
[ɪkˈsaɪzd]

a. 삭제된   deleted
X (ex) 자를 그려 삭제했다고 외워보자.
Certain passages were **excised** from the book. (*v.*)

0836
assertiveness [16]
[əˈsɜːtɪvnəs]

n. 적극성   confident aggression or self-assurance
assert는 '주장하다'는 의미이다. 자신있게(sure → ser) 주장했다고 생각해보자. 따라서 assertiveness는 자신의 주장을 잘 얘기할 정도로 적극성이 있다는 얘기이다.
Chantelle's **assertiveness** stirred up his deep-seated sense of inadequacy. (*n.*)

0837
rag [2]
[ræg]

v. 놀리다, 농담   to tease
랩으로(rap) 사람을 디스, 즉 놀렸다고(rag) 외우자.
I only said it for a **rag**. (*n.*)

Note :

Episode 51

MATCHING Quiz

1. discredit
2. refined
3. enchant
4. detach
5. repudiate
6. slur
7. sordid
8. tenet
9. chasm
10. breach
11. protocol
12. assure
13. abundantly
14. excised
15. assertiveness
16. rag

A. to cut off, sever
B. dirty or vulgar (not sophisticated); lurid
C. to delight, to the point where it seems magical
D. the customs and regulations dealing with diplomatic formality
E. to reject
F. disparaging remark; slander, innuendo
G. break or transgression (as in a set of rules)
H. statement of belief
I. wide space; gulf
J. very
K. deleted
L. to convince, persuade
M. confident aggression or self-assurance
N. to tease
O. to injure the credit or reputation of
P. sophisticated, polished, cultivated

1-O, 2-P, 3-C, 4-A, 5-E, 6-F, 7-B, 8-H, 9-I, 10-G, 11-D, 12-L, 13-J, 14-K, 15-M, 16-N

더 많은 문제를 풀고자 한다면 www.quizlet.com에서 'paul academy seoul' class를 검색

Episode 52: The Socratic Method of Making Friends

838 tenaciously [6]
adv. 끈질기게
persistently; in a recalcitrant manner

839 perennial [3]
a. 지속되는
lasting for an indefinitely long time

840 seclusion [2]
n. 은둔, 고립
isolation

841 guru [4]
n. 전문가
expert

842 pavement [5]
n. 포장도로
a road covered with asphalt

843 autonomy [7]
n. 독립, 자유
independence, freedom

844 denounce [6]
v. 맹렬히 비난하다
to criticize, excoriate

Given everything that had happened during the previous week, the Saturday test, the seventh they had taken so far that summer, had gone quite well. Jake got a 600 in the reading, though his essay score had remained a seven. Greg, when confronted by several students who felt their scores should have been higher, **tenaciously** maintained that the essays were still too short. Still, Ashley had scored well enough to put her near the top of the class (second only to a mysterious private student whose name was now famous for its **perennial** place atop the chart posted in the hallway, but who sat in **seclusion** at the back of the room on Saturdays), so she was suitably happy. Happy enough, it turned out, to jump up and down as she and Jake walked toward the subway to take them to the university.

Apart from a few visits with his father, Jake had never made this trip with another person, and was eager to make his knowledge clear to his new companion. In a way, he had been thankful when TJ had called him the night prior to say he couldn't make it. He could be the **guru**, guiding his charge around campus. He wisely pointed out the good cafes, and the 'interesting' bookstore (which he'd visited once). Ashley was amazed. She was one of those people for whom college is more of an ideal than simply a stepping stone to some adult occupation. As they walked along the leafy **pavement**, she turned to Jake and smiled broadly for the first time since they'd met.

"I can't wait to be a college student! Can you?"

Jake had to admit that escape from the SAT was attractive, but thought more often of the **autonomy** he'd gain from living somewhere far away. How he could sleep in without his mother **denouncing** him, how he could stay out walking and listening to music without having to be home for dinner.

When they got to the familiar office, the Professor was absent, much as Jake expected. He'd left a note to say that he was having coffee with a colleague and "might be some time, so make yourselves comfortable." Ashley immediately began looking at the selection of books on the shelves, even taking a few down to inspect their contents. Jake went behind the desk to **skim** the CDs to play for her. For some reason, he felt an urge to impress her with his **discerning** taste. He selected Miles Davis' *Birth of the Cool* and pressed play. Apparently, however, his uncle had been listening late the night before, so the volume was turned up nearly to maximum, **instigating a bossy** assistant professor to poke his head into the room a few moments after Jake had turned it down.

"What are you two doing here?" he said, suspiciously eyeing the two as if he'd caught them in the midst of some **unethical** activity.

"I'm the Professor's nephew. We're just waiting for him here."

"Oh," he said, again slowly. "Well make sure to keep the music down. This *is* a place of learning, not playing around."

"Yes sir," Ashley said seriously, before the man moved quickly away. Her laugh must have reached him down the corridor, but neither of them minded much. Besides, at that moment, his uncle arrived.

Jake had told him that a few friends who were coming along for their afternoon meeting, but at first the grey-haired teacher seemed slightly upset at Ashley's presence. He assumed at first that she was a student in one of his lectures.

"Are you here for office hours?" he asked.

"No, no," she replied, turning red slightly, "I'm a friend of your nephew."

"Oh, of course!" he shouted as he crossed the border to shake her vigorously by the hand. "How are you?"

"Fine."

"An easy answer. You don't have to be so **verbose**."

"Sorry?" she asked, as **stumped** as the old man had been a few seconds earlier.

---

845 skim 6
v. 훑어보다
to look through

846 discerning 7
a. 안목이 있는
showing outstanding judgment and understanding

847 instigate 2
v. 착수하게 하다, 부추기다
to urge, foment, stimulate

848 unethical 3
a. 비윤리적인, 비도덕적인
corrupt, immoral

849 verbose 2
a. 장황한
characterized by the use of too many words; wordy

850 stumped 2
a. 당황한, 쩔쩔매는
confused, perplexed

| 851 | **humdrum** ³
a. 단조로운, 따분한
boring

| 852 | **rapacious** ⁴
a. 탐욕스러운
inordinately greedy; predatory

| 853 | **galvanize** ²
v. 활기를 북돋다
to energize or inspire

| 854 | **constricted** ⁴
a. 갑갑한, 좁은
small, narrow

| 855 | **rebukingly** ²
adv. 꾸짖듯이
scoldingly, with disapproval

| 856 | **declaim** ²
v. 낭송하다, 읊다
to recite, make a formal speech

| 857 | **idle** ³
a. 나태한
not working or active; doing nothing

| 858 | **hearth** ²
n. 난로, 화덕
a fireplace; fireside

| 859 | **barren** ⁴
a. 황량한
unproductive; unfruitful

| 860 | **savage** ⁷
a. 야만적인
uncivilized

| 861 | **illicit** ³
a. 불법의
illegal, forbidden

| 862 | **enforce** ³
v. 집행하다
to apply, implement, impose

"'Fine' is hardly an answer. And anyway, it's quite a **humdrum** one. Are you happy or bored? Thriving or dying? Sad? Hungry?"

"**Rapacious**," she decided, smiling at Jake as he came around the desk to greet his uncle.

"What's that I hear apart from hungry stomachs? Ah! Miles! Good choice, my boy." He shook Jake's hand as he always did, as though they were long lost friends. He told them that he would order a few dinners to be brought up to the study and began clearing the desk of its usual mess so they would all have somewhere to eat while they talked.

Conversations with his uncle had always been easy, but the presence of Ashley seemed to **galvanize** the old man into a spirit that made the entire afternoon one of the best he'd ever spent in that **constricted** little room. They talked about the SAT, and about words, with Ashley showing off her vocabulary joyfully. Jake realized that she hadn't had anyone else to really talk to in a long while.

"And of course, you remember *mete* and *dole*, Jake," the old man enquired after they had laid their chopsticks down at the end of the meal. Jake had dim memories of having heard the words, but had to claim ignorance this time.

"Oh, come on now," the Professor said **rebukingly**. "The poem we talked about once. 'Ulysses,' it was called."

"By Tennyson," Ashley interrupted, much to the old man's delight.

"Precisely!" Here, he stood up and made an exaggerated impression of a serious actor's face. Then, from memory, **declaimed**: 'It little profits that an **idle** king, by this still **hearth** among these **barren** hills, matched with an aged wife, I *mete* and *dole* unequal laws unto a **savage** race…'" his naturally loud voice boomed across the table at the two students, almost shaking the glasses of **illicit** beer he'd brought to share (the university having **enforced** a strict 'no alcohol' policy).

"It means… to give," offered Jake shyly.

"Well, more or less, I suppose," said the old man. "To share or distribute would be more accurate, of course, but, 'give' is sufficient for now, I suppose. Do *you* know the poem?" he turned to Ashley.

"We studied it last year in school. But I haven't memorized it or anything," she replied.

"Oh well, you must try to memorize some poetry, especially at your age, when the memory has a bit more adhesive to make it stick. I've tried telling Jake that if he ever wants to court a girl, he must try to learn a few poems. Haven't I, my boy?" His eyes twinkled at his nephew, and though Jake enjoyed the fun, he was somewhat **perturbed** by this mention of his private life.

The rest of the afternoon, stretching into the evening, went much the same way. Once it had gotten cool enough to leave the building (and after they had finished the few cans of beer), the Professor offered to walk back to the subway station with them, on the way talking **predominantly** to Ashley about her future plans and offering them both his offer to "entertain you whenever you wish to visit again."

Once he had turned back to the darkness of the campus, it was clear that the Professor's charms had clearly worked on Ashley.

"He's the best, Jake. Thanks for bringing me here today," she said as they **descended** to the subway tracks, where they each again got trains going in different directions.

Jake was a little worried about his uncle telling his father of his friendship with a girl, a fact which would no doubt raise questions about his studies, and worry his mother, who still clung to the **apocryphal** myth he'd created about Susan. However, a few minutes after he got home, he received a text from the Professor, with the elder's usual humor and confidentiality:

Don't worry. I won't tell your father, as long as you two come again soon.

---

863 perturbed [2]
a. 혼란스러운
annoyed or disturbed

864 predominant [10]
a. 분명한, 뚜렷한
prominent; distinct

865 descend [8]
v. 내려가다
to go or pass from a higher to a lower place

866 apocryphal [2]
a. 출처가 불분명한
of doubtful authorship or authenticity; not true

Vocabulary

0838
tenaciously [6]
[təˈneɪʃəsli]

adv. 끈질기게   persistently; in a recalcitrant manner
열 번이나(ten) 찾아와서 물어볼(ask → ac) 정도로 끈질기다고 외우자.
In spite of his illness, he clung **tenaciously** to his job. (*adv.*)

0839
perennial [3]
[pəˈreniəl]

a. 지속되는, 영원한   lasting for an indefinitely long time; enduring or continually recurring.
permanent 의 per- (지속되는)와 ennial 이 붙어서 '영원히 지속되는'으로 외우자.
A pine is a famous tree with its **perennial** leaves. (*adj.*)

0840
seclusion [2]
[sɪˈkluːʒn]

n. 은둔, 고립   isolation
어디에도 포함되려고(include) 하지 않고 고립됐다고(seclude) 외우자.
The **seclusion** and peace of the island (*n.*)

0841
guru [4]
[ˈɡuːruː]

n. 전문가   expert
스승님 아래에서 가장 오래 자란(grew) 학생이 가장 전문가라고(guru) 생각하자.
He's the **guru** in this field. (*n.*)

0842
pavement [5]
[ˈpeɪvmənt]

n. 포장도로   a road covered with asphalt
시멘트로(cement → cement) 채운 포장도로라고 외우자.
The man is painting the **pavement**. (*n.*)

0843
autonomy [7]
[ɔːˈtɑːnəmi]

n. 독립, 자유   independence, freedom
남의 간섭 없이 혼자서 자동으로(auto) 서로와 대화할 수 있는(nom) 자유를 뜻한다.
People want to have greater **autonomy** in their own lives. (*n.*)

0844
denounce [6]
[dɪˈnáuns]

v. 맹렬히 비난하다, 고발하다   to criticize, excoriate, to point out or publicly accuse
de '나쁘게' + announce '알리다'. '비난하다, 고발하다'.
The critic **denounced** the film as terribly boring. (*v.*)

0845
skim [skɪm]

v. 훑어보다   to look through
skip은 건너뛰는 것이지만 알파벳에서 m이 p보다 먼저 오니까 건너뛰는 것보다는 조금 전단계인 훑어보는 것이라고 외우자.
I always **skim** the financial section of the newspaper. (*v.*)

0846
discerning [disə́:rniŋ]

a. 안목이 있는, 통찰력 있는, 명민한   showing outstanding judgment and understanding, insightful; penetrating
'this' is 'cer'tain. 이건 확실하다고 판단할 수 있는 통찰력을 말한다.
The **discerning** art collector immediately recognized the sculpture as a fake. (*adj.*)

0847
instigate [ˈɪnstɪɡeɪt]

v. 착수하게 하다, 부추기다   to urge, foment, stimulate
막대(stick → stig) 하나를 던져서 군중을 부추긴다고 생각하자.
The government has **instigated** a programme of economic reform. (*v.*)

0848
unethical [ʌnˈeθɪkl]

a. 비윤리적인, 비도덕적인   corrupt, immoral
ethic 은 도덕이라는 뜻이므로 unethical은 도덕적이지 않다는(un) 뜻이다.
Unethical behavior is hard to forgive. (*adj.*)

0849
verbose [vəːrbóus]

a. 장황한, 말이 많은   characterized by the use of too many words; wordy
verb는 '말, 단어'를 뜻하므로 단어를 많이 쓴다는 의미이다.
During the **verbose** lecture, the students struggled to find the professor's main points.(*adj.*)

0850
stumped [stʌmpt]

a. 당황한, 쩔쩔 매는, 모지라진   confused, perplexed, unable to solve a problem
상대방에게 차이면(dumped), 대부분의 사람들은 당황해서 어쩔 줄을 몰라 하게 (stumped) 된다.
I am slightly **stumped** by your last question. (*adj.*)

0851
humdrum [hʌ́mdrʌ̀m]

a. 단조로운, 따분한, 평범한   boring, dull; monotonous
지루할 때 내는 하품 소리와 비슷하다.
Humdrum routine (*adj.*)

0852
rapacious [4]
[rəpéiʃəs]

a. 탐욕스러운   inordinately greedy; predatory, disposed to seize by violence or by unlawful or greedy methods
rape는 '무언가를 빨리 가로채 달아나다'라는 의미의 어원이므로 '탐욕스러운'의 의미를 가진다.
Rapacious soldiers looted the houses in the defeated city. (*adj.*)

0853
galvanize [2]
[gǽlvənàiz]

v. 활기를 북돋다, 충격요법을 쓰다   to energize or inspire, to stimulate by or as if by a galvanic current
죽은 개구리 다리를 이용해 전기를 통하게 한 18세기 과학자 Luigi Galvani의 이름에서 유래한 단어이다.
The 9/11 has **galvanized** seriousness of terrorism in North America. (*v.*)

0854
constricted [4]
[kən|strɪktɪd]

a. 갑갑한, 좁은   small, narrow
지나치게 엄격한(strict) 부모님과 같이(con) 있으면 갑갑한(constricted) 느낌이 든다고 외우자.
a **constricted** vision of the world (*adj.*)

0855
rebukingly [2]
[rɪ|bjuːkɪŋli]

adv. 꾸짖듯이   scoldingly, with disapproval
꾸짖으면서(rebuke) 다시(re) 엉덩이를(butt → bu) 차는(kick → ke) 모습을 생각해보자.
The remark provoked a sharp **rebuke** from Iraq. (*n.*)

0856
declaim [2]
[dɪ|kleɪm]

v. 낭송하다, 읊다   to recite, make a formal speech
claim이 '주장하다'는 의미이므로 declaim은 '낭송하다, 읊다'라는 의미이다.
She **declaimed** the famous opening speech of the play. (*v.*)

0857
idle [3]
[áidl]

a. 나태한, 게으름뱅이의   not working or active; doing nothing, lazy; unproductive
idle은 15세기에 '시간을 낭비하다'라는 뜻이었다. 게으름뱅이는 아무것도 하지 않은 채 시간을 낭비하지? 그렇게 외우자.
The lazy student **idled** in his room instead of doing his homework. (*v.*)

0858
hearth ² [hɑːrθ]

n. 난로, 화덕   a fireplace; fireside
난로는(hearth) 집의 심장이라는(heart) 표현을 생각해보자.
The cat dozed in its favourite spot on the **hearth**. (*n.*)

0859
barren ⁴ [bǽrən]

a. 황량한; 불모의   unfruitful; unproductive, not producing; desolate
bare는 '맨, 벌거벗은'이라는 의미이다.
After famine, the **barren** wasteland was left by itself. (*adj.*)

0860
savage ⁷ [sǽvidʒ]

a. 야만적인, 야만의   uncivilized, A wild and uncivilized human being
Brave new world(멋진 신세계)라는 책의 주인공 John Savage는 인디언 보호구역에서 wild하게 생활했다.
When traveling to unknown places, you should be aware of the presence of **savages**. (*n.*)

0861
illicit ³ [ɪ|lɪsɪt]

a. 불법의   illegal, forbidden
illegal과 연결해서 외워보자.
Illicit work must be tackled at the roots. (*adj.*)

0862
enforce ³ [ɪn|fɔːrs]

v. 집행하다   to apply, implement, impose, to put in force
force(힘)으로 enforce 해야겠지?
The king **enforced** the new law by threatening to kill anyone who didn't obey. (*v.*)

0863
perturbed ² [pərtə́ːrbd]

a. 혼란스러운   annoyed or disturbed
disturb가 '방해하다'라는 의미이므로 100퍼센트(per) 방해 받아서 혼란스럽다고(perturb) 외우자.
She didn't seem **perturbed** at the change of plan. (*adj.*)

0864
predominant ¹⁰ [pridάmənənt]

a. 분명한, 뚜렷한, 우세한, 뛰어난   prominent; distinct
라틴어 domin은 '주인이 되어 다스리다'의 뜻으로 접두어 pre와 합쳐져 '먼저 지배하는 뛰어난 능력을 가진 것'을 의미한다. 관련어 domain(영토), dominion(주권, 지배권) 등도 모두 여기서 파생되었다.
The forest is **predominantly** oak. (*adv.*)

0865
descend [dɪ|sɛnd]

v. 내려가다; 내려오다   to go or pass from a higher to a lower place; to come down

죽음(death → desc)과 끝을(end) 향해 내려간다고 외우자.

The old man **descended** the stairs, all the way down to the first floor. (v.)

0866
apocryphal [əpákrəfəl]

a. 출처가 불분명한, 사실이 아닐 듯한   of doubtful authorship or authenticity; not true, untrue; made up

apo(away), 라틴어 crypticus(hidden)에서 '정식 경전으로 인정받지 못하고 멀리 떨어져 숨어 있는'이란 뜻이다.

There are many **apocryphal** stories when it comes to heroes but people believe them anyway (adj.)

Episode 52

MATCHING Quiz

1. tenaciously
2. perennial
3. seclusion
4. guru
5. pavement
6. autonomy
7. denounce
8. skim
9. discerning
10. instigate
11. unethical
12. verbose
13. stumped
14. humdrum
15. rapacious
16. galvanize
17. constricted
18. rebukingly
19. declaim
20. idle

A. not working or active; doing nothing
B. to recite, make a formal speech
C. persistently; in a recalcitrant manner
D. lasting for an indefinitely long time
E. a road covered with asphalt
F. isolation
G. expert
H. to look through
I. showing outstanding judgment and understanding
J. independence, freedom
K. to criticize, excoriate
L. characterized by the use of too many words; wordy
M. confused, perplexed
N. corrupt, immoral
O. inordinately greedy; predatory
P. to energize or inspire
Q. to urge, foment, stimulate
R. scoldingly, with disapproval
S. boring
T. small, narrow

1-C, 2-D, 3-F, 4-G, 5-E, 6-J, 7-K, 8-H, 9-I, 10-Q, 11-N, 12-L, 13-M, 14-S, 15-O, 16-P, 17-T, 18-R, 19-B, 20-A

더 많은 문제를 풀고자 한다면 www.quizlet.com에서 'paul academy seoul' class를 검색

Episode 53

The Boat Race

That Sunday, feeling adventurous, Jake, TJ, Ashley, and Sam planned a picnic to the river. It was to be, as TJ proudly said, "An SAT festival," though there would be only four attendees. They agreed four people could easily be enough for a festival, and arranged for a **culinary** dish (mothers may have helped), and took their bags of sandwiches and soda to the grassy fields looking out onto the blue channel that flowed through the grey city.

There had been a drought for much of the spring, a dryness that had left the **turf** weak and yellowed, but they managed to find a spot which was still green. There, Ashley and Sam laid a few blankets end to end and began their feast, while the other two went to the water's edge to stare out. People do this and we do not know why, but it is most likely an ancient longing to fly or to return to the water. Regardless of the explanation, they stood there in silence for a few moments, TJ counting the beer cans in the shallows and Jake looking to the other side.

"Wish we could do this every day," he said.

"But then how would we improve?" his companion said cynically.

"Dunno. But it'd be better than that air conditioned hell we go to."

"True."

Ashley called out from the blankets. "We're going to eat your food if you stay out there looking like old men staring out into nothing!"

They returned.

"I don't know why you guys wanted to come here," Sam sniffed. He had an allergy to grass seeds, and had suggested they see a movie instead.

"Oh come on, man. Look at that!"

A sailboat had come into view, its mast **rigid** and **glimmering** in the afternoon sun, its smooth form cutting through the waves, its sails **swelling** in the wind as it headed toward the bridge, on which had been placed a statue to **commemorate** the war veterans.

"How are you going to see that while staying inside?"

The taller boy stayed silent besides his sniffing.

"Well, anyway, what do you propose we do now that we're here?" Ashley wasn't sure what boys did at the river, besides playing sports

---

867 culinary [3]
a. 요리의
relating to or used in cooking or the kitchen

868 turf [3]
n. 잔디
grass

869 rigid [8]
a. 뻣뻣한, 단단한
stiff; not flexible

870 glimmering [6]
a. 희미하게 빛나는
gleaming, flickering

871 swell [3]
v. 불룩해지다
to bulge out, as a sail or the middle of a cask

872 commemorate [7]
v. 기념하다
to serve as a memorial or reminder of

873 gape 5
v. (놀라서) 바라보다
to stare with open mouth, as in wonder

874 query 3
n. 의문, 질문
a question, inquiry

875 conducive 2
a. 도움이 되는
useful, helpful

876 buoyant 2
a. 부력이 있는, 물에 뜨는
able to float

877 befit 2
v. 걸맞다
to be proper or appropriate for; suit; fit

878 scheme 7
n. 계획
plan, project

879 brashly 2
adv. 성급하게, 경솔하게
recklessly

880 chide 3
v. 꾸짖다
to scold; reproach

881 impetuous 4
a. 충동적인
characterized by rash action; impulsive

882 prone 7
a. ~하기 쉬운
liable, disposed

883 crude 9
a. 대강의
lacking finish, polish, or completeness

884 tether 3
v. 묶다
to tie

or hitting one another.

"We could build a boat!" Jake said suddenly, the food having revived his spirits after the early morning test and its stresses.

The other three **gaped** at him.

"A boat? Do I look like a carpenter, Jake?" TJ asked.

"Well, I was just thinking of a small one, or maybe two that we could race."

No one had too many **queries** about this, as long as Jake gathered the materials. Jake stood up as they seemed to sink further into the grass, lying down or taking out their phones to text other distant acquaintances.

He looked around for material which might be **conducive** to a project such as this, anything that looked **buoyant** enough to float. Water bottles arranged behind the convenience store seemed to **befit** the project, but he didn't want to be responsible for polluting the river. Then, he noticed a few leaves sitting on the grass in the shade of a tall tree. They were long and wide and curved upwards on the edges like canoes, and he thought that they looked like perfect candidates for the **scheme**, as long as they didn't immediately sink.

He took a few to the edge of the river, **brashly** leaning out over water and almost falling in. He kept his balance, and released one of the 'boats' onto the stream. It floated!

He ran back to the blanket, where the others were and told them of his new boats. They **chided** him for being childishly **impetuous**, but in such a peaceful setting, everyone is **prone** to being a bit childish, and eventually they all agreed to a boat race.

"Are you sure they will work, Jake?" Ashley asked uncertainly, holding one of their temporary boats in her hands to check its weight.

"Oh sure, they should be fine," he replied smiling. At last, he had undertaken a project which didn't involve vocabulary or money or girls. *Why haven't I done this before*? he thought.

TJ suggested that the game was silly, but still managed to make a small thin captain for his boat, and gave the man a cigarette to take on as cargo. Sam, who enjoyed sitting by the water as it had fewer grass seeds, sniffed and made his own **crude** imitation of a boatman.

Ashley, it will not surprise you, took the game even more seriously than the others, and after only fifteen minutes had made a family of figures to **tether** to her vessel, along with a small scrap of paper, on which she **scrawled** a message of hope that their expedition would be a success. She also had placed some **translucent** plastic on the bottom of the leaf to prevent water from coming in.

After half an hour of reviewing the **codified** rules, they all grabbed their boats and sat down near the waterfront. They would release them at this point, and then try to watch their progress as long as they could, declaring a winner when it became clear that one boat had **surpassed** the rest. Amidst much shouting and encouragement, the boats made their way out of the calm water near the edge and moved gracefully downstream.

"Mine is clearly superior," TJ said smilingly, walking on the cement path with a hurried, eager step.

"Where's mine?" Ashley asked worriedly. They all looked and saw that it had become trapped in weeds. She cursed but walked with the others nonetheless.

By the end of it all, Sam's boat had gone the farthest, and they had to return back to the blanket to make sure that their belongings hadn't been stolen. Ashley congratulated Jake on a successful project, and they raced each other back to see who would buy the afternoon ice cream.

Over the river behind them, a cool breeze **foreboded** the **advent** of fall in a few short months.

---

885 scrawl [3]
v. 휘갈겨 쓰다
to write or draw in a sprawling, awkward manner

886 translucent [2]
a. 반투명한
permitting light to pass through but not so clearly visible

887 codified [2]
a. 정리된
organized or arranged systematically

888 surpass [6]
v. 뛰어넘다, 능가하다
to outpace, beat

889 forebode [3]
v. 전조가 되다
to presage, predict

890 advent [3]
n. 도래, 출현
arrival, beginning, coming

Vocabulary

0867
culinary [|kʌlɪneri]

a. 요리[음식]의   relating to or used in cooking or the kitchen
culi + nary 라고 생각하자. culi '커리(카레)' 같은(nary) 것이라고 상상하자. 그래서 culinary는 '요리의'라는 뜻이다.
They had only a few **culinary** tools including a pan, pot, and knife. (*adj.*)

0868
turf [t3:rf]

n. 잔디   grass
잔디가(turf) 터프해서(tough) 잘 뽑히지 않는다고 외워보자.
These roofs were then covered by **turf**. (*n.*)

0869
rigid [|rɪdʒɪd]

a. 뻣뻣한, 단단한   stiff; not flexible
돌처럼(rock → rig) 단단하다고(rigid) 외우자.
The curriculum was too narrow and too **rigid**. (*adj.*)

0870
glimmering [glímərɪŋ]

a. 희미하게 빛나는   gleaming, flickering
glitter는 장식할 때 쓰는 반짝이 가루를 말한다. m 은 t 보다 알파벳에서 먼저 나오므로 그보다 앞단계인 '희미하게 빛나는 것'이라고 외우자.
I saw a light of the house **glimmering** in the distance. (*adj.*)

0871
swell [swél]

v. 불룩해지다, 부풀다   to bulge out, as a sail or the middle of a cask, to grow in bulk, as by the absorption of moisture
swollen(부푼)과 관련된 단어이다.
The balloon continued to **swell** with air and eventually popped. (*v.*)

0872
commemorate [kə|meməreɪt]

v. 기념하다   to serve as a memorial or reminder of
기억에(memory → memor) 영원히 남겨두기 위해 기념한다는 의미이다.
A series of movies will be shown to **commemorate** the 30th anniversary of his death. (*v.*)

0873
gape ⁵ [geɪp]

v. (놀라서) 바라보다 — to stare with open mouth, as in wonder
꼭 원숭이처럼(ape) 놀라서 멍하니 쳐다본다고(gape) 외우자.
His secretary stopped taking notes to **gape** at me. (v.)

0874
query ³ [|kwɪri]

n. 의문, 질문 — a question, inquiry
question과 연결해서 외우자.
Our assistants will be happy to answer your **queries**. (n.)

0875
conducive ² [kəndjúːsiv]

a. 도움이 되는 — useful, helpful, contributing to an end; helpful to
con(함께) do(하다). 함께 하면 도움이 된다.
Rain is **conducive** to plant growth. (adj.)

0876
buoyant ² [|buːjənt]

a. 부력이 있는, 물에 뜨는 — able to float
바다 위에 띄워놓은 표시를 buoy(부표)라고 하지? 그것에서 파생된 말이다.
Salt water is more **buoyant** than fresh water. (adj.)

0877
befit ² [bɪ|fɪt]

v. 걸맞다 — to be proper or appropriate for; suit; fit
fit이 맞다는 의미이므로 befit은 걸맞다는 의미이다.
His clothes do not **befit** the occasion. (v.)

0878
scheme ⁷ [skiːm]

n. 계획 — plan, project
좋은 계획은(scheme) 한 번 훑어봤을(skim) 때 모든 게 분명해야 한다고 외우자.
Under the new **scheme** only successful schools will be given extra funding. (n.)

0879
brashly ² [bræʃli]

adv. 성급하게, 경솔하게 — recklessly
rash가 성급하다는 의미이므로 brash도 비슷한 의미를 지니고 있다.
I **brashly** announced to the group that NATO needed to be turned around. (adv.)

0880
chide ³ [tʃáid]

v. 꾸짖다, 야단치다 — to scold; reproach
I hide to avoid being chided. (혼나기를 피하기 위해서 숨는다)
이 문장을 기억하자.
A grandmother **chiding** a child for his ill manners. (adj.)

0881
impetuous [4]
[ɪmˈpetʃuəs]

a. 충동적인 — characterized by rash action; impulsive
impulse(충동)과 연결해서 외워보자.
It's **impetuous** of you to jump to such a conclusion. (*adj.*)

0882
prone [7]
[proʊn]

a. ~하기 쉬운 — liable, disposed
프로들은(pro) 남들이 하기 쉬운(prone) 실수를 하지 않는다.
Working without a break makes you more **prone** to error. (*adj.*)

0883
crude [9]
[kruːd]

a. 대강의, 천연 그대로의, 미숙한 — lacking finish, polish, or completeness, unrefined; unpolished
crude oil 이라고 들어봤지? 즉 '세련되지 않은, 미숙한 것'을 말한다.
It is **crude** for a lady to bite her nails. (*adj.*)

0884
tether [3]
[ˈteðə(r)]

v. 묶다; 밧줄[사슬] — to tie
tie와 연결해서 외워보자.
With nothing left, Tyron is at the end of his **tether**. (*n.*)

0885
scrawl [3]
[skrɔːl]

v. 휘갈겨 쓰다 — to write or draw in a sprawling, awkward manner
스크롤바를(scroll) 내리면서 휘갈겨 썼다고(scrawl) 생각하자.
Someone had **scrawled** all over my notes. (*v.*)

0886
translucent [2]
[trænsˈluːsnt]

a. 반투명한, 반투명의 — permitting light to pass through but not so clearly visible
luc는 '빛', trans는 '통과한다'는 의미이므로 '빛이 통과할 수 있다', 즉 반투명하다는 뜻이다.
They set **translucent** glass in their bathroom window. (*adj.*)

0887
codified [2]
[ˈkɑːdɪfaɪd]

a. 정리된 — organized or arranged systematically
모든 코드에(code) 정해진 규칙이 있는 것처럼, 규칙에 맞게 정리한다는 (codify) 의미이다.
We can **codify** the system, much better than we do at present. (*v.*)

0888
surpass [6]

[sərˈpæs]

v. 뛰어넘다, 능가하다 to outpace, beat; to exceed
sur(above, over) + pass 이므로 go beyond 라는 뜻으로 자연스럽게 유추할 수 있다.
Usain Bolt **surpassed** the world record again. (v.)

0889
forebode [3]

[fɔːrˈbóud]

v. 전조가 되다 to presage, predict
bode는 '징조'라는 의미로 미리(fore) 징조가 된다는 의미이다.
More rapidly even than he had **foreboded** those changes had occurred. (v.)

0890
advent [3]

[ǽdvent]

n. 도래, 출현 arrival, beginning, coming
beginning of a venture, 즉 '모험의 시작'이라고 외우자.
The new age started with the **advent** of the Internet. (n.)

Episode 53

MATCHING Quiz

1. culinary
2. turf
3. rigid
4. glimmering
5. swell
6. commemorate
7. gape
8. query
9. conducive
10. buoyant
11. befit
12. scheme
13. brashly
14. chide
15. impetuous
16. prone
17. crude
18. tether
19. scrawl
20. translucent

A. stiff; not flexible
B. grass
C. to serve as a memorial or reminder of
D. relating to or used in cooking or the kitchen
E. to bulge out, as a sail or the middle of a cask
F. to stare with open mouth, as in wonder
G. useful, helpful
H. gleaming, flickering
I. plan, project
J. able to float
K. a question, inquiry
L. recklessly
M. to scold; reproach
N. to tie
O. to be proper or appropriate for; suit; fit
P. characterized by rash action; impulsive
Q. lacking finish, polish, or completeness
R. permitting light to pass through but not so clearly visible
S. to write or draw in a sprawling, awkward manner
T. liable, disposed

1-D, 2-B, 3-A, 4-H, 5-E, 6-C, 7-F, 8-K, 9-G, 10-J, 11-O, 12-I, 13-L, 14-M, 15-P, 16-T, 17-Q, 18-N, 19-S, 20-R

더 많은 문제를 풀고자 한다면 www.quizlet.com에서 'paul academy seoul' class를 검색

Episode 54 — Dog Days

891 pertain ²⁸
v. 적용되다
to have reference or relation

892 underlie ¹⁸
v. 내포하다
to lie under or beneath

893 epidemic ³
a. 널리 퍼진
prevalent, widespread

894 paradoxical ³¹
a. 역설의, 자기모순의
self-contradictory

895 perilous ⁷
a. 아주 위험한
dangerous or threatening

896 mandate ²
v. 명령하다
to command, order

897 conceive ¹¹
v. 상상하다
to form a notion or idea of

898 wobble ²
v. 흔들리다
to waver between two points or decisions

899 roam ⁵
v. 배회하다
to wander without purpose

900 clutter ³
v. 막 집어넣다
to fill or litter with things in a disorderly manner

While he'd had a fun weekend with the Professor and then his friends, Jake felt on Monday afternoon that the ordinary order of the universe had seemed to have become turned upside down in the last few weeks. A few months earlier, he had been a regular high school student, and the biggest problems he had to deal with **pertained** to studying, and perhaps his sleep schedule. Now, of course, the **underlying** issue was improving his score, but there were so many other **epidemic** issues that seemed mark of a transition away from childhood to a **paradoxical** state of semi-adulthood. He was too old for childish things and too young for adult things. This transformation was not very clear to Jake at that moment, however, since one has no idea one is changing until months after the first signs present themselves.

Nothing seemed as clear as it once had, and now that he had dealt with the **perilous** world of love and the more boring questions of finances and friendship, Jake was lost. A few minutes after six, having just left the academy, he stood on the sidewalk, unsure of what to do. He could go home, as his mother **mandated**, but surely she wouldn't complain too much about half an hour's delay. He could always claim some subway delay, or an after-class discussion with a teacher. She'd like that, he decided.

Still, he couldn't **conceive** what to do in the meantime. He **wobbled** outside of the school, deciding between a lonely coffee or a walk. He ultimately decided to **roam** around and try to think clearly, though his mind was **cluttered** with **debris**. He walked down toward the subway, then took a sudden right turn through a road. He passed through the dim hallway to the sunlit parking lot behind, thinking suddenly that he'd never known this area existed. He followed the alley behind the academy building, looking up as he sometimes did to the rooftops as they stood out against the bright blue **firmament** of the sky. A pair of black and white birds peered down at him, as though passing judgment.

Jake's imagined dialogue of the rooftop birds, their songs translated to English:

Bird 1: Look at that poor boy down there. He seems lost.
Bird 2: Who cares? It's just a boy. Let's fly over there and **scavenge** some scraps!
1: How can you be so heartless? Sometimes I wonder why I ever married you.
2: Come on, darling. Don't get upset.
1: You don't even look at my feathers anymore.
2: What, did you change it?
1: Well, actually, yes, I did. Maureen and I were cleaning myself all morning yesterday. You never notice anything! Like this boy for instance…
2: So what about the boy?
1: He looks so stupid down there. I wonder if they can talk to each other?
2: They seem almost **astute** sometimes, yes.
1: Probably just pretending. I mean, they can't even fly.
2: Well, maybe someday they'll evolve.

The birds depart.

Jake watched them until they disappeared into the light of the sun. Off to some other adventure, he thought. But the idea of flying was so **captivating**, and something in their freedom **beguiled** him, made him wonder why humans could long for flight, something they've never been capable of.

Now, of course, it is unwise to climb onto strange rooftops, not to mention illegal. But Jake, drawn by the **tantalizing prospect** of looking down at the city and its **inhabitants** as though in flight. Finding the top of the staircase, he pushed at the top door, which was hooked by a small wire to allow smokers to get in and out easily. He ventured out onto the blinding white terrace, happy that no one else had an **equivalent** impulse at that moment. After all, he thought, everyone was probably going home at this very moment.

He spun slowly, absorbing the panoramic view of the vibrant city beneath him. He walked toward the edge and watched the uniform silver-suited businessmen moving in slow steps, sometimes gathering in groups around a trash can to smoke and talk of whatever they usually spoke about (he could only guess), and then the bright

---

901 debris [2]
n. 잔해, 쓰레기
garbage; detritus

902 firmament [4]
n. 창공, 하늘
the vault of heaven, sky

903 scavenge [7]
v. 쓰레기더미를 뒤지다
to take or gather from discarded material

904 astute [3]
a. 약삭빠른, 총명한
intelligent, perceptive

905 captivating [6]
a. 매력적인, 매혹적인
fascinating, attractive

906 beguile [4]
v. 끌다, 이끌다
to allure, entice

907 tantalizing [4]
a. 애타게 하는
exhibiting something that provokes desire, especially that which remains beyond one's reach

908 prospect [9]
n. 가망, 전망
an apparent probability of advancement, success, profit

909 inhabitant [4]
n. 주민
a person or animal that inhabits a place

910 equivalent [11]
a. 동등한
equal in value

912 maneuver [3]
v. 교묘히 이동하다
to change the position according to tactics

912 flicker [6]
v. 깜박거리다
to burn unsteadily; shine with a wavering light

913 unfold [3]
v. 퍼지다
to spread

914 pedestrian [9]
a. 재미없는
lacking in vitality, imagination; commonplace

915 extravagance [10]
n. 낭비, 사치
excessive or unnecessary expenditure or outlay of money

916 enshrine [2]
v. 소중히 간직하다
to cherish as sacred

917 compliant [3]
a. 순종적인
obedient

summer dresses and legs of women as they **maneuvered** through the crowds. Huge cups of coffee, held in their hands, seemed to move independently, as though they too were getting back home to little coffee mug wives and espresso cup children. Turning another way, he noticed that the alleys and backstreets had adopted a slightly more shadowy evening color, and the vivid neon lights of the bars and restaurants **flickered** into life as the shadows began to **unfold**.

He edged closer to the outer walls, which were about three feet high, and took a quick look directly down the full sixty feet to the bottom, feeling suddenly very connected to life and history. If only I had a feather and a bowling ball like Galileo, he thought.

Retreating to the center, he thought again of flight. He wanted so much to go somewhere else, somewhere away from this **pedestrian** repetition, of these expectations. Rooftops, he decided, were like islands, and if only he could have moved this building far away from the city, from the responsibilities of home and academy, he would have gladly done so. He thought of how much happier Jessica would be without her constant worry, and how they would all be better off without the threats of this upcoming test hanging over their heads. He wanted to escape, at least for a few days.

He took his phone out of his pocket and was about to text Jessica, but he stopped himself. What would he say? Come join me on the rooftop? He thought of that last night on her balcony, overlooking the entire city. How boring this would be for her in comparison, he thought. How much higher her heights were. How he longed to get to them, to gain the **extravagance** that so many people seemed to **enshrine** with so much importance, and yet simultaneously he hated the thought of following his father's misery into the world of finance.

There was nothing to be done but go quietly down the stairs and return like a good **compliant** son to get his dinner. However, thoughts of islands and Jessica and escape filled his evening, and he quietly decided that adulthood was not as wonderful as everyone maintained. Life had seemed much easier in middle school, and now the constant requests for his improvement and thoughts of his future haunted him.

However, he was about to discover a much worse element of growing up than the mere status anxiety that currently haunted him.

Vocabulary

0891
pertain [28]
[pərtéin]

v. 관련 있다   to have reference or relation
파트너처럼(partner → pertain) 서로 관련이 있다고 외워보자.
Those laws no longer **pertain**. (*v.*)

0892
underlie [18]
[ìʌndərlái]

v. 내포하다   to lie under or beneath
아래에(under) 깔려있다(lie), 즉 '내포한다'는 의미이다.
These ideas **underlie** much of his work. (*v.*)

0893
epidemic [3]
[èpədémik]

a. 널리 퍼진; 유행병   prevalent, widespread; wide-spread occurrence of a disease in a certain region
demos '사람들이 자주 걸리는 병', 즉 유행병을 뜻한다.
With little medical knowledge Europe suffered from **epidemic**.

0894
paradoxical [31]
[pærədάksikəl]

a. 역설의, 자기모순의   self-contradictory
paradox는 흔히 잘 알고 있는 '창과 방패의 모순'을 뜻한다.
This can produce some **paradoxical** results. (x.)

0895
perilous [7]
[pérələs]

a. 아주 위험한   very dangerous or threatening
peril은 danger '위험'과 연관되어 있다.
Since the journey is **perilous**, be sure to bring a first-aid kit. (*adj.*)

0896
mandate [2]
[mændeit]

v. 명령하다, 명령, 지령   to command, order; charge
mand- '명령'에서 유래했다.
The president gave a **mandate** to stop the war, but the general fired the missile anyway. (*n.*)

0897
conceive [11]
[kənsíːv]

v. 상상하다   to form a notion or idea of, to imagine
'can see've 라고 외우자.
Now airplanes are fairly common, but back in the 19th century people couldn't even **conceive** of a flying machine. (*v.*)

0898
wobble ²
[wάbl]

v. 흔들리다, 동요하다   to waver between two points or decisions, to shake; to quaver
bubble이 가만히 있지 않고 흔들거리는 것을 연상하면 외우기 쉽다.
Her voice **wobbled** with emotion. (*v.*)

0899
roam ⁵
[roʊm]

v. 배회하다   to wander without purpose
빈 방을(room) 정처 없이 배회한다고(roam) 생각하자.
The sheep are allowed to **roam** freely on this land. (*v.*)

0900
clutter ³
[|klʌtə(r)]

v. 막 집어넣다, (너무 많은 것들을 어수선하게) 채우다   to fill or litter with things in a disorderly manner
넣을 때 엄청 많이 넣으니까 clutter는 '너무 많이 어수선하게 집어넣다'라는 뜻이다.
Trash and clothes **cluttered** the messy child's bedroom floor. (*v.*)

0901
debris ²
[də|bri:]

n. 잔해, 쓰레기   garbage; detritus, the remains of anything broken down or destroyed; ruins
de + bristle '털' 이라고 생각하자. 필요 없는 털은 깎아서 버려야겠지? 그러므로 debris는 '잔해, 쓰레기'라는 뜻이다.
The **debris** of the building were all over the place after the bombing. (*n.*)

0902
firmament ⁴
[|f3:rməmənt]

n. 창공, 하늘   the vault of heaven, sky
늘 위에 굳건하게(firm) 존재하는 하늘을 보며 아멘이라고(amen) 말하는 모습을 떠올려보자.
A rising star in the literary **firmament** (*n.*)

0903
scavenge ⁷
[skǽvindʒ]

v. 쓰레기더미를 뒤지다   to take or gather from discarded material, to collect things by searching among unwanted objects
scrap '조각'들을 scrape '긁어내는' 행위라고 생각하자.
We **scavenged** for pretty clothes in every shop in town. (*v.*)

0904
astute [əstjúːt]

a. **약삭빠른, 총명한; 기민한, 빈틈없는**   intelligent, perceptive; keen; shrewd
a + not + stu + pid. 멍청하지 않은 사람은 기민하고 똑똑하겠지?
The child made **astute** remarks about the story that even his teacher had not thought of. (*adj.*)

0905
captivating [kǽptəvèitiŋ]

a. **매력적인, 매혹적인**   fascinating, attractive
captive는 '잡히다'라는 뜻이다. 따라서 어떤 것에 시선을 잡힐만큼 매혹적이라는 의미.
When the captain had a **captivating** voice, so the sailors loved to listen to him sing. (*adj.*)

0906
beguile [bɪɡáɪl]

v. **구슬리다**   to allure, entice
guile은 '속임수'라는 뜻을 가지고 있다. 따라서 beguile은 '속여서 구슬리다'라는 의미이다.
He was **beguiled** by her beauty. (*v.*)

0907
tantalizing [tǽntəlàizɪŋ]

a. **애타게 하는**   exhibiting something that provokes desire, especially that which remains beyond one's reach, enticing
그리스 로마 신화에서 Tantalus라는 인간이 신들의 벌을 받아 턱 바로 아래까지는 물이고 머리 바로 위에는 과일 나무가 달린 곳에 갇힌다. 과일을 먹거나 물을 마시려고 할 때마다 나뭇가지가 위로 올라가거나 수면이 내려가거나 해서 평생 애타 하는 이야기에서 유래.
It is **tantalizing** to see it but not be allowed to touch it. (*adj.*)

0908
prospect [prɑ́ːspekt]

n. **가망, 전망**   an apparent probability of advancement, success, profit; a possibility of happening
pro 는 '앞', spec 은 '보다'라는 어원을 갖고 있으므로 prospect는 '가망, 전망'이라는 뜻이다.
The **prospect** of winning this contest is very low, so I'm not going to get my hopes up. (*n.*)

0909
inhabitant [ɪnhǽbɪtənt]

n. **주민**   a person or animal that inhabits a place
inhabit은 '거주하다'는 의미다. 이미 안에서(in) 지내는 것이 습관이(habit) 되었을 정도로 오래 거주했다고 생각하자.
Yankee' means an **inhabitant** of the northern American States, especially those of New England. (*n.*)

0910
equivalent [11]
[ɪ|kwɪvələnt]

a. 동등한   equal in value
equal과 연결해서 외워보자.
Eight kilometres is roughly **equivalent** to five miles. (*adj.*)

0911
maneuver [3]
[mənúːvər]

v. 교묘히 이동하다; 연습시키다, 계략을 써서 …하게 하다; 책략, 작전 행동
to change the position according to tactics, to scheme; intrigue; a plot
어원적으로는 manual + operate 의 뜻이다. 손으로 교묘하게 조작을 하니까 '책략'을 뜻한다.
His excellent **maneuver** of the handle led to the greatest car stunt ever. (*n.*)

0912
flicker [6]
[|flɪkə(r)]

v. 깜박거리다   to burn unsteadily; shine with a wavering light
flick은 손가락을 까딱거리는 모습을 표현한다. 손가락이 까딱거리듯이 빛이 깜박거린다고 외우자.
The lights **flickered** and went out. (*v.*)

0913
unfold [3]
[ʌn|foʊld]

v. 퍼지다, 펴다[펼치다]   to spread out or lay open to view
un + fold. 접는 것의 반대는 펼치는 것이다.
I took out the map in my pocket and **unfolded** it to find out the location of the monument. (*v.*)

0914
pedestrian [9]
[pədéstriən]

a. 재미없는, 상상력이 없는   lacking in vitality, imagination; commonplace
'보행자'라는 뜻으로 알고 있지? 똑같은 길을 계속 걸어서 '재미없는, 상상력이 없는'이라는 뜻이다.
I put up pretty **pedestrian** numbers. (*adj.*)

0915
extravagance [10]
[ɪk|strævəgəns]

n. 낭비, 사치   excessive or unnecessary expenditure or outlay of money
필요없는 추가적인(extra) 물건까지 항상 사는 것은 낭비라고 외우자.
Going to the theatre is our only **extravagance**. (*n.*)

0916
enshrine [2]
[inʃráin]

v. **(특히 문서상으로) 소중히 간직하다, 모시다**   to cherish as sacred, to protect

en 'make', shrine '성지'. 즉 어떤 것을 성지에 모시듯 소중히 간직하는 것을 말한다.

The record breaking homerun ball was **enshrined** at the hall of fame. (*v.*)

0917
compliant [3]
[kəmpláiənt]

a. **순종적인, 남이 시키는 대로하는, 고분고분한**   obedient, willing to comply

ply- 는 '구부리다'라는 뜻이 있다.

Henry seemed less **compliant** with his wife's wishes than he had six months before. (*adj.*)

Episode 54

MATCHING Quiz

1. pertain	A. prevalent, widespread
2. underlie	B. to command, order
3. epidemic	C. to form a notion or idea of
4. paradoxical	D. to take or gather from discarded material
5. perilous	E. garbage; detritus
6. mandate	F. fascinating, attractive
7. conceive	G. intelligent, perceptive
8. wobble	H. dangerous or threatening
9. roam	I. to allure, entice
10. clutter	J. fill or litter with things in a disorderly manner
11. debris	K. exhibiting something that provokes desire, especially that which remains beyond one's reach
12. firmament	L. an apparent probability of advancement, success, profit
13. scavenge	M. to lie under or beneath
14. astute	N. self-contradictory
15. captivating	O. a person or animal that inhabits a place
16. beguile	P. to have reference or relation
17. tantalizing	Q. the vault of heaven, sky
18. prospect	R. equal in value
19. inhabitant	S. to wander without purpose
20. equivalent	T. to waver between two points or decisions

1-P, 2-M, 3-A, 4-N, 5-H, 6-B, 7-C, 8-T, 9-S, 10-J, 11-E, 12-Q, 13-D, 14-G, 15-F, 16-I, 17-K, 18-L, 19-O, 20-R

더 많은 문제를 풀고자 한다면 www.quizlet.com에서 'paul academy seoul' class를 검색

Episode 55

Loss

918 chimera [2]
n. 불가능한 생각
a wild and unrealistic dream or notion

919 realm [8]
n. 영역
dimension, domain

920 conquer [7]
v. 정복하다
to defeat, overcome

921 subjugate [3]
v. 지배하에 두다
to bring under complete control or subjection

922 rampage [5]
v. 소란을 피우다
to disturb

923 sputter [2]
v. 더듬더듬 말하다
to stammer, falter

924 emanate [3]
v. 내뿜다
to flow out of; waft from

925 quiver [3]
v. 떨다
to shake with a slight but rapid motion

Up until a certain age, death is merely a **chimera**, something that happens to other people, particularly the very old or the poor or those in other countries. It is an alien **realm**, and even on the darkest of days one thinks, in the prime of one's life, that it just might be escapable. Might I be the one to finally **conquer** or **subjugate** it? The drunk thinks as he pours another shot, or the smoker as he lights up once more. At any rate, they say, it will not happen for a long, long time. But sometimes it does happen, and in most cases, one has no time to prepare.

Jake had been making flashcards, listening to Pink Floyd's "Shine On You Crazy Diamond" when he heard someone **rampaging** in the kitchen, even over the wailing guitar solo in his headphones. He heard his father's voice, unusual to hear at seven in the evening as he usually came home well past midnight.

He put his cards down and opened his door to see his father standing in the middle of the room, his phone still held in his hand, shoulders bent forward. He started when he noticed the light from Jake's open door, and turned away from his son quickly to wipe his eyes.

"Where's your mother, son?" he asked in a strange, faraway voice.

"Shopping, I think," Jake **sputtered**, completely confused by this. Not only was his father home from work, but he was showing emotion, openly, without the same odor of alcohol that had **emanated** from him the only other time he'd talked openly with him at the start of the summer.

"When will she be back? I just left her a message."

"What's happened?"

His father looked straight at him, and his lip seemed to **quiver** slightly. His unemotional nature had always seemed to Jake to be a required feature of manhood, but at this moment he could only manage a thin **facade** of control, under which his mind seemed to burst with emotion. As though his legs had suddenly lost all power, he fell backwards onto the sofa, and told Jake to take a seat.

"Your uncle… my brother—" he began, hardly able to go on. But he didn't have to say anything after that. Jake knew.

The Professor was dead.

After those first syllables, Jake's father became **introvert** and went to his office, where Jake saw, just as he came into the room to see if there was anything he could do (after his half-digested lunch had been wiped from the living room), the older man sitting on his large cherry-red leather chair with a bottle of whiskey on the table beside him in an **overtly** sad mood. He barely looked up as Jake softly closed the door and waited for his mother to come home and **rectify** things as she always did.

When she did come home, she went immediately to her husband, passing Jake as though he were a non-person. The groceries lay in the entryway until he decided that the only contribution he could possibly make would be to stow their contents in the refrigerator.

Once she **emerged** a half hour later, she cautioned him not to disturb his father, thanked him rudely for bringing the food, and began to cook dinner, as if it had been any other night. The two of them ate in near silence. After a few bites, Jake suddenly felt angry at her **ostensible** lack of emotion.

"I bet you love this," he snapped. "You always hated him."

"Excuse me?" His mother raised her shining eyes directly at his, her voice carrying a **tremulous** note of rage and injury.

"My uncle. You hated him, didn't you?"

"How dare you," she said, rising from the table to her fullest scary height. They had been eating only a few feet from each other, and at this distance she didn't have far to go to hit him with full force on the back of his head, as she used to do when he was in elementary school. WHACK! He felt once again, for the first time since middle school, the hard points of her rings as they dug into his head. As he gripped the

---

926 facade [6]
n. 표면, 허울
a superficial appearance of something

927 introvert [2]
a. 내성적인, 내향적인
solitary and quiet; diffident; shy

928 overtly [2]
adv. 명백히
apparently, obviously

929 rectify [4]
v. 교정하다
to correct or fix

930 emerge [10]
v. 출현하다
to come forth into view or notice

931 ostensible [3]
a. 표면적으로
based on appearances; seemingly

932 tremulous [1]
a. 살짝 떨리는
trembling or quivering; vibratory

point of impact, she began clearing the dishes.

"You stupid boy," she said, after a long silence. "That's how you're going to talk to your mother after her brother-in-law has died? Don't speak if you don't know what you're talking about."

Jake was sent to his room to text TJ. He felt the urge to call Jessica, but had had enough of women for one day. He pulled out an old Bill Evans CD his uncle had given him for his last birthday and put on "Waltz for Debby" as he finally felt tears hot on his face. He hardly remembered falling asleep.

Vocabulary

0918
chimera [2]
[kaɪ|mɪrə]

n. 불가능한 생각[희망]   a wild and unrealistic dream or notion
키메라가 상상 속에만 존재하는 동물인 것처럼, chimera는 실제로는 불가능한 생각을 의미한다.
In the tangled equation of Balkan politics, neutrality is a **chimera**. (*n.*)

0919
realm [8]
[relm]

n. 영역   dimension, domain
rule과 연결해서 외워보자. 누군가가 지배하는(rule) 영역이 realm이다.
At the end of the speech he seemed to be moving into the **realms** of fantasy. (*n.*)

0920
conquer [7]
[kάŋkər]

v. 정복하다   to defeat, to overcome by force
남아메리카를 정복한 사람들을 conquistadors라고 한다.
An emperor **conquers** a country. (*v.*)

0921
subjugate [3]
[sʌ́bdʒugèit]

v. 지배하에 두다; 정복하다, 복종시키다   to bring under complete control or subjection; to conquer
나폴레옹은 전쟁에서 승리해 돌아온 것을 기념해 개선문이라는 gate를 만들어 그 아래(sub)를 지나가려고 했지.
The Romans **subjugated** many empires beneath them. (*v.*)

0922
rampage [5]
[|ræmpeɪdʒ]

v. 소란을 피우다; 광란   to disturb
산양이(ram) 큰 뿔로 모든 걸 박고 다니면서 광란을 피우는 모습의 사진이 있는 페이지(page)를 떠올려보자.
Gangs of youths went on the **rampage** in the city yesterday. (*n.*)

0923
sputter [2]
[|spʌtə(r)]

v. 더듬더듬 말하다   to stammer, falter
sputter를 발음해 보면 침이 많이 튄다. 준비되지 않고 막 더듬더듬 말을 내뱉을 때 침이 많이 튀는 걸 떠올려보자.
'W-What?' **sputtered** Anna. (*v.*)

0924
emanate [émənèit]

v. 내뿜다, (빛 열 소리 등을)방사하다   to flow out of; waft from, to flow forth or proceed, as from some source
어원인 emanare가 flow out, 즉 '흘러 나오다'라는 뜻이므로 방사하다라는 것과 일맥상통한다.
The explosion **emanated** a bright light that blinded people for a few seconds. (*v.*)

0925
quiver [|kwɪvə(r)]

v. 떨다   to shake with a slight but rapid motion
shiver '떨다'랑 비슷하지? 그런데 앞부분은 quiet '조용하다'와 비슷하잖아. 그래서 조용히, 가볍게 떨리는 거라고 생각해.
When people tell a lie, their eyes **quiver** slightly. (*v.*)

0926
facade [fə|sɑ:d]

n. 표면, 허울   a superficial appearance of something
가짜(fake → fac) 얼굴(face → fac)이라고 외우자.
The **facade** of that building is made of wood. (*n.*)

0927
introvert [|ɪntrəvɜ:rt]

a. 내성적인, 내향적인   solitary and quiet; diffident; shy
overt는 '보이다'라는 의미이므로 introvert는 보이는 게 밖에 있는 것이 아니라 안에(in) 있다는, 즉 내성적이란 뜻이다.
I was an **introvert** and very quiet. (*adj.*)

0928
overtly [ouvə́:rtli]

adv. 명백히   apparently, obviously
overt는 '보이다'라는 의미이므로 overtly는 '확실히 보이게', 즉 '명백히'라는 뜻이다.
He's written a few **overtly** political lyrics over the years. (*adv.*)

0929
rectify [|rektɪfaɪ]

v. 교정하다   to correct or fix
correct와 어원 rect를 공유하는 단어이다. correct가 '옳다'는 뜻이므로 옳게 만들다, 즉 '교정하다'라는 뜻이다.
We must take steps to **rectify** the situation. (*v.*)

0930
emerge [i|mɜ:rdʒ]

v. 출현하다   to come forth into view or notice
새로운 이미지로(image → emerge) 출현한다고(emerge) 외우자.
No new evidence **emerged** during the investigation. (*v.*)

0931
ostensible [3]

[ɑ:|stensəbl]

a. 표면적으로 based on appearances; seemingly
'보이다'라는 뜻의 라틴어 ostendere에서 유래.
The **ostensible** reason for his absence was illness. (*adj.*)

0932
tremulous [1]

[|tremjələs]

a. 살짝 떨리는 trembling or quivering; vibratory
tremble '떨다'와 함께 외우자.
He was in a state of **tremulous** excitement. (*adj.*)

MATCHING Quiz — Episode 55

1. chimera	A. to stammer, falter
2. realm	B. to flow out of; waft from
3. conquer	C. dimension, domain
4. subjugate	D. a superficial appearance of something
5. rampage	E. to defeat, overcome
6. sputter	F. solitary and quiet; diffident; shy
7. emanate	G. to correct or fix
8. quiver	H. to shake with a slight but rapid motion
9. facade	I. apparently, obviously
10. introvert	J. trembling or quivering; vibratory
11. overtly	K. to come forth into view or notice
12. rectify	L. to disturb
13. emerge	M. to bring under complete control or subjection
14. ostensible	N. a wild and unrealistic dream or notion
15. tremulous	O. based on appearances; seemingly

1-N, 2-C, 3-E, 4-M, 5-L, 6-A, 7-B, 8-H, 9-D, 10-F, 11-I, 12-G, 13-K, 14-O, 15-I

더 많은 문제를 풀고자 한다면 www.quizlet.com에서 'paul academy seoul' class를 검색

Episode 56: Grief

933 eccentricity [6]
n. 기이함
an oddity or peculiarity, as of conduct

934 cliché [9]
n. 상투적인 문구
a trite, stereotyped expression

935 genealogy [6]
n. 족보
family tree

936 mishap [2]
n. 사고, 불행
accident

937 notable [5]
a. 주목할만한, 눈에 띄는
noteworthy, distinguished

938 strenuous [2]
a. 힘이 많이 드는
demanding or requiring vigorous exertion; arduous

939 hectic [2]
a. 정신 없이 바쁜
characterized by intense agitation, excitement, and rapid movement

While a few years older than his father, the Professor had never seemed an old man, except for the way his **eccentricities** followed the old professorial **cliché** of the slightly aged academic, and for his grey hair which followed his **genealogy**, and unlike his younger brother, he refused to dye. He was an occasional smoker, for which Jake scolded him, but in the end it hadn't been age or nicotine which had killed him. It was just a **mishap** of fate.

He had been walking home late one night after counseling a few students in his office, the same one with the faded books and pictures and jazz albums, when he saw a former colleague across the road and called him in his **notable** voice. The other man had reported to the police that the Professor looked happy to see him, and had told him to wait so that they could grab a beer or glass of wine at a local bar. They hadn't seen each other in quite some time, as both taught at different universities and had **strenuous** schedules, as well as various personal responsibilities like families (in the case of the colleague) or women (in the case of his uncle).

Neither had seen the car rushing down the leafy avenue, its driver sucking a cigarette while talking on the phone. He had been drinking, the police reported, and claimed later that the car jumped suddenly due to a bump in the road. Either way, no matter who was responsible, the car had hit the professor at nearly full speed, and he had died very soon thereafter.

This story filtered down to Jake gradually over the next few days, whispered by cousins and various members of the university faculty at the watch over the body. Jake's mother, still furious over his comments at dinner, had not said much to him apart from what outfit he should wear to the various ceremonies scheduled to take place, ending with the funeral. He gathered she hadn't told his father about the incident as A) he hadn't been killed yet, and B) the banker was **hectic** with all the blood-stained work of dealing with the official funeral process. The two brothers had been the only members of the family, and both their parents had died quite young. Jake remembered their deaths from his early childhood, when both men had drunk the same whiskey, and had stood quietly at the bodies (both died within a few years of each other, one of lung cancer and the other, as they say, of grief).

His mother's family, a crowd of her sisters (two of them), their bored-looking husbands, and their indifferent children, came too to make their appearances, but Jake wished they hadn't bothered. Most of them came for the required four-hour period, but otherwise they stood outside the hospital **ward** checking their phones and talking about the boring nonsense of their lives. Of course, he sat the entire three-day hour period, watching his uncle's face as though it would spark into a smile at any moment and return to its former joy. His father stayed too, and the two of them took turns to stay while the other slept, or left briefly to get food or use the toilet.

After all rites had been conducted, they were going to have a brief memorial service, for which his uncle had unsurprisingly written a few requests.

"He never made a will," his father said with a sad smile, "but the old man spent a lot of time planning his going-away party." The two of them were standing outside the hospital as the body was being prepared for the funeral, his father shakily smoking a cigarette.

"What did he ask, Dad?"

"Well, there's a few poems to be read, apparently. He wanted you to read the last one." The older man allowed himself another short smile. Having spent so much time staring at his uncle's blank expression, Jake saw for the first time the similarity in the lines of their faces, the echo of his uncle's smile somehow in his father's.

"Also, he asked for a few songs to be played. It doesn't say which ones. Only…" he paused as tears came momentarily into his eyes, "he wrote 'Jake will know what to do.'"

After three days of grieving, Jake felt an **affinity** for his father which he'd until now never experienced. He grabbed him by the shoulder, much like a peer might do, and said "he was a good man, wasn't he Dad?"

---

940 ward [5]
n. 병실
a division, floor, or room of a hospital for a particular class or group of patients

941 affinity [4]
n. 친밀함
sense of friendship or similarity of feeling; kinship

At this, his father couldn't stop his tears from flowing, and Jake left him there on the sidewalk outside the hospital building to weep in as much privacy as the space allowed. Jake texted him to say he was going to the Professor's office to find a few CDs.

Vocabulary

0933
eccentricity [6]

[|eksen|trɪsəti]

n. **기이함**   an oddity or peculiarity, as of conduct
맨 처음 전기(electricity)를 발견했을 때 사람들은 전기를 매우 기이하게 (eccentricity) 여겼다.
As a teacher, she had a reputation for **eccentricity**. (*n.*)

0934
cliché [9]

[kliːʃéi]

n. **상투적인 문구, 진부한 표현(생각)**   a trite, stereotyped expression, phrase dulled in meaning by repetition
"Shoot for the stars(목표를 크게)" 처럼 너무 많이 쓰여 따분하고 진부해진 표현을 말한다. 진부한 표현 때문에 따분해져서 생각 없이 클릭(click)만 하고 있다고 생각하자.
"I avoid cliches like the plague," Minnie boasted, not knowing that she was just quoting another **cliché**. (*n.*)

0935
genealogy [6]

[|dʒiːni|ælədʒi]

n. **족보**   family tree
gene이 유전자를 뜻하므로 genealogy는 누군가의 유전적 지도, 즉 족보를 의미한다.
I've been studying the **genealogy** of my family. (*n.*)

0936
mishap [2]

[|mɪshæp]

n. **사고, 불행**   accident
실수로(mistake → mis) 일어난 사건 (happening → hap), 즉 '사고'라고 생각하자.
The cause of every **mishap** comes from carelessness. (*n.*)

0937
notable [5]

[nóutəbl]

a. **주목할 만한, 눈에 띄는, 저명한**   noteworthy, distinguished, worthy of note
눈에 띄는 중요한 일이 생기면 노트에 기록해야 한다.
The student president has become a **notable** politician. (*adj.*)

0938
strenuous [2]

[strénjuəs]

a. **힘이 많이 드는**   demanding or requiring vigorous exertion; arduous, exhausting
부담(strain)을 많이 받는, 즉 '몹시 힘든'.
The **strenuous** exercise made him breathe roughly and sweat. (*adj.*)

0939
hectic ²

[|hektɪk]

a. **정신 없이 바쁜**   characterized by intense agitation, excitement, and rapid movement
너무 정신 없이 바빠서(hectic) 'heck(젠장)'(→ hec)이라고 욕이 나온다고 외우자.
A **hectic** schedule (*adj.*)

0940
ward ⁵

[wɔːrd]

n. **병실, (환자들을 위한) ~실**   a division, floor, or room of a hospital for a particular class or group of patients
원래 '수호자, 수호하다'라는 의미로 쓰였다. 그러므로 보호 받아야 하는 환자들이 모여있는 곳이 ward라고 외우자.
He worked as a nurse on the children's **ward**. (*n.*)

0941
affinity ⁴

[ə|fɪnəti]

n. **친밀함**   sense of friendship or similarity of feeling; kinship
마치 무한한 시간(infinity) 동안 알아왔던 것처럼 친밀감을(affinity) 느낀다고 생각하자.
Sam was born in the country and had a deep **affinity** with nature. (*n.*)

Episode 56

MATCHING Quiz

1. eccentricity   •   • A. accident
2. cliché   •   • B. demanding or requiring vigorous exertion; arduous
3. genealogy   •   • C. a trite, stereotyped expression
4. mishap   •   • D. a division, floor, or room of a hospital for a particular class or group of patients
5. notable   •   • E. sense of friendship or similarity of feeling; kinship
6. strenuous   •   • F. an oddity or peculiarity, as of conduct
7. hectic   •   • G. characterized by intense agitation, excitement, and rapid movement
8. ward   •   • H. noteworthy, distinguished
9. affinity   •   • I. family tree

1-F, 2-C, 3-I, 4-A, 5-H, 6-B, 7-G, 8-D, 9-E

더 많은 문제를 풀고자 한다면 www.quizlet.com에서 'paul academy seoul' class를 검색

Episode 57 — After the Destruction, a Reckoning

After the short ceremony at the funeral, and Jake and his father had fed the few family members who had hung around, the two of them drove back home, Jake's mother accompanying them. The past few days had brought the two males of the family into a friendly partnership, but had **alienated** her, and she had continued giving Jake the silent treatment.

Her moods had always been a mystery to Jake, though this time he was quite sure he was going to get the beating of his life now that the grieving process had finished. He felt the back of his head, where her rings had dug into his head a few days before, but he knew there would be many more scars to follow now that his uncle was buried and his father had to return to work.

The next day, a Friday, the banker did indeed have to go to the office and sort out a number of problems which had arisen in his absence. For the fourth day in a row, Jake's mother had called the academy on his behalf to excuse her son from attendance, but that morning Jake wished he had agreed to go back, if only to escape her **wrath**.

The wrath, however, was not immediately **imminent** during breakfast, which Jake ate at 9 AM while his mother watched the morning news. A bombing somewhere. Politicians in trouble for corruption. All of it seemed like white noise until she turned it off at 9:30 and headed back into the kitchen, coffee mug still held in her slight white hands.

Jake readied himself for a sudden hit, but no violence came. She simply refilled her cup from the machine and sat next to him at the table, her fingers dancing across the **porcelain** as he warily finished his food.

"Jake, I wanted to explain something to you. I'm not sure you understand something."

---

942 reckoning [2]
n. 계산
count; computation; calculation

943 alienate [18]
v. 소원하게[멀어지게] 만들다
to cause (someone) to feel isolated or estranged

944 wrath [3]
n. 분노
anger or vindictive rage

945 imminent [4]
a. 목전의, 임박한
forthcoming, immediate

946 porcelain [2]
n. 자기
ceramic

947 **ravage** ³
v. 황폐하게 만들다, 파괴하다
to ruin, devastate, destroy

948 **pernicious** ²
a. 치명적인
armful or malicious; having detrimental intentions

949 **pledge** ³
v. 맹세하다
to promise solemnly

950 **propitious** ²
a. 유리한
presenting favorable conditions; favorable

He had nothing to say to this, but merely nodded in agreement. There were a great many things he didn't understand, he'd discovered over the last few months.

"Your uncle was not always as kind as you think he was." She took a long sip of coffee and slid her wedding ring up and down her finger. "He loved you, of course, and spent so much time making sure you were doing well, but for most of his life, there was only your father and him, and he loved your father more than anything. They used to be close as children, closer than most. They were—and your father still is—passionate about life and learning."

Don't ever forget your own happiness.

"But then they took different paths. He followed literature, and decided that learning was his only purpose in life. Your father, however... met me." She turned red.

Jake was again unsure of how to respond. His mother had never spoken to him this way, and he had already had enough 'adult' conversations over the last few weeks. Even hitting was preferable to this, he thought as she continued.

"Before our wedding, he used to visit your father while he was studying for his MBA, saying 'don't marry that bitch and **ravage** your life — live free,' but he stopped after your father told him that we were in love. I remember him, standing in the wedding hall, with a look so **pernicious** it could have killed, as I had to **pledge** my love to this man, your father. And then, a few months later, I was pregnant." Another long sip followed. "You weren't expected, you know, Jake. Your father was a bank clerk when we found out. Not exactly a **propitious** announcement. He was working all day as I was learning how to be a pregnant housewife, all while your uncle kept coming over and drinking, telling the same jokes and telling your father that marriage was a horrible mistake, *while I was in the room.* 'She's not intelligent enough to be a wife,' he'd say, looking straight at me. I mean, I was in love with your father, but my family had always told me this was what I was born to do, give birth to children, take care of them, then die. He never asked me about my dreams, about my aspirations. Obviously, a woman couldn't have had those things, he must have thought. They're for men. But I did have them, Jake. My dreams just became about you once you were born. That's all there was, all there ever would be."

She wasn't going to cry in front of her only child, but Jake could detect a **surge** of tears hiding in her eyes, so said nothing hoping not to **expedite** their arrival. She, after evidently having **enumerated** this long-held list of crimes, had said all she wanted to say, and let the full importance of her words hang in the air…

"What *did* you want to do, Mom?" Jake asked after an uncomfortable silence.

"Oh, I was a real estate agent's secretary," she answered quickly. "I really wanted to sell houses and was even studying for a license. But, once I met your father, I knew I wanted to be his wife. And once you were born, I knew I would be a mother. It was a blessing, really."

She smiled as she said this part, but the **remnants** of the old disappointment seemed obvious between the lines. You weren't expected. I gave up my dreams.

"So… You didn't want me, is that it?" He was almost shaking and he seemed to be forming his own tears.

"No! That's not it at all, Jake. Don't ever think that you were a sacrifice for me. I—we—both love you so much. But you asked what my dreams were, and that was it. I guess it seems petty to you, but it was meaningful to me. And when I saw how much you hated me for disliking your uncle, I knew I had to explain something to you. You can't go on hating your mother, and I don't want to **misguide** my **gullible** son."

The anger went away a little as he considered this, but her usual style had made him unprepared for many secrets. He refused to believe how **regressively** the Professor had acted, nor that his mother had feelings. But there she was, beginning to cry as he eyed her with super coldness over the expanse of the coffee table. He excused himself and went back to his room.

---

951 surge [2]
n. 치밀어 오름, 밀려듦
deluge, flood

952 expedite [16]
v. (진행을) 서두르다
to speed up the progress of; hasten

953 enumerate [7]
v. 열거하다
to mention separately as if in counting

954 remnant [2]
n. 나머지, 잔여물
leftover, residue

955 misguide [6]
v. 잘못 이끌다
to guide wrongly

956 gullible [5]
a. 남을 잘 믿는
easily deceived or cheated

957 regressive [2]
a. 퇴보하는
reverting; retrogressive

Vocabulary

0942
reckoning ²
[|rekənɪŋ]

n. 계산　count; computation; calculation
다시 숫자를 세며(recount → reckon) 계산한다고 외우자.
By my **reckoning** you still owe me $10. (*n.*)

0943
alienate ¹⁸
[|eɪliəneɪt]

v. 소원하게[멀어지게] 만들다　to cause (someone) to feel isolated or estranged
누군가를 외계인처럼(alien) 같은 집단에 속하지 않은 것처럼 느끼게 만든다는 의미이다.
The argument could **alienate** black voters. (*v.*)

0944
wrath ³
[ræθ]

n. 분노　anger or vindictive rage
'타이탄의 분노'라는 영화의 영어 제목이 'Wrath of the Titans'이다.
Envy and **wrath** shorten the life. (*n.*)

0945
imminent ⁴
[|ɪmɪnənt]

a. 목전의, 임박한　forthcoming, immediate, likely to occur at any moment; impending
툭 튀어나온(minent) 것이 안쪽까지 들어와 버렸으니 꽤 임박한 문제라고 생각하자.
As the storm grew worse, the sailers realized they were in **imminent** danger of drowning. (*adj.*)

0946
porcelain ²
[|pɔːrsəlɪn]

n. 자기　ceramic
동양의 항아리들은 모두 porcelain으로 만든 것이다.
His father gave him a rare and precious **porcelain**. (*n.*)

0947
ravage ³
[rævɪdʒ]

v. 황폐하게 만들다, 파괴하다　to ruin, devastate, destroy; to lay waste by pillage, rapine, devouring, or other destructive methods
야만족들이(savage) 모든 걸 황폐하게 만든다고(ravage) 외워보자.
A country **ravaged** by civil war. (*v.*)

0948
pernicious [pərníʃəs]

a. 치명적인, 유해(유독)한 — harmful or malicious; having detrimental intentions, deadly; fatal
per '완전히'와 necis '잔혹한 죽음'을 합쳐서 생긴 단어이다.
The company remained calm despite the **pernicious** comments from its rivals. (*adj.*)

0949
pledge [pledʒ]

v. 맹세하다, 약속하다 — to promise solemnly
국기에 대한 맹세를 pledge to the flag라고 한다.
Japan has **pledged** $100 million in humanitarian aid. (*v.*)

0950
propitious [prəpíʃəs]

a. 유리한, 순조로운 — presenting favorable conditions; favorable
고대 로마의 새점을 치는 복점술(augury)에서 온 말로, 접두어 pro(before)와 piti(fly)의 합성으로 '새가 순조롭게 앞으로 날아가다'는 의미에서 '징조가 좋은'이란 뜻이 되었다.
It is **propitious** that the school festival begins after all of our tests are over. (*adj.*)

0951
surge [sɜːrdʒ]

n. 치밀어 오름, 밀려듦; 밀려들다 — deluge, flood; to move along on the waves
A wave's S-sudden URGE 라고 외우자.
When the store announced that the clothes were special offer, people **surged** into the store and filled it in a second. (*v.*)

0952
expedite [ékspədaɪt]

v. (진행을) 서두르다 — to speed up the progress of; hasten
스피드(speed → xped)를 빠르게 한다고 생각하자.
We have developed rapid order processing to **expedite** deliveries to customers. (*v.*)

0953
enumerate [injúːmərèit]

v. 열거하다, 세다 — to mention separately as if in counting, to name one by one
numer는 '숫자'라는 뜻으로 숫자를 하나하나 세듯이 나열한다는 뜻이다.
When he was asked to **enumerate** three benefits of the policy, he could only list two. (*v.*)

0954
remnant ²
[|remnənt]

n. 나머지, 잔여물   leftover, residue
remain '나머지'와 연결해서 외워보자.
Work is the last **remnant** of his old life. (*n.*)

0955
misguide ⁶
[misgáid]

v. 잘못 이끌다   to guide wrongly
말 그대로 잘못(mis) 이끈다는(guide) 의미이다.
Those inadequate uses of English may **misguide** the initial intention of the promotion and defame the nation. (*v.*)

0956
gullible ⁵
[|gʌləbl]

a. 남을 잘 믿는   easily deceived or cheated
걸리버(Guliver) 이야기에서처럼 소인국, 거인국 같은 이상한 곳에 갔다오면 웬만한 것은 다 잘 믿게 될(gullible) 것이다.
I told you he was **gullible**. (*adj.*)

0957
regressive ²
[rigrésiv]

a. 퇴보하는   reverting; retrogressive
'퇴행하다'는 뜻의 동사 regress의 형용사형이다.
Regressive desire to return to the past (*adj.*)

Voca Hamburger — Episode 57
MATCHING Quiz

1. reckoning
2. alienate
3. wrath
4. imminent
5. porcelain
6. ravage
7. pernicious
8. pledge
9. propitious
10. surge
11. expedite
12. enumerate
13. remnant
14. misguide
15. gullible
16. regressive

A. forthcoming, immediate
B. to ruin, devastate, destroy
C. to promise solemnly
D. to cause (someone) to feel isolated or estranged
E. presenting favorable conditions; favorable
F. to speed up the progress of; hasten
G. leftover, residue
H. easily deceived or cheated
I. reverting; retrogressive
J. to guide wrongly
K. deluge, flood
L. ceramic
M. to mention separately as if in counting
N. armful or malicious; having detrimental intentions
O. count; computation; calculation
P. anger or vindictive rage

1-O, 2-D, 3-P, 4-A, 5-L, 6-B, 7-N, 8-C, 9-E, 10-K, 11-F, 12-M, 13-G, 14-J, 15-H, 16-I

더 많은 문제를 풀고자 한다면 www.quizlet.com에서 'paul academy seoul' class를 검색

Episode 58

The Academic Recovery

A few days after his uncle's memorial service, Jake was still lost in his grief, listening to the same jazz albums so much that, on Friday evening, he overheard his mother talking about him on the telephone to her friend until she realized he'd entered the room. A few minutes after waking, he realized it was Saturday, and thought with a sudden fright about the practice test he was supposed to be taking, and the improving he was supposed to be doing. He rushed into the kitchen to find his mother and father having brunch at the same table where he and his mother had had their brief emotional confrontation the day before. It was still too soon to say anything about it, they both seemed to **tacitly** accept with their silence, but still its **ramifications** hung in the air. Only his father ate fully, but that was just because he had a full day of work to do.

The tension in the room was obvious, but was cut short when the doorbell rang. His mother, looking **taken aback**, glanced sideways at the entryway.

"Probably nothing important. Let's not answer it," she said, the first voice to break the morning's silence. No one moved.

Some people are experts at **concealing** their curiosity, **abstaining** from asking the **shrewd** question, content not to know all the answers. They could let a door ring, or a phone vibrate violently on a cafe table, without needing to know who was calling. Jake was not one of those people, and when the doorbell rung again, he jumped up to answer it, if only to escape the silent brunch his parents obviously weren't enjoying.

When he opened the door, he had expected to find a missionary raising money for some **philanthropic** project, or trying to convert nonbelievers. But he was surprised to find not an old woman but a young man, slightly **ruffled**.

"You must be Jake," he said uncertainly.

---

958 tacit [3]
a. 암묵적인, 무언의
without being said; understood

959 ramification [3]
n. 파문, 영향
a derived subject, problem, etc.; outgrowth

960 be taken aback [3]
v. 깜짝 놀라다
to be taken by surprise

961 conceal [7]
v. 숨기다, 감추다
to hide, keep secret

962 abstain [4]
v. 자제하다
to hold back, cease

963 shrewd [7]
a. 면밀히 살피는, 예리한
probing, penetrating, judicious

964 philanthropic [3]
a. 인정 많은, 박애주의의
charitable, humanitarian

965 ruffled [3]
a. 헝클어진
disorganized or untidy; bedraggled

966 tyrant [5]
n. 폭군
powerful leader who allows few freedoms; despot

967 smear [2]
v. 명예를 훼손하다
to tarnish, slur

968 hubris [2]
n. 자만심
excessive pride or self-confidence

969 somber [2]
a. 어두침침한
gloomy or mournful

"Yes," he responded, warily. This guy could be anyone. A killer, or a friend of Terry's, the **tyrant** of the karaoke room. He maintained his suspicion until the boy began crying.

Well, not crying, exactly, just a sudden breath followed by a swipe at his wet eyes. Jake turned and pretended not to notice, so as not to **smear** the young man's masculine **hubris**. The visitor began to introduce himself quickly thereafter, becoming easier to understand as his crying stopped.

"Sorry about that. I should explain. I was your uncle's student. I saw you in the lecture room. He talked a lot about you in our study sessions. And I missed the ceremony. I wasn't sure if it was family only, or if it was appropriate to join."

He became sad in his blue suit, which had obviously been bought for him in high school, pulling a bit at the sleeves to pull them over his wrists.

"It's OK," Jake responded maturely. He thought of the horrible feeling of grief which his relatives had shown at the funeral, all of them looking very **somber** but basically waiting until they could leave. It was probably best the young sensitive man had not been there, he decided.

"Jake? Who's at the door?" his mother shouted from the kitchen.

Jake was unsure of what to say. Her confession the night before was still fresh in his mind, and something made him unable to mention his uncle to her. Also, he wasn't sure how the young man would feel. Nevertheless, they couldn't keep talking in the entryway (and his curiosity about the boy was still not completely satisfied), so he said what he thought to be the most relevant and appropriate thing to say under the circumstances.

"Do you wanna come in?" he asked.

"Well, I don't want to disturb you. He just talked about you so much, it seemed like I should come to console you. Also," he put his hand into his jacket pocket, pulling out a CD. "I thought I'd give you this. He said you liked jazz, but I never liked the stuff myself. It's rock, so you can throw it away or whatever, but I thought you might like to listen to it."

Jake looked at it, recognizing the name of the artist but unable to quite imagine the music.

"Thanks," he said, then, realizing that the boy probably didn't want to be subjected to his parents, added "why don't we get a coffee sometime?"

"That sounds great. You wanna come to the campus?"

Jake said he would love it, and the two students exchanged numbers and promised to see each other very soon. The boy **galloped** down the hallway, and disappeared into the elevator.

"Well, that was a long conversation," his father said as he got up to put on his jacket.

"He was one of the Professor's students," Jake said as his mother quickly turned to clear away the dishes. "He gave me this." He showed them the CD and then hurried to his room to play it, planning to escape to the campus once more.

---

970 gallop [3]
v. 전력 질주하다
to go fast, race, or hurry

Vocabulary

0958
tacit [3]
[tǽsit]

a. 암묵적인, 무언의   without being said; understood, implied, silent
That's it! 이라고 소리 내어 말하진 않지만 몸짓, 손짓, 눈짓으로 표현한다고 외우자.
Tacit approval with a nod (*adj.*)

0959
ramification [3]
[ˌræmɪfɪˈkeɪʃn]

n. 파문, 영향   a derived subject, problem, etc.; outgrowth
도레미파(re me fa → ra mi fi) 소리가 퍼져나가는 것처럼, 무언가의 영향을 뜻한다고 외워보자.
That's the public policy **ramification** of good health care insurance. (*n.*)

0960
be taken aback [3]
[bi teɪkn əbǽk]

v. 깜짝 놀라다   to be taken by surprise
깜짝 놀라서 뒤로(back) 넘어졌다고(taken) 외우자.
She was completely **taken aback** by his anger. (*v.*)

0961
conceal [7]
[kənˈsiːl]

v. 숨기다, 감추다   to hide, keep secret
conceal하려면 아무도 모르는 통에 조용히 seal (걸어잠그다) 해야지?
She tried very hard to **conceal** her true feelings, but he found out anyway. (*v.*)

0962
abstain [4]
[əbˈsteɪn]

v. 자제하다   to hold back, cease
멋있는 복근을(abs) 만들기 위해 너무 기름기 많은 음식으로 몸이 더러워지는 (stain) 것을 자제한다고 생각하자.
It is a good habit to **abstain** from any kind of abuse. (*v.*)

0963
shrewd [ʃrúːd]

a. 면밀히 살피는; 예리한, 영리한, 약삭빠른   probing, penetrating, judicious; characterized by skill at understanding and profiting by circumstances
원래는 evil, mischievous 등의 나쁜 뜻이었는데 점차 변해서, '다른 사람을 다루는데 기교를 잘 부린다'라고 하여 '기민하고 영리한'이란 뜻으로 쓰이게 되었다.
Ed is a **shrewd** dealer; he sold more cars per year than any salesman this year. (*adj.*)

0964
philanthropic [filənθrǽpik]

a. 인정 많은, 박애주의의   charitable, humanitarian
phil은 사랑, anthro는 사람을 뜻하므로 사람을 사랑하는, 즉 '박애주의의'라는 의미이다. Philip is a philanthropic person이라고 외워보자.
He is doing a lot of **philanthropic** work. (*adj.*)

0965
ruffled [ˈrʌfld]

a. 헝클어진   disorganized or untidy; bedraggled
거칠게(rough → ruff) 다뤄서 머리가 헝클어졌다고(ruffle) 외우자.
He stood there with his hair **ruffled** by the breeze. (*adj.*)

0966
tyrant [táiərənt]

n. 폭군, 독재자   powerful leader who allows few freedoms; despot, oppressor; dictator
Tyrannosaurus Rex와 같은 어원이다. 공룡만큼 난폭한 독재자를 말한다.
The **tyrant** sentenced all of those who opposed him to death. (*n.*)

0967
smear [smɪr]

v. 명예를 훼손하다   to tarnish, slur
smear는 '표면에 문지르다, 바르다'라는 의미를 가지고 있다. 그러므로 '누군가의 명예에 더러움을 묻혀서 훼손하다'라는 의미이다.
The story was an attempt to **smear** the party leader. (*v.*)

0968
hubris [hjúːbris]

n. 자만심, 지나친 자신   excessive pride or self-confidence; arrogant
그리스어로 '신에게 반대하는'이라는 의미이다. 자신감이 넘쳐 신도 몰라보는 경우를 말한다.
Hubris about victory over the weaker team (*n.*)

0969
somber ²

[sámbər]

a. **어두침침한, 음침한**   gloomy or mournful; dull

'아래'라는 뜻의 sub와 '그늘'이라는 뜻의 'umbra'가 합쳐져 그늘 아래, 즉 '어두컴컴한'의 의미이다.

When I saw the doctor's **somber** expression, I knew my diagnosis was not a good one. (*adj.*)

0970
gallop ³

[ǁgæləp]

v. **전력 질주하다**   to go fast, race, or hurry

소녀가(gal) 점프하듯이(leap → lop) 전력 질주했다고 외우자.

She came **galloping** down the street. (*v.*)

Episode 58
MATCHING Quiz

1. tacit • • A. to hide, keep secret
2. ramification • • B. charitable, humanitarian
3. be taken aback • • C. without being said; understood
4. conceal • • D. to tarnish, slur
5. abstain • • E. gloomy or mournful
6. shrewd • • F. to go fast, race, or hurry
7. philanthropic • • G. excessive pride or self-confidence
8. ruffled • • H. disorganized or untidy; bedraggled
9. tyrant • • I. to hold back, cease
10. smear • • J. to be taken by surprise
11. hubris • • K. powerful leader who allows few freedoms; despot
12. somber • • L. probing, penetrating, judicious
13. gallop • • M. a derived subject, problem, etc.; outgrowth

1-C, 2-M, 3-J, 4-A, 5-I, 6-L, 7-B, 8-H, 9-K, 10-D, 11-G, 12-E, 13-F

더 많은 문제를 풀고자 한다면 www.quizlet.com에서 'paul academy seoul' class를 검색

Episode 59: Postmodernism

After meeting his friends in the hallway at the academy that Monday morning and allowing Ashley to **cuddle** him for quite a long time, Jake walked through the next few days like a sleepwalker, hardly noticing much of what was being discussed.

On Wednesday night, however, reviewing some of the material from his missing week, he was surprised to find himself reading something from the academy with real passion. He had been glancing through a reading passage on postmodernism, and had even looked up several of the writers and painters it mentioned in its **litany** on the subject. He spent ten minutes looking at "Nude Descending a Staircase" and decided that Duchamp was obviously insane, but he loved the madness of it, much more than Salvador Dali's crazy paintings with their strange imagery. Then he turned to the literature.

Halfway through one article, he reached for his phone to call his uncle. He pressed the usual button and then stopped suddenly, remembering the loss like injured soldiers are said to scratch at cut limbs, trying to reach an itch that no longer exists. He shut the phone quietly and, drying his eyes, opened a copy of Albert Camus's novel The Stranger that someone had put online. The first line **devastated** him: "Mother died today. Or yesterday. I can't remember."

How strange coincidence can be.

However, as he kept reading the simple prose (he realized he liked Camus if only because it was a lot more **accessible** than any other novel he'd read and much easier than the paintings to understand) he kept thinking how meaningless everything appeared. He was sympathetic to the passiveness of the novel's **protagonist** and thought it extremely similar to his rooftop thinking a few weeks earlier. He kept flipping back to the reading passage: "postmodernists rejected the conservative values of the Victorian **epoch**, preferring to put **credence** in the idea that life had no purpose and there was not always justice, and that God no longer controlled people's fates."

---

971 cuddle [2]
v. 껴안다
to hug tightly, snuggle

972 litany [2]
n. 장황한 설명
a prolonged or tedious account

973 devastate [8]
v. 완전히 파괴하다
to lay waste, render desolate

974 accessible [19]
a. 이해하기 쉬운
easy to understand

975 protagonist [7]
n. 주인공
main character of a novel or play

976 epoch [3]
n. 시대
era, period

977 credence [2]
n. 신빙성
belief as to the truth of something

978 epiphany [6]
n. (어떤 사물에 대한) 직관
a sudden, intuitive perception of the reality or essential meaning of something

979 meager [8]
a. 메마른, 불충분한
in small amount; insufficient; scanty

980 abolish [12]
v. 폐지하다
to do away with

"Yes," he said aloud. Perhaps none of this has any meaning. He read a few more pages of Camus and realized with a secret smile that he had been reading an obviously advanced novel with no difficulty whatsoever, and had been enjoying it. This **epiphany** pleased him enough to forget the darkness of the text, but it couldn't quite hide the fact that he had somehow become a postmodernist in the midst of reading. But who could he tell if not the Professor?

He looked through his **meager** list of contacts, reminding. Names passed, each one carrying a memory, an emotion, or a combination of many such things. Jessica, Sam, TJ, Ashley. Those were the potential candidates with whom to share his newest intellectual breakthrough. He hit a number and waited for the response.

"Don't you know what time it is, Jake?" Ashley's tired voice said.

"No, actually." He looked at the clock and realized with a gasp that it was 1:30 AM. "Sorry. I didn't realize."

"Well, anything important enough to **abolish** time itself from your memory must be important. What's up?" She was joking, but he could tell she was genuinely curious.

"Oh, well, it seems silly to say it out loud now," he admitted.

"Oh come on. You've already woken me up. You could at least share."

"It's just… well… I think I'm a postmodernist."

He had to pull the phone away from his ear she was laughing so hard.

"I'm sorry, Jake. That was just unexpected. You call a girl in the middle of the night to say that you're becoming Albert Camus all of a sudden."

"Yes! That's exactly it! Have you read The Stranger?"

"Yes. Let me guess: everything is meaningless now, right?"

"Yes! Anyway, I guess we can talk about it tomorrow. I just wanted to tell someone."

"That's sweet Jake. Let's talk about it at lunch or something."

"Oh no, can't do that," he said seriously, imagining what TJ would say if he told him he'd found inspiration in a book.

"Oh yes, of course. The peer pressure. Well, what was that college student's name? The one who came to visit you?"

"Victor."

"Let's invite him to hang out. You free on Friday?"

That was almost a joke. She knew his social life was an empty calendar.

"Fine, I'll take that as a yes."

And so they both, once again, had plans to go back to the campus.

Vocabulary

0971
cuddle [2]
[|kʌdl]

v. 껴안다   to hug tightly, snuggle
커플끼리(couple) 서로 껴안고 있다고(cuddle) 외워보자.
The little boy **cuddled** the teddy bear close. (*v.*)

0972
litany [2]
[|lɪtəni]

n. 장황한 설명   a prolonged or tedious account
머리에서 생각나는 말을(line → lit) 아무 거나(any) 하다 보니 장황해졌다고 생각하자.
I have become very frustrated with Peter's lethargy and **litany** of excuses. (*n.*)

0973
devastate [8]
[|devəsteɪt]

v. 완전히 파괴하다   to lay waste, render desolate
악마가(devil → dev) 하나의 주(state)를 완전히 파괴했다고(devastate) 외우자.
The bomb **devastated** much of the old part of the city. (*v.*)

0974
accessible [19]
[ək|sesəbl]

a. 이해하기 쉬운   easy to understand
access는 접근이라는 뜻이므로 accessible은 접근하기 쉬운, 즉 '이해하기 쉬운'이라는 뜻이다.
A programme making science more **accessible** to young people (*adj.*)

0975
protagonist [7]
[prə|tægənɪst]

n. 주인공   main character of a novel or play
'반지의 제왕'에서 프로도(frodo → prota)가 주인공(protagonist)이라는 걸 생각하자.
The **protagonist** is looking for something. (*n.*)

0976
epoch [3]
[|epək]

n. 시대   era, period
era, period와 연결해서 외워보자.
The death of the emperor marked the end of an **epoch** in the country's history. (*n.*)

0977
credence [ˈkriːdns]

n. 신빙성   belief as to the truth of something
credit은 신용이라는 뜻이므로(credit card = 신용카드) credence는 '신임, 신빙성'을 의미한다.
Historical evidence lends **credence** to his theory. (*n.*)

0978
epiphany [ipífəni]

n. (어떤 사물에 대한) 직관, 통찰   a sudden, intuitive perception of the reality or essential meaning of something, insight
티파니(Tiffany)는 여자의 직감을 사용해 갑작스럽게 깨달음을(epiphany) 얻었다고 외우자.
But one day earlier this year i had a sudden **epiphany**. (*n.*)

0979
meager [míːgər]

a. 메마른, 불충분한, 빈약한   in small amount; insufficient; scanty, deficient in quantity or quality; scanty
어떤 것이 meager한 양만큼 있다면 '나(me)'는 eager하게 그것을 더 많이 가지려고 한다.
The **meager** apartment was uncomfortable a big family. (*adj.*)

0980
abolish [əbáliʃ]

v. 폐지하다, 철폐하다   to do away with, to cancel; to put an end to a + 'bomb' + lish 라고 생각하자. destroy와 비슷한 뜻이다.
Ever since the law against cigarettes was **abolished**, people have been smoking left and right. (*v.*)

Voca Hamburger

Episode 59

MATCHING Quiz

1. cuddle
2. litany
3. devastate
4. accessible
5. protagonist
6. epoch
7. credence
8. epiphany
9. meager
10. abolish

- A. to lay waste, render desolate
- B. era, period
- C. in small amount; insufficient; scanty
- D. belief as to the truth of something
- E. easy to understand
- F. to hug tightly, snuggle
- G. to do away with
- H. main character of a novel or play
- I. a sudden, intuitive perception of the reality or essential meaning of something
- J. a prolonged or tedious account

1-F, 2-J, 3-A, 4-E, 5-H, 6-B, 7-D, 8-I, 9-C, 10-G

더 많은 문제를 풀고자 한다면 www.quizlet.com에서 'paul academy seoul' class를 검색

Episode 60

Back to School

981 seduce [3]
v. 유혹하다, 꾀다
to entice, tempt

982 prance [2]
v. 활보하다, 뛰어다니다
to cavort, swagger

983 congenial [2]
a. 화기애애한
agreeable, affable, convivial

984 erratic [2]
a. 불규칙한, 변덕스러운
deviating from the usual course in conduct; eccentric

985 vicissitude [5]
n. 우여곡절
alternating or changing phases of life or fortune

Having been unable to **seduce** Ashley into coming to visit Victor instead of going to the afternoon session, Jake had agreed to go ahead of her and await her arrival in the later evening.

And so, once more, he found himself walking up the leafy road toward the college campus, enjoying the feeling of wandering in secret through the crowd of students as though he was one of them, looking at the same familiar buildings he'd identified for Ashley, places where memories of the Professor still scared him. He'd texted Victor, and they had arranged to meet outside the literature building, from whence they'd journey to the campus cafe and talk. It was Friday, a day of work for most people, but many students seemed to be **prancing** around with nothing to do, a few stood around doorways deep in intellectual conversation and others recounted drunken escapades from the previous night.

When he did arrive, Victor seemed to be in much the same state as he had at Jake's house, still not perfect yet quite fashionable in the semi-informal uniform of the university student. He even wore a slightly old-fashioned hat, which he duly tipped to his new friend as he approached.

"Hope you weren't waiting long, Jake," he said warmly as he clasped his hand in a **congenial** shake.

"No, no. Just got here, actually."

"Oh, good. It's only that we're having quite a heated conversation which began last night and still hasn't quite stopped, even though most of us have slept somewhat. Others haven't, I should warn you, so their behavior might seem mildly **erratic**. Come on, it's this way."

Jake became more nervous when faced with the prospect of meeting some real college students. Wouldn't they see he was really just a kid? Hadn't all of the **vicissitudes** of losing his uncle been enough without this new test to prove his worth? He was about to protest, but they had already arrived at the cafe.

Inside, a number of hung-over students leaned over their books in a state of pure exhaustion, while others who obviously hadn't been out late the previous night engaged in some more pleasant conversations. Walking by a few such tables, Jake **marveled** at how much enthusiasm they had.

When they reached the rear of the cafe, behind the glass divider, he saw that nearly all the available tables and chairs had been taken over for their conversation. A few passionate students were talking over each other on some point of literary translation, and a surprised Jake stood and listened as their conversation continued.

986 marvel [3]
v. 경탄하다
to wonder at, be curious about

Vocabulary

0981

seduce ³

[sɪ|duːs]

v. 유혹하다, 꾀다   to entice, tempt, to persuade or induce
쾌감을 위해 유혹하는 것을 seduce라고 한다.
She **seduced** the indifferent man with her beautiful singing, and made him fall in love with her. (v.)

0982

prance ²

[præns]

v. 활보하다, 뛰어다니다   to cavort, swagger
뛰어다니는 조랑말(prancing pony)을 떠올려보자.
The lead singer was **prancing** around with the microphone. (v.)

0983

congenial ²

[kəndʒíːnjəl]

a. 화기애애한, 마음이 맞는   agreeable in character, affable, convivial
con(together) + genial(genius: spirit)에서 '날 때부터 같은 정신(마음)을 가진'이란 뜻이다. genius(천재)는 본래 라틴어로 '수호신'이란 뜻인데 '태어날 때부터 함께 붙어 있다'는 뜻이기도 하다.
The thank you note ended **congenially**. (adv.)

0984

erratic ²

[ɪ|rætɪk]

a. 불규칙한, 변덕스러운   deviating from the usual or proper course in conduct or opinion; eccentric
쥐(rat)들은 치즈를 보면 흥분해서 불규칙적으로, 변덕스럽게 움직인다.
The weather was quite **erratic**: it was very sunny one day, but snowed the next day. (adj.)

0985

vicissitude ⁵

[vɪsísətjùːd]

n. 우여곡절   alternating or changing phases of life or fortune, variations
우여곡절(vicissitudes)을 겪으면 사나운 행동(vicious attitudes)을 하게 될 수도 있다.
The many **vicissitudes** of life are what makes life truly challenging. (n.)

0986

marvel ³

[|mɑːrvl]

v. **경탄하다**   to wonder at, be curious about

마블(Marvel)사의 어벤져스 슈퍼히어로들은 사람들로 하여금 경탄하게 만든다.

Everyone **marvelled** at his courage. (v.)

Voca Hamburger

Episode 60

MATCHING Quiz

1. seduce •   • A. to cavort, swagger
2. prance •   • B. to wonder at, be curious about
3. congenial •   • C. to entice, tempt
4. erratic •   • D. alternating or changing phases of life or fortune
5. vicissitude •   • E. deviating from the usual course in conduct; eccentric
6. marvel •   • F. agreeable, affable, convivial

1-C, 2-A, 3-F, 4-E, 5-D, 6-B

더 많은 문제를 풀고자 한다면 www.quizlet.com에서 'paul academy seoul' class를 검색

Episode 61: A Future Foreshadowed

987 foreshadow [8]
v. 미리 보여주다
to show or indicate beforehand; prefigure

988 aspire [12]
v. 열망하다
to long, aim, or seek ambitiously

989 repose [6]
n. 안식, 휴식
rest, tranquility

990 reminiscence [10]
n. 추억
remembrance

991 inundate [2]
v. 압도시키다
to overwhelm

992 awe [20]
n. 경외감
amazement and respect

993 milieu [3]
n. 환경
environment; surroundings

"But you can't just censor Burroughs like that! If you lose the sexuality, the entire meaning is lost!" A very angry undergraduate began.

"Yeah, but then you can't teach the book in schools, which is an obvious insult to the author, who **aspires** to reach a broader audience. Anyway, it's only one scene. Can't we just use a different word and allow older readers to understand what it means anyway?"

"No! It has to be clear, its—"

Victor cleared his throat at this point, before the struggle threatened the **repose** of a pleasant afternoon. The two who were talking instantly stopped and turned to the door, where the boy in the hat stood proudly next to his young friend.

"Guys, you remember hearing about Jake? The nephew?"

A wave of happy **reminiscence** suddenly greeted Jake as they all in turn rose to shake his hand, **inundating** him with such warmth that he felt unworthy of the association.

"Your uncle was a great man," one said, offering his chair.
"A visionary," said another.

As he took one of the chairs, Jake enjoyed the **awe** his uncle inspired in them, and nodded at Victor in thanks for treating him to more than a solitary conversation.

As it turned out, the students (nine of them) had all been in the class during the lecture which Jake had seen a few weeks earlier. It seemed an eternity to him, but as he began getting used to this scholarly **milieu**, he began recognizing a few of the faces he had seen then.

A few of them had also been helping the old man to work on his latest book on poetry, which he had expected to publish in January of the next year. Now, they were trying to get the university to print it anyway, which had itself **provoked** a lot of controversy in the department, causing many of them to try to explain to the **bewildered** high school student the problems of the university regulations.

Jake wondered if he had been **deluded** about what it really meant to study. These students were so different from those in high school or the academy. Firstly, they talked a *lot*, and filled their conversations with **allegories** and a great many literary **allusions** to books which he hadn't even heard of. They told stories **embellished** with quotes from writers they all apparently had studied with the Professor (who was always discussed as though he had been the only one at the entire school to truly deserve the title). They were full of knowledge which even Ashley (the smartest person Jake had ever met who was even close to his own age) would be intimidated by.

"So, what about you, Jake?" one of them said. "What are you going to study when you come to university?"

"I… I don't know," he admitted ashamedly, quickly expecting them to **revile** him for his unpreparedness as his mother had often done.

"Terrific," one girl said. "It's so terrible when people are so *sure* of their programs before they've even applied. But I think you should study literature, so you can join us."

"Well, I have been reading Camus lately," he said, remembering his midnight revelation a few days earlier.

"Ah-ha!" One of them said victoriously. "So much better than that nonsense created by Sartre, isn't it? He just wrote in this lengthy way which is so tiring, isn't it?"

Jake had to admit he had yet to read Sartre, which caused a few of them to begin arguing about the relative merits of various authors.

"You don't want all the **flamboyance** of the French," Victor said after a brief (and rare) pause. "Read the Germans. They don't use such flowery, cheap, pseudo-philosophical language. Isn't that right, sweetheart?" He **nudged** the girl sitting next to him playfully. She responded with one unreproducible word that he wasn't her sweetheart. He still smiled.

---

994 provoke [26]
v. 화나게 하다
to anger, enrage, exasperate, or vex

995 bewildered [8]
a. 갈피를 못 잡는
confused or puzzled completely

996 delude [4]
v. 속이다, 착각하게 하다
to mislead the mind or judgment of

997 allegory [4]
n. 우화, 풍자
a symbolical narrative, figurative treatment of one subject under the guise of another

998 allusion [9]
n. 암시
the making of a casual or indirect reference to something

999 embellished [7]
a. 장식된
decorated or added detail

1000 revile [3]
v. 꾸짖다, 매도하다
to admonish, scold

1001 flamboyance [2]
n. 화려함
striking boldness, flashiness

1002 nudge [3]
v. (팔꿈치로) 쿡 찌르다
to push slightly, especially with the elbow

1003 rejoice [2]
v. 기뻐하다
to be glad, express joy

1004 exalt [6]
v. 칭찬하다
to praise, extol

1005 discord [4]
n. 논쟁, 분란
dispute, disagreement, difference of opinions

1006 replicate [11]
v. 복제하다
to repeat, duplicate

Halfway between the discussion of postmodernism and a brief comment about music, Ashley texted to say that she was at the station, asking where she should go. Jake ran out to meet her, if only to warn her about the dense nature of the conversations. They met outside the library.

"It's weird being back here," she said. "That last time was... so recent."

"Yeah, but he would **rejoice** you came back. That *was* the last thing he said to either of us."

She sniffled slightly, even though it wasn't cold. They walked mostly in silence towards the cafe, only stopping at the doorway for Jake to warn her about the conversation.

There was nothing to worry about, of course. They **exalted** her just as they had Jake, and she kept up with the conversation much better than he had, enjoying the atmosphere of intellectual **discord** and heated argument. As the afternoon wore on, they went to a nearby restaurant, where the older students told the younger with tales of college life and the many wonders of its independence (even though they all still lived at home).

At the end of the day, most of the red-eyed college students finally admitted to being tired, and Victor walked back with Jake and his "new girlfriend" (as kept calling Ashley) to the subway station. They shook hands, promising once more that they would keep in touch. Jake finally got a chance to thank him for the CD, which he had played repeatedly during the last few days.

"Don't mention it, my boy," Victor said, perfectly **replicating** the Professor's tone. They laughed with relief, and Jake went to bed that night dreaming of college, Camus, and a future in cafes. He even told his father about the publishing project later that night. The old man just smiled.

Vocabulary

0987
foreshadow [8]
[fɔːrˈʃædoʊ]

v. 미리 보여주다, 전조가 되다   to show or indicate beforehand; prefigure
fore + shadow 인데 fore는 앞이라는 뜻이지? shadow는 그림자. 그래서 미래의 일을 그림자처럼 은근히 알려주는 거야. 그래서 '조짐을 나타내다, 암시하다'라는 뜻이야.
Last night's nightmare seems to **foreshadow** that something bad will happen. (v.)

0988
aspire [12]
[əˈspaɪə(r)]

v. 열망하다   to long, aim, or seek ambitiously
spire는 '높은 첨탑'을 뜻한다. 높은 곳으로 가기를 열망한다고(aspire) 생각하자.
She didn't **aspire** to a career in the music business. (v.)

0989
repose [6]
[rɪˈpoʊz]

n. 안식, 휴식   tranquility, a state of rest
지금 서 있다면, 쉬기 위해서는 다시(re) 포즈(pose)를 취해야 한다.
After a long day, an hour of **repose** may be very pleasant. (n.)

0990
reminiscence [10]
[ˌreməˈnɪsns]

n. 추억   remembrance
remind는 '기억나게 한다'는 의미이다. 따라서 옛 기억을 떠오르게 하는 추억(reminiscence)이라는 뜻이다.
The book is a collection of his **reminiscences** about the actress. (n.)

0991
inundate [2]
[ˈɪnəndeɪt]

v. 압도시키다; 감당 못할 정도로 주다, 침수시키다   to overwhelm; to fill with an overflowing abundance
'in under'를 연상해서 외우자.
The houses was **inundated** by the storm so everything became wet. (v.)

0992
awe [20]
[ɔː]

n. 경외감   amazement and respect
amazing을 awe-mazing이라고 생각해서 외우자.
He speaks of her with **awe**. (n.)

0993
milieu ³
[miːljɜː]

n. 환경　environment; surroundings
군대(military)에 갔다오면 어떤 환경에서도(milieu) 살아남을 수 있다고 외우자.
They stayed, safe and happy, within their own social **milieu**. (*n.*)

0994
provoke ²⁶
[prəˈvoʊk]

v. 화나게 하다　to anger, enrage, exasperate, or vex
계속해서 콕콕 찔러서(poke) 화나게 만든다고(provoke) 외워보자.
There's no need to **provoke** her and press her buttons. (*v.*)

0995
bewildered ⁸
[bɪˈwɪldərd]

a. 갈피를 못 잡는, 당황한　confused or puzzled completely, out of one's element and confused
황야에 버려지면 당황하고 길을 찾기 힘들 것이므로 wilderness를 떠올리면서 이 단어의 뜻을 유추하자.
She was **bewildered** by their questions. (*adj.*)

0996
delude ⁴
[dɪˈluːd]

v. 속이다, 착각하게 하다　to mislead the mind or judgment of
deceive와 연결해서 외워보자.
Don't be **deluded** into thinking that we are out of danger yet. (*v.*)

0997
allegory ⁴
[ˈæləɡɔːri]

n. 우화, 풍자　a symbolical narrative, figurative treatment of one subject under the guise of another
allos(다른) + agoreuein(터놓고 얘기하다). 즉 우화를 통해 다른 주제에 대해 터놓고 얘기할 수 있다는 의미이다.
A political **allegory** (*n.*)

0998
allusion ⁹
[əˈluːʒn]

n. 암시　the making of a casual or indirect reference to something
delude는 속이다는 의미니까, 속이는 대신 반대로 무언가를 암시한다고(allude) 외우자.
Her poetry is full of obscure literary **allusion**. (*n.*)

0999
embellished ⁷
[ɪmˈbelɪʃt]

a. 장식된　decorated or added detail
크리스마스 트리에 종을(bell) 달면서 장식한다고(embellish) 외워보자.
He did not try to **embellish** anything. (*v.*)

1000
revile ³ [riváil]

v. 꾸짖다, 매도하다; 욕하다, 욕설을 퍼붓다   to admonish, scold; to speak abusively
vile 은 '극도록 불쾌하다'라는 단어에서 왔다.
He is **reviled** for his mistake. (v.)

1001
flamboyance ² [flæmbɔ́iəns(i)]

n. 화려함   striking boldness, flashiness
남자아이를(boy) 재미있게 해 주기 위해서 불꽃(flame → flam) 같이 화려한(flamboyant) 옷을 입고 나간다고 외우자.
Their **flamboyance** means they are better suited for the evening. (n.)

1002
nudge ³ [nʌdʒ]

v. (팔꿈치로) 쿡 찌르다   to push slightly, especially with the elbow
견과류(nut)를 팔꿈치로 쿡 찌르면(nudge) 깨지는 않고 팔꿈치만 아플 걸.
He **nudged** me and whispered, 'Look who's just come in.' (v.)

1003
rejoice ² [ridʒɔ́is]

v. 기뻐하다   to be glad, express joy
다시(re) 기쁨을(joy → joi) 느낄만큼 기뻐하는(rejoice) 것이라고 외우자.
The motor industry is **rejoicing** at the cut in car tax. (v.)

1004
exalt ⁶ [igzɔ́ːlt]

v. 칭찬하다; 승격시키다   to praise, extol; to raise in rank, honor, quality, etc
소금(salt)을 음식에 넣으면 음식의 맛이 한층 더 좋아질 때가 많죠.
They **exalted** the prince by calling him the bravest and most heroic man in the world. (v.)

1005
discord ⁴ [dískɔːrd]

n. 논쟁, 분란; 부조화, 불일치   dispute, disagreement, difference of opinions, absence of harmoniousness
DIS(not) + ACCORD(agreement) 동의가 되지 않음, 불일치.
Discord amongst the different social groups is just unpredictable. (n.)

1006
replicate ¹¹ [répləkèit]

v. 복제하다, 모사(복사)하다   to reproduce; to duplicate
replicate는 'duplicate'와 발음이 비슷하므로 같이 외우면 좋다.
The scientists tried to **replicate** his experiment by using the exact same ingredients and methods. (v.)

Note :

Episode 61

MATCHING Quiz

1. foreshadow
2. aspire
3. repose
4. reminiscence
5. inundate
6. awe
7. milieu
8. provoke
9. bewildered
10. delude
11. allegory
12. allusion
13. embellished
14. revile
15. flamboyance
16. nudge
17. rejoice
18. exalt
19. discord
20. replicate

A. to mislead the mind or judgment of
B. to anger, enrage, exasperate, or vex
C. decorated or added detail
D. confused or puzzled completely
E. a symbolical narrative, figurative treatment of one subject under the guise of another
F. to praise, extol
G. to push slightly, especially with the elbow
H. to admonish, scold
I. dispute, disagreement, difference of opinions
J. amazement and respect
K. the making of a casual or indirect reference to something
L. to long, aim, or seek ambitiously
M. striking boldness, flashiness
N. to be glad, express joy
O. environment; surroundings
P. rest, tranquility
Q. to overwhelm
R. to repeat, duplicate
S. to show or indicate beforehand; prefigure
T. remembrance

1-S, 2-L, 3-P, 4-T, 5-Q, 6-J, 7-O, 8-B, 9-D, 10-A, 11-E, 12-K, 13-C, 14-H, 15-M, 16-G, 17-N, 18-F, 19-I, 20-R

더 많은 문제를 풀고자 한다면 www.quizlet.com에서 'paul academy seoul' class를 검색

Episode 62: (Just Like) Starting Over

Summer was nearly over, and the golden light in the afternoon proved to the fact that it had come and gone. Slowly, days began to feel more and more **abbreviated**. Though it was only by a few minutes every day, Jake felt that the golden days of June and July were nothing more than memories now.

As the students prepared to **disseminate** back into their normal lives, there was still a final test to take, and so they appeared once more at 8:45 on Saturday morning, many of them for the last time. Jake would stay for one more week (to **reconcile** the work he missed during his week of sadness), but nearly everyone had elected to go.

For much of the summer, scores had stayed mostly static, with little moments of improvement every now and then. At one point, Jake had achieved a 600 on the reading section (1250 overall), but had dismissed it as lucky since he knew many of the words in the reading. Then it nearly happened again, and he began to recognize that the **synthesis** of events up to that point, the **fleeting** romance, the new friendships, the strange but **auspicious deviations** in his **rapport** with his parents, had somehow **instilled** in him a renewed motivation to improve. And he had. After all, the improvement in score was **predestined**.

Even TJ, who had **scorned** the very idea of studying at the beginning of the summer, had found his scores improving, having reached a point during his brief affair with Chastity when he realized that English vocabulary could be useful for the purpose of chatting.

Jake was glad he had met TJ, and the two had become close over the last eight weeks. They had proven their **valor** in facing the dangerous Cabal, and had dealt with the **repercussions** of that night and many other less dangerous jobs. There was such a **plethora** of memorable events that they overwhelmed Jake with their enormity.

1007 abbreviated [11]
a. 축약된
shortened by omitting letters; substituted into shorter forms

1008 disseminate [2]
v. 흩어지다
to spread out, scatter in different directions

1009 reconcile [10]
v. 받아들이다
to cause to accept or be resigned to something not desired

1010 synthesis [10]
n. 종합, 통합
the combining of the constituent elements of separate material

1011 fleeting [5]
a. 순식간의
passing swiftly; transitional

1012 auspicious [3]
a. 상서로운, 길조의
promising success; opportune

1013 deviation [12]
n. 빗나감, 벗어남, 편차
departure from a standard or norm

1014 rapport [4]
n 관계
relation, connection

1015 instill [2]
v. 서서히 주입시키다
to infuse gradually into the mind or feelings

1016 predestine [2]
v. 운명 짓다
to destine in advance

1017 scorn [13]
v. 경멸하다, 반대하다
to treat with contempt or disdain; reject

1018 valor [3]
n. 용기
bravery

1019 repercussion [3]
n. 파급효과
negative consequence of one's actions

1020 plethora [2]
n. 과다
a large amount

1021 quip [2]
n. 재담, 익살
a clever, witty remark, banter

1022 pundit [3]
n. 전문가, 권위자
scholar, expert, authority

1023 alloyed [2]
a. (합금처럼) 접합된
combined into one

1024 huddle [2]
v. 웅크리다
to curl up, crouch

1025 succor [2]
n. 구조
help, relief

1026 calamity [3]
n. 재난, 재해
disaster

Ashley, too, had been a big part of the summer. Jake knew that now, looking back over their friendship like a film. More than his score had improved over that period.

That morning, the sky was again clear after a heavy midnight rain, which had awoken more than a few students, judging from their tired eyes and listless attitudes. There was less friendly **quip** in the morning, and it all seemed quite similar to the first week, when they had raised questions of originality and had expressed their collective frustration with the scores they'd received.

As the test began, Jake again looked at the passage, which Greg had said he'd chosen specially for their last essay.

It was another passage on Postmodernism. With a smile, he thought of the college-level **pundits** in the cafe a few days prior, and his uncle, whose face appeared throughout the **alloyed** memories and experiences at the academy that summer.

He began to write, looking around to see Ashley **huddled** intensely over her paper, her pencil flying across the page, and TJ staring with confusion at the question before beginning. Some people, he thought.

****

Some people (An Epilogue)

Some people say that, after a major catastrophe, after the damage has been cleared and the survivors salvaged from the remains, they realize that they had an ability they'd never known before, something which had lain quiet in them for some time, but which had never been tested. People who had been too afraid to even say hello to their peers had dived into the destruction to help strangers. Those who had considered themselves too cowardly, either physically or spiritually, had led the **succor** efforts, expertly pulling people out and comforting them on the edge of the **calamity** zone.

That revelation was on Jake's mind when he finally put his pencil down at the end of the last test and sat back with a heavy sigh. In June, he too had tried giving up his responsibility for the tests, as had everyone else, blaming teachers or the difficulty of the vocabulary, but somehow throughout all the difficulty of those weeks, he had emerged triumphant.

Indeed, when it was all over, Jake had had the best test of his summer, as had TJ, who was surprised by his 1200.

"What'd you get?" he asked Jake.

Jake paused for a moment, holding the page close to his face in disbelief.

"1280," he said quietly.

The other boy swore at him, but then smiled. Ashley and Sam appeared a few moments later to complete the group which had supported them throughout the long summer. She, too, had achieved the best score of her summer. Sam, having spent too little time studying, had not done as well (as was the case for many of the students who had looks of panic as they walked out of the building for the last time).

"Well," TJ said with his usual determination. "Now that we're officially **unfettered**, how about a hamburger?"

1027 unfettered [2]
a. 제한 받지 않는
free; liberated

Vocabulary

1007
abbreviated [11]
[əbríːvièitid]

a. 축약된   shortened by omitting letters; substituted into shorter forms
짧게(brief → brev) 만든 거라고 외워보자.
Where appropriate, **abbreviated** forms are used. (*adj.*)

1008
disseminate [2]
[dɪˈsemɪneɪt]

v. 흩어지다, (정보·지식 등을) 퍼뜨리다[전파하다]   to spread out, scatter in different directions
씨앗을(semen = semin) 이곳저곳에(dis → this) 다 뿌려서 퍼뜨린다고 (disseminate) 외우자.
Their findings have been widely **disseminated**. (*v.*)

1009
reconcile [10]
[ˈrekənsaɪl]

v. 받아들이다, 중재하다   to cause to accept or be resigned to something not desired, make peace
recon-nect와 같이 연상하면 외우기 쉽다.
Those two finally **reconciled** after a long fight so their kids can get married. (*v.*)

1010
synthesis [10]
[ˈsɪnθəsɪs]

n. 종합, 통합   the combining of the constituent elements of separate material
광합성이 photosynthesis라고 불리우는 걸 들어봤을 것이다. 빛을 사용해 포도당을 합성하는(synthesis) 과정이다.
A **synthesis** of traditional and modern values (*n.*)

1011
fleeting [5]
[ˈfliːtɪŋ]

a. 순식간의   passing swiftly; transitional, brief
flying처럼 무언가가 날아서 순식간에 사라진다고 해석할 수 있다.
For just one moment, he caught a **fleeting** glimpse of his first love before a train passed in front of his view, blocking her from his sight. (*adj.*)

1012
auspicious [ɔːspíʃəs]

a. 상서로운, 경사스러운, 길조의   promising success; opportune, favorable

auspice(길조, 전조)는 새점을 칠 때 왼쪽으로 날아가는 새(avi = ird)를 보고 (spi) 길조라 생각했다는 데서 온 말이다.

The charity's first fundraiser raised a lot of money and was an **auspicious** beginning. (*adj.*)

1013
deviation [12]

n. 빗나감, 벗어남, 편차   departure from a standard or norm

운전을(drive → dev) 하다가 길에서 벗어났다고(deviate) 외워보자.

The **deviation** from the average is too great to conclude that there is a significant difference between the two data.

1014
rapport [ræpɔ́ːr]

n. (친밀한) 관계   relation, connection; harmony

rap 음악으로 친밀한 관계를 맺을 수 있다.

Rapport between like-minded people is often the beginning of friendship. (*n.*)

1015
instill [instíl]

v. 서서히 주입시키다, 스며들게 하다   to infuse gradually into the mind or feelings, to fill with an idea or feeling

install '설치하다, 넣다'를 연상하자.

The beautiful, rosy sunrise **instilled** a feeling of awe in all of them. (*v.*)

1016
predestine [pridéstin]

v. 운명 짓다   to destine in advance

미리(pre) 운명이(destiny → destine) 결정됐다는 의미다.

I believe that each of us are **predestined** to walk a path in life. (*v.*)

1017
scorn [skɔ́ːrn]

v. 경멸하다, 반대하다; 경멸   to treat with contempt or disdain; reject, contempt; deride

scour(문질러 닦다)와 비슷한 단어. 성질을 긁으면 화가 나 경멸하게 된다.

He **scorned** anything with cilantro in it. (*v.*)

1018
valor [vǽlər]

n. 용기   bravery

용기는(valor) 매우 가치 있는(value) 것이라고 외우자.

He showed **valor** and skill on the battlefield. (*n.*)

1019
repercussion ³
[|ri:pər|kʌʃn]

n. (보통 좋지 못한) 파급효과 — negative consequence of one's actions
concussion은 뇌진탕이라는 뜻이다. 따라서 무언가에 대해 다시(re) 돌아오는 좋지 못한 효과라고 외우자.
The collapse of the company will have **repercussions** for the whole industry. (*n.*)

1020
plethora ²
[pléθərə]

n. 과다, 과잉 — a large amount, excess; overabundance
'매우 많다'라는 뜻의 plenty와 비슷하게 들리며 비슷한 의미이다.
A **plethora** of product choices. (*n.*)

1021
quip ²
[kwɪp]

n. 재담, 익살 — a clever, witty remark, banter
재치있는 입담(quip)과 재치있는 질문(quiz)을 연결해서 외워보자.
Your **quip** about the taxi driver was most humorous. (*n.*)

1022
pundit ³
[pʌ́ndit]

n. 전문가, 권위자, 학자, 박식한 사람 — scholar, expert, authority, one who has authority on a subject; learned person; an expert of the field
어원은 payndit. '배움이 많은 사람'이라는 힌두어이다.
The **pundit** discussed the prince's lessons. (*n.*)

1023
alloyed ²
[ælɔid]

a. (합금처럼) 접합된 — combined into one
아이언맨의 수트는 합금으로(alloy) 만들어져 있다고 생각하자.
Brass is an **alloy** of copper and zinc. (*n.*)

1024
huddle ²
[|hʌdl]

v. 웅크리다 — to curl up, crouch
차력쇼에서 웅크려 있는(huddle) 사람들 몇 명을 허들처럼 뛰어넘는 장면을 연상해 보자.
We **huddled** together for warmth. (*v.*)

1025
succor ²
[sʌ́kər]

n. 구조, 구원(자) — help, relief, aid; assist
succ(ess)와 연관지어서 성공한 사람이 다른사람들을 도와주므로 '구원'이라는 뜻으로 외울 수 있다.
The generous doctor provided **succor** to his poorest patients for free. (*n.*)

1026
calamity [3]
[kəlǽməti]

n. 재난, 재해   disaster, a great misfortune
범죄조직과 손을잡고 그들을 불러(call) 범죄를 저지른다면 분명 훗날 큰 (mighty) 재앙이 올 것이다. (call + mighty = calamity)
The Nepal earthquake was a national **calamity**. (*n.*)

1027
unfettered [2]
[ʌnfétərd]

a. 제한 받지 않는   free; liberated
지방(fat → fet)이 사라져(un) 살 때문에 제한 받지 않는다고 외워보자.
The **unfettered** slaves ran to freedom. (*adj.*)

Episode 62

MATCHING Quiz

1. abbreviated
2. disseminate
3. reconcile
4. synthesis
5. fleeting
6. auspicious
7. deviation
8. rapport
9. instill
10. predestine
11. scorn
12. valor
13. repercussion
14. plethora
15. quip
16. pundit
17. alloyed
18. huddle
19. succor
20. calamity

A. to cause to accept or be resigned to something not desired
B. disaster
C. bravery
D. a large amount
E. to infuse gradually into the mind or feelings
F. a clever, witty remark, banter
G. passing swiftly; transitional
H. departure from a standard or norm
I. scholar, expert, authority
J. promising success; opportune
K. relation, connection
L. combined into one
M. to destine in advance
N. help, relief
O. to treat with contempt or disdain; reject
P. shortened by omitting letters; substituted into shorter forms
Q. negative consequence of one's actions
R. to spread out, scatter in different directions
S. to curl up, crouch
T. the combining of the constituent elements of separate material

1-P, 2-R, 3-A, 4-T, 5-G, 6-J, 7-H, 8-K, 9-E, 10-M, 11-O, 12-C, 13-Q, 14-D, 15-F, 16-I, 17-L, 18-S, 19-N, 20-B
더 많은 문제를 풀고자 한다면 www.quizlet.com에서 'paul academy seoul' class를 검색

Episode 63

Touchdown

1028 aberrant [4]
a. 별난
weird, peculiar

1029 unforeseen [2]
a. 예측하지 못한
not anticipated, not predicted

1030 ecosystem [16]
n. 생태계
biological community

1031 indigenous [8]
a. 원산의, 토착의
innate, inherent; native

1032 pidgin [7]
n. 단순한 언어
casual dialect, simplified form of language

1033 topography [4]
n. 지형, 지형학
changes in elevation

1034 fluctuating [7]
a. 불규칙적인
varying irregularly; shirting back and forth

1035 cartographer [2]
n. 지도 제작자
a map maker

1036 remorse [4]
n. 회한, 후회
guilt, regret

Jake shifted in his seat, trying to find a position that would not make his legs fall asleep. He had been flying for less than an hour, but something about airplane seats gave him pain. He adjusted his earbuds and thumbed his smartphone to find something upbeat and settled on "Good Intentions Paving Company" by Joanna Newsom. Ashley had recommended the song, and despite its somewhat **aberrant** tone, Jake found the artist's voice and lyrics comforting, kind of like Ashley herself. He looked out the window and saw the island approaching.

This **unforeseen** journey into his own childhood was the last thing he wanted to do before going off to college. He questioned the wisdom of vacationing to a tropical island in the summer, when his home town was already hot and wet enough of an **ecosystem** as it was, but his mother had insisted. *You need a vacation, you need to get out of this apartment, and you need to let your mother have a month to herself. Besides, your cousin will be so happy to see you.*

Jake's heart did a little hop in his chest at the thought of William, and rather than deal with the thought, he decided he'd just ignore it. So, the island. Were there **indigenous** people there? Did they speak a **pidgin** English, all mixed up wonderfully with their native tongue? What was the **topography** like of the island? Smooth and flat or **fluctuating**? He saw a tiny island off the coast there. *Don't think about your cousin.* How many islands does it take to make a group of islands? Was two enough? He'd have to ask a **cartographer** to be sure. *Don't feel full of* **remorse** *about your cousin.* They had been close growing up, but then Jake's uncle had had a kind of a emotional **upheaval** and quit his job, buying some **fertile** land here which would allow the organic farm he wanted to start, **cultivating** soybeans, peanuts, and other dry crops and **tinging** his voice with the island's accent. They ate only what they grew, and what they grew was beans. William was a bean farmer's son, and he was not going to go to college.

Jake thumbed through his text message exchanges with his cousin over the last week leading up to the trip. Their back and forth through letters **constituted** a tale laying out Jake's hesitance to make the trip in the first place and William's excitement and barely contained **animosity** at Jake's success and academic prospects. Jake had, after all, scored 1400 on his SAT. When they were young they had been personally **incompatible**, with William's **unrestrained lavishness** a striking **antithesis** to Jake's quiet reserve, but they had never been foes. They had actually managed to get into a lot of **predicament**s together at family gatherings during their elementary school days, back when they were both at the height of youthful innocence and **plausible** deniability. Now, Jake wasn't sure what to expect.

He looked up. A flight attendant was making her way down the aisle and, smiling but not really, she motioned for Jake to remove his earbuds for landing. He, smiling but not really, acted surprised, bowed a little bit in fake embarrassment, and removed them. As soon as she passed he put them back in. He closed his eyes and waited for the plane to land.

Having gathered his luggage from the plane and still feeling **stiff** from the flight, Jake dragged his bag through the doorway to the terminal and instantly saw his cousin. How could he not? William wore a neon green and red Hawaiian shirt and bright orange cowboy boots. He smiled like a maniac and waved a sign decorated with Jake's dreaded childhood nickname.

"Hey! Fish-sniffer! Over here!" cried William.

Half the airport turned to look, perhaps fearing they were the fish-sniffer being summoned. Jake cleared his throat and waved back half-heartedly. 30 seconds into the trip and it was already a mistake. Jake wondered if he had enough money on him to just decide the whole thing wasn't going to work and buy a ticket home.

William ran over and hugged him, tightly. He was very strong, but the hug was warm and friendly. Despite himself, Jake hugged back. It had been a long time.

"It's good to see you, man!" They both said at the same time, and laughed. William offered to take his bag, but Jake waved him off and pulled it along. William clapped him on the back.

"Man, I can't believe you're here. We're gonna have such a great

---

1037 **upheaval** [7]
n. 격변, 대변동
strong or violent change or disturbance

1038 **fertile** [7]
a. 비옥한, 기름진
arable, productive

1039 **cultivate** [10]
v. 경작하다
to prepare and work on in order to raise crops

1040 **tinge** [2]
v. 물들이다
to impart a trace or slight degree of some color

1041 **constitute** [7]
v. 구성하다, 이루다
to form, create

1042 **animosity** [2]
n. 적대감, 반감
hostility, bitterness

1043 **incompatible** [5]
a. 서로 맞지 않는
unable to exist together in harmony

1044 **unrestrained** [7]
a. 억제되지 않은
excessive, uncontrolled

1045 **lavishness** [6]
n. 풍부함, 무성함
exuberance

1046 **antithesis** [7]
n. 정반대, 대조
opposite, contrast

1047 **predicament** [3]
n. 곤경, 궁지
difficult situation, trouble

1048 **plausible** [10]
a. 타당한 것 같은
having an appearance of truth or reason; credible

1049 stiff [6]
a. 뻣뻣한
rigid or firm

1050 grim [6]
a. 암울한, 우울한
somber, stern

1051 wretch [2]
n. 불쌍하고 가엾은 사람
a miserable, desolate person

1052 crass [4]
a. 무신경한, 대충의
coarse, vulgar

1053 grotesque [2]
a. 터무니없는, 기괴한
absurd, bizarre

1054 vault [2]
v. 뛰어넘다
to leap or spring, as to or from a position or over something

1055 agilely [3]
adv. 재빨리, 민첩하게
quickly, nimbly

1056 grasp [14]
v. 파악하다
to understand, comprehend

1057 immurement [2]
n. 감금, 칩거
imprisonment

---

time." He said. Jake smiled and nodded.

William stopped short suddenly, and slapped a hand across Jake's chest, forcing him to halt as well. He turned Jake around and grabbed him by the shoulders, looking him directly in the eye with grave seriousness.

"Cousin. Fish-sniffer. Do you remember *The Ode to Horrible Candy*?"

Jake's eyes widened in horror. Not the Hymn. But before he could say anything, William's resonant baritone had already begun vibrating throughout airport, the voice carrying far and wide thanks to the great acoustics of the building. A sick and falsely **grim** soloist.

"*Amaaaazing taaaaste, how sweeeet and sour...*"

It had been created by the two of them during a late night birthday party sleepover, fueled by a giant bag of convenience store candy, and sung to the tune of "Amazing Grace". It was absurd, childishly dirty, and if one cousin started it, then both had to finish it. It had gotten them kicked out more than one movie theater. Normally, he would never perform in public, but with The Hymn Jake had no choice. He closed his eyes and added his own weak tenor.

"*That made me* **wretch** *and heeeeave...*"

They sang their **crass** little song, gathering a little spectatorship of weary bystanders who formed a little circle around them and watched with curiosity and alarm.

William was an incomparable performer and showman, more than anyone else Jake had ever met, effortlessly able to appeal to a crowd of everyday strangers, even in such **grotesque** circumstances. He glided around the terminal, **vaulting** onto chairs and drawing applause from the crowd, performing like a real professional. Jake enjoyed it himself, until he spotted a couple of elderly guards making their way towards their performance. William had begun to sing to a potted plant, and Jake pulled on his sleeve and nodded toward the exit. William, **agilely grasping** the situation, chose a graceful exit over **immurement** and quickly took off the plant. He bowed deeply to the crowd, who clapped appreciatively as Jake and William ran for the door, singing all the while about bodily functions and **obnoxious** food.

Once outside they couldn't contain their laughter. This dangerously-timed **evocation** of their youth, this calling back into existence a part of himself which he had thought lost, had awoken something in Jake, and he **resolved** to be less of a mindless, fun-hating jerk for the rest of the trip. He smiled at his cousin and followed him to the parking lot, as the warm sun shone down upon them.

1058 **obnoxious** [2]
a. 아주 불쾌한, 고약한
disgusting, offensive

1059 **evocation** [13]
n. 환기, 유발시킴
calling to mind, summoning

1060 **resolve** [7]
v. 해결하다
to come to a definite or earnest decision about

Vocabulary

1028
aberrant [4]
[əbérənt]

a. **별난; 정도를 벗어난**   weird, peculiar; deviating from an accepted standard
라틴어 aberrare는 '정도에서 벗어난'이란 의미가 있다.
The **aberrant** car was sent back to the manufacturer and reformed to fit normal standards. (*adj.*)

1029
unforeseen [2]
[ˌʌnfɔːrˈsiːn]

a. **예측하지 못한**   not anticipated, not predicted
앞서(fore) 보지(seen) 못했으므로(un) '예측하지 못했다'는 의미이다.
Unforeseen occurrences are out of your control. (*adj.*)

1030
ecosystem [16]
[ˈiːkoʊsɪstəm]

n. **생태계**   biological community
eco는 자연을 뜻한다. 따라서 ecosystem은 자연의 시스템, 즉 생태계를 의미한다.
Honeybees are an important part of the **ecosystem**. (*n.*)

1031
indigenous [8]
[ɪnˈdɪdʒənəs]

a. **원산의, 토착의, 고유의**   innate, inherent; native; originating from the place
in(안에) + gen(birth, 탄생) + ous : '안에서 발생하는' → 지역에서 발생하는 → 토착의, 고유한
Indians are **indigenous** people of the American continent. (*adj.*)

1032
pidgin [7]
[ˈpɪdʒɪn]

n. **단순한 언어**   casual dialect, simplified form of language
비둘기들끼리(pigeon → pidgin) '구구'거리는 걸로 의사소통하는 것처럼 단순한 언어를 의미한다.
I tried to get my message across in my **pidgin** Italian. (*n.*)

1033
topography [4]
[təˈpɑːɡrəfi]

n. **지형, 지형학**   changes in elevation
지형의 가장 윗부분의(top) 높이가 어떻게 변하는지 보여주는 그래프라고 (graph) 외워보자.
A map showing the **topography** of the island (*n.*)

1034
fluctuating [flʌ́ktʃuèitiŋ]

a. 불규칙적인   varying irregularly; shirting back and forth
액체처럼(fluid → flu) 가만히 있지 않고 불규칙적이라고 외우자.
Prices are **fluctuating** and very unstable these days. (*adj.*)

1035
cartographer [kɑːrtɑːgrəfə(r)]

n. 지도 제작자   a map maker
topography, 즉 지형을 그리는 지도 제작자라고 외우자.
He was a **cartographer**, explorer and the governor of New France. (*n.*)

1036
remorse [rimɔ́ːrs]

n. 회한, 후회, 양심의 가책, 자책   guilt, regret; self-reproach
'mord'는 'bite'란 뜻이어서 직역하면 '나를 다시 깨물다'라는 뜻이다. 스스로를 깨물어버리는 것이니까 '자책'하는 것이다.
The criminal felt a sudden **remorse** for his sins and turned himself in to the police. (*n.*)

1037
upheaval [ʌphíːvəl]

n. 격변, 대변동, 들어올림, 융기   strong or violent change or disturbance, overthrow or violent disturbance of established order or condition
heaven까지 up '들어올린다'.
The revolutionary elections threw the government into **upheaval**. (*n.*)

1038
fertile [fɜ́ːrtl]

a. 비옥한, 기름진   arable, productive, bearing, producing, or capable of producing vegetation, crops, etc
타일(tile)로 깔려 있는 도로는 비옥하지 않지.
The land was so **fertile** that whenever we planted a seed, a tree sprung up in five seconds. (*adj.*)

1039
cultivate [kʌ́ltəvèit]

v. 경작하다   to prepare and work on in order to raise crops, to promote growth
'정원 등을 자르다, 가꾸다'라는 의미인 cull과 연관지어 생각하자.
The farmer **cultivated** crops by giving them enough water and food. (*v.*)

1040
tinge ²
[tɪndʒ]

v. 물들이다   to impart a trace or slight degree of some color
끝부분(tip → tin)만 살짝 적셔서 물들인다고 외우자.
White petals **tinged** with blue (v.)

1041
constitute ⁷
[|kɑ:nstətu:t]

v. 구성하다, 이루다, …이 되다   to form, create, to compose
con(='with') + statuere(='to set') 함께 셋업을 하는 것이니까 '구성하다'.
Grass **constitutes** most of a cow's diet . (v.)

1042
animosity ²
[ænəmɑ́səti]

n. 적대감, 반감, 악의, 증오   hostility, bitterness, extreme dislike; acrimony
antagonism, antipathy와 비슷한 단어로, anti '반대'의 감정을 말한다.
Religious **animosity** (n.)

1043
incompatible ⁵
[|ɪnkəm|pætəbl]

a. 서로 맞지 않는, 양립할 수 없는   unable to exist together in harmony, not compatible; unable to exist together in harmony
두 가지가 incompatible하면 서로 companion '친구'가 되기 힘들다.
The **incompatible** couple worked really hard to save their marriage, but they just couldn't stay together. (adj.)

1044
unrestrained ⁷
[|ʌnrɪ|streɪnd]

a. 억제되지 않은   excessive, uncontrolled
restrain은 restrict와 같이 '제한하다'라는 뜻이다. 따라서 제한되지 않았으므로(un) '억제되지 않은'이라는 뜻이다.
It was an **unrestrained** attack on workers. (adj.)

1045
lavishness ⁶
[|lævɪʃnɪs]

n. 풍부함, 무성함   exuberance
라벤더(lavender → lav) 향이 집안 어디에서나 풍부하게 풍기고 있다고 외우자.
Architects declared that it was as far as modern **lavishness** and extravagance could go. (n.)

1046
antithesis ⁷
[æntíθəsis]

n. 정반대, 대조   contrast; direct opposite of or to
anti(반대) + thesis(='to place') '정반대'란 의미이다.
Good is the **antithesis** of evil. (n.)

1047
predicament [3]

[pridíkəmənt]

n. 곤경, 궁지, 상태　　difficult situation, trouble, an unpleasant situation that is difficult to get out of
[pre(before) + dic < dict(speak) + a + ment : '앞에 말하게 한 것' → 단언, 단정 → 상태, 상황 → 어려운 상황 = 곤경, 궁지
She faced a major **predicament** when she was late for work on her first day. (*n.*)

1048
plausible [10]

[|plɔːzəbl]

a. 타당한 것 같은　　having an appearance of truth or reason; credible
반대 의견이 너무 타당성이 있어서(plausible) 나를 잠깐 멈추게(pause) 만들었다고 외우자.
Her story sounded perfectly **plausible**. (*adj.*)

1049
stiff [6]

[stɪf]

a. 뻣뻣한　　rigid or firm
stiff는 '시체'라는 뜻도 있다. 사람이 죽으면 몸이 stiff(뻣뻣)하게 굳는 것을 생각하자.
When choosing a stick to use as a staff, always pick a **stiff** one so it will not bend or break. (*adj.*)

1050
grim [6]

[grɪm]

a. 암울한, 우울한　　somber, stern
grin(미소)과 연관지어서 grim은 암울하다고 외우자.
We face the **grim** prospect of still higher unemployment. (*adj.*)

1051
wretch [2]

[retʃ]

n. 불쌍하고 가엾은 사람　　a miserable, desolate person
cockroach와 wretch가 끝 발음이 비슷한 것을 생각해 보자. 집에 바퀴벌레가 있는 사람은 정말 불쌍하고 가엾다고(wretch) 외우면 쉽다.
A thief is a **wretch** who steals the property of others. (*n.*)

1052
crass [4]

[kræs]

a. 무신경한, 대충의　　coarse, vulgar
머저리들(ass)이나 그런 무신경한(crass) 질문을 할 거라고 외워보자.
The **crass** questions all disabled people get asked (*adj.*)

1053
grotesque [2]

[groʊ|tesk]

a. 터무니없는, 기괴한　　absurd, bizarre
흉측하고 이상한 물체를 묘사할 때 '그로테스크'하다는 말을 들어봤을 것이다. grotesque는 '기괴하다'라는 의미를 가지고 있다.
A **grotesque** distortion of the truth (*adj.*)

1054
vault [vɔːlt]

v. 뛰어넘다 — to leap or spring, as to or from a position or over something
금고(vault)를 털기 위해 남의 집 담벼락을 뛰어넘었다고(vault) 외우자.
She **vaulted** over the gate and ran up the path. (*v.*)

1055
agilely [|ædʒli]

adv. 재빨리, 민첩하게 — quickly, nimbly
어린 나이(age → ag) 덕분에 민첩하게(agile) 움직일 수 있었다고 외우자.
He is an excellent soccer player that can run **agilely**. (*adv.*)

1056
grasp [græsp]

v. 파악하다 — to understand, comprehend
어떤 개념을 잡았으므로(grab = grasp) 확실히 파악했다고 외우자.
They failed to **grasp** the importance of his words. (*v.*)

1057
immurement [ɪ|mjʊrmənt]

n. 감금, 칩거 — imprisonment
mural은 '벽'을 뜻한다. 따라서 immure는 '벽 안에 가둔다'는 의미다.
He had but one thought, that of saving his daughter from that awful life of **immurement** and entombment. (*n.*)

1058
obnoxious [əbnάkʃəs]

a. 아주 불쾌한, 고약한, 싫은 — disgusting, offensive, detestable
noxious는 '독성의'를 뜻하므로 '불쾌하다'는 의미로 해석할 수 있다.
My little sister can be really **obnoxious** when she's annoyed: once, she threw my birthday cake into the toilet because she was jealous of all the attention I got. (*adj.*)

1059
evocation [ìːvoukéiʃən]

n. (기억 등의) 환기, 유발시킴 — calling to mind, summoning
목소리(voice = voc)를 크게 내서 기억을 되살려내려고(evocation) 했다고 외우자.
A brilliant **evocation** of childhood in the 1940s (*n.*)

1060
resolve [rizάlv]

v. 해결하다 — to come to a definite or earnest decision about, to settle; to solve
solve는 '풀다'는 뜻으로, 해결한다는 의미이다.
Is there any way of **resolving** that problem? (*v.*)

Note :

Episode 63

MATCHING Quiz

1. aberrant	A. unable to exist together in harmony
2. ecosystem	B. difficult situation, trouble
3. topography	C. somber, stern
4. fertile	D. coarse, vulgar
5. tinge	E. imprisonment
6. constitute	F. disgusting, offensive
7. incompatible	G. calling to mind, summoning
8. unrestrained	H. to impart a trace or slight degree of some color
9. lavishness	I. excessive, uncontrolled
10. antithesis	J. opposite, contrast
11. predicament	K. exuberance
12. stiff	L. changes in elevation
13. grim	M. a miserable, desolate person
14. wretch	N. arable, productive
15. crass	O. to come to a definite or earnest decision about
16. grasp	P. to form, create
17. immurement	Q. weird, peculiar
18. obnoxious	R. rigid or firm
19. evocation	S. to understand, comprehend
20. resolve	T. biological community

1-Q, 2-T, 3-L, 4-N, 5-H, 6-P, 7-A, 8-I, 9-K, 10-J, 11-B, 12-R, 13-C, 14-M, 15-D, 16-S, 17-E, 18-F, 19-G, 20-O

더 많은 문제를 풀고자 한다면 www.quizlet.com에서 'paul academy seoul' class를 검색

Episode 64: An Unexpected Friend

1061 putrefaction ²
n. 부패
decay

1062 hurl ²
v. (거칠게) 던지다
to throw with great force

1063 digress ⁵
v. 주제에서 벗어나다
to deviate or wander away from the main topic

1064 conceptual ⁴
a. 개념적인, 관념적인
theoretical, abstract

William's truck appeared to be thirty years old. Rust covered its wheel wells like a ring of sharp red teeth and traced a bit of **putrefaction** all along the bottom of the vehicle. The vehicle's original color was hard to determine between the rust and dirt. Jake feared for his life. William put his hands on his hips and smiled.

"My baby."

To be fair, it was one more truck than Jake owned. He resolved to be less judgmental and just try to enjoy himself.

William **hurled** Jake's suitcase into the back and they climbed in the cab. Inside it was very hot.

"Woof! That's a tropical climate for you. Let me roll down a window and get some air circulating in here. My baby has 4:40 air conditioning, you know," William said, looking expectantly at Jake. Jake rolled his eyes and took the bait.

"Ok, fine, what is 4:40 air conditioning?"

"4 windows rolled down and 40 kilometers an hour."

Jake groaned but smiled despite himself. William smiled, and turned the ignition. The engine sounded to be in surprisingly perfect condition. William shifted into gear and pulled them out of the parking lot onto the road.

The two made some small talk about little things, girls and school and things. It was a longish drive to the farm, and eventually topics **digressed** into more **conceptual** territory. Jake had forgotten how clever William could be when he was passionate about a topic. Eventually, Jake just sat and listened as his cousin talked at length in a stream of consciousness, jumping from one subject to the next. William drove with one hand on the wheel and gestured at nothing in particular with the other as he spoke.

"The way I see it, cousin, is that we have always been disadvantaged, the both of us. It is hard to pinpoint exactly, but I would say, generally, that we both have something that **snags** us in every situation. You have your nearly **deforming** loneliness, and I never know when to take a hint and relax."

Jake nodded in agreement. William was exaggerating, but he was telling the truth. A long stretch of road marked with speed bumps was making them constantly go up and down, up and down. This **undulation** combined with William's **sagacious** psychoanalysis was making him carsick. Jake sighed deeply.

"What are you soughing about?" William asked.

"Nothing, just a bit tired…" Jake stopped himself and gave a smile. "*Soughing* huh? That's an unusual word for a farm boy."

William laughed.

"Yeah, I've been studying up on my vocab, even if I'm not going to go to school. I'd like to go, but my parents have **vetoed** it. I have no **suffrage**. I don't have a vote." He frowned. "I mean, I want to be a farmer, I do. And we can't afford school anyway, it's just…"

"What?"

"I always wanted to study bugs. I always **adored** climbing trees and looking for them, to see where they live, their little antennae waving. I want to go to the African rainforests and study insects in their natural habitat."

Jake was impressed.

"That is an amazingly specific and well-thought-out plan. I don't even know what I want to study yet. You know they have scholarships, right?"

William's grip tightened on the wheel, and he turned toward Jake.

"You think I don't know that? Of course I know about scholarships! Just because our bookcase at home is **replete** with beans, literally

---

1065 snag [2]
v. 걸려들게 하다
to make entangled with some obstacle or hindrance

1066 deforming [7]
a. 치명적인, 타격을 입히는
crippling, disfiguring

1067 undulation [3]
n. 물결
moving up and down

1068 sagacious [3]
a. 현명한
judicious, insightful

1069 veto [2]
v. 거부하다
to vote against

1070 suffrage [13]
n. 투표권
the right to vote, especially in a political election

1071 adore [11]
v. 흠모하다
to regard with the utmost esteem, love

1072 replete [2]
a. 가득 찬
full, filled

1073 endow 5
v. 기부하다, 주다
to give out, donate

1074 jolt 2
v. 갑자기 마구 흔들다
to move along in a jerky or bumpy fashion

1075 murky 2
a. 탁한, 흐린
foggy, cloudy

1076 dabble 4
v. 튀기다
to splatter, splash

1077 utilitarian 5
a. 실용적인, 실리적인
effective, practical

1078 excavate 2
v. 파내다, 발굴하다
to dig out

1079 paraphernalia 2
n. (특정한) 용품
equipment with a purpose

filled with bags of different kinds of beans, doesn't mean I don't know that schools **endow** scholarships!"

"Hey, I didn't mean anything, I just…"

"You think of college as a right, as some sort of right because your parents are rich and they don't need your help to make money to live, so you can go study communications or French poetry or whatever, but it isn't the same at my house. If I go to college, WHO is going to take care of THE BEANS?"

"Hey! That's not fair! I have my own… Look out!"

There was a goat in the road. William slammed on the breaks. The rear tires of the truck lost traction and began to turn quickly. Jake could actually feel the truck lose connection with the ground beneath them as the truck started what seemed to be an endless 180 degree spin off the side of the road and into the hill on the other side. The windshield broke and Jake **jolted** against his seatbelt. The goat ran down the other side of the hill with a scream. There was a moment of silence as the two boys looked at each other, wide-eyed.

"You ok?" They said together, and then burst into laughter.

Other than the windshield, the truck appeared to be in ok shape. The engine started just fine, but the front wheels were stuck deeply in some **murky**, water in the wetland, and only spun with an useless noise, **dabbling** mud everywhere when William stepped on the accelerator. They both got around to the front of the truck, knee-deep in muck to try to push, but in a bit of comic slapstick, they both slipped and fell at the same moment, landing on their butts in with a splash.

"We'll have to think of something more **utilitarian** than this pushing. She's stuck in there pretty tight," Jake said, hands on his hips, covered in mud. "We'll have to dig it out. Is there anything we can use to **excavate** it?"

"We can use these big sticks as prehistoric **paraphernalia** until the rest of the historical expedition shows up with our shovels," William chuckled, and handed Jake a long bent branch. "Remember we share credit for any uncovered objects."

After a half an hour of hacking away amongst the mosquitoes and heat, both of them had had enough of the hole and retreated to other side of the road to take a rest. They might just have to admit that they were **stranded**. Jake had just sat down next to his cousin with a heavy sigh when they became suddenly aware of the low noise of an approaching vehicle. It had the deep sound of a diesel engine.

"Oh thank god," said William. "Sounds like a big truck. Maybe they can tow us out of here."

The humming grew louder, and then louder still. The sound echoed throughout the area. If this was actually a truck, Jake thought, it was going to be one huge monster of one. Five minutes later, the biggest pickup Jake had ever seen turned around the corner, seeming to shake the earth beneath it. It rolled to a stop next to the boys, twice as tall as they were, making noises like an impatient dragon. The driver's side window rolled down, and with a style that could only have been one person, TJ stuck his head outside and looked down at the two mud-splattered cousins. Jake nearly fell in surprise.

"Well!" TJ said with an enormous smile. "Looks like you two unbelievably lucky!"

William looked at Jake for explanation, but Jake could only shake his head in amazement.

1080 strand ²
v. 오도 가도 못하게 하다
to bring into or leave in a helpless position

Vocabulary

1061
putrefaction [2]
[|pjuːtrɪ|fækʃn]

n. 부패 decay
putrid는 썩었다는 뜻이다. 썩어서 쓰레기통에 넣어서(put) 버린다고(rid) 외워보자. 따라서 putrefaction은 '부패'를 의미한다.
Yeast speeds up the **putrefaction** process. (n.)

1062
hurl [2]
[hɜːrl]

v. (거칠게) 던지다 to throw with great force
공을 너무 세게 던져서(hurl) 유리창이 깨지자 서둘러(hurry) 자리를 벗어났다고 외우자.
He **hurled** a brick through the window. (v.)

1063
digress [5]
[daɪ|gres]

v. 주제에서 벗어나다 to deviate or wander away from the main topic
digress는 di < dis(away) + gress(go) 로 '벗어나 가다'란 뜻으로 '(딴 데로) 빗나가다, 탈선하다'를 뜻한다.
I do not wish to **digress** too far. (v.)

1064
conceptual [4]
[kənséptʃuəl]

a. 개념적인, 관념적인 theoretical, abstract
concept '개념'의 변형.
The book was about the **conceptual** art of future buildings. (adj.)

1065
snag [2]
[snæg]

v. 걸려들게 하다; 예상 밖의 문제 to make entangled with some obstacle or hindrance; a small problem or disadvantage
숫사슴이(stag) 숨겨진 덫에 걸렸다고(snag) 외우자.
We've hit a **snag** with the building project. (n.)

1066
deforming [7]
[dɪˈfɔːmɪŋ]

a. 치명적인, 타격을 입히는 crippling, disfiguring
원래 형태가(form) 아니게(de) 만들 정도로 치명적이라고 외워보자.
The disease had **deformed** his spine. (v.)

1067
undulation [3]

[|ʌndʒə|leɪʃn]

n. 물결   moving up and down
인어공주에 나오는 under('undul') the sea 노래를 떠올려보자.
인어공주는 물결을(undulation) 타고 우아하게 수영을 한다.
The road followed the **undulations** of the landscape. (*n.*)

1068
sagacious [3]

[səgéiʃəs]

a. 현명한, 영리한   judicious, insightful, able to discern with wise perception
어원인 sage는 wise person을 지칭한다.
Sagacious advice (*adj.*)

1069
veto [2]

[|vi:toʊ]

v. 거부하다   to vote against
vote, 즉 투표의 스펠링의 순서를 바꿨으므로 반대투표를 던진다고 외워보자.
I wanted to go camping but the others quickly **vetoed** that idea. (*v.*)

1070
suffrage [13]

[sʌ́frɪdʒ]

n. 투표(권), 선거권   the right to vote, especially in a political election
역사적으로 사람들은 고통(suffer) 끝에 투표권을 얻었다.
To be a true citizen, you should exercise your **suffrage** and go vote. (n)

1071
adore [11]

[ə|dɔː(r)]

v. 흠모하다   to regard with the utmost esteem, love
인형(doll → dore)을 다루듯 애정을 쏟는다고(adore) 외워보자.
It's obvious that she **adores** him. (*v.*)

1072
replete [2]

[rɪ|pliːt]

a. 가득 찬   full, filled
complete는 완성하다라는 의미이다. 다시(re) 완성해서 이제 정말 가득 찼다고(replete) 외우자.
This car has an engine **replete** with the latest technology. (*adj.*)

1073
endow [5]

[ɪn|daʊ]

v. 기부하다, 주다   to give out, donate
사냥꾼 아버지가 아들에게 활(bow)을 주었다고(endow) 외우자.
I hope that the fund will also **endow** a system of bursaries. (*v.*)

1074
jolt ²
[dʒoʊlt]

v. 갑자기 마구 흔든다   to move along in a jerky or bumpy fashion
벼락이(lightning bolt → olt) 떨어져서 깜짝 놀라서 옆에 자던 친구를 마구 흔들어서(jolt) 깨웠다고 외우자.
The truck **jolted** and rattled over the rough ground. *(v.)*

1075
murky ²
[mə́ːrki]

a. 탁한, 흐린   foggy, cloudy, dark and gloomy; thick with fog; vague
dark와 연관지어서 외우자.
The **murky** night *(adj.)*

1076
dabble ⁴
[|dæbl]

v. 튀다   to splatter, splash
비눗방울을(bubble → bble) 터뜨리면 비누거품이 여기저기 튄다고 (dabble) 외워보자.
She **dabbled** her toes in the stream. *(v.)*

1077
utilitarian ⁵
[|juːtɪlɪ|terɪən]

a. 실용적인, 실리적인   effective, practical
utility는 실용성이라는 의미이다. 실용성을 추구하는 사람은 실리적일 수 밖에.
The house is built by **utilitarian** materials. *(adj.)*

1078
excavate ²
[|ekskəveɪt]

v. 파내다, 발굴하다   to dig out, to scoop out
동굴(cave)에서 유물을 발굴한다고 생각하자.
The archaeologist **excavated** an ancient Egyptian tomb from beneath the sand. *(v.)*

1079
paraphernalia ²
[|pærəfə|neɪliə]

n. (특정한) 용품   equipment with a purpose
para(='beside') + pherne(='dowry') 지참금을 항상 옆에 놔두고 있는 것은 특정한 용도에 쓰려고 갖춰놓는 법이다. 그래서 paraphernalia는 (특정)용품 이라는 뜻이다.
A large courtyard full of builders' **paraphernalia** *(n.)*

1080
strand ²
[strænd]

v. 오도 가도 못하게 하다   to bring into or leave in a helpless position
이상한 곳(strange → stran)에 갇혀서 오도 가도 못하게 됐다고(strand) 외워보자.
The strike left hundreds of tourists **stranded** at the airport. *(v.)*

Note :

Episode 64

MATCHING Quiz

1.	putrefaction	●	●	A. to make entangled with some obstacle or hindrance
2.	hurl	●	●	B. to regard with the utmost esteem, love
3.	digress	●	●	C. foggy, cloudy
4.	conceptual	●	●	D. to give out, donate
5.	snag	●	●	E. to splatter, splash
6.	deforming	●	●	F. to deviate or wander away from the main topic
7.	undulation	●	●	G. theoretical, abstract
8.	sagacious	●	●	H. moving up and down
9.	veto	●	●	I. judicious, insightful
10.	suffrage	●	●	J. the right to vote, especially in a political election
11.	adore	●	●	K. effective, practical
12.	replete	●	●	L. to dig out
13.	endow	●	●	M. to bring into or leave in a helpless position
14.	jolt	●	●	N. to throw with great force
15.	murky	●	●	O. crippling, disfiguring
16.	dabble	●	●	P. full, filled
17.	utilitarian	●	●	Q. to move along in a jerky or bumpy fashion
18.	excavate	●	●	R. equipment with a purpose
19.	paraphernalia	●	●	S. to vote against
20.	strand	●	●	T. decay

1-T, 2-N, 3-F, 4-G, 5-A, 6-O, 7-H, 8-I, 9-S, 10-J, 11-B, 12-P, 13-D, 14-Q, 15-C, 16-E, 17-K, 18-L, 19-R, 20-M

더 많은 문제를 풀고자 한다면 www.quizlet.com에서 'paul academy seoul' class를 검색

Episode 65

A Dream of Mimes

1081 delicate [16]
a. 연약한
fine in texture, quality, construction

1082 vanishingly [7]
adv. 사라지게
disappeared from sight without a trace

1083 pseudonym [3]
n. 가명
false name

Still unable to believe the turn of events, Jake climbed up into the cab of the pickup, and, after a brief moment of explanation, William followed close behind. Sure enough, there was TJ, behind the steering wheel, his **delicate** frame contrasting comically with the massive size of the pickup truck.

"Jake! I can't believe it! What are you doing here?"

"I'm taking a vacation that my mother forced on me, but then I could ask you the same thing! What are the odds that you would be driving by in a giant truck at the exact same time that my cousin and I needed one?"

"**Vanishingly** small, my old SAT study buddy, vanishingly small." They both regarded each other with disbelieving smiles. "Oh well!" said TJ after a moment. "No one said that life has to make sense! I will tell you why I am here, but you have to promise to keep it a secret. I'm travelling under a **pseudonym**. In public you have to call me EJ." William raised an eyebrow at this.

"Why on Earth would a high school student need to travel under a false name?"

TJ leaned in and whispered.

"I am studying mime. You can understand my need for absolute silence on this matter."

William and Jake burst into laughter.

"Mime!?" Jake cried. "How would they get you to shut up?"

William shouted with laughter at this. TJ frowned.

"Yes, well, that is very clever but if anyone amongst my parents' circle of friends found out, they would kick my mom and dad out of the country club. Their social group is highly judgmental. My parents have been trying to move up a level in the club **hierarchy**, but to have a son who practices the silent arts would be a great embarrassment and decrease their standing in the eyes of their peers. Nevertheless, they respect my wishes and are giving me one chance to **debunk** their fears about my abilities."

"OK, fair enough," said William, wiping a tear of laughter from his eye. "How are you going to be able to prove them?"

"My aunt is a famous mime critic. If I can prove my talent to her, then my parents will allow me to study at The Grand Mime Conservatory in Paris." His jaw set tightly at this. Jake was impressed.

"She always wanted to be a mime herself but didn't have the talent and became a scientist instead. Mime has always been just a hobby for her." TJ continued. "Now, she lives her dreams through me, but refuses to use her **leverage** to get me a position. I'll tell you, it is a lot of pressure. Especially considering that I only have two moves in my **repertoire**. I have to add to my **trove** of mime moves, and she is teaching me from this book right here."

TJ pulled a massive book from beneath the front seat and set it in front of them. It was bound in rich brown leather and **ornate** all over with beautiful gold images of men dressed like clowns. Stamped on the front in gold was one word: MIME.

TJ's eyes shone with wonder, his voice was hushed. "I really shouldn't be showing this to you guys."

"No kidding," said Jake, but his eyes didn't leave the book.

Inside was a series of images **denoting** the way to do every move within the art of silent expression. A full history of the **medium** of mime, laid out in **painstaking** detail for **posterity**.

Jake looked up, put a hand on TJ's shoulder and smiled.

"This is the stupidest thing I have ever seen."

TJ gasped as if he had been punched and slammed the book shut. He held it tightly to his chest as though it could protect him from

---

1084 hierarchy [5]
n. 계급, 계층
ranking, order

1085 debunk [7]
v. 틀렸음을 드러내다
to expose or excoriate as being false or pretentious

1086 leverage [2]
n. 영향력
influence

1087 repertoire [4]
n. 레퍼토리
collection of skills

1088 trove [2]
n. 수집물
collection

1089 ornate [5]
a. 화려하게 장식된
fancily decorated, elegant, glamorous

1090 denote [3]
v. 나타내다, 의미하다
to represent

1091 medium [18]
n. 매체
an intervening substance

1092 painstaking [8]
a. 공들인
thorough, meticulous

1093 posterity [9]
n. 후세, 후대
succeeding or future generation collectively

1094 malevolent ²
a. 악의적인
hateful, malicious

1095 grandiose ⁴
a. 거창한, 장대한
affectedly impressive, grand

1096 magnitude ⁵
n. 중요함, 장엄함
grandeur, importance

1097 inexplicable ⁶
a. 설명할 수 없는, 불가해한
mysterious, hard to explain

1098 brandish ²
v. 휘두르다
to swing around

1099 preposterous ⁵
a. 말도 안 되는, 터무니없는
ridiculous, absurd

Jake's **malevolent** words. He began to speak, slowly and carefully, peering out from behind the massive book like a child hiding beneath his covers.

"Philistines! You laugh now, but when I enter as a competitor in the Great Mime Showdown and crowned king mime, and listed amongst the **grandiose** roll call of all the legendary mimes, my name full of **magnitude** I can tell you this: you will no longer be laughing." Once he had finished, his chin was a bit higher and his back a bit straighter.

William nodded solemnly.

"Wouldn't that make you a pretty terrible mime, though?"

All three of the boys laughed at this, and TJ slipped the book back under the seat.

"Alright, enough of these brotherly getting-to-know-yous," he said. "Let's get your truck out of the hole, shall we?"

"Do you have some rope, or a chain or something?" William asked.

"My new friend, I am a mime, and thus prepared for such a problem." TJ said with an **inexplicable** smile. "I always have rope." Jake and William exchanged a look of confusion, but stepped out of the vehicle.

TJ climbed down from his side and walked around to the back of the nonmoving truck and turned to the side. He planted his feet firmly, and began to **brandish** his arm around in the air, just as though he was swinging a rope. He let the invisible rope fly and pulled it tight, seemingly satisfied with its security. He walked over to the back of his giant truck and chained the other invisible end around the truck.

"This is **preposterous**." said Jake.

"Yeah, but you saw the book. What if there is something to this mime stuff?" said William.

TJ climbed into the cab of his pickup and started the engine, then drove forward slowly. Jake and William held their breath as the bigger vehicle inched forward, and they watched closely for any sign of movement from the smaller. TJ had driven about a hundred meters down the road before they realized that they had been **hoaxed**. TJ opened the door and climbed out the cab, barely able to stand for his laughing so hard. Jake and William yelled and laughed and ran after him.

"I don't have a rope, guys, sorry," said TJ amidst his laughter. "We'll have to come back later. You guys hungry? I know a great place near my aunt's house. We can get a rope from her."

The cousins nodded their agreement, and they climbed into truck. Together, the young men set off down the road, seeking **nourishment** and a rope.

1100 **hoax** ³
v. 속이다
to deceive, trick

1101 **nourishment** ³
n. 음식물, 영양분
food, nutrition, sustenance

Vocabulary

1081
delicate [16]
[|delɪkət]

a. 연약한   fine in texture, quality, construction
골목길에(alley → eli) 사는 고양이는(cat) 연약하다고(delicate) 외우자.
The eye is one of the most **delicate** organs of the body. (*adj.*)

1082
vanishingly [7]
[ˈvænɪʃɪŋli]

adv. 사라지게   disappeared from sight without a trace
vanish가 사라진다는 뜻이므로 vanishingly는 '사라지는 것처럼'이라는 의미다.
The magician **vanished** in a puff of smoke. (*v.*)

1083
pseudonym [3]
[|suːdənɪm]

n. 가명, 필명   false name
pseudo는 가짜라는 뜻이다. 즉 가짜 이름(name → nym)이라는 의미다.
She writes under a **pseudonym**. (*n.*)

1084
hierarchy [5]
[|haɪərɑːrki]

n. 계급, 계층   ranking, order, any system of persons or things ranked one above another
hierarchy에서는 더 높은(higher) 급에 있을수록 이득이 많다.
There was a clear **hierarchy** in the family: Grandmother was first, Mother second, my dog third, and then me last. (*n.*)

1085
debunk [7]
[diːbʌ́ŋk]

v. 틀렸음을 드러내다, 정체를 폭로하다   to expose or excoriate as being false or pretentious, to expose as false, exaggerated, etc.; ridicule
kick out of bed(bunk) 침대에서 나와 정체를 폭로하다.
The scientist **debunked** the myth about the Loch Ness monster by proving that the pictures were all fake. (*v.*)

1086
leverage [2]
[|levərɪdʒ]

n. 영향력   influence
lever는 지렛대라는 의미다. 지렛대는 적은 힘으로 큰 영향을 줄 수 있게 하므로 leverage는 '영향력'이라는 뜻이다.
They do not have political **leverage**. (*n.*)

1087
repertoire [4]

[|repərtwɑː(r)]

n. 레퍼토리   collection of skills
한 사람이 준비해 둔 여러 가지 기술을 뜻한다.
A pianist with a wide **repertoire** (*n.*)

1088
trove [2]

[tróuv]

n. 수집물   collection of objects
보물(treasure)과 연관되어 있으므로 '발견된 것'이라는 의미이다.
The little mermaid thought her collection of human objects was a treasure **trove**, but the other fish just thought it was a junkyard. (*n.*)

1089
ornate [5]

[ɔːrnéit]

a. 화려하게 장식된, 공들여 꾸민, (문체 등이) 화려한   fancily decorated, elegant, glamorous
ornare는 'prepare, furnish'의 뜻을 갖고 있다.
The fancy palace was famous for its **ornate** designs. (*adj.*)

1090
denote [3]

[dɪ|noʊt]

v. 나타내다, 의미하다   to represent
노트(note)에 확실히 써서 나타낸다고(denote) 외워보자.
In this example 'X' **denotes** the time taken and 'Y' denotes the distance covered. (*v.*)

1091
medium [18]

[|miːdiəm]

n. 매체   an intervening substance
두 물체의 중간(medium)을 이어주는 것이 매체(medium)라고 외워보자.
Television is the **modern** medium of communication. (*n.*)

1092
painstaking [8]

[péinztèikiŋ]

a. 공들인   thorough, meticulous, showing hard work
고통(pain)을 모두 감수하며(take) 공들인다는 의미이다.
Although the work is actually **painstaking**, many people think that it is easy and can be finished quickly. (*adj.*)

1093
posterity [9]

[pɑː|steráti]

n. 후세, 후대   succeeding or future generation collectively
post는 뒤를 뜻하므로 뒤에 올 세대들을 뜻한다.
Their music has been preserved for **posterity**. (*n.*)

1094
malevolent [məlévələnt]

a. 악의적인   hateful, malicious, evil; harmful
mal(bad) + evil 처럼 들린다. 즉 '나쁜, 악의있는'의 의미이다.
Malevolent dictator (*adj.*)

1095
grandiose [|ɡrændioʊs]

a. 거창한, 장대한   affectedly impressive, grand
grand는 웅장하다는 의미이므로 거의 똑같은 뜻이다.
He had the **grandiose** goal of being the first man to travel at a faster speed than light. (*adj.*)

1096
magnitude [|mæɡnɪtuːd]

n. 중요함, 장엄함, 규모   grandeur, importance, size; extent
라틴어 magnitudo '크기'에서 왔다.
The **magnitude** of the earthquake was so great that it destroyed one entire city.(*n.*)

1097
inexplicable [|ɪnɪk|splɪkəbl]

a. 설명할 수 없는, 불가해한   mysterious, hard to explain
설명(explain → expli)할 수 없다는(in...able) 의미이다.
For some **inexplicable** reason he gave up a fantastic job. (*adj.*)

1098
brandish [|brændɪʃ]

v. 휘두르다   to swing around
부엌에서 함부로 물건을 휘두르다가(brandish) 접시를(dish) 깨뜨렸다고 외우자.
I raised my stick and **brandished** it at them. (*v.*)

1099
preposterous [prɪ|pɑːstərəs]

a. 말도 안 되는, 터무니없는   ridiculous, absurd
앞(pre)과 뒤(post)가 구별이 안 될 정도로 '터무니 없다'고 외우자.
These claims are absolutely **preposterous**! (*adj.*)

1100
hoax [hoʊks]

v. 속이다 ; 거짓말[장난질]   to deceive, trick
여우(fox)는 거짓말(hoax)을 잘 하는 동물로 자주 등장한다.
Stop playing a **hoax** on your brother. (*n.*)

1101
nourishment [|nɜːrɪʃmənt]

n. 음식물, 영양분   food, nutrition, sustenance
nutrient(영양분)과 연결해서 외워보자.
Can plants obtain adequate **nourishment** from such poor soil? (*n.*)

Note :

Voca Hamburger
Episode 65
MATCHING Quiz

1. delicate — A. to represent
2. vanishingly — B. succeeding or future generation collectively
3. hierarchy — C. an intervening substance
4. debunk — D. to expose or excoriate as being false or pretentious
5. leverage — E. influence
6. repertoire — F. mysterious, hard to explain
7. trove — G. affectedly impressive, grand
8. ornate — H. to deceive, trick
9. denote — I. fancily decorated, elegant, glamorous
10. medium — J. to swing around
11. painstaking — K. thorough, meticulous
12. posterity — L. food, nutrition, sustenance
13. malevolent — M. hateful, malicious
14. grandiose — N. ranking, order
15. magnitude — O. grandeur, importance
16. inexplicable — P. disappeared from sight without a trace
17. brandish — Q. collection of skills
18. preposterous — R. fine in texture, quality, construction
19. hoax — S. ridiculous, absurd
20. nourishment — T. collection

1-R, 2-P, 3-N, 4-O, 5-M, 6-Q, 7-T, 8-I, 9-A, 10-C, 11-E, 12-B, 13-L, 14-G, 15-D, 16-F, 17-J, 18-S, 19-H, 20-L.

더 많은 문제를 풀고자 한다면 www.quizlet.com에서 'paul academy seoul' class를 검색

Episode 66 — Curry Disease

1102 clan ²
n. 무리, 집단
a group of people, clique

1103 growl ²
v. 으르렁 거리다
to make a low guttural sound

1104 ill-tempered ²
a. 짜증을 (잘) 내는, 화가 난
irritable, grumpy

1105 audacious ⁵
a. 대담한, 무모한
reckless, bold

1106 indignant ⁹
a. 분개한
expressing strong displeasure at

1107 deliberate ²⁰
a. 신중한, 찬찬한
cautious; careful or slow in deciding

Further down the road, having spent some time in loud conversation, the **clan** of boys approached a boring but inoffensive looking little restaurant off to the side of the road. The location's humble situation, and its sign's plain, hand-lettered printing indicated either the best or the worst food they had ever eaten.

"Are you stomachs **growling**? Are you feeling slightly **ill-tempered** and light-headed? These are symptoms of hunger my dear friends!" said TJ. "Soon, they will be cured."

Inside, they greeted a friendly-looking woman, ordered a round of fried pork cutlets and curry, and took a seat.

"So! Jake! What are your plans now that all your tests are finished? Or, as I suspect, are you just drifting along until something pushes you in one direction or another?"

Jake smiled at his friend's directness, but William was taken aback. He let forth with a stream of anger, cursing with **audacious** abandon. After a moment of appreciating this impressive display, Jake put a hand on his shoulder.

"It's just TJ's style, William," he said. "He doesn't mean offense, and I don't get **indignant** about it. And he's right. I need to be more **deliberate** in my choices, making decisions rather than just letting things happen to me."

"Ok, fine, if it doesn't bother you, but that wasn't how we were raised in my house," William frowned. "Where is our food? It is taking forever."

TJ shifted in his seat a little bit and began to get everyone's silverware together from the wooden box and lay it out on napkins. Jake had never seen him so ashamed.

"I'm sorry, William. You too, Jake. I am just not very good with **nuance** or delicacy, and I make up for my nervousness with **bluntness**." He set a small metal glass in front of each of them and poured water into them. "I really want to know, Jake. What is coming up for you? I remember during the story at the academy, there was some **subplot** about how you wanted to be a writer. Are you still interested in that?"

Jake smiled.

"Yeah, I am. But my uncle was always the guy who encouraged me the most in those things, and since he's gone, I don't know, I guess I just haven't felt as strongly about it. I've stayed in my room mostly since graduation. If I were religious, I'd say I became a monk, but since all I've been doing is playing video games and listening to music, I would say I'm more of a worldly **hermit** than a monk."

TJ and William both laughed.

At that moment, the lady came and set three steaming plates of curry and pork in front of them.

"Maybe when I leave home and go to university, I'll feel better. You know, become **displaced**, feel the inspiration from a new location?" said TJ.

Like true pigs, the three boys stuffed themselves on plates of fried pork, rice and thick golden curry until they were satisfied.

Afterward, their bodies shut down. Movement and thought were **inconceivable** due to an overload of **saturated** fat and nutrients. Their conversation became detached and half-hearted.

"What..." William began. His head **drooped**, his chin resting on his neck.

A fly buzzed uselessly against the window pane. Some dishes made noise in the kitchen. A dog barked somewhere far away. Jake rolled his head slowly to the left in order to look at his cousin. William's head rose slightly, but his eyes remained shut.

"...time is it?" William finished. The fly stopped buzzing.

1108 nuance 4
n. 미묘한 차이, 음영
subtlety

1109 bluntness 3
n. 무딤
dullness

1110 subplot 2
n. 부차적 줄거리
a subordinate plot in a novel, play, film, etc.

1111 hermit 2
n. 은둔자
a person who lives alone often far from a community

1112 displaced 2
a. 추방된
removed from the normal location

1113 inconceivable 2
a. 상상도 할 수 없는
unimaginable, unthinkable

1114 saturated 2
a. 흠뻑 젖은; 포화된
soaked, impregnated; containing the maximum amount of solute

1115 droop 2
v. 축 처지다
to hung down, lost strength

1116 smudge ²
n. (더러운) 자국, 얼룩
a dirty mark or smear

1117 compulsory ⁵
a. 의무적인
required, mandatory, obligatory

1118 jaunt ²
n. 짧은 여행
a short journey

"I think it's time to go guys, but…" Jake said. His eyes failed to maintain their connection with those of his cousin and slid their focus instead to a **smudge** of oil on the floor. "…we may need to rest for a while here and regain our strength."

TJ responded with a noise that called to mind a chainsaw left to run unsupervised in an empty steel garbage container until it cuts its own power cord.

After 45 minutes and one cup of **compulsory** coffee forced upon them by an irritated restaurant lady, they climbed back into the truck and continued their **jaunt** into the wilds of the island.

Vocabulary

1102
clan [2]
[klæn]

n. 무리, 집단   a group of people, clique
클래시 오브 클랜스 (Clash of Clans)라는 유명한 모바일 게임이 있는데, 부족 무리끼리 싸우는 게임으로 clan은 '무리'를 뜻한다.
One of a growing **clan** of stars who have left Hollywood (*n.*)

1103
growl [2]
[graʊl]

v. 으르렁거리다   to make a low guttural sound
개가 으르렁거리는 소리를 떠올려보자.
I hope she didn't **growl** at you. (*v.*)

1104
ill-tempered [2]
[ɪl-ˈtempərd]

a. 짜증을 (잘) 내는, 화가 난   irritable, grumpy
성질(temper)이 마치 병(ill)에 든 것처럼 짜증을 낸다는 의미이다.
He has an **ill-tempered** dog that barks at strangers. (*adj.*)

1105
audacious [5]
[ɔːˈdeɪʃəs]

a. 대담한, 무모한   reckless, bold, recklessly brave
auda(AUDIBLE), 즉 사람들이 듣게 만들려면 대담해야 한다.
The **audacious** girl wasn't afraid of lions and even tried to hit them on the head. (*adj.*)

1106
indignant [9]
[ɪnˈdɪɡnənt]

a. 분개한, 성난   expressing strong displeasure at something considered unjust or offensive
라틴어 indignantem은 '참을성이 없는, 내키지 않은'이란 의미가 있다. 따라서, 어떤 것을 잘 참지 못하면 쉽게 화가 나겠지?
He was **indignant** that his rival was offered the job. (*adj.*)

1107
deliberate [20]
[dɪˈlɪbərət]

a. 신중한, 찬찬한   cautious; careful or slow in deciding
델리버거 (deli ber)를 이미 하나 먹었는데(ate) 또 먹을지 말지 신중하게 (deliberate) 결정한다고 외워보자.
She spoke in a slow and **deliberate** way. (*adj.*)

1108
nuance [4]
[nuˈɑːns]

n. **미묘한 차이, 음영**   subtlety, a subtle difference
뉘앙스라고 많이 불리운다.
I had to watch the professor's face very carefully to discern every **nuance** of expression and to see whether he liked my presentation. (*n.*)

1109
bluntness [3]
[ˈblʌntnəs]

n. **무딤**   dullness
몸이 파래질(blue → blue) 정도로 얼어서 감각이 무뎌졌다고(blunt) 외우자.
His **bluntness** got him into trouble. (*n.*)

1110
subplot [2]
[ˈsʌblɑːt]

n. **부차적 줄거리**   a subordinate plot in a novel, play, film, etc.
본 줄거리(plot) 아래에(sub) 깔려있는 부차적 줄거리라는 의미다.
Unfortunately, he passed away before he could complete the script, but not before he chose to add a completely new **subplot** to the film. (*n.*)

1111
hermit [2]
[ˈhəːrmit]

n. **은둔자**   a person who lives alone often far from a community, recluse
I met her. 그녀를 만난 후, 나는 혼자가 되었다. 이렇게 생각하면 외우기 쉽다.
The **hermit** lived in a desert cave to avoid contact with other people. (*n.*)

1112
displaced [2]
[displéist]

a. **추방된**   removed from the normal location
원래 위치가(place) 아닌(dis) 곳으로 추방됐다는(displace) 의미이다.
Gradually factory workers have been **displaced** by machines. (*adj.*)

1113
inconceivable [2]
[ˌɪnkənˈsiːvəbl]

a. **상상[생각]도 할 수 없는**   unimaginable, unthinkable
conceive는 '마음으로 품다'라는 뜻인데 in이 붙으니까 마음으로 품을 수 없는, 즉 '상상도 할 수 없는'이라는 뜻이다.
The accident was so **inconceivable** that no one even though of preparing for it. (*adj.*)

1114
saturated ²

[|sætʃəreɪtɪd]

a. 흠뻑 젖은; 포화된   soaked, impregnated; containing the maximum amount of solute
토요일은(Saturday → satur) 약속으로 가득 포화된(saturate) 상태라고 외우자.
I forgot to bring my umbrella and thus was **saturated** by the pouring rain. (*v.*)

1115
droop ²

[dru:p]

v. 축 처지다   to hang down, lost strength
drop이 떨어지다는 뜻인데 o가 하나 더 붙어서 더 떨어져서 축 처졌다고 (droop) 외우자.
She was so tired, her eyelids were beginning to **droop**. (*v.*)

1116
smudge ²

[smʌdʒ]

n. (더러운) 자국, 얼룩   a dirty mark or smear
진흙이(mud) 묻어서 얼룩을(smudge) 남겼다고 외워보자.
A **smudge** of lipstick on a cup (*n.*)

1117
compulsory ⁵

[kəmpʌlsəri]

a. 의무적인, 강제적인   required, mandatory, obligatory, forced
compel과 연관지어서 외우자.
Compulsory public schooling (*adj.*)

1118
jaunt ²

[dʒɔ:nt]

n. 짧은 여행   a short journey
즐겁고(joy → ju) 재밌는(fun → un) 짧은 여행(jaunt)이라고 외워보자.
Our **jaunt** to Philippines was so exciting, that I went on a longer trip the month after. (*n.*)

Note :

Voca Hamburger — Episode 66
MATCHING Quiz

1. clan
2. growl
3. ill-tempered
4. audacious
5. indignant
6. deliberate
7. nuance
8. bluntness
9. subplot
10. hermit
11. displaced
12. inconceivable
13. saturated
14. droop
15. smudge
16. compulsory
17. jaunt

A. irritable, grumpy
B. to make a low guttural sound
C. a short journey
D. a group of people, clique
E. a dirty mark or smear
F. cautious; careful or slow in deciding
G. reckless, bold
H. expressing strong displeasure at
I. dullness
J. subtlety
K. a subordinate plot in a novel, play, film, etc.
L. a person who lives alone often far from a community
M. removed from the normal location
N. unimaginable, unthinkable
O. soaked, impregnated; containing the maximum amount of solute
P. required, mandatory, obligatory
Q. to hang down, lost strength

1-D, 2-B, 3-A, 4-G, 5-H, 6-F, 7-J, 8-I, 9-K, 10-L, 11-M, 12-N, 13-O, 14-Q, 15-E, 16-P, 17-C

더 많은 문제를 풀고자 한다면 www.quizlet.com에서 'paul academy seoul' class를 검색

Episode 67: Crimes and Sin

The boys stopped at a rest area to stretch their legs.

"In retrospect, it may have been a bad idea to fill up so much at lunch. Why is the most delicious food always so regrettable?" William asked with disappointment. He held his hat belly at either side and walked with a duckish **waddle**. "The human **anatomy** can't take this kind of punishment. My innards are going to **retaliate** for sure."

Jake **grimaced** at the thought.

"Please don't be **vulgar**, William. I don't want to imagine your stomach. And Jake, please do not add any of your usual **obligatory** nonsense to this situation. My stomach is not in the mood for any toilet jokes."

TJ laughed out loud.

"Jake my good man! I'm sure you can **absolve** me for a little toilet humor. Even Chaucer and Shakespeare were fond of them. Can't I make just one? I have a huge storage of barely **obscene** bathroom references. I'll keep it nice, I promise. You will barely even know what I'm talking about."

William and Jake looked at him with a distinct lack of patience.

Daunted, TJ threw up his hands.

"Fine! What if I just—"

Jake cut him off with a wave of his hand.

"No. No looking for escapes. You can't find a way around it. We just aren't in the mood for toilet jokes."

1119 waddle [4]
n. 뒤뚱뒤뚱 걸음
walking with short steps, rocking from side to side, as a duck

1120 anatomy [3]
n. 해부학
the science dealing with the structure of animals or plants

1121 retaliate [3]
v. 보복하다
revenge

1122 grimace [2]
v. 얼굴을 찡그리다
to make an ugly or contorted facial expression

1123 vulgar [10]
a. 저속한, 천박한
lack of good breeding; indecent; obscene

1124 obligatory [14]
a. 의무적인
required as a matter of obligation

1125 absolve [2]
v. 무죄임을 선언하다
to forgive; to free from guilt or blame

1126 obscene [2]
v. 음란한, 외설적인
indecent; vulgar

1127 rambling ²
a. 이리저리 막 다니는
aimlessly wandering

1128 disparity ⁷
n. 차이, 격차
lack of similarity, equality

1129 gaudily ²
adv. 야하게, 화려하게
brilliantly or excessively showy; garish

1130 homogenous ⁷
a. 동질의
akin, alike

1131 shun ⁵
v. 피하다
to avoid, keep away from

1132 compress ⁶
v. 꾹 누르다, 밀어 넣다
to cram, press together

1133 nomadic ²
a. 유목의, 떠도는
traveling from place to place; itinerant

1134 fauna ³
n. (어떤 지역의) 동물들
the animals of a given region

1135 parched ³
a. 바싹 마른
arid, scorched

1136 redress ²
n. 변상, 보상
compensation

1137 recoup ²
v. 되찾다, 만회하다
to get back the equivalent of; regain

1138 defacement ⁵
n. 훼손된 외관, 표면
damaged surface or appearance

TJ hung his head. Though his yearning for inappropriate humor had not been fulfilled, he would find a way to deal with it.

They left the rest area and headed back out on the road for more **rambling** exploration. William expertly guided TJ's massive truck along the curving roads. As evening fell, a sudden **disparity** in color was noticeable as all around them the trees and plants of the island began to lose their **gaudily** green color and turn a boring grey, a **homogenous** mass of sameness in the half-light of dusk.

Jake sat in the small passenger area in the back of the truck cab in order to **shun** the uncomfortable level of closeness caused by having three young men **compressed** into the front seat. He yawned and stretched his arms wide and rolled his neck in a circle to loosen it.

"So, what's the plan, cousin? We've been driving for over an hour now. Where are we headed? These wanderings can't continue forever."

"Certainly not! Our **nomadic** travel will soon be at an end. As you know, I am a bit of a nature fan, and I thought we would enjoy the beautiful plants together for a while."

TJ leaned his head against the passenger side window and glanced out at the darkening trees.

"It has been quite lovely," he said. Jake nodded his agreement.

"Well," William continued, "now that night has fallen, I'd thought we'd check out some **fauna**. We're heading for the zoo."

They drove on for a little while, and being **parched**, Jake grabbed a bottle of water. He twisted the cap and took a deep drink, the cool liquid soothing his dry throat.

"It is getting pretty late, won't the zoo be closed when we get there?" he asked, taking another drink.

"Oh, definitely." William said, eyes still fixed on the road. "In fact, I'm counting on it. We're going to break in."

TJ later demanded **redress** from Jake to **recoup** the cost of the **defacement** to his very un-waterproof leather caused by Jake's reaction.

Vocabulary

1119
waddle 4
[|wɑːdl]

n. 뒤뚱뒤뚱 걸음   walking with short steps, rocking from side to side, as a duck
'와와'(wa)하고 우는 아기가 뒤뚱뒤뚱 걷는 (waddle) 모습을 떠올려보자.
The fat person walked with a **waddle**. (*n.*)

1120
anatomy 3
[ə|nætəmi]

n. 해부학   the science dealing with the structure of animals or plants
그레이 아나토미 (Grey's Anatomy)라는 미국 의학 드라마를 들어봤을 것이다. 의학과 관련해서 anatomy는 해부학을 뜻한다.
The professor's lecture on the **anatomy** was great. (*n.*)

1121
retaliate 3
[rɪ|tælieɪt]

v. 보복하다   revenge
탈리반(Taliban → tali)이 보복성(retaliate) 테러를 강행했다고 외워보자.
We tried to locate them and **retaliate**. (*v.*)

1122
grimace 2
[grɪ|meɪs]

v. 얼굴을 찡그리다   to make an ugly or contorted facial expression
grim은 암울함이다. 암울하니까 얼굴을 찡그렸다고(grimace) 외워보자.
He **grimaced** at the bitter taste. (*v.*)

1123
vulgar 10
[vʌ́lgər]

a. 저속한, 천박한, 상스러운   lack of good breeding; indecent; obscene, indecent; lewd
vulgus-(common people, 보통 사람)을 어원으로 갖는다.
The **vulgar** man ran in the streets naked while shouting swear words. (*adj.*)

1124
obligatory 14
[ə|blɪgətɔːri]

a. 의무적인   required as a matter of obligation
노블레스 오블리제라는 말을 들어보았을 것이다. 부유한 사람들이 그렇지 못한 사람들을 돌봐야 하는 의무를 뜻하는 말로 obligatory는 '의무적인'이라는 의미를 가지고 있다.
It is **obligatory** for all employees to wear protective clothing. (*adj.*)

1125
absolve ²
[əbˈzɑːlv]

v. 무죄임을 선언하다   to forgive; to free from guilt or blame
resolve는 해결하다는 의미이다. 연결해서 사건을 해결해 무죄임을 선언했다고(absolve) 외우자.
The court **absolved** him of all responsibility for the accident. (v.)

1126
obscene ²
[əbsíːn]

v. 음란한, 외설적인   indecent; vulgar; depraved
off seen과 비슷하게 들리므로 너무 음란해 '보지 않게 되는'의 의미로 해석할 수 있다.
He was using **obscene** language and threatening Jim. (adj.)

1127
rambling ²
[ræmbliŋ]

a. 이리저리 막 다니는, 할 일 없이 거니는   aimlessly wandering
amble은 '걷다'라는 뜻이 있다.
He was **rambling** down the road. (adj.)

1128
disparity ⁷
[dispǽrəti]

n. 차이, 격차, 부동, 불균형   lack of similarity, equality, difference; condition of inequality
남극, 북극처럼 정반대에 있어 균형을 이루기 힘들다.
The **disparity** between the giant's height and the dwarf's height is obvious. (n.)

1129
gaudily ²
[ɡɔ́ːdəli]

adv. 야하게, 화려하게   brilliantly or excessively showy; garish
그리스 로마에 나오는 신들처럼(god → gaud) 화려하게 옷을 입었다고 외우자.
She is **gaudily** dressed. (adv.)

1130
homogenous ⁷
[həmɑ́dʒənəs]

a. 동질의   akin, alike
유전자가(gene = gen) 같아서(homo) '동질의'이라는 의미다.
South Korea is a **homogenous** country. (adj.)

1131
shun ⁵
[ʃʌ́n]

v. 피하다   to avoid, to keep away from
sun을 shun하고 싶다고 생각하자.
The man **shunned** himself from repeating his horrible mistakes. (v.)

1132
compress [6]

[kəm|pres]

v. 꾹 누르다, 밀어 넣다, 압축하다   to cram, press together
compress를 하려면 모든 것을 꾹꾹 눌러야 된다(press).
Lily **compressed** all of her bulky clothes into her tiny bag. (*v.*)

1133
nomadic [2]

[noumǽdik]

a. 유목의, 떠도는   traveling from place to place; itinerant, moving from place to place
nomadic 은 유목민이라는 뜻의 nomad와 형용사꼴 ~ic가 합쳐져 생긴 단어이다.
The **nomadic** tribe did not build long-lasting houses, because they would not stay there for long. (*adj.*)

1134
fauna [3]

[|fɔːnə]

n. (어떤 지역의) 동물들   the animals of a given region or period
fauna와 반대되는 flora가 있다라는 것을 꼭 알아두자. 그래서 flora는 단어 안에 flower랑 비슷한 것이 들어있어서 '식물종'이라는 뜻이고, fauna는 그 반대니까 '동물종'이다.
The **fauna** of the region includes lion, eagle, tiger, and wolf. (*n.*)

1135
parched [3]

[pάːrtʃt]

a. 바싹 마른; 목마른   arid, scorched; very thirsty
scorched(불에 그슬린)라는 단어와 연관지어서 외우자.
After walking through the desert for hours without a drop of water, Antoine's throat was **parched**. (*adj.*)

1136
redress [2]

[rɪ|dres]

n. 변상, 보상; 바로잡다   compensation; to amend
re-address(다시 착수케 하다) 함으로써 잘못이나 빚을 바로 잡는 것이다.
John was scolded to **redress** his wrong behaviors and set it upright. (*v.*)

1137
recoup [2]

[rɪ|kuːp]

v. 되찾다, 만회하다, 벌충하다   to get back the equivalent of; regain, pay back
recover와 비슷한 뜻으로 연관지어서 외우면 좋다.
Profit from the bank **recouped** his loss. (*v.*)

1138
defacement [5]

[dɪˈfeɪsmənt]

n. 훼손된 외관, 표면   damaged surface or appearance
얼굴을(face) 좋지 않게(de) 만들어서 훼손시킨다는(deface) 의미이다.
Calling the **defacement** of both public and private property a form of art is not proper. (*n.*)

Note :

Episode 67

MATCHING Quiz

1. waddle
2. anatomy
3. retaliate
4. grimace
5. vulgar
6. obligatory
7. absolve
8. obscene
9. rambling
10. disparity
11. gaudily
12. homogenous
13. shun
14. compress
15. nomadic
16. fauna
17. parched
18. redress
19. recoup
20. defacement

A. revenge
B. the science dealing with the structure of animals or plants
C. indecent; vulgar
D. walking with short steps, rocking from side to side, as a duck
E. lack of good breeding; indecent; obscene
F. required as a matter of obligation
G. to make an ugly or contorted facial expression
H. lack of similarity, equality
I. aimlessly wandering
J. akin, alike
K. to forgive; to free from guilt or blame
L. to cram, press together
M. to avoid, keep away from
N. compensation
O. traveling from place to place; itinerant
P. brilliantly or excessively showy; garish
Q. arid, scorched
R. damaged surface or appearance
S. to get back the equivalent of; regain
T. the animals of a given region

1-D, 2-B, 3-A, 4-G, 5-H, 6-F, 7-K, 8-C, 9-I, 10-H, 11-P, 12-J, 13-M, 14-L, 15-O, 16-T, 17-Q, 18-N, 19-S, 20-R

더 많은 문제를 풀고자 한다면 www.quizlet.com에서 'paul academy seoul' class를 검색

Episode 68: The Cousin Clause

"Break in!?" Jake cried. "Are you crazy!?"

William glanced quickly back toward Jake, then turned his eyes back to the road.

"It's ok! Don't worry about it!" William turned back again hopefully. "My girlfriend's father runs the place. She's brought us in a million times. It's the off-season anyway, so there is only the one guard and he's my buddy anyway. It'll be fine!"

Jake was angry in the back seat. How dare he! To put all their futures at risk like that!

"No! No way!"

"But the animals are so much more active at night! I thought it would be an adventure we could share together!"

A chilly silence fell over the cab. There was only a subtle wind from the truck's air conditioner, the engine and the tires on the road.

TJ looked between the two of his companions and decided not to speak or attempt **diplomacy**. The truck had become a fighting arena. They would kill him, then kill each other, and no one would know that he tried to stop them. It was not his **prerogative** to die an unsung hero. There would be no parties, no parties to **extol** his **august** sacrifice. No ballads would be sung to **bemoan** his passing. His death notice would say that he was killed by his friends while studying to be a mime. That was just terrible. He tried to make himself as small as possible in the passenger seat.

Another moment passed before William spoke, his eyes not leaving the road.

"I'm **invoking** the Cousin Clause," he said. His voice was heavy

---

1139 diplomacy [3]
n. 외교, 사교 수완
the art or science of conducting negotiations

1140 prerogative [2]
n. 특권, 특혜
an exclusive right, privilege

1141 extol [2]
v. 극찬하다
acclaim, applaud

1142 august [3]
a. 숭고한, 고결한
grand, noble

1143 bemoan [5]
v. 한탄하다, 애도하다
to mourn, lament

1144 invoke [5]
v. 호소하다
to appeal to, beseech

1145 oscillate [4]
v. 동요하다
to waver, vibrate

1146 underscore [11]
v. 밑줄 긋다; 강조하다
to underline; stress, emphasize

1147 petition [5]
v. 청원[탄원]하다
to beg, request

1148 camouflage [7]
v. 위장하다
to disguise by means of concealment; dissimulate

1149 rein [3]
v. 억제하다
to hold, restrain

with seriousness though its amplitude **oscillated** in such a way that **underscored** how deeply emotional he was.

Jake gasped. He was trapped. He knew it was useless to **petition** his cousin to change his mind. No attorney or legal counsel could reason their way out of the Cousin Clause. It was absolutely binding. They had made a pinky swear when they were 8. Jake had to do whatever his cousin asked of him. He couldn't believe that William had remembered it and that he himself had forgotten it.

William sniffed loudly and wiped his eyes.

"Look, if you don't want—"

"No! I'll do it." Jake cried, failing to **camouflage** the emotion in his own voice, and reached up and clapped his oldest friend on the shoulder. William turned around and smiled broadly beneath eyes wet and red with the tears he was holding back. Jake **reined** back on tears of his own. Even TJ started crying.

"Just… you gotta promise me that you can get us in and out without being seen."

Somehow, William's smile grew wider.

"Not a problem, cuz. Not a problem. You do this, and I'll be in your debt for life."

Jake smiled right back.

"I already owe you for getting me out of my shell on this trip. Let's do this."

William nodded and turned back to the road. He pushed the accelerator a little harder and the road opened out in front of them.

A few minutes later TJ cleared his throat.

"Uh, just so you guys know, my truck and I are totally in, too." He drummed his fingers on the dashboard and cleared his throat again. "I guess I have no choice but to come along on this adventure, so, uh… let's go commit some minor offenses and stuff together."

William turned up the radio.

As they pulled into the deserted parking lot, night had fallen completely. The zoo sat nestled in a clearing far into a mountain valley. As they climbed out of the cab and made their way to the gate, their way was lit by a single glaring streetlight which shone scarily through a fog which had drifted down off the mountain and **unfurled** itself across the **void** parking spaces. The fog drifted up and around, creating phantoms before their eyes. It was atmospherically **ghastly**.

Jake could have believed they were walking through some mystical wetland, walking through swamp water, holding magical swords to fight a dragon rather than tiptoeing through the parking lot of a commercial zoo to **jeopardize** their futures for fun. He suspected that his fears were baseless, but William's appeal to his childhood sentimentality could not **mend** his **circumspect** nature completely. Jake swallowed nervously and ran to catch up with William and TJ, who had moved to a section of the fence that joined with the mountainside itself. The adventurers stood side by side, staring up together at the fence which towered ten meters above their heads, topped by a loop of rusty sharp wire.

William looked Jake and TJ and rubbed his hands together eagerly.

"Let's do this."

1150 unfurl [5]
v. 펼쳐지다
to unfold

1151 void [2]
a. 텅 빈
empty; vain

1152 ghastly [3]
a. 섬뜩한, 무시무시한
shockingly frightful or dreadful; horrible

1153 jeopardize [2]
v. 위험에 빠뜨리다
to endanger, threaten

1154 mend [2]
v. 수리하다, 고치다
to fix, repair

1155 circumspect [7]
a. 신중한
cautious, careful

Vocabulary

1139
diplomacy [3]
[dɪ|ploʊməsi]

n. 외교, 사교 수완   the art or science of conducting negotiations
영화에서 전쟁 대신 diplomacy(외교)를 해야 한다는 말을 많이 들어봤을 것이다.
Diplomacy is better than war. (*n.*)

1140
prerogative [2]
[prɪ|rɑːgətɪv]

n. 특권, 특혜   an exclusive right, privilege
privilege와 연관지어서 외워보자.
In many countries education is still the **prerogative** of the rich. (*n.*)

1141
extol [2]
[ikstóul]

v. 극찬하다, 칭찬하다, 격찬하다   acclaim, applaud, to praise in the highest terms
ex(up), tollere(raise, 들어 올리다)에서 유래.
The queen **extolled** the knight's courage in slaying the dragon and gave him a medal. (*v.*)

1142
august [3]
[ɔ́ːgəst]

a. 숭고한, 고결한, 당당한; 8월   grand, noble, impressive; majestic
August의 무성한 나무들은 얼마나 august한지(멋있는지) 기억하자.
An **august** group of statesmen (*adj.*)

1143
bemoan [5]
[bɪ|moʊn]

v. 한탄하다, 애도하다   to mourn, lament, to express distress
답답할 때는 moon(달, sounds like moan)을 보면서 한탄해 봐! 마음이 한결 나아질 거야.
When he heard that he would never be able to run again, the marathon runner **bemoaned** his fate. (*v.*)

1144
invoke [5]
[invóuk]

v. 호소하다, 기원하다   to appeal to, beseech, to call on for assistance or protection
어원인 voc- 은 'speaking or calling'이라는 뜻을 가지고 있다.
In times of difficulty, people **invoke** higher powers to help and protect them. (*v.*)

1145
oscillate [4]
[ásəlèit]

v. 동요하다, 흔들리다   to waver, vibrate, to swing back and forth
oscillate에서 l(엘) 2개가 있는 걸 보면서 흔들리면 세상이 두 개로 보인다고 연상하자.
The orangutan **oscillated** between two branches before leaping to the other side of the river. (*v.*)

1146
underscore [11]
[|ʌndər|skɔː(r)]

v. 밑줄 긋다; 강조하다   to underline; stress; to emphasize
밑줄 쫙 치면 강조가 된다.
My superior **underscored** the importance of being in time and said he would punish everyone who comes late. (*v.*)

1147
petition [5]
[pətíʃən]

v. 청원[탄원]하다   to beg, request; to appeal
옛 불어 peticion 은 '요구하다, 청원하다'라는 말에서 유래했다.
The parents of the kids **petitioned** for the bill the pass but government rejected their appeal. (*v.*)

1148
camouflage [7]
[kǽməflɑːʒ]

v. 위장하다; 위장, 속임수   to disguise by means of concealment; dissimulate; concealment
flage를 flower로 연상해서 '너무 예뻐서 꽃밭에서 못 찾겠다'라는 것을 생각하면 위장이라는 뜻을 재밌게 외울 수 있다.
Military **camouflages** are oftenly used to hide the soldiers in secret actions.(*n.*)

1149
rein [3]
[reɪn]

v. 억제하다   to hold, restrain
비가(rain) 오니까 밖에 나가지 않고 행동을 억제하게(rein) 됐다고 외우자.
We need to **rein** back public spending. (*v.*)

1150
unfurl [5]
[|ʌn|f3ːrl]

v. 펼쳐지다   to unfold
unfold와 연관지어서 외우자.
The leaves slowly **unfurled**. (*v.*)

1151
void [2]
[vɔɪd]

a. 텅 빈   empty; vain
'텅 빈'을 뜻하는 라틴어 vocivos 에서 유래.
Void spaces (*adj.*)

1152
ghastly [ˈɡæstli]

a. 섬뜩한, 무시무시한 shockingly frightful or dreadful; horrible
유령(ghost → ghast)을 본 것처럼 섬뜩하다고 외우자.
It was the worst week of my life. It was **ghastly**. (*adj.*)

1153
jeopardize [dʒépərdàiz]

v. 위험에 빠뜨리다 to endanger, threaten
leopard한테 쫓기면 jeopardy한 상황이다.
He would never do anything to **jeopardize** his career. (*v.*)

1154
mend [mend]

v. 수리하다, 고치다 to fix, repair
해리포터 영화에 나온 맨드레이크(mandrake → mend) 약을 먹으면 몸이 굳은 사람들을 고칠(mend) 수 있다.
Could you **mend** my bike for me? (*v.*)

1155
circumspect [sə́ːrkəmspèkt]

a. 신중한, 조심성 있는, 용의주도한 cautious, careful, showing watchfulness, caution, or careful consideration
주위(circum)를 본다(spect)는 뜻으로 조심성 있음을 의미한다.
He was so **circumspect** about everything that he never made a single mistake. (*adj.*)

Episode 68
MATCHING Quiz

1. diplomacy — C. the art or science of conducting negotiations
2. prerogative — D. an exclusive right, privilege
3. extol — F. acclaim, applaud
4. august — G. grand, noble
5. bemoan — E. to mourn, lament
6. invoke — J. to appeal to, beseech
7. oscillate — K. to waver, vibrate
8. underscore — H. to underline; stress, emphasize
9. petition — I. to beg, request
10. camouflage — O. to disguise by means of concealment; dissimulate
11. rein — N. to hold, restrain
12. unfurl — L. to unfold
13. void — M. empty; vain
14. ghastly — Q. shockingly frightful or dreadful; horrible
15. jeopardize — A. to endanger, threaten
16. mend — P. to fix, repair
17. circumspect — B. cautious, careful

1-C, 2-D, 3-F, 4-G, 5-E, 6-J, 7-K, 8-H, 9-I, 10-O, 11-N, 12-L, 13-M, 14-Q, 15-A, 16-P, 17-B

더 많은 문제를 풀고자 한다면 www.quizlet.com에서 'paul academy seoul' class를 검색

Episode 69

Night in the Zoo

The area where the fence was built onto the mountain was clearly not as sound as the rest of the fence. Jake could see that if someone was a bravery **incarnate** and could actually manage to climb up the rocks, it would be fairly simple to **circumvent** the zoo's defenses.

"Are you guys coming up or what?"

William was up the rocks already.

"How did you get up there so fast?" TJ demanded. "I don't have the arm strength to pull myself up."

"It's no problem, just push Jake up here, and then we will both pull you up, like a human **scaffolding**," William said.

TJ did as he was instructed, forming a loop with his hands and boosting TJ up onto the **curb**. Of course, with TJ's **paucity** of strength, Jake was barely able to make it and nearly slid back down the **sedimentary** rock.

"Be careful TJ, I almost **fractured** my neck there."

"Well you are pretty awkward. If you decide to legally attack, I'll just tell the **tribunal** that you **destabilized** me because you need to lose a few kilos."

"Har har," Jake said he and William pulled TJ up onto the rock. "You could stand to put a few on."

"Have you ever seen a fat mime? It's hard to lean against an invisible post if you can't lean against a real one without knocking it over."

William made a quick gesture for them to be silent.

1156 incarnate [2]
a. 인간의 모습을 한
embodied in flesh, especially a human

1157 circumvent [3]
v. 피해가다, 우회하다
to bypass, avoid

1158 scaffolding [3]
n. 비계, 뼈대
a temporary structure for holding workers and materials during the erection of a building

1159 curb [2]
n. 경계
ledge, border

1160 paucity [2]
n. 부족, 소량
scarcity, shortage

1161 sedimentary [3]
a. 퇴적물의
relating to the matter that settles to the bottom of a liquid

1162 fracture [3]
v. 골절시키다, 부러뜨리다
to break, crack

1163 tribunal [3]
n. 재판소
court

1164 destabilize [2]
v. 불안정하게 하다
to make unstable

1165 jest [2]
n. 농담, 장난
joke, witty remark

1166 propel [3]
v. 몰고 가다
to drive, or cause to move, forward or onward

1167 distort [15]
v. 왜곡하다
to twist awry; make deformed

1168 flank [3]
n. 측면
side

1169 defect [4]
n. 부족
deficiency, lack

1170 eerie [6]
a. 으스스한, 괴상한
spooky, frightening

1171 infinitesimal [2]
a. 극미한, 극소의
indefinitely or exceedingly small

1172 ecological [9]
a. 생태계의
environmental, green

1173 inhumane [3]
a. 비인간적인, 잔혹한
brutal, barbarous, savage

"All right, you silly people," he hissed. "Enough with the entertainment routine. Did you steal those **jests** from some movie from the 20s?"

William **propelled** them to a place in the chain link fence that had been dealt a huge blow by a tumbling rock, **distorting** it into a bubble and leaving enough room at the bottom to crawl through. Once on the other side, sliding down was easier than climbing up had been.

Jake brushed dust off the left **flank** of his pants.

"OK, so here we are," he whispered. "Now what?"

William was clearly excited, but still kept his voice low.

"Well, we're going to check out some night animals. That's the whole reason we came here at night."

William led them into the park. The darkened cages, occasional strange animal sounds and the **defect** of lighting made for an **eerie** trip. As they walked, they passed a number of buildings, one with a sign denoting it as the "Gift Emporium". Inside the shadowy window were a number of **infinitesimal** animal dolls, arranged in a parade. This happy **ecological** parade struck a strange contrast with the darkness and strangeness of their surroundings. From the distant cage, some unknown bird gave a harsh cry. Jake shook a little bit, his anxiety high. A little longer down the path and William walked up to an open place and stopped, taking out a pad of paper and a pencil.

"Here's our first stop. In biology they are called *crocuta crocuta*, but you know them as hyenas."

Jake came up to the open place and stood next to William, with TJ close behind. They looked into the enclosure but could see nothing but night.

"They are one of the few mammal species where the female is larger than the male. See, they're **inhumane** predators, and out on the flat grasslands of the African savanna they hunt and eat anything they can get their hands on, including their own young. I think that's why the females are so much bigger than the males, in order to protect the babies."

Out in the open place, Jake heard some movement and what sounded like barking, but he didn't see any hyenas.

"Keep an eye out for anything that looks like social behavior," William said. "I can include it in my observations."

"Observations?" Jake asked. "For what?"

"I'm doing a paper to show my potential as a biologist," William said, scratching the back of his head. "I'm going to apply for college next year."

"That's great!" Jake cried, a little too loudly. Somewhere in the darkness, animals stirred.

"I mean, that's great," he said again in a whisper. "But why don't you do it during the day?"

"Hyenas sleep during the day. As I mentioned, my girlfriend's dad owns the zoo, and he was kind enough to let me come in at night and start my observations. Unfortunately, she decided to become my ex-girlfriend last week and in his **intractable** egoism, her father stopped me from finishing my project."

"Oh, that's just great," TJ said anxiously. "That means if we get caught he's going to send us to jail."

"You've got that right, boy," said a voice behind them. They turned around quickly, and fear took away the color from their faces at once. A middle-aged man was shining an **immense** and nasty-looking flashlight in their faces. "William, what do you think you are you getting up to in here? Arson? You thinking to burn down my zoo as revenge for my daughter deciding that she had enough of you?"

William held his hand up to shield his eyes from the light.

"No sir, Mr. P!" he said. "In fact, my breaking and entering tonight had nothing to do with your daughter, I promise. I'm only finishing up my observations on the hyenas tonight, and I'll never come back here again."

Mr. P lowered the flashlight and approached them. He seemed to have softened a little.

1174 intractable [2]
a. 고집스러운
stubborn, obstinate

1175 immense [6]
a. 거대한
gigantic, enormous

1176 incarcerate ³
v. 감금하다
to confine, imprison

1177 entangle ²
v. 얽매다
to involve in difficulties

1178 prosecute ³
v. 기소하다
to charge

1179 redeem ³
v. (결함 등을) 보완하다
to recover by payment or other satisfaction

1180 degenerate ³
v. 퇴보하다, 악화하다
to worsen, backslide

"Sorry for the inconvenience," William continued. "I hope you don't hold it against us. To be honest, I've barely even thought about your daughter since she dumped me last week. It's almost like we never even dated!"

Mr. P's frown was visible, even in the one A.M. darkness.

Ten minutes later, Mr. P had rounded them up and **incarcerated** them in a single room on the top floor of the Gift Market. He turned to face the boys, who were sitting on a large box of stuffed zebras.

"So," he said, hands on his hips. "I'm not a cruel man, and I know the position you have gotten yourself into as well as you do."

He scanned their faces.

"I don't want to get you **entangled** in trouble with the police, so I am not going to **prosecute**, but you are going to have to do something to **redeem** yourselves so that I know you aren't going to come back here. You aren't going to come back here outside of business hours, are you?"

All three answered at once.

"No sir!"

"You're not going to **degenerate** and I come back tomorrow and find you camping out in the giraffe room or something like that?"

"No sir!"

"Good. Just so that I know that you're serious, you are going to spend the rest of the morning cleaning cages and sweeping animal rooms. I'll have my assistant show you around so that you don't get on the wrong side of a rhinoceros by accident."

He turned to look at William.

"You can start right now by picking up trash around the hyena room until my assistant gets here in an hour."

He threw a pile of clothes and safety equipment at their feet.

"Your wardrobe for the day. Make sure that stuff fits all right. The last thing you want is to leave a space for hippo dung to touch your skin."

He turned and got of the attic's tiny door.

Jake, William, and TJ all shared a look at one another and began to sort out the overalls, work gloves and rubber boots Mr. P had left behind.

"You know, this could be a really great experience," TJ said as he adjusted the tightness of a pair of safety goggles. "Not many people can put 'zoo slave' on their college application."

Jake hopped on one foot as he tried to pull on a rubber boot that went up to his thigh.

"Well, at least we're not handcuffed in the back of a police car," he said, giving up on the boot and sitting down on a box to put it on more easily. "And I bet you're right. I bet I can get a pretty good college essay out of this."

William was already fully dressed and standing next to the doorway with a mop in his hand.

"Come on guys, were going to miss the hyenas' mating time," he said with a slight cry, tapping the handle of the mop on the ground and shifting anxiously. "It's kind of the whole reason we broke in."

He got the door and began to climb down the stairs.

"All right, all right, we're coming," TJ said, following close behind him with his boots clearly on the wrong feet.

Jake hung back a moment and looked out the window as dawn broke and shapes of the zoo began to emerge from the darkness. He could **embark on** make out animals moving in the blue grey dawn and hear the sounds of birds and beasts begin or end their day. He zipped up his overalls and got the door himself, and caught up with William and TJ a little ways down the path. He took a deep breath of the crisp morning air and held it in his lungs. He hoped that all his punishments in life would be so **piquant**. He knew they wouldn't be, that some might break him or **grind** him down. But he thought that as long as he was willing to put on the gloves and **wade** into the mud, that maybe he could at least learn something from them, too.

1181 embark on [3]
v. ~에 착수하다
to start to do something new

1182 piquant [4]
a. 짜릿한, 흥미진진한
interesting, exciting

1183 grind [2]
v. 가루로 만들다
to reduce to dust or powder

1184 wade [3]
v. 물, 진흙을 헤치며 걷다
to walk in water, when partially immersed

Vocabulary

1156
incarnate ²
[ɪnˈkɑːrnət]

a. 인간의 모습을 한   embodied in flesh, especially a human
고대 잉카(Inca) 문명은 인간의 모습을 한(incarnate) 신의 존재를 믿었다고 외우자.
The leader seemed the devil **incarnate**. (*adj.*)

1157
circumvent ³
[ˈsɜːrkəmˌvent]

v. 피해가다, 우회하다, 피하다   to bypass, avoid, to go around
circumvent는 'circum'(around) + 'vent'(come). 즉, '빙 돌아서 오다' → 우회하다 → 〈문제, 실패 등을〉 교묘하게 피하다, 모면하다 순으로 파생되었다.
Mr. Jones has a bad temper, but his peaceful wife **circumvents** him from getting into fights. (*v.*)

1158
scaffolding ³
[ˈskæfəldɪŋ]

n. 비계, 뼈대   a temporary structure for holding workers and materials during the erection of a building
스카프(scarf → scaff)를 마네킹의 뼈대(scaffold)에 둘렀다고 외우자.
Scaffolding has been put up around a building. (*n.*)

1159
curb ²
[kɜːrb]

n. 경계; 제한하다   ledge, border; to restrain
커브(cuve, sounds like curb) 길에서는 속도제한이 있지?
We tried to **curb** my brother's tantrums by threatening to break his toys, but they only grew worse. (*v.*)

1160
paucity ²
[ˈpɔːsəti]

n. 부족, 소량, 소수   scarcity, shortage, not enough of something
음식의 공급이 멈춰(pause → pauc) 부족 현상을 겪고 있다고 생각하자.
There is a **paucity** of information. (*n.*)

1161
sedimentary ³
[ˌsedɪˈmentri]

a. 퇴적물의   relating to the matter that settles to the bottom of a liquid
sed는 '앉다'는 뜻으로 물을 가만히 놔두고 오래 가라'앉히'면 아래에 깔리는 퇴적물을 sediment라고 한다.
The area is composed of **sedimentary** rock. (*adj.*)

1162
fracture ³

[frǽktʃər]

v. 골절시키다, 부러뜨리다; 부서짐   to break, crack; a break
망가져서(rack → rac) 부서졌다고(fracture) 외워보자.
His leg **fractured** in two places. (*v.*)

1163
tribunal ³

[traɪˈbjuːnl]

n. 재판소, 법원   a court; a place or seat of judgment.
옛날에 로마의 tribune이라는 직책은 '호민관'이라는 민중지도자였다. tribune은 많은 결정과 판결을 내렸다. 그것처럼 tribunal은 '재판소, 심사 위원회'라는 뜻이다.
The **tribunal** judged whether he broke the employment law or not. (*n.*)

1164
destabilize ²

[ˌdiːˈsteɪbəlaɪz]

v. 불안정하게 하다   to make unstable
안정되지(stable) 않게(un) 하므로 불안정하게 한다는 의미다.
Terrorist attacks were threatening to **destabilize** the government. (*v.*)

1165
jest ²

[dʒest]

n. 농담, 장난   joke, witty remark
joke와 연관지어서 외우자.
Don't say such a thing even in **jest**. (*n.*)

1166
propel ³

[prəˈpel]

v. 몰고 가다   to drive, or cause to move, forward or onward
프로펠러가(propeller) 돌아가야 비행기를 몰고 갈(propel) 수 있다.
He was grabbed from behind and **propelled** through the door. (*v.*)

1167
distort ¹⁵

[dɪˈstɔːrt]

v. 왜곡하다   to twist awry; make deformed
디스코를(disco → disto) 추다 보면 몸을 이리저리 꼬며 마치 몸이 왜곡되는(distort) 것 같다고 생각하자.
Newspapers are often guilty of **distorting** the truth. (*v.*)

1168
flank ³

[flæŋk]

n. 측면   side
플랭크(plank) 위에서 열심히 운동을 해서 측면(flank) 복근이 발달했다고 외우자.
The enemy's main force pressed on our left **flank**.

1169
defect [⁴]
[|di:fekt]

n. 부족, 결함   deficiency, lack
deficient와 연관지어서 외워보자.
I first thought the machine had a mechanical **defect**. (*v.*)

1170
eerie [⁶]
[|ɪri]

a. 으스스한, 괴상한   spooky, frightening
'겁 많은'을 뜻하는 고전 영어 earg에서 유래.
I found the silence underwater really **eerie**. (*adj.*)

1171
infinitesimal [⁶]
[infɪnətésəməl]

a. 으스스한, 괴상한, 미소한, 무한소의   spooky, frightening, very small
infinitely(무한대로) small(작은)이라고 볼 수 있다.
The **infinitesimal** amount of love left in Jane's heart was killed when John said, "You look as fat as a Christmas pig." (*adj.*)

1172
ecological [⁹]
[|i:kə|lɑ:dʒɪkl]

a. 생태계의   environmental, green
eco는 자연이라는 뜻이므로 ecological은 '생태계의'라는 의미를 가지고 있다.
We risk upsetting the **ecological** balance of the area.

1173
inhumane [³]
[inhju:méin]

a. 비인간적인, 잔혹한, 몰인정한, 무자비한   brutal, barbarous, savage, cruel
인간이(human) 아닌(in), 즉 '비인간적인'이라는 의미다.
Doing scientific experiments on animals is **inhumane**. (*adj.*)

1174
intractable [²]
[intræktəbl]

a. 고집스러운, 아주 다루기 힘든   stubborn, obstinate
tractable(다루기 쉬운)이 아니라는 뜻이므로 다른 사람의 말을 듣지 않는다는 뜻으로 유추할 수 있다.
The little boy was so **intractable** that he wouldn't listen to any of his mother's urgings. (*adj.*)

1175
immense [⁶]
[iméns]

a. 거대한, 무한한, 광대한   gigantic, enormous, very great in degree, extent, size, or quantity
im은 '아니다', mense는 measure, 즉 '치수를 재다'를 뜻하므로 치수를 잴 수 없을 정도로 거대하다고 해석할 수 있다.
The **immense** size of the universe makes it impossible for us to travel to its end. (*adj.*)

1176
incarcerate [3]

[ɪnˈkɑːrsəreɪt]

v. 감금하다　to confine, imprison
고대 잉카(Inca) 문명은 포로들을 감금해 놓고(incarcerate) 나중에 먹어치웠다는(ate) 설이 있다.
He used to be **incarcerated** for 3 months. (*v.*)

1177
entangle [2]

[ɪnˈtæŋɡl]

v. 얽매다, 얽히게 하다　to involve in difficulties, to make tangled; intertwine
entangle은 en(make) + tangle(touch) : '접촉하게 하다' → 뒤얽히게 하다 → 〈남을〉 (골치아픈 일 등에) 말려들게 하다 → 난처하게 하다, 당황하게 하다 순으로 발전했다.
The necklace **entangled** with the bracelet when the jewelry box bounced around in the car. (*v.*)

1178
prosecute [3]

[ˈprɑːsɪkjuːt]

v. 기소하다　to charge
검사를 영어로 prosecutor, 즉 '기소하는 사람'이라고 한다.
The police decided not to **prosecute**. (*v.*)

1179
redeem [3]

[rɪˈdiːm]

v. (결함 등을) 보완하다, 만회하다, 구하다　to recover by payment or other satisfaction, to make up for; make amends for; offset
deem은 '생각하다'라는 뜻인데 re, 다시 생각한 거니까 한번 실패했던 걸 다시 생각해서 '보완하다, 만회하다'라는 뜻이다.
The excellent plot was not enough to **redeem** the weak acting. (*v.*)

1180
degenerate [3]

[dɪˈdʒenəreɪt]

v. 퇴보하다, 악화하다　to worsen, backslide
발전시키지(generate) 않고(de) 악화시킨다는 의미이다.
Her health **degenerated** slowly.

1181
embark on [3]

[ɪmˈbɑːrk-ɔːn]

v. ~에 착수하다　to start to do something new
노아는 신의 계시를 듣고 방주를(ark) 만드는 일에 착수했다(embark on).
I'm about to **embark on** a new journey. (*v.*)

1182
piquant [4]

[ˈpiːkənt]

a. 짜릿한, 흥미진진한　interesting, exciting
산 꼭대기에(peak → piq) 올라선 것처럼 짜릿하다고(piquant) 외우자.
Chicken was served with a **piquant** wild mushroom sauce. (*adj.*)

1183
grind ²   [graɪnd]

v. 가루로 만들다   to reduce to dust or powder
이를 그르(gr) 갈아서 이빨 사이의 음식을 가루로 만들었다고(grind) 외워보자.
He was **grinding** coffee. (v.)

1184
wade ³   [weɪd]

v. 물, 진흙을 헤치며 걷다   to walk in water, when partially immersed
물에(water → wad) 잠겨서 걷는다고 외우자.
He **waded** into the water to push the boat out (v.)

Episode 69
MATCHING Quiz

1. incarnate
2. circumvent
3. scaffolding
4. curb
5. paucity
6. sedimentary
7. fracture
8. tribunal
9. destabilize
10. jest
11. propel
12. distort
13. flank
14. defect
15. eerie
16. infinitesimal
17. ecological
18. inhumane
19. intractable
20. immense

A. indefinitely or exceedingly small
B. environmental, green
C. ledge, border
D. embodied in flesh, especially a human
E. to bypass, avoid
F. a temporary structure for holding workers and materials during the erection of a building
G. scarcity, shortage
H. to break, crack
I. relating to the matter that settles to the bottom of a liquid
J. court
K. joke, witty remark
L. to make unstable
M. to drive, or cause to move, forward or onward
N. deficiency, lack
O. to twist awry; make deformed
P. brutal, barbarous, savage
Q. side
R. gigantic, enormous
S. stubborn, obstinate
T. spooky, frightening

1-D, 2-E, 3-F, 4-C, 5-G, 6-I, 7-H, 8-J, 9-L, 10-K, 11-M, 12-O, 13-Q, 14-N, 15-T, 16-A, 17-B, 18-P, 19-S, 20-R

더 많은 문제를 풀고자 한다면 www.quizlet.com에서 'paul academy seoul' class를 검색

SAT Vocabulary

기출 예상 단어

기출 예상 단어

번호	단어	우리말 뜻	품사	영어 뜻
1185	lateralization	대뇌의 좌우의 기능 분화	noun	Cognitive function that relies more on one side of the brain than the other.
1186	predation	포식, 약탈	noun	Interaction in which one organism captures and feeds on another organism.
1187	countenance	표정, 안색	noun	A person's face or facial expression.
1188	pseudoscience	가짜과학, 가짜의학	noun	Methods, theories, or systems considered as having no scientific basis.
1189	lampoon	풍자	noun	Harsh satire aimed at an individual.
1190	malfeasance	(특히 공무원의) 불법(부정) 행위	noun	Misconduct or wrongdoing, especially by a public official.
1191	rotunda	원형 건물	noun	A circular domed building or hall.
1192	census	인구조사	noun	An official count of the population.
1193	gangway	통로	noun	A passageway, especially a narrow walkway.
1194	mural	벽화(들)	noun	Large paintings made on walls.
1195	ponderous	무거운, 육중한	adj.	Weighty; slow and heavy.
1196	protocol	절차	noun	List of steps to be taken in different situations.
1197	schema	개요, 윤곽; 도식	noun	An underlying organizational pattern or structure; conceptual framework.
1198	scions	자손	noun	A descendant.
1199	turmoil	소란, 혼란, 불안, 동요	noun	A state of great commotion, confusion, or disturbance.
1200	unprecedented	전례 없는	adj.	Without previous instance, never before known or experienced.
1201	veracity	진실성, 정확성	noun	Habitual truthfulness and honesty.
1202	adduce	증거로 인용하다	verb	To bring forward as evidence.
1203	conglomeration	복합	noun	A number of different things, grouped together.
1204	dainty	앙증맞은, 조심스러운	adj.	Preciously delicate or charming.
1205	demure	얌전한, 조신한	adj.	Modest and reserved in manner or behavior.
1206	detract	(가치, 중요성, 명성 따위를) 떨어뜨리다	verb	To take away a part, as from quality, value, or reputation.
1207	expostulatory	타이르는, 충고의	adj.	Of or relating to earnest and kind protests.
1208	holistic	전체적인	adj.	Concerning the whole rather than the parts.
1209	impugne	의문을 제기하다	verb	To challenge as false.
1210	locus	(특정) 위치, 장소	noun	A place.
1211	microbial	미생물의	adj.	Of or relating to a microorganism, especially a pathogenic bacterium.
1212	oversight	실수, 간과	noun	An omission or error due to carelessness.
1213	pillage	약탈	verb	Plundering, looting, taking property by force.
1214	plummet	수직으로 떨어지다; 급락하다	verb	Fall or drop straight down at high speed.
1215	posthumous	사후의	adj.	Occurring or continuing after one's death.

#	Word	Korean	POS	Definition
1216	postural	자세의, 자세를 취하는	adj.	Of or relating to the carriage of the body as a whole.
1217	prerequisite	필요조건; 사전에 필요한	adj.	Required beforehand.
1218	quiver	떨다, 흔들다	verb	To shake or move with a slight trembling motion.
1219	revelers	흥청대는 사람들	noun	People who participate in boisterous merrymaking.
1220	ruefully	슬프게, 비참하게	adv.	Regretfully; causing sorrow or pity, deplorable.
1221	shoal	얕은 물가	noun	A place where a sea, river, or other body of water is shallow.
1222	speciation	종의 형성	noun	The formation of new species.
1223	unorthodox	정통이 아닌, 특이한	adj.	Not conforming to rules or tradition.
1224	usurpation	강탈, 탈취	noun	Wrongful or illegal seizure.
1225	vandalism	고의적 파괴	noun	Deliberate and pointless destruction of public or private property.
1226	abdicate	(왕권, 권리, 의무) 버리다, 포기하다	verb	To give up a position, right, or power.
1227	accretion	축적	noun	Growth in size or increase in amount.
1228	altruistic	자신보다 남을 위하는, 이타적인	adj.	Unselfishly concerned for the welfare of others.
1229	amenable	순종하는, 쾌히 받아 들이는	adj.	Open to influence, persuasion, or advice.
1230	annals	연대기	noun	A record of events; especially yearly.
1231	annulment	무효화, 취소	noun	A voiding, invalidation.
1232	anterior	이전의; 앞쪽의	adj.	Situated before or at the front of.
1233	antipathy	반감, 혐오감	noun	A strong dislike, hostile feeling.
1234	apprehend	체포하다	verb	To seize; to arrest.
1235	appropriation	의회가 승인한 예산	noun	An act of a legislature granting money from the treasury.
1236	axiom	자명한 이치, 원칙	noun	A universally recognized principle.
1237	betoken	나타내다, 표시하다; 전조가 되다	verb	To give evidence of; indicate.
1238	blare	(소리) 요란하게 울리다, 떠들어대다	verb	To emit a loud, raucous sound.
1239	bode	징조가 되다	verb	To be an omen of; to indicate by signs.
1240	brawny	건장한	adj.	Strong, muscular.
1241	brusque	무뚝뚝한, 퉁명스러운	adj.	Abrupt, blunt, with no formalities.
1242	candor	솔직함, 정직함	noun	Honesty, frankness.
1243	congenital	선천적인	adj.	Of or relating to a condition present at birth.
1244	conspecific	같은 종의	adj.	Of the same species.
1245	convulsive	경련성인, 발작적인	adj.	Characterized by involuntary jerky contractions.
1246	coquettish	요염한, 교태를 부리는	adj.	Flirtatious in a teasing manner.
1247	covet	(남의것을) 탐내다	verb	To desire wrongfully; greatly desire.
1248	crux	가장 중요한 부분	noun	A vital, basic, decisive, or pivotal point.
1249	decennial	10년마다의	adj.	Occurring every 10 years
1250	decimation	대량학살	noun	Destroying or killing a large part of.
1251	defecate	배변하다	verb	To void excrement from the bowels.

#	Word	Korean	POS	Definition
1252	dejected	낙담한	adj.	Downcast or sad; depressed.
1253	demarcation	경계, 구분	noun	Act of defining or marking a boundary or distinction.
1254	derision	조롱, 조소	noun	Ridicule; mockery.
1255	desultory	두서없는, 되는대로, 산만한	adj.	Lacking consistency or order, disconnected.
1256	deter	단념시키다, 그만두게 하다	verb	To discourage from acting or proceeding.
1257	detritus	파편	noun	Any disintegrated material; debris.
1258	diabolical	악마 같은	adj.	Devilish; fiendish.
1259	discern	식별하다, 분별하다	verb	To see clearly, recognize.
1260	distended	팽창한	adj.	Enlarged or expanded from pressure.
1261	divest	빼앗다, 박탈하다	verb	To strip or deprive, especially of property or rights.
1262	divulge	누설하다	verb	To disclose or reveal.
1263	doldrums	침체, 부진; 침울	noun	A state of inactivity or stagnation.
1264	ecstasy	무아의 경지, 황홀	noun	Extreme happiness.
1265	emaciation	수척	noun	Abnormal thinness caused by lack of nutrition or by disease.
1266	encomium	찬사	noun	A formal expression of high praise.
1267	endemic	고유의	adj.	Inherent, native; belonging to an area.
1268	equitable	공정한, 공평한	adj.	Fair, just, embodying principles of justice.
1269	ethology	인성학; 행동 생물학	noun	The study of animal behavior, especially of behavioral patterns.
1270	evince	분명히 나타내다, 명시하다	verb	To demonstrate clearly; to prove.
1271	exiguity	근소, 부족	noun	The quality or state of being meager or scanty.
1272	florid	발그레한	adj.	Reddish; ruddy; rosy.
1273	food-borne	오염된 음식을 통해 전파되는	adj.	Caused by eating or drinking.
1274	forsooth	과연, 정말	adv.	In truth; in fact; indeed.
1275	foul	오염, 굴욕	verb	To defile; dishonor; disgrace.
1276	fritter	조금씩 낭비하다	verb	Wasting little by little.
1277	garner	얻다, 모으다	verb	To gather and store.
1278	glib	유창한	adj.	Readily fluent, often without thought or hesitation.
1279	granulate	알갱이로 만들다	verb	To make grainy.
1280	gynecology	부인과 의학	noun	The branch of medicine dealing with the reproductive system in women.
1281	headstone	묘비	noun	The memorial stone marking the head of the grave.
1282	headwork	정신 노동; 사고, 사색	noun	Mental labor; thought.
1283	hefty	무거운, 상당한	adj.	Heavy; weighty.
1284	imbecility	정신박약, 저능, 무능	noun	An instance or point of weakness; incapability.
1285	increment	증가, 인상	noun	An enlargement, increase, addition.
1286	inculcate	되풀이하여 심어주다, 명심시키다	verb	To implant by repeated statement.
1287	indefatigable	지치지 않는	adj.	Incapable of being tired out.
1288	indoctrinate	주입하다, 세뇌시키다	verb	To instill a doctrine, principle, ideology, etc.

#	Word	Korean	Part	Definition
1289	ingrained	(기질, 습관) 뿌리깊은, 깊이 박힌	adj.	Deep-rooted, forming part of the very essence.
1290	insurmountable	극복할 수 없는	adj.	Impossible to overcome.
1291	interject	불쑥 끼어들다	verb	To insert between other things.
1292	intone	(어느 어조로) 말하다, 읊조리다	verb	To utter with a particular tone or voice modulation.
1293	invidious	비위에 거슬리는, 불쾌한	adj.	Hateful, offensive, injurious.
1294	invigorate	기운나게 하다, 상쾌하게 하다	verb	Imparting strength and vitality.
1295	irksome	짜증나는, 귀찮은	adj.	Annoying; irritating; exasperating; tiresome.
1296	iterative	되풀이되는	adj.	Repeating, making repetitions.
1297	jargon	(특정 집단의 전문) 용어	noun	Vocabulary, peculiar to a particular trade, profession, or group.
1298	jut	돌출하다	verb	To extend sharply outward or upward; project.
1299	kudos	영광; 명성, 영예	noun	Honor; glory; acclaim.
1300	laborious	힘든	adj.	Requiring much work, exertion, or perseverance.
1301	lancet	양날의 끝이 뾰족한 의료용 칼	noun	Small surgical tool for making incisions.
1302	laypeople	일반인, 비전문가	noun	People who are not a member of a profession.
1303	levity	(말, 태도의) 가벼움, 경솔함, 경박함	noun	An inappropriate lack of seriousness.
1304	licentiousness	부도덕함, 음탕함, 음란함	adj.	Lacking legal or moral restraints.
1305	limelight	이목, 관심	noun	The center of attention.
1306	looming	(중요하거나 위협적인 일이) 곧 닥칠 것처럼 보이다	adj.	Something unwanted, about to happen soon, causing worry.
1307	lumber	느릿느릿 움직이다	verb	To move slowly and awkwardly.
1308	luminary	선각자, 권위자	noun	A person who is an inspiration to others in his or her field.
1309	mainstay	중심축, 대들보	noun	A chief support.
1310	mangy	지저분한	adj.	Shabby; filthy.
1311	matriculate	(대학에) 입학하다	verb	To enroll at a college or university.
1312	matrimony	결혼, 결혼상태	noun	State of being married.
1313	miasma	독기, 악영향	noun	A dangerous, foreboding, or deathlike influence or atmosphere.
1314	mirth	환희, 유쾌함, 웃음	noun	Merriment; amusement or laughter.
1315	misanthrope	사람을 싫어하는 사람	noun	A person who dislikes others.
1316	mislay	두고 잊어버리다	verb	To lose temporarily; misplace.
1317	misogyny	여성혐오	noun	Hatred of women.
1318	mogul	중요한 인물, 거물	noun	An important, powerful, or influential person.
1319	moor	고정시키다, 정박시키다	verb	To fix firmly; secure.
1320	munition	군수품, 무기	noun	Military supplies.
1321	mutation	변이, 변화	noun	A change in a gene or chromosome.
1322	mutual	상호간에	adj.	Held in common; shared.
1323	neural	신경(계)의	adj.	Of or relating to a nerve or the nervous system.

#	Word	Korean	POS	Definition
1324	neutralize	무력화하다	verb	To make something ineffective.
1325	nucleus	(원자)핵, 중심	noun	The central part, to which other parts are gathered.
1326	obstetrics	산부인과	noun	Branch of medicine concerned with pregnancy and childbirth.
1327	obtrusive	눈에 거슬리는	adj.	Undesirably protruding; imposing one's opinions on others.
1328	opulence	부유, 풍부	noun	Extreme wealth, abundance.
1329	overarching	포괄적인, (전체에 영향을 주므로) 매우 중요한	adj.	Encompassing or overshadowing everything.
1330	parity	동등함	noun	Equality, as in amount, status, or character.
1331	pathogen	병균	noun	An organism that causes disease.
1332	periphery	주변부	noun	A boundary line; perimeter; an outside surface.
1333	perusal	정독; 통독	noun	A careful examination, review.
1334	pitted	(과실의) 씨를 뺀	adj.	Having the pit (of fruit) removed.
1335	plaintiffs	원고, 고소인	noun	Persons filling a lawsuit.
1336	plaintive	슬픈, 불쌍한, 애처로운	adj.	Expressive of sorrow, melancholy.
1337	pollination	수분(작용)	noun	Transfer of pollen from the male reproductive structure to the female reproductive structure.
1338	prattle	(쓸데없이 마구) 지껄이다	verb	To talk in a foolish or simple-minded way; chatter.
1339	predilection	편애, 경향	noun	A tendency to think favorably of something in particular.
1340	primeval	원시의, 태고의	adj.	Relating to the beginning of the first age, especially of the world.
1341	primordial	원시의, 태고의, 옛날의	adj.	Original; existing from the beginning.
1342	procure	어렵게 구하다	verb	To obtain by care, effort, or special means.
1343	proliferate	급증하다	verb	To increase in number quickly.
1344	promulgate	공포, 선포; 널리 알리다	verb	To make known by open declaration; publish.
1345	protract	오래 끄는, 지연하는	verb	To draw out or lengthen.
1346	proximate	가까운, 근접한	adj.	Immediate; nearest.
1347	punctilious	세심한, 꼼꼼한	adj.	Very careful and exact; extremely attentive to etiquette.
1348	punctuality	시간 엄수, 정확함	noun	Promptness or being on time.
1349	regiment	(군사) 연대; 다수, 큰 무리	noun	A unit of ground forces, consisting of two or more battalions.
1350	rekindle	다시 불붙이다, (흥미, 관심) 다시 불러 일으키다	verb	Revive something that has been lost.
1351	repatriate	(본국으로의) 송환, 귀환	verb	To be restored or returned to the country of origin, allegiance, or citizenship.
1352	retardation	지체, 지연	noun	Slowing down of something.
1353	retrospective	회고하는	adj.	Looking or applying to the past or backward.
1354	salient	눈에 띄는, 유명한	adj.	Prominent; of notable significance.
1355	sanguine	낙관적인, 쾌활한	adj.	Cheerfully optimistic; hopeful.
1356	sceptic	회의론자, 의심 많은 사람	noun	A person who questions the validity or authenticity of something supposed to be true.

#	Word	Korean	POS	Definition
1357	scrupulous	양심적인; 세심한, 꼼꼼한, 면밀한	adj.	Exact, careful, attending thoroughly to details; having high moral standards, principled.
1358	senile	노쇠한, 나이 많은	adj.	Showing a decline of physical strength or mental functioning as a result of old age or disease.
1359	seraph	천사	noun	An angel.
1360	shrill	(소리가) 날카로운, 높은	adj.	High-pitched and piercing in sound quality.
1361	shroud	수의	noun	A cloth or sheet in which a corpse is wrapped for burial.
1362	sparse	희박한, 드문드문 있는	adj.	Thinly scattered or distributed.
1363	spearhead	창끝; 선봉	noun	A person, thing, or group that organizes or leads something.
1364	spelunk	동굴탐험을 하다	verb	To explore caves, especially as a hobby.
1365	staunch	확고한, 충실한	adj.	Firm or steadfast in principle, loyalty.
1366	stave	저지하다, 막다	verb	To drive or thrust away.
1367	sterling	훌륭한, 법정 순도의 (금,은)	adj.	Genuine, excellent; made of silver of standard fineness.
1368	stilts	기둥, 지주	noun	Tall, slender supporting posts.
1369	stipulation	계약 조건	noun	A demand or condition of an agreement.
1370	strapped	무엇에 궁한, 돈에 궁한	adj.	To be in need of something, wanting.
1371	substrate	기질	noun	A specific reactant acted upon by an enzyme.
1372	telltale	감추어도 드러나는	adj.	That reveals or betrays what is not intended to be known.
1373	transient	덧없는, 일시적인	adj.	Not lasting, temporary. Lasting only a short time.
1374	tutelage	후견, 보호, 지도, 교육	noun	Instruction, protection, or guardianship.
1375	tween	10세와 12세 사이의 사람	noun	A person between 10 and 12 years of age, too old to be a child and too young to be a teenager.
1376	unassuming	겸손한, 허세부리지 않는	adj.	Modest.
1377	unbidden	요청받지 않은, 예상 밖의	adj.	Not ordered or commanded; spontaneous.
1378	unwieldy	(무겁고 커서) 옮기거나 들기 힘든, 다루기 힘든	adj.	Not easily carried or handled, as from size, shape, or weight.
1379	unwittingly	모르는 사이에; 고의가 아니게	adv.	Without knowledge or intention.
1380	validate	확인하다, 증명하다	verb	To make valid, confirm, substantiate.
1381	weathering	풍화(작용)	noun	The breaking down of rocks and other materials by chemical or physical means.
1382	wily	약삭빠른, 교활한	adj.	Crafty; cunning.
1383	writhing	몸부림치는	adj.	Twisting and turning the body in a worm-like fashion, as in pain.
1384	xenophobic	외국(인) 공포(혐오)증의 (을 가진)	adj.	Having abnormal fear or hatred of the strange or foreign; having fear of foreigners.
1385	behest	명령, 지시	noun	A command or directive.
1386	ecologist	생태학자	noun	A person who studies the branch of biology dealing with the relations between organisms and their environment.
1387	endeavor	노력하다	verb	To make a serious attempt or effort.

1388	**epistemology**	인식론	*noun*	A branch of philosophy that studies the origin, nature, methods, and limits of human knowledge.
1389	**lisp**	혀짤배기소리	*noun*	A speech defect consisting in pronouncing s and z like th.
1390	**locale**	(사건 등의) 현장	*noun*	A place, especially having to do with events related to it.
1391	**mortgage**	저당, 주택 융자	*noun*	A specific type of loan that is used to buy real estate.
1392	**mounting**	뒤를 받치는 재료, 지지대	*noun*	Backing, setting or support.
1393	**prejudice**	편견, 선입견	*noun*	An unfavorable opinion or feeling formed beforehand without reason.
1394	**psychoanalysis**	정신분석(학)	*noun*	Structure of theories concerning the relation of conscious and unconscious psychological processes.
1395	**sapphic**	사포풍의; 레즈비언의	*adj.*	A poetic verse pattern pertaining to Sappho; of or relating to relationships between women.
1396	**succour**	도움, 구제	*noun*	A person or thing that gives help, relief, aid.
1397	**swaddle**	포대기로 감싸다	*verb*	To bind with long, narrow strips of cloth to prevent free movement.
1398	**symposium**	토론회	*noun*	A meeting or conference for the discussion of some subject.
1399	**systemic**	조직의; 온몸의	*adj.*	Pertaining to or affecting a particular body system.
1400	**unawares**	알지못하고 부지중에, 뜻밖에	*adv.*	By surprise, suddenly, unexpectedly.

SAT Vocabulary

Index

A, a

	ID NO.
abashed	30
abbreviated	1007
abdicate	1226
aberrant	1028
abide	342
abject	679
abnormal	685
abolish	980
abridge	316
abruptly	41
absolve	1125
absorb	318
abstaining	962
abundantly	834
abysmal	587
abyss	332
accessible	974
accord	602
accretion	1227
accustomed	170
acquiescence	36
acrimonious	258
acute	239
adage	465
adamant	378
adduce	1202
adhere	421
admonish	345
adored	1071
adorned	66
adrift	717
advent	890
advocate	338
aesthetic	4
affinity	941
affirmation	812
afflicted	750
affluent	481
affront	637
aggregated	334
aggressive	628
agilely	1055
ailment	506
albeit	94
alienate	943
alignment	22
allege	234
allegory	997
allotted	152
alloyed	1023
alluring	74
allusions	998
aloof	454
alternative	688
altruistic	1228
ambiguous	522
ambivalent	585
amenable	1229
amenities	783
amidst	762
amoral	499
amplify	606
amputate	418
anachronistic	712
analogy	186
anarchy	160
anatomy	1120
anecdote	175
anguish	802
animosity	1042
annals	1230
annihilate	508
annulment	1231
anomaly	768
anonymous	763
anterior	1232
anticipated	20
antidote	433
antipathy	1233
antithesis	1046
apex	198
apocalyptic	191
apocryphal	866
appalled	224
appease	492
appraisal	70
apprehend	1234
apprehension	47
apprentice	493
approbation	119
appropriately	32
appropriation	1235
apt	187
arbitrary	793
archaic	784
ardor	554
arduous	86
arid	533
array	311
articulate	367
artifice	572
artisan	365
ascertain	776
ascribe	281
aspect	357
aspire	988
assemble	222
assertiveness	836
assess	277
assimilate	368
assorted	59
assure	833
astounded	228
astute	904
atrocious	192
attentive	416
attest	451
audacious	1105
august	1142
auspicious	1012
austere	328
autonomy	843
avarice	546
aversion	117
avert	15
awe	992
axiom	1236

B, b

baffle	18
banal	408
barren	859
beckon	343
befall	322
befitting	877
beget	630
beguiled	906
behest	1385
belie	6
belittlement	624
bemoan	1143
benefactor	441
benevolent	314
benighted	120
benign	796
beseech	517

betoken 1237	chimera 918	confer 101
bewildered 995	chronic 427	confide 558
bigoted 766	chronicle 773	configured 691
blare 1238	circumscribe 255	confine 37
blatant 90	circumspect 1155	congenial 983
bliss 250	circumstance 215	congenital 1243
bluntness 1109	circumvent 1157	congested 335
bode 1239	civilized 176	conglomeration 1203
boisterously 260	clamorous 180	conjecture 653
bolster 279	clan 1102	conjugated 350
bombastically 676	clandestine 469	conjure 284
brandish 1098	clasp 754	connoisseur 34
brashly 879	cliché 934	connotation 673
brawny 1240	clinical 100	conquer 920
breach 831	cluster 10	conscientious 452
bristling 641	clutch 31	consent 327
broach 372	clutter 900	considerable 386
brusque 1241	coarse 782	considerate 487
buoyant 876	codified 887	consigned 769
burdensome 134	coerced 538	console 261
bustle 627	cognitive 588	conspecific 1244
	coherently 174	conspiratorial 468
C, c	cohesion 589	consternation 25
	collaborate 92	constituted 1041
calamity 1026	colloquial 256	constrain 324
callous 89	collude 788	constricted 854
calumnious 375	colossal 678	consummate 474
camouflage 1148	commemorate 872	contaminating 652
candid 370	commodity 201	contempt 751
candor 1242	communal 519	contemptuous 684
canvass 238	companion 91	contend 530
capacious 347	compatriot 407	contentious 809
capitulate 391	complacent 545	contour 744
capricious 722	compliant 917	contravene 161
captivating 905	complicity 686	contrive 270
cardinal 56	compressed 1132	conundrum 619
caricature 615	comprise 387	conventional 293
cartographer 1035	compulsory 1117	converse 340
castigate 482	concealing 961	conviction 104
catalyst 811	concede 164	convoluted 52
catastrophically 710	conceited 381	convulsive 1245
caucuses 771	conceive 897	coquettish 1246
cease 179	conceptual 1064	corollary 525
celestial 701	conciliatory 797	countenance 1187
censure 236	concoction 516	counterfeit 672
census 1192	concur 548	courtier 75
cerebral 83	condemn 604	covert 560
chagrin 359	condone 500	covet 1247
chasm 830	conducive 875	crass 1052
chided 880	conduit 273	credence 977

453

credible 218	demarcation 1253	discredit 822
criteria 734	demise 369	discrepant 252
crucial 440	demolished 505	discrete 419
crude 883	demoralizing 315	disdain 14
crumble 778	demur 431	disenchanted 674
crux 1248	demure 1205	disillusioned 430
cryptic 291	denigrate 394	disintegrate 109
cuddle 971	denoting 1090	disinterested 700
culinary 867	denouncing 844	dismayed 799
cull 136	depicting 703	disparage 636
cultivating 1039	deplore 209	disparity 1128
curb 1159	deprive 443	dispassionate 214
cursory 216	depute 669	dispel 518
	derision 1254	displaced 1112
D, d	derisive 71	dispute 383
	derive 562	disregard 547
dabbling 1076	descend 865	disruptive 632
dainty 1204	designated 693	disseminate 1008
dearth 105	desolate 655	dissent 27
debased 55	despair 705	dissipate 144
debris 901	despise 423	dissonant 384
debunk 1085	despondent 429	distended 1260
deceit 682	destabilized 1164	distilled 272
decennial 1249	desultory 1255	distort 1167
decimation 1250	detaching 825	distress 753
declaimed 856	deter 1256	diverge 300
decree 42	deteriorate 598	divest 1261
decry 785	detonate 116	divulge 1262
deduce 390	detract 1206	docile 541
deem 302	detritus 1257	doldrums 1263
defacement 1138	devastate 973	dominant 58
defecate 1251	deviations 1013	downplay 425
defect 1169	devious 263	drastic 733
deferential 264	devoid 3	dreadful 780
defiant 123	diabolical 1258	dreary 331
deficiency 478	dichotomy 157	drooped 1115
defied 775	didactic 364	drudgery 609
deforming 1066	diffident 13	
defraud 555	dignity 515	**E, e**
deftly 185	digressed 1063	
degenerate 1180	dilute 610	earnest 43
deity 251	diminish 599	eccentricities 933
dejected 1252	diplomacy 1139	ecological 1172
deliberate 1107	discard 385	ecologist 1386
delicate 1081	discern 1259	ecosystem 1030
delightful 398	discerning 846	ecstasy 1264
delineate 49	disclose 303	edifice 5
delude 996	disconcert 135	eerie 1170
delve 282	discord 1005	egalitarian 399
demagogue 57	discourse 738	egregious 577

elaborate 692	erratic 984	fatal 726
elate 113	erroneous 353	fathom 54
elicit 29	erudite 810	fatigue 166
eloquent 618	erudition 593	fauna 1134
elucidate 732	esoteric 805	fawning 814
elusive 241	espoused 731	feasible 708
emaciation 1265	estranged 317	feign 592
emanated 924	ethology 1269	ferocious 801
emancipation 145	euphemism 243	fertile 1038
embark on 1181	evade 262	fervently 156
embedded 11	evince 1270	fickle 698
embellished 999	evocation 1059	firmament 902
embodied 666	exalted 1004	fissure 719
emerge 930	exasperated 730	flagrant 257
eminent 102	excavate 1078	flamboyance 1001
emit 46	excised 835	flank 1168
empathy 711	exclaim 184	flaunt 411
empirical 608	excruciating 736	fleeting 1011
enact 741	exemplary 253	flicker 912
enchant 824	exemplify 635	flinch 463
enclose 7	exhilarated 404	florid 1272
encomium 1266	exiguity 1271	fluctuating 1034
encompassed 770	exile 629	flustered 95
encumbrance 715	exotic 638	foible 584
endeavor 1387	expatriate 564	foil 289
endemic 1267	expedite 952	folly 208
endorsement 490	expenditure 457	food-borne 1273
endow 1073	explicate 677	foolhardiness 229
enforced 862	exploit 477	foray 240
engender 374	expostulatory 1207	forbear 412
engulfing 196	exquisite 397	foreboded 889
ennobled 393	exterminate 319	foremost 665
enraged 794	extol 1141	foreseen 820
enshrine 916	extraneous 758	foreshadowed 987
ensue 557	extrapolate 578	forged 39
entail 559	extraterrestrial 540	forgo 656
entangled 1177	extravagance 915	forsake 436
enthralled 819	exuberance 325	forsooth 1274
entity 448	exultant 351	fortitude 523
enumerated 953		foster 274
envisaged 695	**F, f**	foul 1275
envision 813		fractured 1162
ephemeral 727	fabricate 458	fragmentary 595
epidemic 893	façade 926	frantic 756
epiphany 978	facet 151	fraudulent 786
epistemology 1388	facilitate 202	fray 524
epoch 976	faction 61	frenetic 494
equitable 1268	fallacious 82	fritter 1276
equivalent 910	falter 520	frivolous 620
equivocally 217	fascinate 551	frugal 444

fugitive	745
furnished	690
furtive	40
fuzzy	675

G, g

gaiety	396
gallant	406
galloped	970
galvanize	853
gangway	1193
gaped	873
garish	84
garner	1277
garrulous	183
gaudily	1129
gauge	278
genealogy	935
ghastly	1152
gibberish	197
glibly	1278
glimmering	870
gloat	326
gnaw	777
grandiose	1095
granulate	1279
grappling	787
grasping	1056
gratified	410
gregarious	195
grieving	507
grim	1050
grimace	1122
grind	1183
gritty	167
grotesque	1053
growling	1103
grudgingly	360
grunt	24
guise	442
gullible	956
guru	841
gynecology	1280

H, h

habituated	567
halting	268
hamper	344
haphazardly	309
hapless	583
harness	759
haste	205
haughty	724
havoc	716
headstone	1281
headwork	1282
hearth	858
heave	570
hectic	939
hedge	521
hedonist	529
hefty	1283
heinous	275
heresy	313
hermit	1111
hierarchy	1084
hinge	346
hoaxed	1100
hobble	415
holistic	1208
homily	162
homogenous	1130
hone	779
hound	532
hubris	968
huddled	1024
humdrum	851
hunched	265
hurled	1062
hyperbole	227

I, i

idiosyncrasy	616
idle	857
idyllic	510
illicit	861
ill-tempered	1104
illuminated	699
imbecility	1284
immense	1175
imminent	945
immobile	568
immurement	1057
immutable	597
impair	471
impart	459
impede	455
impelled	65
impenetrable	153
imperative	73
impetuous	881
imply	246
impoverished	694
improbable	78
improvise	339
impugne	1209
impulsively	62
impute	534
inaccessible	747
inadequate	709
inadvertent	254
inanimate	147
incarcerated	1176
incarnate	1156
incoherent	466
incompatible	1043
incomprehensible	569
inconceivable	1113
incongruous	81
inconspicuous	12
increment	1285
inculcate	1286
indefatigable	1287
indicting	132
indigenous	1031
indignant	1106
indispensable	150
indistinct	561
indoctrinated	1288
indulge	491
indulgent	295
ineffable	395
ineptitude	336
inexorable	177
inexplicable	1097
inextricable	356
infallible	366
inferior	718
infinitesimal	1171
infringe	647
ingeniously	269
ingrained	1289
inhabitant	909
inherent	573
inhumane	1173
injunction	206
innate	304

innocuous 667
innumerable 535
insolent 580
instigating 847
instill................................. 1015
insuperable 774
insurmountable................. 1290
intact................................. 479
interject 1291
intermittently 663
interrogate 63
intersperse 341
intimate 400
intimidating 244
intone 1292
intoxicated 173
intractable 1174
intricacy 552
intrinsically........................ 64
introvert 927
intrude 371
intuition 405
inundating 991
inure 67
invade 108
invariable.......................... 503
invidious 1293
invigorate 1294
invoking 1144
irksomeness 1295
irrelevant........................... 581
irreverently....................... 603
irrevocable 649
iterative 1296

J, j

jargon 1297
jaunt 1118
jeer.................................... 171
jeopardize 1153
jest.................................... 1165
jolted................................ 1074
jubilation.......................... 190
judicious 460
jumble 148
jut 1298
juxtaposed 542

K, k

kudos................................ 1299

L, l

laboriously 1300
lament 38
lampoon 1189
lancet 1301
lapse 130
lateralization 1185
lauded 194
lavishness 1045
laypeople 1302
leap 617
legitimate 79
leverage 1086
levity 1303
licentiousness 1304
limelight 1305
linger 203
lisp.................................... 1389
litany................................ 972
loathe 352
locale................................ 1390
locus 1210
looming 1306
lores 721
lucrative 668
ludicrous 806
lull 760
lumber 1307
luminary 1308
luminous 348
lurching 181
lurid 312
lurking 163

M, m

magnificent...................... 382
magnitude 1096
mainstay 1309
malevolent 1094
malfeasance 1190
malicious 512
mandate 896
maneuver.......................... 911
mangy 1310

manifest 612
manipulate 480
marveled 986
matriculate 1311
matrimony 1312
maxim 432
meager 979
meander 60
meddle 323
mediocre 486
meditate 445
medium 1091
menace 475
mend................................. 1154
mergence.......................... 659
mesmerized 553
methodically 221
meticulousness 143
miasma............................. 1313
microbial 1211
microcosm 226
milieu 993
minimize 789
mirth 1314
misanthrope 1315
miscellaneous 622
mischief 237
misfit................................ 93
misguide.......................... 955
mishap............................. 936
mislay 1316
misogyny......................... 1317
mogul 1318
moor 1319
morbid............................. 818
moribund......................... 748
morose............................. 231
mortgage 1391
mounting......................... 1392
multifaceted 757
mundane 749
munition 1320
murals 1194
murky 1075
muster 795
mutation 1321
mutual 1322
myriad 44

N, n

natter 596
nebulous 528
negate 526
neural 1323
neutralize 1324
nomadic 1133
nomenclature 271
nonchalant 211
nostalgically 290
notable 937
notion 447
notorious 242
nourishment 1101
novice 129
noxious 651
nuance 1108
nucleus 1325
nudged 1002
nuisances 764

O, o

obfuscated 792
obligatory 1124
oblique 17
obliterate 320
oblivious 133
obnoxious 1058
obscene 1126
obscured 200
obsolete 354
obstetrics 1326
obtrusive 1327
ominous 45
omit 461
omnipotent 138
omnipresence 438
omniscient 223
onslaught 21
opacity 743
opine 614
oppressive 16
opulence 1328
opulent 80
ordeal 435
ornate 1089
oscillated 1145
ostensible 931

ostentatious 697
outlandish 305
outmoded 537
overarching 1329
overborne 472
overshadowed 689
oversight 1212
overtly 928

P, p

painstaking 1092
palatial 696
palpable 131
paltry 772
paradoxical 894
paramount 504
paranoia 232
paraphernalia 1079
paraphrase 122
parched 1135
parity 1330
parlor 502
parochial 566
parsimonious 103
partisan 633
pastime 437
pastoral 565
patently 680
Paternal 767
pathogen 1331
patriarch 453
patron 85
patter 621
paucity 1160
pavement 842
peculiar 462
pedant 626
pedantic 111
pedestal 28
pedestrian 914
peevish 816
pelt 23
penetrating 126
pensive 76
perch 467
peregrine 563
perennial 839
perilous 895
peripheral 582

periphery 1332
permeate 358
pernicious 948
perpetrate 752
perpetual 128
personnel 210
perspicacious 737
pertained 891
perturbed 863
perusal 1333
pervaded 761
perverse 139
pessimistic 321
petition 1147
petulant 230
pharmaceutical 288
philanthropic 964
pidgin 1032
pillaging 1213
pioneer 158
pious 247
piquant 1182
pittance 790
pitted 1334
pivotal 307
placid 579
plaintiffs 1335
plaintive 1336
plausible 1048
pledge 949
plethora 1020
pliable 361
plodded 739
plummet 1214
poignant 146
polarized 643
pollination 1337
pompous 683
ponderous 1195
porcelain 946
portentous 283
posterity 1093
posthumously 1215
postulation 388
postural 1216
potent 509
pragmatic 645
prancing 982
prattle 1338
preamble 298

Word	Page
precarious	488
precipitate	373
predate	355
predation	1186
predestined	1016
predicaments	1047
predilections	1339
predisposed	389
predominantly	864
preeminent	439
preempt	212
preexistent	125
prejudices	1393
premature	646
premeditate	755
premise	154
premonitory	97
preoccupation	803
preposterous	1099
prerequisite	1217
prerogative	1140
preside	650
pretext	556
prevail	428
primeval	1340
primordial	1341
pristine	687
probe	681
proclaim	527
procure	1342
prodigy	765
profane	661
profusion	8
proliferate	1343
proliferation	392
promulgate	1344
prone	882
propagandist	155
propelled	1166
propensity	424
prophesy	72
propitious	950
prosecute	1178
prospect	908
protagonist	975
protocol	1196
protocol	832
protract	1345
provoke	994
prowl	401
proximate	1346
prudent	35
pry	742
pseudonym	1083
pseudoscience	1188
psychoanalysis	1394
puffery	489
punctilious	1347
punctuality	1348
pundits	1022
pupil	51
purported	88
putrefaction	1061

Q, q

Word	Page
quagmire	729
quandary	735
quasi	804
query	874
quintessential	48
quip	1021
quirk	611
quiver	1218
quiver	925

R, r

Word	Page
raconteur	781
rag	837
rage	219
raiding	142
rake	140
rambling	1127
rambunctious	498
ramification	959
rampage	922
rapacious	852
rapport	1014
rashly	640
raucous	543
ravage	947
raven	496
reaffirmed	660
realm	919
reap	33
rebel	292
rebukingly	855
rebuttal	446
recalcitrant	141
recede	607
reciprocal	207
reckoning	942
reconcile	1009
recoup	1137
rectify	929
recuperated	807
recur	188
redeem	1179
redress	1136
reel	337
refined	823
refracting	333
refuge	590
refute	294
regimen	124
regiment	1349
regressively	957
rehash	625
reign	670
reined	1149
reiterate	121
rejoice	1003
rekindle	1350
relegated	664
relentless	118
relish	107
reminiscence	990
remnants	954
remorse	1036
render	199
renounce	225
repatriate	1351
repellent	464
repentantly	513
repercussions	1019
repertoire (repertory)	1087
replete	1072
replicating	1006
repose	989
repress	644
reproach	536
repudiated	826
repugnant	213
resilient	544
resolute	658
resolve	1060
retain	514
retaliate	1121
retardation	1352

reticent 634	senile 1358	stifle 662
retrospective 1353	seraph 1359	stilts 1368
revelation 245	serendipitous 112	stipulation 1369
revelers 1219	serenely 549	straddle 301
revere 815	servile 363	stranded 1080
revile 1000	shard 306	strapped 1370
rhetorically 285	shoal 1221	strenuous 938
riddle 310	shrewd 963	stumped 850
righteous 642	shrilled 1360	stupefied 50
rigid 869	shroud 1361	subdued 114
rigorous 434	shudder 349	subjugate 921
roam 899	shun 1131	sublime 413
roguish 654	sinister 723	subordinate 159
rotunda 1191	skim 845	subplot 1110
rudiment 484	skulk 266	substrate 1371
ruefully 1220	sloth 178	subversion 296
ruffled 965	sluggish 591	succinct 69
ruminate 420	slumping 800	succor 1025
ruptured 706	slurs 827	succour 1396
ruthless 287	smear 967	succumb 165
	smudge 1116	suffrage 1070
S, s	snag 1065	sumptuous 702
	snatch 297	superfluous 456
sagacious 1068	snide 98	supplant 511
salient 1354	snobby 204	surge 951
salvage 106	snort 575	surpassed 888
sanction 249	sober 539	surreptitious 169
sanctuary 280	sojourn 728	swaddled 1397
sanguine 1355	solemn 68	swell 871
sapphic 1395	solicitous 2	swindle 259
sardonically 704	somber 969	symbiosis 299
saturated 1114	sordid 828	symposium 1398
savage 860	sparse 1362	synthesis 1010
scaffolding 1158	spearhead 1363	systemic 1399
scanty 821	speciation 1222	
scavenge 903	spelunking 1364	**T, t**
sceptic 1356	spew 470	
schema 1197	spout 605	tacitly 958
scheme 878	sprawl 402	taint 376
scions 1198	sputtered 923	taken aback 960
scorn 1017	squander 713	tame 594
scrawled 885	squint 276	tamper 574
scruple 476	stark 601	tantalizing 907
scrupulous 1357	staunch 1365	tedious 172
scrutinize 99	staving 1366	teeter 115
seclusion 840	stellar 308	telltale 1372
sedimentary 1161	sterile 707	temper 808
seduce 981	sterling 1367	tempestuous 576
seeped 746	stern 657	tenaciously 838
seismic 791	stiff 1049	tenant 449

tenets 829	unfold 913	vulnerable 403
tether 884	unforeseen 1029	
throes 725	unfurled 1150	**W, w**
thwart 182	unorthodox 1223	
timbre 798	unprecedented 1200	waddle 1119
timid 248	unravel 422	wade 1184
timorous 497	unrestrained 1044	wander 9
tinging 1040	unstinting 450	wane 550
toil 149	unwieldy 1378	ward 940
topography 1033	unwittingly 1379	weathering 1381
trajectory 426	upheaval 1037	whim 720
tramp 417	urge 330	wilt 600
tranquil 96	usurpation 1224	wily 1382
transcribe 235	utilitarian 1077	witty 19
transgression 483		wobble 898
transient 1373	**V, v**	wrath 944
translucent 886		wrench 380
transmute 531	vagary 362	wretch 1051
traverse 740	valiant 137	writhing 1383
treachery 501	validate 1380	
tremulous 932	valor 1018	**X, x**
trepidation 1	vandalism 1225	
tribunal 1163	vanishingly 1082	xenophobic 1384
trite 414	vanity 168	
trove 1088	vanquish 26	**Z, z**
truncate 495	vaulting 1054	
tumultuous 623	vaunt 193	zealous 189
turbulence 631	vehemently 220	
turf 868	venerated 77	
turmoil 1199	vengeance 639	
tutelage 1374	veracity 1201	
tween 1375	verbose 849	
tyrant 966	verdict 648	
	verge 714	
U, u	verify 110	
	verity 377	
ubiquitous 87	vernacular 53	
unassuming 1376	versatile 127	
unawares 1400	vetoed 1069	
unbidden 1377	vicissitude 985	
underlying 892	vigor 671	
undermine 329	vilify 233	
underscored 1146	villain 485	
undeterred 571	vindicate 286	
undulation 1067	vituperations 817	
unease 379	void 1151	
unequivocally 267	volatile 473	
unerring 586	voluptuous 613	
unethical 848	voracious 409	
unfettered 1027	vulgar 1123	

Paul's SAT® Vocabulary

지 은 이	김동현
발 행 인	김동현
발 행 처	엘티씨 (LTC)
출판등록	2008년 12월 24일
주　　소	서울특별시 성북구 북악산로 831 201-504
대표전화	02-558-2715
홈페이지	http://www.paulacademy.net
	http://blog.naver.com/paulacademy

ISBN 979-11-86461-06-8 (53740)

※ 이 책은 엘티씨(LTC)가 저작권자와의 계약에 따라 발행한 것이므로 본사의 허락 없이는 어떠한 형태와 수단으로도 이 책의 내용을 이용하지 못합니다.

※ 잘못된 책은 구입하신 서점에서 바꾸어 드립니다.

PaulAcademy
LEARN · TRY · FLY

732	elucidate	설명하다	clarify and explain
733	drastic	극단적인	extreme, intense
734	criteria	기준	standards of judgment
735	quandary	진퇴양난, 곤경	dilemma, difficulty
736	excruciating	몹시 고통스러운	incredibly painful; arduous
737	perspicacious	총명한, 명민한	shrewd, astute
738	discourse	담론	conversation or dialogue
739	plodded	터벅터벅 걷다	walk heavily
740	traverse	가로지르다	cross
741	enact	상연, 연기하다	to represent or perform in or as if in a play
742	pry	캐묻다	to inquire impertinently or unnecessarily into something
743	opacity	불투명	lack of clarity; cloudiness
744	contour	윤곽	silhouette, outline
745	fugitive	덧없는, 사라지는	fleeting, lasting a short time
746	seeped	스미다, 배다	permeate, soak
747	inaccessible	가까워지기 어려운, 접근하기 어려운, 먼	distant, out of reach
748	moribund	빈사 상태의	in a dying state, near death
749	mundane	재미없는, 일상의	ordinary or common (often with negative connotation)
750	afflicted	괴로워하는, 고통받는	suffering, tormented
751	contempt	경멸	disdain
752	perpetrate	(범죄를) 저지르다	to commit (used for crimes)
753	distress	고통, 괴로움	great pain, anxiety, or sorrow; acute physical or mental suffering
754	clasp	움켜쥐다	to seize, grip, or grasp with the hand
755	premeditate	미리 숙고하다	to plan, propose
756	frantic	정신 없이 서두르는	desperate or wild with excitement, passion, fear, pain, etc.
757	multifaceted	다면적인	having many facets, as a gem
758	extraneous	관련 없는	unnecessarily extra; superfluous
759	harness	이용하다	to bring under conditions for effective use
760	lull	소강상태	pause; moment of inactivity
761	pervaded	팽배한	spread throughout; was ubiquitous or omnipresent
762	amidst	~한 가운데에, ~에 둘러싸여	in the middle of, surrounded by
763	anonymous	익명의	not identified by name n.anonymity
764	nuisances	성가신 사람	an obnoxious person, annoyance, pest
765	prodigy	영재	genius at a young age; precocious person
766	bigoted	편견이 심한	prejudiced or racist
767	paternal	아버지의	characteristic or befitting of a father
768	anomaly	변칙	something which doesn't fit a pattern or rule; abnormality
769	consigned	위임된, 위탁된, 맡겨진	assigned, handed over for care
770	encompassed	둘러싸다, 에워싸다	surround, encircle
771	caucuses	회의, 모임	gathering, meeting, assembly
772	paltry	하찮은 사소한	of little importance; insignificant
773	chronicle	연대기	an extended account in prose presented in chronological order
774	insuperable	난공불락의	unable to be defeated
775	defied	거역하다	challenge, confront
776	ascertain	확인하다	check for accuracy
777	gnaw	갉아먹다	wear away, erode
778	crumble	바스러지다	to break into small fragments or crumbs
779	hone	연마하다	to make more acute or effective, improve, perfect
780	dreadful	끔찍한, 지독한	extremely bad, unpleasant, or ugly
781	raconteur	이야기꾼	storyteller (one who recounts)
782	coarse	거친	rude and unsociable; vulgar

#	Word	Korean	English
783	amenities	편의시설	a feature of a house which gives comfort (eg. Beds, plumbing, etc)
784	archaic	낡은, 구식의	antiquated, ancient
785	decry	헐뜯다, 매도하다	criticize
786	fraudulent	기만하는, 사기를 치는	cheating, dishonest
787	grappling	(해결책을 찾아) 고심하다	deal with, cope
788	collude	공모하다	to co-operate
789	minimize	최소화하다	to reduce to smallest possible amount
790	pittance	아주 적은 보수	a small salary
791	seismic	(영향, 규모가) 엄청난	of enormous proportions or having highly significant consequences
792	obfuscated	어리둥절한, 혼란스러운	perplexed and confused
793	arbitrary	임의적인, 제멋대로의	despotic or tyrannical ; referring to randomness
794	enraged	격분한, 화가 난	exasperated, angered
795	muster	모으다, 소집하다	gather or bring together for a service
796	benign	상냥한	benevolent
797	conciliatory	달래는	attempting to placate or behave in an acquiescent manner, conciliate
798	timbre	음색	tone
799	dismayed	낙담한	thoroughly disheartened
800	slumping	털썩 앉은	falling heavily or collapsing
801	ferocious	흉포한, 너무한	violent, brutal, truculent
802	anguish	고민, 고뇌	great suffering or distress
803	preoccupation	집착	obsession or fixation
804	quasi	외견상, 표면상	seemingly
805	esoteric	비전의	mysterious ; hard to understand ; arcane
806	ludicrous	터무니없는	causing laughter because of absurdity
807	recuperated	회복하다	recover, improve in health
808	temper	온화시키다	moderate

#	Word	Korean	English
705	despair	절망	feeling of hopelessness
706	ruptured	파열된	broken apart; exploded
707	sterile	아무 소득이 없는	not productive of results, ideas, etc.
708	feasible	실현 가능한	possible
709	inadequate	불충분한	not adequate or sufficient
710	catastrophically	파멸로, 비극으로	disastrously
711	empathy	감정이입, 공감	feeling of pity or sadness for another person's distress
712	anachronistic	시대착오적인	not fitting the times; from the wrong time period
713	squander	낭비하다	waste, use up
714	verge	길가	edge; brink
715	encumbrance	짐, 폐	burden or hardship
716	havoc	대재앙, 큰 혼란	chaotic situation
717	adrift	표류하는, 떠내려가는	loose from moorings or out of control
718	inferior	낮은, 열등한	lower, less in rank
719	fissure	갈게 갈라진 틈	a narrow opening produced by cleavage or separation of parts
720	whim	일시적인 변덕	an odd or capricious notion or desire; a freakish fancy
721	lores	설화, 전통	folklore, myth
722	capricious	변덕스러운	unpredictable, whimsical, mercurial
723	sinister	사악한	evil ; destructive
724	haughty	교만	overly proud of oneself; supercilious
725	throes	고통, 고투	pain, suffering, misery
726	fatal	치명적인, 해로운	deleterious, deadly
727	ephemeral	일시적인	momentary, short-lived
728	sojourn	체류	trip or brief stay
729	quagmire	수렁	very difficult problem; conundrum
730	exasperated	몹시 화가 난	annoyed and vexed
731	espoused	쓰다, 채택하다	adopt

#	Word	Korean	English
678	colossal	거대한, 엄청난	enormous, huge
679	abject	아주 비참한	hopeless or very low
680	patently	명백히, 틀림없이	obviously; blatantly
681	probe	캐묻다, 조사하다	to search into or examine thoroughly
682	deceit	속임수, 기만	duplicity, deception
683	pompous	거만한	arrogant, pretentious
684	contemptuous	경멸하는	feeling something is inferior or worthy of hatred; dismissive
685	abnormal	비정상의	not normal; deviating from what is usual
686	complicity	공모	partnership in wrongdoing (as accomplices)
687	pristine	아주 깨끗한	in an original, pure state
688	alternative	대안, 선택 가능한 것	(of one or more things) available as another possibility
689	overshadowed	그늘을 드리우다, 빛을 잃게 만들다	make obscure or dim
690	furnished	비치된	decorated, supplied
691	configured	구성된, 배열된	arranged, structured
692	elaborate	정교한	worked out with great care and nicety of detail
693	designated	지정된	to nominate, or select for duty
694	impoverished	빈약한, 힘면 없는	poor, deprived of strength
695	envisaged	예상, 상상하다	imagine
696	palatial	으리으리한	grand, opulent
697	ostentatious	호사스러운	very showy or expensive-looking
698	fickle	변덕스러운	temperamental, capricious
699	illuminated	빛이 비춰지는	supplied or brightened with light
700	disinterested	객관적이, 무관심한	neutral
701	celestial	하늘의, 천외의	heavenly; sublime; ethereal
702	sumptuous	호화스러운	fancy, luxurious
703	depicting	그리다	to represent by or as if by painting
704	sardonically	냉소적으로	sarcastically
809	contentious	논쟁을 조래할	tending to argue or quarrel
810	erudite	학식 있는	learned; scholarly
811	catalyst	촉매	something that motivates or causes activity to occur
812	affirmation	확언	agreement or 'yes' response
813	envision	마음 속에 그리다, 상상하다	imagine or picture mentally
814	fawning	아양 떠는	flattering or sycophantic; trying to gain favor by praising or following
815	revere	숭배하다	respect, worship
816	peevish	짜증 잘내는	argumentative or annoyed; fractious
817	vituperations	혹평	severe criticism, castigation
818	morbid	병적인	suggesting an unhealthy mental state or attitude
819	enthralled	마음을 사로잡는	deeply attracted or fixated on something
820	foreseen	예견하다, ~일 거라고 생각하다	anticipate, predict
821	scanty	얼마 안 되는	very little; insufficient
822	discredit	존경심을 떨어뜨리다	to injure the credit or reputation of
823	refined	세련된, 교양 있는	sophisticated, polished, cultivated
824	enchant	황홀하게 하다	to delight, to the point where it seems magical
825	detaching	떼다, 분리하다	cut off, sever
826	repudiated	거절하다, 거부하다	reject
827	slurs	비방, 중상하는 말	slander, innuendo
828	sordid	비도덕적인	dirty or vulgar (not sophisticated); lurid
829	tenets	주의, 교리	statements of belief
830	chasm	아주 깊은 틈	wide space; gulf
831	breach	위반	break or transgression (as in a set of rules)
832	protocol	외교 의례, 프로토콜	the customs and regulations dealing with diplomatic formality
833	assure	장담하다, 확언하다	convince, persuade

#	Word	Korean	English
834	**abundantly**	아주 풍부한	present in great quantity
835	**excised**	삭제된	deleted
836	**assertiveness**	적극적인	confidently aggressive or self-assured
837	**rag**	놀리다	tease
838	**tenaciously**	끈덕지게	stubbornly; in a recalcitrant manner
839	**perennial**	지속되는	lasting for an indefinitely long time
840	**seclusion**	은둔, 고립	isolation
841	**guru**	전문가	expert
842	**pavement**	포장도로	a road covered with asphalt
843	**autonomy**	독립, 자유	independence
844	**denouncing**	맹렬히 비난하다	criticize, excoriate
845	**skim**	훑어보다	look through
846	**discerning**	안목이 있는	having excellent taste; discriminating
847	**instigating**	착수하게 하다, 남을 부추기다	urge, foment, stimulate
848	**unethical**	비윤리적인, 비도덕적인	corrupt, immoral
849	**verbose**	장황한	wordy, circumlocutory
850	**stumped**	당황한, 쩔쩔매는	confused, perplexed
851	**humdrum**	단조로운, 따분한	boring
852	**rapacious**	탐욕스러운	given to seizing for plunder or the satisfaction of greed
853	**galvanize**	활기를 북돋다	energize or inspire
854	**constricted**	수축된, 조여진	compressed, cramped
855	**rebukingly**	꾸짖는 투로	scoldingly, with disapproval
856	**declaimed**	낭송하다, 읊다	recite, make a formal speech
857	**idle**	나태한	not working or active; doing nothing
858	**hearth**	난로, 화덕	the floor of a fireplace
859	**barren**	불모의	unproductive; unfruitful
860	**savage**	야만적인	uncivilized

#	Word	Korean	English
651	**noxious**	해로운	harmful
652	**contaminating**	오염시키는	affecting negatively
653	**conjecture**	추측하다	assume, guess
654	**roguish**	악당 같은	acting like a rogue; knavish
655	**desolate**	적막한	empty and gloomy
656	**forgo**	포기하다	give up
657	**stern**	엄격한, 단호한	strict, harsh
658	**resolute**	단호한	firmly resolved or determined
659	**mergence**	합체, 융합	coming together or uniting; coalescence
660	**reaffirmed**	확언된, 확인된	acknowledged, affirmed
661	**profane**	불경한	impious or irreverent
662	**stifle**	억누르다	suppress
663	**intermittently**	간헐적	occasionally
664	**relegated**	좌천[강등]당한	sent down to a lower level
665	**foremost**	가장 중요한	primary, most important
666	**embodied**	구현된, 표현된	represented, manifested
667	**innocuous**	악의 없는	harmless
668	**lucrative**	수익성이 좋은	profitable
669	**depute**	위임[위탁]하다	appoint, instruct
670	**reign**	통치기간	the period during which a king or queen rules a country
671	**vigor**	활력	liveliness or energy; earnestness
672	**counterfeit**	위조의, 모조의	made in imitation; not genuine
673	**connotation**	함축된 의미	the associated or secondary meaning
674	**disenchanted**	환상에서 깨어난	free from enchantment, illusion, or credulity
675	**fuzzy**	어렴풋한	indistinct, blurred
676	**bombastically**	과장되게, 허풍스럽게	pretentiously
677	**explicate**	설명하다	explain, expound

#	Word	Korean	English
625	rehash	반복하다	repeat
626	pedant	세세한 것에 얽매이는 사람	a person who overemphasizes rules or minor details
627	bustle	바삐 움직이다	move with a great show of energy
628	aggressive	공격적인, 적대적인	hostile, contentious
629	exile	망명, 추방	expulsion from one's native land by authoritative decree
630	beget	야기하다, 일으키다	create, cause
631	turbulence	격돌, 난기류	trouble and chaos
632	disruptive	지장을 주는	preventing something from acting in a normal way
633	partisan	열렬한 신봉자	an adherent or supporter of a person, group, party, or cause
634	reticent	말이 없는	disposed to be silent or not to speak freely
635	exemplify	예를 들다	illustrate by example; typify
636	disparage	폄하하다	speak of or treat slightly
637	affront	모욕하다	offend
638	exotic	외국의, 이국적인	of foreign origin or character
639	vengeance	복수	violent revenge
640	rashly	성급하게	too hastily; without thinking of the consequences
641	bristling	~으로 꽉 찬	to be thickly set or filled with something
642	righteous	도덕적으로 옳은	morally right or justifiable
643	polarized	양극화된, 나뉜	divided, separated
644	repress	억누르다	put pressure on; control
645	pragmatic	실용적인	of a practical point of view or practical considerations
646	premature	너무 이른, 시기상조의	mature or ripe before the proper time
647	infringe	위반하다	violate, disobey
648	verdict	판결	a judgment, decision
649	irrevocable	변경할 수 없는	not to be revoked or recalled
650	preside	통제하다	control, have authority over

#	Word	Korean	English
861	illicit	불법의	illegal, forbidden
862	enforced	집행하다	apply, implement, impose
863	perturbed	혼란된	annoyed or disturbed
864	predominantly	대개, 대부분	having ascendancy, power, authority, or influence over others
865	descend	내려가다	to go or pass from a higher to a lower place
866	apocryphal	출처가 불분명한	not true; chimerical
867	culinary	요리의	of, relating to, or used in cooking or the kitchen
868	turf	잔디	grass
869	rigid	단단한	stiff; not flexible
870	glimmering	희미하게 빛나다	gleam, flicker
871	swell	불룩해지다	to rise in waves, as the sea
872	commemorate	기념하다	to honor the memory of by some observance
873	gaped	(놀라서) 바라보다	gawk, stare with open mouth
874	query	의문, 문의	objection, inquiry
875	conducive	도움이 되는	useful, helpful
876	buoyant	부력이 있는, 물에 뜨는	able to float (metaphorically, refers to a cheerful and upbeat personality) n.buoyancy
877	befitting	적당한, 어울리는	suitable, proper
878	scheme	계획	plan, project
879	brashly	성급하게, 경솔하게	recklessly
880	chided	꾸짖다	scold; reproach
881	impetuous	성급하게	hurriedly, hastily
882	prone	(좋지 않은 일을 하기) 쉬운	liable, disposed
883	crude	대강의	lacking finish, polish, or completeness
884	tether	묶다	to tie
885	scrawled	휘갈겨쓰다	scribble, inscribe

#	Word	Korean	English
886	translucent	반투명한	permitting lights to pass through but not so clearly visible
887	codified	성문화된(글이나 문서로 나타냄)	to organize or arrange systematically, especially in writing
888	surpassed	뛰어넘다, 능가하다	outpace, beat
889	foreboded	징조가 되다	presage, predict
890	advent	도래, 출현	arrival, beginning, coming
891	pertained	적용되다	to have reference or relation
892	underlying	기저를 그리다	to lie under or beneath
893	epidemic	널리 퍼진	prevalent, widespread
894	paradoxical	역설의, 자가모순의	self-contradictory
895	perilous	아주 위험한	dangerous or threatening
896	mandate	명령하다	commanded, ordered
897	conceive	마음속으로 하다, 상상하다	to form a notion or idea of
898	wobbled	흔들리다	waver between two points or decisions
899	roam	배회하다	wander without purpose
900	clutter	막 어지르다	to find or litter with things in a disorderly manner
901	debris	잔해, 쓰레기	garbage; detritus
902	firmament	창공, 하늘	the vault of heaven, sky
903	scavenge	쓰레기더미를 뒤지다	to take or gather from discarded material
904	astute	약삭빠른, 총명한	intelligent, perceptive
905	captivating	매력적인, 매혹적인	fascinating, attractive
906	beguiled	꼴다, 이끌다	allure, entice
907	tantalizing	애타게 하는	tempting (used for things which cannot be easily obtained)
908	prospect	가망, 전망	an apparent probability of advancement, success, profit
909	inhabitant	주민	a person or animal that inhabits a place, especially as a permanent resident
910	equivalent	동등한	equal in value

#	Word	Korean	English
599	diminish	줄어들다	make or cause to seem smaller
600	wilt	말라 죽다, 시들다	weaken, fade, wither
601	stark	완전한, 극명한	blunt, utter
602	accord	합의	agreement
603	irreverently	비꼿듯이	without respect; impiously
604	condemn	규탄하다	pronounce to be guilty
605	spout	지껄이다, 말씀하다	talk or speak at some length or in an oratorical manner
606	amplify	더 자세히 설명하다	expand in stating or describing
607	recede	사라지다, 물러나다	go or move away; retreat; withdraw
608	empirical	경험에 의한	derived from or guided by experience
609	drudgery	힘들고 단조로운 일	menial, distasteful, dull, or hard work
610	dilute	약화시키다	reduce the strength or force
611	quirk	별난 성격	a peculiarity of action, behavior, or personality
612	manifest	분명하다, 나타내다	make clear or evident; show plainly
613	voluptuous	관능적인	full of luxury, pleasure, and sensuous enjoyment
614	opine	의견을 밝히다	hold or express an opinion
615	caricature	희화/풍자화한 그림	a picture, ludicrously exaggerating the peculiarities of person or things
616	idiosyncrasy	특별한 점	a characteristic, habit, mannerism
617	leap	서둘러 ~하다	move or act quickly or suddenly
618	eloquent	유창한	articulate, distinctive
619	conundrum	수수께끼	problem or puzzle
620	frivolous	바보 같은, 까부는	foolish
621	patter	재잘거리다	babble
622	miscellaneous	이것저것 다양한	having various qualities, aspects, or subjects
623	tumultuous	떠들썩한	boisterous, raucous
624	belittlement	비하, 얕보여김	depreciation; abasement, disparagement

#	Word	Korean	Definition
573	inherent	타고난	in-born or innate; something one has as part of one's nature
574	tamper	간섭하다, 참견하다	meddle, interfere
575	snort	콧귀를 뀌다	express contempt, indignation
576	tempestuous	격렬한	wild, stormy
577	egregious	지독하게 나쁜	outstandingly bad
578	extrapolate	추론하다	deduce, infer
579	placid	차분한, 얌전한	calm, tranquil
580	insolent	무례한, 버릇없는	rude; impudent
581	irrelevant	무관한	not applicable or pertinent
582	peripheral	주변적인	concerned with relatively minor, irrelevant aspects of the subject
583	hapless	불운한	unlucky
584	foible	약점	weakness, flaw
585	ambivalent	결정할 수 없는	being unable to choose between the two
586	unerring	틀림없는, 정확한	accurate
587	abysmal	심히 나쁜, 끔찍한	extremely hopeless, wretched
588	cognitive	인식의	of or relating to the mental processes of perception, memory, judgment, and reasoning
589	cohesion	화합, 결합	the act or state of uniting or sticking together
590	refuge	피난처	protection; a safe place
591	sluggish	느릿느릿한	inactive, lethargic
592	feign	가장하다	fake; affect
593	erudition	학식	academic knowledge
594	tame	재미없는, 맛맛한	dull, insipid
595	fragmentary	부분적인	consisting of or reduced to fragments, incomplete
596	natter	수다	foolish and vapid conversation; chatter
597	immutable	변경할 수 없는	unchangeable; eternal
598	deteriorate	악화되다	degenerate, languish

#	Word	Korean	Definition
911	maneuver	교묘히 이동하다	to change the position according to tactics
912	flicker	깜박거리다	to burn unsteadily; shine with a wavering light
913	unfold	퍼지다	spread
914	pedestrian	재미없는	lacking in vitality, imagination; commonplace
915	extravagance	낭비, 사치	excessive or unnecessary expenditure or outlay of money
916	enshrine	소중히 간직하다	to cherish as sacred
917	compliant	순종적인	obedient
918	chimera	불가능한 생각	an illusion; something not real
919	realm	영역	dimension, domain
920	conquer	정복하다	defeat, overcome
921	subjugate	지배하에 두다	to bring under complete control or subjection
922	rampage	광란, 소란	disturbance, commotion, violence
923	sputtered	더듬더듬 말하다	stammer, falter
924	emanated	내뿜는	flowed out of; wafted from
925	quiver	떨다	to shake with a slight but rapid motion
926	façade	표면, 허울	veneer, appearance
927	introvert	내성적인, 내향적인	solitary and quiet; diffident; shy
928	overtly	명백히	apparently, obviously
929	rectify	교정하다	correct or fix
930	emerge	출현하다	to come forth into view or notice, as from concealment or obscurity
931	ostensible	표면적으로	based on appearances; seemingly (usually contrasted with the way something actually is)
932	tremulous	약간 떠는	trembling or quivering (usually with great emotion)
933	eccentricities	기이함	unique, personal mannerisms; quirks
934	cliché	상투적인 문구	a trite, stereotyped expression
935	genealogy	족보	family tree

#	Word	Korean	English
936	mishap	사고, 불행	accident
937	notable	주목할 만한, 눈에 띄는	noteworthy, distinguished
938	strenuous	힘이 많이 드는, 몹시 힘든	arduous, demanding
939	hectic	정신없이 바쁜	characterized by intense agitation, excitement, and rapid movement
940	ward	병실	a division, floor, or room of a hospital for a particular class or group of patients
941	affinity	친밀함	sense of friendship or similarity of feeling; kinship (like kindred)
942	reckoning	계산, 추정	a judgment
943	alienate	(사람을 소원하게/외지게 만들다)	cause (someone) to feel isolated or estranged
944	wrath	분노	anger or vindictive rage
945	imminent	목전의, 임박한	forthcoming, immediate
946	porcelain	자기	ceramic
947	ravage	황폐하게 만들다, 파괴하다	ruin, devastate, destroy
948	pernicious	치명적인	harmful or malicious; having detrimental intentions
949	pledge	맹세하다	to promise solemnly
950	propitious	유리한	having favorable conditions; having good signs for the future; opportune
951	surge	치밀어 오름, 밀려듦	deluge, flood
952	expedite	더 신속하게 처리하다	to speed up the progress of
953	enumerated	열거하다	to mention separately as if in counting
954	remnants	나머지, 잔여물	leftover, residue
955	misguide	잘못 이끌다	to guide wrongly
956	gullible	남을 잘 믿는	easily deceived or cheated
957	regressively	퇴보하여	reverting
958	tacitly	무언으로	without being said; understood
959	ramification	파문, 영향	a related or derived subject, problem, etc.

#	Word	Korean	English
547	disregard	무시하다, 묵살하다	ignore, pay no attention to
548	concur	동의하다	agree
549	serenely	차분하게	calmly, peacefully
550	wane	줄어들다, 약해지다	subside, diminish
551	fascinate	매료시키다	attract and hold attentively
552	intricacy	복잡한 사항들	complicated matter
553	mesmerized	마음이 사로잡힌, 매료된	hypnotized, captivated
554	ardor	열정	passion; vehemence
555	defraud	속이다, 사기치다	cheat or deceive
556	pretext	구실	something to conceal a true purpose; an ostensible reason
557	ensue	뒤따르다	follow; happen as a result
558	confide	털어놓다	tell a secret to a trusted friend
559	entail	수반하다, 포함하다	involve, require
560	covert	은밀한	concealed; secret; disguised
561	indistinct	또렷하지 않은	not clearly marked or defined
562	derive	얻다, 끌어내다	obtain, glean
563	peregrine	외국의, 외래의	foreign, alien, coming from abroad
564	expatriate	국외 거주자	someone who is living in a country which is not their own
565	pastoral	시골의, 소박한	related to the countryside, outside of the city; rural
566	parochial	편협한	narrow-minded (used for those from rural areas)
567	habituated	길들여진, 익숙한	used to, accustomed to
568	immobile	움직이지 않는	incapable of being moved or moving
569	incomprehensible	이해할 수 없는	impossible to understand or comprehend
570	heave	들썩거리다	cause to rise and fall with a swelling motion
571	undeterred	단념[좌절]하지 않는	not discouraged
572	artifice	책략, 계략	hoax, gimmick

#	Word	Korean	English
522	ambiguous	애매모호한	of doubtful or uncertain nature, difficult to comprehend
523	fortitude	불굴의 용기	bravery, boldness
524	fray	싸움, 소동	fight, battle
525	corollary	필연적인 결과	a natural consequence or result
526	negate	부인하다	deny the existence, evidence, or truth of
527	proclaim	선언하다	to announce or declare in an open manner
528	nebulous	모호한, 애매한	vague, unclear
529	hedonist	쾌락주의자	lover of pleasure (usually immorally); a licentious person
530	contend	주장하다	to assert
531	transmute	변화시키다	transform completely
532	hound	사냥개	a dog trained to hunt a game by sight or by scent
533	arid	건조한	dry; desiccated
534	impute	~에게 돌리다, 전가하다	ascribe, attribute
535	innumerable	많은	many, numerous
536	reproach	비난	blame or criticism
537	outmoded	유행에 뒤떨어진	gone out of style; no longer fashionable
538	coerced	강요된	compelled by force
539	sober	술 취하지 않은	not intoxicated or drunk
540	extraterrestrial	외계인	an alien
541	docile	유순한, 고분고분한	meek, gentle
542	juxtaposed	병치하다, 나란히 놓다	place close together or side by side
543	raucous	요란한 가진	loud and potentially destructive; rambunctious
544	resilient	회복력 있는	springing back, rebounding
545	complacent	자기만족적인	self-satisfied, often not aware of potential danger
546	avarice	탐욕	insatiable greed for riches
960	taken aback	충이 역풍을 받고	taken by surprise
961	concealing	숨기다, 감추다	hide, keep secret
962	abstaining	자제하는	hold back, cease
963	shrewd	면밀히 살피는, 예리한	probing, penetrating, judicious
964	philanthropic	인정많은, 박애주의의	charitable, humanitarian
965	ruffled	헝클어진	disorganized or untidy; bedraggled
966	tyrant	폭군	powerful leader who allows few freedoms; despot
967	smear	명예를 훼손하다	tarnish, slur
968	hubris	자만심	excessive pride or self-confidence
969	somber	어두침침한	gloomy or mournful
970	galloped	전력질주하다	go fast, race, or hurry
971	cuddle	껴안다	hug tightly, snuggle
972	litany	장황한 설명	a prolonged or tedious account
973	devastate	황폐하게 만들다	lay waste, render desolate
974	accessible	이해하기 쉬운	easy to understand
975	protagonist	주인공	main character of a novel or play
976	epoch	시대	era, period
977	credence	신용성	historical evidence lends credence to his theory
978	epiphany	(어떤 사물에 대한) 직관	sudden realization
979	meager	메마른, 불충분한	in small amount; insufficient; scanty
980	abolish	폐지하다	to do away with
981	seduce	유혹하다, 꾀다	entice, tempt
982	prancing	활보하다, 뛰어다니다	cavorting, swaggering
983	congenial	화기애애한	agreeable, affable, convivial
984	erratic	불규칙한	abnormal; characterized by particularly unique quirks or mannerisms
985	vicissitude	우여곡절	alternating or changing phases of life or fortune

#	Word	Korean	English
986	marveled	경이로운	showed amazement at
987	foreshadowed	전조가 되다	to show or ndicate beforehand, prefigure
988	aspire	열망하다	to long, aim, or seek ambitiously
989	repose	안식, 휴식	rest, tranquility
990	reminiscence	추억	remembrance
991	inundating	침수	flooding or overwhelm
992	awe	경외감	amazement and respect
993	milieu	환경	environment; surroundings
994	Provoke	화나게 하다	to anger, enrage, exasperate, or vex
995	bewildered	갈피를 못 잡는	confused or puzzled completely
996	delude	속이다, 착각하게 하다	to mislead the mind or judgment of
997	allegory	우화, 풍자	a symbolical narrative, figurative treatment of one subject under the guise of another
998	allusions	암시	the making of a casual or indirect reference to something
999	embellished	장식된	decorated or added detail
1000	revile	꾸짖다, 매도하다	admonish, scold
1001	flamboyance	화려함	striking boldness, flashiness
1002	nudged	(팔꿈치로) 쿡 찌르다	poke, elbow
1003	rejoice	기뻐하다	be glad, express joy
1004	exalted	칭찬하다	praise, extol
1005	discord	논쟁, 불만	dispute, disagreement, difference of opinions
1006	replicating	모사하다	to repeat, duplicate
1007	abbreviated	줄여 쓰다	to shorten by omitting letters, substituting shorter forms
1008	disseminate	흩뿌려지다	spread out, scatter in different directions
1009	reconcile	받아들이다	to cause to accept or be resigned to something not desired
1010	synthesis	종합, 통합	a complex whole formed by combining
1011	fleeting	순식간의	passing swiftly; transitionary

#	Word	Korean	English
496	raven	먹이를 찾아다니다	seek prey
497	timorous	겁이 많은	full of fear; fearful
498	rambunctious	난폭한	loud and (usually) destructive
499	amoral	도덕 관념이 없는	without moral quality; neither moral nor immoral
500	condone	용납하다	allow; sanction
501	treachery	배반	disloyalty
502	parlor	방, 점, 건물	a room, apartment, or building serving as a place of business
503	invariable	변함없는	without change or deviation
504	paramount	다른 무엇보다 중요한	important, supreme
505	demolished	철거된, 무너진	dilapidated, destroyed
506	ailment	질병	a physical disorder or illness
507	grieving	비통해하는	feeling grief or sorrow
508	annihilate	전멸시키다	destroy the collective existence or main body of
509	potent	강한	powerful
510	idyllic	목가적인; 아주 편안한	rustic; extremely pleasant, simple, and peaceful
511	supplant	대신하다	replace; push away
512	malicious	악의적인	with harmful intentions
513	repentantly	뉘우치며	apologetically, regretfully
514	retain	유지하다, 보유하다	preserve, keep
515	dignity	위엄, 품위	honor, nobility
516	concoction	혼합물	mixture of liquids
517	beseech	애원하다	begged or requested; entreated
518	dispel	떨쳐버리다	disprove (as a theory)
519	communal	공동의	used or shared in common by everyone in a group
520	falter	흔들리다	stumble; move without confidence or skill
521	hedge	울타리	any barrier or boundary

#	Word	Korean	English
470	spew	토해내다	vomit
471	impair	손상을 입히다	weaken; damage
472	overborne	압도당한	dominated, overpowered
473	volatile	변덕스러운	changeable; tending to fluctuate
474	consummate	완료하다	fully complete; bring to a perfect state of completion
475	menace	위협하다	threaten, imperil
476	scruple	양심, 양심의 가책	a moral or ethical consideration or standard
477	exploit	(부당하게) 이용하다	use in an abusive way; take advantage of
478	deficiency	결점, 결함	weakness, flaw
479	intact	온전한	not changed or broken; complete or whole
480	manipulate	조작하다	manage or influence skillfully in an unfair manner
481	affluent	부유한	wealthy
482	castigate	꾸짖다, 책망하다	scold or criticize for wrongdoing
483	transgression	위반	violation of law, command, etc.; infraction
484	rudiment	기본, 기초	basis, foundation
485	villain	악당, 악인	evil person
486	mediocre	평범한	of average value; not overly positive or negative
487	considerate	사려 깊은	thoughtful, mindful
488	precarious	불안정한, 위태로운	uncertain; unstable; insecure
489	puffery	과찬	exaggerated praise; adulation
490	endorsement	지지, 승인	support, backing, approval
491	indulge	마음껏 하다	treat oneself; give in to a temptation
492	appease	진정시키다, 달래다	make peaceful; pacify
493	apprentice	견습생, 도제	a person who works for another in order to learn a trade
494	frenetic	정신 없이 바쁜, 부산한	frantic, frenzied
495	truncate	줄이다, 짧게 만들다	shorten; abridge

#	Word	Korean	English
1012	auspicious	길조의	promising
1013	deviations	빗나감, 벗어남, 편차	the act of deviating
1014	rapport	관계	relation, connection
1015	instill	스며들게 하다	to infuse gradually into the mind or feelings
1016	predestined	숙명 지워진	to destine in advance
1017	scorn	경멸하다	to reject something strongly
1018	valor	용기	bravery
1019	repercussions	파급효과	negative consequences of one's actions
1020	plethora	과다	a large amount
1021	quip	재담, 익살	a clever, witty remark, banter
1022	pundits	전문가, 권위자	scholar, expert, authority
1023	alloyed	(금속처럼) 결합된	combined into one
1024	huddled	웅크리다	curl up, crouch
1025	succor	구조	help, relief
1026	calamity	재난, 재해	disaster
1027	unfettered	제한받지 않은	free; liberated
1028	aberrant	별남	weirdness, peculiarity
1029	unforeseen	예측하지 못한	unanticipated, unpredicted
1030	ecosystem	생태계	biological community
1031	indigenous	원산의	innate, inherent, natural
1032	pidgin	단순한 형태의 언어, 피진어	casual dialect, simplified form of language
1033	topography	지형, 지형학	changes in elevation
1034	fluctuating	변동하는	change continually, shift back and forth
1035	cartographer	지도 제작자	map maker
1036	remorse	회한, 후회	guilt, regret
1037	upheaval	격변, 대변동	strong or violent change or disturbance
1038	fertile	비옥한, 기름진	arable, productive

#	Word	Korean	Definition
1039	cultivating	경작하다	to prepare and work on in order to raise crops
1040	tinging	물들이다, 기미를 띠게 하다	modifying in character or coloring with a slight shade or taste
1041	constituted	구성하다, 이루다	form, create
1042	animosity	적대감, 반감	hostility, bitterness
1043	incompatible	호흡이 안 맞는, 맞지 않는	doesn't fit
1044	unrestrained	억제되지 않은, 거리낌 없는	excessive, uncontrolled
1045	lavishness	풍부함, 무성함	exuberance
1046	antithesis	정반대, 대조	opposite, contrast
1047	predicament	곤경, 궁지	difficult situation, trouble
1048	plausible	타당한 것 같은	having an appearance of truth or reason
1049	stiff	뻣뻣한	rigid or firm
1050	grim	엄숙한, 우울한	somber, stern
1051	wretch	불쌍하고 가엾은 사람	a miserable, desolate person
1052	crass	무신경한, 대충의	coarse, vulgar
1053	grotesque	터무니없는, 기괴한	absurd, bizarre
1054	vaulting	뛰어 넘음	to leap or spring, as toor from a position or over something
1055	agilely	재빨리, 민첩하게	quickly, nimbly
1056	grasping	욕심 많은	greedy
1057	immurement	감금, 칩거	imprisonment
1058	obnoxious	아주 불쾌한, 고약한	disgusting, offensive
1059	evocation	환기, 유발	calling to mind, summoning
1060	resolve	해결하다	to come to a definite or earnest decision about
1061	putrefaction	부패	decay
1062	hurled	(거칠게) 던지다	throw with great force
1063	digressed	주제에서 벗어나다	to deviate or wander away from the main topic

#	Word	Korean	Definition
445	meditate	사색하다, 명상하다	muse, contemplate
446	rebuttal	반박	argument against another
447	notion	개념, 관념	a general understanding, an opinion, view
448	entity	독립체	being or existence considered as independent
449	tenant	세입자	a person or group that rents and occupies land or a house
450	unstinting	아낌없이 주는	generous, magnanimous
451	attest	증명하다	give evidence of
452	conscientious	양심적인	controlled by one's inner sense of what is right
453	patriarch	족장	the male head of a family or tribal line
454	aloof	무관심한, 냉담한	indifferent; disinterested
455	impede	방해하다, 막다	prevent, hinder, obstruct
456	superfluous	필요치 않은	unnecessarily extra
457	expenditure	지출, 비용	the act of expending something, especially funds
458	fabricate	만들어 내다, 제작하다	devise, construct
459	impart	전하다, 주다	make known, tell
460	judicious	신중한	using good judgment; careful
461	omit	생략하다	leave out
462	peculiar	이상한	strange, queer, odd
463	flinch	움츠러들다, 움찔하다	shy away, wince
464	repellent	역겨운	disgusting; driving one away
465	adage	속담, 격언	a traditional saying expressing a common experience or observation; proverb
466	incoherent	앞뒤가 안 맞는	without logical or meaningful connection; unintelligible
467	perch	걸앉다	take a seat
468	conspiratorial	음모를 꾸미는	sharing a secret; acting as accomplices
469	clandestine	은밀한	secretive; furtive

#	Word	Korean	English
420	ruminate	심사숙고하다	think seriously, contemplate
421	adhere	들러붙다	cling, stick fast
422	unravel	풀다	figure out, solve
423	despise	경멸하다, 깔보다	look down on with contempt; loathe
424	propensity	기질, 경향	inclination, disposition
425	downplay	대단치 않게 생각하다	treat or speak of so as to reduce emphasis on its importance, value, strength, etc.
426	trajectory	탄도, 궤적	a curve described by a projectile, rocket, or the like in its flight
427	chronic	만성적인	constant, habitual, inveterate
428	prevail	승리하다	win, triumph
429	despondent	낙담한	very depressed or hopeless
430	disillusioned	실망한, 환멸을 느낀	disappointed
431	demur	이의를 제기하다	refuse or deny
432	maxim	격언	a principle or rule of conduct
433	antidote	해독제	medicine or remedy
434	rigorous	철저한, 엄격한	rigidly severe or harsh, as people, rules, or discipline
435	ordeal	시련	an extremely severe or trying test, experience, or trial
436	forsake	버리다, 저버리다	give up; eschew
437	pastime	취미	something that serves to make time pass agreeably; recreation
438	omnipresence	어디에나 있음	occurrence everywhere; ubiquity
439	preeminent	아주 뛰어난	superior or extremely important
440	crucial	중대한, 결정적인	involving an extremely important decision or result; critical
441	benefactor	후원자	one who gives a charitable donation
442	guise	겉모습	style of dress, general external appearance
443	deprive	박탈하다	remove or withhold something from the enjoyment or possession of
444	frugal	검소한	spending little money

#	Word	Korean	English
1064	conceptual	개념적인, 관념적인	theoretical, abstract
1065	snag	곤란한 일, 문제	disadvantage, difficulty, obstacle
1066	deforming	치명적인, 타격을 입히는	crippling, disfiguring
1067	undulation	물결치는	moving up and down
1068	sagacious	현명한	judicious, insightful
1069	vetoed	거부하다	voted against
1070	suffrage	투표권	the right to vote, especially in a political election
1071	adored	흠모하다	to regard with the utmost esteem, love
1072	replete	가득 찬	full, filled
1073	endow	기부하다, 주다	give out, donate
1074	jolted	갑자기 마구 흔들다	moved along in a jerky or bumpy fashion
1075	murky	탁한, 흐린	foggy, cloudy
1076	dabbling	튀기다	splatter, splash
1077	utilitarian	실용적인, 실리적인	effective, practical
1078	excavate	파내다, 발굴하다	dig out
1079	paraphernalia	(특정한) 용품	equipment with a purpose
1080	stranded	오도가도 못하게 하다	to bring into or leave in a helpless position
1081	delicate	연약한	fine in texture, quality, construction
1082	vanishingly	사라지게	disappeared from sight without a trace
1083	pseudonym	가명	false name
1084	hierarchy	계급, 계층	ranking, order
1085	debunk	들통을 드러내다	to expose or excoriate as being false or pretentious
1086	leverage	영향력	influence
1087	repertoire (repertory)	레퍼토리, 능력이나 기술의 전 범위	collection of skills
1088	trove	수집물	collection
1089	ornate	화려하게 장식된	fancily decorated, elegant, glamorous
1090	denoting	나타내다, 의미하다	represent

#	Word	Korean	Definition
1091	medium	매체	an intervening substance
1092	painstaking	공들인	thorough, meticulous
1093	posterity	후세, 후대	succeeding or future generations collectively
1094	malevolent	악의적인	hateful, malicious
1095	grandiose	거창한, 장대한	affectedly impressive, grand
1096	magnitude	중요함, 장엄함	grandeur, importance
1097	inexplicable	설명할 수 없는, 불가해한	mysterious, hard to explain
1098	brandish	휘두르다	swing around
1099	preposterous	말도 안되는, 터무니없는	ridiculous, absurd
1100	hoaxed	속이다	deceive, trick
1101	nourishment	음식물, 영양분	food, nutrition, sustenance
1102	clan	무리, 집단	a group of people, clique
1103	growling	으르렁거리다	making a low guttural sound
1104	ill-tempered	짜증을 (잘) 내는, 화가 난	irritable, grumpy
1105	audacious	대담한, 무모한	reckless, bold
1106	indignant	분개한	feeling, characterized by, or expressing strong displeasure at
1107	deliberate	의도적으로	on purpose
1108	nuance	미묘한 차이, 음영	subtlety
1109	bluntness	무딤	dullness
1110	subplot	부차적 줄거리	a subordinate plot in a novel, play, film, etc
1111	hermit	은둔자	a person who lives alone often far from a community
1112	displaced	추방된	removed from the normal location
1113	inconceivable	상상도 할 수 없는	unimaginable, unthinkable
1114	saturated	흠뻑 적셔진	soaked, impregnated, or imbued thoroughly or completely
1115	drooped	축 처지다	hung down, lost strength

#	Word	Korean	Definition
393	ennobled	기품이 있는	elevated in degree, excellence, or respect; exalted
394	denigrate	폄하하다	mock or speak badly of
395	ineffable	형언할 수 없는	unable to be expressed in words
396	gaiety	흥겨움, 유쾌함	happiness, hilarity
397	exquisite	매우 아름다운, 정교한	beautiful; superb; of high quality
398	delightful	정말 기분 좋은	giving great pleasure or delight
399	egalitarian	평등주의의	equal or fair
400	intimate	친밀한, 분위기 있는	characterized by an atmosphere conducive to privacy
401	prowl	서성거리다	rove or go about stealthily
402	sprawl	큰 대자로 뻗다	spread out (often covering a wide area)
403	vulnerable	취약한, 연약한	susceptible to being wounded or hurt
404	exhilarated	쾌활하게 하는	extremely excited; exuberant
405	intuition	직감	direct perception of truth, fact, etc.
406	gallant	용감한, 용맹한	brave, courageous
407	compatriot	동포	fellow member of a group or country
408	banal	지긋지긋할 정도로 평범한	devoid of freshness or originality; trite
409	voracious	배가 고파 죽을 지경인	very hungry, ravenous
410	gratified	만족스러운	satisfied, as a desire
411	flaunt	과시하다, 자랑하다	show off, boast
412	forbear	참다, 삼가다	refrain or abstain from
413	sublime	숭고한	heavenly; near-perfect
414	trite	진부한	clichéd; overly-common; banal
415	hobble	다리를 절뚝거리다	stumble, limp
416	attentive	주의를 기울이는	mindful, considerate
417	tramp	떠돌다	patrol, wander
418	amputate	절단하다	cut off
419	discrete	별개의	separate, distinct

#	Word	Korean	English
367	articulate	분명히 표현된	uttered clearly in distinct syllables
368	assimilate	완전히 이해하다, 동화되다	change oneself to fit into an unfamiliar or different place
369	demise	죽음, 사망	death
370	candid	정직한	completely honest, straightforward
371	intrude	방해하다	come or go without permission or welcome
372	broach	이야기를 꺼내다	bring up a topic in conversation
373	precipitate	느닷없는	exceedingly sudden or abrupt
374	engender	발생시키다, 불러 일으키다	produce, arouse, foment
375	calumnious	중상의	of or relating vicious or untruthful statement; slanderous
376	taint	오명, 오점	stigma, contamination
377	verity	진리, 진실	truth
378	adamant	단호한, 요지부동의	determined
379	unease	불안감, 우려	not being easy in body or mind
380	wrench	(마음의) 쓰라림	ache, pain
381	conceited	자만하는	excessively proud of oneself; arrogant
382	magnificent	훌륭한, 웅장한	glorious
383	dispute	논란, 분쟁	a debate, controversy, or difference of opinion
384	dissonant	조화되지 않은	disagreeing, discordant
385	discard	버리다, 제거하다	eliminate, get rid of
386	considerable	상당한, 많은	rather large or great in size, distance, extent, etc.
387	comprise	~로 구성되다	consist of
388	postulation	가정	assumption, hypothesis, inference
389	predisposed	성향이 있는	having a tendency toward some activity or particular object
390	deduce	추론하다	logically infer; surmise
391	capitulate	굴복하다	surrender; succumb
392	proliferation	급증	spread; large amount

#	Word	Korean	English
1116	smudge	(더러운) 자국, 얼룩	a dirty mark or smear
1117	compulsory	의무적인	required
1118	jaunt	짧은 여행	a short journey
1119	waddle	뒤뚱뒤뚱 걸음	walking with short steps, rocking from side to side, as a duck
1120	anatomy	해부학	study of the body
1121	retaliate	보복하다	revenge
1122	grimace	얼굴을 찡그리다	to make a facial expression, usually ugly or distorted, that indicates pain, disgust, discomfort etc.
1123	vulgar	천박한	boorish
1124	obligatory	의무적인	required as a matter of obligation
1125	absolve	무죄임을 선언하다	forgive
1126	obscene	음란한, 외설적인	offensive, indecent
1127	rambling	횡설수설하는, 장황하고 두서 없는	circuitous, long-winded, prolix
1128	disparity	(특히 한쪽에 불공평한) 차이	from disparate; discrepancy
1129	gaudily	(지속하고) 화려하게	brilliantly or excessively showy
1130	homogenous	동질의	akin, alike
1131	shun	피하다	avoid, keep away from
1132	compressed	꾹 누르다, 밀어 넣다	cram, press together
1133	nomadic	유목의	itinerant
1134	fauna	동물상	animal group
1135	parched	바싹 마른	arid, scorched
1136	redress	변상, 보상	compensation
1137	recoup	(쓰거나 분실한 돈을) 되찾다	regain
1138	defacement	외관이 훼손된	damaged surface or appearance
1139	diplomacy	외교, 사교 수완	the art of science of conducting negotiations
1140	prerogative	특전, 특혜	exemption, immunity

#	Word	Korean	English
1141	extol	극찬하다	acclaim, applaud
1142	august	숭고한, 고결한	grand, noble
1143	bemoan	한탄하다, 애도하다	mourn, lament
1144	invoking	호소하는	appeal to, beseech
1145	oscillated	동요하다	waver, vibrate
1146	underscored	말줄 표시	underline
1147	petition	청원, 탄원	imprecation
1148	camouflage	위장	concealment by some means that alters or obscures the appearance
1149	reined	억제하다	hold, restrain
1150	unfurled	펼쳐지다	unfold
1151	void	텅 빈	empty
1152	ghastly	섬뜩한, 무시무시한	intimidating, horrifying
1153	jeopardize	위험에 빠뜨리다, 위태롭게 하다	endanger, threaten
1154	mend	수리하다, 고치다	fix, repair
1155	circumspect	신중한	cautious, careful
1156	incarnate	인간의 모습을 한	embodied in flesh
1157	circumvent	피해가다, 우회하다	bypass, avoid
1158	scaffolding	비계, 뼈대	a temporary structure for holding workers and materials during the erection of a building
1159	curb	경계	ledge, border
1160	paucity	부족, 소량	scarcity, shortage
1161	sedimentary	퇴적물의	the matter that settles to the bottom of a liquid
1162	fractured	골절되게 하다, 부러뜨리다	break, crack
1163	tribunal	재판소	court
1164	destabilized	불안정	instability
1165	jest	농담, 장난	joke, witty remark

#	Word	Korean	English
341	intersperse	흩어 배치하다	scatter here and there or place at intervals among other things
342	abide	머무르다, 깃들다	dwell, reside; stay
343	beckon	손짓하다	signal, summon, or direct by a gesture of the head or hand
344	hamper	막다, 방해하다	block, hinder
345	admonish	꾸짖다, 책망하다	criticize for wrongdoing
346	hinge	경첩	a jointed device or flexible piece on which a door swings
347	capacious	널찍한	able to hold many things; large (as in a space)
348	luminous	선명한, 빛을 발하는	bright, glowing
349	shudder	몸서리치다	tremble with a sudden movement, as from horror or cold
350	conjugated	합쳐진	joined together
351	exultant	기뻐서 어쩔 줄 모르는	very happy, delighted
352	loathe	몹시혐오하다, 싫어하다	hate, abhor
353	erroneous	잘못된	wrong, incorrect
354	obsolete	더 이상 쓸모가 없는	no longer in general use
355	predate	~보다 (시간이) 앞서다	precede in date
356	inextricable	떼어놓을 수 없는	unable to be separated from
357	aspect	측면	part, attribute
358	permeate	침투하다, 퍼지다	pass into or through every part of
359	chagrin	분함	displeasure, annoyance
360	grudgingly	마지못해	reluctantly
361	pliable	유연한	flexible; easy to persuade or control
362	vagary	예측 불허의 변화 [변동]	an unpredictable or erratic action, occurrence, course
363	servile	아부하는, 굽실거리는	obsequious, subservient
364	didactic	교훈적인	educational, teaching
365	artisan	장인, 기능 보유자	a person skilled in an applied art
366	infallible	결코 실패하지 않는	unfailing in effectiveness or operation

#	Word	Korean	English
315	demoralizing	사기를 떨어뜨리는	discouraging, debasing
316	abridge	요약하다, 줄이다	shorten by omissions; diminish
317	estranged	소원해진	alienated; separated
318	absorb	빨아들이다; 빠져들게 만들다	suck up or drink in; engross or engage wholly
319	exterminate	몰살시키다	get rid of destroying
320	obliterate	흔적을 없애다	destroy completely
321	pessimistic	비관적인	having negative thoughts about the future
322	befall	~에게 일어나다	occur to, happen to
323	meddle	간섭하다	intervene, interfere
324	constrain	제한하다	restrain; suppress
325	exuberance	풍부함, 무성함	abundancy
326	gloat	흡족해하다, 고소해하다	relish, rejoice
327	consent	허락, 동의	permission, approval
328	austere	냉정한, 근엄한	severe in manner or appearance; uncompromising; strict
329	undermine	약화시키다	weaken, reduce the intensity of
330	urge	촉구하다, 강권하다	push or force along; impel with force or vigor
331	dreary	음울한, 따분한	depressingly dull; bleak
332	abyss	심연, 깊은 구렁	a deep, immeasurable space, gulf, or cavity
333	refracting	굴절되는	changing the direction of a ray of light, sound, or heat
334	aggregated	전체의, 합쳐진	cumulative, amassed
335	congested	혼잡한	crowded, blocked
336	ineptitude	기량 부족	lack of skill or proficiency
337	reel	비틀거리다	falter, lurch
338	advocate	지지하다	speak in favor; support or urge
339	improvise	즉석에서 짓다	made or said without previous preparation
340	converse	대화를 나누다	talk, chat
1166	propelled	몰고 가다	to drive, or cause to move, forward or onward
1167	distort	왜곡하다	to twist awry; make deformed
1168	flank	측면	side
1169	defect	부족	deficiency, lack
1170	eerie	으스스한, 괴상한	spooky, frightening
1171	infinitesimal	극미한, 극소의	indefinitely or exceedingly small
1172	ecological	생태계의	environmental, green
1173	inhumane	비인간적인, 잔혹한	brutal, barbarous, savage
1174	intractable	고집스러운, 아주 다루기 힘든	stubborn, obstinate
1175	immense	거대한	gigantic, enormous
1176	incarcerated	감금하다	to confine, imprison
1177	entangled	얽어매다	to involve in difficulties
1178	prosecute	기소하다	to charge
1179	redeem	(결함 등을) 보완하다	recover possession
1180	degenerate	퇴보하다, 악화하다, 타락하다	worsen, backslide
1181	embark on	착수하다	commence, begin
1182	piquant	짜릿한, 흥미진진한	interesting, exciting
1183	grind	가루로 만들다	reduced to dust or powder
1184	wade	물, 진흙을 헤치며 걷다	to walk in water, when partially immersed
1185	lateralization	대뇌의 좌우의 기능 분화	Cognitive function that relies more on one side of the brain than the other.
1186	predation	포식, 약탈	Interaction in which one organism captures and feeds on another organism.
1187	countenance	표정, 안색	A person's face or facial expression.
1188	pseudoscience	가짜과학, 가짜의학	Methods, theories, or systems considered as having no scientific basis.
1189	lampoon	풍자	Harsh satire aimed at an individual.
1190	malfeasance	(특히 공무원의) 불법 (부정) 행위	Misconduct or wrongdoing, especially by a public official.

#	Word	Korean	Definition
1191	rotunda	원형 건물	A circular domed building or hall.
1192	census	인구조사	An official count of the population.
1193	gangway	통로	A passageway, especially a narrow walkway.
1194	mural	벽화(들)	Large paintings made on walls.
1195	ponderous	무거운, 육중한	Weighty; slow and heavy.
1196	protocol	절차	List of steps to be taken in different situations.
1197	schema	개요, 윤곽; 도식	An underlying organizational pattern or structure; conceptual framework.
1198	scions	자손	A descendant.
1199	turmoil	소란, 혼란, 불안, 동요	A state of great commotion, confusion, or disturbance.
1200	unprecedented	전례 없는	Without previous instance, never before known or experienced.
1201	veracity	진실성, 정확성	Habitual truthfulness and honesty.
1202	adduce	증거로 인용하다	To bring forward as evidence.
1203	conglomeration	복합	A number of different things, grouped together.
1204	dainty	앙증맞은, 조신스러운	Preciously delicate or charming.
1205	demure	얌전한, 조신한	Modest and reserved in manner or behavior.
1206	detract	(가치,중요성, 명성따) 떨어뜨리다	To take away a part, as from quality, value, or reputation.
1207	expostulatory	타이르는, 충고의	Of or relating to earnest and kind protests.
1208	holistic	전체적인	Concerning the whole rather than the parts.
1209	impugne	이의를 제기하다	To challenge as false.
1210	locus	(특정) 위치, 장소	A place.
1211	microbial	미생물의	Of or relating to a microorganism, especially a pathogenic bacterium.
1212	oversight	실수, 간과	An omission or error due to carelessness.
1213	pillage	약탈	Plundering, looting, taking property by force.

#	Word	Korean	Definition
290	nostalgically	향수에 젖어	desiring to return to the past
291	cryptic	수수께끼 같은	mysterious, difficult to understand; inscrutable
292	rebel	반역자	a person who resists any authority, control, or tradition
293	conventional	관습적인	conforming or adhering to accepted standards
294	refute	논박하다	contradict, deny
295	indulgent	관대한	lenient, permissive
296	subversion	전복, 파괴	the state of being subverted; destruction
297	snatch	조각, 단편	a bit, piece, fragment
298	preamble	서문	introduction, preface
299	symbiosis	공생	the living together of two dissimilar organisms, as in mutualism
300	diverge	갈라지다	depart from; go down a different path
301	straddle	걸터앉다	sit or stand with the legs wide apart
302	deem	여기다, 간주하다	think, regard
303	disclose	밝히다, 드러내다	reveal; betray
304	innate	타고난	in-built; something one is born with, rather than acquired
305	outlandish	기이한	strange; not normal
306	shard	조각, 파편	a fragment, especially of broken earthenware
307	pivotal	중심적인	central, key, essential
308	stellar	별의; 뛰어난	of or relating to the stars; like a star, as in brilliance
309	haphazardly	우연히	by chance; randomly; indiscriminately
310	riddle	수수께끼, 미스터리	a puzzling question, problem; enigma, conundrum
311	array	배치하다, 진열하다	place in a proper order
312	lurid	섬뜩한, 소름 끼치는	gruesome; horrible; shocking
313	heresy	이단; 사상모독	blasphemy, fallacy
314	benevolent	자애로운	generous; with good intentions

#	Word	Korean	English
263	devious	정직하지 못한, 기만적인	with evil or deceitful intention
264	deferential	공손한	respectful; reverential
265	hunched	구부린	bent; not standing straight
266	skulk	몰래 숨다	lie or keep in hiding, as for some evil reason
267	unequivocally	명백히, 분명히	undeniably
268	halting	멈칫거리는	faltering or hesitating
269	ingeniously	재치 있게	cleverly
270	contrive	고안하다, 창안하다	devise, create, invent
271	nomenclature	(학술적) 이름	naming
272	distilled	증류된	processed through vaporization and subsequent condensation, as for purification
273	conduit	도관	a pipe or channel for conveying fluids
274	foster	양육하다, 조성하다	promote the growth of, raise
275	heinous	악랄한, 극악무도한	abhorrent, horrifying
276	squint	눈을 가늘게 뜨고 보다	look with the eyes partly closed
277	assess	재다, 평가하다	estimate officially the value of
278	gauge	측정하다	measure
279	bolster	강화하다	reinforce, strengthen
280	sanctuary	성소, 성역	a sacred or holy place
281	ascribe	돌리다, 탓하다	give credit to; attribute
282	delve	조사하다, 연구하다	investigate, examine
283	portentous	(불길한) 징후가 있는	having bad signs for the future; foreboding
284	conjure	마술을 부리다	magically make something appear
285	rhetorically	수사적으로	related to public speaking
286	vindicate	정당성을 입증하다	free from blame/guilt
287	ruthless	무자비한	without pity
288	pharmaceutical	약학의	pertaining to pharmacy or pharmacists
289	foil	좌절시키다	prevent success of

#	Word	Korean	English
1214	plummet	수직으로 떨어지다; 급락하다	Fall or drop straight down at high speed.
1215	posthumous	사후의	Occurring or continuing after one's death.
1216	postural	자세의, 자세를 취하는	Of or relating to the carriage of the body as a whole.
1217	prerequisite	필요조건; 사전에 필요한	Required beforehand.
1218	quiver	떨다, 흔들다	To shake or move with a slight trembling motion.
1219	revelers	흥청대는 사람들	People who participate in boisterous merrymaking.
1220	ruefully	슬프게, 비참하게	Regretfully; causing sorrow or pity, deplorable.
1221	shoal	얕은 물가	A place where a sea, river, or other body of water is shallow.
1222	speciation	종의 형성	The formation of new species.
1223	unorthodox	정통이 아닌, 특이한	Not conforming to rules or tradition.
1224	usurpation	강탈, 탈취	Wrongful or illegal seizure.
1225	vandalism	고의적 파괴	Deliberate and pointless destruction of public or private property.
1226	abdicate	(왕위, 권리, 의무) 버리다, 포기하다	To give up a position, right, or power.
1227	accretion	축적	Growth in size or increase in amount.
1228	altruistic	자신보다 남을 위하는, 이타적인	Unselfishly concerned for the welfare of others.
1229	amenable	순종하는, 쾌히 받아들이는	Open to influence, persuasion, or advice.
1230	annals	연대기	A record of events; especially yearly.
1231	annulment	무효화, 취소	A voiding, invalidation.
1232	anterior	이전의; 앞쪽의	Situated before or at the front of.
1233	antipathy	반감, 혐오감	A strong dislike, hostile feeling.
1234	apprehend	체포하다	To seize; to arrest.
1235	appropriation	의회가 승인한 예산	An act of a legislature granting money from the treasury.
1236	axiom	자명한 이치, 원칙	A universally recognized principle.

#	Word	Korean	English
1237	betoken	나타내다, 표시하다; 징조가 되다	To give evidence of; indicate.
1238	blare	(소리) 요란하게 울리다, 떠들어대다	To emit a loud, raucous sound.
1239	bode	징조가 되다	To be an omen of; to indicate by signs.
1240	brawny	건장한	Strong, muscular.
1241	brusque	무뚝뚝한, 퉁명스러운	Abrupt, blunt, with no formalities.
1242	candor	솔직함, 정직함	Honesty, frankness.
1243	congenital	선천적인	Of or relating to a condition present at birth.
1244	conspecific	같은 종의	Of the same species.
1245	convulsive	경련성의, 발작적인	Characterized by involuntary jerky contractions.
1246	coquettish	요염한, 교태를 부리는	Flirtatious in a teasing manner.
1247	covet	(남의것을) 탐내다	To desire wrongfully; greatly desire.
1248	crux	가장 중요한 부분	A vital, basic, decisive, or pivotal point.
1249	decennial	10년마다의	Occurring every 10 years.
1250	decimation	대량학살	Destroying or killing a large part of.
1251	defecate	배변하다	To void excrement from the bowels.
1252	dejected	낙담한	Downcast or sad; depressed.
1253	demarcation	경계, 구분	Act of defining or marking a boundary or distinction.
1254	derision	조롱, 조소	Ridicule; mockery.
1255	desultory	두서없는, 되는대로, 산만한	Lacking consistency or order, disconnected.
1256	deter	단념시키다, 그만두게 하다	To discourage from acting or proceeding.
1257	detritus	파편	Any disintegrated material; debris.
1258	diabolical	악마 같은	Devilish; fiendish.
1259	discern	식별하다, 분별하다	To see clearly, recognize.
1260	distended	빵빵한	Enlarged or expanded from pressure.

#	Word	Korean	English
236	censure	비난하다, 책망하다	reproach or criticize harshly, blame
237	mischief	나쁜 짓, 못된 장난	misconduct, wrongdoing
238	canvass	여론조사를 하다	poll; question a group of people to understand the majority opinion
239	acute	극심한, 격심한	intense, crucial
240	foray	약탈하다	ravage in search of plunder; pillage
241	elusive	찾기 힘든	cleverly or skillfully evasive
242	notorious	악명 높은	famous in a bad way
243	euphemism	완곡어법	'good' word used in place of a bad one
244	intimidating	위협하는, 협박하는	frightening especially by threatening someone
245	revelation	폭로	something revealed; also, a realization
246	imply	암시하다	hint, insinuate
247	pious	경건한	religious
248	timid	소심한	lacking in self-assurance, courage, or bravery; shy
249	sanction	허가, 인가	approval, permission
250	bliss	더 없는 행복	state of euphoria or heavenly happiness
251	deity	신	God
252	discrepant	모순되는	differing, not matching
253	exemplary	모범적인	serving as an example (very good)
254	inadvertent	고의가 아닌, 우연의	without intending; accidental
255	circumscribe	제한하다, 억제하다	limit, confine
256	colloquial	구어의	involving or using conversation; informal
257	flagrant	노골적인	intentionally harmful; obviously wrong; blatant
258	acrimonious	신랄한, 통렬한	caustic, stinging, bitter
259	swindle	속이수, 사기	deceit, deception
260	boisterously	떠들썩하게	loudly
261	console	위로하다, 위안을 주다	soothe, comfort, assuage
262	evade	피하다	avoid, circumvent

#	Word	Korean	English
1261	divest	빼앗다, 박탈하다	To strip or deprive, especially of property or rights.
1262	divulge	누설하다	To disclose or reveal.
1263	doldrums	침체, 부진; 침울	A state of inactivity or stagnation.
1264	ecstasy	무아의 경지, 황홀	Extreme happiness.
1265	emaciation	수척	Abnormal thinness caused by lack of nutrition or by disease.
1266	encomium	찬사	A formal expression of high praise.
1267	endemic	고유의	Inherent, native; belonging to an area.
1268	equitable	공정한, 공평한	Fair, just, embodying principles of justice.
1269	ethology	인성학; 행동 생물학	The study of animal behavior, especially of behavioral patterns.
1270	evince	분명히 나타내다, 명시하다	To demonstrate clearly; to prove.
1271	exiguity	근소, 부족	The quality or state of being meager or scanty.
1272	florid	불그레한	Reddish; ruddy; rosy.
1273	food-borne	오염된 음식을 통해 전파되는	Caused by eating or drinking.
1274	forsooth	과연, 정말	In truth; in fact; indeed.
1275	foul	오염, 굴욕	To defile; dishonor; disgrace.
1276	fritter	조금씩 낭비하다	Wasting little by little.
1277	garner	얻다, 모으다	To gather and store.
1278	glib	유창한	Readily fluent, often without thought or hesitation.
1279	granulate	알갱이로 만들다	To make grainy.
1280	gynecology	부인과 의학	The branch of medicine dealing with the reproductive system in women.
1281	headstone	묘비	The memorial stone marking the head of the grave.
1282	headwork	정신 노동; 사고, 사색	Mental labor; thought.
1283	hefty	무거운, 상당한	Heavy; weighty.
1284	imbecility	정신박약, 저능, 무능	An instance or point of weakness; incapability.

#	Word	Korean	English
210	personnel	직원	staff, employee
211	nonchalant	차분한	coolly unconcerned, indifferent, or unexcited
212	preempt	못하게 하다	prevent
213	repugnant	불쾌한, 혐오스러운	nasty, obnoxious, disgusting
214	dispassionate	감정에 좌우되지 않는	phlegmatic, calm, impartial
215	circumstance	환경, 상황, 정황	a condition
216	cursory	대충 하는	hasty, superficial
217	equivocally	모호하게	vaguely
218	credible	믿을 수 있는	believable; tenable; feasible
219	rage	격렬한 분, 격노	pure anger/fury
220	vehemently	격렬하게	with great passion; zealously
221	methodically	체계적으로	with great attention paid to details; meticulously
222	assemble	집합시키다, 모이다	bring together or gather into one place
223	omniscient	모든 것을 다 아는	knowing everything
224	appalled	간담이 서늘한, 몸서리해 하는	filled or overcome with horror, consternation, or fear
225	renounce	포기하다	give up (usually disdainfully)
226	microcosm	소우주 (더 큰 것의 축소판)	a little world, a world in miniature
227	hyperbole	과장	exaggeration
228	astounded	경악한, 충격 받은	amazed, shocked
229	foolhardiness	무모함	reckless and thoughtless boldness; foolish rash
230	petulant	심술 사나운	cranky, moody
231	morose	시무룩한	sad; melancholy
232	paranoia	편집증	baseless or excessive suspicion of the motives of others
233	vilify	비난하다	criticize
234	allege	주장하다	assert, claim
235	transcribe	기록하다, 옮겨 쓰다	copy, rewrite

#	Word	Korean	Definition
1285	increment	증가, 인상	An enlargement, increase, addition.
1286	inculcate	되풀이하여 심어주다, 명심시키다	To implant by repeated statement.
1287	indefatigable	지치지 않는	Incapable of being tired out.
1288	indoctrinate	주입하다, 세뇌시키다	To instill a doctrine, principle, ideology, etc.
1289	ingrained	(기질, 습관) 뿌리깊은, 깊이 박힌	Deep-rooted, forming part of the very essence.
1290	insurmountable	극복할 수 없는	Impossible to overcome.
1291	interject	불쑥 꺼내들다	To insert between other things.
1292	intone	(어느 어조로) 말하다, 읊조리다	To utter with a particular tone or voice modulation.
1293	invidious	비위에 거슬리는, 불쾌한	Hateful, offensive, injurious.
1294	invigorate	기운나게 하다, 상쾌하게 하다	Imparting strength and vitality.
1295	irksome	짜증나는, 귀찮은	Annoying; irritating; exasperating; tiresome.
1296	iterative	되풀이되는	Repeating, making repetitions.
1297	jargon	(특정 집단의) 전문 용어	Vocabulary, peculiar to a particular trade, profession, or group.
1298	jut	돌출하다	To extend sharply outward or upward; project.
1299	kudos	영광; 명성, 영예	Honor; glory; acclaim.
1300	laborious	많은 노력이 필요한, 힘드는	Requiring much work, exertion, or perseverance.
1301	lancet	얇고 가늘 양 끝이 뾰족한 의료용 칼	Small surgical tool for making incisions.
1302	laypeople	일반인, 비전문가	People who are not a member of a profession.
1303	levity	(말, 태도의) 가벼움, 경솔함, 경박함	An inappropriate lack of seriousness.
1304	licentiousness	부도덕함, 음탕함, 음란함	Lacking legal or moral restraints.
1305	limelight	이목, 관심	The center of attention.

#	Word	Korean	Definition
183	garrulous	말이 많은	talkative; sociable
184	exclaim	소리지르다, 외치다	cry out or speak suddenly and vehemently
185	deftly	솜씨 좋게	skillfully; adeptly
186	analogy	비유	similarity or comparability
187	apt	적절한	appropriate (also used to describe a skilled person)
188	recur	마음에 다시 떠오르다, happen again, repeat in one's mind
189	zealous	열성적인	passionate; fervent
190	jubilation	환희, 환호	rejoice, exult
191	apocalyptic	종말론의	catastrophic; destructive
192	atrocious	형편없는, 끔찍한	awful, outrageous
193	vaunt	자랑하다, 허풍 떨다	speak vaingloriously of, boast of
194	lauded	칭찬받는	praised; lionized
195	gregarious	사교적인	sociable
196	engulfing	에워싸는	completely surround
197	gibberish	횡설수설	meaningless talk, babble, prattle
198	apex	정점, 꼭대기	highest point
199	render	만들다	cause to become
200	obscured	무명의, 잘 알려지지 않은	covered or blocked; occluded
201	commodity	상품, 물자	something that is sold for money
202	facilitate	가능하게 하다	make it easier or more likely to happen
203	linger	어슬렁거리다	hang around
204	snobby	거만한, 버릇없는	impertinent, haughty
205	haste	서두름	speed; alacrity
206	injunction	경고	telling someone not to do something
207	reciprocal	상호간의	mutual; a command, order, admonition
208	folly	판단력 부족, 어리석음	a foolish action, practice, idea
209	deplore	깊이 개탄하다, 슬퍼하다	regret with great passion

#	Word	Korean	English
156	fervently	열렬하게	with great passion
157	dichotomy	양분	a pair of opposites
158	pioneer	개척하다	be the first person to open or prepare
159	subordinate	경시하다	place in a lower rank
160	anarchy	난장판, 무정부 상태	lawlessness, chaos
161	contravene	위반하다	come or be in conflict with
162	homily	설교, 훈계	a sermon, an admonitory discourse
163	lurking	숨어 있는	existing unperceived or unsuspected
164	concede	인정하다	give in; surrender; concede
165	succumb	굴복하다	give in
166	fatigue	피로	tiredness
167	gritty	모래를 섞은 듯 불쾌한	consisting of, containing, or resembling grit
168	vanity	자만심	excessive pride
169	surreptitious	은밀한	secretive; furtive
170	accustomed	익숙한	habituated, used to
171	jeer	야유, 조롱	ridicule, scoff
172	tedious	지루한, 싫증나는	boring, dull
173	intoxicated	취한	drunk, inebriated
174	coherently	일관성 있게	making sense
175	anecdote	일화, 알려지지 않은 얘기	a short, amusing story
176	civilized	문명화된, 교양 있는	having a high state of culture and development both socially and technologically
177	inexorable	멈출 수 없는, 가둘없는	relentless, unyielding
178	sloth	나태	laziness, idleness, indolence
179	cease	중단되다	bring to an end
180	clamorous	떠들썩한	loud noise; usually from many voices
181	lurching	흔들리는, 동요시키는	stagger, jerk
182	thwart	방해하다	prevent or stop from happening

#	Word	Korean	English
1306	looming	(중요하거나 위협적인 일이) 큰 닥칠 것처럼 보이다	Something unwanted, about to happen soon, causing worry.
1307	lumber	느릿느릿 움직이다	To move slowly and awkwardly.
1308	luminary	선각자, 권위자	A person who is an inspiration to others in his or her field.
1309	mainstay	중심축, 대들보	A chief support.
1310	mangy	지저분한	Shabby; filthy.
1311	matriculate	(대학에) 입학하다	To enroll at a college or university.
1312	matrimony	결혼, 결혼상태	State of being married.
1313	miasma	독기, 악영향	A dangerous, foreboding, or deathlike influence or atmosphere.
1314	mirth	환희, 유쾌함, 웃음	Merriment; amusement and laughter.
1315	misanthrope	사람을 싫어하는 사람	A person who dislikes others.
1316	mislay	두고 잊어버리다	To lose temporarily; misplace.
1317	misogyny	여성혐오	Hatred of women.
1318	mogul	중요한 인물, 거물	An important, powerful, or influential person.
1319	moor	고정시키다, 정박시키다	To fix firmly; secure.
1320	munition	군수품, 무기	Military supplies.
1321	mutation	변이, 변화	A change in a gene or chromosome.
1322	mutual	상호간에	Held in common; shared.
1323	neural	신경(계)의	Of or relating to a nerve or the nervous system.
1324	neutralize	무력화하다	To make something ineffective.
1325	nucleus	(원자)핵, 중심	The central part, to which other parts are gathered.
1326	obstetrics	산부인과	Branch of medicine concerned with pregnancy and childbirth.
1327	obtrusive	눈에 거슬리는	Undesirably protruding; imposing one's opinions on others.
1328	opulence	부유, 풍부	Extreme wealth, abundance.

#	Word	Korean	Definition
1329	overarching	포괄적인, (전체에 영향을 주므로) 매우 중요한	Encompassing or overshadowing everything.
1330	parity	동등함	Equality, as in amount, status, or character.
1331	pathogen	병균	An organism that causes disease.
1332	periphery	주변부	A boundary line; perimeter; an outside surface.
1333	perusal	정독; 통독	A careful examination, review.
1334	pitted	(과실의) 씨를 뺀	Having the pit (off fruit) removed.
1335	plaintiffs	원고, 고소인	Persons filling a lawsuit.
1336	plaintive	슬픈, 불쌍한 애처로운	Expressive of sorrow, melancholy.
1337	pollination	수분(작용)	Transfer of pollen from the male reproductive structure to the female reproductive structure.
1338	prattle	(쓸데없이 미주알) 지껄이다	To talk in a foolish or simple-minded way; chatter.
1339	predilection	편애, 경향	A tendency to think favorably of something in particular.
1340	primeval	원시의, 태고의, 옛날의	Original; existing from the beginning.
1341	primordial	원시의, 태고의	Relating to the beginning of the first age, especially of the world.
1342	procure	애써서 구하다	To obtain by care, effort, or special means.
1343	proliferate	급증하다	To increase in number quickly.
1344	promulgate	공포, 선포, 널리 알리다	To make known by open declaration; publish.
1345	protract	오래 끌다, 지연하는	To draw out or lengthen.
1346	proximate	가까운, 근접한	Immediate; nearest.
1347	punctilious	세심한, 꼼꼼한	Very careful and exact; extremely attentive to etiquette.
1348	punctuality	시간 엄수, 정확함	Promptness or being on time.
1349	regiment	(군사) 연대; 다수, 큰 무리	A unit of ground forces, consisting of two or more battalions.

#	Word	Korean	Definition
132	indicting	기소하는	accusing of a crime or wrongdoing
133	oblivious	의식하지 못하는	unmindful; unconscious; unaware
134	burdensome	아주 힘든	requiring great effort; arduous; taxing
135	disconcert	당혹스럽게 하다	disturb the self-possession of; perturb; frustrate
136	cull	고르다; 도태시키다	pick, choose
137	valiant	용감한	brave, courageous
138	omnipotent	전능한	almighty or infinite in power, as God
139	perverse	비뚤어진	willfully determined to go counter to what is expected
140	rake	샅샅이 뒤지다, 찾아내다	scour, scrape up
141	recalcitrant	저항하는; 다루기 힘든	resisting authority or control; stubborn, obstinate
142	raiding	습격하는, 급습하는	suddenly assaulting or attacking
143	meticulousness	꼼꼼함	paying close attention to details
144	dissipate	낭비하다	spend or use wastefully
145	emancipation	해방	the act of being free from restraint, influence, or the like
146	poignant	가슴 아픈	causing great pain, agonizingly
147	inanimate	무생물의, 죽은	not alive, not moving (used of physical objects)
148	jumble	뒤죽박죽 뒤섞인 것	a mixed or disordered heap or mass
149	toil	노역, 고역	hard work
150	indispensable	필요한	necessary, basic, crucial
151	facet	측면	aspect, phase
152	allotted	할당된, 정해진	divided
153	impenetrable	들어갈수 없는	unable to be penetrated; also used for anything which cannot be understood easily (abstruse)
154	premise	전제, 주장	argument, assertion
155	propagandist	선전원	a person who deliberately spread information, rumors, etc.

#	Word	Korean	English
105	dearth	부족, 결핍	lack/shortage of something
106	salvage	구조하다	save from destruction
107	relish	즐기다	enjoy greatly
108	invade	침입하다	enter and encroach, infiltrate
109	disintegrate	해체되다	break apart
110	verify	확인하다	confirm as to accuracy or truth by acceptable evidence
111	pedantic	지나치게 규칙을 찾는	overly-fixated on small academic details
112	serendipitous	시기 적절한	happening at a good time, opportune
113	elate	우쭐대다	make very happy or proud
114	subdued	(기분이) 가라앉은	quiet; suppressed or limited
115	teeter	불안정하게 움직이다	move unsteadily; tremble
115	detonate	폭발하다	explode
117	aversion	혐오, 적대감	dislike, antipathy
118	relentless	끈질긴; 가차 없는	incessant, without giving up
119	approbation	승인, 찬성	approval; praise
120	benighted	무지몽매한	intellectually or morally ignorant
121	reiterate	반복하다	state something again, repeat
122	paraphrase	달리 표현하다	restate or reword
123	defiant	반항하는	rejecting, refusing to follow
124	regimen	(결과를 얻기 위한) 요법	a regulated course intended to restore health; a systematic plan
125	preexistent	이전부터 존재하는	existing beforehand
126	penetrating	날카로운; 꿰뚫어보는	sharp; discerning
127	versatile	다재다능한, 능숙한	skillful
128	perpetual	끊임없이 계속되는	continuing forever, everlasting
129	novice	초심자	beginner
130	lapse	실수	mistake
131	palpable	감지할 수 있는	able to be touched or physically felt; tangible

#	Word	Korean	English
1350	rekindle	다시 불붙이다, (흥미, 관심) 다시 불러일으키다	Revive something that has been lost.
1351	repatriate	(본국으로의) 송환, 귀환	To be restored or returned to the country of origin, allegiance, or citizenship.
1352	retardation	지체, 지연	Slowing down of something.
1353	retrospective	회고하는	Looking or applying to the past or backward.
1354	salient	눈에 띄는, 유명한	Prominent; of notable significance.
1355	sanguine	낙관적인, 쾌활한	Cheerfully optimistic; hopeful.
1356	sceptic	회의론자, 의심 많은 사람	A person who questions the validity or authenticity of something supposed to be true.
1357	scrupulous	양심적인; 세심한; 꼼꼼한; 면밀한	Exact, careful, attending thoroughly to details; having high moral standards, principled.
1358	senile	노쇠한, 나이 많은	Showing a decline of physical strength or mental functioning as a result of old age or disease.
1359	seraph	천사	An angel.
1360	shrill	(소리가) 날카로운, 높은	High-pitched and piercing in sound quality.
1361	shroud	수의	A cloth or sheet in which a corpse is wrapped for burial.
1362	sparse	희박한, 드문드문 있는	Thinly scattered or distributed.
1363	spearhead	창끝; 선봉	A person, thing, or group that organizes or leads something.
1364	spelunk	동굴탐험을 하다	To explore caves, especially as a hobby.
1365	staunch	확고한, 충실한	Firm or steadfast in principle, loyalty.
1366	stave	저지하다, 막다	To drive or thrust away.
1367	sterling	훌륭한, 법정 순도의 (금,은)	Genuine, excellent; made of silver of standard fineness.
1368	stilts	기둥, 지주	Tall, slender supporting posts.
1369	stipulation	계약 조건	A demand or condition of an agreement.

#	Word	Korean	Definition
1370	strapped	무엇에 굶주린, 돈에 궁한	To be in need of something; wanting.
1371	substrate	기질	A specific reactant acted upon by an enzyme.
1372	telltale	감추어도 드러나는	That reveals or betrays what is not intended to be known.
1373	transient	덧없는, 일시적인	Not lasting, temporary. Lasting only a short time.
1374	tutelage	후견, 보호, 지도, 교육	Instruction, protection, or guardianship.
1375	tween	10세와 12세 사이의 사람	A person between 10 and 12 years of age, too old to be a child and too young to be a teenager.
1376	unassuming	겸손한, 허세부리지 않는	Modest.
1377	unbidden	요청받지 않은, 예상 밖의	Not ordered or commanded; spontaneous.
1378	unwieldy	(먹겁고 커서) 옮기가 쉽지 않은, 다루기 힘든	Not easily carried or handled, as from size, shape, or weight.
1379	unwittingly	모르는 사이에; 고의 가 아니게	Without knowledge or intention.
1380	validate	확인하다, 증명하다	To make valid, confirm, substantiate.
1381	weathering	풍화(작용)	The breaking down of rocks and other materials by chemical or physical means.
1382	wily	약삭빠른, 교활한	Crafty; cunning.
1383	writhing	몸부림치는	Twisting and turning the body in a worm-like fashion, as in pain.
1384	xenophobic	외국(인) 공포(혐오 증)의(을 가진)	Having abnormal fear or hatred of the strange or foreign; having fear of foreigners.
1385	behest	명령, 지시	A command or directive.
1386	ecologist	생태학자	A person who studies the branch of biology dealing with the relations between organisms and their environment.
1387	endeavor	노력하다	To make a serious attempt or effort.

#	Word	Korean	Definition
79	legitimate	합법적인	authentic
80	opulent	호화로운	fancy; well-decorated
81	incongruous	어울리지 않는	not matching or fitting in
82	fallacious	잘못된	false; untrue
83	cerebral	뇌의	brainy; scholarly, smart
84	garish	야한, 화려한	decorated in a tasteless, cheap way; overly showy
85	patron	고객; 후원자	customer; financial supporter
86	arduous	몹시 힘든, 고된	requiring great effort; taxing
87	ubiquitous	어디에나 있는	occurring everywhere
88	purported	~라고 알려진	alleged, supposed
89	callous	냉담한	emotionally cold; unfeeling (often cruel)
90	blatant	노골적이, 뻔한	very obvious in an offensive or shameless way
91	companion	동반자, 동행	a person who is frequently in the company of another
92	collaborate	협업하다	work, one with another; cooperate
93	misfit	부적응자	a person who is suited to adjust to the circumstances
94	albeit	비록 ~일지라도	although, even though, despite
95	flustered	경황없이하는	confused and slightly annoyed
96	tranquil	고요한	quiet, peaceful
97	premonitory	예고의, 전조의	having bad signs for the future, ominous
98	snide	(은근히) 헐뜯는	sarcastic, hateful
99	scrutinize	면밀히 조사하다	inspect, examine
100	clinical	냉담한	cold, unemotional
101	confer	수여하다	bestow upon as a gift or honor
102	eminent	유명한, 저명한	famous, distinguished
103	parsimonious	인색한, 쩨쩨한	miserly, frugal, avaricious
104	conviction	신념, 확신; 유죄선고	strong belief; a declaration that a person is guilty

#	Word	Korean	English
51	pupil	학생	student, the children who go to school
52	convoluted	대단히 난해한	complex and confusing
53	vernacular	토착어, 방언	language used by a particular or specialized group
54	fathom	헤아리다, 가늠하다	understand; grasp the meaning
55	debased	품질이 저하된	reduced in quality or value
56	cardinal	가장 중요한	central, important, key
57	demagogue	선동 정치가, 리더	a person, especially an orator or political leader
58	dominant	우세한	main, superior, powerful
59	assorted	여러 가지 종류의	various
60	meander	이리저리 거닐다	walk (usually slowly)
61	faction	파벌, 파당	a group or clique within a larger group
62	impulsively	충동적으로	instinctively, without thought
63	interrogate	심문하다	question very intensely
64	intrinsically	본질적으로	naturally, fundamentally
65	impelled	~해야만 하는	compelled
66	adorned	꾸미다, 장식되다	to be made more attractive or beautiful
67	inure	익히다, 단련하다	accustom, habituate
68	solemn	근엄한	very serious
69	succinct	간단명료한, 간단한	concise, blunt
70	appraisal	평가	judgment of value
71	derisive	조롱하는	mocking, contemptuous
72	prophesy	예언하다	predict, foretell, forecast
73	imperative	반드시 해야 하는	necessary, compulsory
74	alluring	매력적인	attractive, charming
75	courtier	(왕을 보필하던) 조신	an attendant at a sovereign's court
76	pensive	수심 어린	deep in thought
77	venerated	존경 받는, 추앙 받는	respected, prestigious
78	improbable	있을 것 같지 않은	unlikely to be true or to happen

#	Word	Korean	English
1388	epistemology	인식론	A branch of philosophy that studies the origin, nature, methods, and limits of human knowledge.
1389	lisp	혀짤배기소리	A speech defect consisting in pronouncing s and z like th.
1390	locale	(사건 등의) 현장	A place, especially having to do with events related to it.
1391	mortgage	저당, 주택 융자	A specific type of loan that is used to buy real estate.
1392	mounting	뒤를 받치는 재료, 지지대	Backing, setting or support.
1393	prejudice	편견, 선입견	An unfavorable opinion or feeling formed beforehand without reason.
1394	psychoanalysis	정신분석(학)	Structure of theories concerning the relation of conscious and unconscious psychological processes.
1395	sapphic	사포풍의; 레즈비언의	A poetic verse pattern pertaining to Sappho; of or relating to relationships between women.
1396	succour	도움, 구제	A person or thing that gives help, relief, aid.
1397	swaddle	포대기로 감싸다	To bind with long, narrow strips of cloth to prevent free movement.
1398	symposium	토론회	A meeting or conference for the discussion of some subject.
1399	systemic	조직의; 온몸의	Pertaining to or affecting a particular body system.
1400	unawares	알지못하고 부지중에, 뜻밖에	By surprise, suddenly, unexpectedly.

#	Word	Korean	Definition
23	pelt	전력질주	running very fast
24	grunt	꿀꿀거리는 소리	a deep guttural sound (as a pig does)
25	consternation	실망	panic; confused worry
26	vanquish	와파하다	defeat, overcome
27	dissent	반대	disorder and disagreement
28	pedestal	받침대	a base or foundation
29	elicit	끌어내다	withdraw; cause to be released
30	abashed	창피한, 겸연쩍은	shy; embarrassed
31	clutch	움켜쥐다	held tightly
32	appropriately	적당하게, 알맞게	suitable or probable in given circumstances
33	reap	수확하다	gather or take
34	connoisseur	전문가	expert
35	prudent	신중한	wise or judicious in practical affairs
36	acquiescence	묵인	to be in agreement; consent; submission
37	confine	국한시키다	enclose with bounds; limit or restrict
38	lament	한탄하다	mourn; regret
39	forged	구축된	to be formed or made
40	furtive	은밀한	secretive
41	abruptly	갑자기	suddenly
42	decree	선언하다	command, ordain
43	earnest	성실한	showing sincerity or serious dedication
44	myriad	무수히 많은	abundant, a very large number of
45	ominous	불길한	having bad signs for the future; threatening
46	emit	내다, 내뿜다	send-out; release
47	apprehension	우려, 불안	nervousness; trepidation
48	quintessential	정수의, 본질적인	typical, classic
49	delineate	기술/설명하다	outline, describe
50	stupefied	얼이 빠진	to be put into a state of little or no sensibility

SAT Vocabulary

번호	단어	우리말 뜻	영어 뜻
1	trepidation	두려움	nervousness; fear
2	solicitous	배려하는	worried or concerned (about someone else)
3	devoid	전혀 없는	without; empty
4	aesthetic	심미적, 미학적인	related to appearance and beauty
5	edifice	큰 건물, 빌딩	building, structure
6	belie	거짓임을 보여주다	create a false impression; contradict
7	enclose	둘러싸다	close in all sides
8	profusion	풍부, 부유	multitude; great number of something, abundance
9	wander	떠돌아다니다	ramble without a definite purpose or objective
10	cluster	묶음, 뭉치	bundle, group, bunch
11	embedded	단단히 박아넣은	sunk deeply; inserted
12	inconspicuous	이목을 끌지 못하는	unnoticeable; hidden
13	diffident	자신 없는, 수줍은	quiet; shy
14	disdain	경멸	strong dislike
15	avert	외면하다	look away from something
16	oppressive	탄압하는	burdening with cruel or unjust impositions or restraints
17	oblique	완곡한, 간접적인	indirectly stated or expressed; not straightforward
18	baffle	당황하게 만들다	confuse
19	witty	익살스러운	comic
20	anticipated	예상된	expected or predicted
21	onslaught	맹공격	an onset, assault, or attack
22	alignment	가지런함	the correct relationship of things with each other

Paul's SAT® Vocabulary

Paul Academy

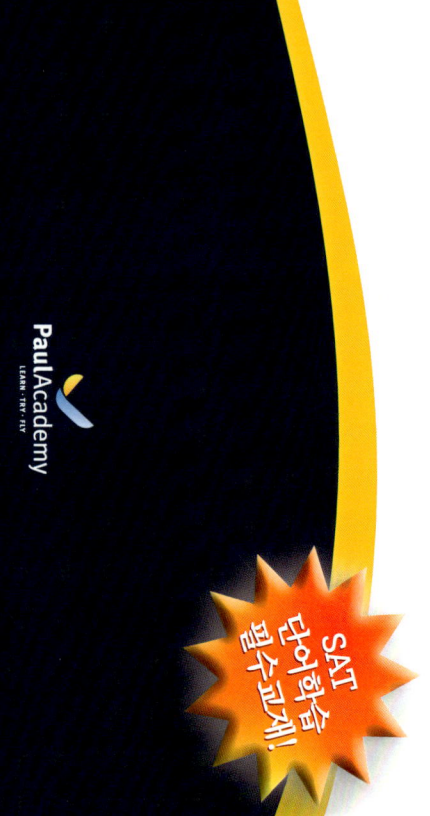

Paul's SAT Vocabulary
단어장

단 한 권으로 SAT 단어학습 종결!

- SAT 소설을 읽으며 문맥 속에서 단어학습
- 각 단어마다 효과적인 단어 암기법 제공
- SAT Official Guide를 포함한 최근 20년간 SAT 기출단어 집중분석
- 풀이카데미의 다년간의 경험과 노하우가 집약된 단어 우선순위 총정리

http://www.paulacademy.net
http://blog.naver.com/paulacademy

Paul's SAT Vocabulary
단어장

저자 Paul Kim(김동환)

SAT 단어학습 필수교재!